Social Research Methods and Statistics

A Computer-Assisted Introduction

Social Research Methods and Statistics

A Computer-Assisted Introduction

William Sims Bainbridge
Towson State University

Wadsworth Publishing Company
Belmont, California
A division of Wadsworth, Inc.

Acquisition Editor: Serina Beauparlant
Editorial Assistant: Marla Nowick
Production: Greg Hubit Bookworks
Print Buyer: Randy Hurst
Designer: John Edeen
Copy Editor: Greg Gullickson
Technical Illustrator: Susan Rogin
Cover: Michael Rogondino
Compositor: Graphics West
Printer: Arcata Graphics Fairfield

*This book is printed on acid-free paper that meets
Environmental Protection Agency standards for
recycled paper.*

1 2 3 4 5 6 7 8 9 10—96 95 94 93 92

Library of Congress Cataloging-in-Publication Data

Bainbridge, William Sims.
    Social research methods and statistics : a computer-assisted
introduction / William Sims Bainbridge.
        p. cm.
    Includes bibliographical references and index.
    ISBN 0-534-13122-0
    1. Sociology—Research—Methodology. 2. Sociology—Research—
Statistical methods. 3. Sociology—Research—Data processing.
I. Title.
HM48.B33 1992
301′.072—dc20   91-42313
                                                          CIP

Contents

Note: Headings beginning with [icon] specifically explain how to use the software that will accompany the textbook.

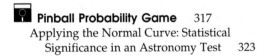

Preface

Students in the social sciences suffer a terrible deprivation: they are seldom if ever able to participate directly in the subject they study. Consider how much more fortunate students are in the so-called *natural* sciences: In biology they examine a wide array of living creatures; in physics they work with electrical circuitry; in chemistry they mix exotic chemicals with often spectacular results; and in geology they collect rocks and fossils for their own personal collections. In this respect, sociology is indeed an *unnatural* science, because science without laboratories is not science at all.

Ideally, sociology's laboratory is society, but a combination of ethical and economic problems limits the extent to which students can experiment with real human beings. Still, a course in social research methods can guide the student through some real-world experiences, and modern computer technology can expand the scope of research training through simulations of data collection and through many kinds of actual data analysis. The purpose of this textbook-software package is to provide the most exciting, most thorough, and most practical introduction to the tools of data collection and analysis used by social scientists.

The key principle is unity: the integration of data collection and data analysis, qualitative and quantitative techniques, methodology and statistics. Among its other challenges, sociology faces a chicken-and-egg problem. Which should come first, the methods or the statistics? I believe that students can learn methods of data collection and methods of statistical analysis simultaneously—step by step—if the educational route is carefully and imaginatively prepared. With the right approach, this is a very practical way to learn how to do social research. The combination of powerful but simple computer programs and several real datasets teaches the student the value of the many research techniques explained in this book: They are all tools to accomplish practical jobs, ways of learning about social reality.

The most common way of doing social research is to ask questions directly of the people under study, through interviews or questionnaires. This book places great stress on survey research, and several survey datasets are included in the software: from the 1860 census of Baton Rouge when a census-taker carried his questionnaire door-to-door, through two separate surveys of over 500 college students each, to a simulated survey of high school students that illustrates principles of sampling. But we shall also learn how to use official government data, how to carry out experiments, and how to perform qualitative observational research in the field. Throughout, I follow five principles that for me define effective teaching of social research methods:

1. Excitement. I love doing research. Several reviewers of the manuscript observed that this comes through in the writing and in the material I have chosen to share with you. It's true. For the sake of my family and the bank that holds my mortgage, I hope that universities and publishers will keep paying me to do sociological research, but I do the work because I love it. I assume you are interested in human beings, and I'll bet there are aspects of society that puzzle or trouble you. Many of you are sociology majors, and the rest are probably majoring in other social sciences or plan careers somehow related to them. Here is a chance actually to be a sociologist for a semester, to ask and answer questions about society, and to gain valuable skills that will serve you well in many kinds of jobs. I hope you have fun, too!

At times, any work gets boring or unpleasant. Some of you may find Chapter 1 a little too philosophical, and others will get impatient in later chapters when I am explaining how to calculate this or that statistical measure. But I have done my best to share my own personal excitement with you and to give you the means for exciting research experiences of your own. I have used many of the software programs and real-world projects in my own classes on research methods, and I am happy to report that students do regularly enjoy exploring the mysteries of society and making their own discoveries.

2. Unified Methods and Statistics. This textbook-software package begins with qualitative methods of research, but the emphasis is on simple quantitative methods. While designing the text so that different instructors can emphasize or deemphasize the statistics, I have combined material that is ordinarily taught in separate courses on methods and statistics. Indeed, I hope that instructors and departments will come more and more to combine the two, perhaps eventually establishing two-semester combined courses. However, this package is also ideal for a course purely devoted to research methods, whether students are expected

to have taken statistics already or will take statistics later.

In a sense, this book is entirely devoted to the methodology of sociological research. The techniques of sociology can be placed into two categories: (1) methods of data collection and (2) methods of data analysis. Statistics, then, is the branch of mathematics that deals with the precise derivation, meaning, and application of specific numerical tools. But you cannot collect data unless you have some idea of how you will analyze them, and you cannot begin analysis until you have collected some data. This textbook-software package combines the two phases of research to make the process much clearer and much more satisfying for students.

The organization of the textbook reflects this combined approach to methods of data collection and analysis. For example, rather than cover questionnaire surveys in one chapter, I have spread them out across several chapters so that we could explore a number of the ways that surveys are administered and that survey data can be analyzed. Several of the programs are based on actual or simulated surveys, because questionnaires are among the most versatile and widely used tools for data collection.

The statistically oriented chapters were structured according to my belief that so-called nonparametric techniques should be studied before parametric techniques. Quantitative data analysis starts with simple two-by-two tables, uses attitude items from questionnaires to expand to seven-by-seven crosstabulations, then employs analysis of variance (ANOVA) as a kind of bridge to Pearson correlations and regression analysis.

Perhaps the most important sequencing comes in the early chapters, where we start with information from individual human beings and then move on to data concerning groups of people. In part, this is a shift from qualitative to quantitative methods, but it is also a shift from the immediate world of human experience to intellectual abstractions. I firmly believe that abstractions lose meaning unless they are grounded in reality. Beyond that, I am convinced that intellect must not be divorced from emotion.

3. Learning by Doing.   Over the years, I have taught courses in field methods, survey methods, and general sociological methodology, working with students from a wide variety of backgrounds. If there is one lesson I have learned it is that students want to do sociological research themselves, rather than to hear about it secondhand. This textbook-software package is a practical means for giving the student stimulating experiences in a wide range of research methods.

At the end of each chapter after the first, I suggest research projects you can do, and most of them use the software included with this book. The rest are projects involving interviewing or observation in real social settings. Most software projects give you a number of choices, and instructors can easily design many projects of their own that explore further the rich datasets and simulations included in the software package. To be sure, the software provides far more opportunities to do projects than any person or class can even begin to try, but this gives instructors the freedom to select or create the set of projects that best serves their educational aims.

At the risk of sounding too proud of myself, I must tell you that I am a seasoned researcher. My articles have appeared in *The American Sociological Review, The American Journal of Sociology, Social Forces,* and more than a dozen specialty journals. I have also published several books based on research; this is my tenth book. The methods I have emphasized in my own work include qualitative field ethnography, both qualitative and quantitative surveys, historical archive research, interviews, statistical analysis of official government data, and even computer simulations. Thus, my aim is not merely to introduce you to research methods, but to invite you to join me in doing research. A good way to share research with you is to give you a truly active role in doing it yourself, through the computer software I have prepared.

4. A Computer-Assisted Introduction.   To accompany this textbook, I have written a set of eleven computer programs and assembled many datasets. This software is not what publishers call ancillary material, extra stuff connected only tenuously to the main text. Rather, my software is fully integrated into the text. It gives you the power to explore the methods of research explained in the book, to gain personal understanding of what they can accomplish, and to create fresh research projects of your own.

Your do not need, however, to sit at the computer while you read the book. Although you will need the book when you are working with the computer, the software is so easy to operate that you will not have to check the instructions very often. I always include illustrations from the computer in the parts of the text that discuss the software, so you can read the text on the bus, in a library, or wherever you want. And I have designed the programs to be extremely *user-friendly*. That is, you will be able to control the computer with easy-to-understand commands. This means usually just pressing a single key that is pictured on the screen so you will have no trouble identifying it.

The software runs on almost any IBM-compatible personal computer. You do not need special graphics capability, except for two optional parts of one program, and you do not need a color monitor. However, the programs make nice use of color if your machine has it, and I have employed every programming trick to make your computer show very good graphs and diagrams, even if it lacks graphics capability. For example, even on simple nongraphics, noncolor machines, one program gives you a decent map of the United States that can display four levels of shading for each of 255 variables across the fifty states.

And the software is fast! By using one of the best available program compilers (Turbo Pascal 5.5), and by writing very efficient computational routines, I have been able to get even very lengthy computations to finish in a fraction of a second. Ask the main survey analysis program to give you a crosstabulation of data from 512 college student respondents, and before you can blink, the screen fills with the crosstabulation and all the appropriate statistics.

The advanced nature of the software actually makes things easier and more intuitive for the student. Several of the programs allow students to see exactly how key statistics were calculated, and to figure results for themselves if this fits the instructor's educational aims. But all the tedious work is performed by the machine, and for courses that do not emphasize the mathematical aspects of research methods, students are offered good, intuitive ways of understanding results. For example, students often have trouble understanding statistical significance based on chi-square. One program offers a set of data-based two-by-two tables, plus the option of inputting one's own table, and shows how to calculate chi-square. Then, if you want, pressing a button makes the computer zip out one hundred or one thousand random two-by-two tables, comparable to the one you are analyzing, calculating their chi-squares. Before your very eyes, you will see how many of these chi-squares based on randomized data achieve various levels of significance, and you will get a clear picture of how the table you are studying compares with distributions you get by chance. Other programs exploit the computer's capacity to produce random numbers to illustrate the logic of sampling, and many other features of the programs expand the traditional functions of software to provide vivid and intuitive introductions to a host of methodological principles.

5. Practical Tools. The various research methodologies and statistical procedures do not exist for their own sake. They are tools designed to accomplish particular practical tasks. But too often, sociology students are forced to study them entirely divorced from their applications. I believe very strongly that it is fruitless to teach students an abstract procedure, unless they already have a use for it that makes it valuable to them. The methods

introduced here are all tools: solutions for practical problems, methods for gaining knowledge, and instruments for enlarging the scope of human creativity.

I always introduce a technique in the context of a goal that we want to reach, something we want to learn from a dataset or some kind of information we are seeking. And the student is encouraged to use the new tool immediately in one of the computer programs or in some real-world exploration. Considered as tools, methodological techniques can be understood and remembered only if they are used. By gaining experience actually using a technique, students gain personal mastery and a realistic sense of accomplishment. Yes, I want you to learn research methods and statistics, but I also want you to like them!

I have great respect for mathematicians, but few sociology students are prepared to become mathematicians themselves, and their interests are frequently very far from the abstract logic and symbols of math. This textbook-software package seeks to solve one of the great problems of university teaching: how to give nonmathematical students clear and correct understanding of basic principles of mathematical tools employed in their field.

Many thanks!   Credit for the original idea for this textbook-software package belongs to Sheryl Fullerton, my first editor at Wadsworth. The editor for this project, Serina Beauparlant, has been remarkably effective in drawing forth from me the best book I could write and in bringing together the best insights of an army of reviewers that have produced a far better book than I could have done alone. While I have learned much from many colleagues, Rodney Stark has taught me far more than anyone else. By taking me on as a research collaborator when I was fresh and inexperienced, he not only gave me a tremendous education in research methods, but he also convinced me that the best way to teach was to enlist someone as a research collaborator, too. The ultimate inspiration for this project, and the most important collaborators in it, have been my students, both in research methods classes and in others with more substantive focus. The best thanks I can offer my former students is to give you, my new students, the most effective and enjoyable educational experience.

My thanks go also to the following reviewers for their helpful comments and suggestions: Ron Anderson, University of Minnesota, Minneapolis; George D. Baldwin, Henderson State University; Steven B. Caldwell, Cornell University; Thomas Conner, Michigan State University; Sheila Cordray, Oregon State University; Richard Dodder, Oklahoma State University; Greg Hoover, Carson-Newman College; David R. James, Indiana University; Bryce Johnson, Southern Oregon State College; William R. Kelly, University of Texas, Austin; Stephen Kulis, Arizona State University; Wm. Alex McIntosh, Texas A&M University; Kenneth J. Mietus, Western Illinois University; William F. Skinner, University of Kentucky; John A. Sonquist, University of California, Santa Barbara.

An Introduction to Social Research

CHAPTER OVERVIEW

We begin our exploration of sociological research and social statistics with two topics that must be covered before anything else: the logic of social research and the ethics of social research. Thus, before we carry out actual social research, we need to consider its *philosophy*. There are two main ways to do social research, the formal-operational approach (which is similar to the approaches of the physical sciences) and the interpretive-advocacy approach (which is more like the approaches of the humanities). In the more systematic formal-operational approach, the sociologist develops a chain of logic rather like a formal proof in mathematics. From a general theory, the sociologist deduces various hypotheses and operationalizes key concepts in these hypotheses with concern for how they can be measured. Before undertaking

a research project, however, it is essential to consider its ethics, to make sure that human beings will not be harmed by participating in it.

Although it is important to understand the philosophical ideas presented in this chapter, real research is usually far less abstract and far more fragmentary. The typical research project aims to uncover some particular facts. Although the information unearthed by any given social science study can contribute to our evaluation of a general theory, usually it takes a whole series of research studies, done by different people applying different methods, to establish the truth or falsity of a general theory.

Because it seeks to be scientific, there is a logic to social research; and because it concerns human beings, there is a morality to it as well. In both science and morality, we strive to achieve ideals. Good social science gains knowledge that contributes to human well-being. To accomplish this, research must be designed carefully, according to a set of logical principles, and it must be conducted in a manner consistent with the rights of the people under study. We begin our examination of these ideals with an overview of the concepts that guide scientific research methodology.

_____ The Logic of Scientific Research

Sociology is a vast field, containing many utterly different schools of thought and research approaches. Put simply, there are two general perspectives on sociological research and how it should connect to theory. I call these the **formal-operational*** and the **interpretive-advocacy** modes of sociological research. This split is not sharp, and I myself have done both kinds of sociology (Wuthnow 1981). It is similar but not identical to the distinction between quantitative and qualitative research, or between the natural sciences and the humanities.

The Formal-Operational Mode

The term _formal-operational_ is taken from the work of Jean Piaget, undoubtedly the most famous and influential psychologist who studied children's development of logical thinking (Inhelder and Piaget 1958). Maurice Richter (1972) introduced into sociology the proposition that the historical development of **science** parallels and extends the cognitive development that takes place in an individual's childhood; the scientific method can thus be seen as the most mature way of learning about reality. Science is both rational and empirical. It is the systematic framing and testing of hypotheses about nature. To the extent that human society is an aspect of nature, it can be studied using this method.

A term often used by other writers to describe what I call the formal-operational approach is **hypothetico-deductive**. The first half of this term refers to the stating and testing of hypotheses about reality, the second half to

* Terms boldfaced in the text are defined in the Glossary/Index at the back of this book.

logical reasoning that deduces the empirical consequences of an hypothesis. For example, consider hypotheses about religion and suicide. Imagine two people, one religious and the other not. Which one should be more afraid of death? In our society, the vast majority of churches teach that there is life after death. Therefore, the religious person should see death as a painful but survivable transition to another plane of existence, perhaps even to a better life than this one. People who are not religious, especially the atheists among them, suspect that death is the absolute end, and therefore they should be more concerned about avoiding it than very religious people would be. This leads to a sociological hypothesis: _Suicide is more common among religious people than among irreligious people._

I am sure you can see flaws in this argument. It is worth distinguishing two very different kinds of error: logical errors and empirical errors. First, the hypothesis at the end of the above paragraph may not follow logically from the assumptions at the top of the paragraph. Generally, it is best to make one's deductions as _formal_ as possible, even to state them in the symbolic language of formal logic, which is a branch of mathematics and philosophy. Even as it stands, however, the paragraph above is somewhat formal, working from some reasonable general principles to a more-or-less logical conclusion.

The second possible error is that the hypothesis may simply not fit reality. However logical it may seem, it must be tested through empirical research. We would have to do a study, comparing religious people with irreligious people, to see if the former really were more prone to suicide than the latter. Easier said than done!

How are we going to distinguish religious people from irreligious people? One way would be to let them decide. We could survey one thousand people (later chapters will tell us exactly how to accomplish this) and ask each one, "Are you religious?" Perhaps some will say yes and others will say no. Ten years later, we return to the research project, find out what happened to each of the one thousand, and count how many committed suicide in each group. I think you can see that there are practical problems in this research design. First of all, it asks us to wait a long time for our results. Furthermore, not many people commit suicide, and out of the 1,000 we select, none of them may do themselves in. Perhaps we need a survey of 100,000 people, or a million.

Practical problems aside, sociologists of religion are not convinced that a simple Yes/No question can properly distinguish religious people from irreligious people. Typically, survey researchers in this field employ batteries of items about religious belief and practice, combining many kinds of information to provide the most solid possible basis for deciding how religious a person is. Several experts have decided that being religious is far from a simple matter, and they have proposed that there are as many as five different kinds of religiousness (Glock and Stark 1965). Clearly, we would have to decide how we were going to define religiousness before we could begin a study such as this one.

Before any hypothesis can be tested, one must decide how to define and measure its concepts, a process called **operationalization**. In the example just given, the **operational definition** of "religious" is answering yes to the question "Are you religious?" In more sophisticated studies, the operational definition might be answering yes to most of a collection of questions about religion, covering such matters as beliefs, prayer, church attendance, and the like.

Many recent studies have operationalized religiousness in terms of membership in a church or other religious organization. Clearly, this is not ideal, because some individuals with powerful beliefs may not belong to a congregation, while some people who do belong may be atheistic members of otherwise religious families. But one advantage of this operational definition of religiosity is that good data already exist about it. Surveys have been done, in a number of different years, reporting the number of members of churches of various denominations in each state, and each county or city, across the United States. It turns out that the rate of church membership varies greatly, being two or three times as high in some places as in others. Government statistics also give suicide rates for different parts of the country, allowing us to compare the "more religious" with "less religious" communities, to see if the former have higher suicide rates.

Let there be no mistake. Researchers climb rather far out on a limb when they do projects like this. The data permit far from the best operationalization of the hypothesis that we can imagine. Indeed, we are now testing a somewhat different hypothesis: *The suicide rate is higher in areas of the United States that possess high rates of church membership than in areas that possess low rates of church membership.* This is related to our original hypothesis, but it takes us on a somewhat indirect route to our research goal and is certainly open to criticism. So, what happens when we let this new hypothesis encounter real data?

Crash! That was the sound of an hypothesis crashing in complete defeat, shot down by data about the real world. Every study of this type that I have seen, including a couple I published myself, failed to find a higher suicide rate in areas with high church membership rates. In fact, studies tend to find the exact opposite. The suicide rate is noticeably higher where the church membership rate is low, not where it is high. Now, we already said that this would not be an ideal test of the original hypothesis, and we might be able to find some twisted logic that would let us weasel out of what appears to be total scientific defeat. But the best evidence we can get certainly does not support the hypothesis that religion encourages suicide.

One could frame several other potentially researchable hypotheses about attitudes toward death: For example, religious people more easily bear the loss of loved ones than do non-religious people. Religious people face their own deaths with greater calm that do nonreligious people. Religious people are more ready to kill their enemies in war than are nonreligious people. This last hypothesis is not very pleasant, and there might be good reason to argue the opposite ("Thou shalt not kill"). But now we have four hypotheses that are all more-or-less logical consequences of the idea that religion makes death seem less terrible. Any of these hypotheses could be the focus of empirical research.

In science, we use the term **theory** to refer to a statement that can generate two or more potentially testable hypotheses. There is no strict distinction between a theory and an hypothesis. You might say that theories are big hypotheses. I define them as hypotheses of great scope, implying many lesser hypotheses. Almost invariably, we cannot test a theory itself, simply because it is too general, but we can logically derive hypotheses from a theory and test them. Sometimes, as in the previous example, we have to work through a chain of hypotheses, operationalizing concepts as best we can until we find an hypothesis that can be tested.

Now you can see the meaning of *hypothetico-deductive*, a term that refers to the following basic process of science. We have a theory. Logically, we *deduce* from this theory various **hypotheses** whose concepts can be empirically operationalized. We perform research, and if the data support the hypotheses, then the theory is also supported. If the data fail to support the hypotheses, then our confidence in the theory is greatly weakened.

I like Piaget's term *formal-operational*, although I give it slightly broader meaning than he did. It stresses that our logic and our methods of research should be as *formal* as possible. We should make all our assumptions explicit. Each step in our logical deductions should be made as clearly as possible, spelled out even in fine detail. The *operational* part does not merely refer to operationalizing concepts in the hypotheses. It also communicates the precise yet dynamic nature of our mental processes. In mathematics, an *operator* is a symbol denoting an operation to be performed, as "÷" tells you to divide one number by another.

Whether you call it hypothetico-deductive or formal-operational, this approach has what we might call a mechanical aspect. That is, much of the work could be done by a machine, such as an appropriately programmed computer. Indeed, computer programs have been written that fairly effectively simulate scientific research (Langley, Simon, Bradshaw, and Zytkow 1987). The computer programs in our software package are going to help us through the "mechanical" aspects, but we still have to work with them imaginatively.

But infrahuman animals cannot do scientific research. It takes a well-developed mind to frame theories, deduce hypotheses, operationalize concepts, systematically collect data, and evaluate the hypotheses in light of the results. Writing about Piaget's work in a highly regarded introductory sociology textbook, Stark (1989:152) notes the development of formal operational thinking in early adolescence: "Eventually ... some people learn to think abstractly and to impose logical tests on their ideas. ... [W]hen they reach the formal operational stage, people can formulate and manipulate theories and logically deduce from these theories that certain things are likely to be true or false. With this comes the ability to think hypothetically—to say 'what if?' and then trace the logical implications of this supposition." You have undoubtedly reached this stage and can understand the formal-operational mode of sociological research.

The Interpretive-Advocacy Mode

Interpretive sociology seeks the human meaning of a social phenomenon. Often, interpretive sociologists say their aim is simply to document what certain situations and experiences mean to their participants (Blumer 1969; Truzzi 1974). Because interpretation is never entirely neutral, and given the history of interpretive approaches in sociology, I add the word *advocacy* to the name for this approach. Many, if not all, interpretive sociologists advocate a particular set of values, politico-economic policies, or other personal commitments through their research publications. Indeed, interpretive research becomes a medium through which sociologists can express their personal feelings as well as those of the people they study.

Thus, it is hard to teach interpretive-advocacy sociology in a general textbook. Simply put, I can't tell you how to do this kind of sociology because I do not know who you are. I do not know your personal values, or your political persuasion, or your aesthetics.

Self-aware practitioners of this approach often urge **reflexivity** or tell their students to include a *reflexive* component in their research and writing. This means to acknowledge that your image of a social phenomenon will always reflect your own standpoint to some extent. What you see will reflect where you look from—literally your perspective or viewpoint. Thus, a sociological essay is always a product of both the writer and the data. You must analyze your own commitments, biases, and habits of perception, perhaps including an analysis of yourself along with the analysis of the phenomenon under study. Reflecting upon your own role as sociologist makes your work reflexive.

Naturally, this means that different interpretive sociologists will have different audiences. We see this most obviously with topics and approaches that have a strong political aspect. For example, political conservatives are unlikely to enjoy reading Marxist sociology. It is not merely that interpretations made from a political standpoint other than your own will offend your values and advocate things that you detest; these interpretations are also likely to seem completely arbitrary and even meaningless to you.

This is not to say that you will like only those sociologists who happen to have exactly your personal beliefs and sentiments. We all like occasionally having our eyes opened to new possibilities and considering slightly unfamiliar insights. But interpretive-advocacy sociology comes in many varieties, each appealing most strongly to the audiences who already share a general perspective with it.

Over the past several years, I have sought a way of bringing together most varieties of interpretive sociology, and I have become convinced that this is possible because they all have something in common: language. The way scholars interpret a social phenomenon is to find the right words to express their impressions of it. Most recently, I have had the marvelous opportunity and challenge of editing the sociology and social psychology sections of the forthcoming *Encyclopedia of Language and Linguistics,* to be published by Aberdeen University Press in collaboration with Pergamon Press. If you are interested in exploring the possibilities for interpretive sociology, you might want to check out the encyclopedia's essays on the sociology of language and some of the particular schools of interpretation: attribution theory, ethnomethodology, labeling theory, sociology of knowledge, symbolic crusades, and symbolic interactionism. If I am right, however, serious interpretive sociology of the future will become very much like linguistics, and this textbook cannot cover that vast academic discipline currently outside the domain of sociology. Therefore, this textbook will emphasize the formal-operational mode of sociological research.

Discovery and Proof

Luck plays a role in scientific discoveries, and the invention of theories and testable hypotheses is as much an art as a science. As A. M. Taylor (1967:ix) says it: "To achieve an advance in knowledge, the experimenter must put the right question, understand the reply, and have the wit to perceive the next step in the argument. Inspiration and imagination, boldness and perseverance are qualities necessary to the scientist no less than the artist, musician, or poet." William Beveridge (1950:44) argues: "That aspect of the scientist's mind which demands convincing evidence should be reserved for the proof stage of the investigation. In research, an attitude of mind is required for discovery which is different from that required for proof, for discovery and proof are distinct processes."

Many influential scientific hypotheses have sprung from the irrational intuition of theorists and researchers, and pure chance has played a significant role in discovery as well. An example of dumb luck from my own research is the discovery that the original records of mental hospitals in the 1860 U.S. census frequently listed the supposed cause of insanity of the inmate, data that could be used to understand the prevailing psychiatric theories of the day (Bainbridge 1984b). I had been scanning endlessly through microfilms of the 1860 census records, hunting for all the utopian communes, because no index to the records existed. Scanning a microfilm roll for Ohio, in search of a particular Shaker community, I stumbled across the records for a mental hospital, and I saw immediately that the causes listed for all the patients' insanity would make a fascinating study. Beveridge (1950) lists six factors that are essential if the scientist is going to be able to exploit chance opportunities:

1. Because lucky accidents are rare, the researcher must invest much time and energy to give them a significant chance of happening. I suppose I was bound to find something interesting in the census records, because my work required me to invest hundreds of hours visually scanning hundreds of the microfilm rolls.

2. When a lucky accident does happen, the researcher has to notice it, and this requires acute powers of observation. Frankly, the microfilm work was so boring that I would pause and scrutinize anything at all that looked unusual on the microfilms, and large institutions stood out like sore thumbs.

3. The researcher must be prepared to interpret the chance observation and recognize its potential significance. The great French biologist Louis Pasteur is reputed to have said, "In the fields of observation, chance favors only the mind that is prepared." Before you can understand the meaning of an unexpected scientific observation, you must have studied the appropriate subject in sufficient depth. As it happened, I had done my Ph.D. oral exam in the sociology and anthropology of mental disorder, so a sudden encounter with unexpected psychiatric data immediately suggested possibilities for analysis.

4. The chance discovery will be lost if the researcher fails to follow up on it. A trip to my university's library, which possessed the published volumes of the 1860 census and other reports of the period, quickly gave me a list of 43 major insane asylums that were in operation by the end of 1860, and within a few days I had located the census records for all but one of them, which undoubtedly opened a few months after the census was taken. Only 17 of these 42 asylums actually listed the supposed causes of insanity for the inmates, so I was lucky to have run across one that did.

5. A discovery may not have an application until several years later; thus, some accidental discoveries may come at the wrong time. Beveridge wrote primarily about discoveries in biology, and many accidental observations in that field could not be followed up until particular research methods had been developed, or theory had advanced to the point where the chance observations had meaning, or it was possible to find a practical application such as the cure of a disease. Had I run across the records for the Ohio mental hospital back in the 1960s, I could have gone no further, because only in the 1970s did the federal government make

available a complete microfilm copy of the entire 1860 census.

6. Finally, Beveridge says, a discovery may have to run a gauntlet of skepticism and resistance on the part of others. Certainly, my little study of madness in the 1860 census encountered no resistance, being accepted for publication by the first journal I sent it to. But on occasion, brand-new science does encounter opposition from members of the general public or even from scientists themselves.

The process of imagining a new theory or discovering a new phenomenon has a strong irrational component, but theory-testing is not wholly rational, despite the necessity of making it as much so as possible. Strictly speaking, scientific research can never prove a theory true. To expect absolute proof is to misunderstand the logic of scientific research.

> Generalizations can never be *proved*. They can be tested by seeing whether deductions made from them are in accord with experimental and observational facts, and if the results are not as predicted, the hypothesis or generalization may be *disproved*. But a favorable result does not prove the generalization, because the deduction made from it may be true without its being true.... In strict logic a generalization is never proved and remains on probation indefinitely, but if it survives all attempts at disproof it is accepted in practice, especially if it fits well into a wider theoretical scheme. (Beveridge 1950:118)

Thus, if theories cannot be proven, they can at least be disproven, and a theory that has resisted several attempts at disproof deserves our respect if not our unswerving belief. In the language of Karl Popper (1959, 1962), a theory that is capable of disproof is **falsifiable**. And every good theory is falsifiable. It must be possible to test a theory, to put it at risk of falsification, before it is of much value for science. If we could

not, in principle, imagine evidence that would disprove a theory, then the theory must not say anything decisive about reality.

A Parable about Brute Facts

Consider the following parable. One day, the word went out in the People's Republic of China that on the following Saturday every citizen was to proceed to a designated field, beach, or hillside in the country, mark out an acre of land, and count the stones and bushes on it, tallying the number of each variety. Over the following week, each of these one billion people was to write a brief report, stating the characteristics of the plot of land that he or she had been assigned and noting how many of each kind of stone and bush was found there. Seven days afterward, the government of the PRC announced proudly that this vast project had produced so much information that it had increased the scientific knowledge of humankind a hundred times. It further proclaimed that China was now the leading scientific nation on Earth and demanded that the Nobel Prizes of that year, and all the prizes for the next century, should be awarded to it.

Would you vote for that? Is scientific knowledge simply a mass of facts, or is science something more than a crude catalog of information? Every successful scientist knows that science is more than just data. Most importantly, it is a set of explanations for data. As Ernest Nagel (1961:4) says, "It is the desire for explanations which are at once systematic and controllable by factual evidence that generates science; and it is the organization and classification of knowledge on the basis of explanatory principles that is the distinctive goal of the sciences."

Young sciences, perhaps including sociology, may not have had the time to find and test very broad generalizations that link a wide range of observations. But when a science has made great progress in discovering and explaining phenomena, it will not merely possess a great number of theoretical notions but a *formal theory*.

Explaining Research Findings with Theories

The word *theory* means different things to different sociologists (Turner 1986). In the interpretive-advocacy mode, it typically is a set of metaphors and analogies that place social phenomena in a meaningful context for the humanist or the advocate. In the formal-operational mode, it is a set of formal propositions, linked by a system of deductions showing how some propositions follow logically from others.

As Richard Braithwaite (1953:22) puts it, "A scientific theory is a deductive system in which observable consequences logically follow from the conjunction of observed facts with the set of the fundamental hypotheses of the system." He further notes that every deductive system consists of a set of propositions of varying scope. Some are very specific statements about relatively narrow facets of reality. Others are the broadest generalizations, linking numerous specific statements.

The sociologist who most forcefully argued that scientific theories should be deductive systems was George C. Homans. According to Homans, science has two aims, discovery and explanation. Discovery is not simply the amassing of brute facts, as in the parable about the People's Republic of China. Rather, "Discovery is the job of stating and testing more or less general relationships between properties of nature" (Homans 1967:7). Although Homans gave examples from the physical sciences, he was quick to argue that sociology was a natural science, as much as physics and biology are, and that regularities in the social behavior of human beings could be discovered in approximately the same way as regularities between atoms or organisms.

A statement about the relationships between properties of nature is called a **proposition**. An example of a sociological proposition is the famous finding of Morselli (1882), introduced into sociology by Durkheim (1897), that Protestants are more prone to suicide than are Catholics. So many sociologists have accepted this

that it has come to be called "sociology's one law" (Pope and Danigelis 1981). Perhaps the best formal statement of this observation is the following proposition: *The suicide rate is higher in Protestant communities than in Catholic communities.*

A proposition like this has two parts. First, the proposition says what the relationship applies to: the suicide rate in Christian communities of the Protestant and Catholic traditions. Using a word borrowed from the terminology of mathematical functions, we can call this the **domain** of the proposition. The domain of the proposition is suicide rates in Protestant and Catholic communities. It says nothing about rates of divorce, larceny, abortion, or about Jewish and Greek Orthodox communities. The properties of nature it addresses are Protestant suicide rates and Catholic suicide rates. We can call these the *terms* of the proposition.

Second, the proposition specifies the relationship between the terms. Here, the relationship is "greater than." The Protestant suicide rate is *greater than* the Catholic suicide rate. The concept *greater than* can be considered an operator in the mathematical sense, because it implies a comparison between the two rates and produces an answer of true or false depending upon the result of the comparison.

Morselli and other writers may have discovered a proposition about suicide rates, but within our own field of sociology, it was Durkheim who explained it. Durkheim asserted that the key difference between Protestant and Catholic communities was that the former were far less well organized than the latter. The typical member of a Catholic community was firmly embedded in stable social relationships with the other members, while Protestant communities tended to possess a highly fragmented and unstable social life. Thus, Durkheim asserted another proposition: *The suicide rate varies inversely with the degree of social integration of the community of which the individual is a part.*

This, too, is an honest-to-goodness scientific proposition. It has a domain: suicide rates across communities of different degrees of social integration. And it asserts a definite relationship—inverse correlation—saying that as social integration increases the suicide rate decreases (and vice versa). The proposition about social integration is more general than the one about Protestants and Catholics. Durkheim also noted that marriage tends to reduce the suicide rate, especially among males. And he argued that political unity, such as that achieved by many communities during wartime, also reduces suicide. Thus, he presented three relatively specific propositions about the suicide rate: one concerning religious tradition, one concerning marital condition, and one concerning politics. These three are all covered by the more general proposition about suicide rate and social integration, because each refers to a specific kind of integration (religious, marital, political).

For Homans (1967:23), "the explanation of a finding . . . is the process of showing that the finding follows as a logical conclusion, as a deduction, from one or more general propositions under specified given conditions." **Formal explanation** of a specific proposition consists in showing that it follows logically from one or more general propositions. Ideally, the logic should be as rigorous as that in mathematics.

The branch of deductive mathematics that college students are most likely to be familiar with is plane geometry. You begin with a set of simple axioms and a few definitions about lines and planes, and from these you begin to derive theorems about triangles and circles. The theorems themselves can then be used to derive further theorems, and the whole deductive system grows until it encompasses a great many facts about plane geometry. In the terminology used here, both the axioms and the theorems are propositions. Propositions can be roughly distinguished in terms of how general or specific they are—the scope of their domains—and the most general propositions are the axioms (Stark and Bainbridge 1987).

Consider Durkheim's explanation of the difference between Protestant and Catholic suicide rates, which can be presented in the following form:

1. The suicide rate is inversely proportional to the degree of social integration of a community.
2. Protestant communities have less social integration than do Catholic communities.
3. Therefore, the suicide rate is higher in Protestant communities than in Catholic communities.

A three-step argument like this is called a **syllogism** (Quine 1982:102–108). The first two statements in this syllogism are its *premises*. The first one is called the *major premise*, the second one the *minor premise*. The major premises in sociological syllogisms are general propositions about a whole category of things (communities in our example). The minor premises are more specific propositions that refer to subcategories within the category identified by the major premise. The third proposition in the syllogisms, which is called the *conclusion*, is deduced logically from the two premises. If both premises are true, and the logic of the deductions is valid, then the conclusion must also be true.

How do these general principles of formal theory apply to social scientific research? In particular, how can empirical research be combined with such abstract considerations? For one thing, it ought to be possible to determine whether suicide rates really are higher in Protestant than in Catholic areas. But three-quarters of a century passed after Durkheim's book on the subject before sociologists seriously considered fresh data on this important point. As I will explain more fully in Chapter 11, sociology then received a bit of a shock when it was discovered that suicide rates were *not* generally higher in areas where many Protestants lived than where Catholics lived.

If the conclusion of Durkheim's syllogism has been proven false, then what happens to his logic and his premises? Clearly, unless the logical deduction of the conclusion from the premises was done incorrectly, one or both premises must be wrong. I think it was the minor premise, the assertion that Protestant communities have less social integration than do Catholic communities. The reason I suspect this is that other evidence supports the major premise. Consider the following similar syllogism:

1. The suicide rate is inversely proportional to the degree of social integration of a community.
2. Church membership provides social integration.
3. Therefore the suicide rate is higher in communities with low rates of church membership than in communities with high rates of church membership.

A number of recent empirical studies confirm the conclusion of this syllogism. The suicide rate does appear higher in communities with low rates of church membership. Thus, Durkheim may have been right about the role of social integration in preventing suicide, but wrong in guessing that Protestant and Catholic communities differed in social integration. His explanation of variations in the suicide rate was logically sound but not empirically correct. A revised version of his syllogism is no better or worse, in terms of its logic, but the revision is far better in terms of empirical adequacy.

Thus, a deductive theory has to pass two tests before it can be judged to be a good one. First, its propositions must form a logical system, with many specific propositions deriving logically from the general propositions. Second, many specific propositions must be empirically testable and must withstand the challenge of real data.

To the extent that a theory is comprised of a rigorously derived set of propositions, it is a powerful tool of sociological research. Its more specific propositions are prescriptions of research topics that should be studied. Are suicide rates higher in Protestant areas than in other areas? Collect some appropriate data and find out! And because they link falsifiable specific propositions to more general propositions, deductive theories allow the general propositions to be tested as well.

The Sociological Process

My friend and colleague Rodney Stark (1989:30–34) has described what he calls "the sociological process," a model of how sociologists construct and test theories. It has eight steps:

1. Wonder
2. Conceptualize
3. Theorize
4. Operationalize
5. Hypothesize
6. Observe
7. Analyze
8. Assess

The first three steps are parts of **theory construction**. The sociological imagination makes us *wonder* about the nature or causes of some phenomenon. But a vague notion that something is perplexing or fascinating is not a sociological grasp of the issue under concern. We must identify and define the elements of the phenomenon and our impressions of it. That is, we must *conceptualize*. Once we have clearly defined concepts, we can place them in formal propositions, statements that explain how concepts are related. To do this, we *theorize*.

Once we have constructed our theory, we turn to **theory testing**, which consists of two parts, **measurement** and *research*. The first step in measurement is to *operationalize*, which Stark says means to "select valid indicators of concepts." As noted earlier, this means finding appropriate ways to measure the concepts in a research setting. Usually a theory is so abstract or general that it is difficult or impossible to test it directly. Therefore, we must *hypothesize*, deducing testable propositions from the theory.

The actual process of research requires us to *observe* and *analyze*, collecting evidence that bears on our hypotheses and systematically comparing it with them. Finally, Stark says, we *assess* the theory in light of our research findings. Perhaps our data entirely support the hypotheses, in which case our confidence in the theory from which they are derived grows substantially. Or perhaps the data contradict the hypotheses, in which case we have good reason to doubt the theory. Often, the results are mixed and may suggest to us a way in which the theory should be revised. Thus the sociological process, as outlined by Stark, loops back upon itself. From our research we gain insights that modify our theories and that often provide new phenomena to wonder about.

If you look at articles in the major sociological journals, however, or books that have been reviewed in the journals, you will seldom find that the authors followed Stark's model. Many writers follow the interpretive-advocacy approach instead. In this case, we cannot expect the model to apply, because it was designed to describe the formal-operational approach. But many other publications also fail to fit.

A chief reason is that most research projects are mere fragments of the sociological process. Once a few sociologists have written about a particular topic, subsequent publications may not need to do any theory construction or to consider issues of measurement. Some of the articles on religion and suicide rates, for example, merely repeated previous research with a fresh dataset. Stark's model may apply to the overall social process of sociology but not to the carrying out of any particular research project.

Other empirical research projects seem to reverse some of the steps in the model. They start with the data, apply some tools of statistical analysis, then try to spin a theoretical explanation around the results. This is often called **inductive** research. Induction is, in a sense, the opposite of deduction. It involves starting with some facts, then using logic to try to make sense of them. This approach cannot test theories, but it can help us construct theories, and it can give us some phenomena to wonder about. Similarly, deduction alone cannot take us very far, because it cannot tell us what to theorize about.

This book will employ both induction and deduction. Some of the projects at the ends of chapters ask you to think up a sociological idea—an hypothesis—and then test it with the data provided. Other projects turn you loose to explore a dataset for interesting facts that then demand explanations. But this is not a textbook in social theory. Its emphasis is on empirical research, so it primarily covers the two steps Stark calls *observe* and *analyze*. At times we shall also examine how to *operationalize* concepts. Although we are not playing the theorist role here, I hope you will often try to think through the meaning of particular research projects to see how they link to theory construction and the testing of formal explanations of social behavior.

The Partnership between Research and Statistics

I have suggested that the interpretive-advocacy mode of sociological research will benefit in the future from an alliance with linguistics, and that the formal-operation mode has already achieved much through an alliance with mathematics. The overwhelming majority of empirical studies performed from this latter perspective are statistical in nature. Therefore, it makes perfect sense to combine research methods and statistics in this textbook and software package.

Recall our discussions of suicide and religion. We spoke of suicide rates and church membership rates. These are statistical concepts. How many Protestants kill themselves for every 100,000 Protestants in the population? This is a question about a rate, and the answer has to be calculated mathematically.

When we compare suicide rates for different areas of the country, we are doing a statistical analysis. To see if the suicide rate is higher in California than in Connecticut, we have to calculate two rates, one for each state, and then compare them. To test the hypothesis that suicide rates are high where church membership rates are low, we have to calculate not only rates for all the areas but a correlation as well.

Thus, it is almost impossible to divorce research methods from statistical methods. In any research project, the two go hand in hand.

The techniques of statistics are practical tools for gaining knowledge, just as are the methods for collecting data. In a research project, one cannot collect the data before one has some idea of how they will be analyzed; and, of course, one cannot analyze data until they have been collected.

Many sociology departments offer separate courses with names like Research Methods and Social Statistics, and there is a never-ending debate over which one students should take first. One argument says, "You need to study research methods first, so you can understand the usefulness of the tools of statistical analysis." But the other argument says, "You need to study statistics first, so you will understand the purpose of many rules for good data collection." I think both arguments are correct. That is, you do need to take each of these two before the other, and the only way to accomplish this is to take them both at once, carefully coordinated so they fit together perfectly.

Many of my colleagues agree that, ideally, research methods and statistics are inseparable and should be taught together. But I know that this ideal is hard to achieve. At many colleges, statistics is taught by the math or psychology department, and thus cannot be combined with methods of sociological research. There are also many other valid reasons that it is impractical to combine methods and statistics at a particular college.

This textbook is designed to work well either in a combined methods-statistics course or in a course devoted to just half of this partnership. It certainly does not assume that students have taken statistics already, although if they have it will be possible to skip the more statistical sections, including some whole chapters. Indeed, there are many ways of adapting this textbook and software package for courses of many kinds, emphasizing different aspects of social research.

Within the formal-operational mode of research, we really should not speak of methods separately from statistics. Rather, we can distinguish methods of data collection from methods of data analysis, acknowledging that in any particular project the two must be combined. Thus, in a very real sense, this entire textbook is about methods of social research. I hope you will agree that the inclusion of at least simple aspects of statistics allows maximum use of the special abilities of microcomputers and helps you experience all parts of the research process.

Writing Proposals and Reports

Sociological research is not a solitary endeavor but a form of communication. If the researcher does not tell others what he or she has found, then the effort invested in the study was wasted. In order to obtain money to do the research, sociologists often submit proposals to grant-giving agencies, and such proposals often foreshadow the reports that will be written when the research is over. Writing a formal proposal can also help a sociologist clarify the aims and methods of his or her study, and colleagues can often be very helpful in suggesting valuable modifications if they see a written plan.

My colleagues R. Guy Sedlack and Jay Stanley shared with me an outline they give students in a course that emphasizes the writing of a research proposal (Sedlack and Stanley 1991). The first of three main sections of a research proposal states the research problem, both naming the research topic and explaining why it is interesting. The second section reviews what earlier writers have said about the problem, considering both relevant theoretical statements and previous research studies, and it zeros in on the particular proposition to be investigated. The third and final section covers the methodology, which includes the overall research design, the sample of the population or other fragment of society that will be studied, the specific means used to operationalize concepts, and the procedures the researcher will employ to analyze the data. There will also be a bibliography listing the publications mentioned in the proposal, and there may be an appendix including such things as the actual text of a questionnaire that will be used.

In many respects, such a proposal can serve as the first draft of a report of the results. That is, if the study is clearly enough designed, the only thing missing that must be supplied for the report is the results themselves. Suppose, for example, that we want to check Durkheim's claim that Protestants are more likely to commit suicide than are Catholics, and we plan to use some recent statistics collected by the government. Our proposal can state the research problem thoroughly, cover the literature and research methods, and even include blank versions of the tables. When we get the results, we can fill the numbers in on the tables and write a conclusion that tells the reader whether Durkheim was right or wrong. Thus, the researcher must have the format of the final publication very much in mind even while writing an initial proposal.

Empirical papers written according to the formal-operational approach often work best if organized according to what is sometimes called the **journal format** (Sociology Writing Group 1991). This format, which takes its name from the fact that several of the leading sociological journals appear to favor it, is designed to communicate the logic and results of studies undertaken to test well-defined hypotheses and theories. It consists of five parts: abstract, introduction, methods, results, discussion.

The **abstract** of a journal article is a short summary of its aims and findings, often stated in a single paragraph and seldom longer than three hundred words. The abstract must be carefully written to tell the reader exactly what the article is about, because many readers will decide whether or not to read the entire article on the basis of this brief summary. The reference periodical *Sociological Abstracts* consists of nothing but the abstracts of thousands of published papers, arranged under subject headings, with information about how to locate the publication itself. If you find it especially difficult to prepare an abstract for an article you have written, then either the article is not by nature a

research report or you have not structured the paper properly in the first place. A good research paper has a small number of key points, arranged in a logical sequence, and thus it can be abstracted successfully. A few journals that take a more humanistic or interpretive approach do not attempt to distill their essays into abstracts, for example the *International Journal of the Sociology of Language.*

The *introduction* usually combines a presentation of the scientific aims of the research with a review of the literature. When we speak of "the literature," we mean previous publications that laid the groundwork for the present study. Often, such a body of literature is so well developed that the researcher need not undertake any new theory construction. A fresh study of suicide rates and church membership would undoubtedly start its literature review with Durkheim, jump quickly to a few publications of the last two decades, then explain how the present study would advance knowledge.

The *methods* section explains how key concepts were operationalized and how appropriate data were collected. Often, the data already exist, and the methods section will refer the reader to other publications. For example, suicide statistics might have come from government publications, which must be cited, while church membership statistics have recently been published by special organizations dedicated to just this purpose. Naturally, the exact content of the methods section will depend on which research methods were actually used, and this entire textbook suggests the kinds of information that might be included.

The *results* section analyzes the data and usually sticks rather close to the data themselves. If two or more sets of data are being used, then there may be subsections for each set. Or, if the topic has two or more particular questions, each may be the subject of a subsection. For example, one part of the results section could report whether the data showed significant differences in suicide rates between Catholics and Protestants, while another part examined differences between church members and persons who did not belong to churches. Tables of numbers are generally found in this section.

The *discussion* evaluates the hypotheses and the theory in light of the data. Often, an author has difficulty separating the results from the discussion, especially if the results are crystal clear. Suppose the theory suggests three hypotheses, and each one is soundly contradicted by data presented in the results section. Then it may be difficult to say anything in the discussion beyond, "As we have just seen, all three hypotheses were soundly contradicted by the data, and thus we have good reason to reject the theory." But often the results are not so clear, and it may be necessary to explain why the present study came to different conclusions from earlier research. The discussion can also contain suggestions for future research and any other observations that bring the essay to a satisfactory conclusion.

Another workable outline is the set of eight steps Stark calls "the sociological process," although as we have noted, a given research project seldom covers all eight. It is worth emphasizing that many publications cover early steps in his model, because they are essays in theory construction rather than theory testing. Very different formats may be necessary if the research is primarily interpretive or descriptive, and exploratory research designed to discover new facts and hypotheses may be very hard to structure logically. Earlier we distinguished deduction from induction. The standard journal and proposal formats tend to assume a deductive approach.

Almost invariably, an agency offering grants prints up a set of guidelines for proposals. Sometimes there are two stages. First, the prospective researcher writes a brief letter, including answers to a few questions about the research, and the agency screens these letters to see which are appropriate studies for the particular source of funds. Second, researchers whose letters seem on target are asked to complete a lengthy formal proposal, following some version of the format discussed here. It may take weeks to write such a proposal. Frequently the agency asks the grant-seeker to include plans for publication and explain how the results will be made public. Often extensive information about the person doing the study is also required, in the form of a personal resumé or curriculum vitae.

A research team invariably includes one or more **principal investigators**, familiarly called *PIs*, the senior members of the team who will have primary responsibility for the project. One of the key factors determining whether the agency is going to provide the money is often the track record of the PI. Indeed, it often seems that the best way to win grants is to have won them in the past. Furthermore, some researchers become extremely adept at guessing exactly what the particular agency wants to hear. Despite much effort by talented and honest grant reviewers and administrators, a sense that grants are more often awarded to "insiders" rather than "outsiders" is widespread among sociologists.

In a sense, every journal and every grant-giving agency has its own "style." When writing an article for submission to a particular journal, it is extremely helpful to read through the past few years of that journal, noting features of articles that it accepted for publication. It is harder to do this for grant proposals, because successful proposals are not published. But research reports based on funded studies are published, and it might be wise to examine some before applying for a grant. Perhaps even more valuable is the chance to confer with colleagues who wrote successful proposals and ask their criticism of a draft you have written. There are even people who do this for a living; one of my best friends, for example, is an anthropologist who for years worked as a proposal editor for a research institute.

In recent years, grant money available to sociologists has declined steeply and steadily. Another main source of research funding is *contracts*. If you have an idea for a research project and you write a proposal seeking money, you are looking for a **research grant**. If the government wants some research done on a particular topic, and you volunteer to do it, you are seeking a **research contract.** Different research teams compete for these contracts, and the contracting agency will give them an outline of how to write their *bid* for the work. Such a proposal will differ from the grant-seeking proposal only in that the topic and relevant literature are already defined for the researcher. Much of the task is convincing the government agency that the particular team has the expertise to do the project successfully.

One set of grant-writing instructions I recently received from the National Science Foundation (1990:7) says:

> *What makes a good proposal?* A good proposal stems from a good project. Other things being equal, the better the project the more likely the proposal is to win an award. Proposers and their colleagues should first think through several iterations of the definition of the project. The best proposals are those to which the reviewers respond, "Of course. I wish I had thought of that!" Few proposals are this striking

and original, but most good ones begin with a good project.

Although you will hear many gripes from sociologists who feel that the grant-giving agencies are insensitive to the value of their particular kind of research, the fact is that the key decisions about grants are made by colleagues through the process called **peer review.** I have often been asked to review grant proposals in the areas of sociology I work in, and every grant proposal is reviewed by several of the proposer's colleagues. Thus the proposal, like the research report, remains an exercise in collegial communication, whatever aspects of a sales pitch it also has.

Because sociology is in all senses a human science—of the people, by the people, and for the people—we must be especially concerned with the implications of our research—both its methods and its findings—for human beings. Thus, the logic of research methodology must be supplemented with consideration of its ethics.

The Ethics of Research

In 1983, I attended a very special reunion at Harvard, organized by a sociologist friend of mine. It commemorated the twentieth anniversary of the firing of two famous faculty members, Timothy Leary and Richard Alpert. This dynamic duo was responsible for much of the psychedelic drug craze of the 1960s, and Harvard fired them mainly because they followed an approach to scientific experimentation that more conservative colleagues found offensive. Although Leary was a psychologist rather than a sociologist, he was a member of the Department of Social Relations, which included the sociology program, and some of his work in social psychology bordered on sociology. The Leary-Alpert research provides an excellent illustration of the ambiguity of

judgments about the ethics of experiments with human subjects.

In 1960, after trying mind-altering mushrooms in Mexico, Leary and Alpert obtained samples of the drug psilocybin and began a series of studies of its *psychedelic* or *consciousness-expanding* properties. Although some other researchers believed that psilocybin mimicked the symptoms of serious mental illness, Leary and Alpert believed it could give the user far greater psychological health and awareness of deeper truths than could be achieved otherwise. This was a basic disagreement about reality. Leary and Alpert acknowledged that the drugs were causing great changes in the undergraduates and other subjects who took them, but they claimed these changes were for the better. Not madness, but increased creativity, greater intelligence, and understanding of life were the results they claimed.

There should be no doubt that the psychedelic movement launched by Leary and Alpert, among others, was a radical, indeed deviant phenomenon. It challenged the very assumptions upon which conventional civilization rested (Wolfe 1969; Weil 1972). As Leary argued in his autobiography, the drugs could free the individual from the snares of a deceitful society and a misguided science:

> Since psychedelic drugs expose us to
> different levels of perception and
> experience, use of them is ultimately a
> philosophical enterprise, compelling us to
> confront the nature of reality and the
> nature of our fragile, subjective belief
> systems. The contrast is what triggers
> the laughter, the terror. We discover
> abruptly that we have been programmed
> all these years, that everything we accept
> as reality is just social fabrication. (Leary
> 1983:33)

Soon, Leary and Alpert were enmeshed in controversy. Harvard made them agree not to experiment with undergraduates, and the Massachusetts Public Health Department demanded that no research be done without the participation of a medical doctor. To this Leary and Alpert objected, citing well-grounded social-psychological justifications. The effects of psilocybin, they said, stemmed not merely from the drug itself but also from "set and setting." A person's **mental set** is the expectations a person brings to the situation. The **setting** is the social cues that tell the person how to interpret the situation. If research subjects were given psilocybin in a medical setting, they would interpret its effects medically, by reacting in psychotic-like terror. But if the subject were given the substance in a spiritually supportive setting, and had a mental set that included the expectation of rapture and enlightenment, the results would be positive (Benson and Smith 1967).

Sociologist Erich Goode (1972) has written about what he calls *the politics of reality*. For Goode, the beliefs of any society are mainly the product of a struggle for power over the minds of its members, and the definitions attached to psilocybin, LSD, and similar substances are both arbitrary and problematic. Thus, the very language with which we speak of these substances shapes our conclusions. To call them "psychotomimetic" (psychosis-mimicking) is to brand them harmful. To call them "psychedelic" (consciousness-expanding) is to brand them beneficial. To doctors, "drug abuse" means taking a drug without a doctor's prescription. Taken to the extreme, Goode's assertion about the politics of experience says that there is no objective way of deciding whether Leary and Alpert were right or wrong. Stressing the interpretive-advocacy mode of analysis rather than the formal-operational mode, it asserts that no interpretive school of thought is inherently superior to the others.

Today, precious few scientists are prepared to endorse what Leary and Alpert did, and few people believe that mystical enlightenment can be obtained from magic mushrooms and laboratory concoctions. However, this may be because Leary and Alpert lost their political battle. Harvard fired them, eventually the police arrested them, and their psychedelic movement dropped from the list of fads that had captured the popular mind. While I was a graduate student at Harvard in the early 1970s, my first teaching job was as an assistant for a psychiatrist who taught a popular class that still promulgated Leary's perspective. A decade later, the class and the psychiatrist were gone. The tide ran heavily against the course that Leary and Alpert had charted.

However much we may despise that course, and however convinced we may be that Leary and Alpert had abandoned the scientific approach, we cannot deny that their work raised very difficult ethical dilemmas. Leary and Alpert thought they were right; and in every generation there will be social scientists who are convinced that the trends of their day need to be resisted, honest and creative people who are prepared to put their own lives on the line and believe deeply that their work does good, not harm. Someday you may find yourself among their small but valiant number. No matter where scholarly consensus draws the line between valid and invalid research, some scholars will be working just across the border.

Ethics of Research on Human Subjects

Moral philosophers have long analyzed the basis of human **ethics**, and a few have offered systems for analyzing the ethical dimensions of particular scientific research projects. Paul Davidson Reynolds (1982:20–21; cf. 1979:43) has suggested that there are seven questions to ask:

1. What rights of various parties associated with the research activity—participants, investigators, society at large—may be affected?
2. What are the costs and benefits of the research program and this project?
3. What are the costs (or risks) and benefits for the participants?
4. What is the expected distribution of the costs and benefits?
5. How has respect for the rights and welfare of the participants been demonstrated?
6. To what extent has the personal treatment of the participants by the investigator(s) approached this ideal?
7. Which social scientist role definition, if any, would be consistent with the major features of the moral analysis?

Reynolds repeatedly stresses that both the researcher and the research subject have rights, and that the society has the right to a considerable amount of information about its members. Much research is necessary to guide government programs, and a variety of social problems cannot be successfully addressed without detailed, repeated scientific examination of their causes. However, people have some right to privacy, and it is generally felt that most kinds of research should be limited to volunteer subjects who have given informed consent.

A familiar exception is the United States census. By law, residents are required to respond fully and accurately to the census, and they do not have the legal right to refuse on grounds that it violates their privacy. In return, respondents are guaranteed that their data will be kept confidential for 72 years after the survey. The government has decided that the harm to individual respondents is negligible and the benefit to society so compelling that compulsion to participate is morally justified.

Most of Reynolds's seven points are clearly stated, but two deserve further comment. As the fourth point notes, both the benefits from research and the human costs of performing it are often unequally distributed throughout the population. Research on the progress of a disease may not at all help the research subjects, who may have recovered or died before the research results are published, but it may benefit later sufferers of the same ailment. Much sociological research concerns social conflict, and the findings may help some groups at the expense of others. Although it may be quite appropriate to conduct research aimed at increasing social justice, the researcher should be aware that groups benefiting from injustice will lose if the research is successful. In the area of deviant behavior and criminology, researchers must be conscious that their research may help either the institutions of social control or the people who wish that control loosened, but probably not both.

When Reynolds speaks of social scientists' role definition, he has in mind distinctions like the one we made between formal-operational and interpretive-advocacy research, but many other distinctions may be made between roles the researcher plays. Reynolds suggests that there are three professional roles social scientists commonly play, and that distinct ethical codes may apply to each: societal agent, social reformer, model citizen. As societal agents we seek to gain knowledge that will benefit society as a whole, but this leaves open the possibility that we can use some force and guile when investigating people who are outside of society, such as criminals. Social reformers in sociology typically seek to improve the lot of disadvantaged groups, and this may mean attacking the privilege and privacy of dominant groups who we may feel are exploiting the downtrodden. The model citizen, in contrast, must set a high standard of behavior and attempt to rise above the conflicts between groups in society.

Code of Ethics of the American Sociological Association

Ethical issues facing sociologists concern much more than just research. In its recently revised *Code of Ethics*, the American Sociological Association (1989) had to consider problems of authorship and plagiarism of publications, conflicts between teachers and students, ethical obligations of employers and employees, as well as matters relating to research. The *Code* also sets up procedures for dealing with ethical disputes of any kind.

The first section of the *Code* states, "Sociologists should adhere to the highest possible technical standards in their research, teaching and practice." Among other things, this means that we must never misrepresent the scope of our expertise. For example, a sociologist who has personally studied only one specialized field cannot claim to be an expert on others. In our publications, we must state results fully and accurately, giving the reader information about findings that contradict the author's theories and stating any qualifications that significantly limit the applicability of our findings. The aim of sociology is gaining correct, reliable knowledge, and it is a violation of scientific ethics to distort results, whether by making false and exaggerated claims or by leaving out critical information.

Of most relevance for this book are the ten principles concerning "disclosure and respect for the rights of research populations." First, sociologists should not mislead research subjects about the nature of the research.

Specifically, the *Code* prohibits not only individual fraud but also the secret gathering of information for governments or other organizations under the cover of sociological research. Part of this must be controversial for some sociologists, who might feel it is appropriate to work secretly for the CIA or other government agencies, and I know of cases in which social scientists have done this. But, certainly, sociology itself would be harmed by such behavior, and the ASA has taken a stand against it. Frankly, the worst that the association could do to someone who did work secretly for a government agency, in violation of this rule, would be to denounce the person and kick him or her out of the association. The person, in turn, could sue the association and a very messy conflict might follow.

Second, research participants have the right to biographical **anonymity**—that is, to privacy about the details of their lives. Exactly what this means, and how it would be applied to famous public figures about whom research might be done, are unclear. But the principle I draw from this is that I, as a sociologist, do not have the right to expose ordinary people to public scrutiny and possible ridicule.

Third—and this is the flip side of point two—we cannot pretend to provide confidentiality for information we take from public sources. This means we cannot promise kinds of privacy we cannot in fact ensure.

Fourth, we must protect research subjects from harm caused by our research and grant them the right to give informed consent, or to withhold participation, when the risks are greater than those experienced in everyday life.

Fifth, we must take into account the research subject's cultural and social situation in getting informed consent and preserving privacy. For example, we must not take advantage of the subject's lack of familiarity with social research to sneak something past him or her.

Sixth, we must anticipate possible threats to confidentiality. This means, for example, that we might want to use code names or numbers, rather than the real names of subjects, on their data in case the data somehow become public.

Seventh—and this is a very sticky point—we must protect **confidentiality** if we have promised it, even if authorities have the legal right to take our data. Let me quote the operative sentence: "Confidential information provided by research participants must be treated as such by sociologists, even when this information enjoys no legal protection and legal force is applied." If I read this correctly, this rule tells sociologists to violate the law, if necessary, to preserve confidentiality. That, I submit, is controversial.

Eighth, although we should acknowledge fully the contributions of co-workers in research ("collaborators"), circumstances may arise in which a collaborator wishes anonymity. If he or she does, we should provide it.

Ninth, in addition to regulations specifically established by the ASA, we should also follow guidelines published by the American Association of University Professors.

And tenth, we must comply with the regulations established by research funding agencies and relevant governments, among them rules requiring research proposals to be checked over by committees for the protection of human subjects.

I noted that points one and seven clearly are controversial, and in part they express the independence of professional sociology from the government. The *Code of Ethics* was developed by a committee, rather than by the entire membership of the association, and some sociologists undoubtedly disagree with some parts of it. As I have suggested, the penalties that the ASA could inflict upon somebody for actions that were lawful are limited.

Whatever the details, the *Code* is the result of considerable discussion among practicing sociologists who have thought deeply about the issues and really want their profession to be ethical. Thus, it deserves respect, whether or not one accepts every single principle in it. Each social researcher has the obligation to consider ethical issues and seek guidance in resolving them. At the very least, that we are social scientists gives us no special right to do things that harm the people we study,

and therefore such ethical practices as preservation of confidentiality and anonymity are vitally important.

Confidentiality and Anonymity

Perhaps the greatest common danger to the human subjects of sociological research is public disclosure of private secrets. In my research on strange religious cults, such as the more-or-less Satanic cult called the Process, which you will learn about in the following two chapters, I was always conscious that some of the individuals I was studying would eventually leave the occult world and reenter respectable, conventional society. When they did so, I felt, they should have the right to cast off their cultic pasts and pretend those years had never happened.

One of the Processeans I came to know best was a young man who had been working on his Ph.D. in one of the physical sciences before entering the group. He had published two scientific articles prior to joining, but threw himself fully into the mystical, communal life of the Process for 15 years. But then, when continuing crisis had convinced several members that the cult's hopes for achieving a supernatural plane of existence were futile, he left. Soon, he obtained an editorial job with a major scientific journal, and on the side he ran a weekly radio show. When my book was published, he interviewed me about it on his program. The only stipulation was that I should not mention the fact that he had been a member.

The most important rule, one followed by most field researchers, all laboratory experimenters, and many in other branches of sociology, is that our publications should not mention our research subjects by name. Often, we invent fake names—pseudonyms—so we can talk about individual research subjects without revealing their names. Perhaps the most famous sociological research subject was the young leader of the street-corner gang studied by William Foote Whyte (1943). Whyte gave this man the pseudonym "Doc," thus protecting him from fame or infamy when the book became extremely popular.

When you are writing a report about a group and need to use pseudonyms, you should draw up a chart listing all the real names with the pseudonyms next to them. Otherwise, you will get hopelessly lost. While writing my book on the Process, I had a chart of nearly a hundred such names. When the book was published, I destroyed it. At times, this effort seemed unnecessary to me, because the cult members had all assumed new names anyway. Now that none of the names is in use, with careful consideration of what I revealed about the individuals in my book, I can tell you from memory two of the name-pairs. The woman I called Sister Amaranth in my book was actually Sister Seraphin. She does not use that name now, and she did not use it before joining the cult. Because the names were supposed to express the person's spiritual reality, I tried to pick pseudonyms with the same flavor, while at the same time disguising the individual's identity. One fellow called himself Mephisto Mephistopheles Santana, but in the book he is Edgar Allan Poe. However, I am not about to tell you the pre-Process names of any of the people, because some of them have returned to those identities.

Anonymity can raise a few problems, even as it greatly solves the issue of subject protection. Years after my Process research, I received a series of phone calls from a man who said he was trying to locate his long-lost brother. My suspicions were aroused when he said his brother had an extensive career in crime before joining the cult, and I thought it possible that the man was lying to me about being the lost Processean's brother, and that he might have been hired to find him for a wicked purpose. The story seemed too pat. The caller said he was a disabled Vietnam veteran, raising his children without either employment or a wife, who had recently promised his dying mother to find her lost son. What tale could be better designed to wheedle the information out of me? After several conversations, the man had me pretty well convinced, but the problem was that

he did not know the pseudonym his brother had adopted in the cult, and my book contained only the second set of pseudonyms I had given members. Thus, I never could figure out exactly who the lost brother was. With great care, I assisted the man in contacting a few former members so he could continue his search. I may never know if I did the right thing.

Often sociologists give pseudonyms to the groups as well as the individuals they study. The literature is filled with reports on towns known only as Yankee City, Middletown, Bay City, Lake City. Usually, the real name of the community is an open secret among social scientists, but the general public is unaware. Whenever sociologists visit Boston, many will intentionally go to William Foote Whyte's "Cornerville" and have a meal at one of the numerous Italian restaurants found there, out of a kind of professional nostalgia.

It is hard to conceal completely the name of an entire community, and usually there are enough clues for the reader to solve the puzzle if he or she really wants to. For example, Hilltown is the pseudonym for a Massachusetts town studied by D. L. Hatch and made famous in an analysis of Hatch's research by George Homans (1950). It took me about ten minutes to learn the real name. I asked Homans, but he wouldn't tell me. I looked in the Massachusetts census, and there it was. The publications had given the exact population of Hilltown for several years, and all one had to do was find a match in government census reports.

A fascinating example is the German town described by William Sheridan Allen (1984) in his book *The Nazi Seizure of Power.* Allen's excellent research had charted how the Nazis won political power in a single community, and his data included personal interviews with participants, as well as documents and the town's newspapers. In the first edition, he gave pseudonyms to the town and all its named inhabitants. But the German press soon figured out the real name of the town, and once that information was public, it was impossible to conceal any longer the identities of the community officials. When I assigned the book in one of my courses, a student who was the daughter of two survivors of Nazi concentration camps called Allen on the phone and asked what the town was really called. He told her, not because he felt a victim of the Nazis had a special right to know, but because the secret had gotten out anyway, and thus Allen had no obligation to conceal it any longer. In his second edition, based on much new information, Allen gives all the real names.

When I originally wrote about the Process, I called it the Power. Two other groups that figured in the story were called the Establishment and Technianity. At that time, a group calling itself the Process still existed, and I felt I should leave it free to work out its own destiny, unhampered by any publicity generated by my book. However, one of the newspapers found at supermarket check-out counters had no difficulty guessing the actual name of the group. Their editorial office contacted me to confirm the guess, but I refused. These journalists were about to publish their speculations anyway, when I worked out a deal with them that I would consent to be the subject of one of their stories, so long as they did not name the group. The story they published ("My Nightmare Year in Satanic Cult!"), illustrated with a very silly picture of me, was filled with inaccuracies, but at least it left the secret unrevealed.

After the book appeared, two reviewers complained that I had limited the scholarly usefulness of the research by not giving the correct names of the groups. Both complaining reviews appeared in British journals. This reflects that the debates over the rights of human subjects had at that time been occurring mainly within American social science, and that the British hadn't yet fully confronted the ethical issues.

Then, the last fragment of the cult still calling itself the Process went out of business. Although the major part of the Process still exists, it uses a quite different name and is located geographically far from its old stamping grounds. Especially because several other authors have identified the group, I feel free to give the correct name now, even though I refused to do so while the group still might be harmed by public disclosure.

My colleague in field research on cults, John Lofland (1966), used pseudonyms for the doomsday cult he studied, its members, and the cities it was in. Years after the research, when Lofland was preparing a second edition of his book, many sociologists felt he should at least name the group, its founder, and its locations correctly, while continuing to protect the identity of individual members. Everybody knew the correct name of the group, it seemed to us, and the leader was a public figure named in hundreds of newspaper articles. Lofland, however, had originally promised the group that he would conceal its identity, and he faithfully kept his pledge in the second edition.

Throughout this book, I will occasionally point out ethical and political problems with particular kinds of research. Except for a couple of projects at the end of Chapters 2 and 3, however, none of the work I suggest for you to do will directly raise moral issues. All the data on your computer disks were originally collected by me, or by the government, and they are offered to you clear of any ethical entanglements. However, the research experiences you can gain through the software should stand you in good stead when you actually undertake research in the real world, and this text will prepare you to think about the ethical issues.

CHAPTER SUMMARY

This chapter outlines the logic and ethics of social research. To begin with, there are two main kinds of sociology: the *formal-operational* type and the *interpretive-advocacy* type. This split is similar but not identical to the distinction between quantitative and qualitative research, or between the natural sciences and the humanities.

Like the natural sciences, the *formal-operational* approach to social research is both rational and empirical. Science is the systematic framing and testing of hypotheses about nature, sometime called *hypothetico-deductive* research. Before any hypothesis can be tested, one must decide how to define and measure its concepts, a process called *operationalization*. The chapter illustrates this process through the theory that religion prevents suicide. In science, we use the term *theory* to refer to a statement that can generate two or more potentially testable hypotheses. Logically, we *deduce* from a theory various *hypotheses* whose concepts can be empirically operationalized. We then perform research. If the data support the hypotheses, then the theory is also supported. If the data fail to support the hypotheses, then our confidence in the theory is greatly weakened.

The interpretive-advocacy approach to social research is similar to literature or political ideology. *Interpretive* sociology seeks the human meaning of a social phenomenon, to document what certain situations and experiences mean to their participants or to *advocate* the writer's values, politico-economic beliefs, or other personal commitments. Thus, interpretive research becomes a *reflexive* medium through which sociologists can express their personal feelings, as well as those of the people they study. Although many sociologists practice the interpretive-advocacy mode of research, the formal-operational mode is more readily taught as a scientific methodology, and thus it will be emphasized in this book.

Luck plays a role in scientific discoveries, and the invention of theories and testable hypotheses is as much an art as a science. However, the process of testing theories is far more rigorous. Every good theory is falsifiable, and it must be possible to test a theory—to put it at risk of falsification—before it is of much value for science. If we could not, in principle, imagine evidence that would disprove a theory, then the theory must not say anything decisive about reality. In the formal-operational mode, a theory is a set of formal statements (propositions), linked by a system of deductions showing how some propositions follow logically from others. *Formal explanation* of a specific proposition consists in showing that it follows logically from one or more general propositions. Ideally, the logic should be as rigorous as that in mathematics.

Rodney Stark described "the sociological process," an eight-step model of how sociologists construct and test theories. The first three steps are parts of theory construction: *wonder, conceptualize, theorize*. Theory testing consists of measurement (*operationalize* and *hypothesize*) and research (*observe* and *analyze*). Finally, we *assess* the theory in light of our research findings.

In formal-operational sociology, there is a partnership between data collection and statistical analysis; together they constitute research. But styles of professional writing are also important. Before a research project is funded, a proposal must be written. The final results are often communicated through the journal format, in an essay consisting of five parts: abstract, introduction, methods, results, discussion.

Whatever approach or writing style is used, social research must attend to ethical issues, especially concerning the people who are studied and whose lives are described in publications. Like other professional organizations, the American Sociological Association has established a code of ethics. Confidentiality and anonymity are among the important principles that protect the rights of human subjects.

KEY CONCEPTS FOR CHAPTER 1

CHAPTER

2 Observation

CHAPTER OUTLINE

Field Observation

Investigating a Deviant Subculture

Research Roles
Ethnographer
Participant Observer
Field Theorist
Covert and Overt Observer
Roles in Group Being Studied

Standard Techniques of Data Collection
Diary of Field Observations
Artifact Collection

Photographic Documentation
Social Maps
Taking a Census

Systematic Observation of Small Groups
Bales's Research
Adapting Bales's Approach

Limitations of Qualitative Research

The Ethics of Field Research

 The Social Map Computer Program

Projects for Chapter 2

CHAPTER OVERVIEW

Observational research performed in the field (some part of the real world) is often called *ethnography* or *participant observation*. Observation may be done either overtly, with the people under observation aware of the investigator's work, or covertly. Because researchers might inadvertently affect the social phenomenon they are studying, they usually seek to be unobtrusive, and their role is a key factor shaping the results. The people under observation play roles as well, such as gatekeeper and native informant.

The standard techniques of qualitative research include a diary of field observations,

an artifact collection, documentary photography, and social maps. Quantitative data can be collected in the field as well, for example by taking a census of people participating in an activity or group or by adapting laboratory methods such as interaction process analysis. Because the field researcher gains much information about private lives, very important ethical issues arise concerning this kind of work.

This chapter introduces the first program in the accompanying software: CULT. It is based on research on the Process Church of the Final Judgement, a communal cult that worshipped several gods. Illustrating social maps, time schedules, and diary keeping, this program gives you an imaginary tour of the cult's chapter house.

Thus, although we will do some of our work with a computer simulation, we begin our examination of sociological research techniques out in the real world, learning about methods that give the researcher the most direct possible contact with people under study. We will look at social settings and listen to what people say spontaneously, through unobtrusive observation. The next chapter will introduce interviewing, a more aggressive technique, and many of the points made there apply here as well, such as advice on how to achieve rapport and how to interact with research subjects. Both observational and interview research can be quantitative, and often the desired end result is a set of statistics that can be used to test theories, but we shall emphasize more qualitative and exploratory approaches. You are encouraged to get out into the field, to observe and interview real people, but our software provides you with programs simulating qualitative research. Although nothing can replace actual field experience, the computer software can give you experience thinking through issues about field research and carrying out a systematic data collection project.

_____ Field Observation

Research conducted in real-world settings, by watching and listening but without intrusive experimental manipulations or formal survey questionnaires, is called **observational research**. Many practitioners of this art use **field research** as a synonym for *observational research*, although others prefer to make a number of fine distinctions among the many research techniques they use when they escape the ivory tower and the laboratory and venture out into the world. Sociologists sometimes casually refer to field research methods as if they were radically different from other approaches, but this is false. *The field is not a method. It is a place.* Although much field research is qualitative in nature, and this chapter will emphasize qualitative approaches, you should be alert to the bountiful possibility for quantitative observational research done in natural field settings.

A great example is provided by a study done in and around Nashville, Tennessee, in 1968, by Lawrence S. Wrightsman (1969). This is one of my favorite studies, partly because it produced an excellent article published in one of the major journals but was dirt-cheap to do. I like clever studies that accomplish much on a shoestring.

1968 was the year of a divisive presidential election campaign. Lyndon Johnson announced he wasn't going to run for re-election, and his vice-president, Hubert Humphrey, was forced to defend Johnson's Vietnam policies despite disagreeing with them. Richard Nixon had returned from a pair of apparently terminal election defeats and was leading the Republican ticket. And George Wallace, governor of Alabama, was making a strong third-party run. Wallace claimed to be in favor of "law and order," but many commentators thought his campaign was really about racism, supported by socially and economically frustrated whites who were angry about the gains blacks had achieved in the civil rights movement.

Wrightsman found a delightfully simple way to test whether Wallace supporters really believed in law and order or were merely using this slogan to cover less admirable values. Nashville had recently passed a law requiring each car registered there to carry a fifteen-dollar tax sticker. Most people dutifully bought the stickers and put them on their cars, but some people defied the law and did not. Wrightsman used presence of the sticker on a car as an operational definition of obeying the law and considered car owners who did not display the sticker to be disobeying the law.

Researchers visited many public parking lots around town, looking for cars with political bumper stickers. They found many sporting pro-Nixon, pro-Humphrey, and pro-Wallace stickers. The researchers checked the license plate to make sure the car was registered in Nashville, rather than belonging to a visitor, and they looked for the tax sticker. If Wallace supporters were really law-and-order people, their cars should have the required tax sticker more often than cars belonging to Nixon and Humphrey supporters.

Out of several hundred Nixon cars registered in Nashville, 86.5 percent had the tax sticker. The proportion was exactly the same, 86.5 percent, for the Humphrey cars. But only 74.8 percent of the Wallace cars bore the required tax sticker. Apparently, Wallace supporters were not really in favor of law and order. Rather, Wrightsman speculated, the Wallace campaign represented defiance of established authority and a rejection of the actions of bureaucrats.

Great care was taken in this study. The researchers were concerned that poorer people might have found the fifteen-dollar sticker a great burden, and that Wallace cars might lack them simply because their owners could not afford them. So they collected information on the vintage of the cars, feeling that owners of new cars would be more able to afford the stickers than owners of old cars. But there was essentially no difference. That Wrightsman's study was cheap does not mean it was scientifically sloppy. With care, good observational research can be done without the investment of much money.

Working alongside Wrightsman, John McCarthy studied the behavior of drivers at a stop sign. Cars with Wallace stickers on them were significantly more likely than Nixon or Humphrey cars to run the sign without stopping. If you have some imagination, are willing to spend some time outdoors, and have a clear theory, you too may achieve great

scientific gains in a systematic but cheap observational study.

Wrightsman's study allows me to make several points. First, observational research is usually **unobtrusive** (Webb, Campbell, Schwartz, and Sechrest 1966), gathering information without disturbing or influencing the people being observed. This is often not true of surveys or interviews, which may ask people to think about matters they never considered before, and it is certainly not true of experiments, which by definition involve doing something to the research subjects and watching for its consequences. Because it is unobtrusive, observational research tells us how people actually behave in real situations, unaffected by the social scientist.

Second, good observational research is systematic. To be sure, much of the work a sociologist does in the field may be exploratory, and we can never predict what new social phenomenon is suddenly going to bite us on the nose. As noted, much of the research covered in this chapter is qualitative, but that does not imply it is unsystematic. Exploration aside, observational research needs to meet the same high standards as other research methods, with respect to systematic collection of data.

Third, observational research requires comparison. Sometimes the comparison is explicit, and the researcher's report draws contrasts between the findings of his or her study and earlier work. When William Foote Whyte (1943) described the well-organized social life in Boston's Italian North End, he explicitly disagreed with the assumption of many earlier sociologists that slum areas were inherently disorganized. Often the comparison is implicit. For example, the field researcher will have read reports of earlier studies of a similar nature and will have them in the back of his or her mind. Before I studied the Process cult (Bainbridge 1978), I had prepared myself through reading *Doomsday Cult*, by John Lofland (1966), and *When Prophecy Fails*, by Leon Festinger, H. W. Riecken, and Stanley Schachter (1956), studies of similar groups.

_____ Investigating a Deviant Subculture

This chapter and the next will draw heavily on an observational research project I did at the beginning of the 1970s, a study of a more-or-less Satanic religious cult called the Process. As I write this, a minor Satanism panic is sweeping the country, and many people believe that a nationwide conspiracy of Satan-worshippers is behind many strange events. For example, just a few days ago our local newspaper reported that a dead goat had been found in a river, and examination of the body revealed that it had been the victim of a Satanic cult. The sexual region had been mutilated and the horns cut off, presumably for later use in weird Satanic rituals. The newspaper said that an anti-Satanism task force, composed of clergy and police, was meeting to decide how best to respond to this threat.

For months, I have been receiving requests to speak at local gatherings on the threat of Satanism to our community, and I was interviewed by one of the TV networks that was preparing a lurid "documentary" about the Satanic Conspiracy. I had to tell both of them that I doubted there was any Satanic threat. To be sure, deranged people may adopt any set of symbols to express the emotional torment they feel, and Satanic symbols have been involved in a few cases across our vast nation. But Satanism exists mainly in the minds of people who are afraid of it, and irresponsible people in the mass media have been trumpeting the idea of a Satanic Conspiracy primarily, I suspect, to build ratings and increase their salaries.

Oh yes, about that goat. Immediately after the newspaper report, a farmer came forward (dare I say "sheepishly"?) and admitted that he had dumped the goat's body in the river. The goat had died from natural causes, and a pack of dogs had caused the mutilation that had convinced a few hysterical people that Satanism was in their midst. The horns had been removed long before so that the goat wouldn't poke the farmer when it got angry at him.

Often, the mass media and the general public perceive minority groups and deviant subcultures through the dark glasses of mythology. Every manner of evil is attributed to strangers, and the popular perceptions of many social phenomena are undoubtedly inaccurate in the extreme. The only way to find out what an unfamiliar group of people is like is to go and look. Responsible field researchers, preferably trained to observe carefully and systematically, must do a reconnaissance of unfamiliar social territory; and if warranted by the topic's relevance for social theory or public policy, they must follow this up with other kinds of research, such as those described throughout this book.

Satanism is a trivial example. I got interested in the Process Church of the Final Judgement not because of images of horror associated with Satan in the public mind, but because I thought that research on it might advance our thinking about deviant subcultures in general, and religious subcultures in particular. I had just completed six months' research on another group that claimed to be very scientific in its approach to spiritual questions, and I thought the emotional and dramatic Process would provide good contrast. A few days of observation revealed to me that the group was polytheistic, that it had several gods, and that each deity represented a different moral code and type of human personality. This added another dimension of sociological interest, because there is some question as to whether a beleaguered minority subculture can afford to have sharply conflicting norms and values within its limited social world.

In fact, I`had briefly investigated several other cults for possible study, including Transcendental Meditation, Hare Krishna, and a couple of local communes. A combination of "field researcher's intuition" and sober analysis had convinced me that much could be learned from the Process, and that it would better repay the great commitment of extended observation than would the other groups. Over the period of five and a half years, I intermittently spent a total of about two years studying the group. I published a scientific book on the Process

(Bainbridge 1978), and the experience gained contributed greatly to my work with Rodney Stark on the theory of religious movements (Stark and Bainbridge 1985, 1987). My later quantitative research on religion was deeply rooted in the earlier observational work.

Much observational research has been done in the sociology of religion, but several other fields have made great use of this approach as well. Community studies, industrial sociology, race and ethnic relations, and medical sociology are only a few such fields. For a century, field research on the conditions faced by disadvantaged groups have contributed to our understanding of poverty, and much of our knowledge about how business organizations function has been based on data collected through direct observation.

This chapter, and the next one on interviewing techniques, will draw heavily on my Process research. Because of all the observational and interview data in my files, I can give you an especially realistic view of the challenges and opportunities of field methods, using examples from the Process. The first two computer programs, the one designed to go with this chapter and the one for the next, will focus on the Process. Frankly, one prime justification is that you, presumably, don't know anything about the cult. Therefore, you can experience the struggles of real research and the thrill of discovery, uncovering the facts about this strange group and trying to make sense of them.

I will tell you just a little. The Process was founded in London, England, around 1963, by a couple who had been trained to be psychotherapists within a widespread pseudoscientific cult that they had just left. Soon, about two dozen people were intensely involved in a process of spiritual discovery using a number of techniques taken from various brands of psychoanalysis and religious cults. The founders were well-educated people, many with backgrounds in the arts, and they invested a tremendous amount of talent and energy inventing—as they saw it—an entirely new civilization.

In 1966, disgusted with the poor response they were getting from staid London society, they left to seek a tropical island paradise where they could build their new civilization. For a time, they lived together in a ruined coconut plantation on the north coast of Mexico's Yucatan peninsula. Socially isolated and completely captivated by dreams of glory and spiritual transcendence, they explored deeper and deeper into the dark recesses of the mind. By the standards of the world they had left, they were going collectively insane. Weird visions came to them, and they adopted radically new identities, attempting to discard their previous natures and transmute into beings elevated above mere humanity. They failed, of course, but it was a grand attempt actually to achieve what many people merely daydream about.

Their wanderings continued into 1969, and they reemerged in London as a particularly striking new religion, complete with fresh doctrines, dramatic rituals, haunting music, and stunning caped uniforms. Having swelled in numbers during their quests, they established branches in Boston, Chicago, Toronto, New Orleans, and New York City. I met them in Boston, in 1970, and began my research. Later, I will explain the computer program that lets you explore the Boston Chapter House, where I first observed the rituals. But before I do, we should consider a number of observational techniques used by researchers studying a wide range of real-world social phenomena.

_____ **Research Roles**

One way to conceptualize a field researcher's work is in terms of the roles he or she may play. Among others, the sociologist may play the roles of ethnographer, participant observer, field theorist, and covert or overt observer.

Ethnographer

Although the field researcher may employ a range of quantitative techniques and may examine any aspect of the social situation, a common role researchers play is to perform ethnography, as many anthropologists do. An **ethnographer** is a trained, professional documenter of the culture of a group. Sociologist William Foote Whyte (1984) has referred to his own qualitative field research techniques as anthropological, and there is no shame in a sociologist drawing upon the extensive experience of practitioners of our sister science. In undertaking my field research on religious groups and aerospace organizations, I was most inspired by the work of anthropologists like Bronislaw Malinowski (1927, 1929, 1961).

Malinowski established a high standard for ethnographic research early in the century. Writing in the *American Sociological Review,* Murray Wax (1972:3) said, "Malinowski must be credited with pioneering personal in-depth field study of a single people," and sociologists as well as anthropologists are greatly in his debt. Among the essential principles were that the researcher must invest a great deal of time in the field, living with the people under study. He or she must learn to communicate with them in their own terms, which may require learning a difficult language. A great deal of data must be collected, and this work must be done both systematically and resourcefully.

As Michael W. Young (1979) summarizes Malinowski's methodological techniques, they fall into three categories. First, the ethnographer must document the structure of the culture under study, amassing a collection of maps, censuses, genealogies, statements of norms, observations of normative behavior, and charts summarizing the customs associated with each societal institution. Second, minute, detailed observations of daily life must be made, both to flesh out the formal structure of the culture and to learn how the human beings who inhabit it experience its important features. Third, the field worker must assemble a kind of library, composed of stories, folklore, narratives of life, ritual scripts, and any other kind of expression by the members of the culture that help us understand what the culture means to them.

Sociological field researchers have often failed to note that anthropological ethnography rests upon a key assumption: The people under study possess a relatively homogeneous, shared culture. If this is true, then the anthropologist can study the culture without worrying very much about obtaining data from a random sample of people or analyzing the relative strengths of different tendencies in the population.

Consider language. When the anthropologist visits an exotic people, in some far-off corner of the world, he or she must typically begin by learning the language. Often, this is done at a mission or a trading post, where a few "natives" happen to be spending time and can be paid to teach the anthropologist their language. This works, because any competent member of the "tribe" the anthropologist wants to study knows the language perfectly well. If a tribe were ever found in which none of the members spoke the same language—an absurdity, to be sure—then the key assumption would be erroneous, and the anthropologist could not learn the linguistic aspects of the culture satisfactorily from one or two key informants. As it happens, in some societies women's language is very different from men's language (Haas 1964), and even though both sexes understand what a person says in either, to study the speech of a single person is not identical with learning the language of the culture.

In complex modern society, it may be thoroughly fallacious to argue that a coherent, unitary culture exists that can be studied through observation of a few individuals in a limited geographic and social setting. Much of the best sociological ethnography has involved deviant subcultures, distinct groups of people with unusual shared beliefs, values, and behaviors. Other good ethnographies have involved religious denominations, which, though not necessarily deviant, usually can be said to possess a well-defined culture. The assumption of cultural unity *may* hold for a subculture, just as it *may* hold for the presumably simple societies classically studied by anthropologists. But often, the phenomenon we call a subculture may in fact be almost as varied as the larger culture itself, and in such cases qualitative ethnography is a highly dubious research approach.

For example, ethnographic studies have been published purporting to describe abortion clinics (in general) based on visiting a single clinic. No justification was given for supposing that the particular clinic was typical, or that observation of it gave the researcher knowledge of a culture it shared with other clinics. You should be skeptical of any ethnographic reports that claim to cover a general phenomenon, such as "the violent gang" or "the cult," if only one example was observed in any great depth. And you should be doubly skeptical if observations were very brief.

Participant Observer

Instead of calling themselves ethnographers, sociologists often refer to themselves as participant observers. **Participant observation** generally means qualitative, field-observational research, and it does not necessarily imply that the phenomenon under investigation is a coherent culture (McCall and Simmons 1969). The term suggests quite plainly that the researcher was not aloof from the phenomenon under study but participated in it to some extent, sharing the experiences of ordinary (non-researcher) participants. Depending on the subject of the research and the researcher's own characteristics and inclinations, the stress may be on participation, on observation, or on any combination of the two.

Many studies have been done by sociology students who had a nonacademic job, out in the "real world," and did their dissertations or other projects on their workplace. Professional experience achieved actually holding down a job in the field may later be a very valuable knowledge base upon which to build a sociological analysis. For example, Pamela McKenzie-Rundle used to be a police

polygraph examiner—a person who interviews suspects using a "lie detector"—and her expertise contributed greatly to a journal article on lie-detector tests written in collaboration with her sociology professor (Davis and McKenzie-Rundle 1984). In one amusing study, a researcher spent eleven days as the Easter Bunny at a shopping center (Hickey, Thompson, and Foster 1988). He learned what it meant to be socialized into a fantasy role—becoming the Easter Bunny—by dressing in a bunny costume and posing for pictures with kids. This is similar to how Howard Becker learned about dance musicians:

> I gathered the material for this study by participant observation, by participating with musicians in the variety of situations that made up their work and leisure lives. At the time I made the study I had played the piano professionally for several years and was active in musical circles in Chicago. . . . I worked with many different orchestras and many different kinds of orchestras during that period and kept extensive notes on the events that occurred while I was with other musicians. I seldom did any formal interviewing, but concentrated rather on listening to and recording the ordinary kinds of conversation that occurred among musicians. Most of my observation was carried out on the job, and even on the stand as we played. (Becker 1963:83–84)

Sometimes the researcher becomes so fully involved as a participant that the research never gets done. In one extreme case, graduate students were sent to observe deviant cults. One came back as a committed member, and another never came back at all. The opposite extreme is pure observation without participation. In the summer of 1970 I documented artistically painted vans and automobiles by wandering through the streets of Boston, photographing psychedelic cars. I never painted my own car, I talked with only one person who had actually done any painting, and I spent one afternoon of observation perched on a foot-bridge across a major highway, a great distance above the vehicles I was studying.

Field Theorist

One of the ways through which participant observation in groups that are not coherent cultures can contribute to the advance of scientific sociology is if the researcher is primarily a theorist who uses real-world experiences to inspire his or her theories. We can describe this as the role of **field theorist**. There is no need for the phenomena observed to be precisely typical of anything, so long as they encourage the field theorist to think deeply. The field is especially good at challenging our ideas, giving us counterexamples that violate our assumptions or logical conclusions, thus forcing us to consider carefully whether our theory is correct and complete. Ultimately, a theory developed through unsystematic observation must be tested by other means.

Covert and Overt Observer

An important distinction concerning participant-observer roles is that between overt and covert observation. When the people being observed are aware that this is happening and understand that the researcher is a social scientist, we speak of **overt observation**. If the people under observation are unaware, perhaps even actively deceived about the researcher's identity and purposes, then we speak of **covert observation**. Many of Becker's fellow dance musicians had no idea that he was also a sociology student, and the Easter Bunny researcher had not informed either the kids or the photographers that he was a sociologist. (Or maybe he really WAS the Easter Bunny, pretending to be a sociologist in order to study US!) I studied the Process cult as a covert observer, pretending to be a depressive piano tuner who had become a real believer, and I maintained that disguise for more than five years. When I do field research on the space program, however, the organizations under study are entirely aware of who I

am and what I am doing, and I frequently obtain an official NASA "press pass" so I can quickly communicate this information to people I meet.

Roles in Group Being Studied

We can also identify roles that members of the group under study may play for you. Very important, especially early in your research, are gatekeepers. A **gatekeeper** is a person with some special authority to keep you out of the group you want to study, or assist you in getting in. In formal organizations, these are people in positions of authority, for example the chief executive officer of a corporation. But the person's authority need not be very great, if he or she has been given special responsibility for dealing with outsiders. Many large school systems have a designated person to deal with researchers. I conducted my last piece of research on one particular religious cult with the help of its public relations officer, rather than with the help of the people actually in charge of the organization. Persons in positions of informal leadership may also be gatekeepers, and you may need to do a little preliminary research around the edges of the group before you can find the best entry gate and determine how best to approach the gatekeeper.

Sometimes you can gain entry with the help of a low-status person who happens to be in the right place and is willing to take a risk for you. This is like climbing in the back window rather than walking through the gate, and I am tempted to call these people *windowkeepers*. One of my students who wanted to study high school students in Japan sought permission from the education minister. This high-status gatekeeper refused to give permission, but my student was able to do the research anyway, with the help of a couple of friendly teachers. Often, you may need the support of some group members before you can convince a gatekeeper. A student of mine who wanted to survey physicians was helped in his contacts with the hospital administration by the fact that his father and several of his father's friends were doctors associated with the administration.

After the gatekeeper, the most important role members can play for you is that of native informant. A **native informant** is a member of the group under study who is willing and able to provide you with reliable information for your research. In a sense, these informants are informal research assistants. Anthropologists make heavy use of native informants, often hiring them to do the job full-time. This can be a little risky, because other members of the group may come to feel that your native informant is a paid spy. Also, too much financial reward for reporting interesting facts can cause some informants to begin making things up, feeding you whatever stories happen to excite you and fit your theories. If you are able to develop considerable rapport with the group, then many of its members will become native informants, and these potential problems will be greatly lessened.

A troublesome role natives often play, especially with overt observers, is that of *exploiter*. The observer often has resources that members of the group under study want. They will ask for rides to distant places, attempt to borrow money, urge you to intercede for them with those in authority, get you to act as a go-between in romantic liaisons, expect you to defend them against their enemies, eat your food, and even sleep in your bed. Aside from the great burden they can place upon you, exploiters can foul up your relations with the other people in the group, at worst completely destroying your research project.

Finally, both the researcher and the researched can become exchange partners. When two people exchange things of value between them, each giving the other something he or she wants in return for something desired, then the two are *exchange partners*. In a sense, this is always the case in overt research. The observer gives something, if only intangible respect and interest, in return for the information. But often the researcher must, in a sense, buy the information or the right to observe by giving the members of the group something they need. In some cases, the researcher must reciprocate the gift of information by sharing the research results. At other times, material payment is required, often in some form other than money. For example, when using photography as a research tool, I frequently gave prints of the best photos to the people I had photographed. One excellent way to get a long interview is to drive the person you want to talk with to a distant destination and chat along the way. And many groups may expect you to participate in the work that real group members are doing if you want to observe it.

Standard Techniques of Data Collection

Sociologists employ many techniques of data collection in the field. Several are used also in other disciplines, including diaries of field observation (anthropology), artifact collections (archaeology), photographic documentation (journalism), social maps (geography), and censuses (demography).

Diary of Field Observations

The classic, anthropological research tool, into which all others connect, is the **diary of field notes**. In its simplest form, this diary will be a chronicle of observations, divided into days and perhaps into separate scenes. If, for example, on a given day studying a particular commune you visited three places (the farmhouse, the hammock roping building, and the swimming hole), each of these three could be a separate scene. Each scene should begin with a statement of the time, date, and place of the observations, with other appropriate introductory information such as a list of the people present, the purpose of the social gathering, and the like. The main section of each of these scenes consists of a chronicle of events and interesting observations, given as much as possible in the exact order they occurred.

If you write your diary actually in the field, you will probably have to do it longhand, just the way the anthropologists do. I know of one anthropologist who carried a small typewriter on his back for months, trekking through the central African jungle, but his physical stamina is greater than mine, and I suspect greater than yours. Contemporary lap-top microcomputers present another option, assuming they won't get stolen where you are likely to go.

If it is feasible to use a word processor, you need to be cautious about editing. Your field notes should probably be preserved exactly as they were originally written. You can always append comments and footnotes when you get added information. For example, if you encounter someone in your work but don't learn his or her name immediately, you can insert an asterisk (*) in your original notes and write the name at the bottom of the page—or use the footnoting function of a word processor. But you should keep your original perceptions and observations in the exact language you used when you first wrote them down.

A diary need not be limited to a simple chronological account of what you saw, hour by hour. I always include some running appendices that are not exactly chronological. For example, I draw a set of social maps, such as are described later in this chapter, adding to them day by day. Studying a religious group, I would have special pages to list the hymns sung in each church service, an estimate of the number of people attending each one, and other details concerning regular events that might conveniently be placed outside the basic chronicle.

Another appendix might be a set of thumbnail sketches of individual people you meet. If you are using an ordinary notebook, for example, you might set aside several pages at the back, writing the name of each person as you meet them at the top of a page. As you get information about the individual, you can write it on his or her page. For example, one day you might learn the formal role the person has in the organization you are studying, and write that down. A few days later, you may learn the person's birthplace and something about what he or she did before joining the organization. Despite the fact that these appendixes are not chronological, you probably will want to date many of the entries you make in them, because the information may change with time.

Although it is often possible to make rough notes while you are watching the events unfold, usually you must make entries afterwards, sometimes even a few hours later when you can get some privacy. This means you must cultivate an accurate memory, something that mainly requires practice, and learn how to take just the crucial notes that will keep you from forgetting when you are actually in the field. After a long day in the field, it can seem an intolerable burden to spend two hours or more writing furiously, and fatigue will both encourage forgetting and motivate you to seek excuses for not having to write it all down. But you do. It is crucial to keep a thorough diary of everything that might conceivably be of use to your study. Perhaps the greatest problem is simply getting yourself to invest enough energy into it. Aware of that, you need to push yourself to keep going and challenge yourself to find the material interesting.

Blanche Geer described her method as follows: "At the end of a six-hour day in the field, I dictated an account of what I had seen and heard, occasionally inserting comments on the material or appending an interpretive summary" (Geer 1964). Some ethnographers, in contrast, do not put any interpretive material in the diary, preferring to keep it a pure record of direct observations. If you decide to incorporate interpretations, you should clearly label them as such, much as a responsible newspaper separates editorial opinions from the straight news articles. But you should be thinking about what you are observing, and saving your tentative interpretations in some form. A way that I personally find quite practical is to begin writing one or two working papers soon after launching the project. A **working paper**, in this context, is an essay that is constantly being modified, updated, and subjected to sharp criticism by the field researcher, to help him or her develop a theoretical interpretation of the data that are piling up.

In my own experience, there usually come several episodes when the field diary is just too tedious to write. At these times, the field situation itself seems boring, and I appear to be learning nothing. But if you really struggle with yourself at these moments of research crisis, you may come up with some of your best theoretical analyses. This is a good time, also, to consider augmenting the diary with other techniques and perhaps reading the diary from the beginning to see if there are insights you have missed or an encouraging progress in your understanding that might reinvigorate your diary writing.

Artifact Collection

Perhaps because they have little else to study, archaeologists are thoroughly conscious of the importance of **artifacts**, material objects created or used by the people under study that may reveal much about them. Sociologists have not been as imaginative or industrious as they might in learning from the archaeologists, but things can speak volumes.

For several years I taught a seminar in field research methods, and collecting artifacts proved to be among the most popular and sociologically interesting projects. One student documented the tools of a professional stonecutter, bringing in several of the smaller tools and collecting pictures of the huge ones. It wasn't enough to know that a particular tool was a hammer; a stonecutter has many hammers. The student interviewed the stonecutter to learn what each tool was used for, and this helped the student learn the many kinds of work this person did for many kinds of clients.

One student surprised us all by bringing a woman FBI agent to class. The collection of artifacts consisted of all the special items an FBI agent carried on her person, which included

two loaded revolvers. You might think there was little of sociological interest to be gained from inspecting an FBI agent's gun, but in fact we learned something very interesting. The type of bullet used in the heavier revolver was designed to cause maximum injury to the person it hit, rather than merely stop the person and permit an arrest, and it might have been judged "illegal" if used in warfare.

Most of the other very interesting artifact collections also reflected particular professions and were of significant monetary value. One student, however, was able to get great sociological mileage out of trash collected after a major sporting event. Of course, ticket stubs and programs contain much information, but so does food refuse. Some plastic tops on fast-food soft-drink cups have little nubs that can be pushed in to mark the kind of drink they contain, so customers can tell diet cola from root beer—a novel medium of communication. A humble example like this reminds us that a substantial portion of our culture is sustained by individually trivial little objects that we use and throw away without thinking about them. Fictional TV detectives are forever solving crimes on the basis of a matchbook they found under the bed, but hardly a sociologist has considered how much real information might be found in such humble items.

Clothing can be considered artifacts, whether the researcher actually collects examples or merely makes drawings and photographs in the field. Women among the Amish ("Pennsylvania Dutch") wear uniform white caps, and it is possible to tell where an Amish woman is from by the design of her cap (Hostetler 1980).

Members of the Process cult wore various badges and jewelry, and I always collected these objects in my research, either by obtaining an example of each or by combining a photograph with a detailed description. Over the years I studied the group, the clothing and badges changed, invariably signaling a shift in social relations. When I first met the group, they were wearing all-black clothing, with a red, Satanic goat's-head badge high on the chest. Then the mass media accused the Process (incorrectly) of having been partly responsible for Charles Manson and his "family" of murderers. The public stigma became so threatening to members of the Process, especially because they made most of their money by begging on the streets, that they changed into bland gray uniforms they made themselves. These proved too dull, and within a few months the group switched again into stunning blue uniforms made for them by a costume company.

A collection of artifacts is useless without thorough documentation. You need to write down when and exactly where an artifact was collected, and to explain as much as you can about the social function, cultural implications, and origins of each object. A famous East Coast museum with a huge warehouse-like room full of African artifacts is embarrassed to admit that many of the artifacts have lost their tags and cannot be identified. A Midwest university recently inherited a rich man's splendid mineral collection and discovered to its dismay that all it had received was a pile of expensive and beautiful rocks, because there was absolutely no accompanying documentation saying what the specimens were and where they had come from. Out of context, an artifact loses most of its scientific value.

Each artifact must be cataloged. Often, it is best to write a number on each piece, using indelible ink, corresponding to a sequential number in the catalog. When I do this with the fossils I collect, I use a two-part number such as 5.12. The first part of the number, before the period, identifies the site where the artifact was collected; the second part of the number, after the period, is the sequential number of specimens collected at that site. Immediately after collecting each item, I enter at least a rough description into a catalog, so the item can be identified without question at any time in the future.

If you cannot write ink numbers on the item, a numbered tag held on by string may be sufficient, but you should consider the most durable way of numbering the item without destroying its value, as ink numbers might do for some art

objects. If the items in a collection are few and varied, detailed verbal descriptions may suffice instead of numbering. Some catalogs contain pictures of the objects, either photographs or drawings. Even photocopy machines will serve to make documentary photos of small objects, especially relatively flat ones, at very low cost. Some recent computer software, notably *Hypercard* for the Apple Macintosh, encourages the user to combine words and pictures in cataloging objects.

Photographic Documentation

Besides being an exceedingly effective way of recording data, photographs can also be useful in communicating the qualities of unfamiliar social settings. Many ethnographies of unusual subcultures include photographs, such as Anderson's (1923) study of hobos and Thrasher's (1927) study of gangs. Although Hostetler (1980:311) notes that photography is forbidden by Amish ("Pennsylvania Dutch") law, his book about them contains many informative photos.

Pictures can be especially compelling when they are arranged to tell a sociological story. Several of my most effective classroom lectures are slide shows based on photos I took in the field. One is a set of pictures of the Process, selected to tell the story of how a person typically joined the cult. It begins with strangers encountering cultists on the street, buying magazines from them, and being invited back to the cult's coffeehouse. Next, the class sees newcomers sitting in the coffeehouse, making friends with other newcomers. These people participate in a variety of cult rituals and other formal activities, such as musical performances. About halfway through, the person being recruited to the cult becomes a formal member and begins doing the work of the cult, begging on the streets, traveling, making things, getting married within the group, and raising his or her children as tiny Satanists. Throughout this sequence of 80 photos runs the theme of social bonds: People first become members of the social group and only later come to adopt the doctrines and the deviant lifestyle.

You should be very cautious about publishing photographs, especially those that zero in on individuals in potentially embarrassing situations. Like any journalist, you have the right to take pictures in a public place. If the setting is not public, or when your pictures highlight a person who is not a public figure, you really should not publish unless the individual in question has signed a consent form explicitly giving you permission to do so. Often, however, you can use photography effectively without actually publishing the photos.

For example, members of the Process cult were kind enough to stage a "fashion show" for my camera, allowing me to document in detail the unusual uniforms they wore. But I did not feel it was fair to publish the pictures, because to do so might harm members who had already left the group and returned to private life. The solution was to hire an artist to turn selected photographs into line drawings that communicated the information about the costumes. The artist altered the faces so that the people would no longer be recognizable.

Many of the pictures I took at the Process were not of people but of things. For instance, I documented all the props and clothing used in the cult's rituals, even employing special lenses to photograph rings and pins while they were being worn. One of the main features of the room used for the cult's rituals was a huge red-and-black face of Satan, made of cardboard and hanging from a black curtain. My photograph of it was redrawn by an artist and included in my book both as an interior illustration, in a page showing all the symbols, and on the book's cover.

One reviewer complained that I must have been sloppy in my research, because one detail of Satan's face was obviously wrong. In traditional pictures, Satan has a five-pointed star on her forehead, with one point directed straight downward. But my illustration showed the star with one point straight up—clearly a mistake, the reviewer said. However, because I had used photography to document exactly how the cult

had depicted Satan, I could prove that the drawings in my book were accurate and that the Process had the star turned just the way I showed it.

If you want to use photography most effectively, study the art and science of picture taking. There are many technical tricks, and this is not the place to discuss them in detail. However, brief mention of a few will communicate the general ideas. Your camera should be sturdy and not prone to breaking down. If you are in the field, far away from a big city, you may not be able to get a broken camera repaired. In purchasing the 35-millimeter camera I used for many years, I took the advice of an anthropologist who had lived for a year in dense African jungle with the same model. It was not automatic, and it required the user to make all the decisions about lens and shutter settings, but that meant it contained few complicated mechanisms that could break. The built-in light meter advised the user but did not control the camera. Years later, the internal light meter did break while I was in a foreign country, but it was a simple matter to set the exposure by hand, guided by a light meter I bought locally.

A variety of lenses can be useful, if you are able to lug them around. A wide-angle lens (28-millimeter focal length) allowed me to document the rooms of the Process chapter house, the one you will visit in the computer program associated with this chapter. Using such a lens, I could stand in the center of each wall of a room, and photograph the entire other wall. The standard 50-millimeter lens is best for all-purpose work, but people's faces and groups of people may be captured better by standing farther back and using a longer-focus lens, perhaps 100 to 135 millimeters. I found that a lens that could zoom from 80 to 200 millimeters served me very well, although it was very heavy and left painful marks on my fingers. I also carried thin diopter lenses that could be screwed on top of my standard 50-millimeter lens. These allowed me to get in very close to small objects, snapping perfect shots of custom-made rings on people's fingers, for example.

When photographing automobiles, I found that an adjustable polarizing filter cut the reflections in window glass. Depending on the nature of your research, you may have to investigate the mysteries of filters and other attachments.

Camera film has been evolving rapidly in recent years, but it still makes sense to carry a variety of kinds. Except for social events that take place outside on bright sunny days, the sociological photographer usually has to cope with dark conditions. I have used film with exposure ratings running from 64 up to 3000, and on several occasions I obtained useful pictures with the light of a single candle flame.

Once, I was caught in unexpectedly dark conditions when I had planned to take several rolls of film. The only way to get the data was to set the exposures as if the film were more sensitive than it really was, and take the film to a laboratory that was willing to "push the film two stops" to get every bit of information out of it. NASA's film laboratory had to do this with a vital portion of the film taken on an Apollo moon flight, because a camera surveying the lunar surface from orbit had been set wrong. By and large, flashguns and bright photoflood lights are not good, because they upset the people you are photographing and render the social moment very far from genuine.

Newspaper photographers carry two cameras. The cameras may differ in the kinds of film loaded into them or in their lenses, or they may use wholly different film formats, depending on the kind of work the photographer typically does. Obviously, if you decide to carry all the camera equipment that might be useful, you will have to lug it around in a truck, so you must decide what to take and what to leave home. If you are following other research approaches at the same time and have to carry other material as well, the problem can be especially acute. Carrying a lot of gear may unnerve your research subjects and can seriously restrict your mobility.

To reduce your load, you will have to learn to improvise. For example, you may have to dispense with a tripod to steady the camera and instead become adept at bracing the camera (or using your shoulder to hold the camera) on a convenient wall or piece of furniture. I have generally limited use of photography to predictable situations, where I could guess ahead of time what pictures might be useful for recording data or communicating to a later academic audience. The convenience of modern, portable video cameras, including the low cost of long-duration tapes, has made them especially attractive for data collection, although the tried-and-true still camera cannot be beat for most purposes. It provides higher-quality pictures for publication and is less likely to disturb your subjects, who may feel threatened by a video recording of all they do and say.

Earlier, I mentioned that I used to give copies of pictures to some of the people I photographed, as part of an exchange relationship with them. If it is not too burdensome, you may find some advantage in taking with you an instant camera, the kind that develops its own pictures. The film is costly, the quality may not be good enough for publication, and you don't get slides for classroom lectures, but you can immediately give copies to the people you are photographing. Another advantage is that you can ask the people to identify exactly what is in an instant photo and what the events depicted mean to them. Then you could paste the picture into your field notes, followed by a detailed description based on what the people told you about the scene. If you simultaneously take photographs with another camera, then you can have both instant documentation pictures and subsequently developed high-quality images.

Although researchers should be encouraged to focus their study on well-defined questions and to aim even their most open-ended explorations toward particular scientific objectives, there is much to be said for comprehensive photographic documentation of all aspects of life in settings that may soon vanish from the Earth (Sorensen 1974). Anthropologists do this when they study a "primitive tribe" whose members are rapidly being assimilated into modern society. In just a few more years, everyone on this planet may be part of a single, global civilization, and then we shall lament all the lost information never collected about all the cultures that have been swallowed up.

Sociologists show far less awareness of the imminent demise of significant social phenomena than do anthropologists, but many parts of "modern society" are vanishing as well, even some of the most "advanced" parts. This is particularly evident for occupations that are being made obsolete by technological advance. For example, just a few years ago, electronic repair workers commonly replaced and resoldered many individual electronic parts. This required great skill and expertise, but now all they often do is unplug one large component, throw it away, and plug in another one straight from the factory. Photo-documentation of work like electronic repair could be very valuable to future social scientists, since some fascinating high-skill professions seem "gone before you know it" in this rapidly changing world. When I performed observational field research at NASA's Jet Propulsion Laboratory in 1986, JPL itself was videotaping in detail how the mission controllers guided the Voyager II space probe, because many of the controllers were about to retire and their professional expertise needed to be captured for future missions before the people were gone.

Social Maps

Maps can be useful to sociologists in many ways. For example, Faris and Dunham (1939) identified social factors that might promote various kinds of mental illness by examining maps of rates of these disorders for 120 subcommunities of Chicago. We will make good use of this approach in Chapter 11, providing fully 255 maps of the United States. But maps of small areas, even of single rooms, can also be of great value. A map of an area used by people, showing who goes where and what they do there, is a **social map**.

Gerald Suttles (1968) used such maps to communicate the interrelations between ethnicity and territory in the "Addams Area" of

Chicago. His study examined the social devices that maintained divisions between groups, among them informal claims to ownership of territory that were backed up by customs and symbolic exclusion, rather than by legally registered deeds. His maps were at various *scales*, that is, they used different measurement scales and covered different sizes of territory. One showed the Addams Area in the midst of other areas, and covered about 12 square miles. Another map showed the city blocks within the Addams Area, which extended less than a mile in its longest dimension, with the locations of 21 neighborhood establishments and other features. A third zeroed in on just one block, "Peanut Park," showing which parts were claimed by different ethnic groups.

Some of Robert Sommer's (1969) research on *personal space*, the ways that individuals socially use and defend small areas around their bodies, incorporates maps of a few pieces of furniture. For example, Sommer analyzes the social meaning of different seating arrangements around a table. People who are casually conversing may often sit next to each other, while those who are competing are apt to sit opposite each other at some distance. A portion of Sommer's data came from simply watching where students sat at tables in a college cafeteria.

John Hostetler's (1974, 1980) studies of the Amish and Hutterites contain several social maps of small indoor areas. For example, a chart of a typical Amish family dinner helps communicate that family members sit in a precisely regulated manner. The father sits at the head of the table, with his wife on his right. The boys sit on the father's left, arranged with the youngest nearest him and the oldest farthest away. The girls are similarly arranged from youngest to oldest on the mother's side of the table. A map of tables arranged for an Amish wedding shows the bridal party sitting in a corner from where they can view all the guests and be seen by them. Hostetler's chart of a Hutterite worship service shows how the men, boys, girls, and women are separated into four distinct groups.

One approach that often reveals unexpected facts about a group or social setting is to ask participants to draw their own maps. Peter Gould and Rodney White (1974) did this both for whole nations and for neighborhoods. In one study, they asked members of three different ethnic groups to draw maps of Los Angeles. Upper-middle-class whites in the Westwood area drew complex maps showing many distant features of their city. Black residents of Avalon drew detailed maps of their own neighborhoods but indicated the rest of the city only in vague terms. And Spanish-speaking residents of Boyle Heights drew highly circumscribed maps of the area around the bus depot. Through their mental maps, these groups had told the researchers which portions of the city they felt were their own and which they knew best.

Two examples from projects done by my students will illustrate what important insights social maps can stimulate. Each of these students had been doing an independent study project concerning a social service agency at which he or she was working. At the beginning of every week, the student would submit some pages of field notes and other material, and at midweek he or she would come to my office to discuss them and plan the observational approach for the next few days. But for all of the students there came a time of temporary burn-out, when they just couldn't see anything worth writing down from their hours at the agency. In each case, a social map got things moving again.

One student was a volunteer at a private agency helping young people work through problems they had with their families. The agency had been founded by a highly energetic older man who had great success getting government funding, but most workers were young, unpaid volunteers like my student. The week when my student's research stalled, he explained that his work was so routine at that point that he just couldn't find anything to write about. This is a common problem. I have experienced it myself in every observational project I have done, and this happens almost periodically in long projects. I asked him, on the spot, to draw me a map of the agency's building, putting in all the details that he could remember.

The building was a wide rectangle, with the front door in the middle leading through a foyer to a large, empty room from which corridors went left and right. Down those corridors were the consulting and meeting rooms in which all the work was done. But before we went down those corridors in our imagination, I asked my student to tell me what was in the large, empty room. "Nothing," he said. "Nothing?" I asked. Well, there's never really nothing in a room, so we went through a list of things that might be there, such as a rug, chairs, pictures on the wall. "Nothing." Then I asked him to imagine, as vividly as he could, that he was in that room and to tell me if he saw anything at all. Finally, he recalled that some paint had been splashed by accident on the floor. That splash of paint turned out to be the clue to the most interesting thing that was going on in the agency.

Paint is highly significant in human affairs, and it is no accident when a particular place gets repainted. Usually, it needs painting for a long time before it actually gets attention, and often the trigger for painting is some social event or process of great interest. It turned out that many volunteers had resigned from the agency in recent weeks, that its creator was seeking a new round of funding, and that new volunteers had to be attracted if it was going to survive. The manager and a few volunteers had reacted to the crisis in part by trying to spruce up the place, and the splashed paint was an almost desperate sign of their attempt to revive the agency.

The other student had been studying a people's clinic, the sort of health center that attempted to mix standard medicine with folk remedies and health fads of the counterculture. When she came in one week with nothing to report, I asked her to do a full set of social maps for her next visit. She brought me an elaborate plan of the two-story frame house that held the clinic, complete with symbols for the furniture. Just off the entry hall was a little room used by a nurse who advised expectant mothers. The map showed that there was a bookcase in the room, a desk, and a chair for the nurse. "Where does the pregnant woman sit?" I asked. "Oh." The student suddenly realized that there wasn't a second chair on her diagram, and she felt pretty sure there wasn't one in the room either. I told her to check closely next time she went.

A week later she reported there had not in fact been a chair for the pregnant women when she did the maps, but that a big couch had been brought in subsequently. I urged her not to stop at this point but to find out how the couch had been brought in. Frankly, the student said, this did not seem very important. Clearly, the pregnant women had needed something to sit on, and the staff of the clinic had simply realized this and provided the couch. But over the next two weeks it turned out that the story of the couch was not simple at all, and it revealed much about what was going on at the clinic.

For weeks, the pregnant women did not have anything to sit on. An extra chair might be brought in from another office but was immediately taken back, and some of the expectant mothers had actually been forced to stand while consulting with the nurse. Then, one of the conventional doctors associated with the clinic had brought in the couch. This was part of his struggle for authority. According to the ideology of this people's clinic, folk healers were as good as standard M.D.s, and a conventional doctor deserved no special status or influence in the group. Aside from any personal resentment this M.D. may have felt about his lack of high status in the clinic, he frequently disagreed with the folk healers who were his colleagues, and the ideology of the clinic denied that his medical training made him better able than they to make decisions about patients. His power play, of which the couch was but one manifestation, failed. He soon quit the clinic, and when he left, so did the couch.

Often, you can learn much from comparison of social maps made at different times. When I

was studying the Process in the early 1970s, I was fascinated by the complex and colorful rituals. The main ritual of the week was the Sabbath Assembly, held every Saturday evening. When I first observed them, Sabbath Assemblies were a carefully crafted dramatic performance. Perhaps sixty people, half in black uniforms of the cult, crammed into a modest space made by combining the living and dining rooms of the Process chapter house. They sat on cushions on the floor, chanting and waiting for the priests to enter.

The hall door would open, and a procession would enter. A water bearer and fire bearer brought two bowls, one filled with water to signify Christ, and the other giving forth flames to signify Satan, two deities the cult believed were joining in a partnership for the end of the world. With the two bearers came two priests. The "sacrifist" wore a purple garment, called a tabard, and represented Christ. The "evangelist" wore a scarlet tabard and represented Satan. The procession moved counter-clockwise around the circular altar set in the middle of the room, until each ritual performer was in his or her place. Then the bearers placed their bowls on stands elevated above the altar, and the sacrifist and evangelist sat on the only two chairs in the room. Figure 2.1 is a pair of maps of the Sabbath Assembly as it was performed in the spring of 1971 and the spring of 1973.

The map at the left shows the arrangement when I first began documenting the ritual in 1971. The letter *A* indicates the altar, a low circular table bearing the cult's symbol and flanked by stands holding bowls of water and fire. The two priests sat on chairs, here marked *E* (evangelist) and *S* (sacrifist), facing each other. Behind the evangelist was a black curtain, carrying a yard-wide red-and-black portrait of Satan, depicted as half man and half goat, marked *G* in the diagram. Behind the sacrifist was a purple curtain carrying an ornate, lobed cross, representing Christ, marked *C*. Various cultists with lesser ritual roles and the members of the congregation were seated on the floor on thin cushions, marked on the map as circles.

FIGURE 2.1
Process Sabbath Assembly

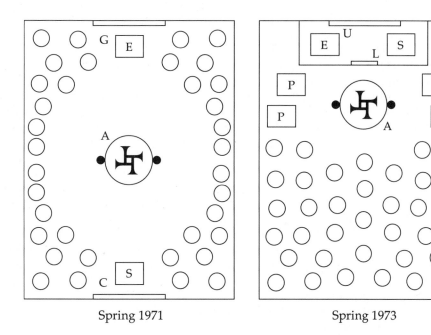

Spring 1971   Spring 1973

The arrangement of things reflected the group's ideology and social structure. Christ and Satan were beings of opposite nature, according to the Process, but they were gradually coming together to destroy the wickedness of mankind and inaugurate a new age. The priests representing them thus sat at opposite ends of the room, facing each other across an altar that held the chief Process symbol, which represented the coming together in common purpose of diametrically opposed entities. The congregation sat in a circle, their backs to the outside world, facing each other. Their focus was on each other, and their physical positioning reflected their great solidarity. Although elevated on chairs above the rest, the priests sat among the congregation; this symbolized that everyone in the room was part of a single community.

Two years later, the doctrines had shifted and so had the social reality of the Process. On the one hand, the group was becoming more fully integrated into the surrounding society, and the social exclusiveness symbolized by sitting in a circle with their backs to the world was no longer appropriate. On the other hand, the priests had become more dictatorial and more remote from common members, often sending the lower-ranked Processeans begging on the cold streets for hours each day while the priests themselves enjoyed the comfort of their chapter house. In addition, the doctrines asserted that Christ and Satan were coming ever closer together. This was perhaps an attempt to revive hope at a time when the cult's mood bordered on despondency. By April 21, 1973, the arrangement of the Sabbath Assembly had shifted radically, reflecting these social and ideological developments, as shown at the right of Figure 2.1.

Now, the two high priests (E and S) were on a raised dais with a lectern (L), separated from the congregation by a wide space filled by the altar (A), by fire and water stands, and by four lesser priests (P) sitting on chairs. The congregation sat on cushions but did not face each other. Instead, they looked forward, toward the priests. Instead of separate symbols for Christ and Satan at opposite ends of the room, a single cross with a red serpent drawn on it hung behind the priests. Called the Unity Cross (U in the diagram), this reflected the coming together of Christ and Satan, but it also reflected the changed social relationship between priests and ordinary members. Weeks later, the altar disappeared and the arrangement became somewhat simpler, but still with the priests separated from the congregation, mediating between the congregation and the deities represented by the cross with a serpent.

Such symbolism is not by any means restricted to weird cults. Standard churches have it, too. In most Western denominations, the symbols of God are at one end of the room, the congregation is at the other, and the clergy operate in the space between, symbolically mediating between the people and their God. An interesting study can be done by visiting Christian churches and mapping where the people and objects are during the Communion ritual. Does the priest (or minister) face the congregation when consecrating the bread and wine, or does he or she face away from the congregation toward symbols of the deity? Where do members of the congregation receive the bread and wine? In some modern churches, a communion rail goes all the way around the front of the church, so that persons taking communion can gaze across at each other. In general, greater social solidarity and equality are probably symbolized by having the clergy and laity facing each other during such rituals. The special status of the priests is usually emphasized by having them face away from the people in the direction of symbols of the deity. In recent years, considerable creative energy has gone into revising rituals and even developing new architectural church designs to strengthen a sense of community between the congregation and the ministers in many denominations.

Taking a Census

Every ten years the federal government takes a census of the entire nation, and we will use much information from such large-scale censuses in later chapters. But you can learn a lot from smaller censuses that you do yourself in the field. When I tell people about the religious cults and social movements I studied in the field in the early 1970s, they often ask me how many people were in them, and it helps communicate a clear picture of these groups by giving a definite answer. But censuses can provide information useful in far more subtle ways as well.

When I was studying the Boston branch of the Process cult, at the end of 1971, I had trouble keeping track of exactly how many members there were, until one of the leaders asked me to take ID photos of all inner members to use in convincing the police that the group was legitimate. The members all lined up, and when the film had been developed I counted the faces. There were 43, 23 of them males and 20 females. Another approach I used was to count people attending various rituals. In April 1971, exactly 50 different persons attended one or more of the Boston group's Progress doctrinal classes. The cheap monthly magazine *The Processeans* included action photos of members living in the main communes in six cities, and in issues spanning 1972 through 1974 I was able to count 92 different faces, exactly half male and half female.

These simple examples illustrate several points. Most obviously, there are many different ways you can count people, and we shall consider more different ways below. Perhaps the biggest problem I faced was the fluidity of the population—people were constantly coming and going—and it was necessary to narrow my count to a particular day whenever possible. Also, you can get information beyond just the number involved, as illustrated here by the information that the group was evenly divided between the two sexes. But these examples also reveal that it is both sociologically interesting and sometimes a problem for the researcher that there can be different definitions of membership. For one thing, somewhat different groups participated in different Process activities, and if I took any one as my only measure of membership, I would miss several people. But also, the Process had a formal ladder of degrees of membership, something that is true informally for almost any group, and when speaking of membership I would have to specify which particular kind of membership I was referring to.

One of the most important uses of censuses is charting changes in membership over time. When I was studying meetings of the Committee for the Future, a private group that was promoting the space program, I found that frequent censuses gave me an excellent picture of the dynamics of the group. The CFF used to hold what it called "Syncon" conventions. A number of people would sign up for a weekend meeting to plan the future of the world. Each person would be registered in a particular task force, a subcommittee that would discuss some aspect of society, such as government, technology, or the environment. After a while, following the Syncon plan, pairs of subcommittees would be combined, and their members would discuss issues common to their topics.

For a 1972 meeting in Washington, DC, 249 people registered to participate, but at the final ceremony I counted only 103. Except for the final ceremony, there was no time when all participants were in the same room at the same time, a fact that made counting them difficult. To estimate the numbers participating in the free-floating meals, I counted dirty dishes. To get the numbers involved in particular task forces, I picked moments when everybody was supposed to be working in them and ran madly from room to room counting and writing my tallies on a clipboard. Tuesday, at 10:15 in the morning, for example, there were 7 people in the technology task force and 12 in the environment task force. Wednesday afternoon at 1:30, when these two task forces had been combined, there were only 14 in the joint technology-environment task force, a loss of 5. Altogether, there were 103 task force participants Tuesday morning and only 75 Wednesday afternoon.

These censuses made it clear that the Syncon was losing people as the hours passed. This was particularly interesting, because the organizers believed that Syncon was a powerful method for achieving consensus among people about the future of human society, and it looked to them that there was greater agreement at the end than at the beginning. The censuses suggest, of course, that what was really happening was that people who disagreed with the organizers' ideas were simply drifting away, leaving those in agreement behind to feel they had achieved consensus. Censuses at three Syncon meetings over a span of more than a year allowed me to chart a decline of interest in the space program and a shift toward mystical and spiritual issues, revealed through a shrinkage in the numbers in the space task force and an increase of those in the "unexplained phenomena" and "nature of man" task forces.

Systematic Observation of Small Groups

Imagine you have set yourself the task of observing the discussions of a small group of six or seven people, writing down who speaks to whom and putting the things they say into some kind of category scheme. How would you do it? What are the things people say to each other? Questions and answers? Questions and answers. That small insight is a start, anyhow.

You could write down the letter Q if somebody asked a question and A if somebody obliged them with an answer. But clearly there is more to a discussion than that. There must be different kinds of questions, with associated kinds of answers, and many things that people say are neither questions nor answers.

Bales's Research

Back in the 1940s, Robert Freed Bales at Harvard developed a slightly more elaborate system for categorizing the communications in discussion groups (Bales 1950; 1970). Called **interaction process analysis**, Bales's technique has been tremendously influential in such varied fields as family therapy and business management. Although many similar techniques have been developed and interaction process analysis is practically an antique, it is still used and is the best example for us to consider here.

Bales and his colleagues did most of their research in a special laboratory rather than out in the field, and as I describe their work, you might want to think how it could be adapted for studying groups in the real world. The lab consisted of two rooms. One was set aside for the people under study, and it offered them chairs and a table to sit around while they discussed a problem the researchers gave them. The other room was for the observers and various equipment they used to record what happened.

A large mirror covered part of one wall of the discussion room, but the research subjects did not pay much attention to it as they engaged in their discussion. This mirror, however, was really a window. Researchers in the observers' room could see through it clearly, even though the subjects could not see them. Probably, you have seen someone with a pair of sunglasses that looked like a mirror, except that the person wearing it could see through it perfectly well. Presidential bodyguards use these glasses because one can't tell which direction they are looking in! The same principle works for the one-way mirrors used in some social science laboratories. The observers have to keep their room pretty dark—no light except that coming through the mirror—and even the glow of a cigarette might be seen by the research subjects. But with care, the subjects never guess that the mirror is really a window through which observers are watching them.

The rooms are also wired for sound. Microphones pick up what the members of the discussion group are saying, and the observers can listen over headphones. Tape recorders were brand new when Bales began his work, and he did not have access to one. However, some of the discussions were captured with wire recorders (a spool of metal wire rather than a reel of plastic tape) and on phonograph disks.

While the discussion was going on, each observer would attempt to categorize whatever each person said or communicated by gestures. The observers had to divide the running flow of speech into what Bales called **unit acts**, the smallest pieces of communication they could perceive, and assign each unit act to one of twelve categories. The observer also had to note who spoke each unit and the person or persons to whom it was directed.

It was extremely difficult for the observers to keep up with the discussion group, and their frantic note taking was thoroughly exhausting. In the early attempts, observers frequently fell behind and missed important things the members of the discussion group were saying. Therefore, Bales devised a machine, called the *interaction recorder*, to help them. It was a mechanical device that moved a roll of paper past a list of the categories Bales had identified. Whenever a member of the discussion group spoke, the observer would write a couple of numbers on the paper roll, right opposite the category that described what the person said. One number identified who had spoken, and the other identified the person spoken to. The interaction recorder automatically marked the paper every minute, so it was possible to know exactly when each unit act had occurred.

Even so, the observers had to be extensively trained and work in high alertness for an hour at a time. Today, we would use video-recorders to tape a discussion that could then be analyzed at our leisure, rendering the one-way mirror unnecessary. However, it may take many hours to analyze the material on a one-hour videotape, so Bales's original approach may have been more efficient than modern techniques, however draining it was for the observers.

The key to interaction process analysis was the system of twelve categories:

1. Shows solidarity
2. Shows tension
3. Agrees
4. Gives suggestion
5. Gives opinion
6. Gives information
7. Asks for information
8. Asks for opinion
9. Asks for suggestion
10. Disagrees
11. Shows tension
12. Shows antagonism

Based on extensive research and development, these categories are not just twelve separate ideas. Instead, they form a tightly organized system. Each one is paired with one of the others, and each is part of a trio of three categories. For example, if somebody asks for a suggestion, this request is put into category 9, "asks for suggestion." Then if somebody else offers one, it is put into category 4, "gives suggestion." Thus, categories 9 and 4 are a pair, asking for a suggestion and giving one. Asking for a suggestion is one of three kinds of question, the others being asking for an opinion (category 8) and asking for information (category 7).

Here's a brief dramatic scene that illustrates the way these categories might be used:

Person 1:   "What shall we have for lunch?" (category 9)
Person 2:   "Let's have pizza." (category 4)
Person 1:   "Where can we get pizza around here?" (category 7)
Person 3:   "There's Pizza Heaven and The Pie Guy." (category 6)
Person 4:   "Which one makes better pizzas?" (category 8)
Person 3:   "I like Pie Guy pies." (category 5)

Together, the six categories of questions and answers constitute what Bales called the *task area* of communication. They move the discussion group toward a solution of the problem before them. The other six categories belong to the social-emotional area, which can be divided into three positive reactions and three negative reactions. The positive reactions strengthen the group's social solidarity and gratify members' emotional needs, while the three negative reactions threaten the group and express frustrations.

This system of twelve categories is based on a theory of communication. Bales believed that human language primarily serves two functions: coordinating social action to accomplish practical tasks and dealing with emotional relations between members of the group. Therefore, he divided the twelve categories into two sets of six: the task area and the social-emotional area. Because he conceptualized group communication in terms of the give and take of person-to-person interaction, he also arranged the twelve categories in six pairs.

Bales predicted that groups attempting to solve problems would go through three phases of discussion (Bales and Strodbeck 1951). First, they would share all the relevant information they had and apply it to their problem. In this phase they would struggle with problems of communication. Second, people would make judgments in terms of their personal values, working with the information developed in the first phases. This entailed problems of evaluation. Finally, the group would decide what to do and assign specific responsibilities to individual members. Here, they would face problems of control. The three phases in Bales's theory gave him the three pairs of question-and-answer categories: communication, evaluation, and control.

Adapting Bales's Approach

I shared these details of the system with you to make a point about any set of categories you might use to describe what people say to each other, or how they interact nonverbally. Every category system is based on some kind of theory, however crude. Bales was very explicit in developing a set of categories with a logical structure, based on clear theoretical statements. His theory may be wrong, but the work he invested in developing it is very much to his credit. If you develop a chaotic set of categories, based on notions that pop into your head at random, then your system is still based on a theory, even if this theory is incoherent and has little or nothing to recommend it. Research without theory is mindless and has little chance of advancing human knowledge.

Some of the research Bales did could have been based on much simpler data collection, and you might consider a simplified version of his approach for a study of your own. Bales and his associates studied stratification in small groups by simply counting how many unit acts each person contributed to the group discussion, not worrying what category the unit acts were in (Bales, Strodbeck, and Mills 1951). For one thing, they found that some people dominated the discussion in essentially every group they studied, and it was possible to work out a formula to predict what proportion of the unit acts would come from the most talkative person, from the second-most-talkative person, and so on down to the person who spoke least. The groups they studied varied in size, and it turned out that members of small groups were more equal in their contributions than members of larger ones. This fascinating discovery suggests that the social power people get from being at the center of communication may be greater the larger the size of the group.

You could try this method in studying a group in the field. One of my students once tape recorded a meeting of the city council where she was living. It was an open, public meeting, and she found that she had the legal right to record it. You could make a tape like this and count how many sentences each member of the council spoke. You could sit at a table with a large sheet of paper divided into big boxes, each box labeled with the name of a council member. As a person spoke, you would put a mark in the box for that person. At the end, you could count up how many unit acts each person contributed. Or, if it didn't cause too much distraction, you could dispense with the tape recorder and keep your tally during the meeting itself, with the boxes for the council members arranged on your paper just as their chairs are, to make it easy for you to find where to make each tally mark.

Much of the research by Bales and his associates analyzed how the unit acts were distributed across the twelve categories, and a graph called the interaction profile was drawn for each person or group. Whatever set of categories you use, you might find similar graphs useful, or stick instead with tables showing what percent of the unit acts fell into each category.

In one study, when each member of the discussion group left the laboratory, Bales asked whether he or she had been satisfied with the way the hour had gone. Then he looked back at the interaction profile to see what had caused satisfaction or dissatisfaction. Groups that produced dissatisfaction in their members tended, not surprisingly, to have had more unit acts in the negative part of the social-emotional area. But negative social-emotional acts can also come simply from getting the task done, Bales found, because progress in solving a practical problem can generate all kinds of interpersonal tension (Bales 1953).

One way of simplifying Bales's system is to work with just two categories, task and social-emotional. Without too much practice, you could probably sit listening to a group discussion and code each sentence in terms of whether it was oriented toward getting the group's job done (task) or toward the emotions and social relations of the members (social-emotional). Some of Bales's research suggested that there were actually two different kinds of group leaders, those who specialized in getting the task done and those who dealt with problems in the social-emotional area. His ideas have been influential in research on the family, and some have suggested that the typical, traditional husband was the task leader for the family, because he was the breadwinner, while the traditional wife was the social-emotional leader, managing relations among all the family members. Of course, we might predict that this sex-based division of labor would have vanished as the roles of women and men became more similar. You could do an observational study of this, watching a family interact and coding the things they say into task and social-emotional categories.

Like all good research ideas, interaction process analysis has its limitations. The observers have to receive such extensive training that we might suspect they would get thoroughly indoctrinated into Bales's theories. If so, they may not be prepared to notice any evidence that conflicts with the theories. Certainly, it would be good to try other category systems, and many sociological theories could give birth to very different categories. But you have to use some such system in doing any systematic observational research, and Bales's approach is a very good example of how to proceed.

Limitations of Qualitative Research

Sociologists who specialize in "methodology" tend to be statisticians, and the essays on methodology published in the most prestigious periodicals tend to be quantitative. To some, this seems a conspiracy of editors against qualitative approaches, but some of those editors have proclaimed themselves innocent of the charge. In reviewing his editorship of *Sociological Methodology* (SM), Samuel Leinhardt (1983) wrote: "If I have one regret it is that I have fared markedly less well than I had hoped in attracting work on nonquantitative methods. In defense I can only say that I was open and committed to the publication of nonquantitative work. I remain steadfast in my belief that SM can and ought to provide publication opportunities for nonquantitative as well as quantitative methodologists, and I hope that future volumes of SM will demonstrate the propriety and utility of this view."

Leinhardt's successor as editor, Nancy Brandon Tuma (1985), seconded his invitation to nonquantitative methodologists: "In fact, manuscripts in which authors take nonquantitative approaches are especially appreciated, not just because they are rare but also, and more importantly, because they demonstrate that sociologists are taking seriously their proper task of understanding *all* social phenomena, some of which are very important but not easily quantified."

The main sociology journals very seldom publish ethnographic research, and this is one of the justifications for special outlets for publications, such as *Journal of Contemporary Ethnography*. One reason journals tend to emphasize quantitative articles is that statistics allow one to communicate much information in a small space. As Blalock (1989:448) has put it, "Quantitative data analyses, being compact, have a competitive advantage over qualitative research when it comes to the journals."

Another reason, unfortunately, is simply that recent sociological ethnographies have tended to be of very poor quality. In the 1960s, when there was so much interest in unusual social experiments and when a number of sociologists declared themselves opposed to mainstream sociology, many participant observation studies were published that were based on very little fieldwork. In a few extreme cases, a single day of observation was inflated by creative writing into a published article. Put simply, standards of research degenerated. Today, a great portion of observational studies submitted for publication were the result of unacceptably brief observation (Emerson 1987).

The other side of this debased coin is that ethnographies to which the researcher does devote a lot of time and effort do not earn him or her much more in the way of scholarly or financial reward. To a very serious extent, participant observation is caught in a vicious circle. Because so much of it is bad, sociology as a discipline does not respect it much. Because the approach is not respected, many good people who might otherwise practice it stay away. And many of the people who continue to do participant observation find themselves fulfilling the prophecy that field research will be of low quality, and that they will go unrewarded for investing more than a minimal amount of effort. Although this is certainly not the way things ought to be, sadly, this is the way they are.

Good nonquantitative observational research can occasionally be used to test theories, but this usually requires that the theory be stated in unrealistically uncategorical terms. For instance, Sigmund Freud believed that the "Oedipus complex" was a universal phenomenon, found in all societies, and that every son is hostile to his father as a rival for his mother's erotic attentions. Bronislaw Malinowski showed that this was untrue, because in the Trobriand society he studied, the family structure was sufficiently different from that in European society that the hostility existed between the son and his mother's brother, while generally warm and supportive relations existed between fathers and sons. Malinowski's Trobrianders were what we call a **counterexample**, a case that goes against the theory. If a theory is stated in universal terms it may be vulnerable to disproof by unsystematically collected data. However, the kind of theory generally found today in sociology, which speaks of weak tendencies operating among a complex collection of variables, cannot be tested except by quantitative research.

Qualitative field research, however, may be a good approach for discovering new phenomena and generating theoretical ideas that may

later be tested by other means, as we noted earlier in our discussion of the role of *field theorist*. One of the most influential sociologists of the previous generation, Erving Goffman, was constantly finding surprising things in his exploratory field observations of everyday life, and his books are an absolute font of ideas about how people interact (e.g., Goffman 1959, 1961, 1963). A number of his empirical claims have been challenged by investigators using other research methods (e.g., Karmel 1969), but Goffman is a prime example of how sociologists often theorize better in the field than in an armchair, high in the ivory tower of their university.

A well-documented example of an idea developed through qualitative field research that was later tested more rigorously comes from William Foote Whyte's (1943) famous study of the "Norton gang" in Boston's Italian North End. Whyte had observed this group of young men for a while and had sketched its social structure. At the top of the hierarchy were Doc (Whyte's key native informant and guide), Mike, and Danny, and this trio tended to include their friend, Long John, among the gang's elite. Lower in the hierarchy were Nutsy, Angelo, Frank, Fred, Carl, Joe, Lou, Tommy, and Alec. An outsider who figured in the following story was Mark.

One of the key pastimes for these men was bowling, and Whyte (1943:18) noted that there was "a close connection between a man's bowling and his position in the group." Near the end of April 1938, a competition was held, to see which of these men were the best individual bowlers. Doc, Danny, and Long John gave Whyte their predictions for how the ranking would turn out, and they unanimously placed themselves at the top. Now, an ethnographer of less imagination might have simply dismissed this as boasting, but Whyte thought more deeply. These three members of the group were essentially predicting that bowling scores would follow the men's social status in the group.

On the fateful evening, the scores came out almost exactly as predicted. One departure was that Whyte himself bowled best. But of the eight Norton men (plus Mark) who showed up for the contest, Danny, Doc, Long John, and Mike all finished in the top half. The bottom half consisted of Joe, Mark, Carl, Frank, and Alec, all low-status members of the gang except Mark, who was not a member. Whyte explains that some of the lower-status members were good bowlers who might have won, but social pressures prevented them from rising above their social status in the group. This pressure took the form of heckling, plus the bowler's own recognition of his proper role in the group.

When George Homans (1950:167, 162) wrote about this match at length in his classic textbook, *The Human Group,* he commented, "Clearly the group, and particularly the leaders, had a definite idea what a man's standing in bowling ought to be, and this idea had a real effect on how he bowled." The key factor, as noted, was the social status of each man, and Homans made much of this in his theoretical analysis. But he also admonished field researchers not to ignore such unexpected indicators of social facts: "Some kinds of behavior that may look trivial to outsiders—for instance, the kind of candy a man eats—are on occasion good signs of social rank."

Before Whyte's ideas could be tested in more systematic research, they had to be clarified and refined. I see really three ideas here, but perhaps you or Whyte would find a different number. (1) When members of a social group make predictions about the performance of fellow members in games, their estimates will be a direct function of the social status of the people judged. (2) When members of a social group play games, their performance will be influenced by their social statuses in the group, so that high-status members will do better than their individual skill might predict, and lower-status members will do worse. (3) Field observational researchers can use both group members' predictions of game performance and actual game scores as indicators of social status. Left out of this analysis is the possibility that social status is partly the

result of how well the men bowled, and both Whyte and his later commentators have seen status as the cause rather than the effect of performance.

The first of these hypotheses was put to the test in a series of experiments done with school children (Harvey 1953; Sherif, White, and Harvey 1955; cf. Sherif and Sherif 1969). First, the researchers would determine social status rankings in a number of groups of kids, sometimes by observing them and sometimes by interviewing them or administering questionnaires. Then the children would play a game. In one version, the game involved throwing darts at a board that did not have well-marked scoring circles. In another version, balls were thrown at a complex target of concentric rings on a big board (a hit on a ring causing an electric light to flash where the experimenter but not the kids could see it), and a cloth was placed over the target so that it would be difficult to tell how many points each ball earned. Indeed, the social status of an individual significantly influenced how the group judged his or her performance in these ambiguous games, and the individuals themselves showed the same tendency to rate their accomplishments higher or lower because of their social status.

Whyte's discovery was no accident. At the time of the bowling contest, he was consciously looking for evidence about social status in the group. Years later he wrote:

As I spent time with the thirteen men, day after day, I became fascinated by the patterns of their activities and interactions. As I became aware that this informal group had a marked and stable structure of leadership and followership, I set about making systematic observations so as to build up data on group structure. Only as a participant would I have been able to associate closely enough with these men to work out the structure of the group. If my information had been limited to personal interviews, this would not have been possible. When I asked one or another of them who their leader was—as I did from time to time—the answer was always the same: "We have no leader. We are all equal." (Whyte 1984:23)

The Ethics of Field Research

A colleague of mine once assigned students in his course to observe an antipornography crusade and report their observations to him; at the time he was a leader of political opposition to the crusade. Another sociologist observed homosexual liaisons in public men's rooms, then copied down the license plate numbers of the men's cars, so he could later visit their homes in disguise to conduct interviews with them. Another repeatedly violated South African law to develop a relationship of mutual trust with black South Africans who were the victims of apartheid. Two sociologists, in two separate studies of deviant cults, became teachers of the group's weird doctrines, using their considerable intellectual talents to inculcate beliefs that they themselves did not accept. A team of eight researchers got themselves committed to mental hospitals, pretending to be disturbed in order to do observational research from the perspective of a patient; in so doing they not only lied to hospital officials and obtained room and board under false pretenses, but their leader published a harsh attack on the profession of psychiatry based on the findings. Were these researchers' actions ethical?

Observers in the field typically learn secrets that would harm people they studied if made public. Often, researchers investigate groups and individuals without first getting permission, and even when permission is sought there remain questions about whether the right people were asked and whether they knew what they were agreeing to. Publications based on good research concerning situations of conflict are bound to disseminate information that will help one side in the conflict and hurt the other. In short, ethical questions abound for the field observer, because he or she is party to situations in which secrecy, power, reputations, and

illusions are key ingredients, and answers to the ethical questions are often hard to find.

An example from my own experience will illustrate some of the moral ambiguities we face, even when we try to follow strict moral codes in doing observational research. I choose a study of my own because it is not my place to talk about ethical dilemmas in the research of any particular colleague of mine, and my colleagues have the right to speak for themselves.

When I was living in Seattle, I discovered one of the most fascinating religious groups I have ever encountered, the Love Family. I was introduced to them by a social worker who was monitoring their treatment of children. (She was doing her own field observations and interviews to determine whether a particular child should be removed from the custody of a parent who was a member and placed in the custody of the nonmember parent.)

The Love Family had come into being at the end of the 1960s, out of a drug-induced transcendental experience of the founder, who subsequently called himself Love Israel. He gave members new names reflecting the virtues of Christ, and it was intriguing to meet people called Logic, Serious, Understanding, and Fresh. Each of these "virtue names" was represented by a hieroglyphic symbol, which might be woven into the person's robe or made into a ring, and some of the religious scriptures were written in this novel sacred language.

The buildings that constituted their commune on Queen Anne Hill were clustered about a space where trolly cars used to turn around years before, and it seemed almost like a self-contained village. The group had modified two adjacent houses until they grew together. Dozens of abandoned windows had been cleaned to the bare wood and nailed together to make a marvelous greenhouse of a structure where much of the work was done. Inside, the houses were decorated with all kinds of art made by members, although the favorite subject was the faces of the group, sometimes carved into the back of a chair or painted on panels, often arranged to spell out "We are one."

Before I romanticize this cult excessively, I should mention that I observed tremendous power differentials. Love Israel gave all the orders, even deciding which men and women should pair off and bear children. There was public concern that children were being abused, although I never saw this happen. Women were treated as servants, and discipline was so strong that Love Israel did not even have to give orders. Once, when we were having tea, he raised the spoon he had finished using into the air, and instantly one of the women took it for washing, not interrupting for an instant what he was saying. At the meals I attended, the women did not speak unless spoken to.

The group did not believe in modern medicine, and thus did not immunize children against diseases. Nor did they believe in using eyeglasses, so members with poor eyesight had to cross the streets on faith. When they bought some old dental equipment it seemed to mark an accommodation with the medical norms of the outside world, but I shuddered to imagine what it would be like for an untrained member to drill my teeth, using dull drills and no anesthetic but faith! Before I began my study, two adult members had died under conditions that roused public suspicions. The rumor was that the two were found unconscious from misuse of drugs required for membership, and that the group had attempted to revive them through meditation rather than by calling the city's emergency paramedic squad.

At the time, the ethics of research with human subjects was a hot issue in sociology, and the federal government had begun issuing guidelines based on experience with medical experiments but extending to all the sciences. I dutifully explained all the ethical issues of studying deviant groups in my submission to the university's human subjects committee. The federal guidelines for research on human subjects were based on two key principles. First, the researcher must obtain the freely given, informed consent of each individual studied. Second, each research subject must have the right to withdraw from the research project, and remove any personal data about himself or herself, at any time. I felt that these two principles, derived from medical research, could not be applied to sociological field research.

Imagine you are studying social interaction in bars, through the time-honored method of sitting on a bar stool and watching what the other people do. The human subjects guidelines meant you would first have to get each person in the bar to sign a consent form. If only one said "no," you couldn't watch. When new persons entered the bar, you would have to rush over and get them to sign as well. Somehow, I didn't think this would work.

The situation with the Love Family was very different. I had explained my project thoroughly to Love Israel, and he emphatically requested that I study his group. He was ready to line the 200 members up and have them sign the forms. Within the group, however, the idea of freely given, individual consent did not exist. He would tell them to sign, and they would do as they were told.

The issue of withdrawing from the research was probably confused because the guidelines were new and nobody understood how to apply this principle from medical ethics to field sociology. If participants in medical research wanted to stop taking the experimental injections, they had the right to withdraw from the study. But as applied to research on the Love Family, this principle was expanded to mean that people who wanted to withdraw could take away any tapes of interviews they had given me or any other personal information. This implied that at any time the cult's leader could change his mind and have his people strip my office of all the data I might have invested months collecting. This was an impossible condition.

Eventually, I decided not to proceed with the research, despite the cult leader's clear request that his group be studied, because I saw no way of doing the study within the current ethical guidelines. The university, in fact, offered me an escape clause from the human subjects procedures, saying that I could do the research outside the aegis of the university, as a private citizen exercising his normal rights. Freedom of the press, guaranteed in the Constitution of the United States, may give sociologists the right to violate some of their own field's ethical standards, if we agree that sociologists are members of the press.

I met the Love Family just when discussion of ethical issues was at its height, both in sociology specifically and in universities in general. Before that time, little attention had been given to the rights of human subjects. Since then, the ethical rules for sociological research have actually loosened considerably, and our field has been coping with the lack of a perfect consensus on the right rules to follow. Thus, I cannot give you a strict set of guidelines. As mentioned in the previous chapter, the American Sociological Association has published a booklet on ethics, giving its guidelines not only for research but also for teaching and publishing. The ASA also has procedures for considering charges of ethical misconduct leveled against members, but it has little power to collect facts about the case or to enforce its judgments. Many sociologists do not belong to the ASA, and it simply does not have the resources, let alone the mandate, to become the police force for sociology.

Although ethical problems may arise in any kind of research, observational field research raises the most obvious ethical problems. I, like many other sociologists studying deviant behavior in the field, have observed crimes being committed. Have you ever committed misprision of a felony? Sounds terrible, doesn't it? **Misprision** is a crime, defined as concealment of treason or a felony by someone not guilty. So, if you are doing research on a deviant group and see a felony being committed,

you also are breaking the law if you fail to report it.

Although it does not happen often, field researchers sometimes have been served with subpoenas demanding them to turn over their data for use in a legal case, and you may have no legal right to refuse, even though you promised to keep the information confidential (Bond 1978). On many occasions while doing observational research in the field, I have seen people being harmed in ways that might not be criminal but made me feel I wanted to stop what was happening or make public some secret information I had collected.

When should the field observer intervene in events he or she observes? I wish I had a general answer to give you, but I do not. I have met many people I liked while doing research on deviant religious cults, and one time I made the mistake of trying to "save" one of my new friends from a cult. He was an English teacher from West Virginia who had just been divorced and moved to Boston to start a new life. Cut off from old friends and familiar environments, he was ready prey for one of the cults that was actively recruiting socially adrift individuals. With care, and I thought great skill, I helped this fellow realize that the cult was not good for him, and he quit. But the next time I saw him, two weeks later, he had joined another cult almost the same as the one I had "saved" him from! That was a good lesson for me.

Before you intervene in a situation you are observing, please make very certain you are not acting from arrogance and ignorance. That was the twin mistake I made when I intervened for the English teacher. I may have felt he was being tricked and brainwashed by the cult, but he apparently felt he was voluntarily undertaking a spiritual quest that would undoubtedly entail some risk and adventure. In my arrogant, self-centered perception of what was happening to him, I failed to grant him full respect as an autonomous human being, and my perception that he was being duped was insulting in the extreme. This is a problem sociologists may often face, when we claim to know what is good for people, and the people themselves have a very different idea.

These are not by any means issues limited to research on deviant groups. Study ordinary families in their homes, and you may wind up affecting relations between family members. Study workers in a corporation, and your research report is likely to affect the balance of power between labor and management.

Although there may be no satisfactory solution to the ethical problems of observational field research, three points should be kept in mind when preparing to do such a study. First, it is essential to respect your educational institution's guidelines for research on human subjects, and the guidelines of the agency, if there is one, that provides financial support for the project. Second, the very presence of ambiguity in ethical standards means that the individual researcher is under heavy

obligations to consider the ethical dimensions of any project very seriously, taking care not to ignore such questions simply because they are inconvenient. And finally, the field observer must be aware that he or she is also a participant in the human drama, placed personally at risk by the sheer fact of being in the midst of real life while doing the research, possessing all the legal and moral rights of every other participant, but in no way more sacred or more sheltered from criticism than they.

Ethical questions may not concern you as you experiment with the first computer program in our set, one that simulates observational research on the Process cult. But as you play this harmless game, you should occasionally ask yourself what the ethical qualities of your moves in the game would be if you were making them in real life rather than on the screen of a computer.

The Social Map Computer Program

How would you like to visit the Process? Unfortunately, my time machine has room for only one person, so you will have to go alone, but I'll brief you before you go on your expedition. Travel back to the spring of 1971 at 46 Concord Avenue, Cambridge, Massachusetts: the chapter house of the Boston branch of the Process Church of the Final Judgement. If you visit this address today, you will find a bland, brick apartment building, but in 1971 there was a large frame house, owned ironically enough by Harvard University but rented by the Process.

If you walked past 46 Concord Avenue a few times, glancing at the house from different sides, you would see that it was a complex structure, with doors at the front and side. In addition to a large basement, you would see that it had three stories. The top one, a bit smaller than the first and second floors, was more than a mere attic, because you could see several large windows nestled under the peak of the roof.

Your assignment, should you choose to accept it, is to investigate the Process chapter house, taking part in cult rituals if you are brave enough, drawing social maps of the four floors of the building, and developing a schedule of the main activities of the week. You can do so through a computer game I have created, designed to give you some practice with simulated but realistic observational field research.

You should start the computer as described in the introduction to this book, and select program CULT, the social map of the Process. Each of the programs on your disks has its own four-letter name, and this name denotes the group you will study. Remember that the disk operating system (DOS) must have been loaded into the computer so that it is ready to run. Then, the right program disk has to be put into the computer—Disk 1 in this case—and you type the name of the program you want, followed by (ENTER).

When the CULT program starts, the computer will ask you what your sex is. Please do not be offended by this question. The computer needs to know your gender, because people get sorted into the two sexes in a couple of minor features of the cult's life. Unlike many other religious groups, the Process was absolutely dedicated to sexual equality, and it gave equal rights and authority to females and males. But it still needed to tell them apart, so please tell the computer which sex you are.

You do this by pressing (M) for Male or (F) for Female. The computer screen will display these two options. You will see the word Male, with the *M* outlined in a little box, like this: (M)ale. And similarly, the word Female has its first letter boxed: (F)emale. As I am sure you have guessed, (M)ale and (F)emale have their first letters in boxes so they will look like keys on the computer keyboard. This is a standard convention with my software. Whenever you see a letter boxed on the screen to look like a key, you can make something happen by pressing the key it depicts. Don't worry about whether to type a capital letter or a lowercase (little) letter. Just press the key.

This is a good time to remind you about another important key, (ESC), because the computer says, "(ESC)ape to QUIT" when it asks you your sex. (ESC) is the ESCAPE key, and it usually sits near the upper left-hand corner of the keyboard. Often, it will allow you literally to escape from the current situation on the screen. It will take you back to the start of the program or to some other starting point. In this program, you can often (but not always) use it to escape from the chapter house. Yes, if the Processeans are about to eat you, you can press the key to save yourself! But actually, they won't try to do that, and the key merely takes you out of the house quickly to save you time.

Pressing a key is an art. No, really. You should give the key a single, swift press. Do not hold the key down, or the computer will think you are pressing it again and again. This is especially true for the (ESC) key, because it is so powerful. If you hold this key down, the computer will escape you from one situation to another; then it may think you want to escape again from that new situation, and it may sweep you off to somewhere else you might not want to go. Just give (ESC) a firm, quick tap.

When the computer knows who you are, it will ask you what day and hour it is. It is ready to take you to the Process chapter house, but it needs to know when you want to arrive. Some days, the chapter house is closed to outsiders. Other days, it is open only during certain hours. And maybe you want to visit for a particular activity that takes place at a particular hour on a particular day. The computer will say:

```
CONTROL PANEL
[H]our: 8 PM
[D]ay: Saturday
```

```
[Q]uit or change programs
press [H] or [D] to set Hour and Day
Press [ENTER] to visit the PROCESS CHAPTER HOUSE
```

If you press (D), the day will change. Pressing (D) once turns Saturday into Sunday. Press it seven times and you go through all the days of the week, getting back to the day you started.

Pressing (H) will change the hour. The program starts out at eight o'clock on Saturday evening, which happens to be a good time to visit the chapter house. Each time you press (H), the hour will increase by one.

Do not press the Q key until you have completed your field research on the Process. Pressing (Q) ends the program, and you will lose much information and social status that you may have acquired while studying the cult. So avoid pressing (Q) until you are really ready to quit working with the computer.

When you have the day and time just the way you want them, press (ENTER). In a moment, a map of the chapter house will appear on the screen. At first, it is not much of a map, just an outline of the house's shape, with two doors. The door on the right is the front door of the house, and the door at the bottom is the side door. If you are able to enter the house and visit various parts of it, the rooms you have been in will appear clearly on the map. As you progress, your knowledge of the house will increase step by step.

Near the front door of the house, you will see a flashing rectangle. This is you. Your chief job is simply to walk around and observe your surroundings. But the rectangle on the screen does not have any legs. How do you walk? The right end of your computer keyboard should have keys with arrows on them: (→) (↓) (↑) (←). These are not the (BACKSPACE) and (ENTER) keys, which may have big left-pointing arrows, but four keys with little arrows pointing in every direction. These are called **cursor control keys**, and the flashing rectangle on the screen is called a **cursor**. If you press one of these keys, the cursor will move in the indicated direction. For example, pressing (↓) moves the cursor (flashing rectangle) downward.

On most current IBM-type computers, the cursor control (arrow) keys are also keys for typing in numbers. For example, (↓) also has the number 2 on it. Some of you may know that there is a special key called the number lock key that makes these keys type numbers. Please don't worry about this. I have written the program so that these keys always act as arrows rather than numbers. (Incidentally, you could move the cursor around also by pressing the even-numbered number keys up above the letters on your keyboard. But that's too confusing for general use.) Just press the key with the correct arrow on it, and the cursor will go where you want.

You can't walk through walls, however. Try running the cursor into the house, and you will find it stops at the wall. Did you bump your head? Also, you can't walk down the street, off the computer screen. For practice, try walking around the house, and take this opportunity to look all around the screen. If you have a color display computer, you will be walking on a green outline which represents the grass around the house. The house itself is blue on computers with color.

Outside the upper right corner of the lawn is a message reminding you of the time, running vertically. It might say "6 Saturday," for example. Below it is a message, also running vertically, telling you which floor of the house the map depicts:

Floor 0 (the cellar), Floor 1, Floor 2, Floor 3 (the attic). Naturally, the program starts out on the first floor (ground floor), but you will get the opportunity to visit the three other stories of the house if you are clever and do successful field research.

Once you have walked around the house, you are ready to consider entering it. Notice again the two doors, each labeled "door." You will encounter many doors inside the house as well. The best way to enter a door is to come straight up to one of the *o*s in the middle of the word and take a step toward it. Sneaking up to the edge of the door—moving in line with the letters and bumping into the *d* or *r*—won't work.

Move to the front door, the one at the right of the screen, and attempt to enter it. Surprise! It's locked. But try entering it, just to see what happens. A large space will open up on the left side of the screen, and a message will appear. This will happen often while you are running the program. In computer slang, we call message spaces like this *windows,* so I'll call them that here. You won't be climbing in or out of actual windows on the house, so when I refer to a window it is a big space that opens up on the left or right side of the screen to give you a message.

While a computer window is open, you cannot move your cursor around on the screen, and you cannot escape by pressing (ESC). Heh, heh: we've caught you! But don't panic. The windows are pretty harmless. Read the messages in them carefully. They may describe some cult activity that you are participating in, or they may just give you information about your surroundings, such as the simple message you get when you attempt to enter the front door. Note that the last thing appearing in a window is an instruction to press a key on the keyboard. For example, the window that opens when you try to get in the front door has "Press (ENTER)" at the bottom of it.

When you follow this instruction, the window will close, the message will vanish, and you will be free to walk around the house again. Often, a window will fill with a new message after you press (ENTER). Read the message, and if the window instructs you to, press (ENTER) again. Some windows have many messages to give. Others, like the one for the front door, have just one.

A few windows have questions in them. Here's one you won't see, but it communicates the idea: "Are you willing to sell your soul to the Devil? (Y)es or (N)o." You would decide whether you wanted to sell your soul to the Devil, and you would press the appropriate key, (Y) for Yes or (N) for No. One other important question that may be asked in windows will become clear when you try to enter the side door.

So, go around to the side door, near the bottom of the screen, and attempt to enter. What happens next will depend upon what hour of what day it is. You may find the door locked. The first time you try to enter the door (whether locked or not), and every time you find it locked, a sign will give you good hints about when you should visit next. Press (ENTER) to get rid of the message. When the window has closed and you are able to walk around the house, you can press (ESC) to return to the questions about day and hour, selecting a better time for your next visit.

But it may turn out that you have visited the Process chapter house at a good time, and you will enter the side door and suddenly find yourself on a flight of stairs. How do you know? A message will appear telling you:

```
You are on some stairs.
Which way do you want to go?
[U]p the stairs
[S]tay on the current floor
[D]own the stairs
```

Thus, the computer will ask if you want to go up, down, or stay on the same level. To go up, press (U). To go down, press (D). To stay on the same level, press (S).

As in a real house, the stairs allow you to go from one floor to another. And remember, there are four floors to the house, so you will need to take the stairs a good deal. Obviously, when you are in the attic, you can't go up the stairs any further, and you can't go any lower than the basement. So you don't always have the choice of (U)p, (D)own, and (S)tay when you enter some stairs. Sometimes it is just (U)p and (S)tay, or just (D)own and (S)tay. The computer knows how the house is put together and will offer you the correct choices.

Suppose you enter at the side door, the computer asks you which way you want to go, and you press (D) to tell it "down." As the message window is closing, the computer will put a map of the basement on the screen. At first, it will look almost exactly like the map of the first floor, quite blank and featureless. This is because you haven't explored it yet. But one feature will be apparent, the stairs themselves. They even look a bit like stairs. And you will see the flashing cursor, which represents you, on the stairs. Since you have decided to go down, you should continue walking. With luck, you will shortly step off the stairs into a room. Every time you enter a new room, the computer will offer you some information about it and add it to the maps.

Be prepared for surprises when you enter doors. Sometimes they will be unlocked, and you can pass right through, discovering a new room. At other times they are locked. Unless you can find a key somewhere, you will probably not be able to enter. At other times, a member of the Process—a Processean, as they call themselves—will encounter you at the door and perhaps send you back where you came from.

Also, if you want to attend rituals and formal activities of the cult, you will have to be in the right place at the right time. First of all, outsiders are not permitted to go into the main ritual room (wherever that is in the house!) by themselves. They are led in by officials of the cult. So outsiders have to wait somewhere else until someone comes to lead them to the rituals. You might ask yourself where outsiders would wait. Of course, you would have to become at least slightly familiar with part of the building before you could have any idea of the answer.

I should tell you that there are three ways to make time pass in this game. One way is to go to the part of the program that lets you change the day and hour, and do so. Another is to take part in a ritual or activity, because each of these typically lasts an hour. The third will remain a little secret. It is very simple, but I will leave it to you to discover. Watch the time indicator at the upper right corner of the screen while you are doing things in the chapter house, and see what might make it jump forward an hour.

If you are in the right place at the right time, a Processean will lead you to an activity. You won't have to press any keys, just watch as the cursor zips around, going through doors, climbing stairs, and so on. You will find that the route takes you outdoors and then back in again. If this seems strange, I must assure you that this is how things were done when I first began participating in the rituals myself. Although I had to simplify some things to get the Process chapter house into your computer and to make it possible for you to play the game successfully, I have kept very close to reality. The program is quite accurate in most sociologically interesting respects.

You deserve a couple more clues about how to negotiate the game. The Process was highly stratified, having a series of levels of status, knowledge, and access. Most parts of the building are off limits to outsiders. Low-ranked members could enter only a few more rooms than could outsiders. Middle-ranked members could go almost anywhere. Thus, you may have to consider joining the cult and gaining status within it if you are going to get a complete set of social maps.

If you play the game right, you can advance as far as the rank of Messenger. There are three higher ranks, which you cannot achieve in this game: Prophet, Priest, and Master. But there are also ranks below Messenger. Messengers do not live in the chapter house; they have their own commune, called the messenger flat, across town. So Messengers frequently visit the chapter house, as you will do if you become a Messenger.

But I should not tell you any more. The game should be fun, and even more important, it should give you realistic practice figuring things out. In doing my actual field research, I had to go through all the stages you will. At first, I had no idea what the activities were, what the social statuses were, or even what the different rooms of the house were used for. Observation and deduction were very important tools for finding out, as was a certain amount of enterprise. But it was also essential to keep good notes and draw social maps as I progressed step-by-step through my research. You will have to do the same. Although the computer will display the outline of any room you have visited, and a set of maps develops on the screen as you explore, these maps do not say anything about what each room is used for, so you may need to draw your own set of maps to supplement the one on the screen.

PROJECTS FOR CHAPTER 2

The first three projects listed below, which are designed to give you experience thinking through the logic of systematic field research, are done on the computer, using the CULT program. The first illustrates social maps, and you should actually draw a set of such maps as you work. The second asks you to explore time in the same way that maps explore space, making a schedule of regular events at the Process cult. The final computer exercise, project 3, asks you to create a diary of field observations, just as if you were performing field research on a real social group.

The remaining four projects are to be carried out in the real world, and students in my course on field research methods have found them excellent ways of focusing a short episode of field work. Project 4 concerns social maps again, but this time sending you into the real world rather than the simulated world of the computer. As discussed in this chapter, photography can be a very valuable research tool, and the fifth project assigns you to use a camera to record a social or cultural phenomenon. This chapter also noted that sociologists can benefit more than they often realize from collecting artifacts, following the example of archaeologists, and the sixth project lets you experience this for yourself. Finally, the seventh project asks you to do a census, counting some set of people or things in the field, thus driving home the points that the field can be the setting for quantitative as well as qualitative research and that field research can be highly systematic.

1. Explore the Process. Using the first computer program, explore the Process chapter house. As you "go" through the rooms, draw a set of social maps on large sheets of paper. Four maps are probably desirable, one for each floor of the building. The maps should explain what each room is and what social function it serves, as well as merely outlining the physical structure of the house. This can be done by putting a room number inside each room on your maps and attaching a set of pages with numbered paragraphs describing the rooms.

2. Make an Event Schedule. Construct a schedule of events at the Process chapter house, obtaining the data by exploring the house using the first computer program. The schedule should list the day and hours of each event, including the times the house is open to the public. The name of the event should be given, along with a brief description.

3. Diary of Field Observations. Write a field observation diary, step by step, as you explore the Process chapter house with the first computer program. Each entry in the diary should cover a visit to the house and should begin with the day and hours of the visit. The diary should state what parts of the house you entered, what experiences you had, and what activities you participated in. You should also include your hypotheses about the Process and tentative explanations of what you see, clearly labeled as your interpretations to distinguish them from direct observations.

4. Social Maps. Based on real research you do out in the field, draw a set of maps of a social environment, with accompanying comments on how social events and activities fit into the spaces and objects outlined on your maps. Many sorts of business establishments lend themselves to this kind of project. For example, the maps of a restaurant would show not only the area where customers eat but also food preparation areas, restrooms, offices, storage areas, and any other spaces.

Social maps of churches of different denominations often reveal much about the organizations, their style of worship, and social composition. In some cases, one would want to add versions of the maps showing where people sit or stand. One can photocopy several copies of an outline sketch of a meeting room, then draw on each the positions of things and people when the room is being used for different purposes. For example, a traditional Russian Orthodox church I once visited did not have seats for the congregation (a fact your maps would indicate), and the men stood on the right side of a wide aisle, with the women on the other. By the middle of a long service, many of the men were found standing and chatting in the entry area, on the front steps, and in the yard. The women at this time began lighting votive candles and circulated around their side of the church in a set pattern to accomplish this. All these facts, indicated easily on half a dozen photocopies of the basic map of the church, would tell much about the traditions and social relations of members.

5. Photographic Documentation. Take and document a series of photographs recording a particular event or set of cultural objects. One hundred shots, equivalent to three rolls of 36-exposure 35-millimeter film, should be sufficient. To save money, there is no need to have enlarged prints made, and either slides or positive contact sheets would be good enough. The photographs should be numbered, as those on contact sheets already are, and should be accompanied by brief written descriptions of each shot. These descriptions should provide just enough documentation to make it completely clear when and where each shot was taken and what it shows. A record of a parade, for example, would show all the marching formations, start to finish, with the pictures numbered in order and accompanied by one-sentence descriptions that named each school band, float, or major celebrity.

6. Artifact Collection. Make a documented artifact collection of 20 or more objects from a distinct sociocultural group or activity unfamiliar to you. If it is not feasible to obtain the actual thing itself, careful three-view drawings with written descriptions of materials, function, and color would be sufficient. Some of the collection items can be borrowed, but you should avoid merely taking a collection already assembled by someone else. The educational purpose of this project is twofold: to gain experience collecting artifacts and to gain practice interpreting the social meaning of objects. In your brief written documentation of each object, you should give some information about its social meaning. Bring your collection to class and display it in a show-and-tell. Depending upon the nature and size of the collection, you may want to pass in to the instructor only the written descriptions.

7. Census. Conduct a three-part observational census of people or things in the field. The result should be one or more clear quantitative tables and a few paragraphs of description telling where and how you got the numbers and what they suggest about the social questions each touches upon. For example, a student once visited three very different neighborhoods and tabulated the kinds of automobiles that were parked near residences. He found that the proportions of different kinds of cars varied greatly, reflecting the different levels of wealth and lifestyle orientations of the neighborhoods. Another possibility is to count people in some public place. How many men, women, boys, girls, old versus young, well-dressed versus scrubby, or other categories of people are in the waiting rooms at bus, train, and plane terminals? Avoid using these examples, but invent your own census-like, quantitative field observation study.

CHAPTER SUMMARY

Research that is done in real-world settings, by watching and listening but without intrusive experimental manipulations or formal survey questionnaires, is called *observational research*. Sociologists sometimes casually refer to field research methods as if they were radically different from other approaches, but the field is not a method; it is a place. This chapter emphasizes qualitative field research, but it is possible to do quantitative research through field observation as well. Good observational research is usually *unobtrusive,* systematic, and comparative. The chief example presented in the chapter is research on the Process Church of the Final Judgement, an unusual religious cult.

Field researchers play various roles. An *ethnographer* is a trained, professional documenter of the culture of a group. A *participant observer* is not aloof from the phenomenon under study but participates in it to some extent, sharing the experiences of ordinary (nonresearcher) participants. A *field theorist* uses real-world experiences to inspire his or her theories and may not need systematic methods. Observers may be either *overt* or *covert.* Research subjects also may play different roles, including gatekeeper, windowkeeper, native informant, and exploiter.

Among the focused methods field observers use are a diary of field notes, working papers, artifact collections, photography, social maps, and census taking. A number of special methods have been devised for observation of small groups, notably interaction process analysis.

Field observation raises many ethical questions, because observers learn secrets that would harm people they studied if made public, and publications based on good research concerning situations of conflict are bound to disseminate information that will help one side in the conflict and hurt the other. Field researchers may find themselves parties to legal disputes, and their records may be subpoenaed, even if they promised to keep the information confidential.

KEY CONCEPTS FOR CHAPTER 2

Interviewing

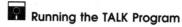
CHAPTER OVERVIEW

Although interviewing is an art, many aspects of it can be learned through practice, instruction, and reading about the experiences of professional interviewers. A key issue is the building of rapport with the person being interviewed, and mutual trust is essential. Raymond Gordon identified eight factors that inhibit communication in interviews and eight factors that facilitate it.

A researcher has to develop the knack of finding the right person to interview and convincing that person to play the appropriate role. An informant provides objective information, while a respondent expresses feelings or opinions. Some interviewees are liars, and one must guard against a variety of factors that can introduce bias into the interview.

Once the interviewee begins answering questions, the answers have to be captured, either by writing them on an interview schedule or by tape recording; although convenient during the interview, recordings must be transcribed before they can be analyzed. Among the varieties of sociologically useful interviews are subculture dictionaries, life histories, and oral histories.

The second software program, TALK, is designed to go with this chapter. It lets you pretend to interview twenty members of the Process cult, learning about them as individuals and piecing together information from several to discover the beliefs, practices, and history of the group. This computer simulation cannot substitute for experience interviewing real human beings, but it does provide excellent practice in designing a series of interviews and combining information from several people.

Interviews and questionnaires have much in common. Each uses a set of questions posed by the researcher and answered by the interviewee. Because of this overlap in methods, we will consider many aspects of question-writing that are important for interviewing in Chapter 7, which is on *survey research,* the systematic polling of the population or of a sample drawn from it. A questionnaire written to guide interviews is called an **interview schedule.** Usually the answers go right on it, just as with a printed questionnaire the interviewee fills out, except that the interviewer will do the writing.

Similarly, field observation and field interviewing are not completely distinct activities. While simply observing, one frequently asks questions, and a series of questions equals an interview. On the other hand, an interviewer cannot help observing the person being interviewed, and many interviews are conducted out in the field. Therefore, many of the principles that apply to field observation also apply to interviewing, and vice versa. The immediately following sections, on gaining rapport and achieving successful communication, apply as much to observation as to interviewing.

Interviews as Focused Communication

Although sociological interviews can be highly rigorous tools of scientific research, at heart they are invariably a completely human process: communication between two people. Essential to this is an appropriate relationship between the parties, conditions conducive to honest and free expression of thoughts and feelings, and the interviewer's awareness of the factors that facilitate or block successful communication.

Establishing Rapport

To get a good interview, you must make the person interviewed feel that it is both safe and good to answer, and thus you must help him or her feel at ease while interested in your questions and motivated to respond correctly. My dictionary defines **rapport** as a relationship marked by harmony, conformity, accord, or affinity. A sociologist might add a dash of excitement and a cup of commitment to this recipe. Perhaps the crucial questions the interviewee will have about you are "Who is that person? What is that person doing?" To a certain extent, you must project the positive image of a good person engaged in a harmless but important task. Erving Goffman has called this **impression management**. The idea is not a new one. In the 1930s, when a team of sociologists studied every aspect of a small Massachusetts town, they found it expedient to present themselves to different people in different ways:

> We made no attempt to explain all our aims to any one person. Since our interests were most varied, all information offered to us was grist for our mill. Most of the older residents were "historically minded" and thought of any social research as historical. To them we were social historians. To the industrialists and some of the businessmen we were social economists, and to many of the older ladies we were students interested in genealogical history. To the members of the various ethnic groups we were fair-minded gentlemen interested in seeing that their groups received their

rightful place in the economic and social study we were making. To those who saw us at entertainments and parties, I fear, we were young men having a good time, not too intent upon our work. Nevertheless, in such gatherings we were able to obtain some of our most valuable information. (Warner and Lunt 1941:43)

In my research on the Process cult, I established rapport by becoming a member of the group and adjusting my apparent personality to fit what the "real" members wanted of me. It is seldom necessary, however, to belong to a group in order to achieve rapport with its members. Blanche Geer suggests that finding the appropriate role is not a matter of becoming positively like group members but, rather, is a "matter of judicious negatives." She says the researcher "should not have the manner or appearance of any group which the informant group distinguishes sharply from itself" (Geer 1964:325). Besides speaking and acting in ways that are nonthreatening, you should cultivate a relatively neutral role, but one that allows you to be highly approachable for the people you want to interview.

Berk and Adams (1970) have written about the problems of establishing rapport with deviant groups, but the principles they identify should apply to most groups you are interested in studying. They begin by emphasizing techniques for establishing and maintaining trust. First, they say the researcher should always be honest with the subjects, partly for ethical reasons and partly because the researcher may easily be caught in a lie, leading to the collapse of the trust essential for good interviewing.

Second, Berk and Adams suggest that the researcher should do some of the work at a time obviously inconvenient for him or her, thus proving great motivation to talk with the subjects. This principle may be expanded to include any effective ways of communicating the fact that the subjects and their interviews are of great importance to the researcher. Third, the researcher should always keep his or her word. Fourth, the researcher should present the reasons for the investigation in as flattering terms as possible, consistent with plausibility.

Berk and Adams then list five techniques for establishing and maintaining respect and acceptance, important qualities for a successful interview. First, although it is important for an interviewer dealing with subjects who speak (in any sense) a different language to communicate in their terms, the interviewer should not adopt the slang style of the subjects unless it is very natural for him or her. The subjects may appreciate the special effort the interviewer makes to learn their language, but they know the interviewer is not a member of their group and may be offended by the interviewer's pretense of membership. Language is the medium of interviews, so one should take care to adopt the right language.

For example, I once had a bath in Baahth. This was in the English city of Bath, which the local residents pronounce *Baahth*. I felt it would be disingenuous to say I took a baahth in Baahth, because every Englishman talking with me would know I was an American who pronounced the word *bath*. But it felt appropriate to pronounce the city's name the way the residents would, just as I might say Köln rather than Cologne when in that German city. So I had a bath in Baahth.

Second, the interviewer must not appear shaken by what he or she hears and sees, even if it is very shocking to the researcher's personal standards. Third, researchers should be aware that the subjects are observing and questioning them, too, and that at times the subject may test interviewers to see what kinds of people they are. Fourth, Berk and Adams advise thinking ahead and trying to anticipate situations that might arise, including possible risks that may threaten the research or even the researcher's personal safety. And fifth, they argue that it is wise to remain neutral when a conflict divides group members into factions.

Finally, whether in a relatively brief interview, a long series of interviews, or extended field observation, it is best to gain the subjects' acceptance before being too obvious about collecting data. Of course, you may learn interesting things from the very first moment, but it would be best not to be seen as grabbing fists full of data until you have established at least some basis of rapport. One way of facilitating this, Berk and Adams say, is to reveal some intimate facts about yourself. Reciprocity is a hallmark of good human relationships, and if you want your interviewees to share themselves with you, you should share something of yourself with them. Naturally, this principle is conditioned by the focus of the research and the nature of the research setting; for example, you don't get a series of interviews with stock brokers off to a good start by talking about the delinquent acts you performed when you were a juvenile, something that might work when interviewing juvenile delinquents.

But it would be too simplistic to say that always, in all research situations, the subjects must feel perfectly comfortable with the researcher. Even when respondents do not want to reveal information, the researcher can often extract it from them anyway, although the techniques effective in achieving this raise ethical issues. A classic example comes from the research E.E. Evans-Pritchard (1937) did on witchcraft among the Azande of central Africa. For a time, Evans-Pritchard considered becoming a witch doctor himself to learn the secrets of that profession, but a European might not easily be accepted into an African secret society, so he used his "personal servant," Kamanga, instead. Kamanga was initiated into the secret society, experienced many interesting adventures, and reported all he learned to his boss.

Meanwhile, Evans-Pritchard was endeavoring to interview various witch doctors, at first meeting with little success. Then information began to flow from Kamanga, and Evans-Pritchard (1937:151–152) used it to great effect: "While Kamanga was slowly being initiated by one practitioner, it was possible for me to utilize his information to draw out of their shells rival practitioners by playing on their jealousy and vanity." At first, people may greet the researcher with a brick wall of silence. "In the long run, however, an ethnographer is bound to triumph. Armed with preliminary

knowledge nothing can prevent him from driving deeper and deeper the wedge if he is interested and persistent."

Often the technique is that of information merchant rather than simple information gatherer. If, like Evans-Pritchard, you are studying witch doctors who possess various secret remedies and magic spells, your chief challenge is learning the first one or two, which you can then trade with other witch doctors to get their spells. Each witch doctor wishes he had the secrets of his competitors. If he is reluctant to give away any of his secrets, offer him an attractive deal—two spells for one, for example. In the end, you will have more magic spells than you know what to do with, and that is great for your research. But what is the impact on the people you have studied? Certainly, information has been spread around that would have been kept secret otherwise. Some witch doctors may gain business and others may lose. In the extreme, the entire system of magic may be upset.

Often you don't need to use any special guile at all. To your surprise, people will tell you all kinds of damaging things about themselves or their organization, even when you least expect it. One day I was prowling around a nuclear power plant—the exact circumstances need not concern us—when I got into a conversation with two of its guards. Note that they had never seen me before and I did not have any credentials that would logically convince them I was to be trusted. But in a few moments they were showing me all the visitors' records in their desk, complaining that nobody in administration cared who had signed into the plant and that the records were never picked up and filed properly as the rules demanded. All I did to provoke this very revealing lecture on the security deficiencies at the nuclear power station was to stand there vaguely helpless, asking the guards how uncredentialled people could get past their gate. What makes it all the more surprising was that the Nuclear Regulatory Commission was staging an inspection at that very moment, so for all the guards knew I was one of the inspectors and the discrediting information they gave me might ultimately cost them their jobs.

General Principles of Interviewing

Raymond L. Gordon (1969) has identified eight factors that inhibit communication in interviews and eight more that facilitate it. With luck and skill, the interviewer can find ways to reduce the effect of the inhibitors and increase the effect of the facilitators, thus encouraging the informant to give the desired information. The eight *inhibitors* are

1. Competing demands for time
2. Ego threat
3. Etiquette
4. Trauma
5. Forgetting
6. Chronological confusion
7. Inferential confusion
8. Unconscious behavior

If your informant has work to do, an appointment to get to, or has been looking forward to some time to relax in private, he or she will be less willing to give you time. These *competing demands for time* may cause the person to refuse an interview in the first place, to end the interview before you have asked all your questions, or to make the answers uselessly brief. Care in scheduling the interview may prevent this problem. Aim for times in the day or week when the particular type of person you want to interview is likely to be free, and if practicable let the person suggest a day and hour. When there is no way to avoid competing with other things the informant wants to do, consider ways of making a successful interview more valuable to him or her, perhaps by stressing the facilitators of communication discussed below.

Ego threat means that some aspect of the interview may threaten the self-esteem of the person. For example, this can happen if the topic of the interview is embarrassing to the interviewee. Care in phrasing your

questions may help, such as adding little phrases that suggest the respondent is just like many other people and therefore need not feel any special embarrassment. One school of thought advocates giving interviewees "unconditional positive regard," responding to whatever they say with a positive and accepting tone. In the extreme, this attempt to encourage interviewees can backfire. They may see through your tactic and be offended by your lack of genuineness, or they may misinterpret your blandness as lack of real interest. Stressing the fact that your motives are professional, rather than personal, and assuring the interviewee of confidentiality can also reduce ego threat.

Conventional *etiquette* prohibits saying certain kinds of things in public or to certain kinds of people. A person may feel inhibited speaking about sexuality, for instance, if the interviewer is of the opposite sex. In many cultures, speaking publicly about some matters is taboo, regardless of the audience. One solution to this problem is to establish a strong impression that an interview is very different from other social interactions and thus is not covered by conventional rules of etiquette. Under some circumstances, you might want to stress your professionalism—such as by donning medical attire for a medical interview—although this tactic runs counter to any attempt to gain rapport by appearing to be the same kind of person as the interviewee. If your interview schedule has some professional sounding sections—for example, a number of detailed factual questions about innocuous matters—you might want to put them in the beginning to get the informant into the role of information-giver, in a setting that seems remote from conventional etiquette restrictions.

If the interview touches on past *trauma* the informant has experienced, the pain and often outright fear that recollection of dreadful events brings can block communication. Here, the pain is not being caused by the interview, as in ego threat, but by the memories themselves. Unless you have proper professional training and experience, it can be a big mistake to try to do therapy during an interview, although a little ordinary human compassion and reassurance would be quite appropriate. You may decide that the information you would gain from probing the traumatic incident deeply are just not worth the pain you would cause your informant, and therefore stop asking about it. But if you decide to persist you will need to handle the traumatic incident carefully, perhaps coming back to it after a few minutes of happier talk about other matters and getting your information in nibbles rather than in big bites.

Sadly, informants may have already *forgotten* much of what you want to learn. At the outset, you should design your study so that it does not place impossible demands upon people's memories. A number of methods have been proposed for stimulating people's memories, but frankly I am rather suspicious of them. The extreme example is hypnosis, occasionally used as a tool to extract information from witnesses to a crime who say they do not remember key details. But no responsible official would rely upon information gained in this way, because it may be totally false despite the informant's conviction that it is true. Hypnosis is only the most dramatic example of the great influence that suggestion can exert on a person's answers to questions concerning matters about which he or she is originally uncertain.

You should strenuously avoid encouraging your informants to imaginatively reconstruct lost memories, and guard against confabulation from informants who are too strongly motivated but can't honestly recall what you want to know. I have found that gently asking questions around a topic can stimulate memories, but this can lead a respondent to misremember a dimly recalled event as being more similar to other, clearly recalled memories of similar events than in fact it really was. Perhaps the best advice is not to base important conclusions on dimly recalled memories, and to make sure the informant feels free to admit having forgotten. Your motto should be "False information is worse than none at all."

Perhaps the most common memory problem for interviews, so prevalent that Gordon placed it in its own category, is **chronological confusion**. One of the most important varieties of surveys, one administered each year to so many respondents that I was even included once, concerns crime victimization. I can recall vividly the phone ringing and the interviewer asking me if I had been the victim of a crime in the previous year. Yes, indeed, my apartment had been burglarized. There was a big footprint on my front door where the thief had kicked it in. My mother's wedding ring, gone forever. But wait. Did that burglary really take place during the previous 365 days, or could it have been 400 days earlier? Now, years later, when I think back, I even wonder whether I actually mentioned the burglary to the interviewer. Is it possible that the interview came before the burglary? All I am sure about is that both took place in the same apartment, and it is possible that I have the chronology completely mixed up. That both memories concern crime and happened in the same place may have caused me to fit them together in my mind.

The problem of exact timing is a major one for the victimization surveys, because they are attempting to discover how common various crimes are, and thus they have to use a time period such as one year, even if informants may be hazy on the dates. Because people may arrange events in their memories in a logical order, they may pull the events out of their actual chronological sequence and greatly distort interpretations of cause and effect. My only advice is to be very cautious about chronological data and to seek external verification whenever possible.

Inferential confusion means coming to a false conclusion about the meaning of past events. In particular, people may confuse the relations between different events, incorrectly seeing one thing as the cause of another or otherwise connecting two things that had nothing to do with each other. Often sociological research focuses on how people interpret events, taking their statements as expressions of ideology or otherwise being very interested in how people understand their world. But too often beginning sociologists expect their informants to analyze objectively the factors that cause events or to place events in a neat set of conceptual categories. Really, those are our jobs as professional sociologists, and we should not expect our informants to do them for us.

I have often faced this issue in my research on cults, because many cult members are addicted to introspective analysis of people and events, having a theory for everything and frequently wanting to talk more about their theories than about the facts they supposedly explain. In the final analysis, the sociologist does the analyzing, and unless you are specifically studying people's inferences, you should avoid encouraging interviewees to do much analysis and guard against confusions that their own tendencies to explain things may cause.

Often a social scientist may want to know about actions and reactions that the respondent is not aware of—what might be called *unconscious behavior*. Included are habits the person may never have thought about, behavior related to nonverbal forms of communication, and acts that occur under extreme emotional distress. If the respondent does not recognize or understand the behavior, it may be impossible to get him or her to talk coherently about it.

Perhaps the best antidotes to the eight inhibitions Gordon listed are his eight facilitators:

1. Fulfilling expectations
2. Recognition
3. Altruistic appeals
4. Sympathetic understanding
5. New experience
6. Catharsis
7. The need for meaning
8. Extrinsic rewards

When people agree to give an interview, they generally recognize that they have entered into an implicit contract. By answering the questions accurately and fully, the person *fulfills the expectations* not only of the interviewer but of the surrounding society, which constantly requires people to meet the demands of roles they adopt.

It can be useful to think of each interview as based on a tacit contract, because this reminds the interviewer that he or she should not violate the terms to which the interviewee has implicitly agreed. If the interviewer causes the interviewee significant psychological pain, or aggressively asks about matters the person had good reason to believe were outside the scope of the interview, the interviewee can legitimately withdraw from the situation. Each party has expectations for the other, and if the interviewer wants the interviewee to follow the rules, the interviewer has to as well. Of course, it is generally not necessary to state a formal contract between the parties, but the interviewer can communicate in many informal ways that the interview will be a serious, safe experience, and that serious, informative answers to the questions are expected.

By *recognition*, Gordon means the attention and respect the interviewer offers that contribute to the self-esteem of the interviewee. As he stresses, the recognition must be sincere, but the interviewer in fact has several reasons for respecting the informant. First, the informant possesses interesting information, or else there would be no point to the interview in the first place. Second, if sociologists are worth their salt, they are genuinely interested in other people, and this interest can be communicated with appropriate words, facial expressions, and tones of voice. Third, the informant is doing a service for the sociologist, and gratitude naturally produces genuine appreciation.

You may be aware that there are communications courses that train people to feign interest in what other people are saying and affection for strangers. I do not recommend these courses, which are usually taught outside the college setting, having taken a couple as part of my field research. Unless you are a great actor, many people will detect that you are a fake.

Unfortunately, in any research project there are down days, when the sociologist is bored with the whole business and can hardly keep awake during the interview, let alone display lively recognition. Personally, I have often found it best to schedule routine work, like data coding, during periods of low enthusiasm and save my time of fullest alertness and enthusiasm for my research subjects. They deserve it.

Altruistic appeals encourage the interviewee to contribute information for a good cause. Because most people still feel there is value in expanding scientific knowledge, they are willing to do a little to advance human knowledge. Indeed, a well-designed sociological interview offers the average person a rare opportunity to participate in expansion of scientific knowledge, and clearly for many people this is a significant motivation. Also, most people are willing to sacrifice some of their time to advance a student's education. My own students have discovered this again and again when I have sent them out to do a project for a research methods class. When you can combine these two altruistic motives—adding to scientific knowledge and advancing a student's education at the same time—most people are positively proud to contribute.

Depending on the nature of your research, other altruistic appeals may also be appropriate. The obvious example is research on disease: "Ultimately we hope this research will help us prevent the disease from which you are currently suffering." Often it is not so easy to express a similar claim for sociological research: "I want to interview you, a racist bigot, because I want to discover how to eradicate racism and bigotry." No, that won't work. But if appropriate, and you share basic values with your informants, you should find the words to enlist them in service of those values.

Sympathetic understanding means sharing the informant's feelings. Gordon believes that people generally desire to share negative as well as positive experiences and emotions. This borders on recognition, which was discussed above, but includes the need to confess one's sins and the desire to air one's gripes. Gordon suggests that people need other people to respond to them, that they seek acceptance and approval. Obviously, the interviewer needs to channel this psychological force in the direction of the needed information, rather than letting the interviewee's feelings take charge.

In my field interviews, when I was studying organized groups by interviewing many individual members, informants frequently filled my ears with complaints and accusations about the other members. To a certain extent, these expressions of anger can be grist for the sociologist's mill; but generally they are of value only as a means for committing the interviewee to the interview, making him or her yield the desired information in return for time bending a sympathetic ear.

For many informants, a professionally administered interview is a *new experience*. Even if they have been on the receiving end of an interview before, it is likely to have been a job examination or some other unpleasant experience during which they were sorely afraid of failure. Thus, a scientific interview can be great fun and full of happy excitement. It can relieve the tedium of the person's ordinary routine and may be a welcome break from obligations that weigh heavily on the interviewee. My students have been surprised to discover how often the people they interview thank them at the end and say they had a marvelous time. The sociologist should probably not make any special effort to inject entertainment into the interview. A well-designed interview study should be interesting enough, and the researcher should realize that the interview is a fresh experience for each interviewee, even though it may become dull and routine for the social scientist giving a series of them.

Catharsis is a concept introduced by the Greek philosopher Aristotle and employed by several varieties of psychologists and scholars of the arts. It is the process by which a person is purged of negative feelings and psychological complexes by expressing them or seeing them expressed through a great work of art. In this conception, the interview is a little like a laxative that empties out the digestive system, though in this case the recesses of the mind are the cavities that get cleared. Many people seldom have the opportunity to get things off their chest, perhaps because the people they share life with will judge them harshly if they speak too openly.

The interviewer is a neutral listener who wants to hear whatever the interviewee says, greeting even the most horrible statements with calm acceptance. Although a desire for catharsis may motivate people to talk actively in the interview, I worry that very strong desires for purgation will distort the interview in two ways. First, it may be hard to get the person to talk about matters of interest to the interviewer that are unrelated to the catharsis sought. Second, the person's intense psychological needs may distort what he or she says, injecting irrelevant meaning into topics that can in some way symbolize the person's deepest agonies. Thus, we should not intentionally stimulate catharsis but exploit this motive whenever it appears, carefully limiting the emotional outpourings so that they don't take over the interview.

The need for meaning may inspire many people to explore their memories and feelings with an intelligent listener who asks guiding questions. Life is a great mystery to most of us, and the interviewee may feel a scientific interview is a perfect setting to make sense of things that have puzzled him or her. The trouble is that he or she may start interviewing the interviewer! "Sometimes I wonder myself why I dropped out of college and joined that commune? What do you think, professor? You're an expert on communes and all, and I've told you a lot about myself. What is the answer? My whole life changed from that point on, and I wish I knew what it all meant." Aside from the possible waste of time, superficial analysis in the interview can distort the information collected. The interviewee can become so fascinated with a new perspective that it will color everything he or she says. Again, I find in these psychological needs danger as well as forces that may motivate a person to cooperate.

Extrinsic rewards can also help gain people's cooperation. Often, especially in psychological laboratory research, people are paid for their time. People may also see an indirect personal benefit to them from the study. Frequently, members of minority groups or somewhat stigmatized subcultures may cooperate with sympathetic interviewers in the reasonable hope that publication of the study will gain the group greater tolerance from the larger society. Parties to a social dispute may hope that the study will advance their cause and help defeat their opponents. Again, if the interviewee is too intensely motivated by the desire for particular rewards, the objectivity and balance of the interview may suffer.

As the past few concepts have illustrated, some of Gordon's facilitators can become inhibitors if they are allowed to dominate the interview. Also, Gordon may have missed one of the most important inhibitors that sociologists commonly confront in their research, *extrinsic costs and dangers*. A person who has committed crimes may reasonably fear that admitting them even to a scientific interviewer may bring the law down on his or her neck. A number of the deviant groups I studied were secret societies, dedicated to preventing outsiders and new members from gaining many kinds of information. Thus, it was very difficult to get inner members to talk about the secret doctrines and practices, because they knew the group would punish them if it became known they had spoken openly to me.

Members of some groups, for example members of the radical political right, have good reason to fear that information given to sociologists will be used against them and that published studies will harm their interests. Not long ago I had the interesting experience of interviewing a sociologist who was studying the Survivalists, a radical right-wing movement. His aim was to nail the Survivalists for the evil and stupid monsters he believed them to be, and he had no interest whatever in considering things from their point of view or extending the slightest sympathy to the members he interviewed. Note that my interview of the sociologist winds up harming his interests, because if you see a harsh report on Survivalists published by a sociologist, you may guess that this person admitted lack of scientific objectivity to me.

Selecting the Right Interviewee

Just as there is a knack in knowing what questions to ask and how to deliver them, it takes skill and imagination to find the right person to ask, but often you just have to think clearly about the obvious. In 1981, while driving through Cloverdale, California, I noticed that the town's fire hydrants were painted with wild designs. I stopped, pulled out my camera, and began documenting them. The plugs had been painted to resemble people—Benjamin Franklin, Casimir Pulaski, Pocahontas—and one was disguised as Snoopy the dog. What was this? There were two clues. First, most of the characters on the fireplugs were heroes of early American history. Second, these characters were painted on fire hydrants. How do you learn about a town's fire hydrants? Go to the fire department.

A five-minute interview with the fire chief revealed that the plugs had been painted a few years earlier by elementary-school kids as part of the bicentennial celebration. He said the kids had gotten carried away, painting more plugs than had been agreed upon and covering up the color-coded tops of the plugs that indicated each one's capacity. When the town had enough money, he added, the pictures would be erased by sand blasting. "We liked them for a while, but the charm wore off."

Sometimes the social researcher acts exactly like a private detective, for example when tracing lost persons. Suppose you are studying a particular organization and need to interview people who were active in it before your project began. Or you may be doing a follow-up survey on a group of people who filled out another survey some years before. This is the task that faced Clarridge, Sheehy, and Hauser (1977). A panel of over ten thousand high-school seniors had been surveyed in 1957 and again in 1964, and they were needed for a fresh survey in 1975. The researchers succeeded in finding 97.4 percent of the 1957 sample, including 99 percent of those who had been surveyed again in 1964. Their prime tool turned out to be the telephone.

I am told that Chicago detectives, trying to find a lost person, tend to drive out to O'Hare airport. No, they don't laboriously walk through all the terminals looking for the person waiting for a plane. Instead, they use a huge set of telephone directories that were set up in one part of the airport and that cover much of the nation. Many public libraries, and university libraries as well, have large collections of phone books. I became very familiar with phone books when I was studying the reception given to astrology around the country, simply by counting the astrologers listed in the *Yellow Pages.*

Clarridge, Sheehy and Hauser first checked the 1957 and 1964 surveys to see what information that had about each individual. A key fact was the names of the parents, and most of the former high-school seniors were readily located through parents who were still listed in the phone book. In other cases, the respondents themselves were found there. At times, the researchers used a city directory to identify people who lived in the respondent's old neighborhood, and calls to them frequently revealed where the person had moved. City directories are published by many municipalities, often annually, and they typically list all the people who live along each street of the town, thus allowing one to identify a person's neighbors. The researchers also called schools, labor unions, professional societies, and the military services. So long as your research project has the funding to cover extensive telephoning, avoid personally running all over the place in search of lost souls. As the phone book advertisement says, "Let your fingers do the walking."

One way to find the right people to interview, obviously enough, is to interview people more-or-less at random in the group under study, asking them who knows what. You have probably often had the experience of encountering a problem with your college registration or course schedule, when it can sometimes take the better part of a day to find the particular bureaucrat (or professor) who can straighten out the problem for you. You visit various offices and call others on the telephone, getting referred from one to the next until, you hope, you find the right person. The same tedious process works outside your college, too. In studying a particular organization, even if you are doing systematic interviews rather than wide-ranging observation, it is important to acquire a couple of native informants who know the social system very well and can help you navigate your way around it.

For a successful interview, you need a willing person who is competent to answer your questions. All too often, the person who has one of these attributes lacks the other, but researchers often add unnecessarily to this problem by failing to consider carefully enough whom to inflict the questions upon. For example, studies of drug use have found a considerable similarity between parental behavior and that of their children when children were the sources of information on the parents. But little correlation on drug use has been found when both the parents and the children were asked about their own drug use (Kandel 1974; Kandel, Treibman, Faust, and Single 1976). You should start with the assumption that the one who can best tell you about a person's feelings or behavior is the person in question. Only if you have

reason to believe the person will lie or is somehow incompetent to communicate the truth to you should you prefer to get the information from someone else.

A distinction is often made between two roles the interviewee may play, informant or respondent. An **informant** gives you objective information. A **respondent** gives you personal opinions, feelings, and attitudes. Of course, there is a sense in which nobody ever tells you the straight facts, no matter how hard they try, and each informant merely provides his or her opinions rather than objective information. Clearly, the roles of informant and respondent blur into each other in many particular interviews, but the distinction is worth preserving, at least in terms of the researcher's goals.

If you want the interviewee to act as a kind of research assistant, giving you simple information that you could have collected through observation if you had only been on the scene at the right time, then you are putting the person into the role of informant. If, however, your chief interest is how the person feels about something, or how he or she interprets the situation, then you are using the person as a respondent. Everybody is competent to be a respondent, but only some people are competent to act as informants about any particular matter.

Interview Bias

Howard Becker (1970:29) cautions interviewers to ask themselves four questions about informants before trusting what they say:

1. Does the informant have reason to lie or conceal some of what he sees as the truth?
2. Does vanity or expediency lead him to mis-state his own role in an event or his attitude toward it?
3. Did he actually have an opportunity to witness the occurrence he describes or is hearsay the source of his knowledge?

4. Do his feelings about the issues or persons under discussion lead him to alter his story in some way?

If the answer to any of these questions is "yes," then you should exercise caution in accepting what the person says as fact. However, a biased interviewee is not necessarily a useless one. Sometimes our research topic concerns such biases, since we often want to learn what people feel. Their distortions of fact may reveal much about their attitudes, but more often than not, biases add little to our research and may even threaten the validity of major findings.

In 1929, Stuart A. Rice alerted the readers of the *American Journal of Sociology* to what he called **contagion bias**, the tendency of the data to be infected by the views of the interviewer. This problem had come to Rice's attention 15 years before, in a massive study of applicants to the New York Municipal Lodging House. The respondents were indigents, people down on their luck and quite out of cash, who had no place to stay and hoped the city would provide them a bed. A dozen skilled interviewers grilled each of 2,000 applicants for half an hour, using a carefully prepared four-page schedule of questions. After the data had been tabulated, Rice noticed that two of the interviewers (call them A and B) had found very different causes for their respondents' poverty.

When interviewer A asked respondents why they were destitute, 34 percent mentioned alcohol as the cause, but interviewer B found that only 11 percent blamed alcohol. The interviewers were also supposed to write down their own opinions about the cause, and interviewer A was personally convinced that fully 78 percent were victims of drink. Sixty percent of interviewer B's respondents blamed industrial problems such as layoff, seasonal work, or a shutdown of the plant where they were employed, compared with 43 percent for interviewer A's respondents. Interviewer B himself thought the real figure was 73 percent. As Rice reports, these huge differences probably reflected very different assumptions the two interviewers held: "After the tabulation had been made, inquiry disclosed that A was an ardent believer in prohibition while B was regarded by his associates as a socialist."

Note two important facts. First, not only did the interviewers differ in their personal explanations for their respondents' destitution, but the respondents themselves placed the blame differently. Second, Rice never accused the interviewers of lying or consciously distorting the data. Apparently, the interviewers almost subconsciously communicated the answers they expected to hear, and the needy respondents willingly obliged.

Just before the United States entered the Second World War, Daniel Katz examined interviewer bias in a survey of opinions about labor-related and war-related issues. The respondents were about 1,200 residents of a low-income area of Pittsburgh, and the interviewers were of two kinds. Half were professional interviewers from the middle social class, while the other half were freshly trained members of the working class. Although the results were almost identical for many questions, for some there were substantial differences in the opinions expressed to the two classes of interviewers.

One item on the survey asked whether there should be a law against strikes in defense industries. Although 65 percent of respondents interviewed by middle-class pollsters agreed, just 54 percent of those with working-class interviewers did so. Another item asked if the Congress should ban membership in organizations that supported other governments, such as the pro-Nazi group called the German-American Bund. Although 91 percent of respondents with middle-class interviewers agreed, just 79 percent of those with working-class interviewers want to ban such groups. Apparently, the working-class respondents were more ready to disagree with the majority if the interviewer were from their own social class. Katz offered three possible explanations for these findings:

(1) Respondents have a tendency, often unconscious, to give the answers they think their questioners expect. (2) In labor disputes, where unionism has been an issue, the white-collar interviewer may meet active resistance in the form of deceit or non-cooperation from the worker who is suspicious of company spies. (3) The white-collar interviewer may unconsciously select his respondents instead of rigorously following his instructions. (Katz 1941:249)

Today, research institutes are quite aware of these problems and carefully train interviewers to minimize them. However, interviewer bias continues to plague surveys on controversial topics. For example, respondents give significantly different patterns of response to interviewers of a different race than to members of their own group. Anderson, Silver, and Abramson (1988a, 1988b) found that black respondents replied differently to questions about race relations, depending on the race of the interviewer. For example, one item measured how close the black respondent felt to blacks in general. In 1984, when the interviewer was black, 100 percent of black respondents felt close to blacks. But when the interviewer was white, only 71.3 percent did so.

An item in five interview surveys from 1964 to 1986 said: "Some say that the civil rights people have been trying to push too fast. Others feel they haven't pushed fast enough. How about you: Do you think that civil rights leaders are trying to push too fast, are going too slowly, or are they moving about the right speed?" In 1964, 31.5 percent of blacks responding to black interviewers felt that civil rights leaders were pushing too slowly, but only 17.7 percent expressed this view to white interviewers. In 1986, 54.3 percent said "too slowly" to black interviewers, compared with 43.9 percent to white interviewers.

The same kind of differences show up when respondents are asked whether they are going to vote or not, and on other issues that may indirectly concern relations between the races. This bias can distort research results in many ways. From 1976 to 1984, researchers had reported, the degree of closeness among blacks in the United States had declined, but detailed examination of the data revealed that what had really changed was the racial balance among interviewers. There were fewer black interviewers in 1984, so more of the black respondents were interviewed by whites and thus expressed less closeness with members of their own race.

When a bias like this turns up, we must not assume that respondents are lying or

that interviewers are pressing for certain kinds of answers. Many black respondents may simply have felt it would be impolite to express too much solidarity with members of their own race in the presence of a white interviewer. And, conversely, they may have felt politeness demanded more solidarity when the interviewer was black. This raises the almost insoluble question of which response is correct, the one given to an interviewer of a different race or the sometimes different answer given to a member of the respondent's own race.

Many researchers believe that a more candid and correct answer will be given to an interviewer of the same race, ethnic group, sex, and social class. But sometimes this may not be the case. For example, the black community has been the focus of many voter-registration drives in recent years, and individual members of the community who don't get around to voting may still feel a considerable obligation to do so. Like most of us, they tend to promise to do the right thing when a member of their community asks them; but, again like most of us, they may not follow through on this promise. When a black interviewer asks members of the black community if they plan to vote, more respondents may incorrectly answer yes than if a white interviewer had asked them.

Social psychologists often use the term **demand characteristics** to describe all the qualities the researcher brings into a situation that might demand a particular set of responses from the research subject. In linguistics, a branch of social science that often examines topics of interest to sociologists, there is much literature on **speech accommodation**, the tendency of a person to adjust his or her speech to conform to the style used by the people he or she is talking with. Thus, the interviewee may begin talking like the interviewer, adopting goals and assumptions implied by the style and setting of the interview. Both demand characteristics and speech accommodation can distort the information gained.

One problem may be in the assumption that people have firm attitudes about public issues. Instead, each person may have a range of responses, depending on the circumstances. The challenge is to select an interview approach that gets data closet in spirit to the scientific question the researcher wants to answer. A visit from the interviewer is not the same thing as election day itself. No interviewer, of whatever race, can get data that are perfectly predictive of whether a person is going to vote. The best we can do is take reasonable precautions, both in training interviewers and matching them with respondents.

A sound approach, when feasible, is to hire interviewers of both races (or social classes, and so on), and assign them at random to respondents. Then, data from interviews in which both parties were of the same race can be compared with data from interracial interviews. If there is no difference, there is nothing to worry about. If there is a difference, one can either take an average or keep the two sets of data separate and try to understand each in its own terms.

Guiding the Interview

Interviews vary tremendously in their forms, contents, and sociological goals. Often you may want to keep an interview as free-floating as possible, drifting from topic to topic according to the interviewee's whim or your momentary intuition that something interesting may happen if you change the topic. Many of the most productive interviews, however, have followed very strict plans, and every good interviewer does a certain amount of formal preparation for each interview.

Often, an interview is really a verbally administered questionnaire. Several national polls that send researchers door-to-door have them follow a precise printed questionnaire, reading the questions aloud exactly as they were written. The hope is that more people will give valid answers verbally to an interviewer than would do so if they were asked merely to check boxes and write replies with a pencil. Furthermore, a higher percentage of potential respondents may consent and follow through when the interview approach is used to administer a questionnaire. For ideas on how to write a questionnaire, see Chapter 7, but a few comments on verbal administration will be appropriate here.

Long questions with a set of complex predetermined response choices may not work well on an interview schedule. When the respondent is filling out a questionnaire himself or herself, there is always the opportunity to look back over a set of choices several times before checking one of the boxes. But when a survey item is administered verbally, the possible answers have to be simple enough for the interviewee to keep them in his or her mind.

On the other hand, questions that encourage the person to talk at length about some topic may work far better in interviews than with printed questionnaires. Few people enjoy handwriting lengthy replies, but many are prepared to talk for a few minutes about topics that interest them. The kind of question that presents people with a fixed set of choices to select from is called a **fixed-choice item**, or sometimes a **forced-choice item**. This type of item is also called **closed-ended**. Instead of a predetermined set of allowed answers, an **open-ended item** gives the respondent a chance to formulate his or her own answer.

Let me share part of an interview I conducted with Mother Juliet, a leader of the Chicago chapter of the Process cult, not because it is by any means a perfect example of how to coax information from someone but because it illustrates how a few little nudges from the interviewer can encourage the person to speak at length. This is the very beginning of the interview, which I start by asking how she joined the Process. Although I have attended a couple of cult activities led by Mother Juliet, I am essentially a stranger to her, so I must proceed cautiously. In braces I will put fresh comments ("{comment}") explaining to you why I said what I did.

JULIET: I met the church in England. I can't remember which year. Either '64 or '65.

ME: Fairly early years? {The period she refers to is clear to me, and I ask this seemingly unnecessary question simply to make her feel comfortable about saying more. Often you can get a person to continue talking, without shifting the conversation to a new topic, by paraphrasing for them what they have just said.}

JULIET: Yes, early days. Through a friend who had met the church before me. It wasn't a church in those days, as you know. I was an actress at the time, and in my own terms quite successful, getting more so.

ME: What kind of work? {She's starting to talk spontaneously now, and I want to encourage her to continue.}

JULIET: Well, I had done a lot of repertory . . . [pauses]

ME: [a questioning expression on my face] {I know what repertory is, and I want to encourage her to go on but do not feel ready to tell her what to talk about.}

JULIET: It's a bit like stock, summer stock, only that they have it going all the time in the cities. And I had done that for several years. At that time I was doing radio, the BBC. I subsequently then did a play in the West End, and television, and this sort of thing, so things were kind of opening up, and it looked like I was going to have a very . . . I was having a successful career, but was becoming better known. So far as that was concerned, it was very good.

But I wasn't totally satisfied. I was very happy to entertain a lot of people at one go. I was not particularly happy with the way I related on a personal level. The idea of a conventional marriage to a doctor or lawyer, a psychiatrist, a whatever, which is what my background would have supposed would happen . . . something like that, and the raising of a family in a conventional setting absolutely—for some reason, I don't know why—just appalled me. I could not imagine that kind of existence as being too fulfilling.

ME: Did the idea of a career in the theater provide a fulfilling alternative? {I do not feel our rapport is strong enough to confront directly the topic of marriage and the role of housewife. This early in the game, to ask her anything about how or why she rejects the "traditional" woman's role could poison the atmosphere—I do not know this would happen, but I decide to be cautious. I want to become her psychological ally concerning any painful conflicts, and not risk irritating her by implying that anyone might criticize her; so I consciously move the conversation along to her theater career, which is interesting to me and, I judge, safer.}

JULIET: Well, yes it did, to begin with, which is why I felt I had an actual calling to be famous as an actress. I was quite presumptuous in that respect. [she laughs]

ME: Somebody has to be famous. {This is an attempt at a joke. We are discussing potentially painful topics for her, and I guess that her laughter is a release of tension, so I try to share the tension reduction with her.}

JULIET: Somebody has to be famous, and it was absolutely bound to be me! Although this obviously got slightly modified with time, in the sense that I didn't immediately hit the headlines as a great star. I nevertheless had faith that one day I was going to be quite well-known.

But still, the more time went on, there was still something missing, I felt. And when I had the opportunity to meet this group of people {the Process} who were already working together, I went along out of interest, because I wanted to see what was happening, what they were doing. And I got very fascinated and subsequently much more interested in inner development than in outer development—if that makes sense.

ME: A theater career would have been in a sense outer development? {She has essentially asked me if I understand what inner and outer development mean, but I don't want to derail the conversation by attempting to offer her formal definitions. She clearly implies that her theater career was outer development, while the Process offered inner development, so this is another example of echoing back what the person has just said, but in a way that is not obvious parroting.}

JULIET: Oh, yes. Of course that was outwardly directed, and therefore it didn't really matter, as far as the hundreds of people (or whatever) were concerned, what the [Juliet's] personal life was doing. It was irrelevant. But a growth of an inner security, inner development—I think the modern phrase is "a growth of inner space"—I had not really considered as an area to develop until that point.

ME: When the friend you mentioned introduced you to the group, did you go with any sense of purpose, or just going along casually to see what was going on? {She has stopped talking, and I must urge her on with another question. I would really like to know something about the friend who introduced her to the Process, because sociological theories of conversion to deviant cults place great stress on the role of intimate social bonds in getting people to join. But I want to give her some choice as to what aspect of the situation to talk about, because I am not yet sure which parts of it might trouble her. So I ask a rather bland question about the degree of her interest when she first visited the

Process, hoping she might quickly tell me something about the relationship with the friend.}

JULIET: I would say I went along from the point of view of interest, a lot of interest, because of what had been happening and what I'd seen happen with my friend. I'd seen some changes happening there.

ME: Is the friend in the church now? {By this point, I have interviewed many members of the cult, and I hoped she would tell me who the friend was so that I could link their interviews, both in my analysis and in the specifics of some questions I might ask Juliet.}

JULIET: Yes, he is. . . . [she pauses and looks slightly uncomfortable]

ME: In the earliest months, what struck you about the group? {I sense that I have made a mistake by pushing too hard about the friend. Another time, when Juliet knows me better and I have some hint of why she is reluctant to name him or describe their relationship, I can come back to the topic, but now I have to get off that topic as quickly and comfortably as I can.}

JULIET: The thing that struck me was the degree of intensity at which the work was being done. The kind of questions the people were asking, and not only asking themselves but asking one another. The degree of intense personalizing that went on, which I was unaccustomed to. One didn't ask those kinds of questions! [laughs] The absolute commitment to truth about self and ownership of the answers. Like owning, "*I* feel this. *I* do X," or whatever. Discovering that people didn't fall apart. I didn't fall apart. In fact, it made me feel a lot stronger, and it made other people feel stronger, too. I thought that it would end up with people not being able to speak to one another at all; in fact it had the opposite effect—[laughs]—which I found very

fascinating. More than fascinating—
otherwise I wouldn't still be here.

I suspect that Juliet emphasized the asking
and answering of intimate, personal questions
in describing her first experience with the
Process because our interview had just gone
through a little crisis. After just a brief time to
establish some rapport, I had asked the direct
question about her friend that seemed to put
her on guard. But then I changed the topic
slightly, signaling to her that it was okay for
her to refuse to talk about her friend. Again, I
do not present this example to illustrate my
frankly moderate talents in interviewing, but
because it is a fairly typical slice of back-and-
forth conversation in which a few often vague
questions encourage the respondent to express
herself at some length about topics important to
my research. In a sense, the respondent is in
charge of the interview, and she does most of
the talking.

Before they can be incorporated in a sociological analysis, open-ended verbal data must
be reduced in some way to manageable form, a
process that is often called coding. In its most
formal sense, **coding** verbal material means iso-
lating parts of it and assigning them to analytic
categories. Note that I identified moments of
tension release in the interview with Juliet.
Tension release is one of the categories of
Bales's interaction process analysis, which was
presented in the previous chapter. How you
code your data depends on your theoretical
approach and substantive focus; for now I will
merely stress that, whatever your coding
scheme, you must be clear on what the verbal
material means to the person uttering it.

Here's an example of miscoding. In 1967,
Larson and Garbin published an article entitled
"Hamlets: A Typological Consideration." All
sociological journal articles are listed in a reference work called *Sociological Abstracts,* and I
encountered this one while scanning through
the section covering the sociology of language
and literature. The abstract stated, "Hamlet
study appears helpful in studying social change
and may aid in the understanding of more
complex and heterogeneous societies."

Fascinating! I'm sure you are familiar with
Shakespeare's play *Hamlet,* and you may know
that other authors wrote about Hamlet as
well, but I was astonished to see that this article
was an analysis of fully 340 Hamlets! Can
you imagine that many dramas about the indecisive prince of Denmark? Well, stop wondering. The article was actually about 340
tiny villages in Nebraska, with populations
running from 10 to 250; villages of this size are
sometimes called hamlets. *Sociological Abstracts*
had seen the word *hamlet,* capitalized because it
was the first word of the title, and erroneously
assumed the article belonged with the studies
of literature.

Getting the Data Down

One of the chief problems in good interviews is
information overload, receiving more data
than you can comfortably handle. In preparing
for an interview, you must decide how you are
going to record the data. Will you write answers down while the person is talking, use an
electronic recorder to preserve the entire interview, or will you attempt to remember the answers and write them down later. This last
method is extremely difficult, although while
doing field observation in many settings it may
not be appropriate to take notes, and writing a
report from memory may be the best you can
do. In such cases it is almost impossible to recall the exact wording of answers, and you
must probably be content to remember factual
information, either separate bits of data or stories that assist you in remembering because of
their clarity and meaningfulness.

In the previous chapter, we discussed interaction process analysis, one of several systematic procedures that have been developed for

coding communicative acts. We noted that the original research used coders who were trained to make the judgments in real time but who were assisted by mechanical devices, and that modern researchers often use sound or video recording to collect the data for future analysis. You may consider employing similar technology to facilitate your interviews, but you should be aware of the practical challenges they present.

When I was interviewing members of the Process, I used a tape recorder, whenever possible, to record the answers. The reason was that I needed all my brain to think up questions. Before talking with a particular cult member, I would not know what topics he or she would be willing and able to discuss. I would take notes during the interview, but they were new questions to ask rather than answers the person had just given. Often a person would bring up two topics at once, and I would write one down for later questioning while urging the person to tell me as much as possible about the other. Ideas for questions may pop into your mind that have little to do with what the person is saying at the moment, but you can scribble down a note to ask the question later, when there is a natural pause in the interview.

If you are going to do serious interviewing, it is worth investing in a good recorder. I have had several over the years, and I now interview with a pair, as in my interviews with sociologists George Homans and David Riesman (Bainbridge 1987a, 1987b). One recorder uses the relatively large music-type cassettes commonly used today and has two cassette decks, so that I can easily copy tapes in the field. This is useful if you are going to be away from your home base for a long time and might need to archive backup copies for security or keep only excerpts of long-ranging discussions or group conversations. The other recorder uses the smaller microcassettes and was primarily designed for dictation by business executives. I run both during the interview, placing them at different spots near the subject. This makes it more likely I will get a good recording of every

word and also prevents loss of material when a tape comes to the end, because the two machines use tapes of different duration.

You should employ the highest-fidelity machines possible, probably with external microphones that can be positioned comfortably where they will catch the speaker's words and not be swamped by extraneous noise. Some interviewers find that stereo recording makes it easier to hear the words when reviewing the tape, despite background noise. The best machine for recording is not necessarily the best for transcribing the tape later on, but if your machines are of high enough quality, you can copy the tapes from your interviewing machine to one well adapted to transcription. If your machine was designed to record music, you certainly do not have to use the very highest-quality music-recording tapes with it, but you should avoid the cheapest tapes. On two disastrous occasions, badly made cassettes went wild during my interviews, wrapping themselves up on the machine's drive spindle and jamming everything royally.

Transcription is the hard part. First of all, most machines are not designed for playing sections of tape short enough that you can write down everything on them. Special transcription tape players, usually employing the microcassette format, have foot pedals and will precisely start and stop, and even back up a tiny bit before starting, so you can catch every word. If comfortable for you, typing the material on a word processor will give you the opportunity to edit it while listening to the tape a second time, perhaps hearing things you missed the first time through.

If your tape player is not designed for transcription, then you have a painful process ahead of you. I have spent dozens of hours working with such a machine, and the best system I have found is to go through the tape a little bit at a time, writing down whatever words and phrases you can, even though they do not form complete sentences, and leaving space between them. Then go through the tape a second time, specifically listening for the missing words that will tie these fragments together. Finally, go through the tape a third time to correct any errors.

A good transcription preserves not only the words but also some of the sounds and actions of the original interview. If the person slams his or her fist on the table to make a point, this noise is part of their answer to your question, and you can include it in your transcription like this: "I feel very strongly [slamming fist on table] that the workers don't understand that we managers have their best interests at heart!" Look at the script for a modern play to see how stage directions are handled. Here's an example from a television play broadcast in 1952, an episode of the science fiction show *Space Patrol*. Commander Buzz Corey, Cadet Happy Osborn, Carol Carlisle, and Tonga (Lady of Diamonds), have just returned to their own century from a visit to ancient Egypt in a time machine, and they are standing in the exact spot they just visited, but now 6,000 years later:

BUZZ: [over shoulder] Happy . . . where is your ray gun?

HAPPY: Huh? [thinks] Oh . . . I lost it in that fight, Commander . . . I remember when it was knocked from my hand it got broken.

BUZZ: [turns around] Like this? [hands Happy his broken ray gun, but now it's all caked over with mud to make it look ancient]

HAPPY: [takes it] That's it, sir. I remember . . . it got broken right here. [then does a take] But, sir . . . this is old!

BUZZ: [smiles] 6,000 years old, Happy.

CAROL: That's what Professor Cartwright dug up . . . in the 30th century.

HAPPY: But . . . but . . . I *just* left it there!

TONGA: [smiles] In 2700 B.C.

HAPPY: [is really confused now . . . studies the gun. . . . and as he does . . . the others . . . smiling . . . slip away] That's my gun. I just left it in Egypt. But that was in 2700 B.C. It was just dug up . . . but that was in the 30th century. It's practically a new gun . . . but it's 6,000 years old. [tries to comprehend. Hits himself in the forehead a couple of times with heel of hand . . . shakes his head . . . then still baffled studies gun again. Speaks deliberately] It's my gun! I left it there in . . . [then glances up, looking directly into camera. Does a slight take as though he's spotted the viewers at home] Well? What are you grinnin' about? Can *you* figure it out?

This TV example shows how you could flesh out a transcription of mere words with actions and expressions, and it suggests that you might adopt standard conventions—like three dots (". . .") for a pause and brackets to enclose remarks ("[remark]")—and employ standard descriptions for common behaviors. For example, a *double-take* is a delayed reaction to a surprising or significant situation. This example has two of these *takes*. You may not be able to fill in as many stage directions as in this scene, and you must decide to what extent to insert interpretations of what the subject is thinking or feeling. Because Cadet Happy was played by an actor who was very good at looking confused, there was never any doubt when he was projecting confusion, but in real life there may be limits to how much you can accurately read beyond the mere words a person speaks. And, of course, your research purposes may not require you to go very deeply into the exact way the subjects express themselves.

If you plan to write down the subject's responses during the interview, one of the best ways is to write directly on a copy of an interview schedule. If the questions for the interview can be thoroughly prepared in advance, you may invest a little effort producing a very clear draft, even adding little boxes to check to indicate certain responses. Other questions can be followed with short spaces where you can write in a word or phrase the interviewee gives in response. In short, like a questionnaire administered directly to the general public, an interview schedule should be designed for maximum clarity and ease of answering. Then you can comfortably mark or write the responses up to speed, without delaying or disconcerting the interviewee. You should be able to save much of your attention and energy for asking the questions and maintaining rapport with the person answering them.

_____ Specialized Interviews

Several types of interviews have been devised by social scientists, and the researcher may select the right one for a particular problem or combine a variety of methods in a single meeting with a respondent. Among the distinct types worth knowing are dictionaries of subcultures, histories of individual lives, and oral histories of collective phenomena. The principles of these methods can be applied to many other kinds of interviews as well.

Subculture Dictionaries

Many subcultures in our society augment ordinary English with jargon, argot, slang, and lingo of their own, and research on these subcultures may need to include a **subculture dictionary**. Every profession has its special terms, as does every deviant subculture. An ordinary word can be used in a special way. For example, *line* refers to a thin row of cocaine crystals in the drug subculture; *barbecue* means slow rotation around the longitudinal axis of a spacecraft in aerospace jargon. But in many cases, the words are unfamiliar outside the subculture. Examples include *wippen,* the mechanism that fits between the key and hammer of a piano, and *gafiate,* which means to defect from the science fiction subculture. Sometimes a key concept is expressed in a phrase, such as being *sent up the river,* which means being incarcerated in a penitentiary.

The simplest form of a dictionary is a set of file cards, or their computerized equivalent, each dedicated to a particular word or phrase and giving its meaning in ordinary English. Some jargon words need to be defined in terms of others in the dictionary, and in some cases you might need to include a picture or diagram as well as a verbal definition.

Good dictionaries usually explain how each of the words is pronounced. If you are assembling a dictionary, you may want to use the system in an ordinary dictionary or the international phonetic alphabet, but you don't have to use fancy phonetic systems for most ordinary sociological purposes. I have been referring to the Process, but do you know how to pronounce this name? It is not PRAH-sess but PROH-sess. I think you get the idea.

For examples of how to develop definitions, we can turn to the subculture of science fiction fans. If you attend conventions of these creative if slightly introverted people and interview them, you will hear some mysterious language. "Egoboo is the one thing which enables a faned to go from one or two issues to an annish." "If you think there's a problem now with new fans making BNFs out of other neofans who've been in fandom maybe four months longer than the first, you should have seen 1966." "The age of the ditto crudzine is almost past. Now mimeo crudzines dominate, with offset crudzines on the upswing." How can the researcher make sense of such nonstandard words?

There are primarily two ways to develop dictionary definitions, and they should be used together whenever possible. First, you can collect many instances in which each word was used and look at the context. Second, you can ask people directly what each word means. You might think the second approach is so much better than the first that it should be used exclusively, but it has several drawbacks. For one thing, most people have trouble framing good definitions; definition-writing is a professional skill. Also, when people attempt to formalize their knowledge, they often simplify or focus on only a few aspects of it. Finally, you simply may not be able to interview some individuals and therefore have to be content with things they have written that incorporate the special language.

What is "egoboo"? One science fiction fan was explaining why so many fans invest so much effort publishing absolutely dreadful mimeographed amateur magazines, and commented: "I believe the underlying factor is a search for egoboo. Egoboo is short for egoboost." Thus, the fan provided a definition of *egoboo*, without even being asked. Similar alertness to what fans are saying spontaneously would reveal that a "faned" is a fan editor, someone who publishes a "fanzine" (fan magazine) that may achieve its "annish" (anniversary issue). A "neofan" is a new member of "fandom," the fan subculture, while a "BNF" is a Big Name Fan, respected by other "fen" (plural of *fan*, just as *men* is the plural of *man*). A "crudzine" is a fanzine of low quality (you can probably guess the etymology of this word).

Etymology is the study of the origins of words and phrases. A subcultural dictionary is not complete without the etymologies of the words. Not only do they amplify the ordinary definitions, but they may suggest something of the style of the subculture. The slang term for being imprisoned, *sent up the river*, derives from the fact that New York City convicts were often sent up the Hudson to Sing Sing penitentiary. *Gafiate*, in science fiction lingo, is derived from the first letters of "Get Away from It All."

Almost all the new words used in the science fiction subculture are elisions or acronyms. An *elision* is the result of dropping something out of a word or phrase. For example, *fanzine* is the result of taking *maga* out of *fan magazine*." An *acronym* is a word made up of the initials of a string of words. For example, BNF is the acronym of Big Name Fan. Did you know that the American Sociological Association used to be called the American Sociological Society? The name was changed when acronyms became popular. We often refer to the American Sociological Association by its acronym, the ASA. What is the acronym of American Sociological Society? Now you understand why the name was changed.

Apparently, the thinking patterns of the science fiction subculture are highly mechanical, because elision and acronyms are not very poetic ways of arriving at new words. Some other subcultures use vivid metaphors instead, what we call figures of speech. In a *simile*, a thing gets a new name taken from something basically very different but resembling it in some way. In the drug subculture, "snow" and "grass" are drugs that look like these common coverings of the ground. *Metonymy* is the figure of speech in which something gets a new name from something that is associated with it. Using "skirt" to refer to a woman or "pants" to refer to a man is an example. Rather similar to metonymy is *synecdoche*, using a part of something to describe the whole, or the whole to describe a part. An example is calling an assassin a "cutthroat," if the particular assassin in fact used some means other than cutting throats to accomplish the crime, because a portion of assassins do cut throats. In fact, the number of mechanisms by which new words can be created in a subculture is vast (Flexner, 1960).

Many sociological studies contain dictionaries of the subculture under study. For example, Edwin Sutherland's (1937) book about a professional thief has a glossary in the back informing the reader that in thief argot a *booster* is a shoplifter, a *moll-buzzer* is someone who steals from the pockets of women, and a *glim-dropper* is a con man who uses an artificial eye as part of his racket. Rose Giallombardo's (1966) study of a women's prison includes a dictionary of inmate terminology in the appendix. She reported that women who failed to fit into the inmate subculture, and who were feared as possible informers, were called *squares*. In contrast, exploitative women who could not be trusted were called *jive bitches*. Most inmates were involved in same-sex "marriages," in which the "husband" was a *stud* and the "wife" a *femme*. I hope these rather colorful and possibly offensive examples convince you that dictionaries do not have to be dull.

Do the words *wonk, meatball, jock,* and *gut hopper* mean anything to you? A generation ago, undergraduates at Princeton University used these words to describe an introverted student who studied all the time, a physically and intellectually unattractive student, an athlete, and a student who took one very easy course ("gut") after another (Friendly and Glucksberg 1970). Do you use these words today? The word *wonk* may have been superceded by *nerd*. I have it on good authority that students at M.I.T. spell *nerd* as *gnerd*. But then I have also heard the opinion that all students at the Massachusetts Institute of Technology are "nerds," so a "gnerd" must be an incredibly obnoxious being. Research on the special slang of college students is not trivial. Because generations of students succeed each other so quickly, the slang may be especially volatile, and colleges may be a very good place to study the processes by which subcultural languages change.

Individual Life Histories

An essay, based on interviews often supplemented with data from other sources, that describes and analyzes an individual's development, conditions, and behavior over time is a **life history**. Howard Becker (1970) has noted that the life history has some of the qualities of a novel or an autobiography. It tells the story of an interesting person's life, usually someone who is not famous and whose identity is concealed behind a pseudonym. As a work of literature, it is often far more colorful and far less objective that other forms of sociological writing, but it is not a novel. Although it is often written from the perspective of the person it is about, it is not really an autobiography either. Becker explains:

> The sociologist who gathers a life history takes steps to ensure that it covers everything we want to know, that no important fact or event is slighted, that what purports to be factual squares with other available evidence and that the subject's interpretations are honestly given. The sociologist keeps the subject oriented

to the questions sociology is interested in, asks him about events that require amplification, tries to make the story told jibe with matters of official record and with material furnished by others familiar with the person, event, or place being described. He keeps the game honest for us. (Becker 1970:64)

In the United States, sociological life histories have tended to focus on deviant individuals, but this approach is frequently used in other countries to study a wide variety of people and social statuses (Bertaux and Kohli 1984). One of the more famous interview studies focusing on a single individual is *The Professional Thief*, by Edwin H. Sutherland. Much of the book is drawn from the words of a man who had spent two decades in this illegal profession, and Sutherland reported how it came to be written:

> This description was secured in two ways: first, the thief wrote approximately two-thirds of it on topics and questions prepared by me; second, he and I discussed for about seven hours a week for twelve weeks what he had written, and immediately after each conference I wrote in verbatim form, as nearly as I could remember, all that he had said in the discussion. I have organized this body of materials, written short connecting passages, and eliminated duplications as much as possible. In this organization I have attempted to preserve the ideas, attitudes, and phraseology of the professional thief. The thief read the manuscript as organized and suggested corrections, which have in all cases been made. (Sutherland 1937:vii)

This description appears to contradict Becker's statement that the sociological life history is not an autobiography. Note how many "autobiographies" of celebrities have the footnote "as told to . . ." followed by the name of a professional writer (e.g., Yeager and Janos 1985). Indeed, many classic life histories have been as much like autobiographies as the sociologist could make them. *The Jack-Roller*, produced by Clifford Shaw (1930), is the story of a delinquent young man, written in the fellow's own words. Indeed, Shaw proudly proclaimed that he had changed nothing but the punctuation, and that the subject had decided on even the organization of the material into chapters. However, the autobiography the boy had originally written was only a few pages long, and endless interviews with Shaw drew the story out to book length.

After the classic books by Shaw and Sutherland, social scientists came less and less to expect that the subject of a life history could produce a satisfactory autobiography without a tremendous lot of help in the actual writing, and a variety of techniques were added to the life-historian's tool kit. Henry Murray (1938; 1981) used to give his subjects a questionnaire that guided them in writing an autobiography, but the resulting essay was used as a mere preliminary to in-depth interviewing, which was often supplemented with formal psychological tests. Following Murray's approach, Smith, Bruner, and White (1956) studied the lives and personalities of 10 men in order better to understand their political orientations.

Barbara Heyl's (1979) life history of a Peoria prostitute is a classic account of a deviant lifestyle, based on carefully verified interviews with a woman pseudonymously called "Ann." Heyl met with her subject weekly from 1973 through 1976, and was thus able to interview her at several different times about the same topics and events. Ann also provided lengthy written statements and analyses of important events in her life. This provided much material for cross-checking of factual details: "When Ann's written statements elaborated on past experiences, they could be compared to interviews covering those occurrences conducted at different times between 1973 and 1976. Any contradictions or irregularities in her accounts could be followed up with further questioning of Ann or others who knew her during the time period in question" (Heyl 1979:4).

Thus, Heyl used primarily three methods that evaluated material from one interview in the light of other information. First, she checked the **internal consistency** of what Ann herself said. If the same event came up in two interviews, perhaps conducted a year or more apart, Heyl could check for inconsistencies and follow up with further questioning in a third interview. It is said that liars need good memories, and casual misstatements are apt to be forgotten quickly. Even if the person consistently avoids telling the truth about a painful matter, he or she may tell different false stories at different times, and thus betray the lack of truthfulness to an alert interviewer. Of course, some people may have standard false stories about something very important to them that they will recall perfectly and tell again and again over the years, so internal consistency is not proof of accuracy. Many errors and deceptions, however, will reveal themselves through inconsistencies.

Second, Heyl was able to secure **external corroboration** of Ann's statements by interviewing other people who were involved in various phases of Ann's life and by checking written documents. Heyl called this part of her research **triangulation**, getting the best fix on an event by collecting different perspectives on it. Among those Heyl interviewed were members of Ann's family, who knew much about her childhood and personal life, and various friends and co-workers who had directly observed her at work. The documents consulted included newspaper stories about Ann's arrests, old letters written by Ann and her family members, Ann's high school yearbooks, marriage and divorce certificates, school transcripts, and medical records.

Third, Heyl spent considerable time with Ann and also visited her place of business, giving her some direct observational data against which to check the information from interviews. It is not necessary to check everything an interviewee says, because a few dozen checks are sufficient to evaluate the person's general accuracy. Also, making it clear to the person that the interviews are being checked carefully in relation to much other information may inspire him or her to high standards of accuracy. Nobody wants to be caught for a liar, and the knowledge that the researcher uses careful evaluation techniques will not only prevent outright lies but encourage the person to state facts precisely and to avoid filling in memory gaps with imaginative reconstructions.

I have often found that people need to have their memories jogged, and that giving them some material about their lives to stimulate recall can be useful. For example, you can sit down with the person's family album and have him or her talk about the pictures, going off on tangents if the person wishes. When I wanted to learn about the trips taken by Robert de Grimston, founder of the Process, I spread a set of maps on the table between us. He found it very useful to trace his route with a pencil, recalling many events that might not otherwise have come to mind.

Back issues of the town newspaper can trigger recollections of private matters that have meshed somehow with public ones; for example, a news article about the Fourth of July parade may remind the informant of the guests who came to the family picnic on that same day. Of course, external sources of information like these that are used to stimulate memories cannot simultaneously be used to evaluate the correctness of those memories, but they can contribute to both richness and accuracy of recall.

Subjects of sociological life histories are usually presented as typical examples of some social category (Burgess 1930) or as standard reflections of particular sociocultural backgrounds (Dollard 1935). Thus, Sutherland's professional thief was taken to be representative of a clearly defined category of persons, and other professional thieves checked over the manuscript for discrepancies with their own experiences. Shaw's jack roller was supposed to be a typical Chicago delinquent, and Heyl's prostitute could tell us how house prostitution in small cities was generally carried on. These projects really rest on a pair of assumptions: (1) the existence of a distinct social category, and (2) the particular case as typical of that category.

Both these assumptions can be questioned. A couple of generations after Shaw interviewed his delinquent, criminologists were challenging the notion that a distinct class of persons identifiable as delinquents actually existed (Hirschi 1969). Alternative views suggested that there was a continuous spectrum of degrees of delinquency from very bad boys to very good ones, with no break in-between, or that sociologists should focus on the conditions that produce delinquent behavior both in boys who do a lot of it and in those who only seldom break societal norms. Ultimately, it is an empirical question whether a particular topic of sociological interest can be profitably studied as a category of persons, a clearly defined social role, or a distinct subculture with identifiable members.

The most influential life histories have probably not, in fact, concerned themselves with completely typical cases. Heyl is quite explicit in saying that "Ann" was far more intelligent and articulate than the average person. Indeed, it takes a talent for self-expression and endless patience to be a good interviewee for a life-history interview. Although the early life-history interviewers asserted that their subjects were entirely typical, there is good reason to doubt this claim. They were both willing and able to become expressive writers, and some of them evolved into something like sociologists. The supreme example is Nels Anderson, who went from being a hobo to being a sociologist who wrote the classic book on hobos (Anderson 1923).

But it may not be important whether subjects of life histories are strictly typical, so long as they introduce the social scientists to fresh experiences and perspectives relevant to the topic under study. Although the detailed examination of a single life is not appropriate data for testing a general theory, it can be especially valuable for suggesting ideas that can be refined and tested through subsequent systematic research on a large sample of truly typical people.

Clifford Shaw (1930:19) noted that life-history data could "serve as a means of making preliminary explorations and orientations in relation to specific problems" and "afford a basis for the formulation of hypotheses with reference to the causal factors involved." After life-history data have helped the sociologist develop concepts and explanation, the focus shifts to other research methods. "The validity of these hypotheses may in turn be tested by the comparative study of other detailed case histories and by formal methods of statistical analysis."

In my own work, I have not found it practical to ask subjects to write their autobiographies, so essentially all the information had to come out through my interviews. As with all in-depth qualitative research on human beings, you have to adjust your methods to the person and to the situation. I often found, however, that a good start was to perform one or two interviews designed simply to block out the chronology of major events in the person's life and the major themes that deserved special attention.

The chronological outline would note where the person lived in each year, schools attended, jobs held, major recreational activities, major family events, (births, deaths, marriages), public roles the person played (in political, religious, and social organizations), and other events and statuses that seemed to mark the course of the individual's life. A list of themes can be developed at the same time, and often there is at least some sense of major themes even before the interviews begin. For example, if the subject is a convicted burglar, then one would probably want to chronicle the burglaries committed, arrests, periods of imprisonment, and contacts with other burglars and fences. If the subject belongs to a religious cult, information about the earlier history of spiritual exploration, including membership both in conventional churches and other cults, would be especially important.

If you were writing the biography of the person or including an account of some portion of the person's life in a larger essay, then you would want to flesh out this chronological skeleton with anecdotes or information about the themes of greatest importance for your research. Thus fleshed out, life-history interviews with several people can be woven together into a history of the group to which they all belong.

Collective Oral Histories

When I was a teenager, I often wondered about a huge, mysterious stone house that glowered over a tiny lake set in a small peninsula that thrust out into Long Island Sound, within walking distance of where I lived. Somebody interesting must have lived in that house, and I supposed the person was rich both because the building was so splendid and because everybody called it the Tod Mansion. Only rich people live in mansions. In the middle of the lake, an island the size of a table supported a pillar decked with a bronze eagle. I am sure your own hometown contains something remarkable that you have probably wondered about. Many years later, visiting the town for nostalgia's sake, I discovered a locally produced book that offered a full account of the Tod Mansion, based on oral histories (Ornstein 1981).

A local cultural organization, Friends of the Greenwich Library, had decided to launch an oral-history project, and more than a hundred people participated, some as interviewers and some as interviewees. The method of writing the book was excruciatingly simple. People who knew something about Tod's Point were interviewed, many of them elderly folk (average birthdate: 1905). After being encouraged to tell all they could remember, they provided extensive personal recollections, apparently in a free-form manner. Then this huge mass of interview material was culled for interesting little snippets that were assembled into the book. The book was organized into five sections, according to the historical periods that best seemed to capture the phases that Tod's Point had passed through: Early History, the Era of the Tods, Acquisition by the Town, Veterans in the Mansion, Greenwich Point–Town Park.

The first section, only a page long, contained short statements from six informants. The first was curator of the local historical society, another a famous author who had written an historical novel about the town. The rest of the book rambles through many impressions and pieces of information, including several maps and historical photographs. The point of land was named after J. Kennedy Tod, born in 1852 in Scotland, who bought it with money gained from running a banking firm. He had no children, and after his wife died in 1939, the town purchased the land and turned it into a beach park. Right after World War II, a group of veterans renovated the mansion and lived in it, but the building was torn down in 1961. Not a model for the serious scholar to emulate, this amateur book about Tod's Point nonetheless proves that a group of untrained but interested folk can produce a valuable oral history.

The obvious organizational structure for a serious **oral history** is, again, the chronicle. Each section of the essay would cover a particular period of time. Although you would want to tell the reader when new seasons, years, and decades began, the calendar may not provide the best periods into which to divide the narrative. Instead, you have to consider whether the history you are covering divides naturally into sections. For example, Bruce Catton wrote the books in his trilogy on the Civil War to cover the beginning phase of the war (*The Coming Fury*), the middle phase (*Terrible Swift Sword*), and the end (*Never Call Retreat*). Some historians of the arts seem to believe that every artist has exactly three periods of development (early, middle, and late)—even poor Mozart, who died in his mid-thirties!

My study of the Process combined observational, interview, and historical methods, and both my research techniques and the historical phases of the group's development determined the chapters I would write. Because an important theme was the birth and development of a novel religious cult, the first chapters covered the group's first seven years, arranged in chronological order and based on interviews and documents. After seven years of radical spiritual and geographical wandering, the cult had just settled down when I encountered it and began extensive observational research. Thus it made perfect sense to devote the middle chapters to an ethnographic description of the group at its height, which was exactly the period I explored most closely in my data collection. Three chapters covered the social structure and lifestyle of the group, its complex theological beliefs, and the psychotherapy techniques it used in the attempt to achieve personal transformation. Three years after I began my research, the cult started to split apart and entered an agonizing period of new wandering, providing the material for two more chapters arranged mostly chronologically.

Chronological order may be dull and unimaginative, but you need very good justifications before you can abandon it. The best histories typically weave a number of intellectual themes throughout a chronicle, rather than abandoning the time stream altogether for a structure based on static topics. Of course, if your purpose is to document a relatively stable social phenomenon, you should structure your essay in terms of its features or the theoretical issues that inspire your interest in it. Histories of individual lives may then find their proper places in terms of a structure that is not primarily chronological.

Before you can write an essay, however, you need material, and we shall now turn to the computer program that allows you to simulate interviewing.

The Interviewing Program

Interviews in a Deviant Subculture

In creating the computerized interview module, I drew on a series of real interviews with real people, and I came to know the 20 Processeans represented on your disk very well. My actual interviews were rather free-floating, including the one with Mother Juliet. Because I spoke with some of these individuals many times, I have done a certain amount of cutting and pasting to prepare the material for you. In some cases I have put words in the respondents' mouths, but I have tried to keep them completely in character. For example, one of the respondents was a leading musician in the cult, and a number of his replies are actually words from Process songs.

Two of the respondents are essentially useless as informants about the Process. One has developed a private religion and is a kind of one-person cult. This person knew a lot about the Process, with which he or she was associated for years, but won't tell you about it. Instead, you will learn about the very unusual motivations and beliefs of this individual. This gives you a realistic experience, one I had often in my research, because every successful cult is surrounded by a flock of would-be cult founders who lack followers and are personally attracted to the cult scene in which they wish they were more prominent.

Another respondent is pretty ignorant about the group. This person's mate was a peripheral member for several years, and one of the mate's childhood chums was an inner member. Both of them are also included among the respondents, and they will give you good

material. However, the ignorant respondent won't admit to being ignorant. You will get vague responses to some questions, evasions, and a lot of straight-faced lies. I really enjoyed knowing this person, who as a friend was completely trustworthy. But ask about the past, and you get wild stories. I always suspected that the person was on the run because of some minor criminal violations and therefore didn't want to talk about the real past. That possibility aside, however, the person apparently wanted a far richer past than reality had provided, and so had fabricated one of exquisite exoticism.

The other 18 respondents will give you solid information. Some joined the Process at the very beginning, one being the founder, so they can tell you much about the full range of beliefs and practices. Others joined later on and can both describe their lives in the cult and the circumstances under which they joined. In each interview, the person answering your questions will shift from moment to moment between the roles of informant and respondent. When not giving you accurate factual information about their group, these persons will realistically express their own personal thoughts and feelings.

Running the TALK Program

To get the interviewing program, start your computer and select the program named TALK. Although the interview material is rich and complex, the TALK program itself is very simple, undoubtedly the simplest of the set. It has only two parts, a menu from which you can select a respondent and the interviewing section itself. When the program starts, the computer will ask, "Whom do you want to interview?" You will be given a list of the 20 cult members, with a letter of the alphabet in front of each name, as shown here in Figure 3.1.

At the bottom of the screen is a message: "Press a letter key ((A) through (T)) to select a respondent or (ESC) to QUIT." To interview one of the cultists, simply press the computer key for the letter in front of his or her name. To interview Mother Isis, for example, you would press (A). To interview Bob Stone, you would press (T). Don't worry about whether to type a capital letter or a lowercase (little) letter. Just press the key.

Figure 3.1
The Twenty Respondents from the Process.

(A)	Mother Isis	(H)	Edward de Forest	(O)	Brother Mark
(B)	Mother Juliet	(I)	Sister Norma	(P)	Sister Semantha
(C)	Father Abraham	(J)	Brother Goliath	(Q)	Sister Rose
(D)	Father Paul	(K)	Sister Moira	(R)	Cher
(E)	Father Moses	(L)	Brother Lot	(S)	Edgar Allan Poe
(F)	Father Cain	(M)	Sister Ruth	(T)	Bob Stone
(G)	Father David	(N)	Sister Roxana		

When you are completely finished working with the program and want either to quit working at the computer or to switch to a different program in the set, press (ESC), the ESCAPE key. It will take you to the program menu. I suggest, however, you do not escape the program in the middle of your interviewing project. The answers change slightly as you work the program, and starting over would defeat this minor advantage of the software, so I suggest you don't temporarily switch out of the program when you are doing a project with it. Finish your project before you quit the program.

Suppose you decided to start with mother Isis and pressed (A). The interviewing part of the program would appear on the screen. The top two-thirds of the screen would be mostly blank, except for the heading "Interview with Mother Isis." A horizontal line runs across the screen below this message, and the bottom third is filled with five of the questions you may ask. It might have been nice to put all 26 questions on the screen for you to consult, but that would have left no room for the answers. Instead, I have put five questions with a quick method of checking any of the others.

A message at the bottom of the screen provides a quick guide: "Press (Home) (PgUp) (↑) (END) (PgDn) (↓) to move questions, (ESC) to leave Mother Isis." Try pressing (↓), and you will see that the computer moves you down the list of questions, one question for every time you press (↓). If you press (PgDn), you move down five questions, and pressing (END) takes you immediately to the end. (↑), (PgUp), and (Home) move you up the list in the same way. You don't have to be looking at a question to ask it, but this part of the program lets you check over the questions right on the screen. Because you might find it more convenient to use a printed version on which you can see all 26 at once, I have provided it here as Figure 3.2.

Note that each question is preceded by a letter of the alphabet, (A) through (Z). To ask a question, simply press the appropriate letter. Again, don't worry about capitals; just press the key. When you select a question, it will immediately appear on the screen, above the horizontal line, and the interviewee's answer will pop right below it. As you ask questions, the old questions and answers will march up the screen. Thus, in selecting a new question, you can look back at the past few questions and answers. So that your eye can quickly tell a question from an answer, the questions are indented a space, while the answers start at the left edge of the screen. On color monitors, the questions will be green and the answers red.

Figure 3.2
The Questions of the Process Interview

(A) When and where did you join the Process?
(B) Were you experiencing trouble of any kind when you joined?
(C) Had you participated in any other unusual religious groups before joining?
(D) Were many of your friends members of the Process when you joined?
(E) What was the Process like when you joined it?
(F) Did you travel much with the Process? If so, where did you go?
(G) How has the Process helped you?
(H) State one of the basic beliefs of the Process.
(I) What kind of work do you do outside the group?
(J) What is your role in the group today?
(K) Describe your greatest contribution to your fellow members.
(L) The Process has many group activities. Which is your favorite?
(M) Could you tell me your greatest frustration?
(N) Can you tell me something about the symbols of clothing of the Process?
(O) Please describe your personal relationship to God.
(P) In terms of the Process, how would you describe yourself?
(Q) Some newspaper articles say the Process is evil. What is your reaction?
(R) What does the future hold for the Process?
(S) Why do there seem to be so many new religions today?
(T) How would you describe relations between the sexes in the group?
(U) Do some members of the Process have more power than others? Please explain.
(V) Which member of the group do you most admire? Why?
(W) What is the greatest problem faced by the Process today?
(X) What questions should I ask other members of the Process?
(Y) Is there anything else you would like to say?
(Z) Define a WORD or PHRASE.

Question (Z), "Define a WORD or PHRASE," deserves special mention now, because you ask it in a different manner from the others. This question allows you to type in a short word or phrase that you want the respondent to define or explain. When you press (Z), the questions will vanish from the bottom of the screen, to be replaced by a simple instruction: "Type what you want defined and press ENTER." Below that is "WORD or PHRASE:" followed by a box 20 spaces long.

Suppose your respondent has just referred to MEDIUMISTICS, a mysterious word that is meaningless for you. Press (Z) to get ready to ask for an explanation. When the 20-space box appears, type "MEDIUMISTICS." Actually, you don't have to use capital letters, because the computer will turn little letters into capitals. Type the word exactly as the respondent gave it to you. Any misspelling, and the person may not recognize the word. Don't forget the S on the end of MEDIUMISTICS. If you type just MEDIUMISTIC, you won't get a proper definition.

If you make a mistake as you are typing, you can press (BACKSPACE) a few times and retype correctly. When the word or phrase is just the way you want it, press (ENTER). The following question will appear just above the horizontal line:

"What does MEDIUMISTICS mean?" The respondent's answer pops just below it. If the person didn't understand your question, perhaps because you mistyped the word, an evasive reply will be the only answer you get. If you did make a mistake, you can press (Z) and ask for a definition of the word again.

Even though each of the 20 respondents has his or her own answer for each of the 25 questions labeled (A) through (Y), often you will get exactly the same definition of a term from different individuals. This is because these words are features of the culture of the cult, and members have learned the same definitions. A few of the terms, however, have somewhat variable meanings or rich meanings that cannot be communicated in a single sentence. The word GOD is an example. If you ask Processeans what GOD means, you may get different answers from different people. But it is also possible, with these special words, to get more than one reply from a single respondent. I won't tell you the other words that work like this, because finding them is part of the game, but be aware that certain key concepts may have more than one definition.

How do you decide which words to get defined? I have provided fat clues by capitalizing the letters of the words that have cult definitions. If you are interviewing Mother Isis, you will find that one of her replies to the ordinary questions has MEDIUMISTICS in the middle, spelled in capital letters. This means that she is prepared to define the term for you. A few of the terms consist of two words, such as NEW BEGINNING, and a couple may have hyphens in them, such as P-CAR. You should type the space or the hyphen just as it appears in the phrase or word.

All words, of course, are capitalized at the beginning of sentences, and thus one-letter words like I or A will look like they need defining. If this software were designed to teach philosophy and we were interviewing great philosophers, it might make sense to have respondents define "I." In philosophical logic, the definition of "A" (as in "A book") can also be challenging. But your Processean respondents will not possess wisdom to share with you about these arcane matters. Just look for words of several letters that are all capitals. If something like "A MESSENGER" comes at the beginning of the sentence, you might ask for a definition just of MESSENGER, but it doesn't hurt to try something just to see what happens.

When you are through interviewing someone, you can press (ESC) to return to the list of 20 Processeans. At that point, you can either select another respondent or escape the program.

Twenty-five Questions about Cultism

I make no pretense that the 25 regular questions for the Process interviews are perfect tools for learning about a religious cult. One reason I chose them is simply that I did have the answers in my field notes, transcriptions of actual interviews, or the literature published by the group itself. Another is that they suit the style of the Process. When you are working with any group, you will have to decide what kinds of questions go over smoothly and which cause bad reactions. The Process was a highly introspective group, always discussing their innermost emotions in public meetings, so they would respond calmly and apparently openly to question M: "Could you tell me your greatest frustration?" Indeed, Process activities often included question-and-answer sessions.

An activity known as the TDC (you can ask a Processean what that means!), always began with a "round of the room." That is, each person in turn, going 'round the room, was supposed to answer a standard question. In this case, the question was "What do you hope to give and to receive this evening?" A person might reply, "I would like to give friendship and receive knowledge." The next person might say, "I would like to give security and receive stimulation." Processeans came to be very ready with answers like these, expressing personal feelings in somewhat global and abstract terms. In a way, this made interviewing them very easy. Processeans were comfortable with almost any kind of question and were skillful at providing answers. On the other hand, I sometimes felt their answers lacked substance and were mere verbal games.

A couple of questions are throwaways: "G. How has the Process helped you?" "R. What does the future hold for the Process?" Now, I am not advising you to pad your interviews with useless questions, but it is advisable to be prepared to ask some questions that respondents will find very comfortable, both to put them at their ease and to get them talking. These questions may not be very close to the topic areas that you really care about, but you may be surprised to learn some important and unexpected things from such questions. The respondent may feel, perhaps only subconsciously, that you are missing something important and will take these relatively unfocused questions as an opportunity to open up new areas of discussion.

The other items were carefully selected, for example: "A. When and where did you join the Process?" This question was essential to provide a context for some of the others. Because the Process changed radically over the years, it is vital to know when each respondent joined to understand the circumstances of their recruitment; also, because the cult wandered all over the map, we must ask where a person joined. Interviewees will be adequate informants about different things, depending upon when and where they joined. Obviously, late joiners cannot tell you about the early days of the group, but old-timers may not know

much about the experiences of recent members either, so both should be interviewed. In the case of the Process, a highly stratified group, when a person joined greatly determined how much power he or she has in the group, so the date of joining is a clue about social status as well.

One subset of questions was intended to get respondents talking about the circumstances under which they joined the cult, thus providing material to test standard sociological theories of recruitment to deviant social movements: "B. Were you experiencing trouble of any kind when you joined?" "C. Had you participated in any other unusual religious groups before joining?" "D. Were many of your friends members of the Process when you joined?"

Perhaps the best summary of sociological theories about cult-joining is the classic article by Lofland and Stark (1966; cf. Lofland 1966; Richardson and Stewart 1977; Stark and Bainbridge 1985). One commonly held sociological theory proposes that people perform deviant acts, from committing crimes to converting to cults, because they are deeply frustrated by failures and problems of difficult lives. The question about "trouble" is a mild way of asking respondents whether unusual feelings of pain or frustration impelled them to join.

Another theory holds that cultists drift through a diffuse subculture of cultism, sometimes called the occult milieu, and are often the children and grandchildren of cult members. Also, the founders of cults may have belonged to several cults before and may use the knowledge they gained in those experiences to create their own novel organizations. One way to find out is to ask if the individual had belonged to similar groups before.

A third theory holds that many forms of deviance spread through networks of friends or along other influential social bonds. A person becomes deviant, according to these theories, because he or she comes under the spell of strange companions, not of strange gods. If this is so, then recruits to the Process will have first developed friendship ties, or other social attachments, with members of the group. Pulled into the cult by these social bonds, they first become members of the social group and only later accept its beliefs and values. Asking about friends who were already members may provide information about this hypothesis.

Although these questions often work perfectly with respondents, and in fact served me well in studying the Process, they sometimes fail utterly. I will never forget one evening I spent at a Hare Krishna temple, waiting for a member to give me the promised interview about how he joined. I let the members wash my feet; I danced and sang "Hare Krishna" before the altar, and I ate a 100-percent carbohydrate meal, waiting for that marvelous interview. Finally the guy told me how he had joined: "Hare Krishna!" That was all he said— just the group's incessant chant. His answer was useless, utterly useless.

In fact, in interviews with members of some groups, any question may fail to work. Some churches and social organizations of many other kinds are based on a rhetoric of saving wayward sheep. Each member has to see himself or herself as a poor soul, saved from the jaws of damnation by the group. With such people, a question about the troubles they suffered before joining may simply trigger an explosion of self-denunciation and testimonials to the healing power of the group. Under such circumstances it is hard to identify members who in fact were suffering from no serious problems when they joined and who exaggerate the ordinary difficulties of life in order to have the kind of tale to tell that membership in their group requires. There is no perfect way to determine that a question has failed for a reason like this, but a good clue is if everybody answers it in about the same way. Then you can be pretty sure you are getting group rhetoric rather than individually candid answers.

One question puts Processeans in the role of social scientist: "S. Why do there seem to be so many new religions today?" I included this question partly to make some points about the

extent to which we can expect our respondents to do our scientific work for us. The question is really one for social scientists to answer, and some have tried, through both theory and systematic empirical research (Eister 1972; Stark and Bainbridge 1985). But members of cults, despite their involvement in a particular peculiar group, are not experts on cultism in general. Thus, you should not expect the replies to social-scientific questions like this to be trustworthy. They can, however, have other, related uses.

For one thing, many respondents in any area of human affairs are alert, intelligent people who have thought about issues that might interest social scientists. Thus, they have their own theories about matters relevant to their way of life. Many Processeans, for example, had a good deal of theories about radical religion. The theories may be less logically worked out than those of social scientists, but often they can be turned into plausible scientific explanations with just a little effort. Sociologists should take such folk theories seriously. These might not be true, but at least they deserve to be considered alongside the traditional theories of sociology and to compete in explaining empirical findings from research.

Whatever their value as quasi-scientific explanations, the theories of nonscientists say much about the thought patterns in the group under study. For many anthropologists, and a few sociologists as well, such **folk theories** are in themselves a prime topic of research. From some sociological perspectives, how people view their world is among the most important subjects of research. The theories about cults that cultists hold express important aspects of the ideology of the *cult milieu*, the cluster of groups and activities that deal in radical ways with the supernatural.

Through their ideas about the current situation in religion, members of cults or of any other religious organizations may express some of their hopes for their own group. These ideas may provide clues about the functions the group serves for members, or the organization's aims in its relations with other groups.

For example, members of Protestant sects, which tend to be intense but culturally conventional religious groups, may tell you that the "mainstream" churches have fallen from grace and have ceased meeting people's spiritual needs. Indeed, because the standard churches may fail to meet people's needs for intense, salvational experiences, their theory about why many new religions are springing up becomes an opportunity for them to express major themes in their own religious commitment.

The following questions may get Processeans to tell you about the group's beliefs and practices: "H. State one of the basic beliefs of the Process." "L. The Process has many group activities. Which is your favorite?" "N. Can you tell me something about the symbols or clothing of the Process?" "O. Please describe your personal relationship to God."

Information about the social structure of the group is likely to come from answers to these: "J. What is your role in the group, today?" "K. Describe your greatest contribution to your fellow members." "P. In terms of the Process, how would you describe yourself?" "T. How would you describe relations between the sexes in the group?" "U. Do some members of the Process have more power than others?

Please explain." "V. Which member of the group do you most admire?" These six questions are pretty harmless, but they have the potential to reveal much about power differentials. In fact, the question that is explicitly about power might work less well than the others. Respondents might deny that there are power differentials. As they describe themselves in terms of the group, however, and even as they merely identify the members they admire, they may give you much information about status differences.

Other items had their own purposes, and you can see whether they were worth asking when you get answers to them. Two at the end give the person an opportunity to get something off his or her chest: "X. What questions should I ask other members of the Process?" "Y. Is there anything else you would like to say?" Items like this may be useful in the middle of interviews as well as at the end. They allow the individual to return to an earlier topic of discussion and amplify upon it. They give an opening for a new topic that you might find unexpectedly interesting. And they give the respondent the feeling that you really care about what he or she thinks, rather than merely demanding information about particular matters that are on your agenda.

PROJECTS FOR CHAPTER 3

The first three projects described below ask you to interview real people, while the rest employ the TALK program that simulates interviews on the computer. The first two projects focus on the life-history interview, a type that I have found very successful in my course on field research methods. Project 1 gives you practice in the safe environment of the classroom by having you divide into pairs to critique your interview technique as you practice it. The second project is an interview of an older person, a nonstudent, whose life you need to sketch in a systematic chronological outline. The third interview has you take the role of linguist and document the special words that members of a subculture use, a job dozens of my sociology students have successfully carried out. These three projects emphasize the sensitivity, poise, and active listening that are required for successful interviews, and thus they employ real interviewees. In addition, you get to invent your own questions and learn which ones are most successful in gaining information while building rapport.

Projects 4, 5, and 6 are designed to illustrate the logic of interviewing sets of people and piecing bits of information together. The fourth project stresses that some people are simply bad interviewees, and that the interviewer has to exercise good judgment in selecting interviewees and in evaluating their responses. The fifth project asks you to create a subcultural dictionary comparable to that in project 3, except that it will employ the responses contained on your software disk rather than those of people you contact yourself. And the final project in this set asks you to discover the beliefs of the Process cult. Although exercises done on the computer cannot give you the sensation of interviewing real people, they do stress that interviews involve far more than simply a personal relationship between you and another person. To interview a group of people, you must plan strategy, collect bits of information, and assemble the fragments of knowledge into a general picture greater than that provided by any one respondent.

1. Life-History Interview with a Fellow Student. Do this project in pairs, each person starting without any preparation except to get ready to write several pages of notes. Take turns asking each other questions in the form of a life-history interview. At the end, each one should have an outline of the other person's life history, but the real point of the exercise is to obtain experience and develop imagination in framing questions.

After answering any question, a student can ask, "Why did you ask that question?" The student who asked it must then explain why he or she asked it, and the two can discuss whether it served its intended purpose and what kind of question might have done better. Do not do this with a competitive spirit; instead, try to help each other gain practice and explore the problem of inventing questions for an interview.

2. Life-History Interview. In a two-hour interview with an older person, perhaps a member of your own family, sketch his or her life's course. Arrange the information in extended outline form, giving the major life events in chronological order with dates (the year, at least) when possible. The purpose is *not* to collect interesting anecdotes or to probe deeply into the person's traumas. Indeed, this should be a completely nonthreatening, straightforward interview designed simply to chart the course of the person's life as objectively as possible.

3. A Subcultural Dictionary. Construct a short dictionary of terms used in a subculture, through interviewing knowledgeable members of the subculture. The dictionary should contain 50 words or phrases and, if possible, verbs and adjectives as well as nouns.

The dictionary should be prefaced with a paragraph that briefly identifies the subculture you studied, states whom you interviewed, and explains how you did the interviews. Use whatever form for the dictionary you find convenient. In the past, most of my students used three-by-five-inch file cards, one item to a card, arranged in alphabetical order and held together with a rubber band. More recently, students have been typing the material on a word processor that lets them put everything in alphabetical order.

4. Bad Informants. As I explained in this chapter, 2 of the 20 Processeans in the TALK program are not very good informants about the cult. One is obsessed by his or her own mystical musings, while the other is pretty ignorant about the Process and likes to make bizarre statements. Your assignment is to find out who these people are. By efficiently asking questions of as many of the 20 as you need, identify the two bad respondents by name and explain what is wrong about the answers you are getting from each of them.

5. A Subculture Dictionary of the Process. To do this, ask questions in the TALK program that are likely to get Processeans to use special words from the language of the cult. Then you can ask your informant to define these terms. Sometimes a definition will give you still more terms you can ask to be defined. The form of your dictionary could be either a set of file cards, one for each term, or a set of written pages produced using a word processor. In either case, the terms should be in alphabetical order.

6. The Beliefs of the Process. Using the TALK program, interview several Processeans to determine the chief religious beliefs of the group. In addition to selecting appropriate items from the list of 25 questions, you will want to follow up by asking for definitions of key terms. For example, you will want to get several Processeans to define "God," and ask them also to define any unfamiliar terms that appear in their definitions. Write a six-page essay outlining the cult's beliefs.

CHAPTER SUMMARY

Although sociological interviews can be highly rigorous tools of scientific research, at heart they are invariably a completely human process: communication between two people. The interviewer must establish rapport, which often demands impression management. Berk and Adams have listed techniques for establishing and maintaining trust, respect, and acceptance. Raymond L. Gordon has identified eight factors that inhibit communication in interviews: competing demands for time, ego threat, etiquette, trauma, forgetting, chronological confusion, inferential confusion, and unconscious behavior. To combat these inhibitors, he has listed eight facilitators: fulfilling expectations, recognition, altruistic appeals, sympathetic understanding, new experience, catharsis, the need for meaning, and extrinsic rewards.

It is important to select the right person to interview, and interviewees may be asked to play various roles. An *informant* provides objective information, whereas a *respondent* provides personal opinions, feelings, and attitudes. A variety of kinds of bias can intrude upon interviews, including: *contagion bias*, the tendency of the views of the interviewer to infect the data. An interview with a member of the Process cult illustrates how the interviewer may guide a free-moving conversation.

Before they can be incorporated in a sociological analysis, open-ended verbal data must be reduced in some way to manageable form through *coding*. One of the chief problems in good interviews is *information overload*, receiving more data than one can comfortably handle. A tape recorder can help capture the interviewee's words, but the tape must then be transcribed, a laborious process.

Among specialized kinds of interviews are subcultural dictionaries, life histories (requiring checks for *internal consistency* and *external corroboration*), and collective oral histories.

The second computer program, TALK, simulates interviews with 20 members of the Process cult. These interviews represent the variety of people one actually would encounter in such a cult, including one person gripped by personal obsessions and one who is so ignorant as to be useless as an informant. The program offers a set of 25 questions that you may ask any of the respondents. You also have the option to ask cult members to define the special words their strange group uses.

KEY CONCEPTS FOR CHAPTER 3

interview schedule   63
rapport   63
inhibitors of communication
    66
facilitators of
    communication   68
informant versus respondent
    72

interview bias   72
coding verbal data   78
tape transcription   79
subcultural dictionary   81
life history   83
oral history   86

Social History

CHAPTER OVERVIEW

Many historians have been influenced by sociology, applying the concepts and research approaches of our discipline in their work, and many sociologists specialize in analysis of historical data. In a sense, of course, all sociologists are historians, because our data always concern the past, and all historians give some attention to social factors. But, whether they work in history departments or sociology departments, some researchers primarily seek to understand bygone eras through systematic social analysis. Whether called social historians or historical sociologists, they work in the rich territory between the two academic disciplines.

Historically oriented sociology, or social history, is a tremendously broad field, so we must emphasize just a part of it. Focusing on the American Civil War, 1861–1865, we will begin to move from qualitative research involving individuals, as in the two previous chapters, to quantitative research. This is a shift from the responses of persons to data about groups. We will make use of perhaps the largest and most widely available set of primary historical data, the original manuscripts of the United States census.

Because the Civil War was a time of many kinds of social conflict, including the discrimination against Irish immigrants that burst out in the New York draft riots, doing qualitative social history requires humane sensitivity as well as difficult scholarly work. Among techniques we shall examine are record linkage and tracking (using census data on the Oneida and Shaker communes) and counterfactual arguments (considering what would have happened if the Confederacy had won the war).

The HIST software program, tied to this chapter, lets you examine the 1860 census of Baton Rouge, Louisiana, seeing the actual names of free residents of the town, both white

and black, and of 340 inmates of the penitentiary. The dataset contains several variables: age, sex, birthplace, occupation, wealth, ownership of slaves, education, and—for the inmates—year and offense for which they were convicted. The computer will quickly count how many people are in each category, and special features of the program allow you to select subsets of respondents and examine statistics just for them. This is the first step toward comparison of different groups and the concept of correlation that receives so much attention in later chapters.

The Old Censuses

Perhaps the largest and most widely available set of primary historical data is the original manuscripts of the United States census. Right after the Constitution was signed, the founders of the nation laid plans for a tally of all its residents. From 1790 until the present, the census has been taken every 10 years, and the range of questions asked has continually expanded. Unfortunately, most of the 1890 census records burned up, but the original pages or microfilms from every other census have survived.

A dozen federal archives around the country house complete sets from 1790 through the 1910 census—thousands of microfilm rolls—available for use by the general public. I have used three of the archives myself, and each day I visited them a couple of dozen Americans came in to hunt for records of their ancestors. Rough indexes telling what roll each county is on for each year are available for all censuses. Furthermore, printed or microfilm indexes of people's names are available for many years. The Church of Jesus Christ of Latter Day Saints (Mormons) in Salt Lake City has undertaken a massive project to help people find their ancestors' records, and many universities and state archives around the country maintain portions of the records. You can even order your own copies through the mail. I paid only $40

for the two films that provided the data I put on your computer disk.

The microfilms were made from copies of **census manuscript schedules**, the forms on which the census-takers wrote as they went door-to-door, so we are dealing with copies of copies. While comparing federally made microfilms of some Massachusetts schedules with the bound volume of actual pages in the Boston State House, I found that both were copies rather than originals. After completing their rounds, the census-takers (or often their wives!) had to make two duplicate copies of the original by hand. Occasional errors crept in during the copying process, and it was clear to me that the copies given to both the federal and state governments had a few copying errors.

Accurate and rich enough for many kinds of serious research projects, the census manuscripts make complete sense even to students who have never touched historical records before. Furthermore, we can look at information about real people. We see their names, their ages and birthplaces, their occupations, and the members of their households. In the previous chapters—especially in Chapter 1, where we discussed the ethics of research on human subjects—we noted that sociologists have to protect the anonymity and confidentiality of living human beings we study in our research. That is not true for the deceased, however, and the federal government opens up the data from each census 72 years after it was taken, letting anyone learn anything he or she wants about the people who were counted.

A final reason for focusing on the old censuses is simply that they are fascinating. Having spent hundreds of hours working with them, I can testify that it can get pretty exhausting to scan thousands of pages of names. As they say about the phone book, it has a great cast of characters but no plot. However, every microfilm roll has something fantastic in it, and with a little imagination we can extract valuable knowledge from the records of every family and town.

In this chapter I will be emphasizing the exciting aspects of historical research. I intentionally selected the topics we consider to be emotionally stirring and intellectually provocative. Indeed, at points we may have to urge each other to calm down and view the data dispassionately, because our primary theme will be social, racial, and ethnic conflict around the year 1860, when the United States had more such trouble than it could handle. In particular, we will zero in on the records for Baton Rouge, Louisiana, capital of a state about to rebel against the Union. We will look at slavery and freedom, hostilities and passions, and inequalities and antagonisms that have left their mark on our society today. We will start in a Southern prison but visit some in the North, too. We will tour communes and visit seventeen mental hospitals, and we will spend some time with ordinary families as well.

Although the main point of the census enumerations was simply to count persons, mid-nineteenth-century censuses secondarily focused on questions about deviance. This was the period in which states and cities were rapidly building prisons, mental hospitals, orphanages, asylums for the mentally retarded, and other institutions. Therefore, questions about crime and mental illness were included to gather information on the extent of need for these institutions. By 1870, interest

had swung from deviance to immigration, and this topic replaced deviance as the focus of special data collection for the rest of the century.

The scientific ambitions of the census designers far surpassed the technical capabilities for analysis of the time, and very little information was actually published, despite the immense quantity and generally high quality of data collected. Tabulation of the 1840 census was marred by blatant inaccuracies, as we explain in Chapter 11, for it was not until the end of the century that mechanical data-processing methods were available (Reid-Green 1989). Undaunted by the problems in 1840, census designers for 1850 switched from recording data merely at the household level to collecting data for every free resident of the country, including every inmate of an institution. Louis Newton Robinson (1911) lamented that by the time he wrote, 60 years after the 1850 census, only four pages of prison tabulations had been published from it. Of the midcentury censuses, the one for 1860 is probably of highest quality, and most of it remains unused by social scientists.

On July 16, 1860, a total of 118 persons languished in the House of Correction at Lawrence, Massachusetts. Among them were 31 convicted of larceny and 31 common drunkards. Thirteen had been convicted of assault, 7 of adultery, 6 of burglary, 4 of violation of liquor laws, 4 of lewdness, 3 of vagrancy, and two each of fornication, bigamy, and breach of peace. Among the 118 were 4 infant children, two of whom had common drunkards for mothers, one whose mother was a fornicator, and one whose mother had broken the peace. Although all 31 of the drunkards had been convicted in 1860, and thus had served only a short time in the prison, 9 of those guilty of larceny had been convicted in 1859, and 2 in 1858.

We know these facts because the county marshal who served as census taker in 1860 wrote them down on his enumeration schedules. Similar data can be found for most other prisons, mental institutions, orphanages, and poorhouses, as well as strewn throughout the pages on ordinary households. Although detailed records of particular institutions are important troves for researchers, the census has the advantages of wide coverage, huge numbers of cases, and simultaneous data from a variety of places. The data are hardly so rich or reliable as we might be able to collect today, but they are adequate for several kinds of scientific study and contain more detail than one might expect.

As a group, the Lawrence inmates were convicted of minor crimes and given short sentences, but we can also report many facts of personal history. For example, the only black inmate at Lawrence was Thomas Slocumb, a 27-year-old barber from New Hampshire, who had been convicted in 1860 of adultery. Daguerreotype artist (photographer) Orville Johnson, also from New Hampshire, had already served a year for passing counterfeit money. Eliza Jones, a 19-year-old factory operative from Massachusetts, had served a year for abandoning an infant child. And Bridget Ryan, a 17-year-old domestic servant from Ireland, was locked up for obtaining goods under false pretenses. Daniel Sullivan, also from Ireland, was a highway robber.

All this anecdotal information may be fascinating and may suggest characteristics of society at the time, but the data in the old censuses will be far more valuable to us if we can use them in systematic analyses to test theories and to describe the general conditions of past decades. It is time now for you to begin doing some historical research.

On July 20, 1860, assistant marshall John Riker visited the Louisiana Penitentiary in Baton Rouge to fill out the census forms. J. F. Hayden was the resident warden (other wardens lived in town), and Riker quickly noted down the information about Hayden's family. Mr. Hayden had been born 35 years earlier in Mississippi, while his 30-year-old wife, Catherine, had been born in Pennsylvania. They had two sons and a tiny daughter just nine months old. The family was relatively prosperous, having $3,000 in real estate and $1,000 in other property, substantial sums at the time. Hayden helped Riker copy information from the records of the 340 inmates. I have copied that same information onto your computer disk.

Start up the HIST program, and you will be able to analyze the data from the Louisiana penitentiary yourself.

The HIST Program

The program that lets you examine the history of Baton Rouge is called HIST. You get it in the same manner as the two previous programs, CULT and TALK. HIST begins by asking you which of three datasets you wish to work with. A **dataset** is a collection of information all of one type or from one source. The first consists of information about 340 inmates of the Louisiana Penitentiary, and we will use it for all our first examples. To get it, press the (1) key. To get one of the other datasets, press (2) or (3).

The two other datasets are 1,024 white residents of Baton Rouge and 328 free nonwhite residents. The white residents, which represent about a third of the white population of the town, are almost what we call a **random sample**. For our purely educational purposes, however, I didn't go to the technical lengths required to get a perfect random sample of census data (Johnson 1978; Perlmann 1979). Instead, I selected about every third white household as I worked my way through the microfilm. The 328 free nonwhites include all the completely nonwhite households in town. I keep using the word *free* to describe them because many nonwhite slaves lived in town, but the census taker never interviewed them.

Once the dataset has been loaded from the disk into the computer, you will get the *main menu*, a set of selections that gives you access to all the modules contained within the dataset:

```
[1] Look at the census
[2] Statistics on a variable
[3] Select/reject in terms of a variable
[4] Undo all select/rejects
[5] Get a different dataset
[ESC] Quit or switch programs
```

To get any of these, just press the appropriate number key, (1) through (5), or the escape key. We will go in order.

Look at the Census

If you press (1) to select the first option from the menu, a portion of the census records appears on the screen, much the way the records look in the original documents and as shown here in Figure 4.1. The old censuses were taken on huge printed forms designed to organize the information, and I have made only a few minor changes in how the information is displayed. The major change, of course, is that the letters are printed in patterns of light on a video monitor, instead of being scrawled in half-legible, fading ink on pieces of darkened paper. Be thankful for the clarity of your computer screen. Some of the handwriting in the original documents is very hard to decipher while a few of the microfilms were photographed poorly and cannot be read at all.

The first inmate on the list is Bairby Williams, a 40-year-old Englishman who was convicted in 1849 of murder. All this information is squeezed on his line of the census. The letters *M* and *W* mean that he was a male of the white race. Women, logically enough, have the letter *F* for *female* after their names. Race was a key issue for Americans in 1860, and there were four categories: W, B, M, and Ind. *W* (or a blank space on the original census manuscripts) stands for *white*, and *B* for *black*. *M* stood for *mulatto*, a term hardly used today but meaning a person of mixed black and white ancestry. At the time, many terms were current for various proportions of black ancestry, and mulatto technically meant 50 percent. The government, however, was interested only in the fact of racial mixture, not the degree, and it applied the term to anybody possessing both heritages. *Ind.* stood for Indian—meaning Native Americans—but the 1860 census ignored Indians who still acknowledged tribal rule. Oddly enough, there was no official designation for Asians, even though Asians suffered discrimination and many already lived in some parts of the country. The time of greatest trouble for Asian immigrants came later in the century, and the U.S. government was not particularly interested in identifying them in 1860.

A message in the upper-left corner of the screen says, "Cases 1–20." This means that you are looking at the first 20 inmates out of the 340 incarcerated in the penitentiary. A **case** is a unit of the thing under study and is often an individual person. You can imagine that the data are on a huge list containing 340 lines of information and that we are starting out at the top of it with the first 20 cases.

Your computer screen has room for data about only 20 people, but I have made it easy for you to "turn the page," so to speak, and see information about others. The method is similar to the one you used to move around the Process house in the CULT program and to scan through questions in the TALK program.

Six keys can quickly move you around in the census records: (↑) (PgUp) (Home) (↓) (PgDn) (End). The first three keys move you up toward the top of the list of 340 inmates. At the beginning, you already are at the very top, so they have no effect. But after you have moved down the list, you can use them to return back up. The last three keys move you down toward the bottom of the list. When you get to the very bottom, of course, they can take you no further. You would use the first three keys to come back up. Here is what each key does.

```
[↑] The "up-arrow" key moves you up one line
[PgUp] the "Page Up" key moves you up 20 lines
[Home] the "Home" key moves you all the way to the top
[↓] the "down-arrow" key moves you down one line
[PgDn] the "Page Down" key moves you down 20 lines
[End] the "End" key moves you all the way to the bottom
```

If you are at the computer, try pressing any of these keys and see how it changes the information displayed. You can keep track of where you are in the list of 340 inmates by checking the message about cases in the upper-left corner. When it says "Cases: 320–340," then you have reached the end. Those of you familiar with computers may wonder whether you have to press the NumberLock key to get the arrow keys working properly. Don't worry: they will work. Incidentally, six of the number keys on the top row of the keyboard will also move you through the list of inmates: (1), (2), (3), (7), (8), and (9). They duplicate six of the keys from the keypad.

If you hold one of the keys down, the computer will think you are pressing it several times and will hustle to move rapidly in the direction you have indicated. It may stumble over itself and start beeping in complaint. Just let go of the key and wait a moment while the machine calms down. The (PgUp) and (PgDn) keys will move you several pages at once if you hold them down, but the computer quickly gets confused and either beeps frantically or zips you to the far end of the list, so you shouldn't hold them down very long.

After you've gone some distance into the list of prisoners, you will begin finding some blacks and mulattos, as well as a few women. Look over the names of the blacks and prepare yourselves for a shock. Many of them lack a last name. They were slaves. Now think about what a last name means in our culture. It is a family name. Slaves had no right to their own family life, to establish themselves and their families as bona fide members of the community, or to receive the tiny grain of respect that is communicated when we address a person by the last name preceded by *Mr.* or *Mrs.*

FIGURE 4.1

The First Page of Census Records for the Penitentiary

				Cases 1–20 Louisiana Penitentiary, 1860		

Name	Sex Race Age	Occupation	Birthplace	Year and Crime of Conviction	
Bairby Williams	MW 40	Laborer	England	1849	Murder
Otto Bernard	MW 33	Seaman	Pennsylvania	1849	Murder
A. H. Tyler	MW 50	Laborer	New England	1850	Murder
James McCawley	MW 47	Laborer	Ireland	1850	Rape (attempted)
Robert Lintell	MW 41	Carpenter	New England	1851	Murder
Joseph Bradley	MW 51	Seaman	New England	1851	Murder
George Quarles	MW 60	Carpenter	Georgia	1851	Murder
James B. Messinian	MW 49		New York	1851	Attempted murder
Octave Leontine	MW 37		Louisiana	1852	Robbery
Michael Kearny	MW 44		Ireland	1852	Murder
Alvarez Benito	MW 41	Cigar maker	Latin America	1852	Murder
Thomas Hicky	MW 43	Carpenter	Ireland	1852	Manslaughter
William Fagan	MW 47	Tailor	Ireland	1852	Manslaughter
H. L. Holmes	MW 32		North Carolina	1852	Murder
Antonio Gueraro	MW 28		Spain	1852	Manslaughter
Virhimi Vincenzo	MW 39		Italy	1852	Murder
Isaac Clift	MW 38		Alabama	1852	Robbery
Michael Purnell	MW 39		Ireland	1853	Murder
Frank Davis	MW 31	Seaman	Mexico	1853	Murder
Stephen Day	MW 39		New York	1853	Manslaughter

To move press: (Home) (↑) (PgUp) (↓) (End) (PgDn) Press (ENTER)

Not all the nonwhites in the penitentiary were slaves, and we can't be sure just by looking at their names. A few had the initials *F.M.C.* after full names, which stood for "Free Man of Color." I have indicated these by an asterisk (*) after the name. Louisiana had a substantial free nonwhite population, especially in New Orleans.

If you are ready for another shock, I must mention six nonwhite residents of the penitentiary whom I left off our list of 340 because they were not convicts. Their names were Emily, Joe Wilson, Eli, Washington, Emeline, and Joseph. Their ages ranged from one through nine, and the census taker had written "born in the penitentiary" after their names. Their mothers were inmates. Five of the six were listed right after female inmates who might have been their mothers, although we cannot be sure because they lack last names. If these women were their mothers, then we can compare the kids' ages with the years their mothers were convicted to guess where they were conceived. Three of the five were conceived after the women I guess were their mothers were convicted; the other two were conceived that same year and thus could also be products of the penitentiary. We must be prepared for many more outrages like this.

As you browse through the list of inmates, contemplating their crimes and the other data about them, you may wonder how many were murderers, or how many were in some other category, and be tempted to start counting. But counting is a job that computers do especially well, and other options in the HIST program will provide you with many interesting statistics summarizing the inmate data.

When you are through looking at the census, press (ENTER), and you will return to the main menu.

Statistics on a Variable

The second option in the program will show you any of nine tables summarizing one or another kind of information about the inmates. It begins with another menu that lets you select the type of information you want:

```
[1] Sex
[2] Race
[3] Age
[4] Occupation
[5] Wealth
[6] Slaves
[7] Birthplace
[8] Year convicted
[9] Criminal offense
[ESC] Return to main menu
```

If you press the (1) key, you will find out how many females and males there are in the pen; pressing (2) will get you the race distribution, and so on. The table on wealth will show that the prisoners had none, although hidden loot from robberies was certainly not counted by the census taker; nor did the prisoners own any slaves. For the penitentiary dataset, the last two items on the menu are year convicted and criminal offense, but for the other two datasets they are school attendance (for young people) and ability to read and write (for persons over age 20). The census taker did not attempt to determine whether the inmates were literate, and none of them was going to school.

We call the nine items listed in the menu variables. A **variable** is a quantity that may assume any one of a set of values. A **value** is a distinct number or category. Take age. People have different ages, and if you ask many people their ages in turn, their answers will *vary*. Thus, age is a variable, and each particular age—such as 18 years old or 48—is a value of the variable age.

Variables don't have to have numbers for their values, although for convenience we like to put data into the computer in the form of numbers. For example, the three racial classifications represented by the inmates (white, mulatto, and black) are the three values of the variable "race," and the various offenses for which the inmates were convicted are the values of the variable "crime."

If you are working at the computer, tell it you want the statistics on a variable. When you get the menu of variables, press (9) to get criminal offense. You will immediately see a table like the one shown in Figure 4.2. The first column of figures shows the number of cases of each crime—how many inmates had been convicted of each one. The middle column translates this into a percentage of the total 340, and the crime itself is listed at the right.

The biggest category is murder, with 86 cases. If you consider the manslaughter and attempted murder cases as well, the inmates seem to be a very dangerous crew. Some inmates were convicted of rape and others of attempted rape, but this didn't seem a very big difference in behavior to me, so all nine rapists and would-be rapists are listed as "Rape (attempted)." The category "Trust violations" includes forgery, counterfeiting, and similar crimes. Because I felt the list would be too long if I classified each of these separately, they are all listed as trust violations.

Twenty inmates were locked up specifically for an attack on a white. Today, it would be illegal and universally considered unjust to take into account the race of the victim in convicting someone of assault. I suspect that many of these were cases of slaves responding in kind to the violence of their masters. In most cases we have no idea how much force the inmate used. Certainly, a slave could receive terrible punishment for minor acts, although the slave's owner had to calculate whether it was more profitable to imprison the slave or force the slave to work

FIGURE 4.2
Criminal Offenses of Louisiana Penitentiary Inmates in 1860

Cases	Percent	Crime
86	25.3	Murder
41	12.1	Manslaughter
37	10.9	Attempted murder
2	0.6	Assault
9	2.6	Rape (attempted)
12	3.5	Robbery
17	5.0	Burglary
19	5.6	Arson
49	14.4	Larceny
21	6.2	Trust violations
20	5.9	Attacking whites
13	3.8	Slave stealing
9	2.6	Horse stealing
2	0.6	Aiding slave
2	0.6	Insurrection
1	0.3	Not known
340	100.0	Total

harder. Often, one slave may have been severely punished to discourage others from resisting their enslavement.

Then there is the strange category of "Slave stealing." The Mississippi penitentiary at Jackson had 186 inmates in the middle of 1860, 14 of whom had been locked up for "negro stealing" and one for "inducing slave to escape." As standard histories of the period before the Civil War make clear, one of the most hotly contested legal issues concerned the escape of slaves. Northern states were sometimes legally forced to assist Southern constables in tracking down and dragging back escaped slaves, while many individuals took great risks to aid slaves in their flight for freedom.

Some of the Louisiana inmates convicted of slave stealing may have been abolitionists, members of the social movement dedicated to the eradication of slavery, but others were simply thieves. Incredible as it may seem, slave stealing actually did go on in the United States in 1860. Often, the stolen slaves were children, less able than adults to resist, escape, or explain their situation to anyone who questioned them. Usually the stolen slaves would be taken a great distance and then sold. For instance, slaves stolen in Louisiana might be taken to Texas for sale.

The two Louisiana penitentiary cases of "Aiding slave" are unclear. For one, Riker wrote down "aiding slave to steal." For the other, he wrote, "aiding slave to ???," and I can't read the last word. It doesn't look like either *steal* or *escape* to me, but this is the only conviction offense that is illegible, so I'm not too worried about it. "Insurrection" presumably means resisting slavery. There's something especially shocking about the fact that the warden has no idea why one inmate is there, but he's been there for years and there seems no hurry to let him out.

The Louisiana penitentiary took prisoners convicted of serious offenses from all over the state, but not all convicts went there. Baton Rouge also contained a parish jail—*parish* is the Louisiana word for *county*—with 18 inmates. Throughout the United States, but especially in the South, there was a practice of leasing out prisoners to work in labor camps. Thus, the penitentiary may have disproportionately contained violent prisoners and those who were unfit for hard labor, such as older inmates. You can't simply compare the offenses of inmates in the penitentiaries of different states, because states varied in their convict-leasing practices. If you were a serious historian of prisons, however, you would seek out all the abundant state records on convictions and sentencing, rather than sticking with the limited data collected for the census.

After you have finished inspecting the table of crimes for which inmates were convicted, press (ENTER) to return to the menu of variables. If you want, you can then press (ESC) to get back to the main menu. But perhaps you want to see information about another variable and will press one of the number keys from the variable menu to get it.

All nine variables have tables, but some of them provide a piece of extra information as well. When you select the age variable, the computer provides a table showing how many inmates were in each of eight age ranges, such as 0–9 years and 10–19. I felt that a list of inmates of each specific year of age would not be as useful as these age ranges. Right below the table is a message about the average age, which was calculated from the original data before the computer put inmates into the age ranges. The table for wealth gives average wealth, as well as the numbers in each of eight categories. Again, the inmates are penniless.

When you select the year of conviction, the computer will show you how many inmates were convicted in each year and also give the average year of conviction. Although one inmate was incarcerated in 1839 and another in 1840, none was convicted 1841–1844.

The table for birthplace is quite large, showing how many were born in 20 different states and several nations. At the bottom left there will be information about what percentage were "native born," that is, born in the United States. When you work with another dataset, you will find that the town of Baton Rouge has many foreign-born residents, including many Irish and Germans, just as the penitentiary does.

The table for occupation is equally large, but most people apparently did not have jobs, if we are to believe the census takers. For example, only 282 (27.5 percent) of the 1,024 people in our free-white dataset had occupations. Unfortunately, despite instructions to get the occupations of all employed persons, the census takers almost universally ignored the jobs of women and tended to ask only about the occupation of the head of the household. For the occupation table, the computer calculates the percentages out of the number employed, and a message at the lower left of the screen says what percent of the total this is.

Select/Reject in Terms of a Variable

If nine tables of cases and percentages were all the program offered you, there would hardly be any point to the program. We could simply print all the tables here in your book and be done with it. But the third option on the main menu gives you immense power to analyze in many different ways.

To select or reject cases in terms of a variable, press (3) from the main menu. You will then get a list of a few of the variables in the form of a select/reject menu:

```
[1] Sex
[2] Race
[3] Age
[4] Wealth
[5] Birthplace
[ESC] Return to main menu
```

For our example, we shall use race, because the three categories of this variable provide the best introduction and practice. When you press (2) from the select/reject menu to work with race, you get the table of information with the word *Select* and a number (1 through 3) printed to the left of each row. Figure 4.3 shows what the table looks like.

Each of the numbers next to "Select" on the screen represents a number key on the keyboard of your computer. Just as with menus, you can make something interesting happen when you press a key that is represented on the screen. Press (1), for example, and the "Select" in front of the 235 whites will change to "Reject." *Select* means that the particular group of people is selected to participate in any

FIGURE 4.3
Select/Reject for the Variable Race

			Information about Person's Race	
		Cases	Percent	Race
Select	(1)	235	69.1	White
Select	(2)	23	6.8	Mulatto
Select	(3)	82	24.1	Black
		340	100.0	Total

analysis you ask the computer to do. *Reject* means that the group gets thrown out and will be ignored in the analysis.

Press (1) a second time, and "Reject" turns back into "Select." Press (2) and you reject the mulattos. Press (2) again, and they are selected again. The same goes for the blacks or for any other group when you are selecting and rejecting on the basis of a different variable from race.

I suggest you reject the whites and then check out some of the statistics on variables. That is, set things so that "Reject" is in front of the 235 whites and "Select" in front of the two other groups. This means that you will be working just with the nonwhites, both subgroups of them. When the selects and rejects are just the way you want them, press (ENTER) and you will return to the main menu. There you can press (2) to get statistics about some of the variables. For example, you can see what offenses the nonwhites were locked up for. Any for slave stealing? Any for attacking whites? You can write down the information you find most interesting and save it for comparison with the whites.

Now, get back to the main menu and look at the fourth option: "(4) Undo all select/rejects." This says what it means. Press (4) and the computer will forget the commands you gave it about rejecting the whites and will prepare to work with the entire dataset of 340 inmates. Next, press (3) to do a different select/reject. This time, leave the whites selected and set "Reject" in front of both the mulatto and black groups. Press (ENTER) and check the statistics again. Now you can see the distribution of offenses for the whites, to contrast with the distribution for nonwhites, which you have already seen. Again, to get the full dataset back, go to the main menu and press (4) to undo the select/rejects.

You can, if you want, do two or more select/rejects in a row. For example, you could first reject all the white inmates, then do select/rejects with the sex variable, perhaps rejecting all the men. You will be left with the nonwhite women. Similarly, you could do a couple of select/rejects to get just the white men under age 40. Keep in mind, however, that too much rejecting and you won't have any inmates left!

When you select/reject on the basis of birthplace, you will find that I haven't given you all 40 birthplace categories to work with, but just three: born in the state of Louisiana, born elsewhere in the United States, and foreign-born.

Whether you do one select/reject or a whole series, each group of inmates smaller than the full 340 is called a data subset. A **data subset** is a portion of a dataset consisting of cases that were selected from it. The great value of the data subsets is that they make it possible for you to compare different groups, and systematic comparison is the key to scientific research.

Get a Different Dataset

When you began the HIST program, the computer asked you which of three datasets you wanted to work with. After working with one, you can switch to another with the fifth option on the main menu. The information for the two sets of free Baton Rouge residents is somewhat different from that for penitentiary inmates. Obviously, the free residents don't have dates and offenses of conviction. Instead, you get information about their social class. I will explain with reference to the dataset on 1,024 whites.

If you select the first menu option, to look at the census, cases 1–20 will appear, with Ufrazie Marsen at the top of the list, a 46-year-old woman. Second is Eugene Z. Marsen. To help you see family relationships, I have put the last name of only the first person in the household with a particular name and used ditto marks instead of the last name for the others. Actually, this is what the census taker did as well, to save himself effort writing out all the names. If you are zipping through the list, you will often find that the last name of the top person on the page is missing. Simply move up a few lines until the whole household is visible, and you can see the name. You can easily see which person is in which household, because the head of each household has a small square in front of his or her name.

The middle columns of the census records are the same as for prisoners, but at the right is the social class information. The column labelled "Wealth" is based on two bits of data in the original records. Opposite the name of the head of the household (and occasionally other people, too), the census taker wrote the value of real estate and of personal property owned by that person or by the family as a whole. I combined these figures to get the total wealth of the household. Then I divided that money up equally among the members of the household, to give an indication of the economic status of each individual in the records, not just the heads of the households.

Ufrazie Marsen had no money—none to share with Eugene, who is probably her son. So the wealth column has $0 for each of them. Josephine Hernandez, third case in the records, had $250 and nobody to share it with, because she lived alone. Michael Myer from France had $3,000. There were three people in his household, so they each have one-third of $3,000—which is $1,000—next to their names. Depending on the kind of research you wanted to do with the old censuses, you might not want to divide up the wealth of the heads of household like this, but for our present purposes it allows us to use wealth conveniently in several kinds of analysis.

To the right of the wealth column are three columns filled with the words *No* and *Yes* under the heading "Slaves? School? Illiterate?" The first one tells whether the household had any slaves or not. This information was not actually on the basic census records but on a separate set of documents known as the *slave schedules*. The census taker filled these out as he went door-to-door with the basic census forms. Whenever he encountered a slave owner, he asked the sex and age of each slave and occasionally got other information, such as that a particular slave was blind. The names of the slaves were never written down, another piece of evidence demonstrating that they were not treated fully as human beings.

The next-to-last column reports whether or not the person attended school within the year. Although I can imagine that a few adults attended school, the census records never indicate this. The census taker's intent was to collect information that might be useful in planning schools for children, so the question was asked only about children. The official census-taker instructions did not say anything about what age groups to cover, but they did say not to count attendance at church Sunday schools.

The final column reports whether the person could read or write, either in English or a foreign language. The original census forms and the official instructions told census takers to collect this information only for persons over 20 years of age. The idea, I am sure, was that persons under 21 might still be learning to read and write in school.

When you are comparing school attendance and literacy of various datasets and groups, you may want to take people's ages into account. Using the select/ reject option, you might select only people under 20 years old when you are interested in the percent attending school, and you might select older people when examining the percent who can read and write.

Not only can you use select/reject to compare various subgroups in a dataset, but by switching datasets you can compare whites with nonwhites, and prisoners with either. Or you can compare a subgroup in one dataset with a subgroup of another—for example, white prisoners with free white adults. The projects at the end of this chapter list only some of the research you can do with the three Baton Rouge datasets. The complete census records of the entire nation provide data for countless research projects, as the following sections of this chapter demonstrate.

Using Quantitative Historical Data

To illustrate how you would do serious quantitative research projects with the old census records, let's consider another of the burning social issues of 1860—hostility toward Irish immigrants. Today, citizens of Irish descent are fully integrated into the mainstream of society, but this was not always so. Persons of Irish ancestry have been top leaders of both the American and Canadian governments in recent years. In other walks of life, they have made substantial contributions and achieved great success. At one time, however, the Irish were the victims of severe discrimination, and they struggled against the most extreme barriers of prejudice.

The heritage of Irish-Americans is marked by immeasurable suffering. The title of one historical survey puts it thus: *Ireland: Land of*

Troubles (Johnson 1980). For a thousand years, Ireland was the victim of foreign conquests, and for centuries the English plundered the country. They stole the Irish land, practically enslaved the inhabitants, and violated every political right. At times they sought to suppress the Irish Catholic church, prohibit education of Catholics, and once or twice seemed bent on exterminating the Irish people. Perhaps a third of the population was massacred at the beginning of the 1640s, and about a million were allowed to die in the famine of the late 1840s. Most who succeeded in reaching America had not only experienced great personal hardship, but they had every reason to distrust other groups and possessed few resources with which to begin a new life.

Sociologist Andrew Greeley has compared the status of Irish-Americans to that of African-Americans. To begin with, he says, the condition of the Irish in Ireland in 1700 was hardly different from that of black slaves in the South at the same time. The history of the two groups differed little until about 1860, he says, the time of most of the census data we are using in this chapter. Although we are all aware of the prejudice and discrimination African-Americans have suffered, most of us have forgotten that the Irish were victims of the same misunderstanding and intolerance a century and more ago. As Greeley reports:

> Practically every accusation that has been made against the American blacks was also made against the Irish: their family life was inferior, they had no ambition, they did not keep up their homes, they drank too much, they were not responsible, they had no morals, it was not safe to walk through their neighborhoods at night, they voted the way crooked politicians told them to vote, they were not willing to pull themselves up by their bootstraps, they were not capable of education, they could not think for themselves, and they would always remain social problems for the rest of the country. (Greeley 1972:119–120)

Although many of these accusations were pure slander, others reflected a failure to appreciate the tremendous damage that had been done to the Irish people by centuries of extreme oppression. In particular, the Irish of earlier generations may indeed have had great difficulties with alcoholism (Opler and Singer 1956; Bales 1962; Greeley 1972). According to what is perhaps the dominant theory, the political and economic oppression the Irish suffered for so long caused extreme emotional repression as well. Finding it unsafe to express their feelings, the Irish were unable to seek or give much emotional support to each other. A substitute might be found in the bottle.

The cultural stereotype of the drunken, brawling Irishman has only recently faded from the popular mind, and not long ago police wagons used for taking arrested persons to jail were called *paddy wagons,* after the Paddies (Irishmen) they carried away. Coming from a land overflowing with suffering and feeling like strangers in a new land that greeted them with hostility, many Irish may have found opportunities blocked to them, and it would not be surprising if they turned to drink.

But did they? The quantitative data I have seen all date from the twentieth century. It would be worth hunting for evidence from a time closer to the Irish immigration. Because the 1860 census gives the birthplace of each resident, and reports for the prisons often give the offenses for which inmates were convicted, we can continue our examination of prison census records to seek information on this point.

The 1860 federal census of prisons in the Commonwealth of Massachusetts clearly shows a connection between alcohol and the Irish, and the records of prison inmates are especially revealing. Because there is no detailed index for the 1860 census, the only way we can find the records of Massachusetts prisons is to scan carefully through the entire 49 rolls of microfilm that contain the state's manuscript census schedules, comprising more than a million lines of data. This labor, however, is rewarded by a trove of data.

For 1,683 male prisoners aged 18 or over, the records gave the primary offense for which the man was convicted and his place of birth. A further 28 were listed as witnesses, while 9 were awaiting trial, 1 was insane, and comments were lacking for 7 cases. A further 25 men were described in ways not useful for our analysis. Eleven were identified merely as convicts, 4 were guilty of "sundry offenses," and 1 was guilty of "violating laws" and another of "misdemeanor." The birthplaces of 8 other men were not given, although their offenses were clearly described.

We can divide the men into four main categories, in terms of where they were born. Almost exactly half were native-born, 493 coming from Massachusetts and 347 from other parts of the United States. The overwhelming majority of foreign-born prisoners were from Ireland: 614 in comparison with the 258 from all other countries. The top of Figure 4.4 shows the distribution by gross offense category.

Most of the descriptions of criminal behavior were easy to understand—for example, the large number of cases identified with such familiar terms as *larceny, burglary,* and *robbery.* A case of "woman slaughter" must be the same as manslaughter. The following can be combined as morals offenses: adultery, house of ill fame, polygamy, bigamy, bastardy, fornication, lascivious cohabitation, and incest. The liquor-law crimes were mainly violating liquor laws, selling rum, and selling liquor. The drunkenness category was composed of drunkenness, common drunkard, drunkard, and intemperance.

Although public concern in 1860 may have focused upon the male prisoners, the figures for women would have caused alarm as well. The Massachusetts prisons held a total of 337 female prisoners aged 18 or above, with adequate descriptions of their offenses and their birthplaces. The bottom of the table shows the offense and birthplace distributions of these women.

The offense categories are the same as for the males, although we see far fewer perpetrators of serious crimes, both in absolute numbers and relatively. Whereas 14 percent of the men were guilty of assault, only 4 percent of the women were. No women at all were convicted of burglary or breaking and entering, in contrast to 15 percent of the men. Where men were guilty of rape, women were guilty of prostitution.

The first thing a leading citizen of Massachusetts might have noticed in data such as these was the sheer number of Irish-born convicts. Although 15.1 percent of the population of the state was Irish-born (Kennedy 1864:227), fully 40.0 percent of the prisoners were. One native-born resident out of a thousand was in prison, compared with 4.4 per thousand for Irish-born and 3.7 per thousand for other immigrants. That the Irish constituted 71 percent of foreign-born residents and 75 percent of foreign-born prisoners would have made them stand out in the public perception of deviance.

The proportion of Irish imprisoned for drunkenness was much higher than for the other groups. Just 5 percent of male prisoners born in Massachusetts were locked up for drunkenness, 8 percent of those born in other states, and 13 percent of immigrants other than the Irish. But the proportion was 29 percent for the men born on the Emerald Isle.

More than half of the female prisoners, 58 percent, were born in Ireland; and of these Irish-born women prisoners, more than half were incarcerated for alcohol-related offenses. Drunkenness accounts for 14 percent of native-born female prisoners but 52 percent of the Irish-born.

We must be very cautious in doing quantitative historical research and do everything possible to verify that we understand what the numbers mean. For example, it could be that native-born drunks were not arrested as often as the Irish-born. This might reflect discrimination in the actions of police, for example. At the time, Massachusetts had well over 200 town poorhouses, and the law said that town residents had a right to stay in their town's poorhouse as long as necessary. Immigrants, however, could be kicked out after a week. Thus, many native-born alcoholics could have lived in the poorhouse, while the only

FIGURE 4.4
Adult Prisoners of Massachusetts, 1860: Birthplace and Offense

Offense for Which Convicted	Birthplace				
	Mass. Native	Other USA	Ireland	Other Foreign	Total
MEN:					
Drunkenness	24	28	176	30	258
Violating Liquor Laws	4	3	17	7	31
Assault	80	23	101	37	241
Murder, Homicide, Manslaughter	17	10	25	7	59
Fraud, Forgery, Counterfeiting, RSG	25	30	12	14	81
Larceny	166	118	131	59	474
Breaking and Entering, Burglary	93	69	45	40	247
Robbery	12	11	30	6	59
Other Crimes	72	55	77	29	233
Total	493	347	614	229	1683
WOMEN:					
Drunkenness	5	9	101	8	123
Violating Liquor Laws	1	0	20	0	21
Assault	0	2	8	4	14
Murder, Homicide, Manslaughter	2	1	0	1	4
Fraud, Forgery, Counterfeiting, RSG	1	3	2	0	6
Larceny	21	12	34	11	78
Breaking and Entering, Burglary	0	0	0	0	0
Robbery	1	1	1	0	3
Other Crimes	28	12	28	20	88
Total	59	40	194	44	337

place a drunken Irishman had the right to stay was jail.

One way to strengthen our analysis is to add other data, presumably without exactly the same potential flaws, and see if the results are comparable. The old census records contain much other information that bears on the question of whether Irish rates of alcoholism were especially high, and two of the better datasets are analyzed in Figure 4.5. The first half of the table compares four groups of inmates from 17 American mental hospitals that told the 1860 census taker the supposed cause of inmates' insanity (Bainbridge 1984b). The analysis excludes inmates listed as idiots and epileptics, because these people were not mentally ill; it also excludes patients for whom no presumed case of insanity was listed.

The lower half of the table gives comparable data for Blackwell's Island Work House in New York City. This was a huge institution, combining the functions of poorhouse and prison. A majority of the inmates were Irish-born, 53 percent of the 679 males and 70 percent of the 769

FIGURE 4.5
Intemperance and Birthplace in the 1860 Census

Birthplace	Men:		Women:	
	Inmates	%Alcohol	Inmates	%Alcohol
SEVENTEEN ASYLUMS:				
United States	778	11.2%	657	1.7%
Ireland	157	38.9%	188	15.4%
Britain	36	36.1%	32	12.5%
Germany	109	18.3%	65	1.5%
BLACKWELL'S ISLAND WORK HOUSE:				
United States	161	36.0%	145	68.3%
Ireland	360	44.2%	535	77.4%
Britain	52	32.7%	51	78.4%
Germany	70	11.4%	20	60.0%

females. Many of those incarcerated there in 1860 suffered from destitution. Ellen Chambers, a 29-year-old native of Ireland, was described as "cross, ugly, and destitute." Irishmen James Mullholland and John Doughherty were in for street begging. Common labels included debauchery, vagrancy, prostitution, disorderly conduct, and idleness. The alcohol-caused cases are all those the census taker listed as due to intemperance.

Clearly, the rates of intemperance are much higher for the Irish-born of both sexes than for native-born inmates. Rates for German-born women are essentially the same as for native-born. Among the males, the German mental patients have a slightly higher rate of alcoholism and the workhouse inmates a slightly lower rate. The rates for those born in Britain (Scottish as well as English) are intriguing. In three out of the four comparisons, British rates are high—on a par with the Irish rates. Some of these people may have been ultimately of Irish extraction, but a future research project might consider the possibility that British society contained the same social conditions conducive to alcoholism as the Irish. However, the British-born inmates are a much smaller group than the Irish, and would have thus seemed far less of a social problem than they.

I stress that caution is essential in doing quantitative social history. It is all too easy to get carried away by a particular dataset or by plausible interpretations. Here, we have used three datasets: Massachusetts prisons, seventeen mental hospitals, and Blackwell's Island Work House. The results support the view that alcoholism was a real problem for the Irish, not just a myth, and qualitative histories of the Irish uniformly agree with this theory. We have merely provided added support to a widely accepted idea. Our data, however, say little about the roots of the alcohol problems. We do note that the sheer fact of being immigrants cannot be at fault, because the Germans were immigrants, too, and were not especially alcoholic. Our interpretation of the oppression the Irish suffered merely repeats what some standard authorities have said, and our own data do not really say anything about it.

Research on treatment of groups other than the Irish can draw profitably on the old records. In 1860, for example, the Philadelphia House of Refuge held 481 inmates of average age 13. It was a juvenile reformatory, and the census taker listed an offense for each of the 232 white boys, 79 white girls, 122 black boys, and 48 black girls. The most common offense was "incorrigibility," with 188 cases, and 104 children were in for vagrancy. Incorrigibility is what is often called a *status offense,* a pattern of behavior that would not be criminal for an adult but is found so troublesome in a child that it leads to imprisonment. The second half of the nineteenth century was marked by a movement that sought to "save" children by locking them up (cf. Platt 1969).

Thirteen blacks, but no whites, were guilty of disobedience. Twenty-three blacks, but no whites, were guilty of stealing. In contrast, 95 whites but only 5 blacks were in for larceny. What is the difference between stealing and larceny? The behavior was probably the same. Stealing is a popular label, while larceny is a legal term, indicating that the whites, but not the blacks, had been processed through the courts or analogous institutions.

In 1850, the Boston House of Correction held 195 males and 129 females, and drunkenness was the most common crime for each sex, followed by larceny. Assault, with 33 cases, was third most common for men, while nightwalking stood in third place for the women, with 21 cases. Nightwalking means prostitution, and Hirata (1979) has shown that the census manuscripts can be used to study houses of prostitution directly. Combining records for Boston's three main prisons in 1860 (Deer Island House of Industry, Suffolk County Jail, Boston House of Correction), we find 23 females locked up for nightwalking and 6 for lewdness. What is the distinction between nightwalking and lewdness? The difference is one of age, not of behavior. The age range of inmates convicted of lewdness was 11 through 16, while the age range for nightwalking was 17 through 33.

You must be cautious in interpreting records such as these; when doing your analysis, it is dangerous to get very far from the actual data you have. For example, one of the most widely discussed social histories of recent years was *Time on the Cross,* by Robert William Fogel and Stanley L. Engerman (1974a, 1974b), a book that sought to revise greatly our picture of slavery in the South. Although the authors presented a complex story, the image one gets from a quick reading is that slavery was not all that bad, and this superficial impression greatly stimulated controversy and publicity. Probably to boost the sales and the influence of the book, the authors published it in two parts, with all the technical analysis locked up in volume 2, while volume 1 was easy for anybody to read.

Scholars have subjected this work to severe criticism, saying that the quantitative analyses were based on fragmentary data subjected to uncritical analysis and often very selective reading of the sources (Gutman 1975; Sutch 1975). Careful quantitative social historians may not write books as famous as *Time on the Cross,* but perhaps they can take satisfaction that their modest publications are as solidly based on fact, logic, and awareness of methodological problems as they can make them.

Quantitative research methods are not magic, and they can be all too easily abused. With care, however, they can contribute greatly to the testing of theories and teach us much about past societies. Often an essential step is to combine information from two or more documents.

Record Linkage

Whenever we try to find information about a person in two different places and bring these two pieces of information together, we are doing **record linkage.** For example, when I wanted to see which residents of Baton Rouge owned slaves, I had to check a different set of forms on a different microfilm roll, the so-called slave schedules.

The process of linking records is basically simple but usually time-consuming. I had to go through both kinds of census record, the population schedules with the free residents of the town all listed, and the slave schedules bearing only the names of slave owners, and check each against the other to see which households held slaves. This was made easier by the fact that the same person, the census taker, had written everything down in the same, clear handwriting. Also, people's names are not entirely stable, especially in the old records. Spelling is often irregular, census takers often hear the names wrongly, and people frequently give just parts of their names. George Washington Carver might appear as George Garver in one record, Washington Carter in another, and G. W. Carver in a third.

Another example of the challenges of record linkage shows that the records may be sufficiently uncertain that they cannot be linked reliably. It occurred to me as I was preparing your datasets that it would be interesting to see which of the men of Baton Rouge enlisted in the Confederate Army, starting a year after the census was taken. A complete list of all Louisiana Confederate soldiers has been published in three huge volumes (Booth 1920). To make things easier, the published military roster lists the soldiers alphabetically. But as I worked I quickly found that I could link very few of the records confidently.

Take Simon Bear, for instance. At the time of the 1860 census, he was a 41-year-old merchant, born like his wife in Germany, with seven children ages 1 through 10. The family is in the white dataset on your computer disk, cases 490 through 498. When I looked in the military roster for Simon Bear, the best I could find was S. Bear. Is that the man or isn't it? Could it be some other Bear? S. Bear enrolled in the rebel army at New Orleans, July 9, 1861, and served as a corporal in Company A of the 21st Louisiana Infantry. He deserted at Memphis, Tennessee, in August of 1863.

We have some extra information, however, to help us decide whether S. Bear and Simon Bear were the same. The Louisiana penitentiary just happened to include S. J. Bear (case 135 in your penitentiary dataset), aged 31 and born in Tennessee. My guess is that it was prisoner S. Bear, not Simon the merchant, who joined up

and later deserted in his state of birth. Other ambiguous cases cannot be decided easily, and guesses are not a good basis for scientific research. I finally decided that I could not do sound research on who enlisted and who did not, solely with the census and the roster lists.

The most serious problem with record linkage is that there may be a systematic bias affecting which individuals' records you can find and which you cannot. Suppose I found more names of wealthy residents of Baton Rouge than poor ones in the army roster. This could simply mean that wealthy persons were more careful about writing their names in full, or that record keepers pay more attention to information about the wealthy. This proved a serious problem for Edward Magdol (1986) when he used record linkage to study the people who participated in the crusade against slavery known as abolitionism.

In government archives, Magdol found several petitions that abolitionists from particular towns had signed, and he set out to locate the signers in tax and property records from those towns, to see if they were from relatively high or low social classes. His main dataset concerned 4,057 people who had signed various antislavery petitions. But he could locate information about only 1,720 of them, about 42 percent, and even that information was often fragmentary. The 1,720 look pretty prosperous, but it seems likely that it was far easier to get information about people who had a lot of property, and thus this picture of prosperity may be quite wrong for all 4,057 and thus for abolitionists in general.

Tracking

Tracking is record linkage across time—for example, taking people from the 1850 census and looking them up in the 1860 records to see what happened to them. It has proven very difficult to track individuals across space and time in the old censuses. One project I was indirectly involved with planned to select 5,000 men from the 1880 census and locate them again in the 1900 census, wherever they had moved. To improve the chances of identifying a man for sure, rather than confusing him with someone else, all the men with very common names were dropped from the list, including all those named Charles, George, James, John, Joseph, and William. Twenty-one common last names were also dropped. But even so, the initial success rate was not encouraging: only 39 percent of the first group tracked could be found again.

It is quite easy, however, to examine the residents of a particular community to see who comes and who leaves over the years (Matthews 1976; Hardy 1989). My own experience along this line was gained working with the census records for the Shakers, Oneida, and other radical communal experiments of the nineteenth century. In some cases I was able to make the first reliable count of the number of members, but the main purpose of my research was to develop research methods and see if sociological theories could be tested.

It has long been thought that religion gives social and cultural unity to a commune, thus allowing it to endure (Noyes 1870; Stephan and Stephan 1973; Bainbridge 1985; cf. Durkheim 1915). However, the most successful of the American nineteenth-century communes, the Shakers, lost members rapidly from 1850 onward, despite intense religious rituals and social support for religious values (Andrews 1953; Desroche 1971; Whitworth 1975). The rules of the Shaker communes forbade anyone from having sexual relations, and the communities had to recruit and hold members from the outside world if they were to avoid vanishing.

The sexual abstinence demanded of all Shakers was a deprivation that the young may have felt more keenly than the old, both because their biological urges may have been greater and because they were typically brought to the Shakers while children, and thus had not personally decided to flee the world (Foster 1981; Kern 1981). Also, the lack of personal autonomy in nonerotic areas of life may have further alienated the young. One way to test this would be to compare the Shakers with another

nineteenth-century commune that permitted sexual activity but was equally strong in attacking members' individuality and personal freedom to make decisions.

Oneida was founded in New York State by John Humphrey Noyes, a sociologist as well as a radical religious visionary. It is famous for having practiced a form of group marriage with exotic sexual practices, while seeking spiritual perfection through such means as education, mutual criticism, and selective breeding (Noyes 1870; Carden 1969; Whitworth 1975). Data on Oneida include those from the branch community at Wallingford, Connecticut, which the 1860 census taker described as a "free love society." Of all the well-studied, long-lived communes of the nineteenth-century, Oneida best deserves description as a utopian experiment.

In 1875, Charles Nordhoff remarked upon the profuse publications of the Oneidans, saying, "They aim to keep themselves and their doctrines before the public. In this respect they differ from all the other Communistic societies now existing in this country" (Nordhoff 1875:266). His point is well illustrated by the 1870 census, which shows 11 men working in publishing at Oneida, out of 104 for whom jobs were reported: 8 printers, an author, a shorthand reporter, and a proofreader. These 11 men comprise 11 percent, compared with only 1 percent in printing at the Amana commune in the same year, while the Shakers and the communes of Zoar, Icaria, Harmony, and Bishop Hill all had much smaller numbers and percentages in printing. Eighteen of the Oneida women also worked in publishing in 1870: 15 compositors, a printer, and 2 women with the description "editrise." With so many of both sexes involved in printing, Oneida was a movement that sought to bring its message to the world, and through its publications to lead society into a radically better day.

The Shaker communes and Oneida must both be described as deviant. Early in its history, the Shakers were as much the focus of public and official controversy as the Moonies or Scientologists are today (Anonymous 1828;

Marshall 1847; Anonymous 1849; Blinn 1901). Ann Lee, the founder, was described as a drunkard and fraud, and many outsiders accused the group of brainwashing their children or other family members. Oneida was the preeminent communal cult of its day, eventually surrendering to the harsh moral criticism and threatened legal attacks of outside opponents (Noyes 1937).

Frankly, the methods of tracking are tedious. For one project, I had to locate the census records for all 21 Shaker communities in 1850 and write down data about each of the 3,842 members on a separate file card. Then I went through the 1860 census records, trying to link each person's records across the decade. Luckily, the records were extremely clear, and each person's name was quite legible. Furthermore, I had information on birthdate and birthplace to help make the matches. Only 1,866 of the Shakers were still there after 10 years, but 1,636 new people had joined, so the total membership was down only a little, to 3,502. I made no attempt to locate the people who were missing, because of the great difficulty of telling them from other people with similar names in the general population. Some had died and others defected from the commune, but one

would have to inspect records the communes themselves kept or death certificates to tell how many departed in either manner.

In another project, I tracked just the members of Massachusetts Shaker communes, but I did this in steps of just 5 years rather than 10. To do so, I combined information from the federal censuses of 1850, 1860, and 1870 with the Massachusetts state censuses of 1855 and 1865, which were available on microfilm at the Boston State House. Figure 4.6 shows what I found.

Here's how to read the table. The four columns on the left report how many members of each sex and age group were listed in the four censuses. In 1850, there were 87 male Shakers aged 0 through 19; they are the 87 listed under "1850" and to the right of "Males: 0–19." I copied their names from the 1850 federal census and then looked them up in the 1855 state census. I found 28 of these 87, which is 32 percent. The right side of the table gives the percentage the commune kept over the five years. This 32 percent appears under "1850–1855" and to the right of "Males: 0–19." In 1855, the state census showed 79 males aged 0 through 19. A few of these are boys who had been in the commune back in 1850, but most

FIGURE 4.6
Membership of Massachusetts Shaker Colonies, 1850–1870

Age and sex group	Number of members:				Percent kept:			
	1850	1855	1860	1865	1850–1855	1855–1860	1860–1865	1865–1870
Males:								
0–19	87	79	65	50	32%	28%	18%	14%
20–49	85	71	50	30	60%	48%	50%	73%
50+	73	74	67	56	71%	68%	57%	63%
Females:								
0–19	91	104	88	80	47%	50%	48%	40%
20–49	136	91	84	64	60%	76%	64%	66%
50+	133	125	123	116	65%	75%	74%	69%

are not. Not only did most of 1850's boys leave the Shakers, but several of those who stayed left the age group by becoming older than 19. For each jump of five years, I had to start with a fresh list of names, then see what percentage of them could be found.

The percentage kept can be called the **retention rate**. Notice that the percentage of boys the Shakers kept drops over the four time periods. From 1850 to 1855, they keep 32 percent. But the retention rate goes steadily downward: 28 percent, 18 percent, 14 percent. The figures for girls hop around a little: 47 percent, 50 percent, 48 percent, and 40 percent. Although the last number is lowest, for girls, the first three are about the same, and we don't have the steady downward trend that we do for the boys. The Shakers apparently did a much better job of holding girls than they did boys.

Figure 4.7 shows similar data for Oneida, but based on just three federal censuses 10 years apart. Although Oneida's retention rates seem much higher than those among the Shakers, they are really much higher even than they look. Remember that the Shaker rates are for 5-year periods, while the Oneida rates are for 10-year periods. At all its branches in 1850,

the Shakers had 618 boys aged 0–19. Only 24 percent were still members 10 years later, compared with a retention rate of 75 percent for Oneida boys over the same period.

Defection rates for Oneida women may be exaggerated slightly for 1870–1880. There was a high rate of marriage shortly before the latter census, and I may have failed to identify all of the women who married, because marriage meant a change of last name. Oneida's system of complex marriage, all adult members being like spouses to each other, came to an end August 28, 1879 (Noyes 1937:164). The 1880 census records for the headquarters community list 89 married persons, 41 (46 percent) of whom had weddings between June 1, 1879 and May 31, 1880.

The chaos of the last days of Oneida communism undoubtedly drove several individuals out. Using the commune's own records, Carden (1969:41) counted 288 members for 1875, an increase of about 30 over the previous decade, while we find only 262 for 1880. On June 23, 1879, John Humphrey Noyes himself fled, responding to a threat of criminal prosecution by outsiders who did not appreciate "free love" or communism. Yet despite all these problems, loss of young men did not become acute.

FIGURE 4.7
Membership of Oneida, 1850–1880

Age and sex group	Number of members:			Percent kept:		
	1850	1860	1870	1850–1860	1860–1870	1870–1880
Males:						
0–19	44	42	22	75%	64%	64%
20–49	43	61	71	81%	82%	68%
50+	8	24	34	63%	83%	71%
Females:						
0–19	39	46	27	87%	85%	56%
20–49	37	59	77	86%	86%	62%
50+	11	27	41	73%	67%	66%

Again, one should be cautious in interpreting results such as these, but they certainly support the theory that restrictions on sexuality cost the Shakers much of their membership.

Oneida, which permitted sexual activity, has much higher retention rates than the celibate Shakers.

_____ Qualitative Social History

The qualitative approaches to social history are almost as numerous as the historians who practice them, a fact that illustrates the difficulty of teaching interpretive-advocacy sociology. I can make a few points, however, using a set of examples spanning centuries but united by common themes. My study of spaceflight (Bainbridge 1976) was a qualitative study; but even when not using statistics, sociologists look for regularities that they can analyze and describe systematically. I found that spaceflight was achieved in the twentieth century by a radical social movement, not as the result of inexorable economic or technological trends.

A simple interaction model describes how leaders of the movement gained support for their projects. There are three *actors* in the model: (1) the *spaceman,* a leader of the movement who wants to bring spaceflight about and is prepared to use almost any means to accomplish this goal; (2) the *patron,* a leading member of the larger society who has considerable resources at his disposal and is relatively free to spend these resources as he wishes; and (3) the *opponent,* a peer of the patron, locked in fierce competition with him and temporarily holding an advantage. These actors can be individual persons or organizations. The spaceman sells the patron on his pet project, claiming it will help the patron in his struggle with the opponent.

Close examination of the development of modern rocket technology revealed at least 14 examples of this process. For example, when Wernher von Braun sold the German army on his rockets at the beginning of the 1930s, the army was at a great disadvantage with respect to its opponent, the Western powers, because they had forced it to accept treaties at the end

of World War One severely limiting German heavy artillery. Von Braun told the army, his new patron, that his rockets could overcome the advantage the Western powers enjoyed.

In another case, von Braun got aircraft manufacturer Ernst Heinkel for his patron, when Heinkel was locked in competition with Messerschmidt, a manufacturer who had the support of the Nazis. Heinkel helped von Braun develop rocket engines in a vain attempt to build high-speed fighter planes. Neither the German army nor Heinkel really gained from the bargain, but the spaceflight social movement advanced considerably.

The analytical framework for qualitative social history is often provided by a general theory or school of thought. For example, a number of writers have argued that many revolutions and civil disturbances in developing countries, including the Vietnam War, were caused by the social dislocations that inevitably flow from the introduction of a capitalist system of economics (Hobsbawm 1959; Wolf 1969). These studies followed the interpretive-advocacy approach described in Chapter 1, rather than dispassionately evaluating this theory in the light of evidence in accordance with the formal-operational approach. Although the authors did not seriously consider alternative explanations, they have been highly influential in contemporary sociology, and many professionals consider their conclusions sound.

Some of the most fascinating qualitative studies of the Civil War have interpreted it in terms of class struggle within each of the two halves of the nation. In particular, both sides resorted to drafting unwilling men into their armies, and both draft systems were perceived as unfair to working- and lower-class people. The military draft is an especially controversial practice, and the stormy debates over the Vietnam War led to its most recent abandonment. How can one ask people to give their lives for a cause that they as individuals may not support and about which their society has not achieved a solid consensus?

In the North, the draft regulations made it easy for a rich man to avoid conscription. There were two ways that money let one dodge the draft. First, it was possible to hire a substitute, a poor man willing to go in the stead of the rich man, for a fee of several hundred dollars. Second, when a man was drafted, he could simply pay the government $300 to have his name crossed off the list. The only disadvantage to paying $300 was that he might be chosen again in a later draft, while a substitute was a permanent solution to the problem. And few working-class men could raise $300.

One example, out of thousands of well-to-do men, was Henry Baldwin Hyde, founder of the Equitable Life Assurance Society, one of the largest companies in America today. In 1863, Hyde was drafted, but he paid a substitute $800 to take his place in the Union Army. Apparently he justified this with the self-serving argument that many men could serve well on the battlefield, but only he could lead his new company to success in the field of insurance. In later life, Hyde referred to the $800 as the best investment he had ever made (Buley 1967:81).

Aside from the great danger of being killed in the war, by bullets or the diseases that were rampant, a poor man with a family would suffer greatly from conscription. Neither in the North or the South was the pay high enough for a soldier's family to survive. Unless they had other sources of income, they would literally starve. On top of this, especially in the North the newspapers were filled with stories of incompetence and corruption of military officers. Early in the war the officers were political appointees, to a great extent, and after the first flush of public enthusiasm there was every reason to avoid enlisting if one possibly could. It is one thing to risk one's life willingly for a cause.

It is quite another to be drafted for a cause one may not believe in, and the justified perception that the officers were totally incompetent would hardly add to a draftee's confidence.

Among the most sociologically interesting and morally appalling episodes of the Civil War were the draft riots in New York City that began on July 13, 1863:

> Policemen were killed, the mayor's house was attacked, streetcar tracks were torn up, and authority of any kind was derided in any way possible; then a colored orphanage was burned, business houses employing Negroes were looted, and towards evening the uproar exploded into innumerable "small mobs chasing isolated Negroes as hounds would chase a fox." Negro fugitives caught by these mobs were hanged, or burned alive, or simply kicked and beaten to death. A number of policemen and private citizens died trying to prevent such lynchings . . . and for three days the authorities could do little more than try to set some sort of limits to the area of violence. (Catton 1965:207)

Luckily, the children in the orphan asylum were rescued before the mob destroyed it. Although working-class men of all backgrounds participated in the riots, the riots occurred primarily within Irish sections of the city and were to a very great extent an assault on African Americans by Irish Americans (Wittke 1956:145; Shannon 1963:57). We have already seen the tremendous hardships suffered by many Irish who immigrated to the United States; during a period of economic crisis, high unemployment, and pitifully low wages (street-sweepers earned a dollar a day) the conditions were almost unbearable.

Although many volunteered for military service only as a way of finding employment, it was soon discovered that a man could not support a family through soldiering. It did not help that pay was often months late, and there was little aid for a family that lost its breadwinner in battle. On top of that, the draft was not only unfair to workers but especially so to residents of Irish districts of New York. Whether because of bureaucratic incompetence or intentional discrimination, draft quotas were set much higher for districts where the Irish lived.

But perhaps the most important fact to note when seeking an explanation of the riots, was that New York City as a whole was very lukewarm about the Northern cause. Both in 1860 and 1864, Lincoln lost the presidential vote in the city by a wide margin. Just before hostilities broke out, the mayor led an abortive movement to have New York City declare its own independence, going neither with North nor South. Merchants and industrialists had many economic ties to the South, where many of their clients and suppliers were. White workers had little reason to want slavery abolished, because capitalists used free blacks as a tool for strike breaking and driving wages down (Lee 1943).

The Confederate draft was equally unfair and the political debates over it provide ample material for a class-conflict analysis (Thomas 1979). First enacted on April 16, 1862, like the Union law it permitted a rich man to hire a substitute. Soon an exemption was added for every owner or overseer of 20 slaves. Partly this was designed to keep the slave-based economy going, as well as to keep the slaves under close enough supervision that they could not stage an uprising. Naturally enough, however, the poor and others who did not own slaves saw it as unjust and began to suspect that the conflict was "a rich man's war and a poor man's fight." At times of desperation the South even attempted to shoot draft-evaders as if they were deserters. That substantial minorities of citizens in the South opposed the war—and majorities in sections where there were few slaves—aggravated the conflict over conscription and the sense that it was the tool of one class to exploit others (Tatum 1934).

The main methodological preparation for a sociologist wishing to do social history from a particular interpretative framework, or following a theme like class conflict, is a kind of intellectual apprenticeship. Usually, scholars with this approach are the students of senior scholars in their school of thought. All of them read extensively in that school of thought and closely study existing studies that can be models for their own work. I am not sure there are any distinctively sociological research methodologies for this work, other than creative adherence to the analytic assumptions of the particular school. Often, however, historical research can benefit from what C. Wright Mills called the *sociological imagination*, and the next section will illustrate some aspects of this almost ineffable quality.

Determinism, Accident, and Individual Action

To many students of the Civil War, both the war itself and its outcome seem profoundly shaped by accident and by the actions of a few individuals. Although some are convinced that the irreconcilable societies of North and South could not have coexisted peacefully, others feel that the war need not have happened. Consider that the trigger for Southern secession was the election of Abraham Lincoln, representing an intensely antislavery political movement. But Lincoln got only a minority of the vote cast. He was able to win only because the opposition was divided among three different candidates, two of them representing factions of a splintered Democratic party. Indeed, the two Democratic candidates together outpolled Lincoln. Had the leaders of the two halves of the Democratic party been able to combine their factions, Lincoln might have been defeated, and the war would have been avoided or at least postponed.

Here's a story for you. At the beginning of September, 1862, the Southern army, under the command of Robert E. Lee, had just chased the Northern army out of Virginia. In his military genius, Lee saw a great chance to end the war. He lead his army north. If Lee could achieve a great victory on Northern soil, several European nations might recognize the independence of the South, perhaps even offering aid. At the very least, the combination of military and diplomatic defeat would strengthen the movement in the North to make peace with the South.

Think for a moment what that would mean. North America would today contain several nations. Between Canada and Mexico would be the United States of America (a half or a third its present size) and the Confederate States of America, of comparable size. Some of today's western states might have wound up comprising their own nations, neutral between Union and Confederacy. The Civil War hardly touched California, although factions there supported both sides, and the state might well have gone its own way without a Northern victory. And at one point Utah sought complete independence. How different the map would look if Lee had succeeded!

And not the map alone. What about people's lives? Would the South have ever ended slavery? One theory holds that economic forces would soon have brought an end to this horrible institution, but this is hard to prove (Catton 1961). What would international relations in the twentieth century have been like without a strong, unified United States?

Back to our story about September, 1862. On the 13th, two Union soldiers rested in the shade of a large tree near Frederick, Maryland. One of them discovered a package lying on the ground, three cigars wrapped in a piece of paper. A glance at the paper revealed that it was a copy of Lee's plan for the invasion. The soldiers showed it to an officer, who just happened to recognize the handwriting and realize that the paper was genuine and of vast importance. Soon, General McClellan, commander of the Northern army, had the plans in his hand, exclaiming "Now I know what to do!" Four days later, Lee's army was forced to flee the battlefield at Antietam, and the Confederacy lost its best chance for victory. Only nine copies of Lee's plans existed, and to this day historians are uncertain how one came to be found by two tired Union soldiers, but that scrap of paper changed history.

A nice story, and almost true. The questionable part is that McClellan was so indecisive a commander that he did not effectively exploit the information contained in those plans, and Lee's forces were heavily outnumbered in any case (Howard 1987). But the incident illustrates forcefully the view that the fabric of history is weak at certain key points, and the tiniest accident or individual decision may lead to radically different outcomes.

However exciting, the story may seem irrelevant to sociology. The Confederacy lost the Civil War, slavery was abolished, and no intellectual speculations about what might have been can change those facts. And yet, informed speculations can be of great value to social science. The technical name for an argument of this kind is **counterfactual**. One analyzes important historical trends in terms of what might have happened if some particular event had not occurred. In the process, one comes to understand better both the historical period in question and the sociological theories one uses to explain it. For the sociologist, general trends of social change are even more interesting to speculate about than the fates of nations.

Ward Moore's (1972) intellectually stimulating novel, *Bring the Jubilee*, imagines what might have happened if the South had decisively won the Civil War. Its last chance was probably the battle of Gettysburg, July 1 through 3, 1863. You can visit the battlefield today, as a tourist, and look down from Cemetery Ridge onto the slope where Pickett made his famous charge. Had Pickett's men been able to break through the Union line, a Confederate victory was quite conceivable. But the closest call in the battle, according to Moore, was the failure of the Confederates to take a hill called Little Round Top before the Union troops occupied it. He imagines that by a very slight change in events, Little Round Top would have been in Confederate hands, and Pickett's charge would have been successful. He then postulates that the Union troops would have fled in panic, and Lee would have seized Washington.

By 1942, the time the novel ends, the world is a very different place from the one we know. For example, without American interference, Germany won the First World War and seized all of Europe. The Confederacy expanded south and west, taking over much of Latin America. The Union was left an underdeveloped country of 26 states, impoverished and primitive. All this is very exciting as speculation, but the part I find sociologically most interesting is Moore's belief that all the technological inventions made by Yankees, such as the telephone and airplane, would not have been invented by somebody else.

Here the novel enters the territory of one of the main sociological theories of history, known as **technological determinism**. As proposed by William F. Ogburn (1922) and other social scientists in several fields (e.g., Leslie White 1959), technological determinism has two main axioms. First, technology is the source of all significant social change. Second, technology is self-generating and is not significantly shaped by nontechnological factors. From this perspective, the telephone and airplane were bound to be invented about when they actually were, and Moore is wrong. If Americans had not invented them, Germans or somebody else would have done so. Indeed, technological determinists describe history as a monumental transformation of society by impersonal forces, and questions of which individuals or nations play the key roles in the drama are of minor importance. For them, technology is the author of history, and social science can describe the general trends with great precision.

One of the more striking examples of technological determinism is the theory that the stirrup caused feudalism (Lynn White 1962). In eighth-century Europe, a social system called feudalism arose. To explain it simply, the king in feudal societies gives land to his dukes. In return for his land, each duke has to equip and provide heavily armored horse warriors, known as knights, to the king's service. Out of feudalism arose the modern world, so it is quite important to know where feudalism came from.

The next time you see a movie about ancient Greece or Rome, watch how the men ride their horses. If their feet are in stirrups, the movie is inaccurate. Stirrups were probably a Chinese invention and entered Europe long after the fall of Rome, perhaps around the year 700. Before stirrups, a heavily armored knight would have fallen off his horse, especially when stabbing someone with his lance. Stirrups made knights possible, but knights were very expensive fighters. Their armor, horses, and assistants cost a bundle, and it was difficult for the king to afford them. The system of feudalism arose as a means of concentrating enough wealth to fund the knights, the ultimate weapon of their time, made possible by the lowly stirrup. As with most great theories of history, there is much room for debate, but this argument illustrates the thinking behind technological determinism in history.

When I wrote my social history of spaceflight, I found that my analysis contradicted technological determinism (Bainbridge 1976). By the 1920s, the technological means for spaceflight had been discovered. Theorists working independently in several nations had found that multistage, liquid-fuel rockets could lift payloads and even human beings into orbit. The problem was that rockets would be very expensive, and no conventional source of money was prepared to invest in such a far-out project as spaceflight.

A weak spaceflight social movement emerged—hardly more than amateur clubs—in Germany, the United States, the Soviet Union, and Britain. The German club was first and most important. Founded in 1927, it was about to die for lack of money four years later when it began negotiating with the German army for support. Under the leadership of Wernher von Braun, the club was able to convince the military to invest in its rockets; but until this young aristocrat used all his charm, logic, and social position to sell the army, the rocket club was failing in its attempt to find a patron.

The rockets von Braun's team built for the German army were really prototype spaceships, and they followed technical approaches very different from the ones best for military purposes. In a sense, von Braun conned the army, and later Adolf Hitler personally, into developing spaceflight rather than effective military technology. Toward the end of the Second World War, von Braun's V-2 rockets impressed the Americans and Russians with the potential of the war rocket, and both nations shortly began developing long-range nuclear missiles based on the German designs. The Germans themselves, however, had not been working on nuclear warheads, and the V-2 was too costly to be an effective way of delivering conventional explosives.

Sometimes a counterfactual historical analysis can be based rather solidly on fact, not just wild speculation. Suppose von Braun had not been able to trick the German army into helping him develop space technology. Like the two atomic bombs dropped on Japan that ended the war, nuclear weapons would have been carried by aircraft, not rockets, at least for several years into the 1960s. But by the early 1960s, technical refinements had made nuclear warheads small and light. Any rocket designed to carry them would have been small, like the Minuteman ICBM of that period, and useless for launching humans and large satellites into orbit. Only because the first ICBMs were huge, based directly on von Braun's technical approaches and developed in the 1950s, when warheads were heavy, were they able to open space for human flight and scientific research. Without von Braun and his effective manipulation of military decision-makers, spaceflight would not have occurred, since no other source of the vast funding needed to develop space technology has appeared at any time during its history.

Whether or not I was right in my analysis of spaceflight, providing a counterexample that showed the limitations of technological determinism and identifying a regular process of strategic interaction that promoted the social movement to explore space is not terribly important, and some writers have disagreed with me (Winter 1983; McDougall 1985). The point is that social history often struggles with issues of determinism, accident, and individual action, and sometimes a mixture of these three factors best explains the course of important events.

Sources of Historical Data

The Baton Rouge census data tell us a little bit about each of 1,692 people, a substantial body of information but tantalizing in what it leaves out. To learn more, we would have to consult a wide variety of records. History books report that Louisiana voted to leave the United States on January 26, 1861, that a Northern fleet seized New Orleans on April 25, 1862, and that Northern troops entered Baton Rouge a month later (Bragg 1941; Winters 1963). Sociologists often rely upon published histories for general information, but serious researchers usually consult many original records as well, especially when details are important.

Consider the information we have about the family that comes last in the white dataset, cases 1,019 through 1,024. T. G. Morgan was head of the household, a 61-year-old lawyer born in New Jersey. He and his wife Sarah had four children: Miriam, Sarah, James, and Henry. The records of slave ownership reveal that Morgan owned eight, from an 80-year-old blind woman to a six-month-old baby girl. Indeed, five of the eight slaves were children. Wouldn't it be interesting to know what happened to the Morgan family, or any other particular family, over the next five years of war?

I do. Neither T. G. Morgan, nor his son Henry, lived to see actual fighting. Henry was killed in a duel. Judge Thomas Gibbes Morgan—for that was his full title and name—died in November 1861 at home, before the Yankee navy seized New Orleans and the Yankee army marched on Baton Rouge. James had entered the U.S. Naval Academy at Annapolis, Maryland, but resigned when war broke out and returned to enlist in the Confederate navy; because the Confederacy lacked ships, he traveled to England, where the Confederacy made a vain attempt to build modern ironclad warships. Miriam and the two Sarahs were in Baton Rouge when the Union troops entered, and made a bit of a stir by wearing tiny Confederate flags on their chests. We know these facts, and many more, because daughter Sarah Morgan kept a diary that her son published 50 years later (Dawson 1913).

A diary like this is called a **primary source**, while published historical summaries are **secondary sources**. The distinction is that primary sources were written at the time or by people who actually participated in the events and described what they did and saw, while secondary sources were written by later compilers, historians, or analysts. The typical college term-paper is based entirely on secondary sources. Almost the only exceptions are papers that rely heavily upon published autobiographies. The manuscripts of the 1860 census are a primary source, as is Sarah Morgan's diary. The published summary of the 1860 census is a secondary source, as are the books recounting the history of Louisiana in the Civil War. Secondary sources are based, ultimately, on primary sources; both histories of Louisiana that I consulted used Sarah Morgan's diary.

Researchers generally prefer to work with primary sources, not only because they are more reliable (they sometimes aren't) but because they get the researcher as close as possible to the actual events and are not shaped by the theories and biases of the scholars who wrote the secondary sources.

There are important exceptions to this rule. A quantitative example is Robert K. Merton's (1970) analysis of 17th-century British leaders who were listed in the *Dictionary of National Biography,* a secondary source compiled years after the 17th century by biographers. Merton tabulated the dates of men working in different fields and found that, over the course of that century, the sciences rose in importance and the churches fell. My qualitative social history of spaceflight was based on a mixture of secondary and primary sources, the latter including autobiographies and documents captured by the U.S. Army at the end of the war (e.g., Dornberger 1952; Heinkel 1953; U.S. Army 1945).

Whether working with primary or secondary sources, the social historian always has to confront the issue of reliability. Can the source be trusted? Here's an example. In 1933 the German parliament building burned down. A single, disturbed individual was quickly arrested, but the event also immediately became historically pivotal. The Nazis claimed that Communists were responsible and threw many of their enemies into prison. Later, documents were published indicating that the Nazis themselves had set fire to the building, in order to have a pretext to end German democracy. Indeed, this was the moment of the Nazi seizure of power. Hitler, representing the party with the largest number of votes, had become chancellor but not yet dictator. By burning the building secretly, then branding the Communists as revolutionary arsonists, the Nazis were able to bar Communist representatives from parliament and enact emergency decrees that vastly increased Nazi power.

But there is a slight problem with this analysis. It has been shown that the documents proving the Nazis were the arsonists were actually forgeries made by a Communist group, and personal diaries of the Nazi leaders show they had no idea the fire was going to happen (Mommsen 1972). The correct analysis was that the Nazis were masters at exploiting accidents that could be useful for them; we would have a false picture of how they seized dictatorial power if we did not know about the forgeries.

Sometimes, historians disagree about the trustworthiness of sources. When I was writing my social history of spaceflight, I made some use of a book by Evgeny Riabchikov (1971), a secondary source on the history of Russian rocketry, but I did not trust it very much. It struck me as a work of Soviet propaganda.

Vague in many places, it often contradicted other sources, mainly in depicting spaceflight as an achievement of the Soviet system rather than of a few individuals and space clubs in Russia. My thesis was that private groups, constituting a tiny social movement, had promoted spaceflight in Russia. Walter A. McDougall (1986) disagrees with me, saying that space exploration was a natural extension of Marxist ideology about technology, and he places far more trust in Riabchikov than I do. This kind of dispute arises again and again in social history, and only deep familiarity with many sources and a critical mind can help you sift truth from falsehood.

Even in the relatively reliable old censuses, quality of data varies. At various times, political chicanery or incompetence caused three of our major cities (New York, Philadelphia, St. Louis) to decide the census had been done so badly that they did it over again. In 1860, several prisons did not give date of conviction, as required by the census enumerator instructions. The Eastern Penitentiary in Philadelphia lists about 450 prisoners by conviction number rather than by name. The occupations listed for the men in New York's Sing Sing Penitentiary are clearly their jobs in the institution, rather than those they held outside. A few prisons fail to give the offense for which each inmate was convicted. This may not be a great loss for the four inmates of the jail in Omaha, or even the 18 in the Baton Rouge Parish jail, but all the very large prisons I found in the 1860 records did give this information. Institutions for juveniles varied greatly in whether they considered their inmates to be incarcerated for crimes they had committed, or to be unfortunates taken in charge for their own good, and thus only about half list offenses (Wines and Dwight, 1867).

In addition to good, common sense, specialized language skills may be very important in utilizing primary sources. When Terry N. Clark (1973) performed his detailed examination of the history of French sociology, he needed a perfect command of literary French. My study of the development of space-

flight in Germany required me to know German. Standard international languages like French and German are usually learned for their own sake, when the student is an undergraduate, but sometimes a scholar has to study a language to do a particular project. Before he could do his historical study of Rumania's domination by the Turkish Empire, Daniel Chirot (1976) had to learn Rumanian.

Even if all primary sources are in English, it may not be the kind of English the researcher knows, and special study may be required. Because handwriting styles were very different a century or two ago, you have to work with the older census manuscripts for a while before you can read them swiftly and surely. For example, in the beginning of the 19th century, census takers wrote the number 2 the way we would write 3, and the number 3 looked like a grapevine. Capital letters in the 1860 manuscripts are somewhat different from the ones we use; for example, capital *K* often looks like *H* with a tiny curl in its right foot.

Words themselves have changed over the years, or even become obsolete. Some occupations have vanished, or nearly so, and thus are no longer familiar to us. There are still blacksmiths around, and I suppose we all know the word, but in 1860 the blacksmith did more than merely shoeing horses; he performed various other kinds of simple metalwork as well. Coopers made barrels. Draymen transported things in horsecarts. Hostlers took care of horses or mules. Sometimes our research takes us so far back in time that even English is almost unrecognizable without special training. George C. Homans (1941), a master of many languages, needed to know Latin and Middle English for his book on English villagers of the 13th century.

Later chapters of this book will frequently draw upon sources of historical data, and a number of the kinds of analysis they introduce can be performed with statistics from the past. The key methodological difference between social history and other forms of sociology is that you cannot go back in time to collect your own data. Lacking control over the techniques by which primary historical sources collected their information, we must become both critical and imaginative in our use of these sources.

_____ History and Social Justice

This chapter has taken the first steps into the realm of quantitative research, using data from the 1860 census. Sociologists may use such data for either of two main reasons. First, they may want to understand the society of a past era. A clearer and more balanced picture may be given by statistics that were collected and analyzed systematically than by diaries and other personal reminiscences that record the experiences of a few very unusual individuals. Second, sociologists often wish to test general theories about human behavior, and historical data extend the range of societies on which this scientific work can be done. For example, information from 1860 may be combined with modern data and contribute to a general understanding of ethnic conflict.

Certainly, our contemporary concerns with social justice have their roots in the struggles of the early 1860s. In 1911, social scientist William James commented that most people of his day were glad that the Civil War had been fought and felt that the cost had been worth it, but that they also believed another vast war was unthinkable because the advance of military technology would cause unacceptable devastation. Ironically, three years after James wrote, the Great War began—the "war to end all wars" that was later called the First World War when victory merely laid the basis for a second, more murderous conflict. In our own era, we may hope that injustice can be conquered nonviolently, and we revere the memory of Dr. Martin Luther King, Jr., for his personal achievements and sacrifice. Abraham Lincoln did not hesitate to expend lives in that cause, including those of many men who did not support it.

The Civil War ended slavery, but it only began the struggle for real freedom and equality of African-Americans. The bloodiest war in American history, it took the lives of about a half-million soldiers, a third of whom gave their lives in a cause we now condemn (Fox 1898; Livermore 1957). Our brief counterfactual analysis offers us little confidence that slavery could have been ended without that tremendous cost in lives, and we can speculate that the economic devastation inflicted on the Old South may have lasted until our own lifetimes.

In 1880, a census taker visited the National Military Home in Montgomery county, Ohio, and found almost 3,500 disabled veterans of the Civil War. Many were blind, and the home's hospital was filled with men suffering a variety of terrible complaints. If you look at the census records—the first 71 pages of enumeration district number 169 on microfilm roll 1052—you will be astonished at this catalog of human suffering. Then, I think, you will be greatly touched to find that the men's lives were not entirely empty. At the time of the 1880 census, a dramatic company of 16 actors and musicians was at the home to provide entertainment. Some of the men were still there 10 years later, when a census of Union Veterans was taken. From this census you can learn where the men were wounded, but you will look in vain in the home's records for disabled veterans of the Confederate army. As former rebels, they had no right to be taken care of and no right to the small mercy of a troupe of entertainers.

Union general William Tecumseh Sherman is reputed to have said, "War is hell," and he certainly did his best to make it so. His policy for defeating the Confederacy was to destroy its economic and social strength, and his famous march through Georgia was as much a war against the civilian population as against the rebel army. Another of Sherman's famous sayings is "The only good Indian is a dead Indian." From realization of the barbarity of our past we may draw the hope that great social progress really can be achieved. America of the 1860s was an alien land, half familiar and half utterly strange. Yet sociologists cannot fully understand their own society without studying the generations that went before.

PROJECTS FOR CHAPTER 4

The first five projects below employ the HIST program and the datasets for Baton Rouge, Louisiana, from the 1860 census. The second project asks you to look qualitatively at the actual census records, while the others ask for comparisons between different groups, made using the program's capacity to generate instant tables of numbers and percentages and to select various subgroups for close analysis. The sixth project sends you out for fresh data, and you should not select this project unless you are sure that such data happen to be available to you. All six are designed to do two things. First, they show you that systematic research, even of a quantitative kind, can be done using historical records. Second, they focus your attention on the ways that sociologists can go from facts about individual human beings to conclusions about groups.

1. Comparing White and Nonwhite Prisoners. This project has three steps. First, use the select/reject option to throw out the two groups of nonwhite prisoners and select just the white inmates. Then inspect their statistics on several variables, such as occupation, year convicted, place of birth, age, sex, and criminal offense. Copy down the tables, making sure you include the percentages. In the cases of occupation and birthplace, which have big tables, you can focus just on the most interesting categories. For occupation, I suggest you definitely write down the percent of laborers and the percent with occupations. For birthplace, definitely get the percent born in Louisiana and the percent native-born.

Second, undo the select/rejects and do new select/rejects. This time, throw out the whites and select the two nonwhite groups. Inspect their statistics, and write down the same information as you did for the white prisoners. Third, write a brief report comparing the two groups of prisoners and noting the ways in which they are most different from each other.

2. Analysis of First Names. Using whichever datasets you wish, look at the first names of people in the census records, especially noting unusual names and spellings. Keep in mind, of course, that many natives of Louisiana were of French descent, and many others were immigrants. I think you will find that a number of the names seem odd, and that some social groups had stranger names than others.

To do this project, you need to compare first names of two or more groups—such as white names with nonwhite names, or names of illiterates versus names of people who could read and write. You will need to find the groups on the census manuscript schedules. Although the computer will show them to you, it will not help you do the counting. So this is a project to get experience in the often tedious job of working by hand with primary sources. You can find the job fun, however, if you really think about the first names and try to decide which seem normal and which seem strange to you.

Relying upon both logic and imagination, how can you explain the strangeness of some names? Don't stop when you have just one or two solutions to the problem, but think of others.

3. School Attendance. Use the two datasets of free residents of Baton Rouge, the 1,024 whites and the 328 nonwhites. By using the appropriate select/rejects and inspecting the appropriate statistics, determine which groups were most likely to be attending school and which not. Naturally, you should compare the two racial groups, but you should also look within a race to see, for example, whether boys were more likely to go to school than girls. Think of other groups that would be worth comparing.

Write a brief report giving your findings and explaining what you think they mean. You should include small tables, showing the numbers and percentages attending school within the groups you compare. Whenever you find a big difference between two groups, you have probably found a factor that explains part of differences in school attendance. For example, if boys were more likely to attend school than girls, you can conclude that gender (or being a boy versus being a girl) was one of the factors that explained why an individual might or might not attend school.

4. Literacy. Following the same procedure as for project 3, find the factors that seem to explain why some of the residents of Baton Rouge could not read or write.

5. The Irish. Both the prison dataset and the dataset of white residents of Baton Rouge contain many Irish. Use the HIST program to determine how the Irish differed from others in data from the 1860 census. Your project should result in a short essay, supported by tables of numbers and percentages, comparing the Irish with other groups. If possible, suggest a sociological explanation for each of the major differences you find.

6. Tracking Residents of a Small Town. For this project, you need access to part of the manuscript census schedules. If the project can be planned a few months in advance, it is not expensive to order copies of the two microfilms that would be required. You need records for the same small town at two censuses, 10 years apart, for example 1850 and 1860. The first census must be no earlier than 1850, because earlier censuses did not record the names of all residents, only of the heads of households. The town should be quite small in population, perhaps just 200 to 400 persons. If the class is large, it might be best to select several small towns and divide class members among them. Having many people collaborate in studying one big town is not wise for a classroom project, because of the great amount of time required to search for individuals in the records.

Each student should get the records of about 40 or 50 people from the earlier census year, let's say 1850. Often it is convenient to photocopy an entire page of the census from the microfilms for each student. Then the student goes through the records for the small town for the later year, let's say 1860, looking for each person in the student's 1850 list. Individuals can be recognized by birthdate, birthplace, and family members as well as name, but data do not always match perfectly. For example, the records might imply that a person was 15 years older after the passage of only ten years. This can happen because the person's age is roughly estimated at one or both censuses. Usually the census taker interviewed only one member of each household, and that person might be wrong about some details of another member's life.

Each student should count how many persons in his or her list were found a decade later and calculate what percentage this is of the original number. Most people missing will have moved out of town or died. To complete a really fine project, class members could then combine their data. Students would write the name, sex, and age of each person from the 1850 list on a file card and mark whether or not the person was found again in 1860. Then the file cards can be sorted into piles according to age and sex (just as in our analysis of the Shakers and Oneida), and the class can calculate what percent of each group is found again after 10 years. Look to see which groups are especially likely to disappear over the decade. Think carefully if there are any problems of research method that might distort some of the numbers. For example, is there any reason that it might be difficult to find girls who were age 16 (in 1850) in the 1860 records?

CHAPTER SUMMARY

Sociologists who examine past eras and historians who investigate social factors practice social history. Perhaps the largest and most widely available set of primary historical data is the original manuscripts of the United States census. This chapter drew on data from the 1860 census of Baton Rouge, Louisiana. The period we will focus on is the American Civil War, a time that is both familiar and almost unimaginably strange for the modern reader. In several archives around the country, microfilm copies are available of *census manuscript schedules,* the forms on which the census takers wrote as they went door-to-door. The HIST software program includes three datasets: information about 340 inmates of the Louisiana Penitentiary in 1860, about 1,024 white residents of Baton Rouge, and about 328 free nonwhite residents.

The software illustrates many concepts and principles. A *case* is a unit of the thing under study, often an individual person. A *variable* is a quantity that may assume any one of a set of values, and a *value* is a distinct number or category within a variable. An important tool of analysis is the capacity to select or reject cases. *Select* means that the particular group of people are selected to participate in any analysis, while *reject* means that the group gets thrown out and will be ignored in the analysis. A *data subset* is a portion of a dataset consisting of cases that were selected from it.

To illustrate serious quantitative research projects with the old census records, the chapter examines hostility toward Irish immigrants. Today, citizens of Irish descent are fully integrated into the mainstream of society, but in 1860 they were the victims of severe discrimination and struggled against the most extreme barriers of prejudice. Census data allow us to see whether Irish immigrants were more apt than other people to suffer from alcoholism. The 1860 federal census of prisons in the Commonwealth of Massachusetts and of Blackwell's Island Work House in New York City do show higher rates of alcohol-related problems for the Irish.

Among the more sophisticated quantitative methods of historical research are record linkage and tracking, which we illustrate with data on the 19th-century religious communes of the Shakers and Oneida. Qualitative historical analysis is illustrated by the spaceflight social movement, which can be understood through a three-person model of strategic interaction. The tremendous ambiguity of historical research is demonstrated through a discussion of the roles of accident and individual action in shaping major events. Counterfactual arguments consider what might have happened if a particular historical event had unfolded in a different way.

Many sources exist for historical data. A diary is a *primary source,* while published historical summaries are *secondary sources.* In addition to qualitative data, the chapter introduces quantitative research, using numerical data from the 1860 census. Sociologists may use historical data either to understand the society of a past era or to test general theories about human behavior.

KEY CONCEPTS FOR CHAPTER 4

CHAPTER

5 Experiments

CHAPTER OUTLINE

The Experimental Method
The Logic of Experimental Social Science
Exploring Experimental Design with a
Computer
Classic Sociological Experiments
Early Experiments on Work Incentives
Does Psychotherapy Help?
Two Communication Experiments from Yale
Field Experiments: Stigmatization of the
Accused
A Field Evaluation Experiment: Recidivisim
of Ex-cons

Laboratory Experiments on Communication
Networks
Survey Experiments
**Ethics of Experimentation with Human
Subjects**

 The Simulated Experiment Program

Projects for Chapter 5

CHAPTER OVERVIEW

The most effective way to study cause and effect in the social sciences is through the experimental method. Many methods of research can help the social scientist learn if two variables are connected, and evidence about the correlation between two variables is essential to evaluate theories concerning them. But a correlation between two variables says little about how they influence each other; it does not tell us which one is cause and which is the effect. In experiments, the researcher has control over one variable and can observe how manipulating it affects another variable. That is, the researcher changes the variable that a theory

identifies as the cause to determine if there is the expected change in the effect. If so, the theory is supported. If not, the theory loses its power to convince us.

The XPER software program compares several different experimental designs taken from actual studies described in the chapter: Pitirim Sorokin's experiments on individualism versus cooperation, Carl Hovland's work on communication and social influence, Schwartz and Skolnik's field experiment on stigmatization, the Transitional Aid Research Project (TARP) on ex-convicts, and Harold Leavitt's classical laboratory studies of

134

efficiency of communication networks. Simulated studies of the value of psychotherapy illustrate several possible flaws in experimental design, including nonrandom assignment to groups and attrition.

_____ The Experimental Method

Instead of the terms *cause* and *effect*, social scientists frequently employ *independent variable* and *dependent variable*. This is especially the case outside experimental laboratories, because researchers want to avoid some implications of cause-and-effect terminology that may be misleading in several contexts.

For one thing, no research study of whatever type can conclusively prove that one variable is *the* cause of another. Typically, any aspect of human behavior is shaped by many factors, not by one alone. Even when we are able to identify a cause of a particular behavior, it may operate only under certain circumstances, when certain other factors are just right. Furthermore, a cause may itself have many causes, each of which is also a cause of the original cause's effects.

Finally, as George Homans (1950:97-103) liked to point out, two social phenomena are often *mutually dependent,* each influencing the other in an endless ring of effects that has no ultimate cause. For example, if people interact frequently, other things being equal, they will come to value each other, and people who value each other will tend to interact frequently. Given a group who value each other and interact frequently, one cannot tell cause from effect. This is like the problem of which came first, the chicken or the egg. (Today, of course, we know the answer: neither the chicken nor the egg, but the dinosaur. But then, which came first, the dinosaur or its egg?)

Mindful of these problems, experimenters and other social scientists speak instead of the relative independence or dependence of variables. **Independent variable** means roughly the cause in a cause-effect relationship.

Often the term is used for a variable treated temporarily like a cause with respect to a particular dependent variable. Variations in the independent variable are said to explain some of the variations in the dependent variable. **Dependent variable** is used instead of *effect*, referring temporarily to a variable that is treated like the effect of a particular independent variable. Variations in the dependent variable are said to be explained by variations in the independent variable. I say "temporarily" because at some other time the roles of the two variables may be reversed in a different sociological analysis.

Sociologists are forever talking about **correlation,** the tendency of two variables to vary together. For example, in my own research, I have found that being unchurched (not belonging to a religious group) and larceny (theft) are correlated. I usually interpret this to mean that participation in church reduces a person's likelihood of stealing from others, perhaps because religion teaches morals (Bainbridge 1989a). That is, I consider religion to be the independent variable and stealing to be the dependent variable: Religion prevents stealing. However, the opposite could be true. People who steal may be uncomfortable among all the conventional people who go to church, or if their wayward ways are known, they may even be kicked out of church. Thus it is possible that stealing is the independent variable and religion the dependent variable.

The theory I was testing in my research, however, was that religion prevents deviance, including larceny. Thus, it was quite appropriate to place lack of church membership in the role of the independent variable and stealing in the role of the dependent variable. And, indeed,

I did find the expected correlation: Being un-churched and stealing tended to go together.

Correlation does not prove causation. As we have just seen, either of the two variables (lack of church membership and stealing) could be the cause of the other. Some sociologists leap to the conclusion that causal theories cannot be tested with correlations. This is false. Recall that the formal-operational approach to sociology does not promise conclusive proof. In our research, we derive testable hypotheses from a theory, then place those hypotheses at risk of disconfirmation in an empirical study. If you predict a correlation between two variables, and you do not find one, then your theory is in trouble. If you find the predicted correlation, then your theory is supported, but it is never proven conclusively, regardless of how good your study is. Correlations can provide powerful evidence on the correctness of a theory.

However, we often wish for more than mere correlation. The correlation between being un-churched and committing larceny can be used to support two very different theories, and it would be nice to have evidence to decide between them. In principle, experimental research can provide such evidence. Ethical and practical considerations make it next to impossible to experiment with the relationship between religion and larceny. But experiments on many other sociological topics are entirely feasible, and experimentation has contributed much to our field.

The word *experiment* is very familiar to us. We often use it loosely to refer to any tentative or exploratory action we might try. In his dictionary of English word origins, Onions (1966) connects the word to two others, *experience* and *expert.* An experiment is an attempt to gain experience about something, and an expert is a person who has gained much experience from many experiments. Through experiments, we learn by experience, thus becoming experts. But that's all pretty vague, and in science we have a very special definition of the word *experiment.*

In an **experiment**, the researcher systematically takes some action and compares its result with the result of taking some other action. Unlike the situation in historical research, for example, the experimenter does something to the people or things under study.

Suppose you come to campus early in the morning and decide to study the importance of sociable greetings via the experimental method. When you encounter someone you flip a coin. If it comes up heads, you say, "Good morning! Have a nice day!" If the coin comes up tails, you say, "Go jump in the lake, you turkey!" You do this over and over, to dozens of people. Assuming you don't lose all your friends by this bizarre behavior, you will learn something about the value of pleasant greetings compared with hostile insults.

The different way you treated people is called the experimental manipulation. In other words, the **manipulation** is the different actions the experimenter takes with different groups of people. The people are called experimental **subjects**, and the different things you have engineered for them to experience are the **experimental conditions**. About half of the people you meet will be in the "good-morning-nice-day" condition. The others are in the "jump-in-the-lake" condition. The experimental manipulation consisted of inflicting one or the other of these two messages on the people you met.

Often, we do something to one group of subjects and nothing to the other. Another morning you could walk to a part of town where there are many strangers. At random, as you pass them on the street, you could say, "Go jump in the lake, you turkey!" to half of them. The other strangers you would pass without saying anything. A group of subjects who don't receive anything special in an experiment are called the **control group**. The subjects who do have something special happen to them are often called the **experimental group**. Later in this chapter, for example, we will consider some experiments that sought to evaluate psychotherapy by providing it for some troubled people and withholding it from others. The people who got psychotherapy were the experimental group, while the people who did not get therapy were the control group.

Experiments with control groups, as such, are usually designed to test whether doing one particular thing—such as giving psychotherapy—has the expected effect. The control group allows us to see how people would behave without the treatment the experimental group receives. Often experiments have several groups, however, with different things done to each one. Comparison between groups of subjects is an essential feature of experiments; a pure control group as such is not essential.

We must define a few more simple technical terms. Although we often speak of doing or running an experiment, a standard term for this is **administering** an experiment. Researchers need the organizational skills of a professional administrator to do successful experiments, so this term is a good one.

Often, researchers repeat an experiment that had been done earlier, usually by other researchers. Such a repetition of an experiment, performed to check earlier results and often to see if they hold under slightly different conditions, is called a **replication**. When a replication experiment gives very different results from the original experiment, we speak of a *failure to replicate*, often implying that something may have been wrong with the original experiment rather than suggesting that the replication was performed badly.

The Logic of Experimental Social Science

There is a common misconception that experiments have to be very "true to life." In this view, the laboratory is simply a cleaner, simpler, more controlled version of the real world. As it happens, several of the experiments described in this chapter are realistic in this sense, and a couple were actually done outside the laboratory setting. But experiments need not mimic natural social settings in all their detail, and too much verisimilitude can get in the way of good science.

Morris Zeldich (1980:532) explains, "The purpose of the laboratory experiment is to create certain theoretically relevant aspects of social situations under controlled conditions." He notes that experiments are intended mainly to test theories, and, as we have said, theories are both abstract and general, applying to more that one kind of situation. Therefore, good experiments tend to test somewhat abstract propositions. Perhaps because human beings have trouble understanding abstractions, laboratory experiments often present people with a more-or-less familiar situation, often dressed up with the furniture and decorations of daily life, but the point of the experiment is likely to be something far more abstract.

I remember an experience I had as a graduate student, when I served as an assistant in a social-psychology experiment. The chief experimenter had me dress up in a clown suit, complete with orange hair and bulbous nose, and cavort among the small children who were the subjects of the experiment. These kids were playing with pieces of a construction toy set, at first building whatever they wanted and later making houses according to plans the experimenter had given them. At a crucial point, I was instructed to steal pieces of the toy set and put them out of reach, in a basket hung from the ceiling. I soon suffered a violent assault from one of the kids.

Now, this study was not about clowns. Nor was it about construction sets, toy houses, or wearing silly costumes. It was a study of frustration and aggression. A standard question in social psychology concerns how people react to frustration of their plans and expectations, and several theorists have argued that aggression against the source of the frustration is the most natural response. Well, the clown in the experiment—that is, I—frustrated the kids by putting pieces they needed to make the house out of reach. One of them did, indeed, react aggressively, attacking me with a hammer she had found somewhere. The point of the experiment was to try to explain which of the kids would react to frustration with aggression, on the basis of various psychological tests they had been given earlier. Thus the experiment was designed to study something abstract, and the particular details of clown and construction toy were used merely as an effective way of studying the abstract topic while working with young children as research subjects.

Another experiment I have been deeply involved with was based on a classic study done by Morton Deutsch and Robert M. Krauss (1960). Using the rather primitive computers available at the time, Deutsch and Krauss brought pairs of research subjects into the laboratory and had them play a game in which they pretended to be operators of trucking companies. When I produced a version of this for the software included in my little book for Wadsworth called *Experiments in Psychology*, I drew a picture on the computer screen consisting of two trucks driving down various roads between pairs of warehouses. Research subjects were supposed to make deliveries as fast as they could, without crashing their trucks, and in some parts of the experiment I gave them gates they could close to prevent the other person from driving his or her truck down the most desirable route.

Now, this study was not basically about trucks, roads, gates, warehouses, or deliveries. It was about the abstract question of what conditions favor or impede cooperation between persons. In particular, Deutsch and Krauss were interested in the effect of potential threats in rendering cooperation less likely. The gate that one person could close to block the other's path was the threat. Cooperation consisted of taking turns using a fast, straight section of road; it was only one lane wide, and the game made truckers go in opposite directions on it. In the version Wadsworth and I published for Apple II and IBM-type computers, one can also experiment with the effect of communication on cooperation, letting the subjects talk with each other or making them play the game silently, and a particular experimental setup can sometimes be used to test more than one hypothesis. The superficial details of an experiment—clown suits and truck driving—should not distract us from the abstract concepts the experiment is really about: aggression and cooperation.

In Chapter 1 we introduced the *formal-operational* mode of sociological research, the principles of which apply especially well to experimentation. We have a relatively general theory. From it we derive hypotheses incorporating a few key concepts that can be operationalized. We do a systematic study, testing hypotheses by putting them at risk of disconfirmation.

"Frustration produces aggression." That's a very simple theory. With the kids in the clown experiment, we could examine a particular instance of frustration. To be frustrated, a person needs a goal that can be thwarted. The kids were given the toy construction set and told that the first one to build a house would win a dollar. Wanting dollars, they began to assemble the toy pieces. I, the bad clown, stole essential pieces, thus frustrating them. And I soon found myself the victim of aggression. The experimental hypothesis was that taking needed construction-set pieces away from kids will cause them to lash out aggressively. It was confirmed.

"Threat impedes cooperation." Another simple theory. In the case of the Deutsch and Krauss experiment, threat consisted of being able to block the other research subject's truck by closing a gate. Cooperation was operationalized as taking turns driving down the fast, single-lane road without wasting time fighting. And, indeed, when research subjects have gates at their disposal, they tend to use them to block the other person, and the resulting lack of cooperation actually makes them both lose the game.

In considering the experiments described in this chapter, make sure you look for the underlying abstract concepts that are being explored and the theory-based hypotheses that are being tested. Some of the studies relate very closely to real-world issues, and two focus on employment conditions faced by ex-cons who have just been released from prison. Many studies done in the laboratory, however, are quite removed from the world of practical affairs—for example, the study of communication patterns in small groups that is the last experiment on your disk. Such a study can give us abstract but general findings that may apply to many settings outside the laboratory. True, we cannot be sure the results of laboratory experiments apply to any particular real-world setting, but that fact gives us reason to learn other research methodologies that can determine whether they do.

If your purpose is to test a general, abstract theory, then the experimental method is a great approach, if practical circumstances and the nature of your theory allow you to use it. If hypotheses derived from your theory fail in the laboratory, then they will probably fail in many real-world settings as well. If your theory passes the test of experimental research, it has sustained a powerful challenge, resisting falsification and deserving an increased measure of respect.

Exploring Experimental Design with a Computer

The software that accompanies this chapter will let you replicate—through computer simulations—several classic experiments. These experiments have the following structure, composed of as many as six parts.

1. Assignment of subjects to groups
2. Test at step 1
3. Phase 1 of experiment
4. Test at step 2
5. Phase 2 of experiment
6. Test at step 3

If there are two or more groups, such as an experimental group and a control group, then the people who are to be the subjects of the experiment must be assigned to these groups. Sometimes we will want to know how the groups differ, even before we have done anything to them, and that is the purpose of the test at step 1, or "Test 1" for short. Depending upon the experiment, it may be a pencil-and-paper questionnaire or some completely different way of collecting data, but in any case we can call it a "test."

Next comes the main body of the experiment, which may be in two phases or one. If there are two parts, we call the first part "Phase 1" and the second part "Phase 2." After each phase comes a test, labeled "Test 2" and "Test 3." Please note that we will use the numbers 1, 2 and 3 for the tests regardless of how many times data are collected during the experiment. If there is only one phase, then there are two steps at which we might do a test; if there are two phases, there can be three tests. But we may skip the first test in some experiments, while using numbers 2 and 3. Again, it will help keep things straight if you think in terms of "Test at step 2" and "Test at step 3," even though to save space the computer may say "Test 2" and "Test 3."

_____ Classic Sociological Experiments

The best way to understand all the principles and details of the software is to look at the classic experiments themselves. Usually I have had to simplify the experiments slightly to fit into this software/textbook package, and I generally use a different number of subjects so that each experimental or control group can be an appropriate size for the projects described at the end of the chapter. I have tried, however, to preserve the spirits of all these great experiments. The full set illustrates many principles, including in some cases the practical limits of experimentation and the controversies that can swarm around questionable interpretations of results.

Early Experiments on Work Incentives

We will begin our tour of experiments with a study, published in the *American Journal of*

Sociology in 1930, that compared "communism" with "individualism" in their capacity to motivate people to work. The researcher was Pitirim A. Sorokin (1930), well-known as a macro-sociologist who studied the rise and fall of whole civilizations, not someone you might expect to do experimental research on small groups of school children. Sorokin was a native of Russia who was deeply involved in the moderate government that temporarily ruled the country after the czar's regime was toppled. When the Communists took power, Sorokin narrowly escaped execution. Coming to the United States, he founded Harvard's sociology department and wrote a number of influential books in a grand style no longer popular today but filled with fascinating ideas about the vast sweep of human history.

His interest in comparing collectivism with individualism began after the Russian revolution impressed the problem upon him and nearly cost him his life. Sorokin wrote (1930:765): "In 1921 and 1922 while in Russia I tried to apply the experimental method for the clarification of the problem whether the communistic or individualistic organization is more efficient. My banishment interrupted the study." The experiments he did, both in Russia and the United States, were complex to the point of chaos and involved neither a large number of research subjects nor substantial periods of their time. I will discuss only part of his work here, in slightly simplified form.

Take a group of school children during their recess, and tell them they are going to play a game. They will carry marbles from one place to another and also fill cups with sand and carry them, too. They will be scored in terms of how many marbles and how much sand they deliver to the goal. The prizes in the game are toys, which children can earn by carrying enough marbles and sand to meet a quota set by the experimenter. That is, every kid who carries a certain number of marbles or cups of sand meets the quota and wins a prize. When you first present this game, you remind the kids that they have a new playhouse, and tell them that the toys they earn will belong to the

playhouse, to be shared by all the kids playing the game. Later, on another occasion, you have them play the game again, but this time you say that each kid can personally keep the toys he or she earns.

If this sounds a little bit complicated, the basic idea can be explained simply enough. You have one group of research subjects, the kids. You study them for two periods of time. In each time period, they play the same game, but the prizes are given out following different principles in the two periods. In the first period, the prizes are *cooperative*—they will belong to the collective playhouse. In the second period, the prizes are *individual*—they will belong to the particular children who earn them. Sorokin found that the kids worked harder, delivering more marbles and sand, when they were earning toys for themselves, as individuals, than when they were working for the collective playhouse. That is, when working for themselves (individual condition), kids were more likely to meet the quota than when they were working for the group (cooperative condition).

The top part of Figure 5.1 shows the outline of this study. There are 24 research subjects, the children who will play your game. Sorokin's research design did not involve assigning them to groups. Instead, all of the children go immediately into the first phase of the experiment, in which they play the game cooperatively, earning toys that will belong to their collective playhouse. Test 2 is data collected at the end of Phase 1, measuring how much sand and marbles the kids carried to the goal. (Remember that "Test 2" is an abbreviation for "Test at time 2," and that we did not have a test at time 1 in this experiment.) Next comes the second phase of the experiment, in which the kids play the game again, but now for toys they can keep individually. Again we tally up the amount of sand and marbles delivered, in the test at time 3.

Do you see any problem with this research design? You might doubt that the play of children can be used to evaluate entire social systems, and the fact that the kids worked harder

FIGURE 5.1
Sorokin's Work Experiment

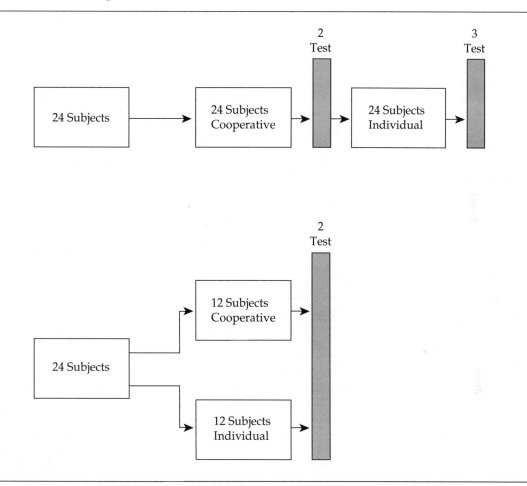

under the individual than the cooperative condition does not prove that "Capitalist" Americans work harder than "Communist" Russians. The Soviet Union is an infinitely bigger experiment than Sorokin's modest study, but it is quite usual in experimental research, as well as in other kinds of scientific study, to examine phenomena that are considerably smaller than the ones we really want to know about. We often experiment with a small group of research subjects and hope to extrapolate from their results to the whole of humanity. The

intellectual leap from the laboratory to the wide world can be a perilous one, and later sections of this book will consider ways to make it safer. This is a problem for all research, which inevitably is somewhat limited in scope, especially small laboratory experiments.

But there is something else about the experimental design that should trouble you. Imagine that you did the experiment in a single day. Phase 1 was done in the morning and Phase 2 in the afternoon. Perhaps the conditions in the morning were very different from those in the afternoon. Maybe it rained last night, and the sand was wet in the morning—heavy and sticky—but dry and easier to carry in the afternoon. Perhaps the kids were still sleepy when they began the experiment, but much more vigorous after lunch in the sunny afternoon. In other words, the differences in work done during the two phases might have nothing to do with the conditions of the experiment (cooperative versus individual) but merely reflect the different times of day when the experiment was carried out.

If you were designing the experiment, how would you prevent this problem from ruining your results? One approach would be to make sure that both conditions were employed over the same hours of the day. On Monday and Wednesday, you could run the kids under the cooperative condition, both morning and afternoon. On Tuesdays and Thursdays, you would run them under the individual condition, and on Fridays you would tabulate the week's data.

But this just pushes the problem with hours of the day onto days of the week. Perhaps the students' class schedules are heavy on Mondays and Wednesdays and light on Tuesdays and Thursdays. If so, they might be more tired when working cooperatively than when working for individual prizes, simply because of the days you picked for the two experimental conditions. Thus, you would have to schedule the experimental sessions very carefully to get a fair comparison between cooperative and individually rewarded work.

Another plan would be to divide the kids into two groups and run the experiment on both groups simultaneously, one group earning toys for the collective playhouse and the other group earning toys for themselves as individuals. The obvious way to do this, employed in a vast number of actual studies, is to take two classes of kids—Mr. Gavigan's seventh grade and Mrs. Johnson's seventh grade, for example—and have one class work under the cooperative condition and the other under the individual condition. But this ignores the possibility that the two classes differ significantly in physical capabilities, desire for a new toy, or

even in the attitudes of their teacher, who may inspire them to work either cooperatively or individually. This observation brings us to the standard design for simple experiments, one that avoids all these problems.

Assign the students at random to two groups. One group will carry the sand and marbles under the cooperative condition, earning toys for their collective playhouse. The other group will do the work individually, earning toys for themselves personally. Run the two groups at the same time, with identical sand, marbles, and other equipment.

Random assignment of subjects to the different groups in an experiment is such a standard approach that you have undoubtedly heard and thought about it already. An alternative is to divide the subjects up in terms of their characteristics. For example, when you have played sports informally—say volleyball—you may have divided up into teams so there was the same number of girls on each team and the same number of boys on each team. This can get very complicated, however, when you are trying to balance two groups in terms of several characteristics simultaneously. Furthermore, it assumes you know which of the subjects' characteristics matter for your experiment and have enough information about the subjects to make reliable judgments about where they should go.

Assigning subjects to the groups at random will balance the groups, without your having to know anything about the characteristics of the subjects or how those characteristics will affect the results. It works best when you have a large number of subjects in each group. With small numbers, bad luck could put all the hard workers in one group and the lazy kids in the other. This is a general feature of using randomness in research. The larger the number of things (such as subjects) randomized, the more confidence you have in the procedure.

The bottom part of Figure 5.1 shows how Sorokin's experiment would look if we divided the kids at random into two groups, each working under one of the experimental conditions. We start with 24 subjects, and random assignment divides them into two groups of 12. You could do this with flips of a coin: heads, and a kid goes into the cooperative group: tails, into the individual group. The two groups are run simultaneously through the experiment, one under each condition.

Practical considerations have frequently prevented researchers from using random assignment, and one of the themes of this chapter is the trouble that failure to assign randomly can cause. For now, it is enough to understand the difference between the two experimental designs illustrated in Figure 5.1. At the top, we have comparison of one group with itself, across two periods of time for which different experimental conditions are in effect. At the bottom, we have random assignment into two groups that undergo different experimental conditions at the same time.

In this chapter, we shall consider many studies in which the subjects were divided into groups and run simultaneously through the experiment. Most of these use random assignment. But we cannot completely ignore Sorokin's approach, using a single group, so here is another example of it.

Ayllon and Azrin (1964) were interested in the power of mere words to influence mental patients' behavior, in comparison with material rewards and a combination of words and rewards. To explore this nest of questions, they did two experiments using female patients in the mental hospital at which the researchers worked. Both experiments were carried out in the dining room of the ward on which the patients resided, and the patients were selected because they usually failed to take a full set of utensils (knife, fork, spoon) when they went through the cafeteria line. The practical purpose of the experiment was to see how the patients could be gotten to use utensils, rather than their tongues and fingers to get the food off the plates—and how to get patients who used just one of the utensils to become more like "normal" people by using all three.

Meals were scheduled so that the 18 patients who were employed as experimental subjects all ate at the same time, with no other patients around, so the researchers could control

carefully what happened. For an initial period of 10 meals (called the "baseline"), the patients were observed to see how often they picked up the full set of utensils, and they did so less than 10 percent of the time. Note that the baseline measurement is equivalent to a "Test at time 1" (or "Test 1") that might be added to the top diagram in Figure 5.1, a measurement of behavior before the experiment really began.

Phase 1 of the experiment itself, which lasted for 20 meals, added a reward for taking the full set of utensils. A patient who did so was automatically offered her choice of candy, a cigarette, a cup of coffee, or a glass of milk. No explanation was given the patients for why some of them were offered these extras and some were not. So few of the patients ever picked up the utensils that they were hardly ever rewarded for doing this, and apparently they never figured out why an occasional patient was offered something extra. The result was that their rate of picking up the utensils did not increase significantly. Apparently—if we can risk a grand generalization from this modest study—rewards alone are not sufficient to modify behavior. The individual has to experience the reward and connect it with the behavior that earned it.

Phase 2, also 20 meals long, added explanatory instructions: "Please pick up your knife, fork, and spoon, and you have a choice of extra milk, coffee, cigarettes, or candy." Now the behavior changed. Most of the time—something like 90 percent—the patients picked up the full set of cutlery. So, the combination of rewards and explanatory instructions did influence behavior in desired directions, even for these chronic mental patients. But this experiment leaves open the possibility that the instructions alone were responsible.

Some months later, Ayllon and Azrin did a second experiment, using 20 patients, also in three phases. Again, a baseline period determined how often the patients picked up a full set of cutlery before any experimental manipulations were administered. Phase 1 involved giving just instructions, no reward. The patients did begin picking up utensils, as they were instructed to do, but the percentage dropped down to an average of 25 percent at the end of this phase. In Phase 2, again both instructions and rewards were used, and the percentage zoomed up to 90 percent and held that high for the duration of the study. Within the limitations of the experiment, then, the combinations of rewards and instructions are more potent than either instructions or rewards alone.

Perhaps you can see that it would be expensive to divide the research subjects into two groups at random. The experimenters' interpretation of their results is quite reasonable, but it is always possible, when comparing a group of subjects with itself at two points in time, that something has changed outside your experiment and caused the difference. We might hope, for example, that many of the patients were improving, perhaps because of the treatments they were receiving in the hospital, and that as they improved they began to behave more and more like "normal" people, eating with a full set of dinner utensils.

One way of guarding against the possibility that results were produced by changes in the subjects or in the environment that had nothing to do with the experiment, is to have several phases and administer the conditions in alternating order upon the subjects. For example, Ayllon and Azrin could have rewarded their patients for picking up utensils for a week, then not rewarded them for a week, then rewarded them for a week, and not rewarded them, and so on for many weeks. If the patients' behavior also switches back and forth between picking up utensils and not doing so, showing what is technically called *reversal* with changes in the experimental conditions (Bushell and Burgess 1969), then we could have great confidence in the results.

Research on mental patients is a very important part of sociology, as well as of psychiatry and psychology, and many important sociological studies have explored both the sociology of deviance and medical sociology. The next experiments we shall consider are also in this area, specifically focusing on the problem of determining the value of psychotherapy, because

this topic will allow us to consider more fully the importance of random assignment and other features of good experimental design.

Does Psychotherapy Help?

First, let me make it clear: I do not intend to answer this question. On the face of it, it is too simple. Many different kinds of treatment go under the general name *psychotherapy,* and many kinds of human problems drive people to the psychotherapist. It is entirely possible that different kinds of psychotherapy are helpful for different kinds of problems. The question is tremendously important. Any treatment that can help reduce human suffering, especially if it preserves human freedom at the same time, would be of great value. Regardless, psychotherapies are based on social interaction and the development of social relationships between clients and therapists, and thus are proper topics for sociologists to study.

Our purpose here is not to answer the question, but to use it to see some of the requirements of good experimental design. Psychotherapy is an especially good example both because it has posed severe challenges to researchers and because lessons learned from studying it may be applied to other important issues. Research to determine the effectiveness of any proposed solution for human problems is often called **evaluation research**. The experimental method is well designed to undertake this vital task. In the following section we are going to identify a great number of problems with experiments on psychotherapy, and those of you who like simple answers to life's problems will find this depressing. Hold onto your hats. Things are going to get stormy for a while.

Go to the library. Check the huge literature on the effectiveness of psychotherapy, and see what conclusion you come to. Some of you may feel the published evidence strongly supports the value of psychotherapy, and you will be enthusiastic about recommending it for your friends and trying it yourself. Others may come away from reading the literature with the pessimistic conclusion that psychotherapy simply does not work and is one of the saddest illusions of our age.

Personally, after reading dozens and dozens of scientific publications, I am entirely uncertain. In my more emotional moments, I feel that the scientific research on psychotherapy is a huge scandal, because scientists have invested vast effort but offer the general public no authoritative advice on whether to rely upon psychotherapy to help them with mental or emotional problems, or whether to avoid it as a waste of time that might prevent them from trying something more useful. Even in my less emotional moments, I am convinced that social science has failed to fulfill its obligations to the public, the main reason being that a host of poorly designed experimental studies have announced strong conclusions on the basis of weak evidence.

The last thing I want to do is to discourage you from seeking whatever kind of help is most convincing to you, personally, when troubles descend upon you. You will have to rely upon people you trust and upon the particular cultural assumptions about human problems that you happen to hold. Research has shown that people's social networks and cultural backgrounds greatly determine whether they will seek psychotherapy or turn, instead, to some other kind of aid such as religion (Larson 1968; Linn 1968). Medical professionals, including those in the field of psychiatry, will confidently refer a patient to practitioners of particular techniques, but they do so greatly on the basis of their own social background, current fads in psychiatry, and their own professional membership (Hollingshead and Redlich 1958; Strauss, Schatzman, Bucher, Ehrlich, and Sabshin 1964). In some respects, psychotherapy is analogous to religion, in that faith is required and faith may be an important part of the healing process (Frank 1961; Stark and Bainbridge 1985).

And yet, you would think that simple experiments could decide the value of psychotherapy, once and for all. You set up a clinic, providing high quality psychotherapy, and

1,000 people sign up for treatment. You divide them into two groups at random, 500 to receive psychotherapy and 500 who will not get it. At the end of a year, you check all 1,000 people again, to see how many have improved. If 80 percent of those who got therapy improved, while only 20 percent of those who got no therapy improved, then you could be confident the therapy worked. However, if the improvement rate was, say, 50 percent in each group, then you know that the treatment was valueless.

Unfortunately, things are not so simple. It is very rare that a clinic or any other treatment facility will let the researcher decide on a random basis who should get treatment and who should not. The therapists already believe their treatment is valuable; otherwise they would not offer it. Instead, people get admitted to treatment on the basis of such criteria as how long they have been on the waiting list, how badly they seem to need help, and how convinced the therapists are that they can help each particular person. The people running the clinic probably feel it would be immoral to dispense help on the basis of a coin flip.

The government, of course, requires the drug companies to subject their new medications to experimental research trials that are completely rigorous. Subjects who volunteer are indeed assigned at random to receive the new medication or not. The ethical argument against withholding treatment from anyone is countered by the scientific argument that until a drug has gone through careful experimental testing, we do not have any solid reason to consider it beneficial. But in the case of psychotherapies, and indeed of social programs designed by sociologists, the government imposes no legal requirement to test the cure to see if it works and lacks severely harmful side effects.

We would not need science at all if the nature of things were readily apparent to any human being who merely looked at the world. There is a host of errors that can convince a person that a particular treatment cures emotional problems. Often, people get better even without treatment; this is called **spontaneous remission**. A person will enter treatment when at a low point in life. Chance or curative influences having nothing to do with the treatment will, thankfully, improve the conditions of many. If they develop a social relationship with the therapist, they may well attribute the changes to the treatment. Certainly the relationship with a therapist can be emotionally charged, and the person may share feelings that he or she had previously kept private. Thus, it is quite natural for both client and therapist to think that improvements were the result of the treatment.

Furthermore, therapists seldom see the many cases of spontaneous remission. They deal with people who are in treatment, not with whose who stay out of treatment. Thus, they are in no position to estimate, even roughly, how much better people in treatment do compared to those who do not get treatment. Some critics of psychotherapy have argued that rates of spontaneous remission are very high, at least for the mild disorders that psychotherapists typically treat (Eysenck 1965; Rachman and Wilson 1980). If so, therapists might be seeing very high rates of improvement merely because of spontaneous remission. If they believed that spontaneous improvement was in fact rare, they would be fully convinced their treatments were responsible for most of the cures they saw. Of course, if rates of spontaneous remission were actually low, and therapists found high rates of improvement among their patients, then the evidence in favor of their treatments would be pretty good.

This would not be true, however, if people were selected for treatment precisely because they had the characteristics that predict spontaneous remission. It is said that the best psychotherapy patients fit "the YAVIS syndrome" (Schofield 1964, Finkel 1976). That is, they are Young, Attractive, Verbal, Intelligent, and Successful. In contrast, people who are "bad risks" for psychotherapy fit "the HOUND syndrome." They are Homely, Old, Unattractive, and Dumb. If your experiment places a lot of YAVIS people into treatment and holds a lot of HOUNDs out of treatment as a "control group," you can expect the people in treatment

to do a lot better than those out of treatment. But this may be because they are YAVIS types, not because they get therapy. People with YAVIS characteristics will probably receive more favorable attention from others in society, and many more routes to happier days will be open to them than to the poor HOUND group.

At the top of Figure 5.2, I have diagrammed a rather full experiment on psychotherapy, with two phases, three tests, and two groups. Imagine that 120 people come to your clinic, seeking therapy. A senior therapist gives each one a two-hour **intake interview**, to determine what the person's problem is and to decide whether to give him or her treatment. Following personal hunches more than formal criteria, the senior therapist lets 60 people immediately into treatment and puts the other 60 on a waiting list. Before treatment starts, a set of psychological tests is administered to all 120. Then Group 1 gets therapy for a number of months. This is the "experimental group." Group 2 is called the "control group," and it gets nothing. Then, at the end of therapy, another set of psychological tests determines how all 120 are doing. To check whether the benefits of therapy last, you have both groups wait another six months and then take the psychological tests all over.

In the previous paragraph, I put quotation marks around "control group" because, strictly speaking, we should not call this group a control at all. It is not comparable to the experimental group because assignments to the two groups were not random. Persons were assigned based on the subjective evaluation of the senior therapist during the intake interview. The results of a study like this will simply not be scientifically valid. Indeed, studies like this, of which there are many in the literature, are even worse than no study at all, because they give many unsophisticated readers the false sense that science has determined the truth. Seeing study after study with flaws like this, the sophisticated reader of psychiatry journals will develop an excessive skepticism of anything published in their pages.

Okay, so let's imagine you have convinced the clinic staff of the necessity for random

FIGURE 5.2
Psychotherapy Experiment

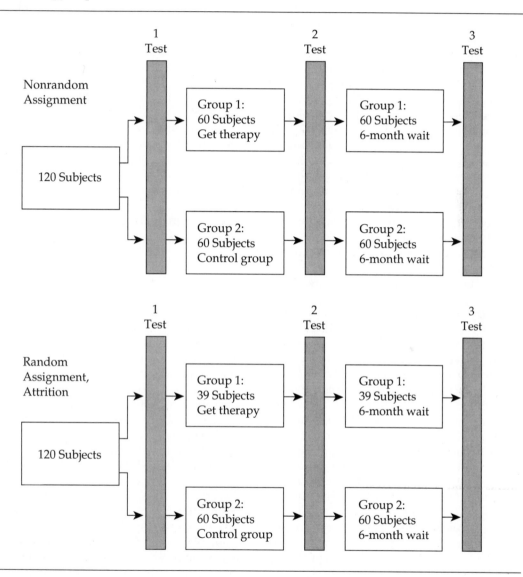

assignment, and you do an experiment with a similar outline, as shown at the bottom of Figure 5.2. You randomly assign 60 patients to get psychotherapy and put the other 60 on the waiting list. And then ... woops! Look at the therapy group in the bottom diagram of

Figure 5.2. It was supposed to have 60 patients, but I see only 39. What happened?

Attrition. When subjects drop out of a study we are doing, such as an experiment, we call their loss **attrition**. Many factors can cause you to lose subjects in a study, but when people abandon a treatment program it is apt to be because they do not like the treatment or sense (perhaps correctly) that it is not helping them. Thus, attrition may remove people who are not getting better from the therapy group, leaving those who improve. On average, the experimental group will appear to be getting better, when all that is really happening is that the worst cases are dropping out of it.

Elsewhere, I have called this process social evaporation (Stark and Bainbridge 1987:257). I define **social evaporation** as the process in which members of a group whose fortunes decline defect from it, leaving behind those members whose fortunes rise or remain constant. Very high rates of social evaporation will destroy a group, but moderate rates increase members' commitments to it, because each remaining member believes the group is improving.

If you want to compare the two research designs of Figure 5.2 with a real experimental design, you might check out a classic and much criticized study by Carl Rogers and his associates (Rogers and Dymond 1954; cf. Eysenck 1965; Rachman and Wilson 1980). In it, the "control groups" were not entirely comparable with the group that got the treatment. Some, for example, were groups of normal people who had not sought treatment and thus would not be expected to improve much from test to test. Even a randomly assigned control group of people put on a waiting list after they sought help is a little problematic, because they may have found help elsewhere when the first clinic they visited refused it.

Social science often faces severe problems when it accepts an assignment from the society to solve a major social problem. Our theories, research methods, and the resources available to us may not be sufficient to complete the mission successfully. Later in this chapter we will see other examples of controversial research on topics of tremendous public concern. The experimental method works perfectly well if you can actually employ it, but when economic, moral, or other concerns prevent you from using random assignment, for example, the

research may collapse. If research is past the purely exploratory phase, then it must be rigorous and carefully done, or there is no point doing it.

Many of the very best experiments have been done away from the complicating concerns of the real world, in university social psychology laboratories. Often the projects were quite inexpensive, but the accumulated knowledge from all such research is tremendously valuable. Out of the vast experimental literature, I will consider just two modest studies, not necessarily perfect but quite competent, that will be of interest to sociologists generally.

Two Communication Experiments from Yale

Around the 1950s, Yale University was a world center for the study of attitude change, persuasion, and communication. Perhaps the central figure in this world was Carl I. Hovland, who collaborated on numerous experimental research projects with many other social psychologists. We will consider two of his experiments, both of them notable for having been relatively inexpensive to do. Together, they illustrate further the range of choices available for experimental design and the necessity of selecting the right approach for a particular scientific problem. Thus, they reinforce two of my mottos: *Brains save bucks. Let the method fit the question.*

The first of this pair of attitude-change experiments concerned the credibility of communicators (Hovland, Janis, and Kelley 1953:31-33). Do you always believe what someone tells you? I hope not. But how do you decide which people to believe? Often we can rely upon long experience with the person, basing present credibility on whether what the person said in the past turned out to be true or not. In the modern world, however, much information comes to us from strangers, and we need some way of evaluating their probable truthfulness. Among the criteria we may use to decide whether to believe people are their apparent intelligence, knowledge of the topic in question, our estimate of their objectivity, and whether we judge them to be good people of sound mind.

This all makes sense, but many things that make sense turn out to be false. The world used to be flat, remember? Much of what we might call folk wisdom, proverbs, and standard notions from popular culture is contradictory. "Look before you leap!" "The early bird catches the worm!" These two proverbs disagree. One tells you to be cautious, the other to move quickly. The proverb about the early bird assumes that you are a bird rather than a worm. If the worm had only stayed in bed, he wouldn't have gotten caught. As with proverbs, so too with popular explanations of human behavior. They may sound good, but until we have tested them scientifically, we cannot be sure they are true.

In the first experiment by Hovland and his colleagues, high-school students were asked to listen to a radio program, supposedly to judge how educational it was. Included in the program was a lecture about juvenile delinquency, in which the speaker advocated extreme leniency in the treatment of delinquents. As part of their task, the high-school students were supposed to say whether they thought the speaker had given a fair presentation of the issue. Altogether, 54 percent said the talk was "completely fair" or "fair," but the students were divided into three experimental groups that gave significantly different ratings. Figure 5.3 shows the outline of this research design, slightly modified as it will later appear in your computer program.

The first group was told that the speaker was a judge in a juvenile court, someone who was a real expert on the topic and highly respectable as well. Among the experimental subjects who thought the speaker was a judge, 73 percent considered the talk fair.

FIGURE 5.3
Delinquency Policy Experiment

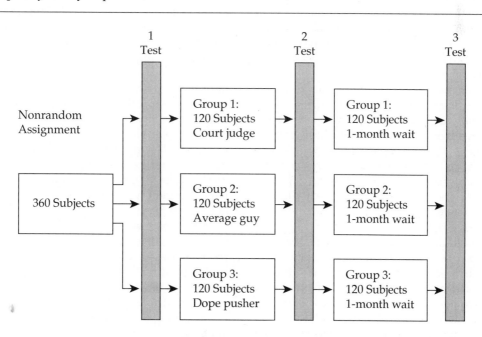

The second group thought the speaker was a member of the radio program's studio audience, someone who might be a decent fellow but lacked any special expertise on the topic. Sixty-three percent of the experimental subjects in this group considered him fair.

The third group was also told that the speaker had been taken from the studio audience, but a chat he had with the program's master of ceremonies revealed that he was an extremely suspicious character. Not only had he been a juvenile delinquent himself, but he was currently awaiting trial for a charge of drug peddling. As he spoke, he expressed great contempt both for the law and for his parents. Only 29 percent of the experimental subjects who heard this version of the radio show thought the talk urging leniency for delinquents was fair.

The experimental groups perceived the judge as slightly more credible than the ordinary person, and the drug pusher as far less credible than both of them. Thus, this study supported popular notions about credibility. The points of greatest interest for us, however, concern the design of the experiment.

Note that there is no control group, as such. If one version of the radio show had a speaker who was not introduced at all and who had no social characteristics that might affect credibility, then the subjects who heard it could be described as a control group. But a speaker with no characteristics is hardly a real person. This study had three different kinds of speakers and three groups of experimental subjects. Such a design is just as valid as one with a true control group, because either way you have the opportunity for systematic comparison of research subjects who experienced different things, depending upon which group they were assigned to.

One thing the experiment lacked was random assignment to the three groups. The researchers felt this was impractical because of the manner in which the subjects were recruited and run through the experiment. Experimental subjects came from 10 high-school classes. Each class sat in its ordinary classroom, listened to a version of the radio program together, and made individual judgments about the speaker. It is possible, of course, to assign the *classes* at random to the three experimental conditions, but not the individual members of the classes.

If you cannot achieve random assignment, you cannot make the experimental groups comparable, but often you can still use other means to determine how comparable they are. In this experiment, the three groups of classes were given a preliminary questionnaire, Test 1, to determine whether their attitudes on delinquency differed significantly. They did not. It was still possible that the classes differed in some other way relevant to the study, but the researchers excluded the most obvious source of bias by measuring the classes' attitudes on the topic of the experiment. Many of the Yale attitude-change studies were done with school classes; however, the experimenters felt their work was somewhat exploratory, anyway. To be sure of their results, one would have to replicate the experiments using adult subjects, as well as following strict rules for random assignment.

Of particular interest to the researchers was the question of whether the attitude changes would last, so a third test was given after a one-month wait. As you might expect, the percent favoring more lenient treatment of delinquents had become more similar across the three groups with the passage of time.

The second attitude-change experiment also used high-school classes, dividing them into two groups. Other aspects of the study were more complicated. The class meeting was devoted to the issue of the voting age, which was 21 years at the time of the study. The experimental session was divided into two phases, as outlined in Figure 5.4.

In the first phase, the subjects heard a speech giving one side of a debate on voting age. Then the students were asked whether they agreed or disagreed with the following statement: "The voting age should be reduced from 21 years to the draft age of 18 years." After that, they all wrote an essay giving their views on the voting age.

FIGURE 5.4
Voting Age Experiment

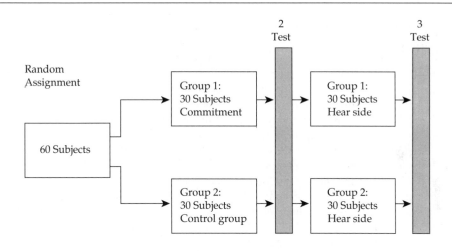

The second stage consisted of another speech, giving the other side of the voting age debate. Finally, the students were asked again to state their view on whether the voting age should be reduced from 21 to 18.

The experimental manipulation concerned the essay the student wrote at the end of the first phase. Because nothing special was done to one of the two groups of students, it can be considered the control group. Members of the other (experimental) group, however, were told to sign their essays and were informed that their essays would appear in the next issue of the school newspaper, for all the other students to see. This study was not about the characteristics of the speakers but about public commitment to a point of view.

The researchers hypothesized that making a public commitment to an opinion reduced the chances that a person would change his or her views subsequently. Students in the experimental group believed their views would be made public in the newspaper, so they probably felt they were making a public commitment as they wrote the essay. According to the theory, this meant they would be much less likely than

members of the control group to change their views in the second phase of the experiment, when they heard the opposite side of the debate.

It is important to note that the researchers did not care which opinion the subjects held. The crucial point was whether the opinion *changed* from the end of Phase 1 to the end of Phase 2—from what we call Test 2 to Test 3. Different classes heard the two sides of the debate in different orders. Among the group that made a public commitment, only 14 percent changed their opinion to agree with the second speaker. In the control group, however, 41 percent did so.

If you wanted to replicate this study, it would be quite practical to use random assignment of individual subjects to the two conditions. You could have them write their essays on special forms. At random, you could give half the students forms that said the essays would be published in the school newspaper, with a special section on the page where the student was supposed to sign his or her name. The other half of the forms would lack these features. Thus, subjects working in the same room together, hearing the same lectures, would be experiencing two different conditions.

Field Experiments: Stigmatization of the Accused

Experimental studies done in natural settings in the world outside the ivy-covered walls of the academy are called **field experiments**. Sometimes the research subjects are not aware that they are being studied. Ordinary people going about their business are suddenly presented with something to deal with. They respond to it, one way or another, and they may never know that a social scientist has observed their reactions and was responsible for whatever disturbed the routine of their day.

A stunning example is an experiment done on the subways of New York City by Piliavin, Rodin, and Piliavin (1969). When they began their study, New York was buzzing with self-recriminations after the infamous murder of Kitty Genovese, whose cries for help had gone unheeded by many New Yorkers who heard her screams for several minutes and did nothing. The experiment concerns "bystander intervention," but of a less spectacular kind than rescue of an assault victim.

For each run of the experiment, a team of four researchers—two men and two women—would board the Eighth Avenue subway express train. Entering by different doors, they gave no sign that they were together or that they were conducting an experiment. Two would sit at one end of the car, serving as observers. One of the men would stagger around, then fall on the floor at the other end. If nobody rushed forward to help, the fourth researcher would pretend to render assistance to this fallen "victim."

The chief experimental manipulation was the appearance of the victim who fell down. Part of the time, he would come in smelling of liquor, carrying a liquor bottle in a paper bag and thus looking drunk. The rest of the time he looked sober and carried a cane. Part of the time the victim was black, and part of the time

white. Can you guess the findings? Seemingly drunk victims got less help than sober ones. The victim's race made no significant difference. Surprised?

One of the neater experiments on stigmatization of deviants was carried out in the field by Richard Schwartz and Jerome Skolnick (1964). Their purpose was to investigate the effects of a criminal record on the employment opportunities of unskilled workers. To the 100 subjects, it did not appear that an experiment was in progress at all. The subjects were the bosses or personnel directors of 100 resort hotels in the Catskill region of New York state. Each of them received a letter in the mail, supposedly from a man who was seeking a job. Enclosed was an employment folder that gave information about the man. Figure 5.5 gives the experiment's outline.

In fact, no one was seeking a job, and the applications had been sent as part of an experiment. Schwartz and Skolnick had divided the 100 subjects at random into four groups and sent each group a slightly different version of the employment application. The 25 bosses in Group 1 got a folder that included the information that the man had been convicted of assault. Group 2 got a folder indicating the man had been acquitted—found innocent—of assault. Group 3 got the same information, as well as a letter from the judge certifying the finding of "not guilty." Finally, Group 4 got folders with no indication of a court record, so this must be considered the control group. Again, all 100 prospective employers got identical applications, except for what was said about the case of assault.

From a certain philosophical perspective, the four different kinds of application folder are the same. In 75 out of the 100 cases, the man was innocent. In the remaining 25 cases, he had served time and thus paid his debt to society. In none of the 100 cases did he deserve to be punished, but would the employers treat the applications the same? In fact, they did not.

In 9 out of the 25 cases where no mention of assault was made, an employer was prepared to talk to the man about a job. This was true in

FIGURE 5.5
Stigmatization Experiment

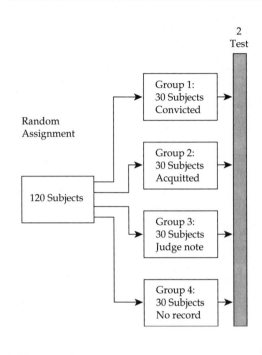

only 6 cases, however, when the man had been acquitted and sent the judge's note, in 3 cases when he was acquitted but did not send a note from the judge, and in only 1 out of the 25 cases when he had supposedly been convicted of assault. Thus, the innocent were stigmatized by an accusation of assault, even when they had been found innocent, and the guilty who had suffered imprisonment were now punished again by difficulty in finding a job.

This experiment, which has a very clean design, concerns a very important issue that might not be validly studied by other means. You could try survey methods, as described in Chapter 7. Mail out questionnaires asking, "Would you be as likely to hire a man the courts had found innocent of assault as you would a man for whom no mention of a court case was made?" I don't know for sure, but I'll bet people would claim they would treat the men equally. They might even say they would give the ex-con a chance, too. Everybody knows that "a person is innocent until found guilty," and everybody might feel a person who has paid his or her debt to society deserves a second chance. Or, to be more precise, everybody knows that we are supposed to feel like this. The experiment showed that, in fact, employers would not treat such people equally, and that perhaps only a field experiment, performed realistically in the real world, would demonstrate the truth about matters where the common ideology about how people are supposed to feel conflicts with reality.

A Field Evaluation Experiment: Recidivism of Ex-cons

Among the most pressing social issues that has drawn the interest of many social scientists is how best to discourage recidivism of convicted criminals. **Recidivism** means commission of new crimes after having been convicted. A key problem is how to reintegrate the convict into society upon release from imprisonment. Perhaps the most famous study on this crucial problem is the TARP experiment, the name standing for "Transitional Aid Research Project." Performed outside the laboratory, in the real world with real convicts, it is an excellent example of a field experiment. Designed to assess the value of various ways of helping the released convict make a successful transition to noncriminal life outside the institution, TARP is also an excellent example of evaluation research.

Evaluation research is sometimes defined as the assessment of the net effects of a social program (Rossi and Wright 1984). Our earlier discussion of research on the effectiveness of psychotherapy examined only a few of its facets. In the 1960s, many government programs were instituted in order to change individual behavior or general social conditions, and there followed a decade-long "Golden Age" of research evaluating these programs. Rossi and

Wright summarize the resultant vast body of scientific findings:

> One of the most important lessons to be learned from all the evaluations initiated during the Golden Age is that it is extremely difficult to design programs that produce noticeable effects in any desired direction. In retrospect, a reasonable summary of the findings is that the expected value of the effect of any program hovers around zero. This conclusion was devastating to the social reformers who had hoped that the Great Society programs would make appreciable (or at least detectable) gains in bettering the lot of the poor and redressing the ills of society. (Rossi and Wright 1984:341)

Make no mistake about it. Many kinds of social programs work perfectly well. If you want to feed hungry children, you can do it. If you want to help elderly people obtain decent medical care, a well-designed government program can do wonders. And if you want to ensure that all citizens have the right to vote and participate fully in the political process, then government is an absolutely essential part of your reform. But if you want government programs to change the behavior of juvenile delinquents, adult criminals, or drug addicts, you may be in for a disappointment. Evaluation research has raised grave doubts about the capacity of relatively modest government programs to eradicate poverty and related social problems.

As you can imagine, this produces an uneasy relationship between researchers who evaluate programs and the political leaders and social reformers who create them. All too frequently, administrators have been able to conceal the truth about their programs by sponsoring incompetent or fraudulent research designed to demonstrate benefits that might not really exist.

There must be thousands of examples, but I have to be cautious in describing the ones I know best, both to protect innocent people who were involved in the frauds and to protect myself and my publisher from possible legal action. Students of mine have been employed by local rehabilitation and education programs to evaluate their effectiveness, but were told in no uncertain terms that the results had to be positive.

In one case, the student was particularly inexperienced and honestly believed that the program must be working. She came to me wondering what she had been doing wrong in her statistical analysis of the experimental results, because the results kept coming out zero. After examining her research methods and finding them basically sound, as gently as I could I suggested to her that maybe the program was really not effective in meeting its goals. Then panic set in, as the student realized that the director of the program was not going to accept these findings and would first demand a revised analysis, then accuse her of incompetence. There is no happy solution in such cases. "In-house" evaluation research, conducted by employees of the agency under evaluation, is frequently a prescription for disaster.

One of the greater embarrassments for our discipline is the case of a nationally famous drug rehabilitation program that was highly praised for its effectiveness by sociologists who had not, in fact, done thorough empirical examinations of it. In one case, I am told, an influential publication praising the program had in great part been written by the program's creator, although only a sociologist was named as the author. In time, the program revealed itself not only as ineffective but dangerous, and it evolved into a weird cult that used violence against its critics. Thankfully for the reputation of sociology, one of those who most vigorously fought to learn and spread the truth was a sociologist who endured all kinds of personal threats and legal problems until, in the end, he received personal vindication, a major professional award, and the satisfaction that finally the truth was known.

Certainly, many government officials really do want to know whether particular programs are working, and much evaluation research has been performed without the political pressures I have just described, but it is equally true that many programs never get seriously evaluated. The disappointments many evaluation researchers have suffered in the past should not deter others from undertaking such research in the future, because our society sorely needs to know which programs work, which do not, and how to improve programs that could work better than they currently do. Of course, evaluation experiments must generally be done out in the real world, rather than in the artificially controlled environment of the academic laboratory. One factor the researcher must contend with in the real world are the political conflicts that rage around practically every government program.

Now we can consider the TARP experiment (Rossi, Berk, and Lenihan 1980), which was conducted in the field—in Georgia and Texas—in 1976. The creators of this vast project had noticed that when convicted felons were released from the penitentiary, they were given essentially no resources to help them get started again in the outside world. Imagine, if you can, that you have just finished serving time in a penitentiary and have just paid your debt to society. The warden shakes your hand and shows you the way to the door, placing a sum of money in your hand as a going-away gift. Stepping outside, you look at the money, realizing that is has to last you until you get your first paycheck from an honest job.

If you were being released in Georgia in 1975, the amount of money you received upon release would be only $150. In Texas, it was $200. How long could you live on that, while looking for a job? You might have had the opportunity to earn a little money while imprisoned, but the wage rates were invariably infinitesimal, and it was almost impossible to save anything. Indeed, in some states, the amount you saved was deducted from the tiny sum of release money, so there was no possibility of increasing your start-off cash by saving. Furthermore, if they were not able to get employment immediately,

released prisoners were not generally eligible for unemployment benefits or any other serious kind of government help. In fact, the assumption was that their families would take care of them and get them started, but some did not have families, and many came from impoverished backgrounds with families unable to help.

What would you do? A few nights in a cheap rooming house, a few poor meals, a few transportation expenses applying for jobs but never getting one, and you are dead broke. If you don't do something quickly, you'll be dead, period. So, with your last five bucks you buy a big knife, and the next night you hold up a gas station, getting enough money to carry on for another week or two. Pretty soon you are back in a life of crime, not looking for a straight job any more, and if you are not careful you'll be back in the "slammer" in no time.

You might never find yourself in this situation, and many of you will be unwilling to muster up much sympathy for the convicted criminals who do. Sympathy aside, however, this situation seems perfectly designed to promote recidivism, to get the convicts back into crime, and to inflict a high crime rate on the society. However you feel about the ex-cons personally, you can see that it is reasonable to consider a program to give them greater financial assistance during the transition period after release, providing them with a greater chance of finding a legitimate job and staying out of jail. That is what the TARP project evaluated. The structure of this experiment was conceptually the same as for the one on stigmatization, so you can look back at Figure 5.5 if you want a rough picture of TARP.

A total of 1,551 prisoners were assigned at random to four treatment groups, and 400 more were placed in a control group that received periodic interviews. Another 2,031 were assigned to a control group that was not contacted personally but whose subsequent arrest records were examined for the period following release. Three of the experimental groups received weekly allowances ($70 per week in Georgia and $63 in Texas) for a period of time, with complex differences in the payment schemes. The fourth experimental group received job placement advice with up to $100 for purchase of tools, special work clothes, or other necessities for a particular job.

The dependent variable was recidivism. Was the person arrested again within a year of release? We can get a quick look at the results of this complicated experiment by combining the four experimental conditions into one experimental group and by combining the two control groups. Because the chance of getting arrested again was significantly different in the two states, however, we should not combine data for them. In Georgia, 49.2 percent of the 775 ex-cons in the experimental groups were arrested again, compared with 48.7 percent of those in the control groups. In Texas, the figures were 38.1 percent and 35.7 percent. That is, in both states more of the ex-cons in the experimental groups were arrested than ex-cons in the control groups. But the experimental manipulations were supposed to reduce recidivism, not increase it!

You might immediately conclude that the experiment failed, but, of course, the research has not failed *as a scientific research project*. It succeeded in carrying out a complex experimental research study in the field, thereby obtaining a great wealth of useful data that can be used to test theories. The results, however, do run counter to the original theory. This massive program, which dispensed over a million dollars to convicts in the experimental groups, hoping to reduce recidivism, did apparently fail. One possible explanation was that the payments might actually have discouraged the ex-cons from seeking jobs, because the payments would stop when their paychecks began.

The study's designers had considered this possibility and had arranged the payment schemes for two of the experimental groups to permit examination of just this possibility. The researchers called these two experimental groups the 100%-Tax group and the 25%-Tax group. In each state, each of these groups had almost exactly 200 research subjects. Members were to receive their weekly payments for as much as 13 weeks. They differed in what happened when they got jobs.

For the 100%-Tax group, 100 percent of weekly earnings would be subtracted from the TARP payment. In Georgia, for example, the TARP payment was $70 per week; so those who earned $70 at a job would get no TARP payment at all. This fact might discourage ex-cons in the group from taking jobs. In the 25%-Tax group, only 25 percent of earnings would be subtracted from the TARP payment. For example, a person earning $70 would have a 25% tax of this amount subtracted from the TARP payment and still receive $52.50 of TARP money. One would expect a lower arrest rate for the ex-cons in the 25%-Tax group, because they should not be discouraged much by the loss of TARP payments from getting jobs.

The results, however, did not support this hypothesis. In Georgia, there was no difference at all in the proportion of the 100%-Tax and 25%-Tax groups who were arrested—49.2 percent for both. In Texas, the 25%-Tax group actually had a higher arrest rate (42.5 percent) than the 100%-Tax group (38.0 percent). The results from comparing these two experimental groups suggest that the reason TARP payments failed to reduce recidivism among all the experimental groups was not that the subjects avoided getting jobs because they knew regular paychecks would end the TARP payments.

The results of this well-designed and expensive experiment may surprise you, but you should not be surprised to learn that they were controversial. When the chief research report was published, it asserted: "TARP demonstrated that the provision of limited amounts of financial aid to released prisoners in the form of minimum unemployment benefit payments for periods of between 3 and 6 months can decrease the arrests experienced by the ex-felons in the year following release by 25% to 50%" (Rossi, Berk, and Lenihan 1980:7). Are you confused? I hope so. You should be.

The results of the TARP study, analyzed in terms of the original experimental design, do not support this optimistic statement at all.

They show no reduction of recidivism in the experimental groups compared with the control groups. However, the authors of the research report employed a different approach, regression analysis, and came up with more positive results. We will explain regression analysis in later chapters of this book. It is a valid statistical technique widely used in sociology. However, a close reading of the TARP research report left me personally quite unsure of whether the researchers had used the technique appropriately.

Other sociologists are not so uncertain in their judgment as I am. In his highly regarded introductory sociology textbook, Rodney Stark (1989:228-230) reports that the original TARP experimental design found no significant difference between experimental and control groups, but then says the researchers "refused to accept the clear results of their own research" and "ransacked their files on those in the experimental group and offered arguments that the program really did help some of them." A more detailed criticism of the TARP study was offered by Hans Zeisel, who had been a member of the project's advisory board (1982a, 1982b; cf. Rossi, Berk, and Lenihan 1985).

The data did clearly show that ex-cons who were given TARP payments were slower to get jobs. Having a job tended to keep an ex-con out of trouble. Rossi, Berk, and Lenihan concluded that getting TARP payments would have reduced crime if it hadn't also discouraged the ex-cons from getting jobs. The trouble I have with this argument is that the 100%-Tax and 25%-Tax groups did not differ in commission of crime, while they should have differed if this were the correct explanation. Interviews seemed to show, however, that subjects in the 100%-Tax and 25%-Tax groups did not understand the differences between their payment schemes. Rossi, Berk, and Lenihan were thus able to argue that this ignorance prevented that part of the experiment from working properly. But to many readers, this sounds like a strained excuse to permit a wobbly argument that TARP worked after all, even though the main experimental results indicated that it did not.

I don't pretend to know where the truth lies; the people who did the TARP study are highly respected social scientists. One point you should take away from this research debacle is that the experimental research approach gives cleaner, more convincing results than do other methods if the experiment is well designed and works properly. The chief controversy concerns interpretation of the regression analysis, not of the experimental findings.

In the ideal, the proper response when you discover that something might have gone wrong in your experiment is to try again, with an improved design. But that was not practical in this case. Do you want to donate another million dollars to pay out to ex-cons in a replication of TARP? Thus, we can fully sympathize with the TARP researchers' decision to attack their data with sophisticated tools of statistical analysis, rather than simply sticking with simple comparisons of arrest rates across pairs of groups. It is an unfortunate general rule in social statistics, however, that the more sophisticated an analytic technique is, the greater the room for error in applying it and controversy in evaluating it. That is one reason many researchers like to stick with the experimental method.

Laboratory Experiments on Communication Networks

A classic kind of social psychology laboratory experiment, performed by sociologists and psychologists alike, involves studying the efficiency of different patterns of communication in small groups. A good example is research Harold J. Leavitt (1951) performed at the Massachusetts Institute of Technology nearly two generations ago. A large number of research subjects were brought into the laboratory five at a time and asked to solve 16 puzzles. Each subject had only some of the pieces of the puzzle, and they all had to communicate with each other to get enough information to solve the problems given them. The experimenter strictly controlled the channels of communication between them, and the point of the study was to compare different patterns of communication in their capacity to produce a quick, correct answer.

The laboratory setup was slightly complicated. The five members of each quintet were not merely sitting around a table, facing each other and chatting openly. Instead, each was isolated from the others in a tiny room. These five rooms were wedge-shaped and fit together like five pieces of a pie. Slots were provided so that the subjects could pass messages written on cards from one of these tiny rooms to another. Depending on the experimental condition that had been assigned to a particular quintet, some of the slots would be blocked, so communication was limited to the slots that were open. In other words, each of the five subjects could communicate with only certain other subjects in the quintet.

Today, we do this kind of experiment using a network of personal computers, or terminals operating off one big computer. Subjects are brought into comfortable little rooms that need not be immediately next to each other. All the communication takes place via computer, and all the communications are preserved on computer disk for instant analysis any way the experimenter wants. When Leavitt did his research, there were no personal computers, and his pie-shaped apparatus of rooms must have been quite spectacular to see, with each room painted a different color and all the communication slots, books of puzzles, and big, colored switches for announcing a problem's solution making the entire scene quite bizarre.

Leavitt compared four different communication patterns, illustrated here in Figure 5.6. Each dot represents a person, and the lines connecting dots represent communication channels. The five subjects in each quintet are labeled A, B, C, D, and E. In the circle pattern, for example, each of the five can communicate with just two others. Person A can exchange messages with B and E, but not with C and D. The chain pattern is similar, except that the two people at the ends, A and E, have only one person to communicate with, being blocked from interacting with each other. The Y and wheel patterns place person C in a position of special importance, at the center of intersecting lines of communication. One can easily imagine other patterns, including a five-pointed star in which each person can communicate with each of the other four, but the particular experiment in question here employed only the four patterns shown in Figure 5.6.

Before we consider the results, think for a moment about the probable processes of communication that will solve the puzzles in each case. With both the Y and the wheel, person C

FIGURE 5.6
Patterns of Communication

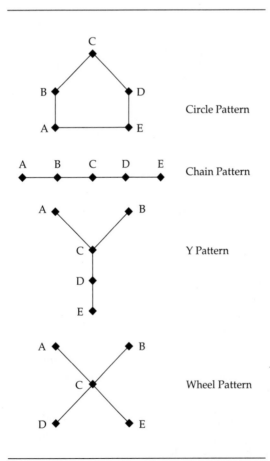

Circle Pattern

Chain Pattern

Y Pattern

Wheel Pattern

may receive all the information, make a decision about the correct answer to the puzzle, then communicate the answer to the other four. Something like that may happen with the chain as well, although subjects B and D may occasionally get the answer first. In the circle, no one is central to the communication pattern, so we would not expect a decision leader to emerge as easily.

Figure 5.7 shows the design you might use for this study. I have increased the number of subjects from Leavitt's original design, because imaginary subjects are cheap enough for us to recruit inside the computer, while Leavitt had to go to great lengths to get enough real people to visit his laboratory in groups of five. I have

also unfolded his design into two phases, as I shall explain shortly, for convenience in programming the simulation of this experiment in your set of software.

We start with 120 quintets (600 individual subjects) and randomly assign them to the four different experimental conditions (circle, chain, Y, and wheel). Note that each experimental group consists of 150 people but only 30 quintets. In experiments like this, we do not focus on the individual's behavior but on the quintet's. In Phase 1, the quintets attempt to solve a number of puzzles, and at Test 2 we tally up how long it took them to get each answer. Those quintets that got each answer in less than a minute, on average, we will call fast.

FIGURE 5.7
Communication Experiment

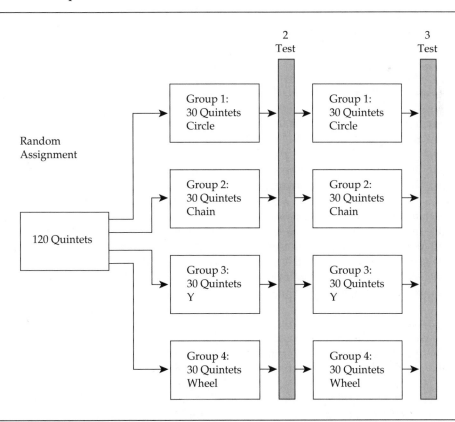

Those that took an average of over a minute we will call slow.

Phase 2 also has them do a number of puzzles, but now we are interested in whether they do them correctly. In particular, we will distinguish quintets that made 2 or more errors on the 16 puzzles from quintets that made fewer than 2 errors. As you may guess, in a real experiment it is far more efficient to combine these phases and count speed and accuracy simultaneously. But the simulated people inside your computer don't mind working a little extra—at least they have never complained to me about it—and I find the picture a little clearer if I separate out these two aspects of the experiment.

Leavitt found that the Y and wheel patterns produced faster answers with fewer errors. Thus the experiment seems to support the common practice in the real world of conferring special authority on certain individuals and placing them at the center of communications. When a club you belong to elects its officers for the next year, it may be doing so out of habit rather than with full awareness of the sociological implications of having leaders. Leavitt's experiment shows that, other things being equal, communication patterns that place special authority in the hands of one person may solve problems more quickly and accurately, at least when there is a definite solution to each one. Of course, the experiment does not consider the social costs of giving some individuals greater power than others, and it does not consider what communication patterns are best when the problem does not have a single, obvious solution.

We have now completed consideration of the experiments that are simulated in your software package. Shortly, I will explain how to control the program and explore these experiments and variants of them you can create for yourself. First, however, we should consider wider issues about experiments, raising yet other studies as illustrations.

Survey Experiments

One very practical way of getting a large number of subjects to participate in an experiment is to present it in the form of a survey, even in a cheap questionnaire sent through the mails. Of course, the experimental manipulation a researcher can achieve in a survey is rather weak, but often it is sufficiently strong to get clear results. In effect, this is what Schwartz and Skolnick did, but their survey had only one question: "Will you consider hiring this man?" Chapter 7 will consider surveys in general, but a few words on survey experiments are appropriate here.

A set of examples is provided by research done by Howard Schuman and Lawrence Bobo (1988) on the issue of whether housing in the respondent's neighborhood should be open to members of all races. In a series of surveys, the researchers used slightly different versions of a question to see which part of the issue affected people's responses. For example, one item said: "Suppose there is a community-wide vote on the general housing issue. There are two possible laws to vote on. One law says that a home owner can decide for himself who to sell his house to, even if he prefers not to sell to blacks. The second law says that a homeowner cannot refuse to sell to someone because of their race or color. Which law would you vote for?" This version of the item was asked of 584 respondents, but another 563 respondents got a similar item that referred to federal legislation about to be voted on by "your representative in Congress." Just as in the laboratory, this experiment used two groups of subjects. The manipulation consisted of whether the question concerned a local referendum or federal legislation.

A small but significant difference did emerge in the results. When the question concerned a local referendum, 42.5 percent said the owner should decide whom to sell to. But when federal legislation was in question, 48.7 percent said the owner should decide. Schuman and Bobo concluded that part of the opposition to fair housing legislation was hostility to coercion from the federal government. Opposition to fair housing laws was weaker when the federal government was not involved.

The same set of experiments also asked whether the respondent would mind if a particular kind of family moved into the neighborhood. In some versions of the questionnaire, the family was black; in others it was Japanese-American. Also, part of the time it was of the same income and education as the respondent. The rest of the time income and education were not mentioned. A Japanese-American family was slightly more welcome than a black family. Interestingly, when income and education were left out of the question, the percent who were uncertain how they would feel went up.

One of my favorite survey experiments was done by Richard F. Larson (1968), who was interested in how psychiatrists and clergy of various religious denominations judge the severity of different kinds of mental problem. His survey included six "case histories," paragraph-long thumbnail sketches of people in trouble, and the respondents were supposed to check a box after each, indicating how severe an emotional disturbance the person suffered from: "none," "mild," "moderate," or "severe." At random, each of the six imaginary people was presented as either male or female. Thus half of the respondents read a story about a withdrawn person named Mr. Thompson, while the other half, selected at random, read a similar story about a withdrawn person named Mrs. Thompson. Twenty years ago, when this study was done, societal norms may have been more tolerant of social withdrawal among women than among men, for Mr. Thompson was more often rated as severely disturbed than was Mrs. Thompson.

Many experiments reported in the scientific journals divide the research subjects into a large number of groups, and thus they appear very complicated to the beginning student. However, these studies are generally far simpler than they might seem. It is frequently a lot easier to create a lot of different experimental groups if you are using surveys that if you have to administer a bewildering range of manipulations in the laboratory.

An entertaining example is an experiment about humor, done by Gutman and Priest (1969). Many jokes describe social interactions in which one person squelches another, responding to an innocent comment by putting the person down with a powerful and well-aimed insult. The two people in the joke can be described as Aggressor and Victim. Often people sympathize with victims, however, and insulting characters are usually not well liked. When, Gutman and Priest asked, is aggression funny?

Their theory suggested that aggression should be funny when Victim provokes the squelch by bad behavior, deserving what the Aggressor dishes out. Also, they suspected people would generally feel comfortable laughing at verbal aggression if the Aggressor behaved in a socially acceptable manner right up until the squelch. We can readily laugh at a good Aggressor putting down a bad Victim, because the squelch is just. Each of the two characters in the story might behave either in a socially acceptable manner or in a socially unacceptable manner. If Aggressor behaves acceptably, while Victim's behavior is socially unacceptable, Aggressor's squelch of Victim can be very funny. However, if a socially unacceptable Aggressor squelches a socially acceptable Victim, our sympathy for the Victim and sense of fair play will reduce our tendency to laugh.

The experiment examined subjects' reactions to the four logically possible combinations of Aggressor and Victim:

1. Good Aggressor and bad Victim
2. Good Aggressor and good Victim
3. Bad Aggressor and bad Victim
4. Bad Aggressor and good Victim

These four possibilities are listed in descending order of how funny they should be, when built into a reasonably humorous joke. So the researchers needed to divide the research subjects at random into four groups, but instead, they divided them into 24 groups. How come?

The problem was the jokes. You can't just say, "A good guy squelched a bad guy," and expect people to laugh. You have to build up a story about the two people, with a little bit of a twist at the end; and that means that research subjects may respond in some complex way to the specific details of the story, rather than to the social acceptability of the characters' behavior. Thus, Gutman and Priest decided to use four different jokes in their research and to vary which one had characters of each type. Here's a version of one, adapted slightly to make it meaningful to sociologists, with two professors as the characters, Alfred Aggressor and Volney Victim:

> Alfred and Volney met at the sociology department picnic, and immediately Volney began boasting about his recent professional accomplishments. When Alfred commented that other members of the department had also published recently, Volney said that their essays had been in minor journals, while his was in the *ASR*, and that they had better shape up if they wanted him to vote for their promotions. Before Alfred could defend his colleagues, one of the graduate students approached them with a plate of dessert pastries. Without thanking the student, Volney wolfed two of them down, then dismissed the student, muttering, "I have to watch my waistline." Alfred observed, "And how lucky you are to have it right out there where you can watch it so easily."

Did you laugh? Should I explain it to you? It's a play on the phrase *watch my waistline*. Well, some people think it's pretty funny, anyway. In this version, Alfred Aggressor comes across as a decent guy, while Volney Victim is thoroughly obnoxious. Here is a different version:

> Alfred and Volney met at the sociology department picnic, and immediately Alfred began boasting about his recent professional accomplishments. When Volney commented that other members of the department had also published recently, Alfred said that their essays had been in minor journals, while his was in the *ASR*, and that they had better shape up if they wanted him to vote for their promotions. Before Volney could defend his colleagues, one of the graduate students approached them with a plate of dessert pastries. Without thanking the student, Alfred wolfed two of them down. Volney smiled at the student but refused the dessert politely, saying, "I have to watch my waistline." Alfred observed, "And how lucky you are to have it right out there where you can watch it so easily."

And how about that one? It is the same joke, as you can see, but with Alfred Aggressor as the bad guy and Volney Victim as the good guy. According to the theory, this version should be less funny than the other. However, you can't expect a story to be as funny the second time, so the researchers gave each research subject four different jokes to judge, one with each of the four combinations of Aggressor and Victim.

Thus, there would be two other versions of this joke, one in which both Alfred and Volney were nice guys, and the other in which they were both bad. Each research subject was given a questionnaire containing all four jokes, one with each combination of Aggressor and Victim. To get all possible combinations of the four versions for each joke required 24 different editions of the questionnaire, with several subjects responding to each version. But this does not mean that the data analysis involved comparing 24 different groups. Instead, there were just four groups to compare, one for each combination of Aggressor and Victim. The first group, for example, would be composed of versions of all four jokes that had a good Aggressor and a bad Victim. The fourth group would include versions of all four jokes that had a bad Aggressor and a good Victim.

Respondents rated the jokes in several different ways, including saying how funny each one was on a scale from 0 (not at all humorous) to 8 (very humorous). On average, the good Aggressor and bad Victim combination got a rating of 4.31. The good Aggressor and good Victim versions of the jokes got 3.92, while bad Aggressor and bad Victim got 3.67. Finally, the same jokes but with bad Aggressor and good Victim were rated 3.32, almost one full humorousness point below the good Aggressor and bad Victim. The researchers were pleased that the data supported their theory, although I personally wish they had found funnier jokes. For our purposes, the point is to see how apparent complexity of research design can actually be a simple technique to make sure the differences between comparison groups are not distorted by, for example, the specific topic of a particular joke. This can be done very efficiently by packaging the experiment in a questionnaire with multiple versions.

The same approach can be used to combine two or more different experiments without adding much to the number of subjects or other investments required. For example, suppose you wanted to study the effect of the sex of Aggressor and Victim on how funny people found the jokes. You could simply add more versions of the jokes, varying the sex of Aggressor and Victim. We might hypothesize that people would laugh more heartily when the Aggressor was of their own sex, and the Victim of the opposite sex, so you would have to ask respondents what their gender was. But a study that merely determined which kinds of jokes the two sexes preferred would not be an experiment. The reason is that in such a study you would not be manipulating the independent variable (sex of respondent). However, a study that examined how members of either sex (or both sexes) responded to versions of the jokes that manipulated the sex of the Aggressor and Victim would be a real experiment.

In a double-barreled experiment that included versions of the jokes with different combinations of good or bad Aggressor and Victim, and that also varied the sexes of the characters, you would analyze the data in two simple ways. First, you would do what we have just described, comparing four groups with different combinations of good and bad characters. Then you would sort the questionnaires afresh into four groups in terms of the combinations of sexes of the two characters. You would be doing two quite separate studies using the same data, studies that are quite compatible with each other. This demonstrates the efficiency you can achieve when you plan your research design carefully.

Ethics of Experimentation with Human Subjects

The experimental method has probably raised more ethical issues that any other, simply because the experimenter takes action with the research subjects and must take responsibility for that action. Although medical experiments may place people's lives at risk, sociological experiments almost never get this dangerous. However, people are frequently embarrassed, feel foolish, gain false impressions of themselves and others, and may generally have an unpleasant time in experiments. Sometimes the subjects may come to feel that they have wasted time and effort, having been tricked into doing so by lies the experimenter told.

A common feature of social psychology laboratory experiments is **deception**. The research subject thinks that one factor is under investigation when another really is. In addition to their moral concerns, experimenters worry that if they use too much deception in too many studies, the typical research subject will become totally suspicious of social scientists and refuse to take experiments at face value, perhaps behaving in deceptive ways themselves when they participate (Cook et al. 1970; Silverman et al. 1970; Golding and Lichtenstein 1970). I remember when my social-psychologist colleague, Richard Emerson, used to visit my big classes to recruit experimental subjects. Because many students were so suspicious of deception, he confronted the issue straight on, promising them that his study involved no deception and begging them to believe him.

The experiment on voting-age opinions done by Hovland et al. at Yale falsely told members of the experimental group that their essays would be published in the school newspaper. The employers in the Schwartz and Skolnick study of stigmatization were even unaware that they were participating in an experiment, thinking instead that the job applications they received were genuine. From their perspective they wasted considerable time and effort—something that may have approached a workweek over the total of 100 employers—deceived as they were by experimenters. Field experiments are particularly open to ethical criticism, because the subjects are not volunteers and did not agree to participate.

The Piliavin, Rodin, and Piliavin study of bystander intervention on New York subways may have caused significant total harm, considering the large number of people who unwillingly and unwittingly became research subjects. You're sitting on the subway, tired and anxious to get home. Somebody falls down in front of you, and you are unsure what to do. Eventually, somebody else comes forward to help the person, so you just sit. That night, when trying to fall asleep, you begin to accuse yourself severely for having failed to help that person. You can't sleep. You hate yourself. That's harm, caused by a field experiment.

Or, you see a person fall down on the subway. The person is holding a bottle and smells of alcohol. The sight disgusts you and confirms your loathing of alcoholics. A little later, you

encounter somebody on the street who is a little "tipsy." You hurry away, so as not to have contact with another "damn drunk" that day. You have become a slightly nastier person, and a group of people depicted in the field experiment has suffered further stigmatization in the eyes of the dozens of innocent bystanders who participated unaware in it.

A solution often employed in the laboratory, not entirely satisfactory in all instances but at least a step in the right direction, is to explain to the subjects what the experiment was really about at the very end and assure them that they did well and should not feel embarrassed. This is called **debriefing**. In the field, this may not be practical.

What are the ethical limits of experimentation in the social sciences? Consider this intentionally provocative and extreme issue: Is it moral to experiment with people's religion? C. Daniel Batson (1977) has argued that social scientific understanding of religion has failed to progress satisfactorily because research has been unable to subject theories to strenuous testing, primarily because the experimental method has seemed both impractical and immoral. Quoting Popper (1959), Batson notes that the experimental method can best subject a theory to risk of falsification:

> Because scientists are hoping that their theories are right (especially in value-laden areas like the psychology of religion), it is important that the falseness, if it exists, be demonstrated as unequivocally as possible. The scientist must not be able to wriggle off the hook by pointing to some additional factors to explain why things did not come out as predicted. Here is where experimentation comes in: a good experiment can produce unequivocal disappointment better than any other research method. (Batson 1977:414)

One of Batson's own studies involved having junior high students on a church retreat read a fake news story supposedly proving Christianity was a hoax. Apparently, some of them believed this fake news report. Even though the researcher debriefed them at the end of the study, announcing that the story was a fake, for a period of time their faith was under a shadow. Is it ethical to do that?

Yeatts and Asher (1979) argued not only that experiments on religion may often be ethical but that it may be unethical not to do experiments. They draw analogies to medicine, where it is unethical to promote cures that have not been subjected to rigorous experimental test. The examples they offer are in the area of religious education, particularly the special programs and religious retreats that have become popular in recent years. They felt it would be quite appropriate to let a number of people sign up for such a program, at random let only half of them actually participate, and compare the results.

But that is pretty tame stuff. Here is a real shocker of an idea: Create a new religion as a social-scientific experiment. We have a lot of sociological literature on new religious movements. Why not test theories on the topic by starting a new religion, or perhaps several religions varying the approach experimentally? I warned you we were going to consider a shocking idea.

In principle, a study that was based on the experimental creation of new religions would be quite legal. You might get into trouble if you faked supernatural events and then collected money from people who believed them, but otherwise you would be quite within your constitutional rights to start new religions. Personally, I've known two people who founded quite radical new religions—one being the founder of the Process—and a dozen or more people who failed in an attempt to do the same thing. The founders of the Process very consciously tried to create a new faith, calling their work "religious engineering." I suspect, however, that most of us would feel that starting a new religion purely as a research study was unethical, even if it was legal and had significant scientific aims.

Would we feel the same way about a social scientist who founded a nonreligious commune

in order to study it? In both cases, the founder is giving a number of innocent people a new faith and lifestyle. Our judgment of the morality of the exercise may not rest so much on the idea that religion is sacred as upon the potential harm done to the research subjects, whose whole lives may be turned upside down. In fact, many sociologists have created communes, either single-handedly or in collaboration with other people, and I have known two very prominent sociologists who did so around 20 years ago.

You might argue that the crucial difference between the cult founders and the commune founders is that the latter did not lie to their followers. The sociologists were quite open about what they were doing, and both really wanted to live in a commune and develop the communal lifestyle for the benefit of all involved. Indeed, their research was primarily aimed at learning how to promote communalism and make it work in modern society. The cult founders, however, were not all that different in their approach. Both were quite candid about the fact that they were creating the religion as they went along, but they were convinced that this was the natural way that all valid religions were founded. They were not conscious frauds. Both were profoundly religious men who strongly rejected the dominant religious traditions of our society and were groping to find an alternative.

My point here is certainly not to sell you on some very dubious practices, and certainly not to recruit you to a cult or commune. Rather, I am suggesting that, if taken to extremes, ordinary scientific principles lead to some very bizarre notions and ethical challenges.

When the ethics of research on human subjects was an especially hot topic a generation ago, some researchers suggested that it was immoral to conduct many kinds of experiment, including those with bland deceptions as well as the more spectacular psychological studies in which subjects thought they were zapping innocent people with electric shocks. An alternative that researchers seriously suggested was to ask the research subjects to play the role required for the experiment, rather than have them actually believe what they were doing. Unfortunately, this idea has little scientific value, because in the end all we would have is information about what these people thought they would do under certain circumstances, rather than data on their real behavior (Freedman 1969). For that information, an opinion poll is a more reasonable approach than costly experimentation.

Ethical questions about experimentation are important, and you should always consider the potential harm your research might inflict upon human subjects. Often, when your research design involves substantial risk of harm, you can find a different design that is more benign but answers the same question. It is possible, however, to go too far in limiting the options for social experimentation. The logical but silly conclusion of *excessive* concern about ethical issues would be to ban research on human beings altogether and do studies only on the simulated people we can create with our computers. With that idea in mind, we can turn now to the software that accompanies this chapter.

_____ The Simulated Experiment Program

The program that explores experimental design is called XPER. When the XPER program begins, the following short menu will appear on your screen:

```
[1]Run a classic experiment
[2]Replicate a classic experiment
[3]Create a new experiment
[ESC] QUIT or change programs
```

The first choice lets you run one of the experiments described earlier in this chapter. The second choice lets you run the same experiment but also gives you the power to decide how many subjects to employ. It also produces somewhat different results (by chance) every time you run it, a realistic aspect of replications. The third choice lets you decide the number of groups, phases, tests, and subjects for an experiment of your own.

If you press either (1) or (2), the computer will ask which classic experiment you want, offering the following menu:

```
[1] Work rates, 1 group 2 phases
[2] Work rates, 2 groups 1 phase
[3] Therapy evaluation, non-random
[4] Therapy evaluation, attrition
[5] Attitudes about delinquency
[6] Attitudes about voting age
[7] Stigmatization of ex-cons
[8] TARP: payments to ex-cons
[9] Communication in small groups
[ESC] Return to main menu
```

Options 1 and 2 give you the two variants of Sorokin's experiment on cooperative versus individual working conditions, outlined in Figure 5.1. Choices 3 and 4 give you two versions of an experiment on the effectiveness of psychotherapy, as in Figure 5.2. The fifth and sixth choices are the two experiments done by Hovland and his associates at Yale, illustrated in Figure 5.3 and Figure 5.4. Option 7, the Schwartz and Skolnick study, is outlined in Figure 5.5, which also gives the structure of the TARP study. Finally, Leavitt's research on communication in small groups is outlined in Figure 5.6 and Figure 5.7.

If you have chosen to replicate, rather than merely run, a classic experiment, the computer will next ask how many research subjects you want to use. It offers these choices:

```
[1] 12 Subjects
[2] 24 Subjects
[3] 36 Subjects
[4] 48 Subjects
[5] 60 Subjects
[6] 120 Subjects
[7] 240 Subjects
[8] 360 Subjects
[9] 480 Subjects
[ESC] Return to main menu
```

If you are replicating Leavitt's experiment on communication in small groups, the menu will say "Quintets" rather than "Subjects," and you might keep in mind that the actual number of people you would need for that research is five times the number of quintets.

Once you have chosen your experiment, and decided the number of subjects if you are doing a replication, the screen will fill with a diagram like those included with this chapter, showing the different parts and stages of the experiment. Look in the lower left-hand corner of the screen for various messages that will tell you what is happening. While running an experiment, all you have to do is press (ENTER) periodically, whenever one of those messages instructs you to do so.

I was not able to flash pictures of the subjects going through the particular experiments on your computer screen. That would have cost a lot of money to pay artists and would have filled up a lot of computer disks. So use your imagination. There will be a little bit of action on the screen during an experiment. For example, the vertical bar representing a test will flash when that particular step in data collection is going on.

At the very end, after you have pressed (ENTER) enough times and the experiment itself has run through, you will get a set of tables like the one shown here in Figure 5.8, which reports results from replicating Sorokin's work experiment with two groups and 48 subjects. This is the simplest kind of table you will get, but the more complex ones merely have more comparisons available across more groups and more tests.

The pair of tables is easy to read. The top table shows the results for Group 1, which followed the cooperative system of reward; kids worked to earn toys for their collective playhouse. Of the 24 kids in this group, 7 met Sorokin's quota by carrying a huge lot of marbles and sand; 11 of these kids did not meet the quota. The bottom table in Figure 5.8 is for the 24 kids in Group 2, who worked under the

FIGURE 5.8
Results of Replicating Sorolin's Experiment (Test 2)

		Cases	Percent
Group 1			
Cooperative	Yes	7	29.2%
	No	17	70.8%
	All	24	100.0%
		Cases	Percent
Group 2			
Individual	Yes	11	45.8%
	No	13	54.2%
	All	24	100.0

Work rates, 2 groups 1 phase: Filled quota?

individual incentive system to win toys for themselves as individuals. Eleven of them filled the quota. When compared in terms of percentages, 29.2 percent of those working cooperatively filled the quota, compared with 45.8 percent of those working individually.

To understand each set of tables, you will have to study the experiment carefully. If you get data for Test 1, its primary purpose will be to see if the different groups start out with different characteristics, something that random assignment is supposed to prevent and usually does. If the groups are very different, the rest of your experiment will be on shaky ground. The results of the experiment will generally be found in tables for Test 2 and Test 3. An exception is Hovland's experiment on attitudes about voting age. If you check my description of it, you will see that the experiment focuses not on the numbers in Test 2 and Test 3 but on changes that individuals exhibit from Test 2 to Test 3. These changes may not show up at all in the simple report of these tests, and for that experiment alone I have added an extra table, which you access by pressing (ENTER) after examining the tables for Test 2 and Test 3.

When you have finished writing down any data you want to remember from an experiment, you can press (ENTER) a final time, to return to the menu. In most of your work, you will go through the program at least twice. First, pick an experiment and run it (not replicate it) once or twice. Every time you *run* one of these classic experiments, you will get the same results. This will allow you to get really familiar with the experiment. Second, replicate this experiment, writing down your results fully. Every time you replicate an experiment, even using the exact same number of subjects, the results will be different. Again, this is a realistic reflection of the fact that things never work out exactly the same a second time an experiment is done.

A final option on the main menu is to create a new experiment. This is a modest simulation that gives you made-up data on a fictitious experiment, so you can't expect to get particularly reasonable results. Invent an experiment of your own, and run this part of the program to go through the motions of actually doing it.

FIGURE 5.9
Control Panel for Simulating Your Own Experiment

```
    Select the experimental conditions you want

    [G]roups: One

    [P]hases: Two

    [R]andom assignment: No

     Administer tests?

    [1]  Before phase one:  No
    [2]  After phase one:  Yes
    [3]  After phase two:  Yes
```

When you select this option, the computer will want to know how many research subjects you intend to use and will present you with the control panel shown in Figure 5.9.

The control panel will start out with the decisions for the last experiment you have been working with; you can change whichever commands you want. To select the number of groups you want, press (G). If the command starts out saying "(G)roups: One," pressing (G) will change it to "(G)roups: Two." Another press of (G) will give you three groups. Press again, and you get four groups. One more press will get you back where you started, with one group.

Press (P) to change the number of phases. There can be either one or two phases. Press (R) to decide whether or not to have random assignment. At the bottom of this control panel are commands to decide which tests to use. In Figure 5.9, the computer is not ready to administer a test at time 1, before the first phase of the experiment, as you can see from the message "(1) Before phase one: No." Press (1) and the "No" will change to a "Yes." Pressing (2) will turn Test 2 on or off, and pressing (3) will do the same for Test 3.

Again, I don't promise that this option to create your own experiment will be very exciting, because the data will probably not make much sense. You will have to write down the experimental conditions the various groups of subjects will experience. Do not expect the computer to understand what your experiment is really about. Nonetheless, this option can provide some amusing practice in designing an experiment.

Sometimes, especially when you are replicating a classic experiment, the results will be fascinating. The theory on which the experiment was based may predict that Group 1 will show a higher percentage than Group 2, but both groups may come out exactly equal. In another experiment, two groups may produce very different figures, and you will conclude that the experimental manipulation really did have the expected result. What can you conclude, however, if Group 1 and Group 2 give very similar but not identical results? Is the theory supported or isn't it? To tell whether the difference in results between two groups is worthy of note, we have to calculate its statistical significance. That is a job for the next chapter, which examines the great usefulness of two-by-two tables in social research.

PROJECTS FOR CHAPTER 5

The seven projects described below, one for each of the simulated experiments in the XPER program, illustrate the logic of experimental research and a number of the problems of experimental design. In addition, you will find it interesting that replications of experiments seldom give exactly the same results as the initial study did. This is a step toward understanding issues of reliability and statistical significance, which later chapters will discuss more fully.

1. Sorokin's Work Experiments. Replicate both versions of this experiment, which compares cooperative with individual work incentives. One version imposes two different conditions on a single group of subjects; the other employs two experimental groups. Do this twice, for a total of four experimental replications, so that you have two replications of each version of Sorokin's study. Make sure you replicate the experiment rather than merely running it, so the results will come out somewhat differently each time.

Your report should include the tables of results from the four replications, a discussion of these results, and your judgment about which version of Sorokin's experiment is superior, giving your reasons for any conclusions you state.

2. Evaluations of Psychotherapy. Replicate the psychotherapy experiment four times. Twice, use the nonrandom assignment version. The other two times, use the attrition version. In a report incorporating tables of the results, explain whether you think these flawed experiments provide a real answer to the question of whether psychotherapy works.

3. Attitudes about Delinquency. Replicate Hovland's experiment about the radio talk on lenience toward delinquents, contrasting the results from four separate replications. Does the dope pusher rank lowest all four times? What about the difference between the judge and the ordinary citizen? In all four replications, do most experimental subjects accept the judge's views, or does the ordinary citizen win in one or more replications? Even if the judge is always better, does the difference in his persuasiveness vary in relation to that of the ordinary citizen?

Write a brief report answering these questions, including the tables of results you got.

4. Attitudes about Voting Age. Run the classic Hovland experiment on attitudes toward voting age; then replicate it once. Read the experiment carefully so you will know which tables offer the results and which are of no interest. Write a report explaining the research design in your own words, and state the results of running and replicating this experiment.

5. Stigmatization of Ex-cons. Replicate the experiment by Schwartz and Skolnick six times, comparing the proportions of men in the four groups that were offered job interviews. Remember that in the original study, men with no mention of assault in their folders did best. Men with a note from the judge certifying their acquittal for assault did less well. Those simply acquitted did worse, and those who were convicted of assault did worst of all. But you may not get exactly this same pattern on each replication. For three of the replications, use only 24 research subjects; for the other three replications use 240. Do you get more stable findings with larger numbers of subjects?

In addition to simply reporting your results, your essay should discuss the advantages and disadvantages of using large versus small numbers of research subjects.

6. The TARP Experiment. Run this experiment about payments to ex-cons once; then replicate it once. Begin your report with your findings, commenting on whatever you find; but complete your report with a discussion of how you might redesign the experiment, suggesting improvements in its methods that might tell us once and for all whether programs like TARP are worth instituting.

7. Communication in Five-person Groups. Run Leavitt's experiment once and replicate it once. Begin your report with a discussion of your results, but then discuss how you might carry such a study out using real research subjects. Describe how you might recruit subjects, manage to get them to the laboratory in five-person groups, and actually administer the experiment on them. Be both imaginative and practical in thinking through the details of actually carrying out laboratory social psychology experiments.

CHAPTER SUMMARY

The most effective way to study cause and effect in the social sciences is through the experimental method. Instead of the terms *cause* and *effect*, social scientists frequently employ *independent variable* and *dependent variable*. The tendency of two variables to vary together is *correlation*, but correlation does not prove causation. In an *experiment*, the researcher systematically manipulates the independent variable, looking for changes in the dependent variable, and thus is in a good position to say whether the independent variable can be a cause of the dependent variable.

People experimented upon are experimental *subjects*, and the different things they experience are the experimental *conditions*. A group of subjects to whom nothing special is done are the *control group*, whereas the *experimental group* undergoes some special treatment. A repetition of an experiment, performed to check earlier results and often see if they hold under slightly different conditions, is a *replication*.

This chapter describes several classical experiments: Sorokin's studies comparing "communism" with "individualism," studies of the effectiveness of psychotherapy, Hovland's research on communication and attitude change, a study of stigmatization by Schwartz and Skolnick, the TARP project to explore recidivism among ex-convicts, and Leavitt's laboratory work on patterns of communication in small groups.

Technical problems with experiments include selection biases if subjects are not assigned randomly to the control and experimental groups, attrition when subjects drop out of a study in midstream, and the practical and ethical difficulties of inflicting powerful manipulations on human beings. Among the special varieties of experiments are field experiments, done in real-world settings rather than in the laboratory, and survey experiments, which are conducted via questionnaires. A common ethically questionable feature of many experiments is *deception,* but experimenters often employ *debriefing* to minimize harm to subjects.

The XPER software program provides practice thinking through the logic of various experimental designs, based on the classical experiments discussed at length in the chapter. The student can run one of these experiments or replicate it, getting somewhat different results each time the experiment is run.

K E Y   C O N C E P T S   F O R   C H A P T E R   5

CHAPTER

6 Data and Dichotomies

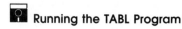

CHAPTER OVERVIEW

Two-by-two tables are powerful tools of theoretical creativity and statistical analysis. Such a table is the intersection of two dichotomies, a cross-cutting of two different two-category schemes for describing observations. Among the classical examples are the Johari window, Robert K. Merton's theory of anomie, and Friedrich Nietzsche's categories of culture. Apparently, this fascination with the number two is not restricted to Western society. It may be universal across human societies, perhaps for the practical reason that division of things into two categories is the simplest system of classification (Lévi-Strauss 1970).

Michael Hannan (1971:9) says, "The history of theorizing in the social sciences demonstrates the prevalence of the tendency to begin theoretical formulations with dichotomies." After a particular theory has been refined, both through conceptual analysis by many scholars and through a series of empirical studies, the dichotomies are likely to expand into dimensions of variation. That is, advanced analysis usually abandons limited two-category conceptual schemes for something more versatile and complex. But the beginning, for theory as for quantitative analysis, is comparison across a pair of categories.

The TABL program lets you analyze a wide variety of two-by-two tables, employing test-pattern simulated data and real data on 19th-century communes, Irish-American and Italian-American mental patients, and inmates of Massachusetts prisons in 1860. The program also contains simulated results from experiments described in the previous chapter, and you can enter fresh data of your own. Basic concepts of quantitative methods introduced in this chapter include frequencies, marginals, column percents, row percents, chi-square, phi, and Yule's Q. You learn the logic behind each of these measures and how to calculate it; the computer program demonstrates how all the calculations are done. A random-number simulation built into the program provides a tremendously clear illustration of the statistical significance of chi-square. Working with very simple yet often real data, you learn the basic concept of correlation and begin to become familiar with measures of association.

_____ Qualitative Analysis with Pairs of Dichotomies

We begin with a set of qualitative examples, showing that the two-by-two table is useful even if one does not undertake statistical analysis, and using it to step from qualitative to quantitative methods.

The Johari Window

Among the most influential two-by-two tables is the infamous Johari Window, invented by Joseph Luft and Harry Ingham back in the 1950s (Luft 1970). The name _Johari_ derives from the originators' first names, and I must admit that the Window struck me as far too cute and painfully superficial when I first encountered it as an undergraduate. Perhaps your reaction will be the same, but I must report that many scholars and administrators take it very seriously. For example, a recent business-oriented textbook called it "perhaps the most useful model for illustrating self-disclosure in groups" (Tubbs 1988), while a reviewer in _Contemporary Sociology_ calls all two-by-two tables "Joharie [sic] Windows" (Melko 1989). Also, in my own experience, the Johari Window turns out to be a very good introduction to two-by-twos for most undergraduates. If it has serious shortcomings, then analyzing them will give you good practice thinking about the general approach it represents.

How well do other people know you? Imagine we could make a list of all the things you know about yourself. Then imagine going through that list and dividing those things into two categories in terms of whether other people know them as well.

Some things are completely public information. Examples might be your name, your approximate height, your gender, and many facts that are on record about you. Luft and Ingham were particularly concerned with the things that come to be known about a person as a result of his or her participation in a group of people who communicate with each other, so this category primarily contains facts that can be directly seen or that have come out in the course of the group's interactions.

Other things you conceal from others. People often hide exactly how much money they have, as well as discreditable acts that would bring condemnation and shame upon them. You may withhold information in order to strengthen your bargaining position. This weekend I plan to have a yard sale, disposing of various items that clutter up the place. I especially need to get rid of a huge glass cabinet we bought at an auction in a moment of bad judgment. Somebody might really want this solid old piece of furniture, so I'm going to put a $70 price tag on it. But, in fact, I would be glad to get rid of it at almost any price. Also, I found two fishing rods on the top shelf of a closet, left there many years earlier by the people who lived in the house before the people who lived there before us. I am not about to tell potential customers that I want to get rid of the fishing gear and cabinet at any price.

If we stopped the analysis right here, we would have two categories, one containing truths about yourself that you let other people know, and the other consisting of truths you conceal. We also have two roles in the analysis, yourself and other people. The two categories concern what other people know. With a slight leap of the imagination, we can imagine two other categories concerning what you yourself know. Although you are quite aware of many truths about yourself, some other truths may be hidden from you.

Imagining a second set of categories like this is a standard analytical step in the approach I am describing.

First, you identify two roles, factors, variables—whatever you want to call them—such as (1) a person and (2) other people. I like to call these the two *elements* of the analysis. Then you identify two categories for one of the elements, such as (1) known and (2) unknown. I call these the **valences** of that element. The third step is to consider whether those valences might also apply to the other element as well. We realized that truths about yourself might be either known or unknown to other people. We now contemplate whether truths about yourself might be either known or unknown to *you*.

The next step in the analysis is to draw a little diagram of the possibilities, in the form of a two-by-two table, and decide what its parts mean. At the left of Figure 6.1 you see a chart of the Johari Window, built on the two

FIGURE 6.1
A Pair of Two-by-two Tables

		Known to Self?	
		No	Yes
Yes		Blind	Open
Known to Others?			
No		Unknown	Hidden

The Johari
Window

		Cultural Goals	
		Reject	Accept
Accept		Ritualism	Conformity
Institutionalized Means			
Reject		Retreatism	Innovation

Merton's
Anomie Theory

elements with their two valences. The window has four windowpanes; sociologists usually call these **cells** of the table. Each cell is a category into which you can put some truths about yourself. The two cells on the right, labeled Open and Hidden, represent the things you know about yourself. Above the table is the question "Known to self?" The Open and Hidden cells have the answer "Yes" above them.

To the left of the table is the question "Known to others?" The Open cell is to the right of the answer "Yes" to this question. The Hidden cell is to the right of the "No" answer. These cells identify the truths about yourself that you are open about or that you keep hidden.

The two cells on the left of the table, labeled Blind and Unknown, are truths about yourself that you are not aware of. Things known to others but not to you go in the Blind box. Other truths are unknown to you or to anybody else: they are in the category of the Unknown. You should go over all four cells of the table, thinking carefully to make sure you understand how each one is defined by the elements and valences that describe it.

Once you understand an analytical scheme like the Johari Window, you can apply it to particular situations. For example, you can pick one of the four cells and try to imagine what truths it may contain. Especially provocative is the Blind cell, the things others know about you but you are not aware of. Sometimes this is called the "bad breath" area, because people are often unaware of their own odors, having become completely accustomed to them. A standard practical joke involves secretly pinning a sign on somebody's back—especially easy if he or she is wearing a thick coat or loose, flowing garment—saying something like "Kick me," or "I'm a turkey." Everybody sees the sign except the person wearing it.

But nice things can also be in this blind area. For example, some people have no idea that they are unusually generous and considerate, while others seem blind to the fact that they are overbearing and obnoxious. The blind area might be referred to as the skeletons in the person's closet, but I believe it is worth noting that most closets contain good things of value rather than dried, useless bones. That is, I think people often overemphasize the unpleasant truths about themselves that people are unaware of, while failing to recognize some of their own positive qualities.

The Unknown area is somewhat controversial. Certainly, there are some facts about yourself that no one knows. Having dinner at a fellow sociologist's house once, I was asked to lie on my back on the floor and place my hands on my chest. The sociologist then placed a full glass of water in my hands and challenged me to place it on the floor beyond my head. I assure you, I had never been in exactly the same situation before, and I was as surprised as the other sociologist when I accomplished the assignment without spilling a drop. Apparently many people find this hard to do, and typically get water all over themselves and the rug. Lest you think I am boasting, I must admit that this previously hidden talent of mine is quite trivial, and I have never found a use for it since. It is a clear example, however, of something that was in my Unknown area. The episode also tells you what a wild time sociologists have in their off-duty hours.

Controversy enters when people start claiming that the Unknown area is positively filled with fascinating things. Alfred Adler (1927, 1929) used to say that each person has a subconscious life goal that can be discovered through intensive psychoanalysis. Supposedly, we are unaware of the hidden goal of our life, but it reveals itself in our compulsions and neuroses, which are distorted attempts to achieve it. The very concept of the subconscious mind brings shudders to many social scientists, who feel it is a hopelessly vague notion, but theories that give an important role to the subconscious acknowledge the vastness of the typical person's Unknown area. One of the key applications of the Johari Window has been in group therapies and encounter groups that have the expressed purpose of bringing the Unknown into awareness through a process of social discovery.

Merton's Anomie Analysis

When Robert K. Merton's typology of modes of adaptation was introduced in the first sociology course I ever took, the instructor said it was the most influential single table in all of sociology. Whether this was strictly true or not, over the years I have encountered Merton's chart again and again, and many sociologists have made it the starting point for their own work. In his analysis of social structure and anomie, Merton (1968) focuses on two elements of social and cultural structures, culturally defined goals (societal values) and legitimate means for achieving them (institutional norms.) The values of the society are the goals worth striving for, while the norms regulate the means people employ in this quest. When the culture is adequately integrated, the norms successfully serve the values, and most people will successfully achieve the goals while conforming to the norms.

In societies like America, however, where large segments of the population are unable to achieve the goals by following the rules, massive deviance will ensue. Perhaps the distinctive American goal is wealth, and the conventional means might be getting a good education and working hard. However, members of the lower social classes and of disadvantaged ethnic groups may be prevented from getting good educations. Working hard will serve them little if the only jobs they can get are menial and manual. Merton uses the traditional term *anomie* to describe a situation in which the norms and values of a society are poorly integrated. I am sure this argument is familiar to all of you who have studied sociology; I remind you of it merely to set the stage for analysis via the two-by-two table.

People for whom the cultural system works will tend to accept its values (goals) and accept its norms (means). People for whom it does not work, who are unable to achieve the goals via the legitimate means, may reject the norms, the values, or both. This is all the conceptual material required for a two-by-two table. We have two elements: norms and values. And each one has two valences: accept or reject. They combine to make the table at the right of Figure 6.1.

Again, we have four cells of the table to label, each one expressing a distinct mode of adaptation to a culture. Those who accept both the conventional goals and the conventional means are conformists, and Merton calls this mode of adaptation *conformity*. Those who continue to accept the norms, while giving up on achievement of the values, can be called *ritualists*. The two really interesting categories, for Merton, are those that involve rejection of the norms and thus lead to deviant behavior.

Merton calls acceptance of the values but rejection of the norms *innovation*, a term that might seem very strange in this context. When Cloward and Ohlin (1960) applied Merton's scheme to juvenile delinquency, they called gangs that used this mode of adaptation simply *criminal*. The chief examples of innovation in the deviance literature all seem to involve violation of the law. The idea is that people adopt new routes to wealth, such as stealing and organized vice, and thus acceptance of the society's values drives some people into crime.

The term *innovation* takes on fuller significance when we realize that Merton's analysis can be applied to science and the arts. I like the example of late-19th-century French painting. Great wealth and honor were showered on a few highly favored artists whose style tended to be fairly realistic, painters who produced endless pictures of historical and mythological scenes, somewhat romanticized but almost photographic in style. Because few young painters could succeed by following this traditional route, some of them turned to innovation, breaking all the rules of conventional painting in producing very unphotographic Impressionist art, but thereby eventually achieving the conventional success that would have eluded them had they followed the standard norms (cf. White and White 1965).

For many people, however, innovation doesn't work. In a sense, they suffer two doses of anomie. First, they cannot achieve society's values by conventional means. Second, they cannot achieve society's values by unconventional means either. So they give up, seeking no goals and thus following no norms. Merton calls them *retreatists,* for they have retreated from the struggles of normal life. Among their ranks are the "psychotics, autists, pariahs, outcasts, vagrants, vagabonds, tramps, chronic drunkards and drug addicts" (Merton 1968:207).

Where are you in this two-by-two table? Before you answer, I should tell you that many fine sociologists had difficulty placing themselves in one of these four boxes. Although Merton's analysis seemed to have put a number of empirical facts in perspective and brought together several sociological concepts in a simple logical structure, it also missed something important.

What about people who march to a different drummer? What about those who seek a consistent set of values, and follow a strict set of norms in doing so, but whose values and norms are not the conventional ones? What about those, to use a somewhat oversimplified example, who seek social equality rather than personal wealth? Their means may be political agitation, giving speeches and writing essays, and even promoting a revolution. They do not merely reject society's norms and values; they also substitute something else. For them, Merton invented the category of *rebellion.*

If there is a chief drawback to two-by-two tables, it is that they make it difficult to think outside their constraining categories. And, indeed, when Merton presented his theory, he did not use this kind of table. Instead, he listed his modes of adaptation in a column, with plus or minus signs after each, under columns labeled "culture goals" and "institutionalized means." For example, "innovation" was followed by "+, -." The plus signified that the innovator accepted the culture goals, and the minus signified that he or she rejected the institutionalized means. After rebellion, he put "± ±," signifying rejection of prevailing values and norms and substitution of new ones.

If you want, you can argue that Merton fouled up a nice, clean analysis by adding

rebellion. Soon, drug addicts will say that they are rebels, too, substituting the value of getting high for that of getting ahead. Once you break open a tight conceptual scheme, like a two-by-two table, there's no clear stopping point. The whole conceptual system may come apart, leaving you with a pile of intellectual junk. Or, you might feel that Merton was justified in escaping from the mental prison of fourfold boxes. But as this classic sociological example makes abundantly clear, there is a price to pay for a very tight conceptual scheme as afforded by two-by-two tables. You may be forced to ignore very important parts of reality, or you may unintentionally distort reality grievously to fit it into your boxes.

Classical Research on Culture

Even very great thinkers, however, can sometimes achieve insights with two-by-two tables that they might otherwise have missed. An example from over a century ago that still has some relevance today is the typology of cultures proposed by Friedrich Nietzsche (1872; cf. Bainbridge 1985a). Usually described as a philosopher, Nietzsche worked in the fields of linguistics, cultural history, and anthropology. Thus he has some claim on the title of social scientist, if not precisely of sociologist. His first book described three kinds of human culture, the Apollonian, Dionysian, and Buddhist. The first two names come from classical Greek deities, while the third, of course, refers to one of the world's great religions.

Each of these three terms can be used to describe an entire society, or it can describe the style of an individual's personality. William James (1963; cf. Maslow 1969) thought people came in two basic varieties, tough-minded or tender-minded, and these concepts parallel Nietzsche's distinction between Apollonian and Dionysian. An Apollonian person or culture is intellectual and rational; perhaps you would call them "cool." A Dionysian person or culture is emotional and intuitive, or "warm." Alvin Gouldner and Richard Peterson (1962) applied this dichotomy in a sociological study of technology, and Ruth Benedict (1934) used it in an influential book on the patterns of cultures. The Buddhist style of person or culture has received far less attention in social theory, perhaps because it seemed alien to members of Western societies. For Nietzsche, it meant the attempt to transcend reality altogether, a detachment lacking both emotion and intellect.

So many writers have whittled Nietzsche's rich conceptual scheme down to just the two Western categories, Apollonian and Dionysian, that I hesitate to suggest a different approach. In many scholars' minds, Ruth Benedict among them, the concepts Apollonian and Dionysian came to mean simply ascetic and sensual—frigid and sexy, to be plain about it—and the extremes of celibacy and orgy were all that the words implied. But Nietzsche had a far richer and far more sociological set of meanings in mind.

According to Nietzsche, each of the three types demands a different relationship to self and to other. While the Dionysian seeks to submerge in the group, the Apollonian is the principle of individuation. The Buddhist rejects both self and other, withdrawing into mystical contemplation. Nietzsche's Buddhist is not, of course, the ordinary citizen of an Asian land who follows the Buddhist faith at some distance, but the monastic Buddhist virtuoso who has left the world and abjures personal pleasure, thus someone who rejects or minimizes concern for both self and other. These three types can be placed into three of the four cells of a two-by-two table.

One of the two variables would be orientation toward self. Do you emphasize the importance of the self, or do you minimize your individual importance? The other variable would be orientation toward other persons or the group. Do you give great importance to the group, or do you not? You can draw the table yourself, if you want practice in thinking such tables through. The Apollonian maximizes the self and minimizes the group. The Dionysian minimizes the self and maximizes the group. The Buddhist minimizes the self and minimizes the group. Any insights yet?

Remember, there are four cells in a two-by-two table, and Nietzsche's cultural types fill only three of them. An empty cell remains: maximizing the self and maximizing the group. This may be a hard trick, but it logically follows from the analysis.

I suspect that Nietzsche was groping, in some of his later writings, to find a synthesis of individual and group, a fourth type in which both self and other were stressed. His famous cultic testament, *Also Sprach Zarathustra* (1885), is the story of a messiah-philosopher who achieves the greatest wisdom and enlightenment while living in seclusion and detachment (Buddhism) for 10 years on a mountain accompanied only by an eagle (Apollonian power) and a serpent (Dionysian passion). He descends to seek followers and fellow philosophers but fails to find them. I cannot say that Nietzsche, or his semimythical Zarathustra, could have succeeded in realizing their majestic dream if they could only have drawn a two-by-two table. But they never articulated the possibility that what they hunted so painfully and so long was the fourth box in the table, the possibility that an individual could retain a sense of autonomous self while living cooperatively within a group.

More down-to-earth, two-by-two tables can help students grasp fine distinctions made by various theories in the behavioral sciences. Akers's (1985) sociology textbook on deviant behavior, which follows what is called the *social learning* approach, provides a good example. This school of thought, which is greatly based on behaviorism in psychology, always centers its analysis on the ways that rewards and punishments influence behavior. One of the key behaviorist technical terms is *reinforcement,* "the process whereby a response-contingent stimulus has the effect of strengthening the response" (Akers 1985:43). I can translate that into English with an example.

You are one of my students, and you hand in an assignment that was especially well done. I give it an A grade and return it to you with abundant praise. Humans find praise rewarding (Homans 1974), so you will be more likely to work hard on your next assignment, too. My praise (including the A grade) has reinforced your tendency to work hard. This is often called *positive reinforcement*, because your behavior was reinforced by something positive (rewarding) that happened. But suppose that, instead of praise, I had calmly given you a note that exempted you from the final exam, because you had done so well. Here, something that would have been punishing (the exam) was removed. Technically, this is called *negative reinforcement*, because something punishing was removed rather than something rewarding being added.

Note that negative reinforcement does not mean punishment—a common mistake students make with these ideas. Many professionals also find this use of terminology extremely confusing, and several sociologists close to Akers's viewpoint do not use it (e.g., Homans 1974; Stark and Bainbridge 1987). To clarify the ideas, Akers resorted to a two-by-two table. Again, you can try drawing the table I am about to describe to gain practice in making them.

One element of the table is *behavior* (response), and the other is the *stimulus.* Under behavior, the two valences are "behavior increases = reinforcement" and "behavior decreases = punishment." The two valences

for the stimulus are similar but not identical: "positive" and "negative." The cell for positive stimulus and behavior increases is labeled "positive reinforcement." Negative stimulus combined with behavior increases give you "negative reinforcement." A positive stimulus that makes the behavior decrease is positive punishment, or the inflicting of punishment on someone. A negative stimulus causing decrease of the behavior is negative punishment, or the taking of a reward away from someone. When a parent spanks a kid for doing something against the parent's wishes, we can speak of positive punishment. When the parent instead takes some privilege away from the kid, such as not letting him or her watch a favorite TV program, that is negative punishment. Precisely because these distinctions are difficult to understand, Akers used a two-by-two table to help clarify them.

The chief use of two-by-two tables in sociology, however, is not the qualitative cross-classification of categories. This section has prepared us to think in terms of pairs of concepts and to label the variables, valences, and contents of the boxes. But the greatest utility of two-by-twos will become apparent only when the tables become quantitative, a step made easy through the fifth of our computer programs.

_____ Running the TABL Program

The computer program written for this chapter is the first one that employs really serious statistical analysis. Therefore, we will have to talk about it at some length. However, you do not need to be sitting at the computer while we do this. I have included illustrations in this chapter that show exactly how the computer screen would look if you were sitting at it, so you can learn the general principles wherever you happen to be reading this book. Later, when you want to try the procedures for yourself, and when it is time to do one of the projects at the end of this chapter, you can work while sitting at the computer.

I have called the program that lets you work with two-by-two tables TABL. To get it, start the computer, insert the appropriate disk, and type TABL(ENTER). The menu of the TABL program has nine choices, in addition to (ESC), which lets you escape the program altogether:

```
[1] Examine a two-by-two table
[2] Explain calculations
[3] Do 1 random table
[4] Do 100 random tables
[5] Do 1000 random tables
[6] New test table
[7] New historical table
[8] New experiment table
[9] Input fresh data for table
[ESC] QUIT or switch programs
```

The first five choices in this menu perform various kinds of analysis, while the last four select a particular two-by-two table to be analyzed. I want to explain the analysis choices at length, but we need to select some data to work with while discussing them. Therefore, we'll consider choice 6 briefly; first, the test tables.

When you press (6), you will get a picture like that in Figure 6.2, which shows 26 two-by-two tables, labeled A through Z. These tables are not based on any real data but were designed to show various possible patterns you might find. For example, table V is the extreme case of a table with no data—zeros in all four cells—while W has all 120 of its cases in one cell. For our present purposes, two-by-two C is a good choice, so if you are working at the computer, simply press (C). This will give you the data I shall describe in the following pages.

Analyzing a Campus Survey

Now it is time to take a closer look at a two-by-two table. To examine a two-by-two table, you first select one, as we have just done, and then go to the main menu and press [1]. You get something very much like what I show here in Figure 6.3. In the upper-right corner is a big version of two-by-two test table C.

The table is a bare-bones presentation of data, and the "two-by-two animal" will make more sense if I give meaning to it. In fact, as I have explained, the test-table data did not come from any real study but were cooked up as good illustrations. Let's pretend, however, that they did come from a study, one you might have done on your own college campus.

Are men more conservative than women? Some studies seem to indicate that this is the case, although the results depend to a great extent on how you define *conservative*. Men tend to show greater support for military expenditures, for example, while women are more likely to attend church. Thus, depending on how you defined conservatism, you might find that one or the other sex was more conservative. But let's imagine you had done a complex study of political views, with several different measures of political orientation. Now you want to analyze the data.

Look at the two-by-two table itself. Each cell contains a number expressing the number of cases in it: 20, 40, 40, and 20. Near the lower-right corner of the two-by-two is the number 120. This means that you are working with data on 120 people. At the top of the table you see the letters F and M, which identify the sexes of the 120 people. The two cells that constitute the left half of the table contain the women, while the two cells on the right contain the men. At the bottom of the table, you see "60" on the left (under the "F" cells) and "60" on the right (under the "M" cells). These numbers tell us that there are 60 women and 60 men.

To the left of the table you see abbreviations for the two standard political orientations:

FIGURE 6.2
Test Tables

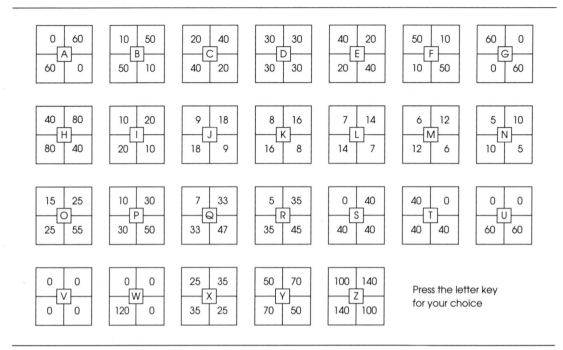

"Con" (Conservative) and "Lib" (Liberal). The two cells at the top of the table represent the political conservatives, while the two cells at the bottom represent the political liberals. To the right of the conservative cells you see "60," and you also see "60" to the right of the liberal cells. Therefore, the 120 people include 60 conservatives and 60 liberals. The numbers at the bottom of the table and along the right side, four 60s, are called the **marginals** of the table, perhaps because they are written on its margins. Because the word *marginals* is used often in talking about tables, you should become familiar with it.

The information at the left side of the computer screen, as shown in Figure 6.3, helps you interpret the particular table you are working with. In this case, it says, "Two-by-two table about sex and political orientation." This tells you the topic of the table. Below that, the computer identifies the two dichotomous variables:

"Variable X: Sex of student. Variable Y: Conservative or Liberal." When you are working with the historical and experimental data available to this program, these descriptions of the variables will be especially useful, making sure you understand what the abbreviations at the top and left side of the table mean.

Note also the message in the lower-left corner of the screen: "[D]isplay:Frequencies." **Frequencies** are the numbers of cases in each category, here the numbers of people in each cell of the table. That the D is highlighted in a little box means that something will happen if you press the D key. If you are seated at the computer, press [D] and see what happens. The message will change to "Column percents," and the numbers in the table will suddenly become percentages. Look carefully, and you will see that these percentages add up to 100% vertically. That is, they tell you the percent with each political orientation among members of

FIGURE 6.3
A Two-by-two Table

F ← X → M

	Con			
Two-by-two table about sex and general political orientation		20	40	60
	Y ↑			
Variable X: Sex of student Variable Y: Conservative or Liberal	Y ↓ Lib	40	20	60
		60	60	120

chi square: 13.33
significance: .001
phi: 0.33
Yule's Q: 0.60

|D|isplay: Frequencies

each of the sexes. One third (33.3%) of the women are conservatives, while two thirds (66.7%) of the women are liberals. Men show the opposite pattern, two thirds being conservative (66.7%) and one third (33.3%) liberal. **Column percents** are percentages calculated within each column of figures, just as in this example.

If you were to press [D] a second time, you would get what we call **row percents,** percentages calculated within each row of figures. You could see what percentage of the conservatives were men, for example, or what percentage of the liberals were women. And you can press [D] a third time to get total percents, the percentage of the total 120 respondents who are in each cell. Finally, you could press [D] again to return to the frequencies.

Look back at the table again. Does the pattern of numbers tell you anything? Just 20 of the 60 women are conservative, while fully 40 of the 60 men are conservative. This seems to

support the proposition that men are more likely than women to be conservative, but suppose the difference had been smaller. Suppose 28 of the women had been conservative, compared with 32 of the men. Would we still be able to conclude that men were more likely to be conservative?

Imagine you were storming around your college campus, clipboard and pencil in hand, finding 60 women and 60 men and asking each one whether he or she was liberal or conservative. Clearly, chance alone would influence to a large degree which 120 people you were able to ask. Some people wouldn't be on campus when you did your survey. Others would be in class when you knocked on their dorm rooms. And even if you used a careful, systematic procedure to select people to study, you couldn't expect the 120 you surveyed to represent perfectly either your college or the nation as a whole. Thus, your data will be a little different from what an identical study done with different people might find, and chance will play a role in exactly how many of each sex are conservative or liberal.

If there were exactly as many female conservatives as male conservatives among the 120 you studied, you might have to conclude that the sexes really did not differ in their general political orientations after all. If there were *almost the same* numbers of conservatives in the two sexes, you would probably come to the same conclusion. On the other hand, if the numbers were *very different,* you would probably conclude that the sexes do differ in their tendencies to be liberal or conservative.

The problem is that these two criteria for judgment, "almost the same" and "very different," are not precisely defined. How similar do the numbers have to be for you to say they are almost the same? How different do they have to be before you would call them very different? Or, to put the issue another way, how different do the numbers have to be before you could conclude that the sexes really are different in their political tendencies, and that the difference was not just the result of the luck of the draw in finding people to answer your survey?

This is where the concept of **statistical significance** comes in. For the past two chapters, especially in the previous one, we have been squinting at tables, hoping that the different patterns we saw were scientifically solid. Now we are going to begin to develop some highly accurate statistical tools for deciding the statistical significance of such differences. In a way, the job will take us several chapters to accomplish, but, thankfully, we won't concentrate on statistical significance for long at a stretch. Instead, we will leave the topic and then return to it periodically, getting an ever deeper understanding as we see how significance is evaluated in many different situations.

Statistical *significance* is not the same thing as scientific *importance*. If you are studying a trivial topic, your results will be unimportant no matter how solid they are in a statistical sense. No, *statistical significance* means simply that a certain pattern in the data was unlikely to have come about by mere chance alone.

Suppose we are playing cards, you and I, some game in which aces are very valuable. I deal out the cards, and your hand is pure junk. Already having good reason to believe that I am a cheat, you grab at my cards and get a glimpse of four aces. "Now, I've got you, you crook! You have been dealing yourself all the good cards by trickery, but now I have proof!" Perhaps your next act is to draw your revolver and shoot me dead, counting on the sheriff's hatred of cardsharps to keep you from being arrested. But was I really guilty? Did I really cheat in dealing out the cards? Unless you actually saw me cheat, it is hard to be sure. Four aces may be very rare, but just by chance a player will occasionally be dealt them. If you already suspect me of cheating, then the four aces are certainly good evidence in support of your suspicions, but they are not absolute proof.

I can imagine an ironic television short story in which a wild-west gambler decides never to cheat again, and he sits down for one last game of cards, just for fun. All the other players suspect him of being a cardsharp, but he has decided to quit cheating, so he is not worried that they will get mad at him even though they ask him to deal and have sly expressions on their faces. Then he deals out the first hand, and he draws a royal flush! Next hand, full house. In the third hand, fingers trembling, he deals himself four aces! Although he knows this is just wild luck, it must look like cheating to anybody watching the game. The other players begin to finger their guns, and a commercial interrupts the story, just before you see whether they shoot him. Perhaps in the second half of the show, you see him desperately trying to cheat in such a way as to lose disastrously, betting his farm and all his other possessions and happy to lose everything but his life.

In social science, as in life itself, we can never be sure. It is always possible that the data have arranged themselves, entirely by chance, in a pattern that confirms all our theories. We always run the risk of betting on the wrong numbers. But science is never a matter of certainty, just of ever-increasing confidence and plausibility.

Although a scientist must be content with something less than certainty, he or she can nonetheless make judgments about whether the data really support a given theory with great precision. That is because we can work with the exact probability that the particular pattern in the data could have come about entirely by chance. Right below the two-by-two table on the computer screen, or in Figure 6.3, are the brief messages "Chi square: 13.33. Significance: .001." The first part, concerning chi-square, reports a calculation the computer did on the figures in the table that will allow it to assess statistical significance. We will shortly consider chi-square, one of the most widely used coefficients in all social-science statistics. For now, note that it was a step the computer had to take before arriving at the significance number, 0.001.

This message tells us how likely it was that the pattern in the data was the result of chance alone. The number, 0.001, is the same as $\frac{1}{1000}$. This means that there was less than one chance in a thousand of getting this big a difference between the political orientations of the women and the men surveyed in a random sample, if in fact the two sexes did not differ in politics in the population from which the sample was taken.

There are several ways we could investigate this further. For example, if this were a course in mathematical statistics, we might spend a few weeks deriving a bunch of formulas, proving not only that the computer did its calculations right but also explaining how we know what to expect pure chance to give us in a run of data. But sociology students do not generally take much math in college (whether they should or not is a question I do not want to touch) and at the very least, this is not a math course.

One point we could make is that mathematicians have kindly done a lot of these calculations for us and developed something called the **chi-square distribution**. Essentially, this is a table of numbers called chi-square, with other numbers stating how likely it was that data would give you each size chi-square that was listed. Standard social statistics books have this table in the back. For various homework problems, you would be taught how to calculate chi-square, you would be given some data from which to calculate it, and then you would be asked to look up in the back of the book what the significance of that chi-square was. The computer figured a chi-square of 13.33 for our table, doing some calculations that I will explain later. Then the computer looked this up in an invisible table of the chi-square distribution it has in its memory and determined that such a big chi-square would come up less often than once in a thousand times, entirely by chance.

Worry about the calculation part later (but don't worry much). Let's focus on the "once in a thousand times" part now. Three related choices on the menu of the "TABL" program let you see what I mean by "chance" and how we can compare real data with figures we might have gotten by "dumb luck."

Random Tables: 1,100,1000

Choice 3 on the program's menu puts your two-by-two table on the screen, over at the right, just as before, but then it puts a similar table over on the left. Figure 6.4 shows what happened once when I asked my computer to do this. The table on the right is labeled "table based on actual data." The new one, on the left, is a "table based on random simulated data." The left-hand table, just like the real one on the right, has a total of 120 cases, and the marginals are exactly the same as well. But the numbers in the cells are quite different. Instead of 20, 40, 40, 20, you see 29, 31, 31, 29. If you were to run this on your computer, you would probably get somewhat different figures for the random simulated table.

I wrote a little section of the computer program to produce random data, almost as if the computer were flipping coins. If you want to think of it in terms of coin flips, take a penny and a dime out of your pocket (or any two coins of different type). Toss them up, and see how they land. You have just produced random data for one simulated person. If the penny is heads, the person is female. If the penny is tails, the person is male. So, too, for politics. If the dime is heads, the person is conservative. If the dime is tails, the person is liberal. If you did this 120 times and wrote down the random, simulated data for all 120 flips of your pair of coins, then you would have data like that the computer puts in the left-hand two-by-two table.

Below the left-hand table, in Figure 6.4, you see a chi-square of 0.13, much smaller than the 13.33 chi-square for the right-hand table. This is the first hint about what chi-square means. Put very crudely, a very even or unsurprising pattern of numbers will produce a very low chi-square. A very uneven or surprising pattern of numbers will give a big chi-square. And notice the significance message: "significance: n.s." "N.s." stands for "not significant." The computer checked a chi-square of 0.13 in its chi-square distribution table and found that a chi-square this small was very likely by chance, and thus not statistically significant.

FIGURE 6.4
Random Data and Real Data

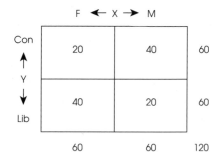

Table based on random simulated data

	F ← X →	M	
Con	29	31	60
Lib	31	29	60
	60	60	120

(Y axis: Con ↑ Y ↓ Lib)

chi square: 0.13
significance: n.s.
phi: 0.03
Yule's Q: 0.07

Table based on actual data

	F ← X →	M	
Con	20	40	60
Lib	40	20	60
	60	60	120

(Y axis: Con ↑ Y ↓ Lib)

chi square: 13.33
significance: .001
phi: 0.33
Yule's Q: 0.60

Of course, the random simulated data *were* produced by pure chance; but remember, the statistical significance of the right-hand table was described as less than one chance in a *thousand.* For a completely convincing demonstration, we would have to look at a thousand of these simulated tables. This sounds like a lot of work, but the computer is ready to do it for you. That is where options 4 ("Do 100 random tables") and 5 ("Do 1000 random tables") come in.

If you press either (4) or (5) when the main menu is on the screen, you will get the standard table of your actual data on the right side of the screen, just as with a single random table. The left side of the screen, however, will summarize information from 100 or 1000 similar two-by-two tables produced in the manner I have just described. To save time, the computer will not print all of each random table on the screen, just the chi-square from each.

Figure 6.5 shows what I got one time when I called for 1000 such tables. If you want to try this, be my guest. However, 1000 tables takes a while for the computer to crank out, so you might consider running just 100 tables, if you are just taking a casual look at how this part of the program works. If you plan to create 1000, or to create a few thousand in sets of one thousand, I suggest you bring some other work to the computer (perhaps, if I may suggest, reading other parts of this textbook). On the other hand, you may want to look at the left-hand edge of the screen as the computer runs, because it will display the chi-square for each random table as it simulates it, and you can get an intuitive sense of the chi-square distribution by watching these numbers stream by.

FIGURE 6.5
1,000 Random Tables

No.	chi²
978	0.12
979	0.05
980	0.48
981	0.01
982	1.26
983	3.92
984	0.70
985	0.00
986	0.05
987	0.02
988	0.02
989	2.02
990	0.23
991	1.86
992	1.08
993	0.54
994	1.19
995	4.02
996	0.13
997	0.13
998	0.65
999	0.04
1000	2.68

Analysis of 1000 simulations

Maximum chi²: 10.91

Average chi²: 0.95

Significance	Simulations
n.s.	954
.05	46
.02	15
.01	7
.001	1

F ← X → M

	F	M	
Con	20	40	60
Lib	40	20	60
	60	60	120

chi square: 13.33
significance: .001
phi: 0.33
Yule's Q: 0.60

When the computer finally stops working and gives you a picture like that in Figure 6.5, the last 23 chi-squares (numbered 978 through 1000) will stay on the left side of the screen. In the particular run displayed here, two of these last chi-squares were "statistically significant" at the 0.05 level. Random table number 983 achieved a chi-square of 3.92, and number 995 achieved 4.02. If you check a table for the chi-square distribution, you would find that the 0.05 level of statistical significance is achieved by any chi-square of 3.84 or above. These two tables achieved that, so they are significant.

But wait a moment! Didn't we say that they were randomly generated tables, and thus that their chi-squares were all achieved by pure chance? So how could they be significant? Doesn't statistical significance mean significantly different from what you would expect by chance?

There is no contradiction here. The 0.05 level of significance means you would expect to get—on average—one chi-square as big as 3.84 about every twenty times you calculated them. Figure 6.5 lists 23 chi-squares, so there's a good probability of getting a "significant" one, and we happened to get two. Other times we tried this, we might get three "significant" chi-squares in the last 23, or none. But on average, we would get one "significant" chi-square for every 20 we calculated.

Near the bottom-center of Figure 6.5, you see a section labeled "Significance Simulations." The first row of this table says: "n.s. 954." Again, the abbreviation "n.s." stands for "not significant." This means that out of the 1,000 chi-squares we calculated from the thousand two-by-two tables of random data, 954 failed to reach 3.84 and be counted as significant. Right below this, we see: ".05 46." This tells us that 46 of the chi-squares, like number 983 and 995, were equal to or greater than 3.84, and thus were counted as significant at the .05 level. Naturally, these two numbers together include all thousand chi-squares calculated (954 + 46 = 1,000).

Below that is ".02 15." This means that 15 of the random tables reached the .02 level of statistical significance (which is achieved by a chi-square of 5.41, according to the table for the chi-square distribution). You would expect this to happen, just by chance, once out of every 50 tries, or 20 times out of 1,000. Our 15 is actually somewhat less than the 20 you would expect by chance, but that's what we mean by *chance*. You can't tell exactly how the numbers will come out for any particular table, or for any set of 1,000 tables, but *on average* or *in the long run*, 2 percent of random chi-squares would achieve the .02 level of significance.

All 15 of the tables that reached the .02 level are included among the 46 that reached the .05 level. Thus, there are 31 tables (46 - 15 = 31) that reached the .05 level but failed to reach the .02 level. Similarly, all 7 of the tables that reached the .01 level are included among the 15 reaching .02 and the 46 reaching .05, and the one table that reached the .001 level of statistical significance reached the other levels as well.

For a two-by-two table, a chi-square of 6.64 is sufficient for the 0.01 level of statistical significance, and we would expect this to happen once in a hundred random tries, or 10 times out of 1,000. We got only 7 chi-squares this big, but in other computer runs we would get numbers greater than 10; the average would be 10. And finally, a chi-square of 10.83 achieves the .001 level, one chance in a thousand that it was the result of pure chance. As it happens, we did get exactly one chi-square this big in our 1,000 random tables.

The chi-square for that particular random table was 10.91. I know this because the computer puts the maximum chi-square for the run right above the table giving the chi-square distributions, along with the average chi-square for all 1,000. A chi-square of 10.91 is only slightly bigger than the 10.83 required to achieve the .001 level, and it is noticeably smaller than the 13.33 achieved by the table of data on the right side of Figure 6.5. To see if I could get a chi-square as big as 13.33 entirely by chance, I ran this part of the program eight times, to get 8,000 randomly generated tables, and for two of those tables the maximum chi-square was bigger: 14.86 and 16.42.

Work with this part of the software a bit, and I think you will understand the basic idea of statistical significance quite well. This should also give you some caution about statistical significances around .05 or .02 when you are examining a large number of two-by-two tables. Just by chance, some weak statistically significant results will emerge out of any real research done with lots of variables that produce lots of tables, just as out of our random data. Two things can guide you in evaluating situations like this. First, be especially concerned if the weakly significant associations are difficult to explain and inconsistent among themselves. Second, demand more stringent tests of significance, perhaps the .001 level or better.

Simple, straightforward experimental studies, done with very few variables, may be convincing if results reach the .05 level. Say an experimenter recruits a small number of research subjects, divides them at random into two groups, applies an experimental manipulation with one of the groups and measures the outcome in terms of a single, dichotomous variable. A simple study like this would produce data for only one two-by-two table, and in such a case you might be content with the .05 level. To achieve a high level, such as .01, the experimenter might have had to recruit far more subjects and to invest vastly greater effort experimenting on them. That might be too much to ask.

If the study has zillions of variables, however, potentially producing multizillions of two-by-two tables, there is always the worry that the researcher selected a small number of these tables that happened by chance to reach the .05 level and published them, leaving heaps of tables with small chi-squares on the computing room floor. If the researcher is very scrupulous, and promises this was not done, we might believe him or her. Otherwise, it is good to be skeptical of weak levels of significance based on data that permitted a large number of potential tables.

In conclusion I must mention a very minor point about the random tables our software produces, a point that will be of no interest to most of you but must be put on the record. When you inspect just one random table, by pressing (3) from the menu, the table will be created in such a way as to give exactly the same marginals as in the table based on your actual data. I have found that if you went to the incredible labor of doing this 100 or 1000 times, you would not get exactly the chi-square distribution we have been talking about. But I felt that a random-data table with the same marginals would be easier to understand and to compare with your actual data, and would convey a greater sense of how patterns in the cell frequencies can vary independently of the marginal distributions. However, when you call for 100 or 1000 chi-squares from random tables, by pressing (4) or (5) from the menu, the computer will produce invisible tables that have the same number of cases as in your table of actual data, but that do not necessarily match the marginal distribution. These chi-squares will exhibit the chi-square distribution, within the limits of chance, and are far quicker for the computer to calculate than if the computer had to duplicate the marginals as well as the total number of cases.

Calculating Chi-square

Now that we have some sense of why chi-square is useful, we need to understand how it is calculated. Sometimes, you may need to figure chi-squares by hand, although I advise you to employ a pocket calculator, if not a computer, because the numbers you have to work with can get pretty big. More important, however, is to begin learning the logic behind the statistics we use, and a couple of the ideas in chi-square will play important roles in other measures we will encounter in later chapters.

Using the TABL program, select the test tables, and when the 26 tables appear on the screen, press (C) to select the third one in the top row, labeled "C." Return to the main menu and select "Explain calculations." Shortly, the right side of the screen will show the table, and the left side will fill with a mess of numbers showing how the computer did its calculations. Figure 6.6 gives this formidable picture.

Don't panic! Don't let some of the huge numbers, mathematical formulas, and apparent complexity disturb you. We are going to go through this topic carefully, step by step, and there won't be too much to memorize. Also, the big numbers on the left side of the screen shouldn't scare you, because you won't have to recalculate them. The computer has already done the hard work for you, and the screen provides all the information we need to understand how three different statistics were calculated.

Let's think the problem through logically. You have some data about sex and politics, with particular numbers in the four cells of the two-by-two. To start, you need to compare these numbers with what the pattern would be if the sexes did not really differ at all. So, let's think for a moment about what a no-difference pattern would look like. Among the 120 people—both sexes combined—60 people are conservative. This is exactly half. If the sexes really did not differ, we would expect to see the same proportion of conservatives among the 60 women. If half of the women were conservative, that would mean 30 female conservatives. The same logic holds for the men. If the sexes did not differ, then we would expect to see the same proportion of conservatives among the men as among the whole 120. Again, half should be conservative, which means 30 conservative men.

Look back in the four cells of the table again. There are three numbers in each cell. We already said that the top one is the number of cases in that cell in your data. The middle number, right under it, is the number we would expect if men and women did not differ in their politics. Analyzing things, we already decided there should be 30 conservative women and 30 conservative men. Notice that the middle numbers in the cells are indeed 30. The numbers are stated as 30.00, rather than just 30, because sometimes our calculations will come up with fractions. These numbers are called the *expected frequencies.*

FIGURE 6.6
Calculating Chi-Square

	Observed	Expected	O − E	$(O - E)^2$	$(O - E)^2/E$
A	40	30.00	10.00	100.000	3.33
B	20	30.00	−10.00	100.000	3.33
C	20	30.00	−10.00	100.000	3.33
D	40	30.00	10.00	100.000	3.33
				$\Sigma((D - E)^2/E)$ =	13.33

N = 120
AD = 1600   BC = 400
AD − BC = 1200   AD + BC = 2000
P = (A + B)(C + D)(A + C)(B + D) = 12960000
$(AD - BC)^2$ = 1440000
$N(AD - BC)^2$ = 172800000

$$chi^2 = \frac{N(AD - BC)^2}{P} = \frac{172800000}{12960000} = 13.33$$

$$phi = \frac{AD - BC}{\sqrt{P}} = \frac{1200}{3600.00} = 0.33$$

$$Q = \frac{AD - BC}{AD + BC} = \frac{1200}{2000} = 0.60$$

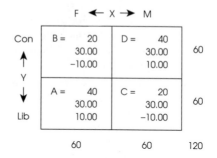

chi square: 13.33
significance: .001
phi: 0.33
Yule's Q: 0.60

Pause for a moment and think over how we calculated the expected frequencies. We started with the proportion that was conservative among the whole 120. We got this by dividing the number of cases in the conservative row (60) by the total number of cases (120). This was 60/120 or 1/2. Then we multiplied this fraction by the number of cases in one of the columns of cells, for example the 60 women. This gave us an expected frequency of 30 female conservatives. We summarize this in a simple formula for E, the expected frequency:

$$E = \frac{(row\ total) \times (column\ total)}{total\ number\ of\ cases}$$

To figure out the expected frequencies for all four cells of the table, you would have to use this formula four times, once for each cell. In our example, the calculating was very easy, because the numbers were nice and round and divisions (male/female, conservative/liberal) were equal. Sometimes the calculations are considerably messier, and the expected frequencies are seldom identical, as they are in this case. Although the method by which we came up with the expected frequencies was very simple, it deserves to be remembered. We will use this exact technique again, when we deal with tables much bigger than two-by-two in later chapters.

The actual data in the cells of your table are called the *observed frequencies*. To this point, then, we have observed frequencies of 20, 40, 40, 20, and we have expected frequencies of 30, 30, 30, 30. The next step is to compare them. This is a very key concept in statistical analysis, one we will use again and again throughout this book. Our purpose is to compare the data we actually got with what we would expect if there were no real difference (in politics) between the groups we are studying (women and men). The obvious first step in comparing the observed frequencies with the expected frequencies is to figure how far apart these numbers in each cell are, something we accomplish by subtracting.

Look at the two-by-two table again. The top one of the three numbers is the observed frequency. The middle number is the expected frequency. The bottom number is the difference, figured by subtracting the expected frequency from the observed frequency. In the upper-right cell, for example, the observed frequency is 40 and the expected frequency is 30. Thus, the difference is 10.00 (40 - 30 = 10). For the upper-left cell, the answer is -10.00. Yes, that's right, *minus* ten (20 - 30 = -10).

These numbers tell us the differences between the observed and expected frequencies in the four cells: -10, 10, 10, -10. To understand how far apart observation and expectation are for the table as a whole, we should combine them. But if you just add these four numbers, you get zero, which isn't a reasonable result. One way to get rid of the minus signs is to square the numbers. Remember from high school algebra that when you square a number you multiply it by itself. $(10) \times (10) = 100$. $(-10) \times (-10) = 100$.

But there is one more thing we want to take into account, as well as getting rid of the minus signs. Throughout social statistics, again and again we find it best to compare proportions rather than the "raw" numbers themselves. Ten students in Professor Parson's class fell asleep. Twenty students in Professor Weber's class fell asleep. Does this mean that Weber is more boring than Parsons? Not necessarily. Parson's class has just 20 students, while Weber's has 100. So, 50% of Parson's students fell asleep, compared with only 20% of Weber's. By the same token, we want to turn the difference between the observed frequency and the expected frequency into a proportion of something. And the best "something," statisticians decided, was the expected frequency. Then we would have numbers that described how far the observations diverged from our expectations, as a proportion of the expectations.

So, for each cell of the table, we subtract the expected frequency from the observed frequency. Next we square that difference, to get rid of minus signs. Then we divide the result by the expected frequency. We follow these thee steps for each of the four cells of the table, giving us four numbers. Now, finally, we can combine the numbers simply by adding them together. The result is called chi-square. The whole process can be described by the following formula:

$$\chi^2 = \Sigma((O - E)^2/E)$$

Again, don't panic. Yes, it looks like Greek to me, too. In fact, it is Greek, or at least two of the letters in it are. The symbol at the left, which looks like an X taking a walk, is simply the Greek version of the letter X, called chi. You won't see it in any of the displays on your computer screen, because a basic IBM computer doesn't have chi among the symbols it can print. And to save my publisher's printers a little trouble, I won't use it much in the text of this book. If you want to remember this Greek letter, you might be interested to know it has religious significance. It is the first letter in the Greek word "Christ," and it looks like a cross. In addition to the ancient Christian symbol of a fish and the familiar cross symbol, chi (combined with the Greek letter rho to make the "Chr" part of Christ) is also an ancient religious symbol.

The "2" after the chi makes it chi-square. The next thing, after the equals sign, is a capital Greek letter sigma, simply the Greek letter "S." This is one of the most common Greek symbols in mathematics, and most IBM-type computers will print it on the screen. It stands for "sum," meaning to add up a bunch of numbers. If you squint at the sigma, you can see it's a kind of angular letter S with an extra zig-zag at the bottom; and since the first letter of *sum* is an s, you ought to have no trouble remembering it. It tells you to add up everything in the parentheses that follow.

The O and E in the formula are ordinary English letters. O stands for *observed*, while E stands for *expected*. "O - E" means the observed frequencies minus the expected frequencies. "$(O - E)^2/E$" means to square this and divide the result by the expected frequencies. Now the sigma comes into play: "$\Sigma((O - E)^2/E)$" means to do these calculations for each cell in the table, then sum up the results. That's what I already explained to you in words.

Now it's safe to look at the mass of numbers on the left side of Figure 6.6. At the top, in a table, you see all the calculations we have done. A glance at the two-by-two will reveal that each cell is labeled with a letter: A, B, C, D. The four rows of the table at the left are identified with these letters, one for each of the cells. The first two columns show the observed and expected frequencies. The third shows the difference, O - E. The fourth column squares these numbers, $(O - E)^2$. And the final column divides the results by the expected frequencies, $(O - E)^2/E$. For each cell in our two-by-two, this happens to be 3.33. Right below row D is the formula we have been discussing, $\Sigma((O - E)^2/E)$, followed by the sum of the four final numbers from the cells, 13.33. This is the chi-square we have been hunting.

As the previous section explained, we don't immediately stop when we get the chi-square. We have to look it up in a table to find the corresponding significance level. The computer display, on the right just below the two-by-two, saves us that effort and reports a significance of 0.001. This means there is less than one chance in a thousand that the male-female political difference in our data was merely the result of bad luck in selecting individual people to study. So, we could have pretty strong confidence in any real data that produced a two-by-two table like this.

A Second Formula for Chi-square

I should tell you that there are other formulas for calculating chi-square with two-by-two tables. One, which you will frequently see in statistics books, is

$$\chi^2 = \frac{N(AD - BC)^2}{(A + B)(C + D)(A + C)(B + D)}$$

The letter N stands for the total number of cases, in our example 120. The letters A, B, C, and D stand for the number of cases in the appropriately labeled cells of the table. Again, you see these letters in the upper-left corners of the two-by-two's cells. This formula, which is mathematically equivalent to the one we just studied, can make for easier calculation, but it ignores the concept of expected frequencies, a really key idea that I thought we should cover. I won't attempt to explain why this formula gives the same results as the earlier one, and we won't try to derive it mathematically from the other. The two formulas really do give the same results, and just to prove it, I wrote the statistics demonstration part of the program so that it calculates chi-square twice, once by each method. The "chi square: 13.33" printed right under the two-by-two was figured using this second formula, while the "$\Sigma((O - E)^2/E) =$ 13.33" on the screen was produced by the first method.

Aside from ease of calculation (and having one fewer confusing Greek letter in it!), the chief merit of the second formula is that it leads us on to the two other statistics we shall consider, phi and Q.

The middle section of the left-hand side of the computer screen (or Figure 6.6) shows how we calculate by this second method. "N = 120" tells us that the number of cases is 120. "AD" tells us to multiply the observed frequency in cell A by the observed frequency in cell D. The result is 1600, because $40 \times 40 =$ 1600. Similarly, BC = 400. And AD - BC = 1600 - 400 = 1200. Note that A + B and C + D are the two numbers at the bottom of the two-by-two, the total number of women and of men. Also, A + C and B + D are the two numbers at the right of the two-by-two, the total number of conservatives and of liberals. Running out of space on the computer screen, I let P = (A + B)(C + D)(A + C)(B + D), the product of these four numbers in the margin of the two-by-two table. The computer tells me that P = 12960000, that $(AD - BC)^2 = 1440000$, and that $N(AD - BC)^2 = 172800000$.

The following formula and calculation at the left side of the screen gives the same final result we calculated earlier:

$$\chi^2 = \frac{N(AD - BC)^2}{P} = \frac{172800000}{12960000} = 13.33$$

You can see why we let computers do our calculating for us. The example we have been working would not be too difficult to figure by hand, because it employs round numbers. The typical two-by-two, however, of which there are many in our dataset, lacks round numbers and would give us the fidgets with so many digits to figure.

Phi and Yule's Q

Although chi-square helps us decide if our results are statistically significant, it does not tell us how strong the pattern in our table is. That is a job for two other statistics, **phi** and **Yule's Q**. They are the first of several **measures of association** we will consider, coefficients that tell us the strength and direction of an association between the variables we are studying.

The *strength* of an association between two variables will be defined more precisely later in this book, but two ways of thinking about this important concept can be sketched roughly now. First, the strength of association between two variables is how strongly they influence each other or are influenced in tandem by other variables. Second, the strength of association between two variables is the extent to which knowing the category into which a case falls for one variable helps you predict which category if falls into for the other variable. Thus, one way of thinking about the strength of association between two variables is in terms of the strength of influence operating between them; the other is in terms of the information that one variable gives the researcher about the other. It makes good intuitive sense, however, to talk about how strongly two variables are related.

Measures of association express the strength of the relationship in terms of a number that can be close to zero, close to one, or in between zero and one. A number near zero expresses a very weak correlation. A number near one expresses a very strong correlation. Other numbers, between zero and one, express varying degrees of moderate association.

The **direction of an association** can be explained best with the example we have been using, a hypothetical two-by-two table about sex and politics. Suppose I tell you that more men than women tend to be conservative. This is what we call a **positive correlation**: men and conservatism go together. But suppose the research results had come out quite differently, and we found to our surprise that FEWER men than women tend to be conservative? This would be what we call a **negative correlation**: men and conservatism part company.

Measures of association express the direction of the relationship through the sign, plus or minus, that comes before the number. A plus sign says that the two variables are positively correlated, and a minus sign says that they are negatively correlated. For example, if we discovered that the correlation between being male and being conservative is +0.33, we would know there is a moderate tendency for more males than females to be conservative. The plus sign tells us that male and conservative go together. The size of the number, 0.33 in this case, suggests a moderate relationship between these two variables. Had the correlation come out - 0.33, then we would know there was a moderate tendency for males NOT to be conservative, compared to females.

So, how do we calculate some of these measures? Figure 6.6 gives us the formulas for phi and Q, two widely used measures that will help me introduce principles we shall examine in greater depth in later chapters. Phi is closely related to chi-square, as the following version of its formula makes clear:

$$\text{phi} = \frac{AD - BC}{\sqrt{(A+B)(C+D)(A+C)(B+D)}}$$

A different way to calculate phi is to divide chi-square by the number of cases and take the square root of the result. But that approach doesn't tell you the direction of the relationship, and leaves you to decide for yourself whether to put a plus or a minus in front of the result. The formula above gives you both degree and direction of the association, expressed as phi. For our hypothetical sex and politics table, the answer is +0.33.

Yule's Q, another popular measure of association, has an even simpler formula than the one for phi:

$$Q = \frac{AD - BC}{AD + BC}$$

There is no square root to worry about, and far less multiplying to do! Of course, in the modern days of computers, a measure doesn't have to be easy to calculate to make us prefer it. The point is to get the best measure for our particular research purposes, perhaps to test a particular kind of theory. Our choice of measures is crucial because the formulas for phi and Q give very different results. Although phi is 0.33, Q is 0.60 for the hypothetical sex and politics data.

Before you become exasperated and consider throwing the science of statistics out with tonight's garbage, let me quickly point out that we often have alternative ways for measuring things in ordinary life. Distance can be measured in both miles and kilometers, and soft drinks can be bottled in either quarts or liters. Many American thermometers express temperature in both Fahrenheit and Celsius. There are good reasons that phi and Q should give somewhat different results. They have somewhat different meanings.

A good way to explain this is in terms of *perfect association*, the strongest possible coefficient you can get, either +1.00 or -1.00 (Loether and McTavish 1976:198-202). To get a perfect association of 1.00 with phi, all of the cases have to be in two diagonally opposite cells of the table. For example, all of the women would have to be liberal and all of the men conservative. This is called the *restrictive definition* of perfect association. With Q, you could get 1.00 if all the women were liberal and most men were conservative, but some men were liberal, too. Q uses a less restrictive definition of perfect association. That is, Q can reach 1.00 if one of the four cells in the table is empty, while phi requires two empty cells that are diagonally opposite each other.

Think again for a moment about the elusive but crucial concepts *cause* and *effect*. When we say that eating a lot is a cause of fatness, we do not deny that fatness can have other causes, too. Lack of exercise also contributes to fatness. Assume for the moment that these are the only two factors that matter: eating too much and getting little exercise. Each can be described as a **necessary condition** for fatness. If you eat a lot but get lots of exercise, you may not get fat.

If you exercise little but avoid eating very much, you may not get fat either. So, eating too much is not in itself a **sufficient condition** for fatness. You also need to exercise little before you will get fat.

Suppose, again, that all the women were liberal, but men could be either liberal or conservative. Then being male would be a necessary condition for conservatism. But it would not be sufficient, something proven by the fact that some men are not conservative. Apparently other factors, about which we have no information, determine which men are conservative and which are liberal. Assuming for a moment, however, that no women are conservative, these other factors that are required to make men conservative have no effect on women.

You could suppose for sake of discussion that women could be either liberal or conservative but that men could only be conservative. Then being female would be a necessary but not sufficient condition for being liberal. Before you object that politics and sex don't work this way, let me quickly admit that we find very few necessary or sufficient conditions in sociology. The point of this discussion is to think about the alternative meanings that perfect association can have, to give us the basis for understanding why measures like phi and Q can give us different results.

When pressed to think of real sociological examples of necessary but not sufficient conditions, I turn to the sociology of deviance. At least as the crime of rape used to be defined, you had to be male to commit it. No women were convicted of rape, and most men were not, either. But some men were found guilty of this wicked crime, so being male was a necessary but not sufficient condition for committing rape. Also, you can't commit incest unless you have a family, because this crime involves sexual relations with certain family members. Most white-collar crimes, such as embezzlement, are violations of trust. If nobody trusts you with their money, you can't embezzle, so being entrusted with money is a necessary but not sufficient condition for embezzlement.

Can there be *sufficient but not necessary conditions?* Sure. Being convicted of homicide is a sufficient but not necessary condition for going to jail. It is sufficient (at least I hope it is!) because the authorities are bound to lock you up if you are convicted of homicide. But they'll also lock you up for other crimes, so homicide is not necessary for you to be incarcerated. Any of these crimes may be a sufficient condition for imprisonment, but none of them is necessary. Assuming our criminal justice system really is just, committing a crime is a necessary but not sufficient condition for getting imprisoned. You also have to get caught!

Finally, are there *necessary and sufficient conditions?* It is hard to think of any in sociology that aren't just tautologies. If, in our sex and politics example, all the women were liberal and all the men were conservative, then being male would be a necessary and sufficient condition for conservatism, and being female would be a necessary and sufficient condition for liberalism.

Phi reaches 1.00 only when one variable is a necessary and sufficient condition for the other. Q is more forgiving. It reaches 1.00 when one variable is a necessary condition for the other variable. It also reaches 1.00 when one variable is a sufficient condition for the other variable. Like phi, Q reaches 1.00 when one variable is both necessary and sufficient. Because it is quicker to get to 1.00, Q tends to be bigger than phi, even when the data are not close to either necessary or sufficient conditions. Which one you would be best advised to focus on, in analyzing real sociological data, depends on what kind of theory you are testing. If your theory suggests that one thing is a necessary condition for another, but not sufficient, use Q. Likewise, if the theory says one thing is sufficient for another, but not necessary, use Q. But if your theory uses a very restrictive definition of cause, asserting that one thing is both necessary and sufficient for another, then use phi.

I must admit to you, however, that many researchers use one or the other out of habit, or because it compares better with other measures they employ, or for other reasons I cannot even imagine. I have explained one good way of deciding which measure to use, and my explanation clearly shows that both phi and Q are valid ways to assess an association, even though they give somewhat different results. In later chapters we will introduce other measures that are more appropriate for tables that are bigger, with more cells and categories than the two-by-twos we consider here. Some of you will already have heard of two of them, Pearson's r and gamma. In the two-by-two table, it happens that phi and Pearson's r are the same thing, and Q and gamma are the same. Thus, learning about phi and Q here will help us understand later material as well.

Input Fresh Data for a Table

The final choice on the main menu, selected by pressing (9), allows you to put new data into the computer, creating a fresh table of your own. You do this by typing in the numbers to go into each of the four cells of the table, with the limitation that no cell frequency can be greater than 250. Sorry, those of you with data for big tables that need analyzing will just have to use a full-featured statistics package! But many two-by-twos from actual research have fewer than 250 cases in each cell, and I added this option mainly to help you learn about working with your own data and to give you the freedom to experiment with cell frequency patterns that I may not have thought to include among the test tables, and that did not happen to emerge from our historical or experimental data. Press (9) from the menu, and you will get what I show here in Figure 6.7.

Look over Figure 6.7 or your computer screen a moment. Notice that the left side of the screen has two two-by-twos, a big one and a small one, while the right side of the screen has instructions on how to enter data. The big two-by-two table is the one into which you will enter data. The small two-by-two table tells you how to select the cell you want to write in at any given moment. The big table shown in Figure 6.7 has zeros in all the cells and zeros for its marginals. If you are working at the computer, and you want to input completely new data but the table already has numbers in it, simply press (P) to purge the table of data that happen to be in it already, and every number will change to zero.

The number in one of the cells of the big table will be highlighted in a small rectangle. In Figure 6.7, this is true of the zero in the lower-left cell. This means that the computer is ready for you to type the number that should actually be in that cell. If I typed "15," for example, by pressing (1) and (5), the zero in the lower-left cell would be replaced by 15.

One of the great features of this big table is that, as you enter data in each cell, the marginals and the total will automatically change, giving you the correct figures at any point. If you start with a table full of zeros and put 15 in the lower-left cell, then the left-hand column total will also become 15, as will the lower row total and the grand total of all cases. And as you add numbers to the three other cells, the marginals and grand total will always be up-to-date. This feature allows you to keep track of all aspects of the table as it grows, perhaps adjusting some of the cell frequencies if you are seeking a particular pattern of marginals.

Once the first cell is just the way you want it, you have to move to the next cell. The small table on the screen handles this for you. Notice that it contains the letters A, B, C, and D, labeling the cells just as we do in calculating chi-square and other statistics. The computer starts you in cell A of the big table. To move to cell B, simply press (B) on the computer's keyboard. When you have finished with cell B, you might press (C) to hop over to cell C, and pressing (D) will get you into cell D. If you want to go back to a cell, just press the appropriate letter, as diagrammed in the little table. You can change numbers, as you are working on them, by pressing (BACKSPACE), and you can putter over a table as long as you want, until it is just right.

When you are through putting your data into the computer, and there are no more changes to make, press (R) to register your data. This will return you to the main menu, where you might decide to press (1) or (2) to see how the new table looks and learn the summary statistics the computer would calculate for it. If you decide the table is all wrong, and just want to give up on it, you can press (ESC) instead. If you had earlier put other data into this option, (ESC) would let you work with it again, so long as you had not registered new data subsequently. And again, pressing (P) would purge the table and turn all its numbers into zeros.

Many of you will wonder what happens if you press (ENTER). Nothing. I decided that some of you would expect to press (ENTER) after typing in each cell of the table. The computer doesn't need you to do this, however, because either hopping to a different cell or registering the table tells it quite plainly enough that you are finished typing in that cell. Some of you might guess that pressing (ENTER) would be the way you return to the main menu. Because inputting data for

FIGURE 6.7
How to Input Data

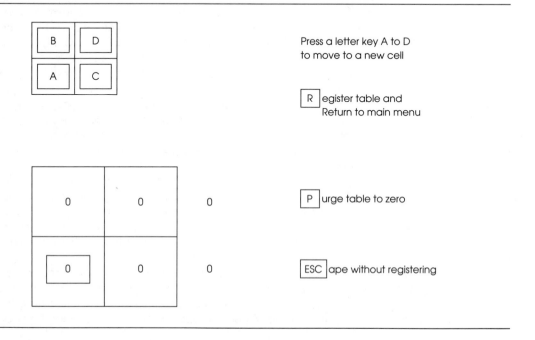

Press a letter key A to D
to move to a new cell

R | egister table and
Return to main menu

P | urge table to zero

ESC | ape without registering

a two-by-two is not exactly like anything else we have done so far in these programs, I was concerned that this was a likely spot for people to make errors. So press (ENTER) to your heart's content, or don't press it at all. It doesn't do anything.

Others will wonder why I don't use the cursor control keys, the ones with arrows on them that you first used to move around the Process chapter house and that scrolled you through the census data from Baton Rouge. Here's the problem. Many IBM-type computers, including all of the original IBM-PCs, have the cursor control keys all tangled up with number keys. To tell the computer whether you mean numbers or arrows when you press them, you must first set the "number lock" key right. But many of you are unfamiliar with computers, and others (like me!) own Apple computers or other brands that don't have this problem at all. Consequently, throughout this textbook/software package, I have avoided mixing up the number keys with the cursor control keys. Part of a program that has you type in numbers will not also require you to press the arrow keys.

As in making menu selections, I suggest you use the row of number keys up above the letters on your keyboard to input data here. Depending on your model of computer, the numbers at the right, on what we call the keypad, may be tangled up with the arrows, so I advise you to avoid them for inputting. Incidentally, as I have mentioned before, parts of my programs that do use the arrow keys do not require you to set the number lock key in any particular way. In writing my programs, I have tried to simplify control of the computer as much as possible. Some of you may not be familiar with computers, while others, like myself, are more familiar with types of keyboard other than the one IBM unfortunately foisted upon the world in 1981.

I believe the system for hopping from one cell to another will be easy for you to figure out. We have already labeled the cells with the letters A through D, and it might be good to think about them in this way for a little longer. Once you have input your fresh data, the first five options on the main menu can be used to analyze them.

Datasets for Two-by-Two Analysis

Now that you understand how to run the TABL program, we should explain the real data available for it through options 7 and 8 on the menu. These are of two kinds, historical data similar to and partly drawn from the material presented earlier in this book, and some of the experimental data from classic experiments offered in the program for the previous chapter.

Historical Data

Chapter 4 introduced us to a variety of fascinating historical data, and a number of two-by-twos derived from it are listed in Figure 6.8.

Included are data on the utopian communes of the 19th century, innovative groups that have received attention from historians and social scientists all out of proportion to their tiny populations and that have had almost negligible direct influence on the course of national events. One reason sociologists have found them interesting is that such radical communal experiments provide extreme contrast to the ordinary towns that so greatly outnumbered them, raising the issue of which features of conventional society are really necessary conditions of social life. In particular, the communes seem to have lasted for years without the institution of private property. However, essentially all of the

FIGURE 6.8
Twenty-Six Historical Tables

[A] Religion, commune lasting 10 years	[N] Building ownership, success
[B] Religion, commune lasting 20 years	[O] Communal dwellings, success
[C] Religion, commune lasting 30 years	[P] Irish-Italian, homosexuality
[D] Religion, commune lasting 40 years	[Q] Irish-Italian, sex, sin, guilt
[E] Religion, commune lasting 100 years	[R] Irish-Italian, behavior disorder
[F] Oral abstinence, success	[S] Irish-Ital., authority attitude
[G] Celibacy, success	[T] Irish-Italian, alcoholism
[H] Austerity, success	[U] Drunkenness, Irish/Massachusetts
[I] Physical participation, success	[V] Drunkenness, Irish/all USA
[J] Financial contribution, success	[W] Drunkenness, Irish/foreign
[K] Property signed over, success	[X] Drunkenness, Irish/non-Irish
[L] Property returned, success	[Y] Drunkenness, USA/non-I foreign
[M] Labor compensated, success	[Z] Drunkenness, USA/foreign

19th-century experimental communes perished, leaving open the possibility that conventional norms were, after all, the right ones for successful communities to have.

Some communes lasted much longer than others, however, and several social scientists have attempted to discover which factors were associated with their relative success. Prominent among the suspected causes of communal longevity is religion (Noyes 1870; Nordhoff 1875; Bainbridge 1985a), as we noted in Chapter 4. Two Shakers, Calvin Green and Seth Wells, wrote about the communism of their group in 1823: "Here the rich and the poor all fare alike.... It is certain that nothing short of divine wisdom could ever have devised a system of equalization, so just and equitable, and yet so contrary to the partial, aspiring and selfish nature of man" (Green and Wells 1823:62). In short: Human beings cannot achieve equality without God's direct help. Later writers, however, argued that the faith, commitment, and powerful social rituals of religion might support voluntary communism, whether the deity was actually involved in the experiment or not.

Karen H. Stephan and G. Edward Stephan (1973) tested the idea that religion contributes to longevity of a commune, using historical data about 143 American utopian communities founded between 1776 and 1900. Of these, 71 were religious in nature, while the remaining 72 were nonreligious experimental communities founded by one or another secular, socialist movement. Their original journal article reported on two variables: (1) whether or not the commune was religious, and (2) how many years the commune lasted. The first was a dichotomous variable: religious versus nonreligious. The second, longevity, was not dichotomous, but we can treat it that way. For purposes of this chapter, I went through the data on longevity of the communes, **dichotomizing** them—dividing them into two groups—in five different ways.

One time, I dichotomized the 143 communes into those that had lasted 10 years or more, versus those that had gone out of existence before their 10th birthdays. When you work with the dataset for the TABL program, you will find that one of the tables reports this dichotomization against religious/nonreligious. You will be able to see how many of the religious communes made it to their 10th birthdays, compared with the number of nonreligious communes that did so. When we pick a number, like 10 years, to be the dividing line when separating the cases into groups, we call it a **cutting point**.

Another time, I dichotomized with a 20-year cutting point. That is, I divided all the communes into those that lasted 20 years and those that died before age 20. I also dichotomized in terms of 30 years, 40 years, and 100 years. When you explore the dataset, perhaps selecting a project at the end of this chapter that asks you to work with it, you can compare results for the five different longevity cutting points I used. Is religion significantly related to success of utopian communes?

Rosabeth Kanter (1972) also studied the 19th-century American communes, but she chose to emphasize factors other than religion in explaining the longer lives of some communes. Although her full theory is rather too complex to cover here, it centers on a set of six *commitment mechanisms,* features of a commune's culture that serve to bind individuals to it. We can think about these in the following way.

Each utopian commune is like part of an experiment. The founders of the commune decide on a set of rules for life in it and provide it with a number of other features that affect commitment to that life. Then people live in this artificial society for a while, and depending partly on the way it was set up, they devote themselves to it or they abandon it. For example, the founders of a commune might or might not demand great sacrifices of the members. Listing sacrifice as the first of her commitment mechanisms, Kanter predicted that communes demanding members to sacrifice would therefore produce more commitment than communes that did not demand sacrifice.

The theoretical support for this analysis of sacrifice was Leon Festinger's *cognitive dissonance theory* from social psychology (Festinger and Carlsmith 1959). As Kanter puts it: "Sacrifice operates on the basis of a simple principle from cognitive consistency theories: the more it 'costs' a person to do something, the more 'valuable' he will consider it, in order to justify the psychic 'expense' and remain internally consistent" (Kanter 1972:76). More about the theory later. Now we will concentrate on how Kanter tested it.

Her data came from historical reports and other publications about 30 19th-century American communes. She divided them into two groups, successful and unsuccessful, in terms of how long each lasted, in about the same manner that Stephan and Stephan did their analysis. Nine of the communes (including the Shakers and Oneida, which we mentioned in Chapter 4) lasted 25 years or more, covering an entire generation of human lives. These she defined as successful. The other 21, which dissolved before their 25th birthdays, Kanter counted as unsuccessful. So, there is one of the dichotomous variables required for a two-by-two: successful versus unsuccessful.

To get the other variable, Kanter took data from the historical record. Indeed, she compiled information for dozens of other variables, several of which she considered to be indicators of sacrifice. I suppose you could study modern communes by asking members a simple question: "Does your commune require you to sacrifice a lot, or not?" But you could not do this with groups and individuals that are long gone. Instead, Kanter considered a number of the particular things that sacrifice might require a person to give up.

One thing communes commonly gave up was sexual intercourse. Have I got your attention, again? Many 19th-century communes required celibacy (abstaining from sex), at least for some period of their history. Another kind of sacrifice Kanter tabulated she called "oral abstinence." This meant abstaining from such things as alcohol, tobacco, coffee, tea, rich foods, or meat. Another kind of sacrifice was austerity in living conditions. A few communes took over comfortable existing buildings, while others made their members build their own homes, often with only the poorest raw materials. Kanter considered having to build one's own house to be a good expression of austerity.

We often refer to data like these as indicators or measures. An **indicator** is a piece of specific information that reflects a more general, underlying reality. A *measure* is essentially the same thing, in the present context. You might say celibacy is a particular kind of sacrifice; a commune that demands it is probably demanding other sacrifices as well. Oral abstinence and residential austerity are other indicators of sacrifice. These three indicators give you tables F through H among the historical two-by-twos.

Investment was the second of Kanter's commitment mechanisms. If you put something into the community—whether it be money or labor—and must stick with the community to enjoy the benefits of that investment, then you have a stake in the community and will be committed to its success. I have included tables based on five indicators of investment in our dataset. One, Kanter called "physical participation:" the requirement to live in the commune in order to be a member of it. Some communes might allow you to live in a nearby town, or even to operate your own farm in the vicinity, and yet be counted part of its grand social experiment.

The second indicator of investment was whether the commune required a financial contribution for membership. A third indicator concerned whether you signed all your property over to the commune when you joined, or whether you could retain possession of it personally. When I briefly studied the modern Love Family commune in Seattle, I was fascinated to learn that someone had joined while owning a house in Hawaii that immediately became the Hawaii branch of the cult, and the Seattle branch owned a pile of guitars that had previously belonged to people who had joined. For the Love Family, turning over property to the group meant everything from houses to guitars.

The fourth and fifth indicators of sacrifice concerned whether a defector got back some of the investment he or she had made. One concerned whether the commune returned a person's property when he or she left the cult. If a defector was paid for work done, then his or her labor was compensated. These are measures of the irreversibility of the investment, and Kanter's theory held that a person would not be so strongly committed if he or she could get part of the investment back without having to stay in the group. Thus, these two indicators of investment operate in the reverse way from the first three. If the commune demanded physical participation, financial contribution, and property transfer, then it showed evidence of the investment commitment mechanism. However, if the commune returned property and labor to defectors, Kanter saw the investment as weak.

Two other indicators having to do with communal sharing of buildings were connected to Kanter's *communion* commitment mechanism. One was simply whether the buildings were owned by the community as a whole, rather than being the property of individual members and their families. The other concerned whether members lived together in communal dwellings, somewhat like college dormitories. Kanter predicted that both kinds of residential sharing would be associated with success of the commune. We will return to the research on communes shortly, to consider special issues of two-by-two analysis, but now we must describe the other historical tables in the dataset.

In Chapter 4 we briefly discussed the proverbial connection between alcoholism and Irish ancestry, scrutinizing some data drawn from the original manuscripts of the 1860 United States census. We well return to those days of yesteryear shortly, but first we come 90 years closer to the present. Among the most influential studies of ethnicity and alcoholism in America was one Marvin K. Opler and Jerome L. Singer (1956) carried out over 30 years ago. The subjects of the research were 60 male mental patients, hospitalized in a New York City institution. All were Catholic and of similar social-class background, their ages ranging from 18 through 45. Thirty of them were Irish-Americans, and 30 were Italian-Americans. Opler and Singer scrutinized their psychiatric records and administered various psychological tests to them, trying to learn whether their different ethnic backgrounds shaped their mental problems.

Note that all 60 were considered deeply troubled, and there were no significant differences in the severity of problems between the two groups. Opler and Singer believed, however, that the men's cultural backgrounds might have given them problems of different kinds. The typical family structures in Ireland and Italy were believed to be significantly different, so that family relationships might either cause or at least color psychological disorders. Furthermore, when people face great problems, they may fall back upon the solutions their cultures favored. Thus, mental patients may struggle with their diseases in ways that reflect their ethnic backgrounds.

In keeping with psychoanalytic theories prevalent in psychiatry at the time, Opler and Singer thought that sexual difficulties might be implicated in many apparently nonsexual mental disorders, so they looked for evidence of sexual imbalance. In 54 of the 60 cases, they thought they saw evidence of homosexuality, but of two kinds. So-called *overt homosexuality* manifested itself as actual erotic acts directed at members of the same sex. *Latent homosexuality*, in contrast, did not involve real sexual behavior but merely fantasies or expressions of homosexual feelings. We should note that researchers today might not be so quick to diagnose homosexuality, and some of the evidence from psychological tests and reports of the patients' dreams might not impress skeptical researchers today. But even if Opler and Singer read too much into some of the men's acts and fantasies, they were applying the same standard of judgment to both ethnic groups, so any difference between the groups was undoubtedly real, even if we might describe it differently today.

Another sex-related bit of data concerned what can be called *sex, sin, guilt ideology*. This is a belief that many people have about sex. If you feel strongly that sexual intercourse is sinful, and thus feel guilty about your own sexual feelings, then you exhibit this belief. Can you guess which ethnic group, Irish or Italian, was more likely to possess sex, sin, guilt ideology? And

which was more apt to express homosexual feelings through overt action?

Well, of 27 Irish-Americans in whom Opler and Singer believed they could see evidence of homosexuality, all were latent and none were overt. In contrast, of 27 Italian-Americans who supposedly showed evidence of homosexuality, 20 had attempted overt homoerotic acts, while only 7 had suppressed their feelings and were merely latent. Can you deduce the pattern of sexual ideology from this? Here, Opler and Singer felt they had data on all 60 patients. Twenty-eight of the Irish-Americans, but only 9 of the Italian-Americans, felt that sex was sinful and thus suffered guilt over their own sexual feelings.

Apparently, Italian culture encouraged acting on one's sexual feelings, while Irish culture discouraged it. Two other variables in the data support this interpretation. Far more of the Italian-American mental patients were said to exhibit *behavior disorder*, which I like to define as the "disease" of behaving in ways doctors dislike. In contrast, the Irish-Americans were far more often described as *compliant to authority*. That is, the Italian-American patients disturbed the quiet routine the hospital staff preferred, while the Irish-Americans did pretty much what they were told.

Finally, we return to the topic of our 1860 data, alcoholism. Although only one of the Italian-American mental patients had evidence of prior problems with alcohol in his hospital records, nearly two-thirds of the Irish-American patients did. One interpretation among many is that Irish culture represses free expression of emotions, and that under stress Irish people turn to the bottle.

All of the variables in the Opler and Singer dataset are dichotomous. The 60 mental patients are divided into two groups: Irish and Italian. Each of the five personality and behavior characteristics divides the 60 into a different pair of categories—alcoholic versus nonalcoholic, for example.

Our alcoholism data from the 1860 census, like the final tables from some of our more complex experiments, divide the data into more

FIGURE 6.9
Twenty-Six Experiment Tables

[A] Work rate, 2 phase	[N] Voting age, change 2-3
[B] Work rate, 2 groups	[O] Stigma, no record or judge note
[C] Therapy, non-random, test 1	[P] Stigma, no record or acquitted
[D] Therapy, non-random, test 2	[Q] Stigma, no record or convicted
[E] Therapy, non-random, test 3	[R] Ex-cons, job help/control
[F] Therapy, attrition, test 1	[S] Ex-cons, taxed $$$/control
[G] Therapy, attrition, test 2	[T] Ex-cons, untaxed $$$/control
[H] Therapy, attrition, test 3	[U] Slow communication, Y
[I] Delinquency policy, test 1	[V] Slow communication, chain
[J] Delinquency policy, test 2	[W] Slow communication, circle
[K] Delinquency policy, test 3	[X] Communication error, Y
[L] Voting age, test 2	[Y] Communication error, chain
[M] Voting age, test 3	[Z] Communication error, circle

than just two categories. I have selected two-by-two comparisons that should be of interest. Four of the tables compare Irish-born with people born in places other than Ireland. One compares Irish with natives of Massachusetts. Another compares them with natives of all the United States. Another compares Irish-born with persons born in other foreign countries, and the last compares Irish-born with everybody else, U.S.-born plus non-Irish foreign-born. Finally, a table compares U.S.-born with these non-Irish foreign-born, and another compares U.S.-born with all foreign-born, Irish included.

Earlier in this chapter, I urged you to be cautious about statistical significance when the data analysis examined a large number of tables and only a few reached a weak level of significance. Here, of course, my purpose was to provide you with lots of material for exploration, but there was an underlying theoretical question that makes a couple of these comparisons worth examining. If Irish levels of alcoholism were high, was that because they were Irish or simply because they were immigrants? If you wish, you can consider this more closely for one of the projects at the end of this chapter.

Experimental Data

The final set of two-by-two tables included in your software were derived from the experiments in the previous program. Thus, the research studies and the variables have been discussed thoroughly already, and there is no need to reconsider them here. Figure 6.9 lists the 26 tables of experimental data. If you read the previous chapter closely, you should have no difficulty telling which is which. For some of the more complex experiments, I have included only the most interesting comparisons. If you want, however, you can use the data input option of the TABL program to enter other comparisons you might want to check for statistical significance. The experimental data included in this program came from replications I ran myself, so if you want to analyze data from your own replications, you will have to input them yourself.

Analytical Caution

If quantitative research were very easy, dozens of sociologists wouldn't get to write textbooks on how to do it. There are a couple of potential traps I should tell you about, which are well illustrated by the historical data on 19th-century communes.

The analysis of statistical significance, using chi-square, is based on a few simple assumptions. One of them is that the cases are completely independent of each other. For the Stephan and Stephan data, however, this may not be true. Here I am not accusing them of doing anything wrong in their research, but I have intentionally misused their data slightly in order to make the following point.

The dataset does not really contain information about 143 communes. Some of them are really the same commune under different names. Take Oneida, for example. The main branch was at Oneida, New York, but there was a substantial satellite commune in Wallingford, Connecticut. Stephan and Stephan not only listed both separately among their 143; they also counted the original, temporary setup in Vermont. So, in a sense, there were not 143 communes but only 141 (subtracting the Connecticut and Vermont aspects of Oneida), and only 69 rather than 71 religious communes, because Oneida was in this category.

But that's not all. Included among the 143 were a slew of Shaker communities, all descended from the movement Ann Lee established two centuries ago near Albany. Indeed, if you count the Shakers only as one case, the number of communes that lasted a century drops from 13 to 2, because it included a dozen Shaker colonies along with the Harmony commune. On top of that, the list considers separately all the fragments of two short-lived socialist movements, the Owenites and Fourierists, that happened to be set up in different locations. Kanter considered the Shakers as just one case and Oneida as one other case. However, her short list of 30 counts 3 Fourierist and 4 Owenite communes as separate cases, because they had been founded by somewhat separate groups of people within these two social movements.

Before we could have great confidence in the statistical significance of the findings in the study by Stephan and Stephan, we would have to go through the list of communes carefully

and cross out any duplications, so that, for example, Oneida and the Shakers might be represented as single cases. Before this, however, we would have to use good judgment and sociological theory to decide how separate two communes had to be before we considered them really independent. After cleaning out the list in this way, chi-square could give us a proper estimate of the statistical significance of the power of religion to strengthen utopian communities.

If you want an example that clarifies why we need the cases to be independent, imagine that we had carefully tabulated data on 100 communes of the 1960s and had a preliminary table that showed no difference between religious and nonreligious communes in their capacity to survive until the 1980s. Then we added the Process, described in Chapters 2 and 3. But say we didn't add it as just one case of a religious commune that lasted. Suppose we counted each location where the Process was ever established as a separate case. Frankly, I don't know how many different places the Process visited for a time, but the list includes London (England), New Orleans, Nassau (Bahamas), the Yucatán (Mexico), Cambridge (Massachusetts), Waltham (Massachusetts), New York City, Washington (D.C.), Los Angeles, Chicago, San Francisco, Toronto, Rome (Italy), Paris (France), Munich (Germany), and perhaps a few dozen other locations. Pretty soon, our table would be loaded up with "cases" of successful religious communes, and the chi-square would indicate a statistically significant tendency for religion to be associated with success. But, of course, the Process "cases" we added would not be independent of each other, so the independence assumption of chi-square would be violated.

Another problem you should be alert for is that the ordinary chi-square distributions published at the backs of ordinary statistics textbooks, and incorporated in our computer program, may not be accurate for some tables. As a rule of thumb, the ordinary chi-square distribution is not right if the expected frequency for one of the cells of the table is less than five. Our TABL program watches for this problem and puts a message under the table warning you if the expected frequency in any cell is less than five. If this happens, the chi-square and the estimate of statistical significance reported will not be accurate. Indeed, they could be very wrong.

Note that the table of data could have a cell with fewer than five cases without causing any trouble. Indeed, a perfect 1.00 phi requires that two diagonally opposite cells have zeros in them. The problem is with the expected frequencies, not the observed frequencies. In general, sociologists perform an uncharacteristic research act when this happens to one of their tables—they give up. Under some circumstances, it may still be possible to salvage the analysis by using modified chi-square distributions or other means, but I urge you to be extremely cautious about evaluating the statistical significance of any tables where cells have expected frequencies less than five. Usual chi-square tests of significance are certainly not appropriate in such circumstances.

Finally, we have to talk about cause and effect again. In the previous chapter, there was seldom any question about which of two variables was cause and which effect. The experimental manipulation was always the independent variable (cause), and the difference measured between groups at the end concerned the dependent variable (effect). Indeed, the great strength of experimental methods, we said, was their capacity to identify cause and

effect unambiguously. But this is not true of other methodologies.

Consider Kanter's *sacrifice* commitment mechanism. She says that people become committed to a commune *because* they have sacrificed for it. Doesn't this sound backward? It seems more reasonable to say that people sacrifice to a commune because they are committed. Thus, Kanter makes sacrifice the independent variable and commitment the dependent variable. I am suggesting, however, that commitment is the independent variable and sacrifice the dependent variable. Kanter's position is far from absurd, and some psychology experiments done in laboratories indicate that things can work the way she says. However, my view is at least as plausible. Can you find out which of us is right, using some of our two-by-two tables based on her data? No. Sorry, you can't. As we said earlier, correlation does not prove causation.

If we abandon the naive optimism that a scientific study can conclusively prove a theory to be true, then we are not too unhappy to learn that correlation does not prove causation. Correlations in line with a theory do strongly support it, even though we can imagine other reasons for them than the causal relationships we hypothesized. Of course, we will always look for other ways to test a theory, and we will constantly attempt to invent other theories to test. Although science may never give us the final answer to our questions, it is the best means known for improving our reliable understanding of the world and for reducing our ignorance.

PROJECTS FOR CHAPTER 6

The six projects outlined below give you practice working with two-by-two quantitative tables, both to gain experience with some simple statistical measures and to see how hypotheses can be tested quantitatively with data. The first three projects emphasize statistical significance (measured via chi-square), phi, and Yule's Q. The fourth and fifth projects employ real historical data taken from studies discussed in Chapter 4, and the sixth uses simulated experimental data from runs of the program described in Chapter 5. You will use the TABL program for all of them.

1. Statistical Significance and the Number of Cases. Other things being equal, the more cases there are in your dataset the easier it will be for patterns to achieve statistical significance. Test tables H through N, included in the dataset of two-by-twos, were designed to let you examine this principle. Table H is based on fully 240 cases, while table N has only 30, and the ones in-between have various intermediary numbers of cases. But all of these tables have exactly the same patterns in terms of the percent of cases in each cell. That is, the strength and degree of the correlations between the two variables are the same for all seven of these tables. Check the chi-square and significance for each of these tables, and write a brief report discussing the impact of the number of cases on statistical significance of your results. You may wish to include test tables X, Y, and Z in your analysis as well.

2. Strength and Degree of Statistical Relationships. Although test tables A through G all contain 120 cases, the distribution of these cases in the cells differs tremendously across this set of seven. Examine the statistics for each of these tables, especially phi and Yule's Q, and write a brief report explaining how the tables differ and stating what the statistics say about the relationship between the two variables in each of these tables.

3. Comparison of Phi and Yule's Q. Test tables O through W (plus tables A, D, and G) provide good material for exploring the differences between phi and Yule's Q. Examine the statistical analysis for each of these tables, and discuss in a brief report how phi and Q differ in what they say about each of these tables. When do phi and Q give the same result? When does one of them reach 1.00, while the other lags behind? Which one tends to be bigger? Why?

4. Explaining Success and Failure among 19th-century Communes. Using the data from the study by Stephan and Stephan and the study by Kanter, explore the question of which factors gave strength to the utopian communities. In addition to tables of data, your analysis should include six pages (typewritten, double-spaced) of discussion. This discussion should highlight the differences you find between communes with various features (commitment mechanisms), but it should also mention any limitations to your statistical analysis, such as those outlined in this chapter.

5. The Myth of the Drunken Irishman. Using the data in historical two-by-two tables P through Z, explore whether or not there is a significant statistical correlation between alcoholism and being Irish. Consider the following alternative hypothesis: Alcoholism is caused not by being Irish, specifically, but by being a member of an immigrant ethnic group. Can you test this alternative hypothesis with the data provided? Write a report to accompany your tables of statistical analysis.

6. Statistical Significance in Convict Research. The experiment about stigmatization of ex-cons and the TARP experiment, both discussed in the previous chapter, gave results that showed differences between various groups. Use the TABL program to analyze the statistical significance of these differences, and write a brief report stating which turned out to be significant and which were not. Six of the tables you will need are already included in this program, experimental-data tables O through T, but you may want to replicate the actual experiments, copy down any other two-by-two comparisons you want to check, and enter these data with the input option.

CHAPTER SUMMARY

Dichotomies, divisions of things into a pair of categories, are very useful tools of sociological analysis with both qualitative and quantitative research methods. Two-by-two tables are based on simultaneous analysis in terms of two dichotomies. Among the most influential two-by-two tables is the infamous Johari Window, a model for illustrating self-disclosure in groups. Robert K. Merton's typology of modes of adaptation and anomie can be understood in a new way by casting it as a two-by-two table. Similarly, we can understand Friedrich Nietzsche's classical theory of cultures, which classifies people and societies as either Apollonian (cool) or Dionysian (warm), as a pair of qualitative dichotomies.

The TABL program teaches the first steps in quantitative analysis, introducing simple statistics including chi-square, phi, and Yule's Q. It displays a two-by-two table containing data the student selects or types in. *Marginals* are the numbers around the edge of the table, reporting how many cases fall into each half of each dichotomy. The *cells* of a table are the boxes inside it that report how many cases are in each intersection of categories. *Frequencies* are the numbers of cases in each category, either marginals or the numbers of cases in each cell of the table. *Column percents* are percentages calculated within each column of figures, whereas *row percents* are calculated for each row.

This chapter introduces the concept of statistical significance for the first time. *Statistical significance* means that a certain pattern in the data was unlikely to have come about by mere chance. An important tool for determining statistical significance is the *chi-square distribution.* The TABL program illustrates this clearly by producing as many as 1000 tables of random data, giving the chi-square for each, to compare with the pattern and chi-square from a table of real data. For example, we see that about 50 times out of 1000, purely random data will give us a chi-square that is significant at the .05 level.

The chapter and the TABL program both show how simple it is to calculate chi-square. The key concept is a comparison, for each cell, of the *expected frequency* and the *observed frequency.* Understanding two ways of calculating chi-square makes it easy to see how phi and Yule's Q are calculated. Phi and Yule's Q are *measures of association,* coefficients that tell us the strength and direction of an association between the variables we are studying. Phi employs the *restrictive definition* of perfect association, while Q is more permissive in defining a perfect correlation of 1.00. We understand the difference between phi and Q through the concepts of *necessary condition* and *sufficient condition* of a cause for an effect. Phi reaches 1.00 only when one variable is a necessary and sufficient condition for the other. Q is more forgiving, reaching 1.00 when one variable is a necessary condition for the other variable; it need not be sufficient.

Datasets available for the TABL program include a number of "test pattern" tables, historical data related to Chapter 4, and experimental data related to Chapter 5. There is also an option to type in fresh data of the student's own choice. Discussion of these data introduces the concepts of *cutting point, indicator, measure,* and the *independence* of cases.

K E Y   C O N C E P T S   F O R   C H A P T E R   6

Survey Research

CHAPTER OVERVIEW

This chapter introduces methods of question-naire writing and survey research. It illustrates several survey formats such as fixed-choice items, agree-disagree (Likert) items, preference scales, semantic differential, screening questions, and contingent questions. Techniques of administration include mailed surveys, door-to-door interviews, telephone surveys, and CATI (Computer-Assisted Telephone Interviewing). We learn that researchers are seldom able to survey entire populations, but instead must employ a variety of samples: purposive, convenience, snowball, quota,

simple random, systematic, categorical, stratified random, proportional, cluster, and multistage. Ways of evaluating the quality of survey results include response rate and margin of error.

Much research using survey data is done by people other than those who created and administered the original questionnaire. Often this is called *secondary analysis*, which Hyman (1972:1) defines as "the extraction of knowledge on topics other than those which were the focus of the original surveys." Generally, the same skills and knowledge are required for secondary analysis as for original survey studies. Although you do not get to write the questions or select the sample of respondents, you need to understand these matters thoroughly, or you may commit serious errors in using data that reflect the responses of a particular sample to a set of questions. It is not just a matter of whether to trust the original researchers or not, whether to accept their items and data, but how to evaluate what new uses the dataset may properly be put to.

The SAMP program simulates the creation, administration, and analysis of a questionnaire survey to as many as 500 respondents in each of eight different cities, with features that illustrate principles of random sampling. Based on a famous study of juvenile delinquency by criminologist Travis Hirschi, this survey gives very realistic results, both in percentages and in two-by-two tables. You can select items from a list of 40 to test several different theories and compare results from any number of different samples.

Varieties of Questions

You will get to do some secondary analysis shortly, using a computer program that simulates administering a questionnaire to random samples of respondents. Although you will not be able to write your own items, you will have the power to select which of a long list will be included. In principle, however, the first step in survey research is creating a set of questions that will survey your sociological purposes.

Fixed-choice Formats

The variety of questions that have been used in surveys is practically infinite, although a few types have been used widely in many research projects and will repay examination here. First of all, not all the "questions" in surveys have a question mark at the end. Some present the respondent with a statement and request him or her to judge it, perhaps by expressing personal agreement or disagreement. Therefore, it can be misleading to talk exclusively about the "questions" in a survey, and we often use the term *item* to refer to each little part of the survey that collects one bit of data for the researcher.

Chapter 3 noted the difference between open-ended items, which lead the respondent to provide spontaneous answers from one word to many words in length, and closed-ended items, which offer a short list of preset choices to select from in giving the answer. Although our discussion of interviewing said much about open-ended items, our focus here will be on the closed-ended type, also called fixed-choice or forced-choice. The typical item of this type offers the respondent boxes to check. Here's one from a survey done by my colleagues Charles Y. Glock and Rodney Stark (1966):

Which, if any, of the following magazines do you read regularly? Check each one which you regularly read.

[ ] Reader's Digest
[ ] Saturday Evening Post
[ ] Ladies Home Journal
[ ] Time
[ ] Newsweek
[ ] Saturday Review of Literature
[ ] Christian Century
[ ] Life
[ ] American Legion Magazine
[ ] New Republic
[ ] Esquire
[ ] Others _____ (please write in)

An item that asks the respondent to select from a list of various distinct alternatives, like this list of magazines, is called a **menu item**. There are many ways you can make use of such data. For example, if you wanted to know which respondents were avid readers of magazines, you could go through the questionnaire and count how many magazines each person read. Or, if you were interested in a particular magazine, you could focus just on whether people read that one or not. For example, you might have been employed by Time, Incorporated, to do market research on its magazines, *Time* and *Life*. So you would see how many people read each of those two magazines, and probably look at various subgroups among respondents to see which of them were especially likely to read *Time* and *Life*. Also, you might want to compare the figures for *Time* with those of its chief rival, *Newsweek*.

Note that this particular item allows the respondent to check any number of boxes, from none up through the total number provided. This is quite appropriate, given the nature of the question, but more often researchers ask the respondent to check just one box. This prevents vacillating respondents from hedging their replies, and makes it far easier to handle the data. In a sense, the excerpt from the Glock and Stark questionnaire, above, is really 12 items, and that is how the researchers treated it. Each magazine is a separate question: Do you read *Time?* Do you read *Newsweek?* Once the answers to these 12 check-a-box questions are in the computer, you can ask the machine to count how many magazines each person reads, saving you the labor.

Here's another example from the Glock and Stark questionnaire:

What is your favorite kind of television program? Place an X in the right hand column beside the kind of TV program you like *best*. Then in the left hand column, put an X by the kind of program you like *least*.

	Like least (one only)	Like best (one only)
Westerns	[ ]	[ ]
Comedies	[ ]	[ ]
Drama	[ ]	[ ]
Detective	[ ]	[ ]
Movies	[ ]	[ ]
Popular music	[ ]	[ ]
Variety shows	[ ]	[ ]
Symphony and concert music	[ ]	[ ]
Religious programs	[ ]	[ ]
Panel shows	[ ]	[ ]
News	[ ]	[ ]
Current events	[ ]	[ ]
Sports	[ ]	[ ]
Quiz	[ ]	[ ]

In a sense, this is a set of 14 questionnaire items, one for each of the 14 kinds of television program. Seen that way, each of the 14 items has three possible answers: like lease, like best, and like neither least nor best. From another perspective, this is just 2 items. One asks for the respondent's favorite kind of TV program, the other for the least-liked kind of program. What Glock and Stark were really interested in was the response given for religious programs, because their study concerned American religion. A different way they could have asked would have been with agree-disagree items, like the following:

Please check the appropriate box to indicate how much you agree or disagree with the following statements:

1. In the long run, discoveries made in our space program will have a big payoff for the average person.

    [ ] Strongly Agree [ ] Agree
    [ ] Not sure [ ] Disagree
    [ ] Strongly Disagree

2. The United States is spending too much money on space, so appropriations for the space program should be reduced.

    [ ] Strongly Agree [ ] Agree
    [ ] Not sure [ ] Disagree
    [ ] Strongly Disagree

3. I like *Newsweek* magazine better than *Time*.

    [ ] Strongly Agree [ ] Agree
    [ ] Not sure [ ] Disagree
    [ ] Strongly Disagree

4. I like *Time* magazine better than *Newsweek*.

    [ ] Strongly Agree   [ ] Agree
    [ ] Not sure   [ ] Disagree
    [ ] Strongly Disagree

5. I read many magazines each week.

    [ ] Strongly Agree   [ ] Agree
    [ ] Not sure   [ ] Disagree
    [ ] Strongly Disagree

6. By and large, my favorite kind of TV show is religious programs.

    [ ] Strongly Agree   [ ] Agree
    [ ] Not sure   [ ] Disagree
    [ ] Strongly Disagree

The first of these items, which Irene Taviss (1972) created for a survey on attitudes toward technology, has proven very useful in my research on the space program (Bainbridge 1986:159). You cannot place too much weight on single agree-disagree items, because responses to them may partly reflect whether the respondent is an agreeable person. Chapter 3 discussed possible biases that can arise in interviews, and we have to worry about biases with pencil-and-paper questionnaires as well. **Response bias** is the tendency of a respondent to answer questions in a particular way, regardless of what the question specifically is about. A very common bias is **acquiescence**, the tendency of a respondent to agree or disagree with whatever a survey item says, regardless of its content. A tendency to agree is called **yea-saying**, and a tendency to disagree is called **nay-saying**. (Couch and Keniston 1960, Block 1965, Berg 1967).

One way to handle acquiescence is to include statements of essentially opposite meaning in your list of agree-disagree items. Although the first statement in the set of six, above, expresses support for the space program, the second expresses lack of support. You can compare how each of these items correlates with others in the questionnaire, and if the pattern is the same (except that the directions of the associations are opposite), then you can be confident that acquiescence is not fouling up your results.

The third and fourth statements in the list of six are exact opposites. Logically, someone cannot agree with both of them, and you should be suspicious of any respondent who did. Items that are such perfect opposites of each other should be used sparingly, for two reasons. First of all, they can waste a lot of space in the questionnaires; and they require the respondent to spend more time on the survey, because for each topic you are interested in you must insert two items rather than just one. But worse than that, respondents get upset when they encounter obvious duplication like this, concluding that the researcher does not trust them (true!) and complaining at the waste of their time. If you have a very long list of items, you can separate two like this, perhaps by several pages, so the respondent probably will not notice. Such items provide very direct measurement of acquiescence bias, information that may be useful in evaluating a respondent's replies to other items as well.

The fifth item, about reading many magazines, is probably a bad question. People undoubtedly differ in their definition of "many magazines," and those who read only one or two may feel that two are many. Also, the item probably hints that people should read a lot of magazines, and it implies a comparison with how much other people read. To appear sophisticated and intelligent, the respondent may check an agree box, regardless of how many magazines he or she actually reads. The Glock and Stark method, making respondents commit themselves about a list of specific publications, probably gets more valid answers. The tendency of a respondent to give socially acceptable answers to questions, putting himself or herself in a good light, is called **social desirability bias** (Crowne and Marlow 1960, Edwards 1967, Phillips and Clancy 1972).

The last of the six agree-disagree items attempts to get the information Glock and Stark wanted about religious TV programs. Probably, more people would agree with it than would check "religious programs" as their favorite in the Glock and Stark questionnaire. Because their survey focused heavily on religion, Glock and Stark worried that the church members who were their respondents would automatically express enthusiasm for religious programming; so their approach sought to reduce this tendency a bit by surrounding religious programs with more than a dozen other alternatives. Undoubtedly the people who told Glock and Stark that religious programs were their favorite were very keen on this type of show, and identifying these people was the job the researchers wanted done.

Agree-disagree items are often called Likert items, after Rensis Likert, the social scientist who developed systematic methods for using them. As with many other types of items, when writing agree-disagree items you have to decide what the fixed responses should be. You must decide how finely to measure agreement and disagreement. You could just offer two boxes, labeled Agree and Disagree, or six boxes, labeled Strongly Agree, Slightly Agree, Agree, Disagree, Slightly Disagree, Strongly Disagree, or some other number with perhaps different adverbs describing the degrees of agreement. Partly, this may depend upon how salient the phenomenon under study is to the respondents. If they have very clear opinions about it, then perhaps they can handle several response choices expressing fine degrees of feeling.

You also must decide whether to have a middle box, perhaps labeled Not Sure or Neutral. Because a middle box can serve as a cop-out for respondents who are reluctant to express an opinion, some researchers avoid using it, preferring to force their respondents to take a stand on the issue. On the other hand, neutrality and uncertainty are quite possible attitudes to hold. If a respondent doesn't know how he or she feels, or is quite sure that he or she doesn't care about the topic in question, forcing agreement or disagreement is artificial.

One of the most troublesome problems in writing check-the-box questionnaire items is how to handle "don't know" and "no opinion." Questions that are written to encourage these responses will elicit far more of them than questions written to discourage them. Howard Schuman and Stanley Presser (1978) conducted a series of experiments to investigate this, administering alternative versions of several questions in a series of questionnaires. For example, one question asked respondents whether they agreed or disagreed with the following statement: "The Russian leaders are basically trying to get along with America." About one respondent in seven (15.2 percent) responded "don't know," even though this choice had not been offered to them. A different version of the survey asked the question thus: "Not everyone has opinions on these questions. If you do not have an opinion, just say so. 'The Russian leaders are basically trying to get along with America.' Do you have an opinion on that?" This version encouraged respondents to admit they had no opinion, and more than a third (37.6 percent) did so.

My habit, in the many surveys I have done using agree-disagree items, is to use five responses, including a neutral one in the middle. The researcher must decide, however, on the basis of past experience and guesses about how respondents will react to the topics of the survey.

Preference Scales

Another common item type is the preference scale, usually in the form of a set of numbers from which the respondent selects one to express how much he or she likes a particular thing. A **scale** is an item or combination of items that measures a respondent characteristic along a graduated series of points, usually assumed to be equal distances apart. We will make extensive use of this type in later chapters. Here is how we might write preference items for the kinds of TV program:

Following are several kinds of television programs. Please tell us how much you generally like each one. After each one, circle the number that indicates how much you like it. Circle "0" if you do not like that kind of program at all. Circle "6" if you like it very much—as much as you possibly could. Otherwise, circle the number in-between that best expresses how much you like the particular kind of TV program.

Westerns	0 1 2 3 4 5 6
Comedies	0 1 2 3 4 5 6
Drama	0 1 2 3 4 5 6
Detective	0 1 2 3 4 5 6
Movies	0 1 2 3 4 5 6
Popular music	0 1 2 3 4 5 6
Variety shows	0 1 2 3 4 5 6
Symphony and concert music	0 1 2 3 4 5 6
	0 1 2 3 4 5 6
Religious programs	0 1 2 3 4 5 6
Panel shows	0 1 2 3 4 5 6
News	0 1 2 3 4 5 6
Current events	0 1 2 3 4 5 6
Sports	0 1 2 3 4 5 6
Quiz	0 1 2 3 4 5 6

To give just a hint of how we can analyze responses to such items, let us look at how 1,439 college students rated four kinds of popular literature, two movies, and two TV shows; these data come from my study of the ideologies of science fiction (Bainbridge 1986:178). Figure 7.1

shows how the students responded, dividing them into the 48 percent who were female and the 52 percent who were male. The form of the preference items was exactly as I have just described, and the table gives the mean (average) response on the 0 to 6 scale, along with the percent who gave high ("5" or "6") responses. Female students on average rated "best-selling novels" about a point higher than did men, and they rated "stories of love and romance" almost two points higher. These are huge differences between the sexes in their preferences for these genres of popular literature. The ratings were about the same for "spy and detective novels," while men rated "science fiction novels" two points higher than did women.

The purpose of these four questions was to learn if men really did like science fiction, on average, better than women, something that people who worked in this field of literature constantly asserted. But if I just asked people to say how much they liked "science fiction novels," I wouldn't know if the differences I found sprang from differences in attitudes toward "science fiction" or toward "novels." Thus, I had to include items about other types of novels, and together the data from these four items confirm that science fiction appeals to more men than women.

FIGURE 7.1
Preferences by 1,439 College Students

	Mean Preference		Percent High Score	
	Women	Men	Women	Men
POPULAR LITERATURE				
Best-selling novels	4.12	3.14	44.2	20.2
Stories of love and romance	4.06	2.20	45.4	6.7
Spy and detective novels	3.08	3.27	24.2	25.1
Science fiction novels	1.42	3.58	6.8	35.6
MOTION PICTURES				
Star Wars	4.68	4.98	63.7	71.3
Close Encounters	4.11	4.40	49.6	55.2
TELEVISION PROGRAMS				
Star Trek	3.73	4.55	42.2	60.2
Battlestar Galactica	3.00	3.45	25.8	32.6

Of course, some women like science fiction quite a lot, and a chapter of my book on science fiction looked at the recent importance of women writers in the field. The third column of Figure 7.1 show that 6.8 percent of the women gave science fiction novels a high rating of "5" or "6" on the 0-to-6 preference scale. Although this is far less than the 35.6 percent of the men, it confirms that some women are SF fans. This fact, in turn, should remind us that averages and similar summary statistics express a general tendency and do not apply to all the cases.

Perhaps you have heard the term *sci-fi*, which Forrest J. Ackerman coined in the 1950s by analogy with *hi-fi* (high fidelity music recordings). Although many people use this term to refer to science fiction, dedicated science fiction fans and the professionals who produce it despise *sci-fi* and prefer *SF* instead. For them, *sci-fi* means junky, popular movies and TV shows that steal their ideas from SF literature. But whatever the prejudices of SF fans against it, *sci-fi* is probably more popular than *SF*, which means it reaches a wider audience. Thus, we might expect the sex differences in preferences for sci-fi movies and TV shows to be less than those for SF literature. That is exactly what the bottom part of Figure 7.1 reveals. On average, the sci-fi is more popular than are science fiction novels, and the sex differences are less.

The Semantic Differential

To show the variety of ways in which scale items can be created, we will consider one more commonly used format, the pair of opposites. This format achieves its greatest influence through an approach to the measurement of meaning called the **semantic differential**, invented by Charles E. Osgood (Osgood, Suci, and Tannenbaum 1957; Osgood, May, and Miron 1975; Osgood 1976). If you were using this technique to study respondents' feelings toward religious TV shows, you might include a questionnaire section like this:

Think, for a moment, about RELIGIOUS TELEVISION PROGRAMS. Perhaps you frequently watch this kind or program, or perhaps you seldom do. But, in either case you must have some image of what these shows are like. With this image in mind, go through the following twelve pairs of opposite words, deciding where RELIGIOUS TELEVISION PROGRAMS are, on the scale between each pair of extremes. For each pair of opposites, circle the ONE number that best describes the image you have.

Good	7	6	5	4	3	2	1	Bad
Beautiful	7	6	5	4	3	2	1	Ugly
Nice	7	6	5	4	3	2	1	Awful
Honest	7	6	5	4	3	2	1	Dishonest
Large	7	6	5	4	3	2	1	Small
Strong	7	6	5	4	3	2	1	Weak
Heavy	7	6	5	4	3	2	1	Light
Rugged	7	6	5	4	3	2	1	Delicate
Sharp	7	6	5	4	3	2	1	Dull
Hot	7	6	5	4	3	2	1	Cold
Active	7	6	5	4	3	2	1	Passive
Fast	7	6	5	4	3	2	1	Slow

This might fill a page of your questionnaire, and the next page could include the same set of 12 scales but ask the respondent to judge SCIENCE FICTION TELEVISION PROGRAMS or some other shows of interest to you. You would then be able to compare how the respondents tended to describe programs of different kinds. A few days before I wrote these lines, a TV evangelist was convicted on charges of financial fraud, and many people have come to doubt the honesty of religious TV programs. By the time you read this, a measure of trust in religious broadcasters may have been reestablished, but can anybody trust science fiction? Does *Star Trek* present an honest or a dishonest view of the human future? Your analysis would not be limited to comparing the two kinds of television on each of the twelve items, because a general theory underlies them.

Using statistical procedures like those described in Chapter 14, Osgood found that these

12 items measured three different dimensions of human meaning. The first was *evaluation,* represented by good-bad, beautiful-ugly, true-false, and kind-cruel. A *potency* dimension emerged in such distinctions as hard-soft, strong-weak, heavy-light, and masculine-feminine. And an *activity* dimension revealed itself in scales like fast-slow, active-passive, and excitable-calm. Thus, following procedures explained at the end of this book (in Chapter 14), you could combine items expressing a particular dimension of meaning and compare types of TV shows along the dimension.

Writing Your Own Survey Questions

"Ask a silly question," the old saying goes, "and you'll get a silly answer." This maxim applies nowhere more forcefully than in questionnaire surveys. Unless you ask the right questions, phrased in the right manner, you will fail to learn what you need to know. A few really bad questions can ruin an entire questionnaire, because they may confuse or anger the respondents so much that they fail to respond properly to the well-designed questions. To a certain extent, question-writing is an art, but we can offer a few points as reasonable guidance for creating your own questionnaire items.

Avoid knee-jerk items. A **knee-jerk item** is one that elicits an almost automatic, conventional response from most respondents. Proverbially, everybody is supposed to be in favor of motherhood and apple pie, and even apple-haters may check the "yes" box when asked, "Do you like apple pie?" If you really want to learn respondents' pie preferences, you may have to embed an item about apple pie in a series of questions: "On a scale from 0 to 10, how much do you like . . . pumpkin pie, cherry pie, custard pie, apple pie, mince pie . . ." Even some very standard questions, frequently employed in professional surveys, may produce knee-jerk responses from many people. For example, most Americans profess to believe in

God, and there seems considerable social pressure to profess faith even if, in fact, one does not have it.

For example, Demerath and Levinson (1971) asked 62 introductory sociology students at the University of Wisconsin if they believed in God, and 53 of them said "yes." But the researchers also had the students answer a question asking them to pick one of five rather complex views about God. In response to this second question, none of the 53 "believers" checked the box saying: "When one speaks of a god or a supernatural, one speaks of an illusion. I do not believe in a god. I do not believe in a supernatural." If any had chosen this alternative, we would have to worry about the validity of this survey or the respondents' reading skills, because this choice would directly contradict the students' claim to believe in God.

However, 6 of the 53 "believers" picked the following vague reply: "The notion of a supernatural force is unclear and perhaps false. Yet this concept has helped to account for man's creativity, man's accomplishments, and man's love." And another 9 chose this view: "Whether or not there are powers of a higher nature than man should be pondered. But to know the answer for sure one might have to be a supernatural himself." Thus, 15 of the 53 who claimed to believe in God while responding to a simply phrased, knee-jerk item, revealed little faith when offered more complex alternatives. The remaining 38 were probably real believers rather than mere knee-jerkers, because they checked the box for one of the following two replies: "That a God exists is unquestionable since His spirit and His works are directly experienced by all of us." "Although one can never receive any real evidence of Him, I have no doubts of God's existence."

Another piece of advice is to be sparing in your use of questions about controversial matters. If there are too many, the respondent will throw down the questionnaire and stamp on it. Short of that, irritation with the survey may cause him or her to start giving capricious answers. Introduce items about controversial matters in such a way that each response will seem socially acceptable. One traditional method has been to insert little phrases into the question or responses implying that reasonable and respectable people might give any of the answers. Here's an item developed years ago by that master of survey research, James A. Davis (1961:33):

Which of the following comes closest to the way you think about yourself?

[1] I don't like the phrase particularly, but I guess you'd have to call me an "intellectual."

[2] I consider myself an educated person, but not really an "intellectual."

[3] I haven't had too much education, so I can't really call myself either an "intellectual" or an "educated person," but I am pretty serious in my approach to things.

[4] I guess I'm sort of a "low brow" when it comes down to it.

The first response begins with an apology letting the respondent excuse himself or herself for professing to be that pretentious creature, an intellectual. The second response lets the person boast about his or her intellectual accomplishments without claiming to be an intellectual. The third allows the person to claim to be a serious person, thus worthy of respect, despite the lack of education and intellectuality. And the fourth response encourages the respondent to be candid about intellectual deficiencies, "when it comes down to it."

Personally, I suspect that many respondents today are rather put off by too much weaseling around in a survey item, and Davis's item might not work so well now as when it was first used back in the 1950s. When writing your own survey items, you will have to seek your own way of encouraging candor on items about touchy subjects like level of education. In a more recent item asking respondents to say where they stood on the political spectrum, Davis and Smith (1986) began by noting,

"There is a lot of talk these days about liberals and conservatives." Respondents were shown a scale that ran from extremely liberal to extremely conservative and were told it represented "the political views that people might hold." These phrases suggest it is okay to be either liberal or conservative, or to be at any point on the political scale. This political item has proven very effective, and we shall use it in the next chapter.

This example suggests another important point. You don't have to write all the items yourself. There are several advantages to appropriating items that other researchers have already used. For one thing, the item has already proven itself in successful research. For another, you can compare your results with those of the social scientist who wrote the item, thus placing your respondents in a larger context. If you are working in an established field of research, on a topic that was the subject of several highly respected earlier surveys, then you should look to those surveys for suitable items. Also, guides have been published that list and often evaluate groups of items that have been used in a variety of studies (Robinson, Rusk and Head 1968; Robinson, Athansiou and Head 1969; Robinson and Shaver 1969; Sweetland and O'Connor 1983; Keyser and Sweetland 1984).

When you write fresh items, you must make sure that your respondents will find them clear and unambiguous. If some of your respondents think an item means one thing, while the others think it means something else, your data will be garbage. Very complicated items might have to be broken apart into sets of simpler ones. If you are at all unsure of how well an item measures a concept of crucial importance to your study, then you should include one or more back-up items seeking the same information by different means.

A pilot study may be essential to help you perfect your survey. If possible, you should find respondents similar to those who will complete your final survey. Have them fill out a draft of the survey, just as the final respondents will, but ask them to mark any questions they found ambiguous and to write in any suggestions about changes in wording or other matters that might improve the questionnaire. If your pilot study has enough respondents, you should look at the numbers who gave each response to all the items. You may find that some items are not working well because everybody checks the same box, perhaps the one labeled "don't know." To get the most out of this pilot study, you might do an in-depth interview with some respondents, right after they filled it out. This might coax out of them further useful suggestions or doubts about some of the items. The pilot study can also check the methods you plan to use to administer the survey.

Techniques of Administration

When you write your questionnaire, you must have a clear idea of how it will be administered. It is worth distinguishing different modes for actually giving the questionnaire to a person.

First, you may use traditional written questionnaires, printed on paper. These may be sent through the mail, or handed to the respondents if that is convenient, as it is when they are all in one place, such as a school or factory. It can be very difficult to get people to respond by mail, however, and you may have to send follow-up letters and second or third copies of the survey (Dillman 1978). The **response rate** is the fraction of people given a survey who actually complete it. It is difficult to get a high response rate on mail surveys. On the other hand, there may be no other practical way of reaching a large number of geographically dispersed respondents.

Second, you can administer the questionnaire through interviews, going to each respondent's home and asking the questions verbally. The interviewer will work from an interview schedule, as described in Chapter 3. A complex question or set of questions could be printed out on a card handed to the respondent, and it may be good to show a pictorial representation of any subtle scale you want him or her to use in responding. The chief disadvantage of this approach is cost. You have to go to where each respondent is, invest much of your time getting the survey completed, and perhaps come back several times if the person is not at home the first time you call. A key advantage is that the response rate tends to be high. People who might never get around to completing a mailed questionnaire will do the job quickly and thoroughly when the interviewer is sitting in their living room asking the questions face-to-face.

Telephone surveys have some of the advantages of at-home interviews, without the cost of driving to the respondent's home. Items that will work well on printed pages, however, may not do so well over the phone. When a respondent is working with a page of a printed questionnaire, he or she can glance back at the directions, and a sweep of the eye will cover all the response categories. But over the telephone, it is not possible for the respondent to do this. Also, it may not be possible to administer very long questionnaires over the phone, because you have neither the moral suasion of face-to-face conversation to keep the respondent answering nor the speed of check-the-box printed surveys. A very new approach that has greatly facilitated telephone interviewing is called **CATI**: Computer-Assisted Telephone Interviewing. The interviewer sits at a microcomputer or the terminal of a mainframe computer while calling respondents on the phone. A special program has been written to flash the questions on the computer screen. The interviewer reads the questions off the screen, and when the respondent selects an answer, the interviewer need only press a key to enter the data. If you want to try this out at low cost, you can do simple CATI with the software package included in my textbook on survey research (Bainbridge 1989b).

Getting the data into the computer is one of the chief practical problems for large surveys. For printed surveys, data entry personnel have to sit at computer keyboards, reading the surveys and pressing keys to enter the responses. If the items on the page look about the same, this can be confusing work, and often it is advisable to print the questionnaire in a way that facilitates data entry as well as respondent answering. Precoded questionnaires are questionnaires with small code numbers for each response choice printed on every copy to guide the data entry personnel. It also helps to have good software. Again, my survey research software (Bainbridge 1989b) includes a good program for data entry from printed questionnaires, one I used myself for the data accompanying several chapters of this textbook. It puts guides on the screen to help you find your place if you need to check anything, and can emit several musical tones to mark the ends of sections or pages, so you need not look up in order to monitor where you are.

Another approach for data entry from printed forms is to have respondents answer with "op-scan" or "mark-sense" forms. These are specially printed questionnaire forms that can be run through optical scanners to enter their data directly into the computer without typing. You have probably answered many of your school tests using these forms. Although I have used these successfully with college students, I have my doubts that nonstudents are familiar enough with them to do a good job of responding.

Finally, we can now use the CATI approach without the telephone. Respondents can sit at the keyboard of a microcomputer and press appropriate keys to answer questions that appear on the screen. Naturally, this requires bringing the respondent to a computer, or a computer to the respondent. Today, many people have still not used computers, so each respondent might need a few minutes to work with a program designed to make them familiar with the keyboard and the process of answering questions.

Pictures can accompany questions, and the computer can do a lot of odd jobs, such as inserting the respondent's name or other information into the questions. One question asks, "What is the name of the first school you ever attended?" The respondent types in the name, say "Grassy Plains School." "And what is the name of the next school you attended?" "Old Greenwich School." Now the computer can insert this information into other questions: "How old were you when you left Grassy Plains School?" "On a scale from 0 through 6, how much did you like Grassy Plains School?" "All things considered, did you like Grassy Plains School better than Old Greenwich School?" "After Old Greenwich School, did you attend any other schools?"

Often questionnaires contain screening questions and contingent items. **Screening questions** are items that separate people into subgroups that receive different contingent questions. **Contingent questions** are items that only a subgroup of respondents is supposed to answer. For example: "What is your present marital status? [ ] Single [ ] Married [ ] Divorced [ ] Widowed." If a person checks the "Married" box, he or she is then directed to answer a number of questions about his or her spouse, but an unmarried person should not answer these questions. On a printed questionnaire, this can be awkward. In interviews, the interviewer can worry about which item to administer next. With a computer, the program can be set to jump directly from each answer to a screening question to the appropriate contingent questions.

If your respondents are all in one place, then computer administration can be very efficient. It can never replace person-to-person interviewing for the warmth and commitment to responding that a living, breathing human being can give, but its place in survey research is already great and will undoubtedly grow in coming years. Computers also play an important role in selecting samples of respondents.

Varieties of Survey Samples

The target group of people the researcher wishes to know about is called the **population**. It may consist of all the people living in a given area (city, state, nation), or of some subgroup such as voters or computer owners. For practical reasons, we usually study a population by drawing a sample of respondents from it. A **sample** is a subset of people in the population under study, often selected by random numbers, whose responses to a survey are used to estimate how the entire population would have responded if all members had been surveyed. A sample that does a good job of capturing the pattern of responses you would get from the population is said to be a **representative sample.**

The number of different kinds of samples is almost infinite, but a few distinct types are worth discussing because they illustrate the range of possibilities (cf. Kish 1965; Babbie 1973). My computer-assisted textbook on survey research (Bainbridge 1989b) provides practice with some of these, using a pair of realistic computer simulations.

A **purposive sample** consists of a set of cases that the researcher has carefully considered and that in his or her judgment will serve the needs of the research. At present, my wife is doing her doctoral dissertation on the topic of mad women in world drama, comparing, for example, mad female characters from English drama of Shakespeare's time with those in Japanese Noh drama of about the same period. Although she is considering all the plays that fit this description, she cannot analyze all of them in detail in her dissertation. Therefore, she will select examples that she feels are representative of various styles for close discussion, making the decisions on the basis of her scholarly knowledge of the subject. When I selected members of the Process to interview, I similarly used the purposive approach, choosing a wide variety of people to get a range of information about different kinds of involvement in the cult, and interviewing every single one of the original members that I could find.

A **convenience sample** is a subset of the population that the researcher polls simply because these persons were easy to contact. "Person in the street" interviews are like this. To get tape to fill time in its nightly news program, a television station sends an interviewer and a camera person to a central downtown spot, or a busy shopping mall, and poses a newsworthy question to people who pass by. There is no reason to believe that these people are representative of the general public. Their chief virtue is their low cost in both time and money, so they are especially appropriate for pilot studies and informal explorations. The subjects in most laboratory experiments are convenience samples, typically college students. Researchers hope that techniques of scientific experimentation, such as random assignment to groups, obviate the necessity of obtaining more representative samples. However, the findings of many laboratory experiments are of very questionable objectivity precisely because the subjects were chosen for convenience rather than because they were representative of the population at large. The results could conceivably have come out very differently with subjects obtained by very different methods.

In a **snowball sample**, the researcher begins with some individuals who are appropriate informants and then asks them for referrals to other appropriate informants. I am very familiar with this idea, because I used to be a professional piano tuner. Whenever I tuned a family's piano, I asked them for the names of some friends who owned pianos. Then I would call these people up on the phone and ask if their pianos needed tuning, too. That I had just done the job for their friends gave me an entrée and inspired the people I called to hire me. Sometimes researchers merely get names and addresses from the first people contacted, and other times they ask these people to introduce them personally and vouch for them.

In sociology, snowball samples may be necessary whenever the target population is rare and there are no lists of its members or other efficient ways of finding each person separately. As my example of finding families to hire me to tune their pianos illustrates, the snowball method may also serve to convince prospective informants to participate. This may be especially helpful with members of deviant subcultures who need some reassurance that you are a sympathetic person and that it is safe to talk to you. If their friend, a fellow deviant, had a good experience with you, they are more apt to accept you themselves.

A **quota sample** sets targets for how many people are to be included from each of several categories. Early election polls often relied upon convenience samples that included too many prosperous, educated individuals. One consequence was that the polls predicted Republicans would win elections that Democrats in fact won. The classic example is the 1936 presidential election, when a series of polls done by *Literary Digest* predicted a win by the Republican, Landon. The magazine had obtained a huge sample, fully 2,376,523 respondents, but it had used convenience methods that failed to reach many of the kinds of people who put Roosevelt back into the White House. Polls that used the quota approach were more accurate (Gallup 1976).

To draw a proper quota sample, you need to know two things: (1) which major groups in the population differ in terms of the information you want, and (2) how many people are in each of these population groups. For example, you might know that professionals (doctors, lawyers, etc.) tend to vote for Republicans, while factory workers vote for Democrats. You could inspect data from the census to see what portion of the population was professionals and what proportion was factory workers. Then you would set quotas for your sample that reflected the proportions of these two occupational groups in the population. To predict a national election, you would also have to set quotas for the different geographic regions of the country, and a really serious study might require a very complex set of overlapping quotas. The approach works very poorly if you are ignorant of some major divisions in society that are strongly related to your key questions, or if you lack good information on the numbers of people in each subgroup of the population.

A **simple random sample** is created using random numbers or other chance-based procedures that select individuals from the population at random. Each member of the population has an equal chance of appearing in the sample, and every combination of a given number of individuals also has an equal chance. The usual approach is first to obtain a list of the members of the population—for example, all the students enrolled in a school you are studying. Then the names in the list are numbered and random numbers are used to draw the sample. The traditional source of random numbers was special published books in which page after page was filled with meaningless figures (Rand Corporation 1955). Some researchers have used the phone book, taking the last few digits of the numbers on a page they have flipped to at random, but this procedure may give very biased results if the phone company fails to allocate the numbers randomly in the first place. A very convenient source of random numbers is a program in my software package on survey research (Bainbridge 1989b) that uses your computer to produce random numbers in a range you select.

Simple random samples are free of prejudice. The very fact that the sampling procedure uses meaningless numbers protects against systematic biases in the selection of informants. Not only does a reasonably large simple random sample represent well the population as a whole, but many of the statistical procedures sociologists employ in analyzing survey data assume that the sample was obtained by this method.

A **systematic sample** is a cheap imitation of a random sample; it saves a little time in actually drawing the sample but gives you less confidence in your results. Suppose you had before you the list of all residents of a small city, what is often called the town directory and sold to anyone who wants it at the town hall. One way to draw a sample would be to take the first name on each page. This is a systematic sample, because you would be using a simple system to select the names. Unfortunately, it would also be a very poor sample. Such lists often begin each page with a new household, with the "head of household" named first. Your sample might have too many males, too many parents, too many employed persons, too many of certain age groups, and too many with other characteristics we cannot even begin to imagine, because your system of selecting names unintentionally resonates with the system that was used in drawing up the list.

There are various ways of improving systematic samples. For example, if you selected every 50th name throughout the list, you might not get too many heads of households. Or you could count forward in the list using a random number table, skipping however many names added up to the next random number on the list. As you can see, however, the more complex the system gets, the more effort you must invest into the systematic sampling, until you might as well use simple random sampling.

Categorical samples combine the best features of quota sampling and simple random sampling. At the outset, the researcher identifies categories of people in the population, just as in quota sampling, and decides how many of each are needed. Then, the researcher draws a random sample for each of these categories separately. For example, when Travis Hirschi studied delinquency among high school students, he wanted to make sure that enough members of the chief ethnic minority, blacks, filled out the survey to permit reliable analysis of that group. Therefore, he **oversampled** blacks, which simply meant asking a higher proportion of them to complete surveys than of the majority groups.

Suppose you were studying a city with 10,000 high school students, seeking their opinions about the educational system. You wouldn't want to give all of them questionnaires, so you decide to draw a sample. School records show that 8,000 students are white and 2,000 black. If you printed up 2,000

questionnaires and used a simple random sample, probably about 400 blacks would complete them—one-fifth of the sample because they are one-fifth of the population. But you might decide you need 1,000 questionnaires from blacks to have a reliable picture of their views on the system and their experiences in school; so you draw a sample of 1,000 from the black category, one-half of these students. And to get an equal number of whites, you sample one-eighth of the white students.

Really, this is like taking two separate samples, one for blacks and the other for whites, and this is how the software connected to this chapter will approach categorical sampling. Each set of 1,000 questionnaires comes from a simple random sample of the particular ethnic group. Such a sample is large enough to represent each category of student with fair reliability. However, the total pile of 2,000 questionnaires does not represent the 10,000 students of the entire population, because it overrepresents the views of minorities. But it is an easy matter to **deflate** the minority statistics just the right amount to make the full study representative.

One way is to take a random sample! Because you have data from one-eighth of the white students, you need data from one-eighth of the black students, but you have data from one-half. Simply take one-fourth of the blacks' questionnaires at random, giving you 250, and combine them with the 1,000 white questionnaires to get 1,250 surveys, a sample that well represents the whole population of high school students. This method has the advantage that you can validly use any normal statistical procedures with these 1,250 surveys, just as if you had taken a simple random sample of 1,250 in the first place.

Doing so, of course, throws out data from fully 750 black students that might provide both greater variety and greater solidity to the findings. Another way of combining the black and white samples is to use a *deflation factor*, sometimes called a *fudge factor*. For example, here's how to calculate age. Suppose the average age of the 1,000 whites is 15.6, and the average age of the 1,000 blacks is 15.2. You might think you get the average by adding these two numbers and dividing by two, to get 15.4. That is wrong, however, because the 1,000 white respondents represent 8,000 in the population, while the 1,000 blacks represent only 2,000. On average, each white is 15.6, so the whites' total age is $8,000 \times 15.6 = 124,800$. On average, each black is 15.2, so the blacks' total age is $2,000 \times 15.2 = 30,400$. Add these two numbers to get the total number of years the 10,000 students have been on Earth ($124,800 + 30,400 = 155,200$). Divide this by the number of students in the population ($155,200/10,000$) to get the average age, 15.52. This is a little cumbersome, and you have to use slightly different methods with different kinds of data, but modern computers can do the work painlessly.

Often you will see the term **stratified random sample** used to describe what I call a categorical sample. I have to admit that I hate this term, *stratified*, because I feel it causes endless confusion for students, and I did not use it in my book on survey research (Bainbridge 1989b:67). However, other professionals use it widely, so (I give up!) you should know and understand it. The term simply means that you have broken the population down into subgroups and are using random methods, to some degree, to sample them separately.

The term *stratification* has also been used to denote breaking the dataset down into component categories during the analysis phase of the research (Rosenberg 1968:26). The words *stratified* and *stratification* come from *strata*, which means "layers." Sociologists commonly use the term *stratification* to refer to the system of social classes that divides society into layers differing in wealth, power, and prestige. Sometimes a survey study does treat social classes or minority groups differently during the sampling, but often the "stratification" is done in terms of groups that have nothing to do with the "stratification" of society. Thus, I think the term is unfortunate.

A **proportionate sample** is a categorical sample that sets quotas for the groups of respondents that match the groups' distribution in the population. Thus, it is a random sample to which you have added the requirement that the sample contain exactly the same proportions of certain key groups as the population. This may provide a slight improvement over a simple random sample in making precise predictions about the population.

These combinations of quota and random sampling usually involve a little more work than random sampling alone. One method of drawing such samples is actually to proceed as if you were doing a simple random sample but to stop accepting particular types of respondents once their categories were full. If you begin your work with a list that has all the needed information on it, the added effort may be just a few minutes of office work. If you do not have enough information to begin with, however, you may wind up contacting several people toward the end of your work that turn out to be wrong for your remaining quotas, and have to pass them by without completing collection of their data.

A **cluster sample** saves time and money because it contains individuals who are clustered together into groups. For example, suppose you wanted to survey 1,000 public school students in a city with 50,000 of them, 500 attending each of 100 schools. You could get a list of all 50,000 and use random numbers to mark off the names of 1,000, entirely at random. That would mean a tremendous amount of driving around, taking you to most of the 100 schools. Or you could start with a list of the schools and use random numbers to select just two of them, with a combined student population of 1,000. If you did this, you would have to visit only two schools, a vast reduction in the effort required. The set of respondents at each school would be called a *cluster*.

But perhaps you can immediately see the disadvantage. The two schools selected might be highly atypical. The town where I first attended school had just four schools: a small high school, two grammar schools with one class for each of the eight grades, and a one-room schoolhouse where two dozen students of all ages learned together. If your sample of two schools consisted of a high school and a one-room schoolhouse, it would not include any typical students like my sister and me, who attended the conventional grade schools.

Cluster samples are very commonly used in survey research, although they are usually not so vulnerable to extreme bias as in my school example. Many national polls follow this approach, sending interviewers to perhaps 100 locations to find about 15 respondents at each. For many purposes, this is not much worse than a simple random sample. The General Social Survey, the most famous annual sociological poll, has been short of money in some years and was forced to use cluster sampling. In other years it had enough money to carry out random samples of individuals.

In work we did on the religious geography of America, Rodney Stark and I examined regional differences revealed in national polls that employed clusters. Our greatest uncertainty concerned the Mountain region (Montana, Idaho, Wyoming, Colorado, New Mexico, Arizona, Utah, and Nevada). I've been in only six of these eight states, but anyone who knows anything about American geographic variations knows that these states vary greatly in religion and most other facets of social life. Both of the national surveys we used had polled clusters of individuals in just three of these states. Although both surveyed Arizona and Montana, one polled clusters in Colorado, while the other did so in Utah. Colorado and Utah are next to each other, but their populations are very different, and the two surveys gave very different pictures of Mountain religion. Utah is the most religious state, so when it is included the region looks religious, while when Colorado replaces Utah, the region appears substantially less religious. The surveys would have given a more accurate picture if they had been based on simple random samples, rather than the cheaper cluster samples.

To draw a **multistage sample**, the researcher carries out the selection in two or more phases. Suppose you want to survey 1,000 students out of 50,000 at the 100 schools mentioned before.

Each school may have 20 classrooms with 25 students in each, for a total of 2,000 classes. In a two-stage sampling procedure, you could start with a list of the 2,000 classes and draw a sample of 100. Then, from each of these classrooms, you would draw a sample of 10 students. In the first stage, you sample classes; in the second, you sample students from these classes. Or you could implement a three-stage sampling procedure. First, draw a sample of schools, then draw a sample of classes from the selected schools, then draw a sample of students from the selected classes. You could draw random samples at each stage or use some other procedure. For example, you could select classes by following a pure quota system, to get classes of the right grade levels to represent the population, then draw simple random samples of students within each selected class.

Area sampling starts not with a list of potential respondents but with information about neighborhoods and other social units in which the respondents will be found, and it almost always uses multiple stages. Suppose you were sampling residents of a state. Often the first step is to inspect census data telling you how many people live in each of the state's sections. Although you could start by taking a sample of the state's counties, high precision may require you to work with *census tracts*, the smallest territorial divisions about which the government keeps data. So you draw a sample of census tracts. Then you obtain a detailed map of census tracts, or town directories, and draw a sample of street blocks within each tract. Then you find one or more dwellings on each block and send an interviewer to each location to find a respondent. When the interviewer arrives at the right address, quota techniques are often used to decide which person to take as a respondent. And the interviewer may be given careful instructions on where to go next if he or she does not find a suitable respondent at the address. The principle, as you can see, is to sample places rather than people, because we often have more precise information on places than we do on the people who dwell within them.

A **census** is the ideal sample, if you are not concerned with cost, because it includes the entire population. Having discussed sampling at length, it is time for us to do some sampling using your computer software.

 ## The SAMP Program

This simulation shows how sociological questionnaires are designed, administered, and analyzed. One of the best and most influential questionnaire studies was created by criminologist Travis Hirschi (1969) to examine the causes of juvenile delinquency. Hirschi carefully wrote a large questionnaire, administered it to over 2,000 high school boys, and collected other data on the respondents from their school and the police. Our SAMP program allows you to replicate Hirschi's research with several samples of young respondents from high schools in six different American cities and two Canadian cities.

Travis Hirschi says that the study of deviant behavior has traditionally been oriented toward three types of sociological theory, and that the purpose of his research was to test the explanatory power of each one in comparison to the others:

> According to *strain* or motivational theories, legitimate desires that conformity cannot satisfy force a person into deviance. According to *control* or bond theories, a person is free to commit delinquent acts because his ties to the conventional order have somehow been broken. According to *cultural deviance* theories, the deviant conforms to a set of standards not accepted by a larger or more powerful society.
> (Hirschi 1969:3)

In a later section we shall examine these three theories closely and mention a few lesser theories that are also incorporated in our survey program. For now, however, it is important only to note that Hirschi's questionnaire and ours were designed to test hypotheses carefully derived from standard theories; thus they are instruments for evaluating the empirical support for major sociological theories, following the logic outlined in Chapter 1.

I must emphasize that the SAMP program is a simulation. We don't really have data from surveys in eight cities. Instead, I developed special programming tricks to generate fictional data that would illustrate Hirschi's real findings, and those of some later studies, in a clear and educationally valid way. The next chapter will introduce a survey that real people actually filled out, and you will be able to analyze that dataset using a rather more advanced statistical program than this one. One reason for using simulated data is to offer strong, clear results from a modest analysis. You should not worry about whether real high schools are as delinquent as ours. Indeed, please be aware that the findings you gain from research with these simulated data may not reflect social patterns in the real world, although I designed many of them to reflect what Hirschi himself found in his pioneering survey.

Another reason we are going to use simulated data is that they allow us to get excellent practice drawing random samples. To accomplish as much with real data would require surveys filled out by many thousands of respondents—perhaps ten or twenty thousand—and that would fill both disks that come with this textbook.

The six cities we will study are identified by pseudonyms, and you shouldn't worry too much what actual places they represent. In addition to following Hirschi's general findings and incorporating a few findings from later research in the same tradition, I have kept the social characteristics of six real cities in mind when creating the part of the program that simulates data. At times, I have simply used my imagination. I hid a few cute surprises in the data, and I hope you enjoy investigating the fictional world on your computer disk. Your findings will be realistic enough to give you some of the experience that real—and fabulously expensive—surveys would provide.

When you start the program, it will begin by asking you which items you want in the survey, and it will show you a list of 40 to choose from. As shown here in Figure 7.2, the 40 cover many aspects of a young person's social life and behavior, including questions about delinquent acts and items that operationalize hypotheses derived from Hirschi's three theories. You can select as many as 20 items for your survey, or as few as 1. In choosing them you get a little of the experience a real researcher has in writing a survey.

As the instructions on the computer screen say, you select an item for your survey by typing in its number and pressing (ENTER). When you do so, the item's number will be marked in a box, to help you keep track of which you have already chosen. If you make a mistake and want to drop one from your list after you have chosen it, simply type its number and press (ENTER) again. The box will disappear,

FIGURE 7.2
Questions in the Delinquency Questionnaire

1	Respondent is male	21	Father's occupation higher status
2	Respondent is black	22	Respondent always tries hard
3	Likes school	23	Frustrated about the future
4	Mother supervises closely	24	Feels few opportunities available
5	Good communication with father	25	Has friend who smokes marijuana
6	Low aptitude test scores	26	Attends church often
7	Drinks alcohol	27	Believes God punishes our sins
8	Smokes cigarettes	28	Smokes marijuana
9	Family moved recently	29	Wears make-up
10	Mother and father divorced	30	Watches violent TV programs
11	Thinks of self as delinquent	31	Listens to loud rock music
12	Wants to be like friends	32	Is sexually experienced
13	Teachers like respondent's friends	33	Picked up by police
14	Police have picked up friends	34	Has stolen inexpensive items
15	Thinks breaking the law is okay	35	Has stolen valuable items
16	Respects best friends' opinions	36	Has driven car without permission
17	Believes in living for today	37	Has vandalized property
18	Has many friends	38	Has beaten someone up
19	Father attended college	39	Committed one or more such acts
20	Mother attended college	40	Committed two or more such acts

leaving the chosen items, which are all marked with boxes. Note that a message on the screen keeps track of how many items are currently selected. Later, when we return to the theories that Hirschi's research sought to test, we will consider how to decide which items to include.

When you have finished selecting items, press (ENTER) an extra time. This tells the computer you are finished and will access the following menu of places where you could do your research, asking you to select one:

(1) Bay City, California
(2) Rainfall, Washington
(3) Desert City, Utah
(4) Dixie, Georgia
(5) Sound Cove, Connecticut
(6) Truckton, Illinois
(7) Westport, B.C.
(8) Paris, Quebec

The names of all these cities are pseudonyms, fictitious names that conceal the cities' actual identity. Although my data will not exactly match those you would get from actual cities, I had real cities in mind when preparing this program. Bay City, California, was actually the place where Hirschi did his research, while one of Hirschi's colleagues, Joseph Weis, has done similar research in Rainfall, another West Coast city. Research similar to Hirschi's, but focusing on the possible effect of religion in deterring delinquency, has been done in Desert City and Dixie. Sound Cove, Connecticut, is an example of a booming, high-tech, small city that has gained great economic importance in recent years, while Truckton is one of the economically depressed "rust-belt" cities of the industrial Middle West. Westport is a lively city on Canada's west coast, while Paris is the traditional heart of French Canada. Indeed, if we were doing a real survey, we would probably want to translate it into French before administering it in Paris.

To select a city, simply press its number on the menu. Once you have done so, the computer will ask which of nine different plans you wish to follow for sampling the students in the city's high school:

(1) 10 teenagers
(2) 100 teenagers
(3) 500 teenagers
(4) 500 boys
(5) 500 girls
(6) 500 white boys
(7) 500 white girls
(8) 500 black boys
(9) 500 black girls

The first three choices give you samples of different sizes, which will let us explore the effect of sample size on the quality of research findings. These samples contain both boys and girls, including students of both European and African descent. Hirschi's own research included respondents from these groups, but his book considered just the boys. He also had some Asian-American respondents, but so few that he left them out of his analysis. We shall find that the samples of particular groups not only can be used rather like the select/rejects of Chapter 4, but will also illustrate some principles of sampling.

When you have made your selection, the computer will go ahead and do the research. As it does, you can keep track of its progress by watching the screen, where the following messages will appear: DRAWING RANDOM SAMPLE, ADMINISTERING QUESTIONNAIRES, ENTERING DATA INTO COMPUTER. Before we consider how to analyze the data, we should examine more closely how several of the items operationalize one or another theory of delinquency.

Testing Delinquency Theories

Strain theory says that all teenagers want to achieve success, to fulfill the American (and Canadian) dream. The standard route to success is to get a good education and the high income it can bring, but youngsters from the lower social classes find it especially difficult to succeed. The result is great frustration, which may express itself in vandalism or other delinquency (Cohen 1955). Also, if poor kids decide they never can gain wealth by legitimate means (getting a good education and working hard), they may turn to the illegitimate means of crime (Merton 1957; Cloward and Ohlin 1960). The 40 items from which you can build your questionnaire include six that measure social class or the deprivation-caused frustrations that strain theory holds are responsible for delinquency:

19 Father attended college
20 Mother attended college
21 Father's occupation higher status
22 Respondent always tries hard
23 Frustrated about the future
24 Feels few opportunities available

Items 19 through 21 measure high social class, so strain theory predicts that respondents who answer "no" to these questions will tend to be delinquent. A kid whose parents attended college and whose father has a higher-status occupation will not be delinquent. Such teenagers have a good chance of following in their parents' footsteps and thus can achieve the good things of life by legitimate means. Having given up on a conventional career, the delinquent will not try hard in school and in other conventional activities. The essence of strain theory is frustrated hopes: the kid who is frustrated about the future and feels that few opportunities are available may become delinquent.

Strain theory assumes that people tend to follow society's norms, unless exceptional circumstances drive them into deviance. In contrast, control theory assumes that anybody might deviate, unless restrained by a strong bond to society. The key idea of control theory is that strong attachment to other people and commitment to conventional institutions like school will prevent kids from engaging in delinquent acts. Ten items measure aspects of control theory:

3 Likes school
4 Mother supervises closely
5 Good communication with father
6 Low aptitude test scores
7 Drinks alcohol
8 Smokes cigarettes
9 Family moved recently
10 Mother and father divorced

18 Has many friends
32 Is sexually experienced

A kid is strongly attached to a parent if his or her mother provides close supervision and the kid enjoys good communication with his or her father. According to control theory, these personal bonds will inhibit delinquency, as will bonds to friends. If a family has moved recently, or if divorce has broken the family, then many social bonds will tend to be weaker, and the teenager is apt to be freer to deviate. Teenagers who like school are attached to their teachers and have invested a good deal of effort in doing well. They would lose this investment if they became delinquent. But teenagers with low test scores at school may do poorly in classes, be rejected by teachers, and stand to lose very little if they violate the law. A kid who drinks alcohol, smokes, and is sexually experienced (at least in many communities) has clearly broken with the restrictions of childhood and does not submit to the controlling force of the norms adults want children to follow.

Cultural deviance theory assumes that there is a delinquent subculture of kids who influence each other to commit delinquent acts. Seven of our questions bear on this theory, some more directly than others:

11 Thinks of self as delinquent
12 Wants to be like friends
13 Teachers like respondent's friends
14 Police have picked up friends
15 Thinks breaking the law is okay
16 Respects best friends' opinion
17 Believes in living for today
28 Wants to be like friends

A member of a delinquent subculture thinks that breaking the law is okay, because lawbreaking is part of the subculture. Commitment to a conventional future career that requires self-denial for years is not part of the delinquent culture, whose members believe in living for today. Because delinquent friends reinforce these opinions, we would expect that a delinquent's friends have often been picked up by police and that teachers do not like these friends (Sutherland and Cressey 1974). Some versions of cultural deviance theory argue that the delinquents are really playing a standard role in the subculture—that of delinquent—and thus that they should think of themselves as delinquents.

Mere evidence that delinquents have delinquent friends, however, does not prove that association with these friends caused the kids' delinquency. Perhaps, as the old saying goes, birds of a feather flock together. That is, teenagers who are already delinquent individuals come together, not trusting each other very much, because the "good kids" reject them. Therefore, if cultural deviance theory is true, we should expect that delinquents would be just as likely as nondelinquents to respect their best friends' opinions and to want to be like their friends.

This brief discussion was based on Hirschi's far more extensive analysis; if you want further details, you should read his fine book. I have added a few miscellaneous items, not all related to the three major theories, to give you a greater variety of hypotheses about delinquency to test:

1 Respondent is male
2 Respondent is black
26 Attends church often
27 Believes God punishes our sins
25 Has friend who smokes marijuana
30 Watches violent TV programs
31 Listens to loud rock music

The first two of these items, sex and race, are variables that can be the basis for your samples, so it was essential to include them. Since time began, however, people have noted that males are far more likely to violate the law than are females, and it will be interesting for you to study the patterns of delinquency across the two sexes. I might have included the question about race among the strain theory items, because strain theory holds that disadvantaged groups will be forced into delinquency. But sociologists have also suggested that members of minority groups are often unfairly accused of crimes. Getting samples that are all-black or all-white will let you see if the same factors produce deviance in these two different parts of our population.

Some sociologists have suggested that religion deters deviance. In part, this is a version of control theory, but while Hirschi's original data supported control theory as described above, they did not show that religious youngsters were less delinquent than nonreligious youngsters (Hirschi and Stark 1969). Rodney Stark, who worked with Hirschi in analyzing the religion data and with whom I have frequently collaborated, has discovered that the power of religion to deter deviance depends on the strength of religion in the community.

This is a subtle idea, so let's examine it closely. According to Stark, in communities where most kids are religious and go to church, those who aren't religious will tend to be delinquent. In such communities, your survey would find that religion prevented delinquency. But in cities where organized religion is weak, where few teenagers attend church, religion has little if any power to deter delinquency. That is, in communities where religion is weak, religion cannot deter deviant behavior, even among religious youngsters. Several research studies have already supported these propositions, which are of such great theoretical importance that I like to call them *Stark's Law*.

A scientifically provocative complication appears in several survey datasets. In communities of weak religion, churchgoing does not deter stealing, vandalism, and assault—crimes for which there is an identifiable victim. But in these same irreligious towns, churchgoing does seem to deter early sexual experience and marijuana use, acts that violate parents' wishes but do not of necessity harm anybody seriously. I do not have an easy explanation for all this, and if you explore the role of religion in your surveys you will be working on the cutting edge of sociological research on deviance.

Although the question about having a friend who smokes marijuana could have been included among the items connected to cultural deviance theory, we have just seen that marijuana-smoking may be significantly different from other kinds of delinquency, such as stealing, vandalism, and assault. Thus, different theories may explain it than explain other kinds of delinquency. If, for example, cultural deviance theory fails to explain theft, it might still explain mild drug use.

Finally, there has been much public concern in recent years over whether television violence and wild rock music teach kids to value deviant behavior. To test theories of delinquent behavior, of course, you also need questions about delinquency itself:

28 Smokes marijuana
33 Picked up by police
34 Has stolen inexpensive items
35 Has stolen valuable items
36 Has driven car without permission
37 Has vandalized property
38 Has beaten someone up
39 Committed one or more such acts
40 Committed two or more such acts

Hirschi did not use any questions about smoking marijuana (it was uncommon in Bay City at the time), but I have included this popular form of deviance here. Although teenagers who have been picked up by the police may not have been charged with a criminal offense, this item is a good general measure of delinquency. The next five items specify particular crimes that harm another person: stealing inexpensive items, stealing expensive items, driving a car without permission, vandalism, and assault. The last two items are based on counting how many times the respondent said "yes" in answer to these five questions. If the person admits to one or more of these acts, he or she is counted as a "yes" for item 39. Two or more such acts give him or her a "yes" for the final item.

Analyzing the Delinquency Data

When the computer has finished administering a survey, it will give you the main menu of the program:

```
[1]  Data from one case
[2]  Statistics for one variable
[3]  Crosstab of two variables
[4]  Select new research site
[5]  Select new sample
[6]  Create new survey
[7]  Add second sample
[ESC] QUIT or change programs
```

The first three options let you look at the data in various ways, while the other four give you the power to compare one group of respondents with another and to administer new questionnaires.

Data from One Case

When you select the first option on the main menu, by pressing (1), the computer will remind you of how many people responded to your survey, and it will ask you to select one of them by typing the person's number. For example, once I was working with a random sample of 500 teenagers from Bay City, California, and wanted to inspect a few cases. The computer told me I had 500 to work with, so I could type in any number from 1 through 500 to get one case. Figure 7.3 shows what I saw when I selected case number 222.

At the top, you see the number of the case, and the nature of the sample is shown in the lower left-hand corner. The items I selected for the questionnaire are listed in order. For example, the first item is "1 Respondent is male." The last is "38 Has beaten someone up." You will notice that the numbers are from the full list of 40 possible items, so there are gaps in the numbering. Because I thought it would confuse things to renumber the items as they stand in your questionnaire, each item always has the same number out of 40, regardless of where it stands in a particular questionnaire.

In front of each item is the answer the respondent gave. The respondent said "Yes" to being male but "No" to being black, so we know he is a white boy. He doesn't like school, sad to say, as his "No" answer to the third item indicates. One clue comes from item 6: he has low aptitude test scores, having done poorly on the school's scholastic aptitude exams. See what else you can tell about this boy. Is he religious? What is his family life like? And, most important of all, would you call him a delinquent?

The boy seems very much out of control. Despite his mother's close supervision and his religiousness, he admits to quite a list of misdeeds. Think about his religion for a moment. Here we have a religious delinquent. Does that disprove the

FIGURE 7.3
Data from One Case

Data from case 222

Yes	1	Respondent is male
No	2	Respondent is black
No	3	Likes school
Yes	4	Mother supervises closely
No	5	Good communication with father
Yes	6	Low aptitude test scores
Yes	7	Drinks alcohol
Yes	8	Smokes cigarettes
No	9	Family moved recently
No	10	Mother and father divorced
Yes	26	Attends church often
Yes	27	Believes God punishes our sins
Yes	33	Picked up by police
Yes	34	Has stolen inexpensive items
No	35	Has stolen valuable items
Yes	36	Has driven car without permission
Yes	37	Has vandalized property
Yes	38	Has beaten someone up

Bay City, California—500 teenagers   Press(ENTER)

theory that religion prevents delinquency? Well, it certainly shows that in one case, at least, religion failed. In many other cases, however, it might have succeeded. It is almost never possible to test a theory on a single case. So many factors shape a person's behavior that some individual somewhere will have almost any conceivable combination of characteristics, even some that seem utterly contradictory. To test whether religion generally prevents delinquency, we would have to look at many cases and look for trends.

When you have finished looking at the data for one individual respondent, press (ENTER) and you will get the main menu again. At that point, you can decide to inspect another case or choose one of the other options.

 ## Statistics for One Variable

The second option on the menu shows you how all your respondents replied to a particular item. For example, we just saw that a particular Bay City, California, respondent was a churchgoer. Does this mean that all respondents attend church often? To see, press (2) to select statistics, and the computer will show you a list of the items in your questionnaire. Type the number of the item you want and press

FIGURE 7.4
Statistics on Question 26: Attends Church Often

Bay City, California
500 teenagers

Answer	Cases	Percent
Yes	132	26.4
No	368	73.6
Total	500	100.0

(ENTER). Something like Figure 7.4, which shows church attendance for my sample of 500 Bay City teenagers, will quickly appear.

This simple table reveals that only 132 of the 500 respondents attend church often. This is only 26.4 percent of the total, a relatively small minority, down near a quarter of all the respondents. Because a fairly large random sample of teenagers in the Bay City area completed our survey, we have to conclude that the churches are weak in this city, but this might not be true for other cities in our list. If you want to see really high levels of church attendance, try Desert City or Paris. We also see that respondent 222 was not typical: He is one of the minority who attend church often in Bay City, California.

Crosstab of Two Variables

Perhaps the most important part of our survey analysis examines how variables are connected to each other. In previous chapters we developed an understanding of two-by-two tables and some simple statistics that summarize what is going on in them. We can now use that knowledge to very good effect.

Press (3) from the main menu, and the computer will list the items in your questionnaire and ask you to choose one. Do so, and you will have selected the item that is to be variable X in a crosstab analysis. A bright box will appear around the item's number, to remind you which one you chose. Then the computer will ask you to type in a second item's number, to be variable Y. For example, variable X could be number 26, "Attends church often," and Y could be number 27, "Believes God punishes our sins." Figure 7.5 shows a crosstab of these two items.

Notice that the two variables are described at the top, as is the sample to which the survey was administered. The table is similar to ones we have seen before, but slightly more complicated because its cells contain several pieces of information at once. In other programs, you press (D) to change what is displayed in the cells, but I thought it would be good to have a little practice reading the kind of crosstab that many serious statistical packages generate. So there is no display option here. Instead, each cell shows how many cases it contains, expressed both as a raw number and as two kinds of percentage. You should examine this table closely so that you will understand the tables you get in your own simulated research.

First, look at the raw numbers, both in the cells and at the right and bottom margins. See the number 500 near the lower right-hand corner of the boxes? That is the total number of cases, the 500 teenage respondents from Bay City, California. To the left of that is the number 132, representing the 132 respondents who attend church often, just as Figure 7.4 reported. You can tell that this is what the 132 represents, because the message at the top-right of the boxes says "Yes" for Variable X, which is "Attends church often." And the 105 cases in the upper-right little box are the people who attend church often and also believe God punishes our sins—they answered "Yes" to both questions represented in the crosstab.

The top percentage in the same cell, 79.5%, tells us what percent 105 is of 132. Note that each cell of the crosstab has two percentage figures in it. The one on top is the column percentage—the percent of cases in the column that the cases in the cell represent. The bottom percentage in each cell is the row percentage—the percent of cases in the row that the cases in the cell represent. If you forget this, the marginal percentages will remind you.

Look at the figures under the two-by-two table. Below the right-hand cells are three numbers: 132, 100.0%, and 26.4%. We just noted that the 132 refers to the

FIGURE 7.5
A Crosstab

X: Attends church often
Y: Believes God punishes our sins

Bay City, California
500 teenagers

		Variable X		
		No	Yes	
	Yes	86 23.4% 45.0%	105 79.5% 55.0%	191 38.2% 100.0%
Variable Y				
	No	282 76.6% 91.3%	27 20.5% 8.7%	309 61.8% 100.0%
		368 100.0% 73.6%	132 100.0% 26.4%	500 100.0% 100.0%

chi-square: 129.87
Significance: .001
phi: 0.51
Q: 0.85

132 people who responded "Yes" to question X, people who attend church often. The 100% is the column percent these 132 represent: 132 is 100% of 132. The 26.4% is the row percent: 132 is 26.4% of the total in the row (368 + 132 = 500). Similarly, note the information to the right of the top-right cell: 191, 38.2%, 100.0%. The 191 refers to the total people in the top row (86 + 105 = 191), those who answered "Yes" to question Y, about believing God punishes our sins. The 38.2% is the column percent, reflecting that 191 is 38.2% of 500. The 100.0% is the row percent, because 191 is 100.0% of 191.

Below the crosstab itself are summary statistics: chi-square, the significance of chi-square, phi, and Q, as the previous chapter explained. Clearly, there is a strong connection between attending church often and believing that God punishes our sins. Both phi and Q are strongly positive, and the chi-square is highly significant. But think it through in terms of percentages. Of the people who do not attend church frequently, only 23.4 percent believe God punishes our sins. Among those who do attend often, however, 79.5 percent believe this. These observations come from examining the column percentages.

Or you can look at the row percentages. Of those who reject the idea that God punishes our sins, only 8.7 percent attend church often. But among those who do believe in divine punishment, 55.0 percent attend often.

Note that it is hard to say which of these two variables is the independent variable and which the dependent variable. Logically, it could go either way. Going to church can make you believe, or belief can bring you to church. If you have identified one variable as independent, you should find the percentage in terms of it. That is, select the variable you consider to be independent first, as variable X, and compare column percentages in the two-by-two table. Because our crosstab offers percentages in terms of both variables, you must decide for yourself which set is more relevant for the hypothesis you are testing.

Creating and Administering New Surveys

Three options on the main menu allow you to do another survey, either starting from scratch or merely getting a different set of respondents. Be careful in selecting these options, as they will wipe out any dataset you have been working with.

If you do want to start from the beginning, you can press (6) to create a new survey. This has the same effect as starting the program over, and you must select a new set of questions from our list of 40. If you press (5), you will merely obtain a new sample from the same city, using the same set of questions. Pressing (4) lets you switch to a different city, without having to select items all over again. If you select new questions, you must also choose a research site and a sample. A new site always demands a new sample.

If your research project calls for comparing two or more samples, these commands allow you to switch to a new sample, after you are sure you have written down the information you want from the first one. For most purposes, however, there is a better way, one that employs the final option on the menu.

Add Second Sample

If you press (7) from the main menu, you will keep the most recent sample you have been working with and add a second one to it, allowing you to compare the two directly with regard to statistics about variables and crosstabs. The new sample can be from the same city or from a different city. It can follow the same sampling plan or a different one. Select this option and the computer will go through the usual routine for selecting a city and sample. From then on, when you select options (2) and (3) from the main menu, data from both samples will appear on your screen.

For example, I told the computer to draw a sample of just 20 teenagers from Bay City, California. Then I pressed (7) to add a second sample. This time, I asked for 500 teenagers from Bay City, California. Figure 7.6 shows a comparison of statistics for one variable, the sex of the respondents.

The right side of the table shows the old sample, 20 teenagers. Fully 65.0 percent of these were male, 13 out of 20. In the larger sample of 500, however, only 48.0 percent are male. The population of Bay City teenagers from which the computer draws its sample happens to be exactly 50 percent male. The first sample, therefore, gives too high an estimate of the male population (65 percent versus 50 percent), while the second sample gives too low an estimate (48 percent versus 50 percent). But the second sample is much closer to the population itself, only 2 percentage points off, compared with a 15-point error for the small sample. Most of the time, a large sample will reflect the population better than a small sample, and you can verify this through your own experiments, comparing samples of 20, 100, and 500 respondents from the same city.

Figure 7.7 shows how two samples look in the crosstab option. Here, I have chosen two different samples of the same size from the same city. The crosstab on the left side is based on one random sample of 500 Bay City teenagers; the crosstab on the right is based on 500 different Bay City teenagers. The variables I have chosen to be X and Y concern whether the respondent smokes marijuana and whether he or she has stolen inexpensive items. These are both acts of deviance, and one might expect them to correlate positively. Bad kids smoke grass, and bad kids steal. Right?

Wrong. Neither sample shows a significant correlation between smoking grass and theft. Apparently, for Bay City teenagers at least, these are two entirely

FIGURE 7.6
Statistics on Question 1: Respondent Is Male

Answer	Bay City, California 500 teenagers		Bay City, California 20 teenagers	
	Cases	Percent	Cases	Percent
Yes	240	48.0	7	35.0
No	260	52.0	13	65.0

separate kinds of deviance. If this is the case, one would expect different causes to produce the two kinds of deviance, and you can undertake a simulated research project to determine what they are.

Note that the numbers in the two crosstabs are all slightly different. The one on the right gives a positive Q of 0.08, while the one on the left gives a negative Q of -0.13. This illustrates clearly that each coefficient based on sample surveys is just an estimate. The estimates vary because the samples draw respondents with some-what different characteristics from the larger population. I wrote this simulation so that the correlation between marijuana and petty theft would be dead zero in the Bay City population, a Q of exactly 0.00. The 0.08 and -0.13 are estimates that are close enough to zero that their differences from zero could be due entirely to chance. Indeed, I know they were due to chance because I know exactly how I wrote the simulation program.

In real research we seldom if ever know the actual numbers for the entire population, and we have to make do with samples. If I saw either of these crosstabs of marijuana and theft, however, I would conclude that the coefficients were effectively zero. Not only are these numbers very close to zero, but our measure of statistical significance, based on chi-square, gives "n.s.," or "not

FIGURE 7.7
Two Crosstabs

X: Smokes marijuana
Y: Has stolen inexpensive items

Bay City, California
500 teenagers

| | Variable X | | |
	No	Yes	
	87	57	144
Yes	31.1%	25.9%	28.8%
	60.4%	39.6%	100.0%
Variable Y			
	193	163	356
No	68.9%	74.1%	71.2%
	54.2%	45.8%	100.0%
	280	220	500
	100.0%	100.0%	100.0%
	56.0%	44.0%	100.0%

chi-square: 1.60
Significance: n.s.
phi: -0.06
Q: -0.13

Bay City, California
500 teenagers

| | Variable X | | |
	No	Yes	
	85	78	163
Yes	31.0%	34.5%	32.6%
	52.1%	47.9%	100.0%
Variable Y			
	189	148	337
No	69.0%	65.5%	67.4%
	56.1%	43.9%	100.0%
	274	226	500
	100.0%	100.0%	100.0%
	54.8%	45.2%	100.0%

chi-square: 0.69
Significance: n.s.
phi: 0.04
Q: 0.08

significant." One of the projects at the end of this chapter calls for you to draw two identical random samples and note that your results will be slightly different but essentially the same.

Comparisons between samples of different populations may reveal even bigger differences than between samples of the same population. First of all, we expect different cities to have different social characteristics. This difference may be either augmented or diminished by the random difference the sampling introduced. An interesting example that lets us understand the logic of statistical correlation a little more deeply is shown in Figure 7.8, which presents data from samples drawn from the (simulated) teenage populations of Paris and Rainfall.

The X variable is whether the family moved recently, and the Y variable is whether the respondent attends church often. Much real research indicates that one of the factors that most affects church membership is geographic mobility. People who move away from home leave their church congregation as well. In a new town, it may take them a long time to get into a new congregation. This is not a simple matter of knocking on the door of the church nearest their new home. Sociologists of religion have found repeatedly that the factor most responsible for connecting a person or family to a new church is the development

FIGURE 7.8
Crosstabs in Two Cities

X: Family moved recently
Y: Attends church often

Paris, Quebec
500 teenagers

		Variable X		
		No	Yes	
	Yes	265	90	355
		75.7%	60.0%	71.0%
		74.6%	25.4%	100.0%
Variable Y				
	No	85	60	145
		24.3%	40.0%	29.0%
		58.6%	41.4%	100.0%
		350	150	500
		100.0%	100.0%	100.0%
		70.0%	30.0%	100.0%

chi-square: 12.59
Significance: .001
phi: −0.16
Q: −0.35

Rainfall, Washington
500 teenagers

		Variable X		
		No	Yes	
	Yes	67	63	130
		36.4%	19.9%	26.0%
		51.5%	48.5%	100.0%
Variable Y				
	No	117	253	370
		63.6%	80.1%	74.0%
		31.6%	68.4%	100.0%
		184	316	500
		100.0%	100.0%	100.0%
		36.8%	63.2%	100.0%

chi-square: 16.41
Significance: .001
phi: −0.18
Q: −0.39

of bonds of friendship with people who already belong. The first friends one makes in the new town may belong to different churches, or they also may be fellow newcomers without church affiliation. Thus, it is reasonable to consider "moving" to be the independent variable and "attending church" to be the dependent variable. Because the theory says that people who move are less likely to attend church, we look for a significant negative correlation between variables X and Y in the data.

Indeed, the summary statistics beneath the two crosstabs tell almost identical stories. On the left, the phi is −0.16, while on the right it is −0.18. The Q on the left is −0.35, while on the right it is −0.39. Both chi-squares are significant at the 0.001 level. But—and perhaps this is surprising—if you look at the numbers of cases in the cells of the two crosstabs, you will see that the patterns are very different.

By far the fullest cell in the left-hand crosstab is the one in the upper-left corner, with 265 cases in it. But the fullest cell in the right-hand crosstab is the one in its lower right, with 253 cases. What is going on?

The trick is that the two cities differ tremendously in their overall rates of moving and of church attendance. Although only 30.0 percent of Paris teenagers' families moved recently, 63.2 percent of Rainfall teenagers' families did. And 71.0 percent of Paris teenagers attend church frequently, compared with only 26.0 percent in Rainfall. I should emphasize again that these data are entirely synthetic, produced by my computer program rather than derived from real surveys, but differences of this kind and magnitude are entirely realistic. Cities can differ this much from each other on key social variables.

Although the migration and religion conditions are very different in the two cities, the connection between these variables is essentially the same. This is not always true for real cities, by any means. Sometimes variables are associated in very different ways in different social environments. Often, however, the same sociological rules apply in two very different communities, and the correlations found in real research can be very similar, even when the levels of the two variables are quite different.

In Chapter 12, we will consider correlations coming from data about whole cities rather than from individuals, but a hint of that kind of analysis can be seen here. Rainfall is high in moving but low in church attendance. Paris is low in moving but high in church attendance. This is the essence of negative correlation.

Another point should be made, concerning how to read the percentages in either crosstab. Our theory identifies moving as the independent variable. Moving influences church attendance, according to the theory, not the other way around. In the tables, moving is variable X, and we have said you should always find the percentage in terms of the independent variable. That means looking at the column percents, not the row percents, in Figure 7.8. Consider Paris. Of those who have moved, 60.0 percent attend church often. But of those who have not moved, 75.7 percent attend often, a larger proportion. Think it through yourself for Rainfall.

Practice with the projects at the end of this chapter will prepare you well for the more complex crosstabs and statistical analysis of following chapters. The projects all use samples of teenagers, of both sexes and both races, but you certainly may experiment with the samples from one or another of the subgroups of the population. Chapter 13 will draw upon this feature of the SAMP program.

Margin of Error in Random-sample Surveys

In the previous chapter, we considered how chi-square could help us measure the statistical significance of a relationship—that is, the probability that a difference revealed in a two-by-two table could really just be zero, having been inflated by pure chance in the process of sampling the population. Now we can consider something very similar, the margin of error in results from a survey done using a simple random sample. Because you will be able to explore this topic using the SAMP program, this section of the book deserves to be here, right after you have learned to use this part of our software. We will define margin of error a little later, but the term is employed very often, even in reports on opinion polls broadcast on television news shows, so you should become familiar with what it means.

Here's an example from a popular opinion poll (Bezilla 1988). In the spring of 1985, the Gallup organization did a survey of American youth, and one of the more interesting questions concerned sex education: "From what source have you, yourself, received the most accurate information about sex?" The largest group, 40 percent of the respondents, answered that they had gotten the most accurate sex information from their parents. Other answers were friends, 25 percent; teachers, 20 percent; books or articles, 15 percent; religious workers, 4 percent; and doctors or nurses, 2 percent. Clearly, parents seem most important, but how reliable is this 40-percent figure?

All statistics from random-sample surveys are just estimates of the real value in the population. Thus, Gallup estimates that 40 percent of the population got their most accurate sex information from their parents. To be sure, we know for a fact that 40 percent of the poll respondents gave this answer, but it is possible that the percentage would be somewhat different if we were able to poll the entire population, perhaps 37 percent or 45 percent.

What is the margin of error in this 40-percent estimate?

Knowing that few of its readers are trained in statistics, the Gallup organization offered a brief appendix in their report explaining how to figure the probable size of the error introduced by chance, during the sampling process. The key factor determining the sampling error is the size of the sample. A table in the appendix to Gallup's report indicates that for a sample of 1,000 respondents, the margin of error of this 40-percent figure is just 4 percentage points. But for a sample of only 100, the margin of error would be 12 percentage points, three times as big.

To explain, let's start with a sample of 1,000. Gallup says the margin of error is plus or minus 4 points. This means that we are reasonably sure that the real percentage—in the population, not in the sample—is between 36 and 44. That is, the population's percentage is about what the sample's percentage is, plus or minus 4 points (40 − 4 = 36; 40 + 4 = 44). For a sample of 100, the margin of error is considerably larger, and we can be reasonably sure only that the population's percentage is within the range from 28 through 52 (40 − 12 = 28; 40 + 12 = 52). Clearly, a large sample gives us more confidence that our estimate is about right than does a small sample.

What do we mean by "reasonably sure" that the population's percentage is within this margin of error? If we took many, many random samples of the given size, 95 percent of them would be within the margin of error of the correct percentage in the population. The best way to illustrate this is through a little study I just did, using our SAMP program.

I created a tiny questionnaire of just one question: "Is the respondent male?" Then I asked the computer to give me a sample of 100 teenagers living in Bay City, California. Checking the results, I discovered that 55 percent of these respondents were male. Does this tell me that exactly 55 percent of all teenagers in Bay City are male? No, it does not. Probably, the real figure is close to 55 percent, but I do not really know how close or which side of 55.

Next, I asked the computer to give me a different sample of 100 teenagers from the same city. This time, 53 percent were male. That is very close to the 55 percent I got with the first sample, and we would expect repeated random samples to give very similar results, more similar the larger the samples were. A third sample came out at 54 percent. Now it really looks like we are getting a clear fix on what proportion of Bay City teenagers are male. Our three samples are 53, 54, and 55, suggesting that 54 percent is about the right figure. But when I tried a fourth sample, I got only 44! Three more samples gave 51, 47, and 48. To this point, I had done seven separate samples, getting results from 44 percent to 55 percent, with an average of 50.28. Clearly, the very first sample I tried, and indeed the first three samples of 100, would have given me a somewhat false idea of what proportion of teenagers were male.

Over the course of a couple of hours at the computer, I did 100 samples. The average percentage turned out to be 49.67, or to round it off, about 50 percent. That is, I now estimate that teenagers in Bay City are about 50-50 male and female. (Indeed, when I wrote the computer simulation program that produced these numbers, I intended for the sexes to be equal in number. But, of course, the researcher seldom knows the exact percentage in the population, and must make estimates based on the sample.) Having done 100 samples, I could examine their distribution; that is, I could

compare them and see how many samples gave each particular result.

The lowest estimate from any of these samples was 38, the highest 61. Had I drawn even more samples, some would probably have given even more extreme results than these. But only one sample out of 100 gave a result of 38 percent, and only one gave 61 percent. Most of the samples gave estimates much closer to 50. In fact, out of the 100 samples, 67 (or two thirds) were in the range from 45 through 55. Ninety-seven of the samples fell between 40 and 60, and 94 fell between 41 and 59. So about 95 percent of the samples were between 41 and 59. This suggests that the margin of error (from 50) was about 9, because $50 - 9 = 41$ and $50 + 9 = 59$.

In real research, of course, you cannot work with 100 samples—this would be far too expensive to be practical. Instead, you would rely upon various mathematical techniques to calculate the margin of error around the results you got with your single sample. Later chapters will explain more of the logic of error estimation, but for now we can conclude with a definition of margin of error: The **margin of error** of a particular estimate from a survey that employed a simple random sample is the range around that estimate in which 95 percent of samples would fall, if you drew a very large number of samples from the population. Of course, you could set a criterion different from 95 percent—for example, a more demanding one such as 99 percent or 99.9 percent. But researchers widely accept this 95-percent criterion, which gives you great confidence that the real number is within the margin of error.

P R O J E C T S   F O R   C H A P T E R   7

The SAMP program, a simulation of quantitative survey research, was inspired by a real study done by criminologist Travis Hirschi. Thus, one of its chief aims is to give you a taste of the stages of real questionnaire research. Another aim, however, is further experience with simple methods of quantitative analysis. The first project—which my class in research methods found quite easy to do—compares the stability of results from samples of different sizes, providing the insight that larger samples give more consistent results than smaller ones, but that reasonably large samples are almost as good as censuses of the entire population. The second project, which is another example of sampling, uses many questionnaire items rather than many samples. The remaining four projects challenge you to test four theories about juvenile delinquency. You must select questionnaire items, select a sample, and interpret the results.

1. Samples of Different Sizes. Select 10 questions for a short questionnaire, and administer it three times to a sample consisting of both races and both sexes. The first sample should consist of 10 teenagers, the second of 100 teenagers, and the third of 500 teenagers.

For each sample, determine what percent of respondents answered "yes" or "no" to each of the 10 questions. Draw up a big table comparing these percentages for all three samples. Then write a brief essay describing the results and explaining why one of the three samples is more trustworthy than the others.

2. Two Large Samples. Create a short questionnaire of about a dozen questions and administer it to two samples of 500 teenagers from the same city. That is, draw two identical random samples. Make a table showing the percentages that gave each response to each item, allowing you to compare the two samples.

Write a brief essay explaining why the two samples differ somewhat in their responses and outlining what you feel you now know about the population from which the two samples were drawn.

3. Strain Theory. Following Hirschi's conceptualization, create a questionnaire to test strain theory's explanation of juvenile delinquency. This will require you to select the right items to represent strain theory and to measure delinquency. Use just one sample, of 500 teenagers, from a city of your choice. Write an essay summarizing your findings.

This project can be especially exciting when combined with the following two. The class would be divided into thirds, each group testing one of the three theories Hirschi identified. Then the groups would present their findings in class, concluding with a great debate concerning which theory the data best support.

4. Control Theory. Use the same instructions given for project 3, above, but focus on control theory as an explanation of deviance.

5. Cultural Deviance Theory. Use the same instructions given for project 3, above, but focus on cultural deviance theory as an explanation of deviance.

6. Does Religion Deter Delinquency? Create a brief questionnaire including the items about religion and the measures of delinquency. Administer it to samples of 500 teenagers in all eight cities. For each city, examine crosstabs that will tell you whether religion deters delinquency, and write down the summary statistics (chi-square, significance, Q, and phi). Then write an essay stating your findings, with special emphasis on the question of whether you got the same results in all eight cities. If you got very different results in some of the cities, try to explain why.

CHAPTER SUMMARY

The term *survey research* refers very generally to the systematic collection of data about an entire population, whether by questionnaires or some other means. Practical considerations often force us to study a sample that we believe represents the population well. *Secondary analysis* using survey data is research with different aims from those for which the questionnaire was originally written, often done by people who played no role in designing or administering the survey.

Although questionnaire items have an almost infinite variety, it is possible to identify several common types: menu items, agree-disagree statement items, preference scales, and the semantic differential. A *knee-jerk item* is one that elicits an almost automatic, conventional response from most respondents, and it contributes nothing to a good survey. *Screening questions* are items that separate people into subgroups that receive different contingent questions. *Contingent questions* are items that only a subgroup of respondents is supposed to answer.

Several kinds of response bias can also detract from surveys, including *acquiescence* (yea-saying and nay-saying) and *social desirability bias*. A low response rate reduces the value of a survey. There are a number of techniques for administering surveys, including printed questionnaires, verbal interrogation using interview schedules, and *CATI* (Computer-Assisted Telephone Interviewing).

A *sample* is a subset of people in the population under study. There are several kinds of samples: purposive samples, convenience samples, snowball samples, quota samples, simple random samples, systematic samples, categorical samples or stratified random samples (often with oversampling), proportionate samples, cluster samples, and multistage samples.

The SAMP program illustrates a number of features of sampling and analysis of survey data. It is a realistic simulation of an actual research study on juvenile delinquency, performed a number of years ago by criminologist Travis Hirschi. It also provides practice in thinking through the logic of social research, because the student can test hypotheses derived from three competing theories of delinquent behavior: *strain theory, control theory*, and *cultural deviance theory*.

The student creates a survey by selecting as many as 20 yes-no items from a list of 40, then selects a research site in one of eight cities and a sample of teenagers. The student can draw many different samples for comparison, with two of them appearing at once on the computer screen in two-by-two crosstabs with simple statistics attached.

A question on sex education from the Gallup Poll explains the concept of *margin of error*. Margin of error is the range around an estimate from a survey that employed a simple random sample in which 95 percent of samples would fall, if one drew a very large number of samples from the population.

KEY CONCEPTS FOR CHAPTER 7

CHAPTER

8

Methods for Handling Survey Variables

CHAPTER OVERVIEW

This chapter introduces a new dataset, based on questionnaires filled out by 512 college students, and offers you a set of simple tools for gaining a truly fascinating wealth of results. Extending your familiarity with good methods for creating and administering a survey, it offers realistic experience working with variables in a variety of ways, including recoding. Beginning with concepts of central tendency (mean, median, mode), it introduces levels of measurement (nominal, ordinal, interval, ratio) and discusses problems such as skewed distributions and missing values. Building on the two-by-two tables introduced earlier, it expands the concept of crosstabulation to encompass tables of any size.

The 87-item student opinion survey that provides the data for this chapter and the next was administered in the wake of the explosion of the space shuttle Challenger, and it includes several items tapping respondents' attitudes toward the space program. The majority of the items are preference questions, and 30 of these let students express their feelings about particular academic subjects, such as sociology. Thus, you will learn about variables and crosstabulations while working with material that is very meaningful to you, since it concerns how fellow students evaluate the college courses they are taking.

The XTAB program is a clean, simple, but full-featured statistical package that gives you

power to examine the student opinion data in many different ways. This chapter teaches you how to use the following options: data from one case, statistics about one variable, histogram for one variable, summary statistics about 1 through 10 variables, crosstab of two variables, recoding a variable, selecting or rejecting cases on the basis of a variable, and drawing a random sample. We must begin with an introduction to the dataset, consisting of 87 variables for the 512 respondents. We will use these data not only in this chapter but also in Chapter 9, which teaches us how to calculate the statistical measures introduced here and explains the logic underlying them. Appendix B lists the items in the questionnaire. Now we shall take a brief overview of the research based on this instrument.

The Student Opinion Survey

On January 28, 1986, I was one of a few dozen people with press credentials visiting Jet Propulsion Laboratory, the chief planetary exploration base of the National Aeronautics and Space Administration. I had been there in 1981, when the Voyager II robot spacecraft flew past the planet Saturn, and now Voyager had encountered Uranus, a mysterious world never before seen close up. JPL was enjoying a rare moment of public attention, and the place was alive with intellectual excitement. For more than a decade, weak funding for deep-space exploration had prevented achievements like the missions to Mars of the late 1960s and early 1970s, and Voyager had actually been launched way back in 1977. In May of 1986, the space shuttle Challenger was scheduled to send JPL's long-delayed Galileo probe to the planet Jupiter, the first American interplanetary launch in 10 years. So many of us turned with special interest to watch NASA's private TV coverage of Challenger's January flight.

A little over a minute after lift-off, Challenger exploded, killing its seven-person crew and devastating the staff of JPL. The crew was

practically a cross-section of American society. There were two civilians among them, a schoolteacher and an employee of an aerospace corporation. There were two women, an Asian-American, an African-American, Christians of various denominations, and a Jew. Many at JPL knew crew members personally, and all immediately realized that their own careers had suffered a near-fatal blow. They did not know when or how the Galileo probe, in which many had invested more than a decade of their lives, could complete its mission. College professors and graduate students in many fields of science would have to wait many years for the data they needed for their projects, and employees of an already-faltering space program had good reason to fear for their jobs.

A year before, I had been asked to testify before a presidential commission that was charting a possible grand future for the space program. Although personally committed to vigorous exploration of space, I did not feel that the private views of a sociologist were of much worth, so I declined to testify. But when the Challenger disaster forcefully raised the long-simmering debate over the future of spaceflight, I decided it was time for a sociological research project to outline the goals our culture imagined that spaceflight might achieve for humanity (Bainbridge 1990b). Altogether, I administered about 4,000 questionnaires, and the data we shall work with came from a survey that 1,007 students at Harvard University filled out during the spring following the Challenger explosion.

Much of the survey consisted of open-ended questions, asking respondents to express their views on the value of the space program and various particular space projects. A second survey, administered in the fall, consisted entirely of closed-ended items based on the written comments collected in the spring. This second space questionnaire provides the data for use with Chapter 14. A few closed-ended items in the spring survey had come from national polls and were designed both to get respondents thinking about the issues and to collect a little quantitative data. And I had also included a set of 68 preference questions—items asking respondents how much they like something—on an experimental basis.

The first 32 of these preference questions, which concerned academic subjects the college students might have studied, are ideal for our educational purposes here. The instructions said: "Following is a list of various subjects which are taught at universities. Please tell us how much you like each one of them, whether you have actually taken a course in it or not." For each one, the respondents were supposed to mark a number on a seven-point scale. The bottom of the scale (represented by the number 1 in our dataset) means "do not like the subject at all." The top of the scale (the number 7) means "like it very much." The subjects range from Anthropology to Zoology and are listed in Appendix B. As we work with these data, you can think which of the subjects you particularly like or dislike, and compare your feelings with those of our respondents.

Another 36 items asked respondents to rate a wide variety of things on the same seven-point preference scale. When I wrote the survey, I had just published a book on science fiction literature (Bainbridge 1986), based on preference-question surveys I had administered to participants at an SF (science fiction) convention. The quantitative part of that research had found that there were primarily three branches of SF literature, each having a different view of the future and of the relationship society has with science and technology. I included 12 items in the spring 1986 survey, four for each of the three factions of science fiction. Without having a very serious research purpose, I was interested to see if the correlations I had found for SF fans would hold up for college students with a wider range of interests.

The *Hard-Science* faction in science fiction is very optimistic about the future, believing advanced science and technology can accomplish almost anything. People who like this variety also like "fiction based on the physical sciences," "stories in which there is a rational explanation for everything," "stories about new technology," and "stories about scientific progress." Indeed, these four preference items pretty much define what Hard-Science SF is.

The *New Wave*, in contrast, is "fiction based on the social sciences," "avant-garde fiction which experiments with new styles," "fiction that is critical of our society," and "fiction which deeply probes personal relationships and feelings." The third category, often called *Fantasy*, includes "stories about magic," "tales of the supernatural," "myths and legends," and "fantasy stories involving swords and sorcery."

Some of these items might seem a bit weird to respondents who are not fans of SF, so I began the section of the survey with some more familiar kinds of fiction that might get varied ratings from different groups: "spy and detective stories," "stories of love and romance," "science fiction stories," "television soap operas like Dallas and Dynasty," and "war stories." Similar items had been tried out in an earlier questionnaire discussed in the previous chapter and reported in Figure 7.1. After the 12 SF items came a half-dozen that might resonate with one or another of the factions: "factual science articles," "poetry," "utopian political novels and essays," "Feminist literature," "the holy Bible," and "essays critical of American society."

Because the military aspects of the space program are politically controversial, I included a few preference items about political issues: "President Ronald Reagan," "electing a woman as president of the United States," "the Republican Party," "the Democratic Party," "investment in South Africa," and "the Equal Rights Amendment." Investment in South Africa was a particularly hot controversy on campus at the time, and a student group had erected a simulated South African shanty town in Harvard Yard to protest the university's investments.

Mostly for fun, I included "advanced technology," "IBM personal computers," and "Apple personal computers." Both types of PC might be considered advanced technology, but Apple had been waging an advertising campaign depicting IBM users as mindless robots and asserting that Apples were the right machines for warm, breathing human beings. I wondered if respondents would actually rate the two brands of computers differently.

One of the items about space adapted from national polls asked respondents if they would go on the first trip to Mars themselves. I have always suspected that such speculative, unrealistic questions are at best opportunities for people to express fanciful self-images, and might not say anything about either support for space exploration or real willingness to undertake risks. To explore this further, I included four risk items: "driving very fast in a car," "complete personal security," "taking physical risks," and "taking risks in your relationships with people."

To complete the dataset, the computer helped me create eight extra items to add to the 79 that came directly from the survey. They are numbered 80 through 87, and we will explain each when we make use of it.

Although 1,007 students were kind enough to fill out the survey, I decided to use just 512 of them for this text/disk. The number 512 was convenient for the computer language in which I was writing my programs, and is about half of the total available. As is usually the case in scientific research, practical considerations made me work with a sample rather than the whole set—to save space on your disk and to make the calculations go faster when you use the statistical analysis programs. Because they parallel decisions you might have to make when you do a survey, I will explain the decisions I made in selecting respondents.

Some students did not fill the questionnaires out completely or conscientiously. Only 978 of the 1,007 got all the way through and completed the last page. When you do surveys or systematic interviews, you will have to decide what to do with these incomplete responders. Often, you will decide to throw all their data out, and hope that these people are not very different from the complete responders you keep in your sample. They may be especially cantankerous or disagreeable people, but society is composed of all types. Therefore, you might want to include whatever items these people answered, leaving them out only when they failed to answer a particular question of interest. Because our purposes here are educational, to gain some experience analyzing real data, we don't need to worry about whether our findings are perfectly representative of the college. So I threw out the 29 worst responders.

One of the questions of greatest interest came from a national poll, the General Social Survey (Davis and Smith 1986), and I mentioned it in the previous chapter. It asks people to place themselves on a very simple seven-point political scale from "extremely liberal" to "extremely conservative." Now, some very reasonable and responsible people just can't answer this GSS question. For example, a few students couldn't care less about politics. One wrote in the margin of the questionnaire, "My politics are *nil* or perhaps: being nice to other people." Another just wrote, "none." The middle response on the scale was "moderate, middle of the road," and I'm sure many people with no interest in politics would pick this one. Some especially conscientious, apolitical respondents, however, might feel this wasn't the correct choice, and might decide it was best to leave the answer blank.

In contrast, some students who are highly interested in politics might feel they are mixtures of extreme liberalism and extreme conservatism. The platform of the Libertarian Party seems to many like a selection of ideas from the two ends of the ordinary political spectrum. Although it has been a very small force in American politics, this party did achieve the third highest vote for presidential candidate in the 1988 election. One respondent wrote, "I'm a Libertarian; this scale won't fit my political beliefs." Another echoed, "I am a Libertarian. I believe in conservative economics and foreign policy, but I have liberal social beliefs." Two marked double responses, adding labels to clarify them. One was a liberal on domestic/fiscal issues and slightly conservative on foreign/monetary issues. Another was socially liberal but conservative in economic and foreign policy. And one admitted, "I'm schizophrenic. I oppose abortion and the death penalty; guns and peace marches."

Still others simply couldn't express their political feelings through such a simple question. "Cannot generalize," wrote one next to the item. Another asked, "What are your criteria?" Here are some other comments: "I don't understand this," "I don't have 'general' political views, just views on particular issues," "I don't like labeling myself." Others seemed a bit irritated: "I reject such labels; they are too limiting." "Only robots and morons easily fit into a neat category."

But 947 of our 978 good responders were able to select a choice for this question, and I doubt that they were robots or morons. On the other hand, the 31 who couldn't give a conventional answer to the question deserve respect, and for most purposes you would want to include their answers. I have dropped them from consideration merely to give us the largest possible number of straightforward responses to this item, among our target 512.

When you administer a questionnaire, some members of your sample will fail to respond. Suppose you mail out 1,000 surveys and only 500 come back. That is 50 percent of what you attempted to get, a proportion we can call the *response rate*. But a few who return the questionnaire will fail to answer the questions, or do so in an obviously uncooperative way. I have received unanswered questionnaires with poignant messages like "Sorry, he's gone blind and can't help you," or "Grandma died last week, so I'm sending back her questionnaire." If 25 of our 500 questionnaires were clearly ruined in these ways, you should throw them out. Then you would be working with 475 out of the original target of 1,000, for a response rate of 47.5 percent. But if you reject another 25 good responders because they gave odd answers to your key question, you should say so in your report, or do analyses using their data as best you can, rather than pitching them out and having a 45-percent response rate. They responded, but just not in the most convenient way for analysis.

So I pared the 1,007 surveys down to 947. To select the final 512, I used sampling just the way you do when sampling a population in preparation for administering a survey. I treated the 947 questionnaires as the *population* and I drew a smaller *sample*. As the previous chapter showed, there are several ways to do sampling, and you have to decide the best approach for your particular project. If we want an unbiased representative sample, the simple random sample might be most appropriate. But in the present case, keeping our educational aims in mind, a combination of quota sampling and proportional random sampling will give us both a useful sample and fresh practice thinking about sampling.

First, I used *quota sampling* to get equal numbers of women and men. Only 320 of the 947 were women. This happened both because Harvard has more male students than female students and because I administered my questionnaire to people who volunteered to express their views about spaceflight, a topic more men than women care about. In the general population, and at American colleges, the sexes are about equally represented, so I set a quota of 256 for each group. This required me to sample

80 percent of the women compared with 41 percent of the men.

Second, I wanted samples that reflected the political distribution within each sex, so I used *proportional random sampling* based on the GSS political question. By chance, a simple random sample might have a slightly different distribution on the political question, and the proportional random sample sticks closer to the population's distribution. As I explained in the previous chapter, this approach works only when you know the distribution in the population and have practical methods for doing the sampling, as we certainly do in this case. The final result was 512 good responders, equally divided between the sexes, with the same political distributions within each sex as in the original set of questionnaires.

Running the XTAB Program

There are 10 choices on the menu of the XTAB program—numbered from zero to nine, so you get each one by pressing a single key—and we will explore them in order. As usual, the computer lists the options and says, "Press the number key for your choice."

(0) Data from one case
(1) Statistics about one variable
(2) Histogram for one variable
(3) Summary statistics about 1–10 variables
(4) Crosstab of two variables
(5) Analysis of variance
(6) Recode a variable
(7) Select/reject on basis of a variable
(8) Draw a random sample
(9) Undo all recodes, select/rejects, samples
(ESC) Quit or switch programs

Data from One Case

The first option, data from one case, gets us familiar with the variables and how to identify them. It does so by showing us how a particular respondent answered the items in the questionnaire. When you press (0) from the menu, the computer announces, "You have 512 cases." The cases, of course, are the 512 students whose questionnaires constitute our dataset. The computer asks, "Which one do you want?" To select one of the respondents, type a number from 1 through 512 and press (ENTER). For our example, we will inspect case number 1. We type (1) and press (ENTER). The computer will display the data from case 1, as shown here in Figure 8.1.

Much of the screen is filled with 87 words or short phrases, often containing abbreviations. These are the **variable names**, descriptions of our 87 variables that

FIGURE 8.1
Data from Case 1

Value	#	Item	Value	#	Item	Value	#	Item
6	1	Botany	3	25	Engineering	1	73	Space civilians
3	2	Astronomy	4	26	Sociology	2	74	Manned space pro
7	3	Foreign language	5	27	Literature	1	75	Space station
4	4	Law	5	28	Medicine	2	76	Defense satellit
4	5	Political scienc	7	29	Zoology	3	77	Mars project
6	6	Music	4	30	Architecture	2	78	Go to Mars
6	7	History	5	31	Sciences	1	79	Contact ETs
4	8	Classics	1	32	Humanities	3	80	Random data 1
4	9	Physics	6	33	Spy stories	4	81	Random data 2
4	10	Geology	1	34	Love stories	7	82	Liberalism
2	11	Business	4	35	Science fiction	1	83	Apple fan
7	12	Biology	2	36	Soap operas	4	84	Spaceflight supp
6	13	Chemistry	7	37	War stories	1	85	Physical science
6	14	Art	4	38	Physical sci. fic.	6	86	Life sciences
3	15	Mathematics	6	39	Social sci. fic.	3	87	Social sciences
2	16	Economics	4	40	Magic stories			
4	17	Education	6	41	Rational stories			
7	18	Anthropology	3	42	Avant garde			
6	19	Nursing	7	43	Supernatural			
6	20	Oceanography	5	44	Technology story			
6	21	Social work	3	45	Critical fiction			
3	22	Drama	1	46	Myths & legends			
6	23	Psychology	1	47	Progress stories			
4	24	Communications	3	48	Feelings fiction			
			3	49	Swords & sorcery			
			4	50	Science articles			
			5	51	Poetry			
			5	52	Utopian essays			
			7	53	Feminist liter.			
			4	54	Holy Bible			
			5	55	Critical essays			
			1	56	Ronald Reagan			
			6	57	Woman president			
			1	58	Republican Party			
			4	59	Democratic Party			
			2	60	South Africa			
			7	61	Equal Rights Am.			
			4	62	Advanced technol			
			6	63	IBM PCs			
			4	64	Apple PCs			
			6	65	Driving fast			
			3	66	Personal securit			
			7	67	Physical risks			
			5	68	People risks			
			3	69	Student category			
			1	70	Sex			
			1	71	Conservatism			
			3	72	Space funding			

are short enough so all can fit on the screen. In front of the labels are two sets of numbers. Immediately next to the labels, highlighted in tall boxes or strips—dark letters on bright background on most computers—are the variable numbers, running from 1 through 87. The other numbers are the variable values for the particular respondent.

A *value* is the number assigned to a particular response to a question. For example, the value for the first item, Botany, is 6 for the first respondent. This is high on the preference scale from 1 through 7, meaning that she likes Botany quite a lot. Her value for Astronomy, in contrast, is 2, very near the bottom. Look over items 1 through 68 in Figure 8.1, and you will see what this particular respondent loves and hates. Sociology, item 26 near the top of the second column, got a 4 rating, which is near the middle of the 1 through 7 scale.

She gives a 7 to five academic subjects: Biology, Anthropology, Literature, Medicine, and Zoology. She also loves soap operas, "feelings fiction" (fiction that deeply probes personal relationships and feelings), Feminist literature, the Equal Rights Amendment, and taking personal risks. Clearly, some of these are logically connected. Botany, Biology, Medicine, and Zoology are academic subjects concerned with life. Soap operas concern feelings. Feminists usually support the Equal Rights Amendment.

It is not terribly surprising that she gives identical ratings to Ronald Reagan and the Republican Party, which he headed at the time of the survey. As it happens, she hated them equally and gave both 1 ratings, the bottom of the scale. You should have no trouble making sense of the variable values for the 68 preference questions. They are simply the numbers of the preference scale, 1 through 7.

To understand the values for other variables, you need to look at the questionnaire itself, Appendix B at the back of this book. For several items, the values are given next to each possible response. On question number 69 about student category, a value of 1 means the respondent is a freshman. A 2 indicates a sophomore. Because the value for student category is 3 for the first respondent, we know she is a junior.

How do we know she is a she? Her value for sex is 1. When I wrote the questionnaire, I gave respondents two boxes, labeled "Female" and "Male," to indicate their gender. Because the "Female" box came first, I tagged it as value 1. Value 2 means male. This is entirely arbitrary. But once we've decided which number means which sex, we have to stick with our decision, or endless confusion will result.

Item 71, conservatism, is the key political question from the GSS, as I mentioned above. Recall that the respondent was supposed to mark a number, from 1 for "extreme liberal" to 7 for "extreme conservative." Apparently, our respondent is an extreme liberal, because her value for this variable is 1. Note that I have named the variable "Conservatism." I did this because conservatives are asked to mark the high numbers on the scale, and the bigger the number the more conservative the respondent. This does not in any way suggest that conservatism is better than liberalism. Again, the particular values merely reflect the way the question was originally written. By calling the item "Conservatism," we can more easily recall what the value numbers mean. Later, we shall see how this Conservatism item can be transformed into a Liberalism scale.

Variables 72 through 79 are the questions about the space program, each one written with a different set of responses. To understand their values, you must consult the questionnaire. Again, the special variables numbered 80 through 87 will be discussed later.

One of the main principles of this book is that students and researchers need to keep closely in touch with their data, no matter how abstract or subtle their theories and methods of statistical analysis are. And this first option on the menu lets you see the actual data for any one of the 512 respondents. When you are through looking at it on your computer, press (ENTER) to return to the menu.

Statistics about One Variable

The second option on the menu shows how all the respondents answered one of the questions. When you select this option, by pressing (2), the computer will show you the variable names, numbered 1 through 87, and instruct, "Enter the number of the variable you want." This means you should find the variable in the list, type its number, and press (ENTER). Our first example will be Sociology, which is item number 26. You type 26 and press (ENTER). Figure 8.2 shows what you would get.

Much of the screen is filled with a simple table showing the distribution of cases across the values. You must have seen many like it in books, newspapers, and in social science classes. There are three columns of numbers, labeled Value, Cases, and Percent. As we just explained, a value is a number representing a particular response to a question on the survey. Anyone who has a value of 7 for Sociology has given it the highest preference rating. He or she likes it very much. Social scientists use the word *case* for each of the things they have data about. Here, a case is a person. Each of the 512 respondents to the survey is a case. The table tells us that 37 of them gave Sociology the top rating of 7. Eighty gave a rating of 6, and 109 gave a rating of 5. This distribution of cases for the various values is often called the *frequencies*.

FIGURE 8.2
Statistics for Variable 26: Sociology

	Value	Cases	Percent	Mode?	Cases: 512
Like very much	7	37	7.3%		Good cases: 508
	6	80	15.7%		Missing cases: 4
	5	109	21.5%		Median: 4.00
Range: 1–7	4	124	24.4%	Yes	
	3	72	14.2%		Dispersion: 0.97
	2	48	9.4%		Mean: 4.19
Do not like	1	38	7.5%		Variance: 2.66
Total		508	100%		Standard deviation: 1.63

The upper right-hand corner of the screen says, "Cases: 512. Good cases: 508. Missing cases: 4." First, this reminds us that the full dataset has 512 cases or respondents. But not all of them may have answered the question about Sociology. In fact, there are only 508 good cases, respondents who marked one (and only one) of the numbers on the preference scale for Sociology. Four respondents failed to do so, and they are the 4 missing cases. Look back at the table, to the very bottom of the cases column, and you see the number 508 again, identified as the total.

The figures in the percent column are percentages out of 508, not 512. Of the 508 people who answered the question, 7.3 percent of them gave sociology the top rating of 7. And almost exactly the same proportion, 7.5 percent, gave sociology the worst rating of 1. The numbers in the percent column should add up to 100%. If you went to the trouble of adding them up by hand, you would find that the percents in this table do total exactly 100%. Occasionally, the percents in a different table will really total 99.9 or 100.1—although the total at the bottom always says 100%—because the computer has to round off the figures to the nearest tenth of a percent, and sometimes this introduces a tiny error.

On the left of the table is a message, "Range : 1–7." The *range* of a variable is the set of values it can have, and our preference scale runs from 1 through 7. To remind you of the meaning of the values for the preferences questions, the computer prints "Like very much" to the left of value 7, and "Do not like" to the left of value 1.

Other information on the screen gives the mean, median, and mode, three different kinds of average. The kind of average you probably are most familiar with is the **mean.** To calculate it, you would add up all the scores the 508 respondents gave to sociology and divide by the number of cases. The total number of points given sociology happened to be 2,130. Divide that by 508 and you get about 4.19, which is the mean.

The **median** is the value for the middle case, if the cases are ranked in terms of their values. Imagine a long, straight street. We bring in the 508 good respondents in a dozen buses (the 4 missing cases must be off in a bar somewhere). Then we line them up. First, the 38 who gave sociology a 1 rating stand in a row along the side of the street. Then, after them in the same row we line up the 48 who gave sociology a 2 rating. We continue in the same way until all 508 people are in one line, about a half-mile long. Then you start counting at one end. You walk down the road until you find the middle person. Then you write down that person's rating for sociology, which happens to be 4, and this is the median.

Of course, there really isn't a middle person in a line of 508, because 508 is an even number. The middle comes right between person number 254 and person 255. They happen to agree about sociology, both giving it a 4 rating, so there's no difficulty deciding what the median is. With an odd number of good cases, there always is a middle person, and his or her value is the median.

What do you do when you have an even number and the two people on either side of the middle disagree? One alternative is to split the difference and say the median is halfway between them. If one of the two middle people gave sociology a 4 and the other gave it a 5, you could decide the median was 4.5, halfway between 4 and 5. Sometimes the two middle people are quite far apart—for example, if you were lining them up in terms of their bank accounts—and there are a variety of standard ways of deciding exactly where to place the median when these complications arise. With our data, however, this almost never happens, and the median is easy to calculate and to understand.

The **mode** is the most common value. Sociology got a 4 rating from 124 people, a larger number than chose any other value. Notice "Mode?" at the top right edge of the table. Look under it and you will find the word "Yes" next to value 4. This means that 4 is the mode. Sometimes two or more values will be tied, and there will be two or more modes. If you want, you can think of the mode as the most fashionable responses, since the word *mode* is sometimes used to refer to fashions in clothing. In a sense, it is the standard response, the one the most people give.

Often, as in the case of preferences for Sociology, the mean, median, and mode are very close together, even identical. But sometimes, they can be quite far apart. Imagine we asked the 512 respondents what their annual incomes were. A hundred of them might say "zero dollars" because they were unemployed. The other 412 would name a great variety of income figures. So the mode would be "zero dollars," because that was the most common response. But the typical respondent earned something, and the mean and median might be in the thousands of dollars.

Suppose 411 of the respondents earned various amounts around $10,000, but one respondent owned all of Saudi Arabia's oil and earned a billion dollars a year. The median would be near $10,000, but the mean would be around $2,000,000. To get the median, you look for the middle person. So, counting from the bottom end, you first pass the 100 with zero income, then work your way through some of those earning around $10,000 until you find the middle. To calculate the mean, however, you add together all the incomes and divide by 512. The billion-dollar income of one person gets spread around to make everybody look rich.

There is nothing wrong in having a mean, median, and mode that are very different numbers. Each is telling you something different, and together they give you a fuller picture than any one of them could provide.

The table shows you three other statistics that we shall not discuss at length here: dispersion, variance, and standard deviation. All three are measures of how spread out the cases are across the values; the bigger the number the more spread out they are. But these three bits of information won't be very useful to you until we have discussed them in detail, a job we won't do in this chapter. Dispersion will come up in Chapter 9, while variance and standard deviation will come up in Chapter 10.

Histogram for One Variable

If you try the histogram option, it will practically explain itself. Figure 8.3 shows what you would get if you asked the computer for a histogram of Sociology ratings. A **histogram** is a simple bar graph that lets you visually compare the numbers of people who have each value on the variable. Each bar in the histogram is labeled with a number at the bottom. The bar at the far left represents the people who

FIGURE 8.3
Histogram of a Variable

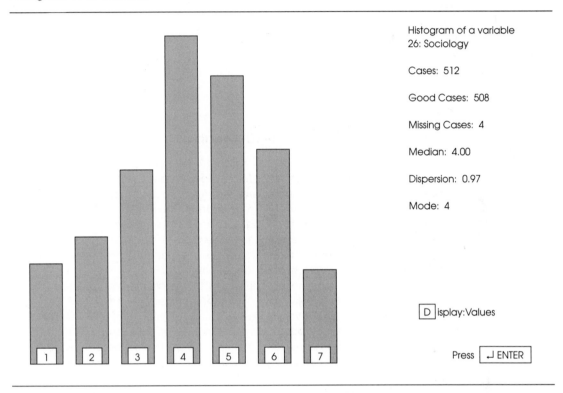

Histogram of a variable
26: Sociology

Cases: 512

Good Cases: 508

Missing Cases: 4

Median: 4.00

Dispersion: 0.97

Mode: 4

[D] isplay:Values

Press [↵ ENTER]

gave Sociology a low rating of 1. The bar at the right is for the people who gave it a 7, indicating that they love Sociology.

A glance shows you that the 4 bar is the highest, and information to the right of the bars reminds you that the median and mode are both 4. The bars get shorter and shorter the farther they are from the 4 bar in the middle. But bars 5 and 6 are noticeably taller than bars 3 and 2, indicating that more people gave responses on the high side. When a histogram is somewhat unbalanced like this, we say that the distribution is **skewed**. Other variables in this survey dataset are far more skewed than this, with most respondents bunched at one end of the distribution. If a variable is not skewed at all, the histogram will be perfectly symmetrical.

The mean, which you get with the statistics on a variable, provides one way of measuring skewness. For Sociology the mean is 4.19. When the mean is high, the distribution is skewed toward the high end. When the mean is low, it is skewed toward the low end. In Chapter 11 we will learn more about distributions, but for now the picture the histogram provides is quite clear enough.

You might want to know how many people are represented by each bar in the histogram, but I did not want to clutter the graph with many numbers. Notice "(D)isplay:Values" near the lower-right corner of the screen. The "Values" part tells you that the numbers at the bottom of the bars currently express the values, 1 through 7. The D of Display is highlighted in a box, which means you can change the display by pressing the D key. If you press (D) once, the value numbers will be replaced by the number of cases each bar represents—124 cases for the 4 bar. A second press of the (D) key will give you the percents, rounded off to the nearest whole percent, and a third press of (D) will take you back to the values.

Summary Statistics about 1–10 Variables

One way to compare two variables is to check the statistics for the first one, write them all down, then get the statistics for the second one and look back and forth between your paper and the computer screen. This can get awkward, especially when you want to compare three or four at once. The fourth option on the menu lets you compare as many as 10 variables on the screen at once. You get a pair of tables—and the screen can be absolutely covered with figures if you choose many variables—but the information is easy to understand because it is all taken from the familiar second menu option, statistics about one variable.

When you press (4), the computer will begin asking you for the numbers of the variables you want. First, it says, "Enter the number of the item that should be variable 1." As usual, pick a variable you want from the list, type its number, and press (ENTER). Then the computer asks for item 2, item 3, and so on. After item 10, it will automatically stop asking for more. If you want to stop before 10, however, simply press (ENTER) an extra time. You can select any variables you want, in any order.

Figure 8.4 shows how the first 10 items would look in this thick pair of tables. The table in the top half of the screen gives the number of good cases, the number of missing cases, and the frequencies. Check the first row. For Botany there are 508 good cases and 4 missing cases. Seventy-two people gave Botany the lowest rating of 1, while 10 gave it a top 7. In the second row you will see that there are 511 good cases for Astronomy, while only 1 person failed to rate Astronomy.

The table in the bottom half of the screen lists the range, median, mean, dispersion, and variance for each of the selected variables. Each preference question used the same seven-point scale, so the ranges are all 1–7. However, if there were some subject nobody liked—Spelling, for example (a subject not actually in our list)—its range would be smaller, perhaps only 1–6 or 1–5. The range the computer gives always runs from 1 to the highest response actually given. You can look at the questionnaire in Appendix B to check the range of possible responses.

If you want to compare the modes of the variables, it is easy enough to look for them in the frequency distributions that fill the upper-right quadrant of the screen. Botany's mode is 3, because 122 cases have that value, while the second largest number of cases is 115. What is Astronomy's mode? Well, it has two modes, 4 and 5, because these two values are tied with 118 cases each.

I shall explain dispersion in the following chapter. Although I shall explain variance in Chapter 10, you can get a quick idea of what it is about by looking at the information for Physics and comparing it with information for a couple of other

FIGURE 8.4
Summary Statistics for the First Ten Variables

| Good Variable | Missing Cases | Number of cases with the value: | | | | | | |
	Cases	1	2	3	4	5	6	7
1 Botany	508	4	72	108	122	115	58	23	10
2 Astronomy	511	1	16	39	84	118	118	85	51
3 Foreign language	511	1	20	31	40	79	108	132	101
4 Law	509	3	28	53	60	105	97	109	57
5 Political science	511	1	26	41	65	90	91	105	93
6 Music	511	1	17	35	64	93	118	84	100
7 History	511	1	12	14	25	79	114	143	124
8 Classics	508	4	18	58	93	117	102	74	46
9 Physics	511	1	90	65	88	92	73	67	36
10 Geology	512	0	74	102	113	117	59	30	17

Variable	Range	Median	Mean	Dispersion	Variance
1 Botany	1–7	3.0	3.17	0.95	2.16
2 Astronomy	1–7	4.0	4.45	0.96	2.34
3 Foreign language	1–7	5.0	5.00	0.95	2.69
4 Law	1–7	5.0	4.46	0.97	2.87
5 Political science	1–7	5.0	4.69	0.98	3.06
6 Music	1–7	5.0	4.78	0.96	2.73
7 History	1–7	6.0	5.34	0.92	2.11
8 Classics	1–7	4.0	4.25	0.97	2.50
9 Physics	1–7	4.0	3.66	0.99	3.45
10 Geology	1–7	3.0	3.28	0.96	2.45

variables. Physics has the largest variance, 3.45. I said that variance is a measure of how spread out the distribution is. Notice that the mode for Physics is 4 but that only 92 people chose this response, the lowest for any mode in the list. The least popular response to Physics is 7, liking it very much, and 36 people gave this response. But if you look through the frequencies for the nine other variables, you will see that the least popular response always has considerably fewer than 36 people choosing it. The Physics distribution is the most spread out of the 10, as the high variance shows.

Crosstab of Two Variables

This fifth option on the menu, the crosstab of two variables, is by far the most complicated, but also the most useful. You should be quite ready to understand most aspects of crosstabs, because they are simply an expanded version of the two-by-two tables we have been working with for the past few chapters. Previously, each variable had just two values, such as Yes or No. Now, each variable can have as many as 7 values, so we have to be ready to cope with seven-by-seven tables. Thankfully, the computer will do most of the work for us.

When you select crosstabs by pressing (5), the computer will ask you for two variables. It will call the first one you select *variable X*, the second one *variable Y*. If you are testing an hypothesis with an independent variable and a dependent variable, select the independent variable first; it will be X. Our first example will use variable 58 (liking the Republican Party) as X and variable 71 (the GSS political conservatism item) as Y. I am not testing a causal hypothesis, but merely demonstrating how the program runs, so we really aren't worried about which variable is independent and which dependent.

It certainly makes sense to guess that people who like the Republican Party tend to be conservatives and that conservatives tend to like the Republican Party. These are only tendencies, however, and individuals may hold a variety of attitudes toward these political concepts. The crosstab will show us whether in fact there is a connection between the two, and various statistics that come with it will measure the strength of this connection. Figure 8.5 shows the Republican-conservative crosstab.

First, I should mention that this crosstab is based on 511 good cases; one case is missing. For a crosstab, the good cases are the people who answered *both* of the questions. Anybody who fails to answer one of the questions is thrown into the missing data category and will not contribute to the other information on the

FIGURE 8.5
Crosstab of Republican and Conservativism

Good cases: 511
Missing cases: 1
r: 0.75
z: 16.90
Significance: .001

Gamma: 0.74
z: 14.43
Significance: .001

Tau-a: 0.50
Tau-b: 0.62
Tau-c: 0.59
D(X→Y): 0.60

Chi-square: 445.77
df: 36
Significance: .001

Variable X: Republican Party

		1	2	3	4	5	6	7	
	7	0	0	0	1	0	1	5	7
	6	0	0	0	4	9	13	14	40
	5	3	2	7	23	26	18	10	89
	4	3	5	14	21	4	4	2	53
	3	22	16	35	26	9	0	1	109
	2	67	47	27	19	4	2	0	166
Variable Y: Conservatism	1	34	10	2	0	1	0	0	47
		129	80	85	94	53	38	32	

[D] isplay frequencies   [C] alculate   Press [↵ ENTER]

screen. Remember that I selected our 512 respondents so that all of them gave valid answers to the conservatism item from the General Social Survey. But one, apparently, failed to rate the Republican Party, and the crosstab will be based on the 511 who did.

The crosstab itself is the rectangle with 49 cells that fills the right half of the screen. **Crosstab** is short for **crosstabulation**, a table that runs two variables across each other. Let's start at the top. See the words "Variable X: Republican Party," and below them the numbers 1 through 7. These numbers, and the columns of cells under them, refer to the seven values the Republican variable can take, the seven responses from 1 ("do not like") to 7 ("like very much").

Look down the first column of cells, under value 1 for the Republican Party. At the very bottom is the number 129, which tells us that 129 respondents gave the Republican party a rating of 1. Eighty respondents rated it 2. If you look below the right-hand column of cells you will see that only 32 people gave the Republican Party a top rating of 7. So the numbers across the top of the rectangle are the values for Republican Party, and the numbers across the bottom are the frequencies, each one under the proper value.

Now look along the left edge of the rectangle of cells, and you will see the numbers 1 through 7 again, running from bottom to top. These are the values for the conservatism variable. Running up the right edge of the rectangle are their frequencies. Way over at the right, in line with the bottom row of cells, is the number 47. This means that 47 respondents have a value of 1 on the conservatism scale. They are not conservative at all. Indeed, these were the people who marked the "extremely liberal" response to the GSS political question. Only 7 people marked "extremely conservative," and they are represented by the number 7 to the right of the top row of cells.

So far, we have discovered that the 49-cell rectangle is framed by the values for the two variables and their respective frequencies. This is the same kind of information we found around the familiar two-by-two tables of earlier chapters. As before, the frequencies are often called the *marginals,* perhaps because they lie around the margin of the crosstab.

As with two-by-two tables, the numbers in the cells of the crosstab tell us how many cases have each possible combination of values for the two variables. The number 5 in the upper-right corner represents the 5 extreme conservatives who love the Republican Party. The number 34 in the lower-left corner represents the 34 extreme liberals who hate the Republican Party. The other two corner cells contain zeros. This tells us that nobody who hates the Republican Party is an extreme conservative, and nobody who loves it is an extreme liberal. Other numbers strewn throughout the 49 cells represent various other shades of opinion.

Sometimes the picture is clearer when the contents of the cells are expressed as percentages rather than as raw numbers. As in some of the previous programs, you can get percentages with the (D)isplay command. When the crosstab comes on the screen, a message on the screen says, "(D)isplay:frequencies." This means that each cell contains the number showing how frequently respondents gave the corresponding combination of responses to the two variables.

If you press (D) once, the message changes to "(D)isplay:column percents." A second press gives you row percents. This is exactly the same as with our two-by-two tables in previous chapters, but if you have any question how the percentages are calculated, look for the "100%" statements below or to the right of the cross-tab. When the 100%s are at the bottom, they mean that each column of percents adds up to 100 vertically. If they are to the right, then each row adds up to 100% sideways. A final press of (D) and you get total percents, with each cell showing what percentage of the total good cases it contains.

As with two-by-two tables, if you have an independent variable, it is best to find the percentage in terms of it. To keep things straight, I suggest you always let X be the independent variable and get the column percents. Then you can compare across the columns. For example, you can then compare the percentage of those who love the Republican Party and are extreme conservatives (15.6%) with the percentage of those who hate the party and are extreme conservatives (0%). But there is no reason not to check all four display options when inspecting a table, and you can go from one to another endlessly, if you like, by pressing (D).

Analysis of Variance

Analysis of variance will be explained fully in Chapter 10. Although it is included in the XTAB program, it has connections to the parametric statistics discussed later in this book, and thus forms a kind of bridge from the material discussed here to the rather different approach discussed later. It is like a hybrid between a crosstab and a normal curve, which I shall explain in Chapter 10. Now, we need to spend a little time explaining aspects of the coefficients presented with a crosstab. This material will also be essential for understanding analysis of variance.

_____ Choosing the Right Tool for Different Kinds of Data

The left-hand side of a crosstab screen, such as that shown in Figure 8.5, is filled with coefficients: r, tau-a, tau-b, tau-c, gamma, Somers' D, and chi-square. You have seen chi-square before, when we were examining two-by-two tables in Chapter 6 and Chapter 7. The other statistics are measures of association (correlation coefficients), similar to phi and Yule's Q, which we also first encountered in Chapter 6, and information about statistical significance. In principle, all of them can range from −1.00 through 0.00 to +1.00. A significantly positive number means a positive correlation. A significantly negative number means a negative correlation. And a number near zero means no correlation at all. You should recall those

general ideas from our earlier work. Chapter 9 will reexamine correlation from the perspective of crosstabs.

You are probably wondering why there are so many different coefficients. Each has its own strengths and weaknesses. For example, for technical reasons that must wait until the next chapter, tau-a and tau-c have a lot of trouble getting all the way to +1.00 or −1.00, and they tend to be closer to zero than tau-b or gamma. Somers' D makes a distinction between the independent variable and the dependent variable. That's why I put the arrow (X →Y) after D on your screen, to emphasize that X was the independent variable and Y the dependent variable. If Republican Party is X, the independent variable, and conservatism is Y, the dependent variable, Somers' D is 0.60. But if you called for the crosstab the other way around, with conservatism for X and Republican Party for Y, Somers' D would come out 0.63.

Details such as these deserve thorough treatment in the next chapter, but we can address the question of which coefficients are right for which kind of data before we learn how the calculations are performed. As a practicing researcher, I often think there are two kinds of data—expensive data I can't get without a big research grant, and cheap data I can easily collect myself. In considering what association coefficient to use, however, there are four kinds of variables: nominal, ordinal, interval, and ratio. These are often described as four different **levels of measurement**.

Think for a moment about the different kinds of questions we ask in surveys. There are many different question formats and hundreds of different kinds of answers. We can ask the same question in many different ways. For example, suppose we wanted to see how people felt about funding for the space program. Here are four different ways we might ask:

1. In general, which of the following statements comes closest to how you feel about funding for the space program?
    [1] Although I favor space exploration, the current budget deficits require us to cut back in most areas, including space.
    [2] Other needs come first, such as feeding the hungry and housing the homeless, so I would delay space exploration until we had solved more of our problems here on earth.
    [3] Personally, I am not much interested in the space program, so I wouldn't mind seeing its funding reduced.
    [4] Space exploration is one of the most important investments we can make in the future of our economy, so I would like to see funding increased.

    [5] If we don't explore space, some other country will, so we must increase funding to keep the U.S. ahead.
    [6] Funding must be increased, because the gains to scientific knowledge and human understanding of the world around us are of incalculable value.
    [7] I really don't have an opinion on the proper level of space funding.

2. Should the amount of money being spent on the U.S. space program be increased, kept at current levels, or ended altogether?
    [1] Decreased greatly
    [2] Decreased
    [3] Decreased slightly
    [4] Kept the same as it is now
    [5] Increased slightly
    [6] Increased
    [7] Increased greatly

3. Compared to this year's appropriation, what would you like to see done with the funding for the space program next year?
    [1] Decreased by $3 billion
    [2] Decreased by $2 billion
    [3] Decreased by $1 billion
    [4] Kept the same as it is now
    [5] Increased by $1 billion
    [6] Increased by $2 billion
    [7] Increased by $3 billion

4. How much money do you feel the federal government should give to NASA (the National Aeronautics and Space Administration) next year?
    [1] No money at all
    [2] $2 billion
    [3] $4 billion
    [4] $6 billion
    [5] $8 billion
    [6] $10 billion
    [7] $12 billion

Read each of these carefully, especially the seven responses offered for each, and think about how the answers relate to each other. Note that when we put the data into the computer we just enter a single number for each respondent's answer to a question: 1, 2, 3, 4, 5, 6, or 7. The computer is a "dumb" machine and doesn't understand what the questions are really about. Although the numbers the computer sees may be the same, these four questions are of radically different types, requiring somewhat different treatment. Each exemplifies a different level of measurement.

Nominal Survey Items

Of the seven responses to the first space-funding question, three want funding increased and three want it reduced. But there is no hint how much funding should be changed, neither in dollars nor even in general qualitative terms. Also, although the three responses that want funding reduced differ greatly in meaning, it's hard to say which one would cut the program most. Nor can we decide which of the three responses about increasing funding involves spending the most dollars. Taken together, the answers to this complex question tell us something about what the respondent wants done about funding, but they seem aimed more at discovering the respondent's justifications than anything else.

When I wrote this question, I had no particular reason for putting the first three responses in the order you see, and I listed responses 4, 5, and 6 simply in the order they popped into my mind. I see no basis for ranking them in any particular order. The "no opinion" response comes last because survey researchers often find that people will use a response like this as a cop-out, when they could just as well express a more definite opinion; giving all the other choices first increases the chance that the respondent will pick one.

This variable is at the nominal level of measurement. **Nominal variables** put cases in categories, but the categories are not in any particular order. Another example would be any of the standard questions about religious tradition. "Please check the box that best indi-

cates your religious background: [1] Protestant [2] Catholic [3] Jewish [4] Other." These responses could have been offered in any order. It is common to see them in this order, because most Americans will check the first box, some will check the second, and few will check the last two. But there's nothing very logical about this order. We could have put Jewish first, because it is the most ancient of the three traditions, or we could have put Catholic first because it has more adherents worldwide and comes first in the alphabet.

With nominal variables, we are using numbers to represent the responses, but we have no right to do anything with these numbers we could not do with the names. I could have written my crosstab program to work with words like Protestant, Catholic, Jewish, and Other, instead of with the numbers 1 through 4. But the datasets would take up much more space on your disk and the calculations would go more slowly. Aside from these matters of convenience, using numbers rather than names to identify the categories of nominal variables does not accomplish a lot.

We cannot do much arithmetic on numbers that are the values of nominal variables. For example, even though we gave the number 3 to Jews and the number 1 to Protestants, it doesn't mean very much to divide this 3 by this 1, or to subtract one from the other. In what way are Jews three times Protestants? In what way are Jews 2 more than Protestants? (No, this is not the place for ethnic jokes.) In no way at all, so far as I know. The numbers in nominal variables should be considered names, and nothing more.

However, once you have created a crosstab with two nominal variables, it is quite appropriate to look at the column or row percentages and at chi-square. The numbers in the cells of the crosstab are honest numbers, counts of how many people fall into the particular pair of cross-cutting categories, and the calculations for percentages and chi-square can quite validly be done for them. However, none of the measures of association on the crosstab screen are appropriate for nominal variables.

Ordinal Survey Items

Responses to the second space question, in contrast, do come in a logical order. I have assigned the value 1 to "decreased greatly," the number 7 to "increased greatly," and all the responses in-between have numbers that run in order from the lowest NASA funding up to the highest. This means that the item is what we call an ordinal variable.

Ordinal variables put cases into categories that are in a logical order. Examples abound in survey research. Standard agree-disagree items give respondents a set of choices—for instance, boxes ranging from "strongly disagree" through "neutral or no opinion" to "strongly agree."

One of my earliest questionnaires about the space program, which 225 registered voters filled out, presented a list of 49 possible justifications for the space program, including the following four: "Space exploration adds tremendously to our scientific knowledge." "Space technology produces many valuable inventions and discoveries which have unexpected applications in industry or everyday life." "Raw materials from the moon and other planets can supplement the dwindling natural resources of the Earth." "Society has a chance for a completely fresh start in space; new social forms and exciting new styles of life can be created on other worlds." Respondents were supposed to read each of the 49 justifications and say how good a reason they thought it was for continuing the space program. Four responses were offered: [1] not a good reason, [2] slightly good reason, [3] moderately good reason, and [4] extremely good reason.

Clearly, these four responses are numbered in the correct order, with the worst justifications getting a rating of 1, and the best ones a rating of 4. But it is not appropriate to do many kinds of arithmetic with these numbers, just as was true for nominal variables. An extremely good reason is better than a slightly good reason, but is it exactly twice as good? That is, does it make sense to divide this 4 by this 2? Certainly not. The series of numbers specifies

the order of the responses, but it does not measure how far apart any two responses are. It is an ordinal scale.

How is the temperature today? Check a box: [1] cold, [2] cool, [3] warm, [4] hot. This is another ordinal scale. Cool is warmer than cold, but we do not know how many degrees there are between them. Further, we do not know that the temperature difference between cold and cool is the same as the difference between warm and hot. Cold might be 30°, cool might be 50°, warm might be 80°, and hot might be 90°. The temperature differences people have in mind might be quite irregular. All we know is the order of the four temperature responses.

If you look *ordinal number* up in a dictionary, you will probably see the words *first*, *second*, *third*, and *fourth* used to illustrate the concept. This is how we count when we are merely announcing the order things come in without measuring the differences between them. Although we can't do much ordinary arithmetic with the numbers in an ordinal scale, once they are in a crosstab we can analyze them with many different measures of association: tau-a, tau-b, tau-c, gamma, and D. The only measure of association the crosstab program provides that we cannot use is r.

Interval Survey Items

The third of our four space-funding questions asks people by how many billions of dollars we should decrease or increase the appropriation. The seven responses are in order from "decreased by $3 billion" to "increased by $3 billion." What's more, each answer is exactly $1 billion more than the last one. Therefore, this item is an interval variable.

Interval variables measure a quantity along a scale consisting of equal steps or intervals. Common thermometer scales are a good example. The difference between 79° and 80° is exactly the same as the difference between 80° and 81°, and the difference between 10° and 20° is exactly the same as the difference between 90° and 100°. You can validly add and subtract with these variables. If it is 80° and it gets 10° hotter, we know it is exactly 90°.

But it is not valid to multiply and divide the numbers in an interval scale. Perhaps by instinct, we avoid saying things like, "Today is twice as hot as yesterday." Oh yes, today could be 80°, and yesterday might have been 40°, but 80° is not really twice as hot as 40°. The reason is that the zero point on most of our scales is not where it should be. There is a temperature called absolute zero, which is really a point of no temperature, at about 460° below zero Fahrenheit and 273° below zero Celsius (centigrade). A lower temperature than this is physically impossible. Although scientists often use a temperature scale called Kelvin or absolute that has this for its zero, ordinary temperature scales have faulty zero points, so it is wrong to multiply and divide in them.

All the measures of association that are good for ordinal variables are also good for interval variables, but one more is also good: r. In Chapters 12 and 13 we will find that r has many advantages and that many other useful statistics are related to r. When they can, sociologists use r rather than the various taus or gamma.

Ratio Survey Items

The fourth space-funding question asks people how much should be spent, from $0 up to $12 billion, with responses progressing in equal steps of $2 billion. Here we have a proper zero—no funding at all, zero dollars and zero cents. Six billion is exactly half of twelve billion. This item gives us a ratio scale.

Ratio variables measure a quantity along a scale consisting of equal steps or intervals, starting from a zero point. Data about how much money people have, how old they are, or how many children they have qualify as ratio variables. It is valid to calculate a ratio between two variables of this kind, that is, dividing one by another. For example, you could divide the money in your bank account by the number of people in your family, to get the ratio of dollars per person. On an interval scale, it is proper to

add and subtract, but you can't multiply and divide. With ratio variables you can do all four. Any statistical measures appropriate for interval-level data are also good for ratio-level data, and our crosstab program has no special statistics that work only with ratio level data. When we reach Chapter 12, this kind of measure will take on special importance.

Practical Distinctions among Kinds of Variables

In addition to the four levels of measurement, we can use a distinction between continuous and discontinuous variables to describe different kinds of data. A **continuous variable** is one that can take on a near-infinite number of different values within its range. Age is the best example. How old are you? Few of us know how old we are exactly, but we can instantly say how many full years have passed since we were born. An we can quickly figure out how many months old we are—multiply our age in years by 12 and add the number of months since our last birthday. It takes more effort to calculate how many days old we are, but everybody knows how to do it. There are 24 hours in a day, 60 minutes in an hour, and 60 seconds in a minute.

I just made the calculation, and unless I made a mistake, I am 1,522,834,226 seconds old. If our clocks were really good, we could add fractions of a second. Think how a check-the-box questionnaire item would look if it asked people for their exact age in seconds! There would have to be two or three billion boxes! An absurd idea, but it illustrates that we can measure time as finely as we want.

A **discontinuous variable** consists of a relatively small number of distinct categories. These are also called **discrete variables** (not to be confused with *discreet*, which means modest and prudent) because the variable's values are individually separate and unconnected. An example is the number of children a person has. I have five, and a year ago I had only four. But at no point in the past two years did I have

4.5 children, let alone a really fine fraction like 4.14159265358979. Occasionally we hear that the average family has 2.5 children, or something like that, and a sick cartoon was once published showing a family with two and a half children. Children are a great joy, but they are also a discontinuous variable.

When writing the computer programs, I had to be very clear about what kinds of variables I was working with. Pascal, the computer language I wrote in, makes very strong distinctions between a number of kinds of variables, and each program has to begin with a list of all the variables that identifies which kind each one is. When several variables are thrown together into a mathematical formula, they all have to be of exactly the right kind, or the result will be wrong and the computer program may even crash.

Among the kinds of variables Pascal defines are *real number* variables, *integer* variables and *Boolean* variables. The term **real number** sounds as if it might mean almost anything, but technically it refers to continuous variables that can be expected to include fractions. Integers are whole numbers that cannot include fractions, and thus they are discontinuous variables. Boolean variables can take on only two values, "true" or "false." They are named after George Boole, who wrote on the mathematical analysis of logic.

In quantitative research, we generally use real numbers and integers. Although non-quantitative researchers seldom consider the fact, qualitative research often uses Boolean variables. In their research, they determine whether the phenomenon under study possesses certain features or not. Do members of the Process cult wear special uniforms? Yes, that's true; they do. The value of the Boolean variable "uniforms?" for the Process is "true." Do Processeans drink blood? No. The value of the "drink blood?" variable is "false." If we start thinking about qualitative research this way, however, we realize that much of it is really quantitative after all.

Boolean variables are functionally equivalent to integer variables that have only two values: 1

and 0. The Boolean value "true" is equivalent to the integer value "1," and "false" is equivalent to "0." In a sense, much complex quantitative research boils down to an ultimate Boolean question: "Do the data indicate that our hypothesis is true or false?" And deep inside, your computer stores all its information, all the different kinds of variables, as strings of 1s and 0s.

Conceptualized in Boolean terms, all analysis that contributes to formal-operational sociology is quantitative; and in terms of modern mathematics and philosophy, all formal logic is quantitative. Interpretive-advocacy sociologists typically use the term *quantitative* to refer to research that uses elaborate statistical measures, but this is a very limited usage of the word. Boolean analysis is just as quantitative as are complicated crosstabulation and multiple-regression analysis. As noted, Boolean variables are a special case—or special interpretation—of integer variables. Real numbers differ from integers only in that they add fractions, which could as easily be represented as the division of one integer by another. (In a strict mathematical sense, not all real numbers can be represented in this way, but as a practical matter the computer cannot precisely represent a real number that cannot be expressed as a ratio of integers.)

Conceptually, it is important to understand the distinction between real numbers and integers, continuous and discontinuous variables. For present purposes, the point of this distinction is to show the limits of crosstabs. Our program's crosstab table can have as many as seven columns and seven rows, but imagine what kind of table we would need if our X variable were the person's age in seconds and the Y variable were his or her weight in milligrams. I suppose that nobody would have exactly the same age or weight as anybody else. That means the table would have to have a column for each of our 512 respondents, and a row for each one, too. There would be 262,144 cells in that monster table. The computer on which I am writing this textbook has enough memory for me to program a crosstab that big into it, but certainly not enough room on the screen to display it. Furthermore, the computer would take forever to calculate all the measures of association from such a table. Our seven-by-seven crosstabs are not only easier for the human eye to comprehend but for the computer chip to calculate. As a practical matter, therefore, sociologists often stick to discontinuous variables with a small number of categories.

As it happens, one of our measures of association can readily be calculated without making a crosstab or doing any other lengthy preparation: r. This is one of r's great advantages and one of the reasons social scientists are especially fond of it. Many researchers use r or other interval-level measures for ordinal data, a practice that is technically incorrect. They argue, however, that the errors introduced are probably small (Boyle 1970; Vigderhous 1977). Years ago, few sociologists used any measure of association except r, but the other methods have increased in popularity as all the methods for working with them have been developed. Because modern statistical packages quickly calculate a wide range of statistics, there is little excuse today for using the wrong ones.

You might ask whether r is appropriate for the items in our survey of 512 students. The preference items are written as interval scales, in six presumably equal steps from 1 (do not like) to 7 (like very much). One could debate the fine technical point of whether respondents psychologically perceive each of these steps as being of the same size. It is a reasonable assumption that they do, however, and one could raise similar quibbles about almost any other kind of data.

The political question is more problematic. If we presented respondents with a seven-point scale from extremely liberal to extremely conservative, but left out the political labels between these extremes, then the item would qualify as an interval scale on the same basis as the preference scales. The General Social Survey did attach labels to all seven steps, but it is not clear that the difference between, say, extremely liberal and liberal is exactly the same as the difference between liberal and slightly liberal.

Thus one is on somewhat weaker ground in using r with the political question. Many researchers would do it, and many journal reviewers would accept it, but others would not be convinced.

The items about the space program are not well suited for r. Take the last one, number 79: "Do you think we should attempt to communicate with intelligent beings on other planets, perhaps using radio?" In addition to a "no opinion" box, respondents were offered three possible answers: yes definitely, yes perhaps, and no. It is impossible to say how the difference between "yes definitely" and "yes perhaps" compares with the difference between "yes perhaps" and "no." For some respondents, "yes perhaps" might be halfway between the other two responses, in terms of strength of enthusiasm for contacting ETs. If we knew that everybody interpreted the responses that way, it would be safe to use r; but since we have no reason to believe that these three responses form an equal-interval scale for most respondents, we'd better stick to gamma or the various taus.

Paradoxically, r may be perfectly appropriate for the questionnaire item about the respondent's sex. Although you may get an argument from some professionals, it is widely considered okay to use r with dichotomous variables, those with only two response categories. I don't know how to measure the difference between females and males, but because we don't have a third sex to worry about there is no need to quantify it. There is only one interval in a scale composed of two items, so there can be no question about such a scale having intervals of different sizes. Later, in Chapters 10 through 12, we will consider other criteria for deciding when r is the best measure of association to use; but on the basis of level of measurement alone, there is no reason not to use it with dichotomous variables.

Remember, the computer does not know the level of measurement of each of the variables. That is something you have to keep track of. Like the big, expensive, full-featured statistical packages, my software will blithely assume that all variables are appropriate for every coefficient, and will calculate some that are utter nonsense. Computers make it possible for us to achieve hitherto unattainable speed and accuracy in our calculations, so we should protect that precision by using only the very most appropriate statistics. Beware and be alert.

_____ Data Management Options

Among the most powerful tools of statistical analysis are techniques that have nothing to do with correlations or statistical significance, but instead give the sociologist the power to transform variables' values and to work with particular subsets of respondents. We became familiar with selects and rejects way back in Chapter 4; the XTAB program offers a similar option. We have also gained practice in drawing random samples, a procedure we can apply to the 512 survey respondents. The power to recode the values of a variable is something new.

Recode a Variable

Among the most important methods of handling data is **recoding**. To _recode_ a variable means to change some of its values, following a systematic plan. The idea is best explained through an example, such as variable 76, which is based on the following questionnaire item:

> Recently, there has been much talk about building a system of space satellites to defend against nuclear attack. Do you think research on this idea should continue, or should research stop?
>
> (1) Research should continue
> (2) Research should stop
> (3) No opinion

Respondents were about equally split between the first two answers, 231 feeling research should continue and 247 wanting it stopped. The item refers indirectly to part of President Reagan's Strategic Defense Initiative (SDI), often called Star Wars after the popular movie about outer-space battles. But the item does not mention Reagan or SDI directly, and it talks about research, not about construction or deployment of an actual satellite defense system.

If all 512 respondents had selected answers 1 and 2, this item would be a simple dichotomous variable, such as we have been analyzing for the past several chapters, and we would not need to do any recoding. But respondents actually fall into four categories, not two. Twenty-two of them checked the third box, indicating they had no opinion about the issue, and 12 of them failed to check any of the three boxes. The dozen who did not give a proper answer are missing cases, and the XTAB program automatically drops their data from its analyses, but the 22 without an opinion complicate things immensely.

We can handle the situation by recoding the variable. If you are at a computer, select the recode option, and when the computer asks what variable you want, tell it number 76, defense satellites. The computer will immediately display the material shown here in the top half of Figure 8.6. The bottom half of Figure 8.6 is an outline of the steps you could take in recoding variable 76.

To do our recoding, we use a version of the frequencies table from the program option that shows us statistics about a variable. Notice that the table at the top right of Figure 8.6 looks very much like the one from "statistics about one variable." It has three columns of figures. The first consists of the numbers 0 through 9, representing the values that the variable might have. The middle column shows how many people got each value for the variable. You see that 231 gave the "1"

FIGURE 8.6
Recode a Variable
Recode values for variable 76: Defense satellites

Recode values for variable 76: defense satellites

Press + or −
to move the recoding
arrow up or down.

Press a number key
to recode the cases
to its value.

Press ↵ ENTER to register
your recodes, or press
ESC to escape.

9	0	0.0%
8	0	0.0%
7	0	0.0%
6	0	0.0%
5	0	0.0%
4	0	0.0%
3	22	4.3%
2	247	48.2%
1	231	45.1%
0	12	2.3%

Recode →

Examples of how to recode the variable:

Value	I	II	A	B	C	D	E	F
9	0	0	0	247	247	0	0	0
8	0	0	0	0	0	0	0	0
7	0	0	0	0	0	0	0	0
6	0	0	0	0	0	0	0	0
5	0	0	0	0	0	0	0	0
4	0	0	0	0	0	0	0	0
3	22	0	22	22	0	247	247	0
2	247	247	247	0	22	22	34	281
1	231	231	231	231	231	231	231	231
0	12	34	12	12	12	12	0	0

response, while 247 gave "2," and 22 gave "3." Twelve others have a value of zero (0) for variable 76. These are the people who failed to answer properly. The right-hand column of figures expresses these numbers as percents of the total. The XTAB program keeps track of missing values by coding them as zero, and it drops any respondent who has a value of zero from an analysis involving the variable.

One way of cleaning up variable 76 so we can work with it would be to throw out the 22 people with no opinion. We could pretend that they, like those who failed to answer properly, had missing values for the item. The recoding module of the program makes this easy to do. Although the instructions on the left side of the screen tell you how to do it, I will explain now at length.

Notice that there is an arrow on the recoding screen (for Figure 8.6) just to the left of the value 0, with the word "Recode" and "+" and "–" attached to it. This is the recoding arrow. The first thing to learn is how to move it to point to the value and group of respondents you want to recode. The screen instructions say, "Press (+) or (–) to move the recoding arrow up or down." If you press the computer's "+" key, the arrow will move up, step by step, until it reaches the top. Each time you press (+), it moves to the next higher value. Pressing (–) takes the arrow down a step, to the next lower value.

NOTE: There is another way to move the recoding arrow, which some of you may find more natural. First, you have to make sure that the NumberLock key is off, so the keypad at the right end of the keyboard is set to produce cursor movement rather than to print numbers. Then you can use the (↑) and (↓) key, the up and down arrow keys, to move the recoding arrow up or down. The trick, of course, is to make sure the NumberLock key is off, something that may not be so easy for those of you who are not used to working with IBM-type keyboards.

This is the only point in my programs where you might have to use both number keys and the cursor control keys ((↑) and (↓)) on the computer's numerical keypad. If you are not especially familiar with the IBM keyboard, I suggest you use (+) and (–) to move the recoding arrow around, and forget about the troublesome NumberLock key required to use (↑) and (↓). In either case, it will be easiest to type the numbers themselves with the typewriter-like set of number keys up above the letter keys.

We want to recode the 22 people at value 3, changing their responses into zeros, and thus turning them into missing values so the computer will ignore them when doing its analyses. We do this in three steps.

Step 1. Move the arrow until it points to the group you want to recode. In our example, press (+) or (↑) until the arrow points at value 3 and the 22 people who had no opinion about defense satellites.

Step 2. Press the key that represents the new value you want these cases to have. In our example, you would press the 0 (zero) key to turn them into missing values, which are represented by 0. When you do this, the 22 cases immediately vanish from value 3 and are added to the 12 already at 0. The bottom-left part of Figure 8.6 shows this. Column I shows how the 512 cases are at the beginning, with 22 at value 3 and 12 at value 0. Column II shows the result—34 people at value 0, representing the 12 who were already there plus the 22 moved down from 3.

Step 3. Press (ENTER) to register the recodes. This tells the computer to go ahead and make the changes, and in a flash it returns you to the menu. But if you decide you don't want to complete the recode after all, press (ESC) and you will escape from the recoding module without changing the variable at all. The frequencies table tells you what would happen if you went ahead with the recode. If you decide you don't like what you see, however, you can prevent this from happening by pressing (ESC). If you like what you see, press (ENTER), and the computer will carry out the sequence of recodes you have typed in, whether it is just one recode, as in our example, or a long series of them with the variable.

Now, if you inspect statistics about variable 76, there will be only 478 good cases, 231 of them giving response 1, and 247 giving response 2. There will be 34 missing cases. You can investigate the political aspects of SDI by crosstabbing it with variables such as conservatism, liberalism, Republican Party, Democratic Party, and President Reagan. An interesting crosstab is that between this recoded version of variable 76 and variable 70, sex. Because sex is already a dichotomous variable (female and male), and we have turned defense satellites into a dichotomous variable, you will get a familiar two-by-two table. Do men tend to favor SDI research more than do women? Check it out.

If you have already made a recode and the data have been transformed according to your instructions, it is possible to undo the changes. Option 9 on the menu accomplishes this with a simple press of the (9) key. If you are trying out our examples on the computer, you should do this, because we should consider alternative ways of recoding variable 76. For that we need to return the data to their form at the beginning.

Perhaps you don't want to throw out the 22 respondents who had no opinion about SDI research. But clearly they are in the wrong place. "No opinion" should be somewhere between favoring SDI research and being against it. The way we recoded the responses originally, however, no opinion has value 3, while favoring and opposing have 1 and 2. It would make much more sense if "no opinion" were value 2 and opposing were value 3. Then the values 1, 2, 3 would represent a logical sequence of responses: continue, no opinion, stop.

Columns A through F at the bottom of Figure 8.6 show one way of getting "no opinion" between "continue" and "stop." First, we have to move the 247 people who oppose SDI research out of the way. They are sitting at value 2, where we want to put the 22 with no opinion. So the first step is to move the recoding arrow to value 2. Then you could press (9) to move the 247 up and out of the way to value 9, as shown in column B of Figure 8.6. These 247 are just visiting there, and we'll move them again in a moment.

Next, we move the recoding arrow to value 3 and press (2). This moves the 22 with no opinion to value 2, where we want them, as shown in column C.

Then we have to move the arrow up to 9, where the 247 respondents are visiting, and press (3) to move them where we want them. Column D shows the result. When you do a recode, you absolutely must keep track of what you are doing. You should write down what the values mean now: 1 = continue SDI research, 2 = no opinion, 3 = stop SDI research.

We might want to go further. Some of the 12 people who failed to answer the question properly checked both the continue and stop boxes, writing in comments about the circumstances under which they would do one or the other. Perhaps some of those expressing no opinion had similarly complex views. Thus, there is some justification for combining the 12 currently with value 0 into the 3 category with the 22 who checked the no-opinion box. If you do this, as shown in column E, you have to remember that value 2 no longer represents "no opinion" (or "stop" as it did originally). Perhaps it means "mixed opinion" or "other responses," somewhere between "continue" and "stop."

Finally, you might be interested merely in comparing people who definitely support continued SDI research with the people who hold all the other views. Column F is the result of recoding the 247 people currently sitting at value 3—those who want research stopped—and adding them to category 2. Now we have a dichotomous variable with 231 cases who want research continued and 281 who do not. The 281 include 247 who definitely want research stopped plus 34 other people who did not go this far but failed to support continued research.

Most of the space-program questions need some kind of recoding before you can use them effectively in crosstabs. Most crucially, you have to decide where to put the "no opinion" people. There is no single, set answer to this question. It depends on your research purposes. The most obvious thing to do is to put them between positive and negative responses. Two of the questions have "yes" and "no" answers, and respondents with no opinion should be comfortable between these two. Or, again, you might want to compare just those in favor of the particular space project, and add those with no opinion to the negative group.

Two questions deserve a little comment, variables 79 and 72. One asks, "Do you think we should attempt to communicate with intelligent beings on other planets, perhaps using radio?" Four responses were given: yes definitely, yes perhaps, no, and no opinion. By recoding, you could rearrange them into the following order: yes definitely, yes perhaps, no opinion, and no. I think this puts "no opinion" in the right place.

One question didn't have a cop-out "no opinion" response: "Should the amount of money being spent on the U.S. space program be increased, kept at current levels, or ended altogether?" There were four responses: increased, kept at current levels, decreased, and ended. Only 7 people felt that the space program should be ended altogether, and you might consider adding them to the 74 who felt funding should be reduced. There are two justifications for this, although neither one is so convincing that we must agree with the recode. First, 7 is a very small number of respondents to have way out on a limb. Second, we did not give supporters of the space program a couple of responses (such as "increase funding somewhat" and "increase funding tremendously") to show the degrees of difference in opinion that "decreased" and "ended" do.

But there is another way you could recode the space-funding variable, with a completely different justification. As it stands, the values go 1 = increased, 2 = kept at current levels, 3 = decreased, and 4 = ended. Thus, the bigger the number the less support for the space program. When a crosstab shows a negative correlation—such as between liking astronomy and space funding—it really means a positive association. Obviously, this is confusing. The crosstab gives us a negative correlation when we would expect a positive one, simply because the values of the space-funding item are arranged so that high numbers mean negative feelings rather than positive ones. It would make much more sense to recode this item so that support for the space program was expressed through high numbers and opposition through low numbers.

This is not hard to do. Select the recode option and variable 72 about space funding. Recode the 195 people at value 1, the strong supporters of the space program, up to 9 to get them out of the way. Then recode the 7 who want funding stopped to 1. Next, move the people visiting up at value 9 to 4, where they belong. At this point we are halfway done, having fixed values 1 and 4. Now move the 222 people with value 2, those who want space funding kept the same, up to value 9, where they can be the visitors for a while. Seventy-four people who want funding reduced are at 3, so move them down to 2. And finally, bring the 222 visiting up at 9 down to 3. Now the values are logical: 1 = end funding, 2 = reduce funding, 3 = keep it the same, and 1 = increase funding.

You might consider applying these principles to the other space variables. Even the variables with no problems might benefit from recoding for certain kinds of analyses. For example, you might want to **collapse categories** for the key political variable. We now have people arranged in seven categories, from extremely liberal to extremely conservative. You might want them in just three categories: liberal, moderate, and conservative. I hope you can figure out how to do this, on the basis of the above instructions.

Have you noticed a variable in the list, number 82, called "liberalism"? Try crosstabbing it with variable 71, conservatism. You will see a perfect negative correlation. The reason is that liberalism is a recoded version of conservatism. The data are the same. Recall that when I introduced conservatism earlier in this chapter, I said that it was an arbitrary decision to give high numbers to conservatives and low ones to liberals. We could have done just the opposite, and the only problem we might get into is remembering what the numbers mean. By calling the variable "conservatism" and giving the highest number to extreme conservatives, we keep the meaning of the item and its data straight in our mind.

Variable 82 simply reverses the numbers and uses the opposite political label. Here is how they go: 1 = extremely conservative, 2 = conservative, 3 = slightly conservative, 4 = moderate—middle of the road, 5 = slightly liberal, 6 = liberal, and 7 = extremely liberal. The political data make perfect sense either way, while most of the other variables have a logical direction to them.

Before we leave recoding, I should make clear how the computer handles values 8 and 9. These values are provided as temporary places to put groups of respondents while you are in the midst of recoding; the crosstab has no room for values of 8 or 9. If you leave some cases coded to 8 or 9, they will not participate in other analyses you do, but will behave just as if they had been assigned the value of 0. When you return to the recoding module, however, you will find the cases still visiting where you left them. Thus, three different values really can represent missing values: 0, 8, and 9. They are what we call **missing values codes**.

I gave the program this feature both for your convenience and to give a taste of the complex recoding that is possible with full-featured statistical packages and computer languages. If you are recoding just one variable, it is convenient enough to undo the recodes when you want to try a different approach, pressing (9) from the menu. But if you have invested time and energy into recoding some variables, and now want to experiment with recodes on another one, it might help a lot to be able to move some cases to values of 8 or 9, rather than adding them to the missing cases already at 0, because you can quickly go back and move them again if you decide to.

Select or Reject on the Basis of a Variable

We first encountered selects and rejects back in Chapter 4, and they continue to be a most useful procedure, even with crosstabs. They operate essentially the same way in our XTAB program as they did in HIST, but they apply to all of the variables rather than just a few, and they have slightly more subtle applications. To do select/rejects, press (7), then pick the variable you want to work with. A table of the variable's values, cases, and percents will appear, with the word "Select" to the left of each value.

The screen instructions say, "Press number keys ((0) to (7)) to select or reject cases with the values of those keys." If you press a number key in this range, the word "Select" to the left of the corresponding value will change to "Reject." Press the number key again to turn "Reject" back to "Select," if you wish. To register the select/rejects and throw out all the rejected cases, press (ENTER). If you decide not to go ahead with them, press (ESC) instead.

For example, if you want to work just with the female respondents, get the select/reject option and pick variable 70 (Sex). The table will show that 256 respondents have a value of 1 (female) and 256 have a value of 2 (male). Reject the males by pressing (2). Then press (ENTER). From now on, you are working just with the females.

Suppose you want to analyze just the female liberals. Follow the instructions above to kick the males out. You might check the statistics on the sex variable to make sure you did the select/reject correctly. Then do a second select/reject, using variable 71, conservatism. A new frequency distribution will appear on the screen, showing the political orientations of the 256 women. You want to reject the moderates and conservatives, those having values of 4, 5, 6, and 7. To do this you press (4), (5), (6), and (7). Then press (ENTER), and you will be working with only the female liberals.

You might wonder why I make it possible to reject the respondents with a value of 0 (zero), if there are any for the particular variable. You might think this would be a waste of effort, because 0 represents missing values, and these people won't participate in statistical analyses of that variable anyway. The point is that if you reject people with a value of 0 for a particular variable, they won't be part of analysis of any other variable, either.

When the computer does a crosstab of two variables, X and Y, it automatically (but temporarily) rejects any cases with missing values on either X or Y. This is called **pairwise deletion**, dropping cases with missing values on either or both of a pair of variables. If you then do a crosstab of variables W and Z, there will be another pairwise deletion. Some respondents who did not participate in the crosstab of X and Y will show up in the one for W and Z, and vice versa.

But perhaps you want to see the correlations linking all four of these variables, and you want the statistics to be calculated on exactly the same respondents for each crosstab. You should use **listwise deletion**, dropping all the cases with missing values on any variable in your list. To accomplish this, you would use select/reject for each of the variables in your list, rejecting the people with a value of 0 on each one.

When you have done one select/reject and start to do another, the computer will ask you, "Do you want to undo the existing select/rejects or samples?"

The responses offered you are (1) Yes and (2) No. If you are doing a series of select/rejects that all depend on each other, then the answer is no, and you should press (2). If you want to start from scratch, however, and get back to the full dataset of 512 cases before selecting/rejecting, press (1). Of course, you can also do this with the undo command from the menu, but that option takes a few seconds because it reloads the original data from your disk, so this approach saves you time. You have the same choice with the sampling option, described below.

Draw a Random Sample

In the previous chapter, we learned much about sampling a population, discovered that there are many kinds of samples—even different varieties of random samples—and gained practice with a valuable selection of sampling techniques. The XTAB program has a sampling option as well, which is useful mainly in demonstrating issues of statistical significance that we will encounter later on. It could not be easier to use.

When you choose this option from the menu, by pressing (8), the computer will tell you how many cases you are working with and explain that the sample can be any size from one case up through the total number of cases. Type in the number of cases you want in the sample and press (ENTER). A very efficient sampling procedure will give you a real random sample of the desired size in a split second. You can check it by looking at the statistics about any variable. The sample is as close to random as the computer can make it, and you will get a slightly different subset of respondents each time.

Rejects and samples are cumulative. That is, both the select/reject procedure and the sampling procedure work by throwing out cases. You can combine select/rejects and samples in any order. The way to restore discarded cases is with the undo option that concludes the menu.

Undo All Recodes, Select/Rejects, and Samples

When you are sure you have learned all you want to about a particular subset of respondents or a particular set of recodes, press (9) from the menu and the computer will restore the original data. The computer accomplishes this by loading the data up from the disk again, so you have to make sure the disk is still in the machine. There is no simple way to undo the undo command, so make sure you want it before pressing (9). The only way to restore undone recodes and select/rejects is to do them over again, but there is no way to regain a particular lost random sample.

PROJECTS FOR CHAPTER 8

The nine projects that follow give you wide experience in working with variables from a real survey dataset, using the XTAB program. They examine variables one at a time, leaving crosstabulations and correlations for the following chapter. In the first project, you inspect responses from individual respondents. The second project asks you to compare your own responses to two items with those of our 512 college-student respondents. The third focuses on the issue of missing cases (missing data), which can highlight poorly written questionnaire items or controversial issues. The fourth examines variable distributions and averages. Projects 5 and 6 concern the very important techniques of value recoding that let you transform a variable for maximum effectiveness. The final three projects illustrate levels of measurement, examine once again the variability in random samples, and view the uniqueness of individual respondents. Although you may not want to do all nine of these projects, trying a few of them will give you a greater understanding of the concept of "variable" and prepare you to use variables in the variety of ways that the remainder of this book will introduce.

1. Comparing Two Respondents. Using the first option on the XTAB menu, inspect the questionnaires filled out by two respondents 250 ID numbers apart. If you select person 51 for your first case, for example, you would pick 301 for the second. If your first case is 400, the second would be 150.

For each of the two cases, inspect the answers the person gave to the questions, trying to get a picture of the kind of person the respondent is. For example, you will be able to describe his or her political views. You will see some of the things the person especially likes, including academic subjects. Because of the particular academic subjects the person favors, you may even be able to guess what profession that person plans to enter.

In your report, describe each person in about a page, referring to specific answers he or she gave on the questionnaire. Then write a page comparing the two, noting what they have in common and how they differ. Do you think the two would get along, in terms of shared interests? Or are these two respondents very different individuals?

2. Your Best and Worst Subjects. Go through the list of 30 college subjects in the XTAB dataset and select the subject you like best and the subject you hate most. You will find the list of subjects in Appendix B, but you will be using the basic statistics program, where they are also listed.

Next, decide your personal preference ratings for the two subjects on the scale from 1 ("do not like") to 7 ("like very much"). Note, however, that you do not have to give the subjects the extreme ratings of 7 and 1, unless you really love and hate them this much. But if they really are the courses you like best and least, you cannot give more extreme ratings to any other subjects.

Use the "Frequencies on one variable" option on the main menu of the basic statistics program to see how the 512 students rated your best and worst subjects. You should copy down the two sets of information, just as they appear on the screen. On each table, you should mark the value you personally gave the subject, using a star ("*"). At the bottom of the page put a footnote explaining what the star means: "* my personal preference rating of this subject."

Finally, write a brief report comparing your ratings with those of the 512 students. What percentage of the students gave the same rating as you did to each subject? What percentage gave higher ratings? Lower ratings? On average, do the students rate your best subject higher than your worst one?

3. Items with Missing Cases. Using the fourth option on the XTAB menu, summary statistics about 1–10 variables, examine variables 1 through 79 to see which have the most missing cases. Perhaps you will find that six or eight items are missing information on more cases than the other items. Then inspect the full wording of each one in Appendix B to see if you can explain why a number of people failed to give a proper answer. There are at least three reasons that this might happen.

First, the question may be poorly written. The responses offered may overlap, making it hard for the respondent to select one. Or an important possible response may have been left out. Or both the question and its responses may have some flaw of logic that prevents people from answering. Some of the national polls from which the spaceflight questions came were written hurriedly in the days following the Challenger disaster, and one or two items might be poorly written. Several of the preference questions were experimental, and a few might be failures. If many people can't answer a question, a number of them will try it, anyway. So when several fail to answer, we know that more answered halfheartedly and with difficulty.

Second, some questions may not be relevant for some respondents. A few students may be completely unfamiliar with certain academic subjects, and others may not have been exposed to soap operas or science fiction. A few will have come recently from distant countries and not really know how the two main American political parties differ. When we intentionally include such questions in a survey, we often add a "no opinion" response. For example, in one survey I had a set of preference questions about movies. Respondents who had seen a particular one were supposed to rate it on a seven-point scale. Those who had not were supposed to check a "have not seen" box.

Third, some questions may be about highly controversial subjects. Some respondents may get hostile and write a nasty note to the researcher, rather than checking one of the boxes. Others will withhold any kind of response, not wanting their opinions to be on the record even in an anonymous survey.

Write a brief analysis of each questionnaire item (among numbers 1–79) that has many missing cases, explaining why you think this happened for each of these items.

4. Inspecting Variable Distributions. Examine the histogram and "statistics about one variable" for the set of variables listed below. Explain how the measures of central tendency (mean, median, and mode) for each were calculated. Say what these different averages tell you about the variable, and explain why the three are different for a given variable.

Use these variables:

56 Ronald Reagan
60 South Africa
61 Equal Rights Amendment
70 Sex
71 Conservatism
72 Space funding
81 Random data 2

5. Recoding the Space Items. Select option 6 from the XTAB menu to recode a variable. Keeping notes on what you are doing, recode items 72 through 79, the outer-space questions, to get rid of bad responses, to get responses in a logical order, and to combine some of the valid responses into reasonable, large categories.

Write a report showing the frequencies you wind up with for each of the eight space items and justifying briefly each of the recoding decisions you made.

6. Recoding to Dichotomize Items. Select 10 variables in the XTAB dataset, including some that are not preference items. Use the recode option to collapse the set of categories for each variable to just two, and discuss your reason for selecting a cutting point to dichotomize the variables. Then examine and discuss the summary statistics for each variable that are given in the "statistics about one variable" option.

7. Levels of Measurement of Survey Items. Select a standard sociological questionnaire, such as the General Social Survey, and see if you can find several examples of items representing each of the four levels of measurement. For each one, state your reasons for deciding it belongs to a particular level of measurement.

8. Random Samples of Respondents. Select one variable to study out of those in the XTAB dataset. One at a time, draw 10 random samples with 100 respondents in each one. After drawing each sample, inspect the statistics about your chosen variable and write them down. When finished, create a table that compares these summary statistics across the 10 samples with the statistics you get using the full 512 respondents. Discuss the variation you see in the statistics, and what it implies about research done with relatively small random samples.

9. Respondents Who Agree about Several Variables. Select three variables in the XTAB dataset, and select one of the 512 respondents. Then use the select/reject and other options in the program to find out how many other people agree exactly with the chosen respondent on the three items.

For example, respondent number 1 gives the following preference ratings to the first three items in the survey: 6 (variable 1—botany), 3 (variable 2—astronomy), and 7 (variable 3—foreign language). The select/reject option tells me that a total of 23 persons rated the first item at 6, and it allows me to reject all of the people who gave any other response, including those 4 who failed to give a valid answer to this question. Then I use select/reject again to get rid of the 20 people who did not agree with respondent number 1 about astronomy, who rated astronomy a 2. This leaves me with only 3 respondents, and when I use select/reject again, I find that just one other respondent rates the three items exactly the way the first respondent does.

Finally, I can examine other variables, using several program options, to see what the characteristics of these two respondents are. I learn, for example, that both are women. One is a junior who describes her politics as extremely liberal. The other is a graduate student who considers herself a political moderate.

With the key respondent and three variables you select, carry out a similar exercise. If you find no other respondents who agree with your key respondent, you may want to try again, either with a different key respondent or with different variables. When you find two or more respondents who agree exactly on three variables, describe them briefly, as I did in my example.

CHAPTER   SUMMARY

This chapter goes beyond dichotomous variables and demonstrates how to work with survey items having several answer categories. The survey that provided the dataset for this chapter and for program XTAB was part of a study of the goals of the space program, begun immediately after the disaster that destroyed the space shuttle Challenger and its crew. XTAB is a simple but full-featured statistical program for analyzing survey data; it teaches the main principles by which social scientists make sense of fixed-choice responses to questionnaires.

Using data from 512 college-student respondents to the survey, the XTAB program analyzes 87 variables, each identified by a *variable name*. Most of these variables are preference items with a range of 1–7; the *range* of a variable is the set of values it can have. The distribution of cases across the various values is the *frequencies*, and three kinds of average are *mean*, *median*, and *mode*. A histogram is a simple bar graph that compares the numbers of cases that have each value on a variable. When a histogram or frequency distribution is unbalanced, we say that the distribution is *skewed*.

The heart of the XTAB program is the two-variable crosstabulation, or *crosstab*, a table that runs two variables across each other. By convention, they are called *variable X* and *variable Y*. The many-cell rectangle of the crosstab is framed by the values for the two variables and their respective frequencies. This is the same kind of information we found around the familiar two-by-two tables of earlier chapters.

Four kinds of variables are commonly found in surveys: nominal, ordinal, interval, and ratio. These are often described as four different *levels of measurement*. *Nominal variables* put cases in categories, but the categories are not in any particular order. *Ordinal variables* put cases into categories that are in a logical order. *Interval variables* measure a quantity along a scale consisting of equal steps or intervals. *Ratio variables* measure a quantity along a scale consisting of equal steps or intervals, starting from a zero point. In addition to the four levels of measurement, a distinction can be made between continuous and discontinuous variables. A *continuous variable* is one that can take on an infinite number of different values within its range. A *discontinuous variable* (also called a *discrete variable*) consists of a relatively small number of distinct categories, often a short sequence of integers.

Among the most powerful tools of statistical analysis are data management techniques that transform variables' values or work with particular subsets of respondents, such as the select and reject options we encountered in the HIST program. Among the most important methods of handling data is *recoding*, changing some of a variable's values according to a systematic plan. Recoding can reverse the direction of a variable—for example, transforming a conservatism scale into a liberalism scale—and it can *collapse categories* to reduce the number of values the variable can take. *Missing values codes* are values that represent the failure of a respondent to answer a question properly, or any other situation in which a case lacks valid data for a variable. *Pairwise deletion* is dropping cases with missing values on either or both of a pair of variables. *Listwise deletion* is dropping all the cases with missing values on any variable in a list.

KEY CONCEPTS FOR CHAPTER 8

Nonparametric Measures

CHAPTER OVERVIEW

This chapter introduces the chief nonparametric measures of association that belong to crosstabs, both symmetrical and asymmetrical, plus complex chi-square. These techniques are especially appropriate for analysis of data from surveys, because most question formats do not generate numbers with the right characteristics for parametric measures.

Quantitative information about some characteristic of a population is called a **parameter**. For example, the average age of residents of Toronto, Canada, is a parameter. The percent who are under age 18 in Toronto is also a parameter. We could speak of a set of such numbers, precisely describing the age distribution in Toronto, as the age parameters. Usually,

however, sociologists are not able to get perfect, complete information about an entire population, and we are forced to work with statistics that are mere estimates of the parameters, usually based on samples of the population rather than the population as a whole.

As we will find in Chapter 12, some measures of association, such as r, assume that the distribution of the variables' values in the population has a certain shape, usually the normal curve to be described in Chapter 10. That is, the r correlation coefficient assumes something about the relevant population parameters that may or may not be true. Thus, it can be risky to use a measure of association that makes these assumptions, even though we shall see that such assumptions give parametric measures of association quite a number of useful features. Because the measures I will explain in this chapter, such as tau and gamma, do not require you to make any assumptions about the shapes of the parameter distributions, they are called **nonparametric**.

The XTAB program includes all the measures discussed here, and the chapter employs many examples done with XTAB to explain further how to get the most out of analysis with crosstabulations. The program not only calculates all these measures, but, if desired, it can show how it did them, to help students learn how to calculate the coefficients themselves. Shortly, we will learn how to do the calculations. First, however, we should get an intuitive idea of how correlations look in a big crosstab. We did this for two-by-twos, and now we can expand our intuitive understanding to include even very big crosstabs.

An Intuitive Approach to Crosstab Correlations

In the previous chapter, we looked at a crosstab containing a positive correlation between liking the Republican Party and being a conservative. If you look back at Figure 8.5, you can see the correlation with your own eyes. The cells with big numbers in them run from the lower-left corner up and to the right, almost reaching the upper-right corner. If you squint or use your imagination, you can see that most respondents are along a line connecting these two corners. This pattern expresses a positive association between the variables. For the two-by-two tables we analyzed in previous chapters, a positive association was expressed by big numbers in the lower-left corner and upper-right, but then we had only four cells to worry about. Here, the many cells near and between the corners come into play as well.

The line of cells containing big numbers doesn't have to run exactly from one corner to the other, and there can be gaps and twists in it. As we have seen repeatedly, sociological data are shaped by many accidental factors as well as by the social laws that provide regularity to human relations. But the idea that a positive association between X and Y is shown by a line of full cells, from lower left to upper right, is a good start toward understanding crosstabs.

If you're having trouble seeing that line, take a look at Figure 9.1. It shows rough sketches of 6 crosstabs, and the one between Republicanism and conservatism is the first in the set.

To make a clearer picture, I have thrown the numbers away and shaded in the cells to show how many respondents are in each one. Empty cells look empty. Cells with 20 or more people in them are black. The other cells have shadings representing how full they are, from 1 to 19 people. Perhaps now you can see the bold (but somewhat irregular) line of full cells running from lower left toward the upper right.

Right below the sketch of the Republican-conservative crosstab in Figure 9.1 is a picture of a perfect positive correlation, for comparison. We almost never see a crosstab like this in sociology. If you choose the same variable for both variable X and variable Y, you will get something like this, but it won't be scientifically informative. Try it. Ask the computer to give you a crosstab in which conservatism is the X variable and is also the Y variable. The screen will show a picture of a perfect positive correlation. Aside from giving you this picture, crosstabbing conservatism with itself accomplishes nothing. All the interesting correlations are somewhat less than perfect.

Of course, coefficients can be negative as well as positive. For example, we might expect a negative correlation between liking the Democratic Party and being conservative. The 512 questionnaires were filled out in the state of Massachusetts at the time Michael Dukakis was governor. In the 1988 presidential election, President Bush continually accused Dukakis of

FIGURE 9.1
Crosstabs

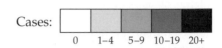

Cases: 0 1–4 5–9 10–19 20+

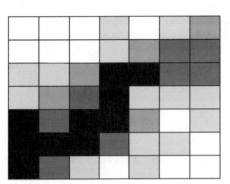

Positive Correlation:
Republican and Conservative

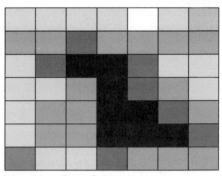

Negative Correlation:
Democratic and Conservative

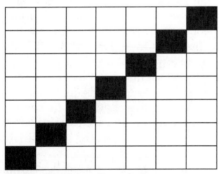

Perfect Positive Correlation

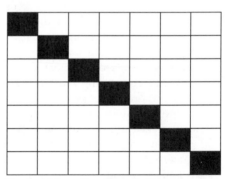

Perfect Negative Correlation

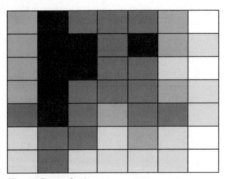

Zero Correlation:
Conservative and Sciences

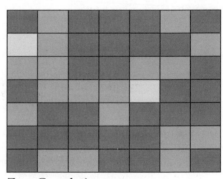

Zero Correlation:
Two Random Variables

being a liberal, even using the code phrase "L word," as if "liberalism" were an unspeakable sin. In some parts of the country, the Democratic Party may include a number of conservatives, but in Massachusetts it is clearly liberal.

So, respondents who like the Democratic Party should tend to be liberal. Not all of them will be, but a strong tendency in this direction should be apparent in the data, since liberal is the opposite of conservative. Democrats at Harvard or in Massachusetts should tend *not* to be conservative. Figure 9.2 is a crosstab of Democratic Party and conservatism that shows this is indeed the case.

The measures of association run from − 0.45 to − 0.28, all on the negative side. If you look at the crosstab itself, you will see that not a single conservative respondent loves the Democratic Party. That is, the cell in the upper-right corner of the crosstab is empty. There are zero cases in the cell in the lower-left corner as well, indicat-

ing that no haters of the Democratic Party are extremely liberal. But the two other corner cells have cases in them, and the fullest cells run in a rough line from the upper-left corner to the lower-right corner.

The pattern is not quite so clear as for the Republican Party. The gamma between Republican Party and conservatism was 0.74, while the gamma for Democratic Party and conservatism is − 0.44. Not only is gamma negative for Democratic Party, but it is smaller. That is, −0.44 is closer to zero than is 0.74. Thus, the association between liking the Democratic party and being conservative is weaker as well as negative.

When comparing two correlations, we always have two characteristics to look at: (1) the sign on the coefficient (whether it is + or −), also called the **direction of association**, and (2) the size of the coefficient (how far from zero it is), also called the **degree of association**. A negative correlation could be just as strong as a

FIGURE 9.2
Crosstab of Democrat and Conservatism

Good cases: 510
Missing cases: 2
r: −0.45
z: −10.09
Significance: .001

Gamma: −0.44
z: −6.24
Significance: .001

Tau-a: −0.28
Tau-b: −0.35
Tau-c: −0.33
D(X→Y): −0.35

Chi-square: 173.25
df: 36
Significance: .001

Variable X: Democratic Party

Variable Y: Conservatism

		1	2	3	4	5	6	7	
7		3	1	1	1	0	1	0	7
6		8	6	11	9	6	0	0	40
5		4	13	24	31	14	1	2	89
4		1	4	6	21	13	6	2	53
3		3	5	7	38	37	12	7	109
2		2	7	8	42	45	42	19	165
1		0	3	3	15	9	9	8	47
		21	39	60	157	124	71	38	

[D]isplay frequencies   [C]alculate   Press ↵ ENTER

positive one; for example, -0.74 is just as strong an association as $+0.74$. In the case of the two political parties and conservatism, however, the coefficients are of different sizes as well as signs.

This makes sense. In Massachusetts, the Democratic Party was in the majority. I recall the 1984 election, when I was living in Cambridge, and there wasn't even a Republican running for Congress from that district. The only choice the ballot offered was between a Democrat and a Communist! As the majority party, the Democrats must include a number of moderates, even in a liberal state like Massachusetts. This will bring the coefficient closer to zero. Also, in some parts of the country the Democratic Party has a significant conservative wing, and many of our respondents had come from those areas, visiting Massachusetts only to go to college.

Because it is weaker, the association between Democratic Party and conservatism is harder to see in the crosstab than the one between Republican Party and conservatism. Figure 9.1 shows the crosstab graphically, in the upper-right corner, and below it a hypothetical perfect negative correlation. I think the band of dark rectangles is apparent in the Democratic/conservative crosstab, running from upper left to lower right, but not quite getting into both corners.

We have discussed positive and negative correlations, but quite a few of them come out zero or so near zero that they might as well be. The two pictures at the bottom of Figure 9.1 show two crosstabs with essentially zero correlation. The one on the left has variable 71 (conservatism) for X and variable 31 (liking the sciences in general) as Y. Some people think that scientists tend to be liberal, but at least in terms of the political distribution among our respondents, this is not so. If you try this crosstab yourself, you will find that all the coefficients come out 0.01. This is really the same as zero.

The picture in the lower-right corner of Figure 9.1 shows a crosstab with variable 80 (Random data 1) as X and variable 81 (Random data 2) as Y. These two variables didn't really come from the questionnaire. Instead, my computer created them out of thin air. To make variable 80, it gave each respondent a number from 1 to 7, chosen at random. Then it gave each respondent a second random number, 1 through 7, to make variable 81. These two variables are quite meaningless data, but they can be used to illustrate what a zero correlation looks like. You can crosstab them with any of the real variables if you want, but don't expect big correlations.

The coefficients for the crosstab between the two random variables are not exactly zero, however, running from 0.03 to 0.05. But these numbers are so close to zero that they prove there is no correlation between the two random variables. When you compare the pictures of the two zero-correlation crosstabs at the bottom of Figure 9.1, they look quite different. Why is this?

The picture of the crosstab between conservatism and liking the sciences has some black cells, containing lots of cases, but the crosstab between the two random variables does not. The reason is the way the variables are distributed across the values 1 through 7. Take conservatism, for example. In the conservatism/sciences crosstab, there are only 7 extreme conservatives. In the picture in Figure 9.1, they are represented by the right-hand column of cells. Because there are only 7, no cell in the column could possibly have more than 7 cases, let alone the 20 cases required to make the cell black in the picture. In contrast, 166 respondents were in the liberal category, represented by the second column from the left. And with so many respondents in this column, five of its cells have 20 or more cases and got colored black. The cases are distributed far more evenly across the values of the random variables, preventing any cells from having as many as 20 cases.

Thus, you have to be a bit careful when visually interpreting the pattern of cases in the cells of a crosstab. That a few cells may contain a lot of cases does not prove a correlation between the variables. The full cells have to be lined up, running roughly from one corner to the opposite one. And the final proof of a correlation is not in what your eye sees but what the computer calculates. Only the measures of association can really tell you what the relationship between the variables is.

Nonparametric Correlations

Above chi-square in a crosstab, you will see a number of other pieces of information. The other coefficients are all **measures of association**, r, gamma, tau-a, tau-b, tau-c, and D. In honor of the statisticians who invented or developed them, some are often called **Pearson's r, Kendall's tau, and Somers' D**. In Chapter 6 we met two similar coefficients, phi and Yule's Q. Now we have a larger selection, and it is time to explain how we calculate them and say something about how we decide which one is most appropriate for our data and research question.

All the measures of association show how strongly and in what way the two variables are related. In principle, each one could be any number from -1.00 through 0.00 to $+1.00$, although in social research we never see coefficients very close to -1.00 or $+1.00$. Notice that each coefficient came out somewhat differently for the Republican/conservative crosstab: 0.75, 0.74, 0.50, 0.62, 0.59, and 0.60. These numbers are similar but not the same. All are substantially on the plus side, and they all indicate a positive correlation between the variables. The formulas used to calculate them are all different, but the five nonparametric measures are based on similar logic.

Calculate Five Measures of Association

When you are working with the crosstab part of the XTAB program and a table appears on the screen, there will be a command at the bottom center: (C)alculate. This is an option to make the computer show how it has calculated some of the coefficients. If you press (C), the computer will erase the information on the left side of the screen, flash the message "select coefficient," and present you with a menu:

```
[1] Gamma
[2] Tau-a
[3] Tau-b
[4] Tau-c
[5] Somers' D
```

To learn how the computer calculated any of these five, simply press the appropriate number key ((1) through (5)). In an instant the computer will replace the menu with the information you want. After looking it over, you might want to switch to a different coefficient. To do so, simply press (C) again. The short menu of five coefficients will reappear, and you can select another one.

It is going to take us a while to examine the five coefficients, understand how each one was calculated, and get some sense of what each one means. To tie this lengthy discussion together, we will consider one particular crosstab: sociology crosstabbed with psychology.

Do you like sociology? Woops! Perhaps that is a dangerous question. I mustn't get you thinking too deeply about why you are using this book, taking this course, or (heaven forbid) majoring in this subject. I shall assume you do like sociology. But as you know, some people don't like sociology, and the same goes for psychology. Both are sciences of human behavior, and they are linked by social psychology. It makes sense that people who like one of these subjects will tend to like the other.

We can confirm this hypothesis by looking at a crosstab in which sociology is the X variable and psychology the Y variable. A total of 508 respondents rated both sociology and psychology on the seven-point preference scale, and the computer finds that there is a correlation between liking sociology and liking psychology. It expresses this association through six coefficients. One of them, called r, will be discussed in Chapters 11 and 12. I included r in the XTAB program because you may want to use it to do projects belonging to those two chapters. But we need the background of Chapter 10 before we can fully understand r, so we will not examine it here. The other five coefficients are Somers' D, gamma, and three varieties of tau. For the sociology-psychology crosstab, these coefficients are as follows:

Gamma = 0.47
Tau-a = 0.32
Tau-b = 0.39
Tau-c = 0.38
$D(X \rightarrow Y) = 0.39$

Notice that all of the coefficients are positive and that they range fairly narrowly from 0.32 to 0.47. Each of them says that there is a substantial positive correlation between liking sociology and liking psychology. Two of these coefficients happen to be the same, Tau-b and D, but this is coincidental, and you should not expect any of these coefficients to be exactly the same, even though they tend to be close to each other. You may at first find it annoying that we have to contend with five measures of association, rather than just one, but there is good reason for this. Each of the five considers the association between sociology and psychology in a slightly different way. Depending upon the precise nature of the hypothesis you are testing, one of these would be better than the others.

I like to think in terms of a workbench analogy. Years ago, I used to be a professional piano tuner, and I also repaired and rebuilt pianos. The toolboxes I lugged from door to door were filled with tools, some of them only slightly different from each other. A few were improvised, such as the ice pick I used to adjust the capstan screws on the backs of some grand-piano keys. The nipper I used to cut off dowels at the right lengths to be hammer shanks had originally been manufactured as toenail clippers for dogs, and a medical syringe made for injecting drugs into human arms served to inject a stiffening liquid around the piano's tuning pins. But then you should have seen my screwdrivers!

I had dozens. There were fat ones and slim ones, very long ones and very short ones. A couple were bent sideways for fitting into narrow spaces. Most had straight, chisel-like blades, but others were of the plus-sign Phillips type, and still others were technically called wrenches but worked just like screwdrivers. Each screwdriver or wrench was designed for turning a different kind of screw.

Sometimes I could make a screw turn with the wrong driver, but this risked chewing the screw's slot or head and making it unturnable. I am sure you have employed a screwdriver when you lacked a chisel, to chop away some wood, but this doesn't work well. A professional piano tuner needs a variety of precisely designed tools, each to do a particular different job. My many screwdrivers were all intended to drive screws—just as the various measures of association are all intended to measure associations—but the particular kind of screw or association determines precisely which tool you need.

We will begin with **gamma**. I find it easier to explain than some of the others, and once we understand it the others will be easier. Furthermore, we have already learned a little about gamma, because it is the same thing as Yule's Q. When we use gamma on a simple two-by-two table, we call it Q.

Calculating Gamma

Imagine for a moment we wanted to learn if height correlated with weight, in a hundred college students chosen at random. Let me state a likely hypothesis: weight correlates positively with height. One way to test this would be to create a two-by-two table, as we did in Chapter 6. First, check each person and decide if he or she is tall or short. That is, we could dichotomize the group into tall and short. Similarly, we could dichotomize the group into heavy and light. We could draw a huge two-by-two table on the ground, and ask each person to stand in the appropriate cell. The tall, heavy ones would stand in one square. The short, light ones would stand in the square diagonally opposite the tall, heavy ones. The tall, light ones would go into the third square, and the short, heavy ones would fill the last one. We could count how many were in each square, and then we could calculate Yule's Q (also known as gamma). Here's the formula, as we learned it in Chapter 6:

$$Q = \frac{AD - BC}{AD + BC}$$

The letters A, B, C, and D in the formula refer to the numbers of people in each of the four cells of the two-by-two, as shown at the top of Figure 9.3. Cell A might represent the short, light people. Then D would be the

FIGURE 9.3
Labeling Crosstab Cells

B	D
A	C

E	F	G
B	D	H
A	C	I

k	l	m	n	o	p	q
Z	a	b	c	d	e	r
Q	R	S	T	U	f	s
J	K	L	M	V	g	t
E	F	G	N	W	h	u
B	D	H	O	X	i	v
A	C	I	P	Y	j	w

tall, heavy people. Taken together, groups A and D are the people who fit our hypothesis. The short ones are light and the tall ones are heavy. So AD has something to do with data that support the hypothesis.

In contrast, B and C are groups of people that contradict the hypothesis. B might be the group who are short but heavy, and C would be the ones who are tall but light. So BC has something to do with data that contradict the hypothesis, and AD-BC says something about whether the data support the hypothesis, on balance, or contradict it. I guess we need to define those somethings.

Correlation is all about comparisons, and one way to define a correlation is in terms of the possible two-person comparisons you could do with the data. At the moment, in our imagination, we have 100 students standing in the four cells on the ground. There are many, many possible pairs you can make with 100 people, and it would be just too much work to do it physically, but imagination (like computers) can make difficult tasks easy. John is short and light. Take him for the moment. Now take one of the tall, heavy guys, such as David. That's one pair in which the comparison of their heights and weights support your hypothesis. In your imagination, write that down: "John and David—one pair supports the hypothesis." Send David back to his cell, keeping John for the moment, and get another tall, heavy person, say Carol. Now you can compare John with Carol. He's short and light, while she's tall and heavy. So that's another pair that supports the hypothesis, bringing the total in support to two.

You would keep on pairing tall, heavy people with John until you had done so for all the tall heavies. Then you would send John back to the short, light cell, and take the next short, light person, say Barbara. Now you would pair Barbara with David, Barbara with Carol, and so on and so on. Eventually, you would have paired every short, light person with every tall, heavy person, and counted how many of these pairs there were. This is a tremendous lot of work, with 100 students standing dutifully in the cells of the two-by-two while pairs march around for you to count them. There is an easier way to determine how many pairs support your hypothesis. Simply multiply the number of short, light people by the number of tall, heavy people.

If you think this through, you will see that the imaginary process of taking pairs of people and counting gives the same result as multiplying. The number of pairs each short, light person participates in is simply the number of tall, heavy persons you have; and the total number of these pairs is the number of short, light people times the number of tall, heavy people. In the formula for Q (gamma), that is represented by AD.

By the same token, BC represents the number of people that directly contradict your hypothesis: pairs combining a short, heavy person with a tall, light person. In real sociological research, we always have a few pairs of cases that contradict the hypothesis. But if you have many comparison pairs that support the hypothesis, and only a few that contradict it, then on balance you can say that the data support the hypothesis. The simplest way to determine the balance of evidence is simply to subtract BC (the contradicting pairs) from AD (the supporting pairs). If AD is greater than BC, then the result will be a positive correlation. If AD is less than BC, the correlation will come out negative. And if AD and BC are the same size, then the correlation will be zero.

So AD-BC tells you whether your hypothesis is supported or not. It would be nice, however, to know how strongly it is supported, and to get this information in a form that permits you to compare the correlation with correlations concerning other variables with quite different numbers of cases and comparison pairs. The strategy for accomplishing this is exactly the same that we use when calculating proportions.

Proportions allow us to compare groups of very different sizes, in terms of the fraction of cases in each that have a particular characteristic. As you know, proportions are calculated by dividing the number of cases with the particular characteristic by the total number of cases in the group. If we have 100 students, and 54 of them are women, then the proportion female is $\frac{54}{100}$ or 0.54.

By what should we divide AD-BC to get an informative proportion? AD and BC refer to the numbers of comparison pairs that relate directly to the hypothesis under test, AD being the supporting ones and BC the contradicting ones. The total number of comparison pairs in question, both supporting and contradicting, is AD + BC. So that's the way we calculate Q: (AD – BC) /(AD + BC).

I hope the logic of this is clear enough for the two-by-two table we have been imagining. To apply the same kind of thinking to a larger crosstab, such as the seven-by-seven you get when you crosstab sociology with psychology, you merely have to be prepared to do a lot more comparing and counting.

People are not just tall or short; some are medium in height. And some folks are average in weight, too, rather than being either light or heavy. So you could divide the 100 students into nine groups rather than four, in terms of two trichotomies rather than two dichotomies. Look at the middle crosstab in Figure 9.3, and you will see a three-by-three table. The numerator in the two-by-two gamma is AD - BC. What should the numerator be for a three-by-three?

In a two-by-two, AD represented all the comparison pairs that clearly supported the hypothesis of a positive correlation between height and weight. In a three-by-three, AG also is a set of comparison pairs in support of the theory, and so is DG. Every person in cell G is both taller and heavier than every person in D or in A. And that's what counts for the comparison pairs that support the hypothesis: one person in each pair is both taller and heavier than the other.

If you think about it, you will see that everybody in cell F is taller and heavier than those in A. The same is true for everybody in cell H, and other comparisons should be added: BF, BG, CG, CH. So the total number of comparison pairs in which one person is both taller and

heavier than the other is AD + AG + DG + AF + AH + BF + BG + CG + CH.

Similarly, you can figure the total number of comparison pairs in which each person is both taller and lighter than the other, the pairs that directly contradict the hypothesis of a positive correlation between height and weight. In the two-by-two, this was simply BC; but in a three-by-three, we have to add ED, EI, DI, FH, EH, EC, FI, BI. So instead of just BC we have BC + ED + EI + DI + FH.

To get the formula for gamma on three-by-three tables, you just substitute these strings of letters for the simple ADs and BCs in the formula.

For two-by-two tables:

$$Q = \frac{AD - BC}{AD + BC}$$

For three-by-three tables:

$$\gamma = \frac{(AD+AG+DG+AF+AH+BF+BG+CG+CH) - (BC+ED+EI+DI+FH+ED+EI+DI+FH+EH+EC+FI+BI)}{(AD+AG+DG+AF+AH+BF+BG+CG+CH) + (BC+ED+EI+DI+FH+ED+EI+DI+FH+EH+EC+FI+BI)}$$

The idea is simple enough, but the formula looks like a pain to calculate. To save space, instead of writing "gamma" I put the Greek letter γ, which is gamma, the Greek equivalent of G. Naturally, we are glad to have the computer to do the counting, multiplying, adding, subtracting, and dividing for us! If you think this would be fun to calculate by hand, you should try a seven-by-seven table, as sketched at the bottom of Figure 9.3. This table is so big that I ran out of capital letters to label the cells and had to use the lowercase (little) letters as well.

First, you would take the people in cell A of the seven-by-seven and note that the people in the following cells are both taller and heavier: l, a, R, K, F, D, m, b, S, L, G, H, n, c, t, M, N, O, o, d, U, V, W, X, p, e, f, g, h, i, q, r, s, t, u, and v. So, to begin with, you would have to calculate Al, Aa, AR, AK, AF, AD, Am, Ab, AS, AL, AG, AH, An, Ac, At, AM, AN, AO, Ao, Ad, AU, AV, AW, AX, Ap, Ae, Af, Ag, Ah, Ai, Aq, Ar, As, At, Au, and Av. And that's only the beginning! I'm not even going to attempt giving you the full formula for gamma on a seven-by-seven table. It would fill pages.

The concept is not difficult, however, only the detailed calculations. You check each cell in the table and note what other cells contain people who are both taller and heavier. For each such pair of cells, you multiply the number of people in one by the number of people in the other, to get the number of comparison pairs of people the two cells represent. You do this with all the appropriate cells, then add up the results of all the multiplications. This will give you the total number of comparison pairs of people in which one was both taller and heavier than the other.

Traditionally, this number is called N_s. The N stands for the word *number,* and the s stands for *same.* You can think of these as the comparison pairs in which the two people differ on both variables in the *same* way. Being taller is like being heavier. Both are a way of being bigger. In the pair John and David, David's height is greater than John's, as is David's weight. Because David's height and weight differ from John's in the same way, this pair of people is one of those included in N_s. In a two-by-two table, $AD = N_s$.

The other pairs we have been considering are called N_d pairs, with the d standing for *different.* They are pairs in which height and weight differ in a different way. A short, heavy person and a tall, light person would be the example for a two-by-two. Here, when height is greater, weight is less. In a two-by-two, $BC = N_d$. By using these general concepts, N_s and N_d, we can quickly transform the formula for Q into one for gamma, regardless of the size of the table:

For two-by-two tables:

$$Q = \frac{AD - BC}{AD + BC}$$

For tables of any size:

$$gamma = \frac{N_s - N_d}{N_s + N_d}$$

Now that, I submit, is pretty neat! Human beings never, ever have to do all the actual counting and figuring. Computers do it for us, swiftly and effortlessly. If you ask the computer to show you how it calculated gamma for the crosstab of sociology and psychology, it will report the following figures:

$$N_s = 64825$$
$$N_d = 23228$$
$$N_s - N_d = 41597$$
$$N_s + N_d = 88053$$

$$gamma =$$
$$(N_s - N_{d)} / (N_s + N_d) =$$
$$0.47$$

If you want, you can check the arithmetic with a hand calculator. In all my programs, I have the computer round off the final answers to a convenient number of decimal points. If you actually divide 41597 by 88053 you will get something like 0.472408663. Rounded off to two decimal places, however, that is the 0.47 the computer gives you for gamma. You might think it would be more precise to report gamma to three or four decimal places (0.472 or 0.4724). But the random errors introduced in getting the sample of 100 students, and in doing the actual height and weight measurements, are probably bigger than the 0.002 or 0.0024 you would be adding. It is misleading to report results to many decimal places, implying far more accuracy in your research than is warranted. Sociologists seldom report correlation coefficients like gamma to more than two decimal places, and 0.47 is the right way to report this result.

You might wonder how high or how low gammas can go. The answer is that gammas run in the range from -1.00 through 0.00 to $+1.00$. Look at the formula and think about this for a moment. N_s and N_d are numbers of comparison pairs. Conceivably, you could have no pairs at all in one of these two groups, and either N_s or N_d would be 0. But N_s and N_d cannot be less than zero, and in most cases one or both of them will be positive whole numbers. Suppose that N_d equals zero. Then you can cross it out of the formula, out of both the numerator and the denominator, and you are left with the following: gamma = N_s/N_s. The result of this division is simply 1.00.

Imagine that N_d slowly grows. Then $N_s - N_d$ gradually grows smaller than $N_s + N_d$ and the result of the formula will be less than 1.00. At a certain point, $N_s = N_d$, and the result will be 0.00. If N_d is greater than N_s, the result will be less than zero.

To find the lower limit that gamma can reach, imagine that $N_s = 0$. Then the formula becomes $- N_d/N_d$. Note the minus sign. The result of this simple division is $- 1.00$. So the lowest that gamma can get is $- 1.00$, and its full range is from $- 1.00$ to $+ 1.00$.

One way I like to think of gamma and similar measures is as a tug-of-war. The one year I went to a summer camp, I experienced a massive one. One night there was a cook-out, and by the camp's ancient tradition (my father had attended it), the evening ended with a ritual tug-of-war. A huge rope was brought out, long and thick. A handkerchief was tied in the middle, and two parallel lines were sketched far apart on the ground. The rope was laid straight, perpendicular to the lines, and we were all made to grab the rope, half on one side, half on the other, facing the center. Then, on a signal, we pulled as hard as we could. The rope snapped taut. The handkerchief fluttered in the air and began to move—the other way. Yes, my side lost, and despite there being nearly a hundred kids on my side, I have always taken that defeat personally. If only I had pulled harder.

Well, I think you have the image of a tug-of-war, but now imagine that instead of kids on each end of the rope you have comparison pairs from our calculation of gamma. On one side of the handkerchief are the N_s pairs, pulling as hard as they can, while on the other end the N_d pairs are pulling in their direction. Which side will win depends on how many pairs there are on each side. If N_s is bigger than N_d, then gamma will be positive. But if N_d is bigger than N_s, gamma will be negative. If N_s equals N_d, gamma will come out zero. The denominator of the formula, $N_s + N_d$, represents all the pairs that are tugging on the rope.

A final comment about gamma will prepare us to consider the alternatives to it. Although $N_s + N_d$ represents all the pairs that are pulling on the rope—all the pairs that contribute directly to either a positive or a negative correlation—they are not all the pairs that exist in the crosstab. At the summer camp, a few kids just sat and watched. In a crosstab, too, there are usually many possible comparison pairs that do not wind up in $N_s + N_d$. If you want to take them into account in calculating your correlation, you might want to use tau-a rather than gamma.

Tau-a

Just as gamma is the Greek letter G, tau is the Greek letter T. You can write it as T or τ, but usually we just write "tau," especially because there are different taus, labeled a, b, and c, and it can be confusing to mix Greek and Latin letters. The first kind of tau we shall consider is closely related to gamma. Indeed, both are proportions with $N_s - N_d$ for the numerator. The only difference is in the denominator. Gamma, as we have seen, has $N_s - N_d$ for its denominator, all the pairs that push toward a positive or a negative coefficient. Tau-a's denominator is the total number of pairs, including those that sit by the sidelines in the tug-of-war.

Recall the 100 students patiently standing in the cells of a big two-by-two table. John and Barbara were short and light, while David and Carol were tall and heavy. In creating N_s we counted how many pairs combined a short, light person with a tall, heavy person. Among these were the pairs John-David, John-Carol, Barbara-David, and Barbara-Carol. But two other pairs are possible with these four people: John-Barbara and David-Carol. John and Barbara are in the same cell of the crosstab, and neither is taller or heavier than the other, at least as indicated by the cell they are standing in. The same goes for David and Carol. These two pairs are *tied* for both of the variables.

In a three-by-three or larger crosstab, there are usually some cases that are tied on one variable but not on the other. Tied pairs, whether tied on one variable or both, do not contribute to either N_s or N_d, but they do represent possible comparisons you could make between cells of the table and cases of the dataset. Thus, one could argue that they should be included in the calculation of a measure of association. Tau-a includes them in the denominator. Here is how the formulas for gamma and tau-a compare:

$$\text{gamma} = \frac{N_s - N_d}{N_s + N_d}$$

$$\text{tau-a} = \frac{N_s - N_d}{T}$$

T, in the denominator of tau-a, stands for the total number of comparison pairs of any kind that you could get from your particular crosstab. If you were feeling especially masochistic, you could figure T, cell by cell across your crosstab, doing an immense number of multiplications and additions. But there is no need. There is an easier way.

If you have N cases in your dataset, then the total number of unique pairs is given by a simple formula: $N(N-1)/2$. For the 100 students patiently standing in their cells, $N = 100$. Thus, $N - 1 = 99$. And $N(N-1)/2 = 100(99)/2 = 4{,}950$. For the 508 survey respondents who rated both sociology and psychology on the seven-point preference scale, $N = 508$. And $N(N-1)/2 = 508(507)/2 = 128{,}778$.

If you ask the computer to show you how it calculated tau-a, it will give you some information that looks very much like the information for gamma:

$$N_s = 64825$$
$$N_d = 23228$$
$$N_s - N_d = 41597$$
$$T = 128778$$

$$\text{Tau-a} = (N_s - N_d) / T = 0.32$$

At this point the similarity between gamma and tau-a should be clear, but we should stress the differences. Above, we showed that gamma can range from -1.00 to $+1.00$, but tau-a usually cannot get all the way down to -1.00 or up to $+1.00$. This is because T is usually considerably bigger than $N_s + N_d$. In the typical crosstab, many comparison pairs will be tied on one or both variables. None of them will be included in $N_s + N_d$ but all will contribute to T.

This makes gamma sound superior to tau-a, because it can be any number over the full range of -1.00 to $+1.00$. And not only will tau-a be limited to a range close to zero, but the precise range of tau-a depends on the proportion of all the comparison pairs that are tied on one or both variables, and that is something you cannot know until you actually look at the crosstab and calculate the totals. One of my colleagues prefers gamma simply because it is big. He is physically big, and he likes research results that are big, too, but that is not a really good reason for preferring gamma.

In fact, gamma is often, in a sense, too big. When most of the comparison pairs are tied on one or both variables, gamma may be based on a very small proportion of the total. Suppose we had a two-by-two on height and weight, with 100 students, but only one of them was tall. Suppose further that this tall person was the only heavy student in the bunch. So, only two of the four cells in the two-by-two would have any students in them. Ninety-nine students would be in the short, light cell, and one would be in the tall, heavy cell. To calculate N_s, you simply multiply 99 by 1 to get the number of comparison pairs of a short, light person with a tall, heavy person. The one tall, heavy person gets paired off with each of the other 99. To calculate N_d, you multiply the numbers in the two other cells of the two-by-two, but both of them are empty: 0 times 0 equals 0. So, $N_s = 99$ And $N_d = 0$. Gamma, for this extreme example, comes out 1.00.

To calculate tau-a, you use the same numerator, 99. The denominator, however, is the total number of possible comparison pairs, including pairing of each of the short, light people with each of the others. Above, we calculated that the total number of possible comparison pairs for 100 cases was 4,950. This gives a tau-a of 0.02 because $99/4,950 = 0.02$ exactly. What a difference! From the same crosstab we get a gamma of 1.00 and a tau-a of 0.02! In a situation like this, we would have to conclude that gamma gives a distorted impression of the association between the two variables.

When I speak of gamma as sometimes misleading, I am thinking of how the reader of a research report may interpret this coefficient. Typically, published reports leave out all the details of how coefficients were calculated and just give the final result. Therefore, the reader won't know when an extreme situation exists, like the one just described. To judge whether gamma is misleading, you have to examine the steps in calculating it and decide if $N_s + N_d$ is very small compared to T. The author of the report should do this, and it is a mistake simply to grab the coefficients the computer calculated and shove them into a report.

One solution is to report both gamma and tau-a. Another simply is to use good judgment, inspecting the crosstab itself to see if it contains an unusual pattern and checking $N_s + N_d$ to see if it is much smaller than T, but you should also think carefully about the nature of your hypothesis. A little later in this chapter we will suggest a way of thinking of some of the coefficients that helps decide which one to use.

I am sure you have noticed that the XTAB program gives you three different measures of association named tau, including tau-b and tau-c as well as tau-a. Although we will not spend as much time on tau-b and tau-c as we did on gamma and tau-a, the two other taus deserve some discussion.

Tau-b and Tau-c

The denominator in the formula for tau-a includes all possible pairs of cases, but the cases that are within single cells of the table are pretty uninteresting. To make it clear what I mean, we should note that there are really three kinds of tied pairs.

First, there are pairs that are tied on the X variable but not on the Y variable, pairs we can symbolize thus: T_x ("tied on X"). For example, suppose that Max and Morris both give sociology a rating of 3 on the preference scale, while Max rates psychology at 2 and Morris rates psychology 4. If sociology is the X variable, then these two men are tied in their preferences for X (sociology), although they differ in their preferences for Y (psychology).

Second, there are pairs that are tied on the Y variable but not on the X variable, pairs we can call T_y ("tied on Y"). If Cornelia rates sociology at 3, while Connie rates sociology 5, and they both rate psychology at 4, then the pair Cornelia-Connie would be included in T_y. They have different preferences for sociology (X), but are tied in their preferences for psychology (Y).

Third, there are pairs that are tied on both variable X and variable Y, which we can call T_{xy}. If Porter and Philip both rate sociology at 3 and psychology at 4, then the pair Porter-Philip is in the T_{xy} category. The denominator of tau-a, T, includes these three kinds of tied pairs, as well as the two kinds of nontied pairs that constitute the denominator of gamma. That is, $T = N_s + N_d + T_x + T_y + T_{xy}$. Tau-b has the very same numerator as gamma and tau-a ($N_s + N_d$), and its denominator makes use of all the types of pairs except those tied on both variables, T_{xy}.

Now, I'm sure you can think of a simple way that you could create a denominator like this, including all the pairs except T_{xy}. For reasons of their own, however, the mathematicians decided to do something a little complicated, and the formula looks like this:

$$\text{tau-b} = \frac{N_s - N_d}{\sqrt{(N_s + N_d + T_x)(N_s + N_d + T_y)}}$$

I can't fully explain here why the denominator is so complicated (a further hint will come in Chapter 12), but I can tell you that it is a kind of average of $N_s + N_d + T_x$ and $N_s + N_d + T_y$. For the usual kind of average, the arithmetic mean, you add two numbers together and divide by two. The arithmetic mean of A and B is (A+B)/2. The mean of 2 and 4 is (2+4)/2 = 3. But for a kind of average known as the *geometric mean*, you multiply the two numbers instead of adding them. The geometric mean of A and B is the square root of A times B. Suppose A = 2 and B = 4. A times B equals 8. The square root of 8 is 2.83, so this is the geometric mean of 2 and 4. Their arithmetic mean is 3, but their geometric mean is 2.83. The denominator of the formula for tau-b is the geometric mean of $N_s + N_d + T_x$ and $N_s + N_d + T_y$.

If you ask the computer to figure tau-b for the crosstab in which sociology is the X variable and psychology is the Y variable, you will get

$N_s = 64825$
$N_d = 23228$
$N_s - N_d = 41597$
$T_x = 16810$
$T_y = 19000$
$N_s + N_d + T_x = 104863$
$N_s + N_d + T_y = 107053$

Tau-b =
$(N_s - N_d)/$
$\overline{\sqrt{(N_s + N_d + T_x)(N_s + N_d + T_y)}} =$
0.39

Although tau-b is widely used in sociology, it has a serious disadvantage. Its range is greatly affected by the shape of the crosstab. That is, if the number of rows in the crosstab is not equal to the number of columns, tau-b cannot reach − 1.00 or + 1.00, regardless of how cooperative the tied pairs are. That has led some researchers to prefer tau-c, which is calculated by a method that explicitly counts how many columns and rows there are.

Actually, tau-c is concerned only with one or the other, columns or rows, whichever one is fewer. A crosstab in which sex is the X variable will have only 2 columns of cells, because there are just two sexes. A crosstab with sex for X and sociology for Y will have 2 columns and 7 rows. The smaller of these two numbers (2 or 7)

is 2. This number, which plays an important role in the formula for tau-c, is called M. So for the crosstab of sex against sociology, M = 2. The crosstab of sociology against psychology has 7 columns and 7 rows, so M = 7.

The tau-c formula also makes use of the total number of cases, N. Note that I said *cases*, not pairs. For the sociology-psychology crosstab, the number of cases is 508, the number of respondents who rated both academic subjects. The formula for tau-c is

$$\text{tau–c} = \frac{2M(N_s - N_d)}{N^2(M - 1)}$$

Tau-c is not bothered by the shape of the table and can, in principle, reach − 1.00 or + 1.00 for a rectangular crosstab like sex against sociology. Here is how the tau-c calculation looks for the sociology-psychology crosstab:

$N_s = 64825$
$N_d = 23228$
$N_s - N_d = 41597$
Rows = 7
Columns = 7
M = lesser = 7
N = 508

Tau–c =
$2M(N_s - N_d)/N^2(M - 1) =$
0.38

You can check the crosstab for sex and sociology yourself, using the computer. Most of the crosstabs that naturally come from our dataset are square—for example, 7 columns by 7 rows. But in addition to the naturally rectangular crosstabs, like sex against sociology, you can create others by recoding 7-value variables to give them fewer categories. Please watch out for one thing, however, when using tau-c calculated on recoded variables. If you have a value for one of the variables and no case involves that variable—for example, if nobody at all rated sociology a 3 but did rate it 2 or 4— then the computer will figure wrong results for tau-c. If you wind up with variables like this, you can recode them to close up any gaps, and tau-c will be accurate again.

All four of the measures we have considered so far, gamma and the three taus, are what we call *symmetrical* coefficients. That is, it doesn't matter in what order you select the two variables. If sociology is your X variable and psychology your Y variable, the gamma will be 0.47. If you select these academic subjects in the reverse order, with sociology for Y and psychology for X, the result will be the same, 0.47. One important measure related to these four, however, does not have this property. This is Somers' D, which makes a distinction between the independent variable and the dependent variable.

Somers' D

If you like gamma and tau-a but can't decide between them, you may want to consider Somers' D, which has a formula very similar to both (Somers 1962). Here are the three formulas for you to compare, with the T in the tau-a formula written out as $N_s + N_d + T_x + T_y + T_{xy}$:

$$\text{gamma} = \frac{N_s - N_d}{N_s + N_d}$$

$$\text{Somers' D} = \frac{N_s - N_d}{N_s + N_d + T_y}$$

$$\text{tau-a} = \frac{N_s - N_d}{N_s + N_d + T_x + T_y + T_{xy}}$$

The denominator of Somers' D includes the pairs tied on the dependent variable (T_y), but not the pairs tied on the independent variable (T_x) or those tied on both variables (T_{xy}). Or, as Somers (1962:804) himself puts it, the denominator of D's formula is "the number of pairs of observations that are not tied on X, regardless of their status on Y." Thus, D will come out slightly differently, depending on which of the two survey items was selected as X and which as Y. That is why the crosstab on your computer screen shows it like this: $D(X{\rightarrow}Y) = 0.39$. The "$X{\rightarrow}Y$" in parentheses is meant to remind you that 0.39 is the Somers' D in which X is the independent variable

and Y the dependent variable. Here's how the computer calculates Somers' D for sociology→psychology:

$$N_s = 64825$$
$$N_d = 23228$$
$$N_s - N_d = 41597$$
$$T_y = 19000$$
$$N_s + N_d + T_y = 107053$$

Somers' D =
$(N_s - N_d)/(N_s + N_d + T_y)$
   0.39

If you selected psychology to be variable X and sociology to be variable Y, however, the calculations for psychology→sociology would be slightly different:

$$N_s = 64825$$
$$N_d = 23228$$
$$N_s - N_d = 41597$$
$$T_y = 16810$$
$$N_s + N_d + T_y = 104863$$

Somers' D =
$(N_s - N_d)/(N_s + N_d + T_x) =$
   0.40

The difference is not great, 0.40 compared with 0.39, but some crosstabs will give you distinctly different Ds, depending on which of the two variables is taken to be independent. Clearly, Somers' D is appropriate when your theory specifies which variable is the cause of which. With sociology and psychology, it is hard to find a theory that says which of the two should be independent and which dependent. Liking either of these two academic subjects could inspire a person to like the other.

But if you were examining the connection between sex and preferences for sociology—perhaps hypothesizing that women are more likely to rate sociology high than are men—you would have a definite independent variable. Liking sociology does not change your gender. Your gender, and perhaps differences in childhood socialization that may be partly determined by gender, will affect how much you like sociology. So if you were examining the association between respondents' sex and their preferences for sociology, the Somers' D you would want would be sex→sociology, not sociology→sex. And because Somers' D distinguishes the independent variable from the dependent variable, you might use it instead of gamma or tau-a when your theory told you which variable should be which.

One final note about Somers' D will add a little further understanding to tau-b, which might strike you as having a funny formula. Tau-b is really the geometric mean of the two Somers' Ds that can be calculated from a crosstab. If you enjoy algebra, you can multiply the two formulas for the two Somers' Ds, take the square root, and you will get the formula for tau-b.

Although gamma and the taus are symmetrical measures, Somers' D is an asymmetrical measure. As we said, it comes out differently depending on which variable you select for X and which for Y. You might keep this idea in mind, because we will use it again in Chapter 11 and Chapter 12. There, we will see that the r coefficient is symmetrical, while the coefficients called *regressions* are asymmetrical.

All five of the coefficients we have discussed have $N_s - N_d$ in the numerators of their formulas, and thus they follow a similar conception of how to measure the strength of a correlation, positive or negative. My tug-of-war metaphor applies to all of them. When $N_s = N_d$, all of the coefficients will be 0.00. Most of the time, however, you can expect them to be different from each other.

Incidentally, whenever the denominator of a formula turns out to be zero, the computer will balk at completing the calculation. It is a basic rule of mathematics that you cannot divide numbers by zero. Whenever this happens, the regular report of the coefficient on the crosstab will give 0.00. But if you are suspicious that the denominator might have been zero, ask the computer to show you the calculation. It will report the zero, along with the message "Denominator is ZERO so we can't calculate!"

Perfect Correlations

As we have mentioned, one of the problems in interpreting the five coefficients is that tau-a cannot usually reach 1.00 in crosstabs. To make this point clear, we can look at four real crosstabs you can create with the XTAB program. Each one is an autocorrelation, the result of correlating a variable with itself, so we would expect to get perfect coefficients of 1.00. Figure 9.4 shows the five coefficients that resulted from each of these crosstabs.

First, I tried crosstabbing sex by sex, letting variable 70 be both the X and Y variables. Logically, your sex should correlate perfectly with your sex. No, this is not an invitation for various obscene jokes. I merely note that being male is the same thing as being male, and being female is the same as being female. An autocorrelation is a **tautology**, a useless repetition of the same information. But, as you can see at the top of the first column of numbers in Figure 9.4, tau-a is only 0.50 for the crosstab. Although the other coefficients achieve 1.00, the weakness of tau-a is immediately apparent.

The second crosstab I examined correlated preferences for sociology (variable 26) with itself. Again, tau-a is well short of 1.00, but tau-c doesn't quite achieve 1.00, either. The way tau-c is calculated doesn't fully ensure it can reach 1.00, but it will come very close if the crosstab is an autocorrelation. Political conservatism (variable 71) gives a similar result—tau-a well short of 1.00 and tau-c a little short—while the three other coefficients do achieve 1.00.

The same principles apply for negative correlations. Two of the variables in the XTAB dataset allow us to examine a perfect negative correlation. Variable 82 (Liberalism) is a reversed, recoded version of variable 71 (Conservatism). The final column of Figure 9.4 shows that we get exactly the same numbers as in the third column, but with a minus sign in front of them.

The very different behavior of tau-a, and the slightly different behavior of tau-c, are not restricted to perfect 1.00 and −1.00 correlations.

FIGURE 9.4
Four Autocorrelations

Coefficient	Sex by Sex	Sociology by Sociology	Conservatism by Conservatism	Liberalism by Conservatism
Tau-a	0.50	0.83	0.80	− 0.80
Tau-b	1.00	1.00	1.00	− 1.00
Tau-c	1.00	0.97	0.93	− 0.93
Gamma	1.00	1.00	1.00	− 1.00
Somers' D	1.00	1.00	1.00	− 1.00

There is an effect through the ranges of these coefficients. As we noted above, the only point at which you can count upon all five to agree is at a perfect 0.00 correlation.

Statistical Significance of Nonparametric Measures

Ideally, each of the measures of association should be accompanied by its own test of statistical significance. Although I have included such tests for both r and gamma, we cannot properly appreciate them until Chapter 12, after we discuss z-scores and the normal curve

in Chapter 10. Complex chi-square gives an estimate of statistical significance, but as we shall see shortly, it is not appropriate to use it to interpret the measures of association. I contemplated including the test for tau-b, but the formula for it is a beast—something we absolutely could not make sense of here—and it would unnecessarily slow down the display of the other information. When you use a full-featured statistics package, all the coefficients will be accompanied by their appropriate tests of statistical significance. For our purposes here, the tests for r and gamma are enough.

Complex Chi-square

If you look down the list of coefficients accompanying a crosstab, such as those in Figure 8.5 and Figure 9.2, you will notice one that seems familiar: chi-square. However, the particular number you see for the Republican/conservative crosstab is 445.77, far larger than we ever saw with two-by-two tables. And the chi-square for Democratic/conservative is pretty big, too: 173.25. The meaning of this chi-square is the same as for the ones we calculated in previous chapters. It reflects how different the contents of the cells are from what we would expect by chance. To determine the

statistical significance of the difference, we can look the chi-square up in a table giving the chi-square distribution. Why, then, is the number so big?

Chi-square is affected by the number of cells in the crosstab, and here we have 49 cells rather than the 4 in a two-by-two table. If statisticians hadn't found a shortcut, we would have to have a different table of chi-square distribution for every possible size of table—one for two-by-two, one for three-by-two, another for four-by-two, four-by-three, and so on, including seven-by-seven.

This shortcut involves a concept known as *degrees of freedom*. No, this is not a political doctrine about incomplete liberty, but a way of describing the freedom that data have to vary. The concept does not arise in isolation, but only in connection to certain measures, such as chi-square. In the abstract, the concept **degrees of freedom** refers to the number of cases, scores, or categories that are free to vary. In the concrete, the degrees of freedom of a crosstab tell us which chi-square table to use when assessing statistical significance by this measure.

In a sense, chi-square is not a single distribution but a whole family of distributions. The chi-square distribution we examined in our discussion of two-by-two tables in Chapter 6 was the right one for two-by-two tables, but it is not appropriate for tables with larger numbers of cells. We often call this case *simple chi-square*, and the chi-squares derived from bigger tables **complex chi-square**. But the concept is really the same. Only the degrees of freedom and the typical range of the chi-squares differ.

The number of degrees of freedom for a crosstab is simply figured by the following formula:

$$\text{degrees of freedom} = (R - 1)(C - 1)$$

In this equation, R is the number of rows of cells in the crosstab; C is the number of columns of cells. Our two crosstabs involving political party and conservatism are seven-by-seven tables. Thus, the number of rows is 7 and the number of columns is also 7. The number of degrees of freedom is 36, because $(7 - 1)(7 - 1) = (6)(6) = 36$. Because the crosstab display announces this number, you don't have to calculate it yourself, even though this is easy to do.

A four-by-five table has the same number of degrees of freedom as a three-by-seven table, because $(4 - 1)(5 - 1) = 12$, and $(3 - 1)(7 - 1) = 12$. If you have a set of statistical tables and you know the number of degrees of freedom, you can look up the statistical significance of a given complex chi-square. Actually, to save space, such tables usually cram several different degrees of freedom onto the same page, and

a small difference in degrees of freedom when the degrees are large usually doesn't matter. The number of degrees of freedom in a two-by-two table is just 1. Most of the tables you will run with the XTAB dataset have 36 degrees of freedom.

The method for calculating complex chi-square is identical to the first of two methods we introduced for calculating simple chi-square, back in Chapter 6. I will illustrate it with the crosstab of Democratic Party by Conservatism, shown here in Figure 9.2. The calculations themselves are shown in Figure 9.5.

Clearly, if Figure 9.5 tells us nothing else, it states most forcefully that it is great to have computers to do the calculations for us. It took me about an hour to produce the table, with the help of a hand calculator. The computer takes less than a second. The table has 49 rows of information, one for each cell of the crosstab. The first two columns tell you which column and row of the crosstab the table row refers to. The columns are the values for preference for the Democratic Party. So, the first handful of data, for column 1, refers to the respondents who hated the party, giving it a rock-bottom preference rating of 1.

I have arranged the crosstab row information, within each column, in descending order (from crosstab row 7 down to 1), to make it very comparable to the crosstab itself, which is given in Figure 9.2. For example, the first line of numbers is for the cell in the upper-left corner of the crosstab, those who rated the Democratic Party at 1 and said they were extremely conservative. The third column of information in Figure 9.3, labeled "E-Formula," shows how I calculated the expected frequency for this cell: (21)(7/510). This is calculated just the way we did for two-by-two tables. Recall that the formula to compute this expected frequency is

$$E = \frac{(\text{column total})(\text{row total})}{\text{total number of cases}}$$

The total number of cases is 510, the number of people who validly answered both of the questions for the particular crosstab. The total

FIGURE 9.5
Calculating Complex Chi-square on Figure 9.2

Column	Row	E-Formula	Expected	Observed	O-E	$(O-E)^2/E$
1	7	(21)(7/510)	0.29	3	2.71	25.32
1	6	(21)(40/510)	1.65	8	40.32	24.44
1	5	(21)(89/510)	3.66	4	0.34	0.03
1	4	(21)(53/510)	2.18	1	−1.18	0.64
1	3	(21)(109/510)	4.49	3	−1.49	0.49
1	2	(21)(165/510)	6.79	2	−4.79	3.38
1	1	(21)(47/510)	1.94	0	−1.94	1.94
2	7	(39)(7/510)	0.54	1	.046	0.39
2	6	(39)(40/510)	3.06	6	2.94	2.82
2	5	(39)(89/510)	6.81	13	6.19	5.63
2	4	(39)(53/510)	4.05	4	−0.05	0.00
2	3	(39)(109/510)	8.34	5	−3.34	1.34
2	2	(39)(165/510)	12.62	7	−5.62	2.50
2	1	(39)(47/510)	3.59	3	−0.59	0.10
3	7	(60)(7/510)	0.82	1	0.18	0.04
3	6	(60)(40/510)	4.71	11	6.29	8.40
3	5	(60)(89/510)	10.47	24	13.53	17.48
3	4	(60)(53/510)	6.24	6	−0.24	0.01
3	3	(60)(109/510)	12.82	7	−5.82	2.64
3	2	(60)(165/510)	19.41	8	−11.41	6.71
3	1	(60)(47/510)	5.53	3	−2.53	1.16
4	7	(157)(7/510)	2.15	1	−1.15	0.62
4	6	(157)(40/510)	12.31	9	−3.31	0.89
4	5	(157)(89/510)	27.40	31	3.60	0.47
4	4	(157)(53/510)	16.32	21	4.68	1.34
4	3	(157)(109/510)	33.55	38	4.45	0.59
4	2	(157)(165/510)	50.79	42	−8.79	1.52
4	1	(157)(47/510)	14.47	15	0.53	0.02
5	7	(124)(7/510)	1.70	0	−1.70	1.70
5	6	(124)(40/510)	9.73	6	−3.73	1.43
5	5	(124)(89/510)	21.64	14	−7.64	2.70
5	4	(124)(53/510)	12.89	13	0.11	0.00
5	3	(124)(109/510)	26.50	37	10.50	4.16
5	2	(124)(165/510)	40.12	45	4.88	0.59
5	1	(124)(47/510)	11.43	9	−2.43	0.52
6	7	(71)(7/510)	0.97	1	0.03	0.00
6	6	(71)(40/510)	5.57	0	−5.57	5.57
6	5	(71)(89/510)	12.39	1	−11.39	10.47
6	4	(71)(53/510)	7.38	6	−1.38	0.26
6	3	(71)(109/510)	15.17	12	−3.17	0.66
6	2	(71)(165/510)	22.97	42	19.03	15.77
6	1	(71)(47/510)	6.54	9	2.46	0.93
7	7	(38)(7/510)	0.52	0	−0.52	0.52
7	6	(38)(40/510)	2.98	0	−2.98	2.98
7	5	(38)(89/510)	6.63	2	−4.63	3.23
7	4	(38)(53/510)	3.95	2	−1.95	0.96
7	3	(38)(109/510)	8.12	7	−1.12	0.15
7	2	(38)(165/510)	12.29	19	6.71	3.66
7	1	(38)(47/510)	3.50	8	4.50	5.79

number of cases in the particular row of the crosstab is 7. You can see that "7" to the right of the top row of the crosstab in Figure 9.5. The column total is 21, the total number of respondents who rated the Democratic Party at 1. In the crosstab itself, you can see that number just below the lower left-hand corner. The formula above suggests I should write the calculation this way: $((21)(7))/510$. But I think this equivalent way makes the meaning clearer: $(21)(7/510)$. Here's why.

How can we decide what frequency to expect in the cells of crosstab column 1? This is equivalent to deciding the expected distribution of the 21 cases in the left-hand column across the column's cells. The only basis we have for deciding is the actual distribution for all 510 cases. Just 7 of the 510 cases are in the top crosstab row. Expressed as a proportion, this is $7/510$. We would expect to find this same proportion of the 21 cases in the top cell of the left-hand column. That is, we expect to find $7/510$ of 21 cases, or $(21)(7/510)$. This happens to come out to 0.29 cases, as shown in the "Expected" column of Figure 9.5.

So, we have to calculate the expected frequencies for all 49 cells, as I have done in Figure 9.5. We want to compare these with the actual "Observed" frequency in each of those cells, information that the next column of the table provides. The formula for chi-square (χ^2) considers the square of the difference between observed and expected frequencies as a proportion of the expected frequency. Then it sums up this number for all the crosstab cells, as represented by the Greek letter sigma (Σ), which stands for summation in the following formula:

$$\chi^2 = \Sigma((0 - E)^2/E)$$

Figure 9.5 has columns labeled "O-E" and "$(O-E)^2/E$," which give you the steps in this calculation. Finally, to get chi-square, you have to add up all 49 numbers in the "$(O-E)^2/E$" column. When I do this, I get almost exactly the chi-square the crosstab itself gives, 173.25. But in doing the divisions and squares with my hand calculator, I introduced lots of little rounding errors, which keep my result from being exactly what the computer so swiftly got.

I think it would repay your time to look through Figure 9.3 carefully and see how all the numbers were derived from the crosstab itself, in Figure 9.2. It would probably be good for you to figure some complex chi-squares by hand, and your instructor may decide to give you an assignment to that effect. Once you understand chi-square fully, however, there is never any need to go through all these tedious calculations. We can let the computer do the dreary drudgery for us, leaving our minds free for more interesting things.

Once you have a complex chi-square and the associated degrees of freedom, you can look up the chi-square in a statistical table and see whether the pattern of frequencies in the crosstab is significantly different from what you would expect to get just by chance. To save you time, the computer will flash an estimate of statistical significance as part of this chi-square information. Let me stress, however, that I have not hidden a chi-square table away inside the XTAB program for the computer to consult, so the estimate is only very approximate. Full-featured statistical analysis packages, such as you would use for serious professional work, do include such chi-square tables (although you never get to see them), so they can give you highly accurate reports about statistical significance. Our rough estimates will serve for purely educational purposes.

Sometimes researchers use chi-square as a means for evaluating the statistical significance of other coefficients, such as taus and gamma. This is not strictly appropriate. Although it is possible to extract a phi from complex chi-square, such a phi would not really be a correlation coefficient, as a phi based on a two-by-two table can be said to be. The reason is that chi-square responds to any marked departure from a random pattern of frequencies in the table's cells, not just to ones that reflect simple correlations.

For example, I can imagine a political party called the Radical Party. It's a little like the real Libertarian Party in that it includes people from both ends of the political spectrum but leaves out many from the middle. This Radical Party is really extreme. It consists only of extreme liberals and extreme conservatives. Shall I admit to you that I founded a party like this back in the eighth grade in the early 1950s? It was called the Caprocialists (Capitalist-Progressive-Socialists) and may have been a contradiction in terms, but many fellow students joined until the school authorities banned our innocent party because they did not want serious political debate about any issues. The chief idea was that nobody discussed anything important at the school or really cared about social and political issues, so those few who did should form a common front against the dull majority, regardless of the tremendous disagreements among Caprocialists. At least we cared.

So imagine a Radical Party like that, composed of extreme liberals and extreme conservatives. Crosstabulate that party against conservatism. There would be no correlation. The Radical Party is not a liberal party. It is not a conservative party. But because it is an extreme party, with no moderate members, the crosstab pattern will be very far from what you might expect by chance. Therefore, chi-square could be large and statistically significant, without there being any correlation—as our measures of association define a correlation—between the two variables.

_____ The Concept of Dispersion

A measure of dispersion is included in both the histogram and the menu option for statistics on a variable of the XTAB program. The **dispersion of a variable** is the extent to which the cases are spread out across the variable's values. If all the cases have the same value, then dispersion will be 0.00, but if the cases are spread equally into the available categories, then the dispersion is 1.00. In Chapter 10 we will learn about variance, another measure of the spread of the distribution that is especially suited to interval or ratio variables. But because the measure of dispersion included in XTAB works with nominal and ordinal variables, it is appropriate to discuss it here.

First, I should emphasize that there are several ways to measure the spread of cases across a number of categories, each with its own logic. Let's consider one that I did not include in the program but that is easy to understand and can get us started on the topic. For this section, I am going to employ three variables from the dataset that have very different degrees of spread, humanities (variable 32), soap operas (variable 36), and war stories (number 37). Conveniently, exactly the same number of respondents gave valid preference ratings for these three variables, so the calculations will be perfectly comparable. The number of good cases is 511, which has the added accidental advantage that it is evenly divisible across the seven values of the variable—a convenient coincidence but not one that the measures we are going to use require. Figure 9.6 shows the frequencies for the three variables, along with the percentages of cases in each category.

The humanities are so well liked, with a mean rating of 5.87 on the 1 to 7 scale, that the overwhelming majority of cases are concentrated in the top three categories, and less than 10 percent are left over for the values 1 through 4. In contrast, soap operas are more hated than loved, and the bottom values have far more cases than the top ones. War stories show a third pattern, very even across six of the seven categories. Certainly one can see at a glance that respondents are more dispersed in their judgments of war stories than in their judgments of either the humanities or soap operas, but it would be useful to be able to capture dispersion in a single number for each variable that would allow clear, direct comparison.

FIGURE 9.6
Frequencies and Percents for Three Preference Items

Value	The Humanities		Soap Operas		War Stories	
	Cases	Percent	Cases	Percent	Cases	Percent
7	157	30.7	27	5.3	36	7.0
6	198	38.7	26	5.1	67	13.1
5	107	20.9	46	9.0	78	15.3
4	36	7.0	52	10.2	86	16.8
3	8	1.6	71	13.9	86	16.8
2	3	0.6	90	17.6	74	14.5
1	2	0.4	199	38.9	84	16.4

One way to think about dispersion would be to consider how many respondents would have to change their answers for there to be identical numbers at each value. For the 511 respondents who gave valid answers to these three questions, that would mean there would be 511/7, or 73, in each of the 7 value categories. One could then go through the 7 categories and see how many people would have to move out of each if the categories were to be balanced. For the humanities, three categories would have to give people up: 5, 6, and 7. The top category would lose 84, because $157 - 73 = 84$. Altogether, these three top categories would lose 243. Expressed as a proportion of the total 511, this is 0.48 of the respondents (48 percent).

This figure could be considered a measure of how *far from* an even dispersion the variable was. Because this is the opposite of dispersion, you might want to subtract this number from 1.00. This would give you 0.52 as a measure of how dispersed the data were. The comparison figure for soap operas is 0.72, and for war stories it is 0.92. Perhaps this was obvious from the raw frequency distributions in Figure 9.6, but now we have definite numbers that tell us war stories are more dispersed than soap operas, which in turn are more dispersed than the humanities. I'd like to call this dispersion measure D, but the crosstab already has a D, Somers' D. So let's call dispersion measures S, for "spread"—telling us how evenly spread around the cases are. This first one will be

S_1. It tells us what proportion of the cases do not have to move in order to achieve perfectly even dispersion.

One flaw of S_1 is that its range is a bit uncertain. The highest it can get is exactly 1.00, a very easy number to remember and a maximum very dear to the hearts of statisticians. The minimum value it can achieve, however, depends on how many categories there are. If there are seven categories, and all the cases are bunched up in one of them, then $6/7$ of the cases have to move to achieve perfect dispersion, and only $1/7$ can stay put. Thus, S_1 for a case like this would be $1/7$ or 0.14. For 7 categories, it can't get any lower than this, but for 5 categories the minimum S_1 is $1/5$ or 0.20. And for 100 categories, it is $1/100$ or 0.01. This means it would be hard to compare the dispersion of variables that have different numbers of response categories.

A second dispersion measure, S_2, can be proposed that gets around this problem because it has a range of 0.00 to 1.00 regardless of the number of categories. Here is its formula:

$$S_2 = 1 - \frac{K(M)}{N(K-1)}$$

N is the number of cases, which is 511 for the three variables we are considering. K is the number of categories the given variable has, seven for each of these three. And M is the number of cases that have to move to achieve a perfectly even dispersion. If no cases at all have to move, then $M = 0$ and S_2 will equal 1. You would never have a situation in which all of the cases would have to move to different categories, because at least one category will contain N/K cases that can stay put. So, at maximum, $M = N - N/K$ cases that have to move. A moment's simple algebra shows that $K(N - N/K) = N(K - 1)$. Then the numerator of the fraction will equal the denominator, and S_2 equals $1 - 1$, or 0. By this measure, the dispersions for humanities, soap operas, and war stories are 0.44, 0.67, and 0.83.

I rather like S_2. It will not be hard for you to calculate it directly from the frequencies table of one of the variables, but I have included a slightly different measure in the software, one that several social statisticians have proposed in one form or another (Hammond and Householder 1962; Loether and McTavish 1976; Mueller, Schuessler, and Costner 1977). Because it is the measure used in the software, we will call it simply Dispersion, and its formula is

$$\text{Dispersion} = \frac{K(N^2 - \Sigma f_i^{\,2})}{N^2(K - 1)}$$

As in the formula for S_2, K is the number of categories and N the number of cases. The quantity f_i is the frequency in one of the categories—the number of cases in the category—and

$\Sigma f_i^{\,2}$ tells you to add up the square of the numbers of cases in each category. I will show how to calculate this for our three variables, using Figure 9.7.

N^2, which appears in both the numerator and denominator of the dispersion formula, is 511 times 511, or 261,121. Again, K is 7, and $K - 1 = 6$. For the humanities, $\Sigma f_i^{\,2}$ is 76,675. Putting all these numbers into the formula gives a dispersion of 0.82. For soap operas and war stories, the dispersions are 0.90 and 0.99. Although these are exactly the numbers the software shows, do not compare them with the numbers we calculated for S_1 above. This is a very different measure of dispersion, one that we must understand in its own terms.

I am sure, however, that you have noticed the similarities in the formulas. Both have K in the numerator and $N(K - 1)$ in the denominator. But the logic behind the software's dispersion measure has some affinity with that for the nonparametric correlation coefficients, discussed at length above. Remember that we used comparison pairs of cases in figuring gamma, Somers' D, and the various taus. Here we are working with just one variable at a time, but we can do something similar.

Consider all the possible pairs of respondents. Many of these pairs have different values on the variable. That is, they are in different categories. If the variable has high dispersion,

FIGURE 9.7
Calculating Dispersion for Three Preference Items

Value	The Humanities		Soap Operas		War Stories	
	Cases	Squared	Cases	Squared	Cases	Squared
7	157	24649	27	729	36	1296
6	198	39204	26	676	67	4489
5	107	11449	46	2116	78	6084
4	36	1296	52	2704	86	7396
3	8	64	71	5041	86	7396
2	3	9	90	8100	74	5476
1	2	4	199	39601	84	7056
Total	511	76675	511	58967	511	39193

then the number of pairs of respondents who have different values for the variable will be at its maximum. Pairs that are not different in value are in the same category. So, if most of the respondents are crammed into a couple of categories, then fewer of the total number of possible comparison pairs will have different values. The measure of dispersion is the ratio of the number of pairs with different values on the variable to the total possible number of different pairs there would be if the cases were evenly dispersed across the categories.

I just worked through the algebra and confirmed for myself what the statistics textbooks tell me. The number of comparison pairs in which the two individuals have different values on the variable is $N^2 - \Sigma f_i^2$. And the maximum possible number of such pairs, if the cases were spread perfectly evenly across the categories, is $N^2(K-1)/K$. Divide the first of these by the second, and you get the dispersion formula given above.

Clearly, there are many ways of measuring dispersion. Here, it is important to have at least one way of doing it that is appropriate for nominal and ordinal data. Equally important is to understand the concept of dispersion itself, and to realize that we may often want to measure the way cases are spread out across the values of a variable, perhaps as a prelude to comparing two variables.

A Modest Research Project

It is time to put together some of the things we have just learned and use them to answer a couple of simple research questions. I suspect you will not find the results of the following research project tremendously surprising, but the procedures we follow illustrate how the techniques of this and the previous chapter are actually applied in specific situations.

As you have gathered by now, one of my chief sociological research interests is space-flight, and I originally created the XTAB dataset as a by-product of a major, multiquestionnaire study of the ideology of space (Bainbridge 1990b). If there had been sociologists on Earth 500 years ago, one of their chief preoccupations would have been understanding the opening of a new world, the American continents, to European civilization. Today, we may be on the threshold of yet another new world, potentially grander even than the Americas: the solar system.

Seriously, now, think about the future, 500 years from now. Will humanity still be forging its destiny on this single world, within a radius of a mere four thousand miles, a world perhaps overpopulated and exhausted in resources? Or will humanity dwell on a dozen worlds beyond Earth, with names like Rhea, Hyperion, Iapetus, Miranda, Oberon, Triton, Ceres, and Mars? These places all actually exist, and they are complex and fascinating environments; the question is whether humans will ever make them home. In 500 years, there will be a definite answer to this question. Although the question may seem fanciful today, in the future there will be a concrete reality, either one way or the other. How we get from the present to either of these two radically different alternative futures should be a major topic of current sociological concern. I am sorry to report that it isn't.

Anyway, why would anybody want to go to Mars? The XTAB survey included the following item, which is variable 78: "If you were asked to go along on the first rocket trip to the planet Mars, would you want to go, or not?" Among the 512 respondents, 283 said "yes," while 196 said "no," 27 had no opinion, and 6 failed to answer the question validly. To be sure, this is a somewhat funny question, because a Martian expedition is not currently funded, and even NASA's most optimistic plans call for a generation to pass before one is launched. Thus, we do not begin with great confidence that people will answer this question in a meaningful way. But let's give analysis a try.

To start with, we have to recode this item. At present, "yes" is coded "1," "no" is coded "2," and "no opinion" is coded "3." Perhaps "no opinion" should be moved between the other choices. Noting that about half of the respondents said "yes," I have decided on a different approach: combining the three other responses into one. It might be nice for the item to measure positive sentiments about a Mars trip, so our crosstabs will be easier to understand.

Using the recode option of the XTAB program, I temporarily moved the 283 yes responses up to a value of 9, so I could move the others around without interference. Then I recoded all the other responses to a value of 1. Thus I combined the 196 who said "no" with the 27 who had no opinion and the 6 who did not answer validly, and gave all of these 229 respondents a value of 1. Then, I recoded the 283 who answered "yes" to 2. This gave me a Mars-trip variable in which there were 229 people (coded 1) who did not express an interest in going to Mars, and 283 people (coded 2) who did want to go. Now, our dependent variable is ready for analysis, and we need to identify the independent variables.

I had included four items in the survey specifically to help me understand variation in the Mars-trip item. I theorized that respondents might vary in what we might call risk-aversion, the tendency to avoid risks in life. Surely, flying across millions of miles of space to the planet Mars will be risky. But there are different kinds of risks—for example, the danger of damage to self-esteem in disastrous love affairs—and after the Challenger disaster people probably think of spaceflight in terms of physical risk. So, I included among the preference items "taking physical risks" (variable 67). Concerned that this item might be too abstract, I also included a preference item about a very real risk that respondents might often take, "driving very

fast in a car" (variable 65). For contrast, there is "taking risks in your relationships with people" (variable 68). Finally, to balance these items asking how much people like risks, I needed a general item that measured how much they preferred to avoid risks, "complete personal security" (variable 66).

But a flight to Mars is more than just a damn-fool stunt, attractive to the daredevil instinct in some of us. It would also be a tremendous intellectual adventure and an opportunity for scientific discovery. Perhaps people who like astronomy (variable 2) and physics (variable 9) would be especially interested in voyaging to another planet. The Mars expedition would also be a tremendous engineering challenge that people who like engineering (variable 25) as an academic subject and those interested in advanced technology (variable 76) might favor. Finally, flight to Mars has been a dream of science fiction since early in this century, and people who like science fiction (variable 35) should be especially in favor of it.

Now that we have prepared the dependent variable through recoding, and have selected a short list of potential independent variables that might contribute to an explanation, we can proceed to do a series of crosstabs. In each one, the dependent variable will be willingness to go to Mars, and the independent variable will be one of those we just selected. We start with variable 67, preference rating of physical risks, and we get a crosstab with the following correlation information:

r: 0.24
z: 5.43
Significance: .001

Gamma: 0.32
z: 3.45
Significance: .001

Tau-a: 0.13
Tau-b: 0.21
Tau-c: 0.26
$D(X \rightarrow Y)$: 0.16

Chi-square: 33.73
df: 6
Significance: .001

This pile of coefficients clearly indicates that liking physical risks is associated with willingness to fly to Mars. All three significance estimates are beyond the .001 level, pretty good support for the theory that risk-orientation predicts interest in participating in a Martian expedition. These facts should encourage us about the validity of the Mars-trip item, because the data strongly support a very reasonable hypothesis about it. The only reservation we might have is that the different coefficients are not exactly the same, and we have not decided which ones to pay attention to. We'd better do that.

Our old friend chi-square is not the ideal measure here, because in complex tables with more than one degree of freedom it does not immediately lead to a correlation coefficient—and that is what we need, a measure of the correlation between the two variables. Pearson's r might be good, although we have not yet laid a basis for understanding it, as we shall do in Chapters 10, 11, and 12. After that introduction to r, we might have much to debate about whether r would be appropriate or not. For now, let's stick with the nonparametric measures.

Gamma is a good one, completely appropriate in the present case. However, we might also want one of the taus, because taus take into account comparison pairs that are tied on the variables. Which tau? Probably not tau-a. In fact, sociologists generally avoid tau-a because it is incapable of filling the full range between -1.00 and $+1.00$. Tau-b can do that, but it is designed for tables that are square in shape, having exactly the same number of rows and columns. This leaves us with tau-c, which is designed for rectangular tables. In addition, we should consider Somers' D, because our theory makes a definite distinction between independent and dependent variables.

In a journal article, you might want to settle on just one of these three valid choices to save printing space, something the journal editors are always screaming for. But here we have some room, so Figure 9.8 will show gamma, tau-a, and the appropriate Somers' D. Often, the sociologist has to settle on just one measure out of several appropriate ones, either to save printing space or to keep tables and text uncluttered and thus easy to read. One way of deciding is to follow whatever tradition happens to exist in the particular line of research, to use the same measures earlier publications did. Naturally, you want to use the best and mathematically most appropriate measure. If there are several, however, the proper choice may

FIGURE 9.8
Predictors of Willingness to Go to Mars

Preference for	Gamma	Significance	Tau-c	Somers' D(X→Y)
Taking physical risks	0.32	.001	0.26	0.16
Driving very fast in a car	0.26	.01	0.22	0.13
Taking risks with people	-0.06	n.s.	-0.05	-0.03
Complete personal security	-0.20	.05	-0.16	-0.10
Astronomy	0.27	.01	0.22	0.14
Physics	0.18	.01	0.15	0.09
Engineering	0.25	.01	0.21	0.13
Advanced technology	0.31	.01	0.24	0.16
Science fiction	0.36	.001	0.30	0.18

be made entirely on the basis of your readers' habits.

There is nothing wrong with this. When beginning students learn that some measures are quite wrong for certain kinds of data and certain hypotheses, they sometimes jump to the incorrect opinion that there is always just one right statistical measure. Not so. Keep in mind that statistical tables are not merely—or even primarily—a method of making scientific decisions. Most importantly, they are a medium of communication from the writer to the reader, and one basic rule of writing is always to write in the reader's language. The reader will understand your argument best if you use the statistical procedures and measures that are most familiar in the particular field of research. This does not mean using inappropriate statistics, and it should not prevent you from using a relatively new measure if to do so greatly improves your research. This rule is good, however, for it stresses that statistics are a medium of communication in sociology as well as a tool for testing hypotheses.

Figure 9.8 shows that the four risk variables correlate just the way we predicted with willingness to go to Mars. Physical risks have the strongest association as measured by each of the coefficients, with driving fast in second place among the four risk measures. Taking risks in relationships with people does not correlate at all; it concerns a very different kind of risk. And complete personal security has a significant negative correlation with willingness to travel to Mars. This correlation is a bit weaker than the two significant positive correlations, probably because personal security undoubtedly includes avoidance of nonphysical risks—as with financial security, for example, for many respondents.

I leave you to ponder the pattern of correlations among the other five preference variables: astronomy, physics, the sciences, engineering, and science fiction. I do not think explanations will be difficult to find. I do, however, want to press the quantitative analysis slightly further. We have not looked at the crosstabs

themselves, and I believe it is important to glance at a couple of them. Students sometimes look at correlation coefficients like the 0.32 gamma for physical risks and the 0.36 gamma for science fiction and feel they are pretty measly. Certainly $0.32 isn't a significant amount of money, and you may not be used to thinking of 0.32 of anything as worth noting.

Figure 9.9 shows, however, that gammas of 0.32 and 0.36 can reflect quite substantial differences in people's responses. The figure has a small table for each of these two independent variables. If you scan across the top row of percentages in each little table, you will see that the percentage of respondents wanting to go to Mars increases substantially as you go from a low preference rating for physical risks or science fiction to a high rating. The pattern is not perfectly even, and we would expect random fluctuations simply from the relatively small numbers in each column, but the difference from the left of each table to the right is huge. Of those who abhor physical risks (rating them a "1"), only 27.3 percent would be willing to go to Mars, compared with 76.5 percent of those who love such risks (rating them a "7"). And for science fiction, the change is almost as dramatic, more than doubling from 31.6 percent to 75.8 percent. Because it expresses what is going on throughout the cells of a table, rather than focusing just on the extremes, gamma is slightly larger for science fiction than for physical risks.

I believe we have made our point. A simple research project, using the statistical techniques covered in this chapter, has given us a very clear picture of factors that shape survey respondents' feelings about going on a trip to Mars. Perhaps you feel, however, that the topic was not really important, not a worthy test of our methods. Well, then, let's examine a spaceflight-related topic of more immediate human impact.

Variable 76 in the XTAB dataset is based on responses to the following item: "Recently, there has been much talk about building a system of space satellites to defend against nuclear attack. Do you think research on this idea should continue, or should research stop?" The topic is clearly the Reagan administration's Strategic Defense Initiative (SDI), otherwise known as the Star Wars project. The idea was to develop a multilevel, multi-approach system to defend the United States (and perhaps its allies) against nuclear missiles. Among the ideas were surface-based defenses such as "smart rocks" (steerable but warheadless projectiles) fired from electric rail guns (gunlike electromagnetic launchers) and long-range laser and charged-particle beams. In the popular mind even more than in actual planning, however, Star Wars was to be space-based, and that is what the wording of the question was intended to get respondents to consider.

Note that the item's wording does not include any of the following phrases: *Reagan administration, Strategic Defense Initiative, Star Wars,* or even *military.* I felt that these would add their own intense connotations, perhaps muddling the results. For example, I included a separate item asking how much respondents liked President Reagan, which we can crosstab against this satellite defense item if we want.

Also, the public debate on SDI at the time of the survey often distinguished between mere research on the possible technologies and actual deployment of an operational system. Some people felt that actual deployment would be provocative and might even violate the ABM treaty, which limits defenses against ballistic missiles. They might simultaneously believe, however, that the United States should continue with research, at the very least so that potential opponents could not gain a technical advantage. In addition, there was great controversy over the feasibility of a missile defense, a question research might resolve. Thus, the particular wording of the question would probably have gotten a higher level of positive responses than would an item about actual deployment of an SDI or one that used any of the political trigger words, like *Reagan* or *Star Wars.*

Out of the 512 respondents, 231 felt that research should continue. A slightly larger number, 247, felt research should stop, while 22 had no opinion, and 12 did not give a valid answer. Again, I considered it wise to recode the item, following the same procedures I used for the Mars-trip item. After recoding, we have 231 people who want research to continue (value 2 on the variable) and 281 who do not express such support (value 1 on the variable).

Again, we need a theory. Why not one similar to our Mars-trip analysis? Shouldn't

FIGURE 9.9

Risk Taking, Science Fiction, and Going to Mars (percent)

| Go to Mars? | Preference for physical risks | | | | | | |
	1	2	3	4	5	6	7
Yes	27.3	37.0	39.7	60.2	58.6	62.4	76.5
No	72.7	63.0	60.3	39.8	41.4	37.6	23.5
N =	22	46	78	88	116	109	51

| Go to Mars? | Preference for science fiction | | | | | | |
	1	2	3	4	5	6	7
Yes	31.6	43.5	43.8	47.6	58.4	65.6	75.8
No	68.4	56.5	56.3	52.4	41.6	34.4	24.2
N =	38	62	64	84	77	90	95

attitudes toward physical risks condition people's responses to a missile defense? But how? Think freely, for a moment, uninfluenced by your own opinions about such a missile defense. Imagine two sociologists, Leroy Left and Rodney Right. Leroy is personally convinced that SDI is a terrible idea. He says it destabilizes the international situation. It threatens the Russians and might even cause them to launch a preemptive attack, if they thought the United States were about to succeed in creating a missile defense. Therefore, SDI is a great risk. Only people who like risks would tolerate SDI. Thus, Leroy would theorize that there should be a positive correlation between liking risks and favoring SDI.

Rodney, on the other hand, happens to be a supporter of SDI as well as a sociologist. He views the "balance of terror" and "mutually assured destruction (MAD)" that have existed between the Soviet Union and the United States as inherently risky. When President Reagan suggested that technology might provide a way out of this terribly risky situation, Rodney thought this was a great idea. When asked to provide an hypothesis to our research project, Rodney predicted a negative correlation between liking risks and supporting SDI, because

in his mind SDI would reduce risks rather than increase them.

It often happens that sociologists' personal feelings and private political commitments shape the theories they construct. If they are good social scientists, however, both Leroy and Rodney will welcome good data and accept sociological conclusions based on proper statistical analysis of them. Figure 9.10 shows the coefficients the risk variables achieved in crosstabs with satellite missile defense. Only driving fast in a car has a statistically significant gamma, and the failure of physical risks to achieve one gives me great doubt whether it is the risky aspect of breaking the speed limit that is involved. In short, neither Leroy nor Rodney has proven right, although the correlation with driving fast gives modest support to Leroy's position. One possibility, of course, is that people in the general public divide up very much as Leroy and Rodney do, some feeling that SDI is risky, others feeling that it reduces risks. A more subtle research project would be needed to explore the possibility that these two opposed factors were simultaneously at work.

The table continues with the rest of the variables we used to predict interest in going to

FIGURE 9.10
Predictors of Support for Missile-defense Satellites

Preference for	Gamma	Significance	Tau-c	Somers' D(X→Y)
Taking physical risks	0.12	n.s.	0.10	0.06
Driving very fast in a car	0.22	.05	0.18	0.11
Taking risks with people	− 0.06	n.s.	− 0.05	− 0.03
Complete personal security	0.02	n.s.	0.02	0.01
Astronomy	0.06	n.s.	0.05	0.03
Physics	0.04	n.s.	0.03	0.02
Engineering	0.17	.10	0.14	0.08
Science fiction	0.10	n.s.	0.08	0.05
Advanced technology	0.20	.05	0.15	0.10
War stories	0.33	.001	0.28	0.17
Political conservatism	0.60	.001	0.50	0.31
Ronald Reagan	0.62	.001	0.52	0.33

Mars. Star Wars does not, however, seem a natural expression of interest in astronomy, physics, or science fiction. One might have thought otherwise; for example, a high level of advanced physics would be required to find missile targets and shoot beam weapons at them. Modest correlations do appear for engineering and advanced technology, perhaps reflecting the tremendous engineering accomplishment that a functioning SDI would represent, or resulting from lower confidence in SDI on the part of respondents who doubt that there are engineering solutions to international problems.

Figure 9.10 includes three other variables: preference for war stories (variable 37), political conservatism (variable 71), and preference for President Ronald Reagan. Suddenly we see huge and highly significant correlations. People who like war stories like Star Wars. Political conservatives and supporters of SDI's patron, Ronald Reagan, believe that research on a satellite missile defense should continue.

The two political items seem to explain just about everything happening inside the missile-defense variable. Among extreme political liberals, only 17 percent feel research should continue. Among the tiny category of seven extreme conservatives, 100 percent do. And the proportion is 82.5 percent among those who are merely conservative without being extreme in their conservatism. Fully 185 respondents loathed Reagan, giving him a rock-bottom preference rating of "1," and only 22.7 percent of these wanted research to continue. In contrast, 81.5 percent of extreme Reagan lovers did so.

If you want to explore these issues more deeply or wish to see the details of the analysis summarized here, you can use the XTAB program yourself. To be sure, you would have predicted the political differences on Star Wars, but you might not have guessed that they would so completely overwhelm the other theories. In any case, one piece of scientific research is worth a dozen good guesses. Our modest research project on willingness to participate in the first expedition to Mars and on satellite missile defense has illustrated the great value and convenience of the statistical techniques introduced in the previous chapter and explained closely here.

PROJECTS FOR CHAPTER 9

Each of the following six projects is a realistic research study, testing hypotheses about relationships between variables by using the XTAB program. Thus, a key aim of these projects is to give you experience framing a sociological question and evaluating possible answers empirically. In addition, these projects help you become familiar with a variety of frequently used measures of association: r, tau, gamma, and Somers' D. You will see that these coefficients are valuable tools of research, not merely mathematical abstractions.

1. **Attitudes Toward Risks.** In our modest research project, we employed four variables (numbers 65 through 68) measuring people's preferences for certain kinds of risk: taking physical risks, driving very fast in a car, taking risks with people, and complete personal security. What other preference items might some of these four correlate with? Frame hypotheses and test them through crosstabs. Your report should include tables of results from the crosstabs, as well as a theoretical argument explaining why certain of the risk variables should be associated with other preference items in the XTAB dataset.

2. Random Crosstabs. The purpose of this project is to explore crosstabs based partly on random data, to get a sense of the statistical significance of a measure of association, as we did for two-by-two tables when the computer automatically produced 100 or 1,000 random two-by-twos. Select one of the two random variables, variable 80 (Random data 1) or variable 81 (Random data 2). Also, select one of the measures of association given by the XTAB program: r, tau-a, tau-b, tau-c, gamma, or Somers' D. Then check the 68 crosstabs in which the random variable is X and one of the preference questions is Y. For each, write down the chosen coefficient.

What is the range of these 68 coefficients? That is, how far on the negative side of zero, and how far on the positive side, are the most extreme coefficients? If a calculator is at hand, you may wish to calculate the mean and the standard deviation of the 68 coefficients. Keep in mind that all of these crosstabs are meaningless, because the X variable is entirely random. Note that with this many coefficients, even based totally on random data, some of them can be quite substantial. Do any of the 68 strike you as big? If so, keep this lesson is mind as you evaluate similar coefficients based on more meaningful data in the future: Chance results can be mistaken for meaningful results, and tests of statistical significance are one way of gaining proper perspective on them.

3. Politicized Subjects. Perhaps you were sitting peacefully in a college class one day, when suddenly you were struck by the feeling that what the professor was giving you was political propaganda, most likely of a kind you disagreed with. This project asks you to use the crosstabs part of the program to see which subjects have significant political bias in the minds of our 512 student respondents.

You should first look through the list of 30 academic subjects and find five that you suspect are politically conservative and five that look politically liberal. Then run a crosstab for each with item 71 (conservatism) as variable X and the subject as variable Y. If there turns out to be a strong positive correlation between political conservatism and the subject, then conservatives tend to like the subject, perhaps because it is biased in their direction. If the correlation is strongly negative, then political liberals are the ones who like the subject, perhaps because it leans in their political direction. In making your judgments, you may want to use gamma, since it comes with an estimate of statistical significance.

To complete this project, write a brief essay reporting the correlation between conservatism and each of the 10 subjects, trying to explain why it came out the way it did—positive, negative, or nearly zero.

4. Explaining Support for Various Aspects of the Space Program. First, do project 5, at the end of the previous chapter, to get space items 72 through 77 in good shape for analysis (ignore items 78 and 79 for this project); these are your dependent variables. Then search through the other items in the survey that you suspect might distinguish supporters of the space program from people who are less enthusiastic about space exploration; these are your independent variables. Do several crosstabs, each one tabulating an independent variable against a dependent variable.

Write a report explaining your theories and stating whether the measures of association you got support or contradict them. For the sake of simplicity, you will probably want to use just one of the several measures of association. I suggest that gamma might be a good choice.

5. Types of Popular Fiction. Try to explain which groups of respondents tend to like the following five types of popular fiction: "spy and detective stories," "stories of love and romance," "science fiction stories," "television soap operas like Dallas and Dynasty," and "war stories." These five items from the questionnaire (items 33 through 37) will be your dependent variables. Using crosstabs, find other variables (considered independent for purposes of this project) that correlate with them and help you explain who likes which types of popular fiction.

6. Mysterious Crosstabs. Some pairs of variables give very interesting crosstabs, in which one can learn much about the two variables and their relationships simply by examining the pattern of cases in the cells. Below are listed five such crosstabs, each one a bit odd and challenging. A couple may simply have difficult-to-see positive correlations in them. Inspect each one and describe it in a section of a short essay on the art of interpreting crosstabs. Make sure you consider what each pair of variables means and why you might expect the variables to be correlated. Look at the pattern of cases in the cells, however, and see if it tells you something beyond what a mere correlation coefficient would. Here is the list you should use:

> X = variable 52 (utopian essays) and Y = variable 55 (critical essays)
> X = variable 47 (avant garde) and Y = variable 47 (progress stories)
> X = variable 31 (the sciences) and Y = variable 32 (the humanities)
> X = variable 28 (medicine) and Y = variable 19 (nursing)
> X = variable 53 (Feminist literature) and Y = variable 54 (Holy Bible)

CHAPTER SUMMARY

The kind of measure of association often best for survey items is nonparametric. Quantitative information about some characteristic of a population is called a *parameter*. Measures, such as tau and gamma, that do not make any assumptions about the shapes of the parameter distributions are *nonparametric*.

Correlations can be negative as well as positive. When comparing two correlations, we always have two characteristics to look at: (1) the sign on the coefficient (whether it is + or −), also called the *direction* of association, and (2) the size of the coefficient (how far from zero it is), also called the *degree* of association. In Chapter 6 we met two coefficients, phi and Yule's Q. Here we examine the following nonparametric measures: gamma, tau-a, tau-b, tau-c, and Somers' D. In principle, each one could be any number from −1.00 through 0.00 to + 1.00, although in social research we never see coefficients very close to −1.00 or + 1.00.

A command on the XTAB program displays the steps by which each of these nonparametric measures was calculated. Each measure considers the association in a slightly different way. Depending upon the precise nature of the hypothesis under test, one would be more appropriate than the others. One way to define a correlation is in terms of the possible comparisons between pairs of cases that could be made with the data. A comparison between two cases could support the hypothesis that a positive correlation exists between the variables. The number of such pairs is designated N_s, representing all the comparison pairs in which the two cases differ on both variables in the *same* way. Other pairs support the hypothesis of a negative correlation (instead of a positive correlation), and they are called N_d pairs, those in which the variables vary in a *different* way. Still other pairs may be tied on one or both variables. Gamma is $(N_s - N_d)/(N_s + N_d)$. It is a kind of tug-of-war, in which the N_s and N_d pairs compete to determine if the coefficient is positive or negative, and no other pairs take part in the contest.

Tau-a is similar to gamma, also having $N_s - N_d$ as the numerator of its formula, but the denominator is the total number of possible pairs of cases in the data. This means that tau-a has difficulty getting to $+1.00$ or -1.00. Although tau-b and tau-c also have $N_s - N_d$ in their numerators, they have still other denominators. Gamma and the three taus are what we call *symmetrical* coefficients; that is, they do not make any distinction between the X and Y variables, producing the same results regardless of which of a pair of questionnaire items was called X and which Y. Somers' D is asymmetrical, making a distinction between the independent variable and the dependent variable.

It is possible to calculate the chi-square for a table with many cells, just as it is for two-by-two tables. However, tables of different shapes have different characteristic chi-square distributions. This is because they differ in their *degrees of freedom,* the number of categories that are free to vary. Complex chi-square can be used to determine the statistical significance of departure of observed cell frequencies from the frequencies expected by pure chance, but this is not a good way of evaluating the statistical significance of a measure of association. The nonparametric measures of association have their own tests of statistical significance, and the XTAB program includes one for gamma. It is also possible to examine the dispersion of cases across a nonparametric variable.

The chapter includes a modest research project that tries to explain why some respondents say they are willing to fly to the planet Mars. One explanation is that the survey item about flying to Mars is so frivolous that respondents fail to respond seriously. Another is that only people who enjoy taking risks would want to go. Perhaps people who like astronomy and physics want to visit another planet. The Mars expedition would be an engineering challenge, favored by people who like engineering and advanced technology. Finally, people who like science fiction should be especially in favor of it. After testing these hypotheses, the chapter concludes with a brief research project explaining support for the Strategic Defense Initiative (SDI), otherwise known as the Star Wars project.

KEY CONCEPTS FOR CHAPTER 9

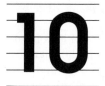

The Normal Curve, ANOVA, and Confidence in Research Results

CHAPTER OVERVIEW

This chapter examines a number of concepts connected to the normal curve, such as variance, standard deviation, and standard scores. We learn more about statistical significance, and see how useful the normal distribution is as a model of sampling probability. We enter the realm of parametric statistics, preparing for the correlations and regressions that are the topics of the next three chapters. After a dynamic introduction to the concept of the normal distribution, we will learn about those immensely useful measures of dispersion,

variance and standard deviation. Finally, we will learn about two methods for estimating the statistical significance of the differences between means: analysis of variance (ANOVA) and t-tests.

We begin with dynamic illustrations of the normal curve, contained in the GRAF program of your software package. These are two versions of a pinball probability game, one that will run on essentially any IBM-compatible microcomputer and the other requiring basic graphics capability. Visually, the game demonstrates the binomial distribution and illustrates features of the normal curve.

Special options in the XTAB program illustrate the analysis of variance (ANOVA) and t-tests.

Pinball Probability Game

You may wonder what a pinball game is doing in the middle of a serious book on research methodology and statistics. There is, in fact, a good historical justification, because some of the earliest mathematical work on probability (the basis for modern statistical analysis) concerned gambling odds. The particular pinball game I have created illustrates one way of deriving the normal curve that is mathematically sound but also visually interesting. It is part of the GRAF program.

There are actually two versions of the game. One will work on any IBM-compatible computer, while the other requires a graphics capability. Both give exactly the same statistical results, but the graphic version produces a nice picture of results and makes a stronger visual connection to the normal curve. A simplified nongraphics version of this game was published in my textbook/software package, *Survey Research* (Bainbridge 1989b). Both present versions illustrate the origins of the normal curve and help you learn about variance and standard deviation.

You should check whether your computer has a graphics capability. If it is your own machine, there should be no question, because you will know what you paid for when you bought it. If it belongs to a computer center, however, you should ask someone who knows. Your computer will also check as it runs this program, and it will advise you if it thinks it lacks graphics. However, IBM compatibles differ so much that I do not have absolute confidence in the routine I wrote into the program to check the kind of machine you have, so you should definitely check. If the program thinks that your machine lacks graphics, it will say: "WARNING! Your computer seems to lack the capacity to display graphics. If this is so, you cannot run the GRAPHIC version of the pinball game or the SCATTERGRAM. Check your computer . . . Does it have graphics? (Y)es (N)o Press (Y) for Yes or (N) for No."

Unless you have very good reason to believe that your computer DOES possess a graphic capability, you should press (N). An attempt to run graphics programs on nongraphics machines will cause your computer to crash (metaphorically) or to seize up. If your computer is a stand-alone machine, this is no disaster. You will simply have to start it over again from scratch. If it is hooked into other machines, however, you may cause them trouble, too, depending on how the hookup was done. The computer lab my undergraduates currently use has some ganged machines, four keyboard-and-screen combinations hooked up to a single central processor. If one of the four students using one of these highly undesirable units does the wrong thing, all four students will suffer the same disaster. That can lead to fistfights.

Shortly, the main menu of the GRAF program will appear on the screen. If your machine lacks graphics, the menu will be:

```
[1] Pinball probability game (Normal Curve) PLAIN version
[2] Regression analysis of two regional variables
[ESC] QUIT or change programs
```

The second option goes with Chapter 12, where we learn about regression analysis, so it should not concern you now. If your machine possesses a graphics capability, the menu will be longer:

```
[1] Pinball probability game (Normal Curve) PLAIN version
[2] Regression analysis of two regional variables
[3] Pinball probability game (Normal Curve) GRAPHIC version
[4] Scattergram of two regional variables
[ESC] QUIT or change programs
```

The fourth option, scattergram, is also for Chapter 13, so wait until then to try it. When you choose either version of the pinball game, a new menu appears:

```
[1] Run tracer balls (or Run slow balls)
[2] Run 10 balls
[3] Run 20 balls
[4] Run 50 balls
[5] Run 100 balls
[6] Run 500 balls
[7] Run 1000 balls
[8] Run 4000 balls
[9] Run 15,000 balls
[ESC] Return to main menu
```

As the menu suggests, you have 15,000 balls you can run through. That can take a long time, however, so you should stick with smaller numbers at first. If your computer has graphics capability, the first choice will say "Run tracer balls." If your machine lacks graphics, it will say, "Run slow balls." Either way, the first choice is designed to help you understand how the game works, so we should begin with it. I will first describe the PLAIN version of the game; then I will use the GRAPHIC version to discuss the statistical meaning of both versions of the game. If you do not have graphics, do not worry. I will show you a couple of pictures of how the graphic version looks.

When it appears on the screen, the plain version of the pinball game looks like Figure 10.1. If you have taken the first menu option, to run slow balls, a little ball will dribble down the left edge of the screen, starting from the left side of the message "Press a key to stop." In Figure 10.1, the ball is shown about halfway down, on the left. It is about to begin rolling to the right. In a moment it will strike a bumper in the shape of an arrowhead (<). As in real pinball games, the ball will bounce. It will go either up or down a little, but will keep moving to the right untill it strikes another arrowhead, bounces again, and keeps moving to the right. Eventually, having bounced up and down 12 times, it will lodge over at the right in a ball bin.

When it gets to the right, each ball will be counted, and its bin will show how many balls have landed in it during the course of the game. Figure 10.1 shows

FIGURE 10.1
The PLAIN Version of the Pinball Game

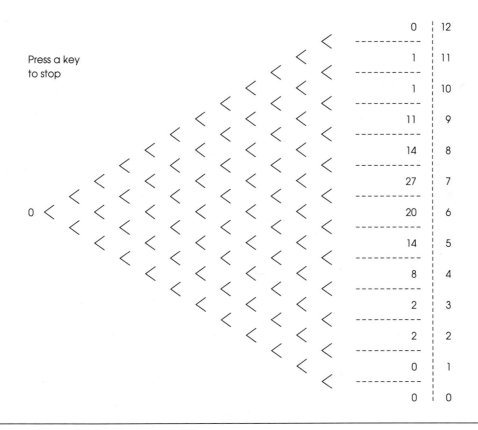

how the game looked one time after I had run 100 balls. At that moment, the middle bin had exactly 20 balls in it. The bin just above the middle had 27, and the bin just below the middle had 14. There are 13 bins altogether, and to the right of them are numbers 0 through 12, showing how many times a ball had to bounce upward to get into the particular bin.

The GRAPHIC version of the pinball game looks somewhat similar, except that the bins for the balls are at the bottom of the screen and the arrowheads point up-ward. I felt it was more realistic to have the ball roll downward, being bounced left or right by the arrowheads, and that is how the graphic version shows the game. (I could not draw it that way for the plain version, because of the limited possibilities for display on the computer screen.) So, in the graphic version, you see a triangle of arrowheads at the top of the game and a set of 13 bins to hold the balls, la-beled 0 through 12, at the bottom. A ball comes in at the top and bounces down through the array of arrowheads, until it comes to rest in one of the bins. Figure 10.2

FIGURE 10.2
Graphic Pinball Game

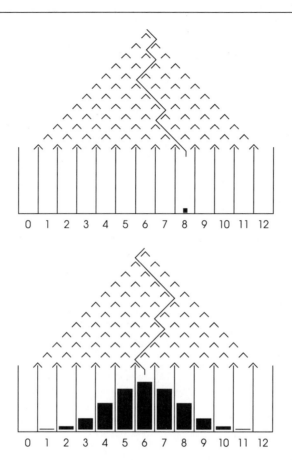

shows the graphic version, which I will not describe in detail. If you are using the plain version, you need only think about the balls rolling to the right and winding up in bins at the right, instead of balls dropping downward as in the graphic version.

In the graphic version, each ball appears right above the top arrowhead and bangs into it. The ball then bounces either left or right, entirely at random. I swear, there is an exactly 50-50 chance that the ball will bounce either way. After its first bounce, the ball will bang into one of the two arrowheads in the second row, again bouncing either left or right. This continues for a total of 12 rows of arrowheads, until the ball comes out at the bottom and falls in a bin.

The first choice on the graphic pinball menu gives you tracer balls. These are like military tracer projectiles—not an appealing concept for many of us, but the best metaphor I could think of. Tracer projectiles could be quite spectacular when fired at night, for example in World War II air defense. The gunner needs to know where the shells are going, so he can aim his anti-aircraft gun at its target. So every

10th shell would be a tracer projectile, containing a special chemical that marked its flight path with a trail of smoke or fire (smoke for the day, fire for night). When you see old movies of air attacks, and the guns on the ground are spitting out lines of fire that arc way up into the air, those are tracers. If you don't like this military metaphor, you can think instead of the slime trails snails leave as they crawl across the glass of an aquarium. Well, I said I had trouble finding an appealing image!

With the tracer option, the ball leaves a trail as it bounces down through the thicket of arrowheads. That is the zigzag line you see weaving its way through the arrowheads in the diagram. As you actually run the program, each tracer ball will leave such a trail, which will vanish in a second or two, to be replaced by the next tracer. As the balls drop into the bins at the bottom, they will pile up; so after a while you can see which bins are more popular, because they will have bigger piles of balls in them.

In the plain version of the pinball game, the first menu option is slow balls; they move so slowly through the thicket of arrowheads that you can watch each bounce. Because there is no room on the screen to show all the balls as they pile up in various bins, I show you the numbers of balls in each bin instead, as in Figure 10.1.

Why would one bin wind up with more balls than another? To be sure, the balls bounce by pure chance, so you might expect some random fluctuation in how many wind up in the 13 bins. As you actually run the program, however, you will find there is also great consistency in where the balls go. Many of them will pile up in the middle bins, and very few in the bins near each end. The reason is that there are far more ways the ball can get to a middle bin than to one on the end.

The numbers next to the bins in the graphic version of the game tell you how many times the balls bounced to the right on their way down in the graphic version of the game. To get in the left-hand bin, a ball has to go through the whole series of arrowheads without bouncing right even once. It must bounce left 12 times. In contrast, to get into the right-hand bin, a ball has to bounce to the right each of the 12 times. This happens only very rarely.

You might be interested in how many different routes there are through the arrowheads. One way to find out would be to watch the tracers go through the game and draw each different zigzag path until you were sure you had them all. But this would take a very long time—weeks, I suppose. I have saved you that effort by calculating the numbers of different routes leading to each bin, shown in Figure 10.3.

We already saw that there is just one route to each of the end bins. The ones just inside the ends, numbers 1 and 11, are almost as easy to figure out. To get into bin 1, a ball has to bounce left 11 times and right 1 time. There are 12 bounces, and the bounce to the right can come at any of these. So there are exactly 12 routes to bin number 1, depending upon which point in its course the ball takes its one bounce to the right. Similarly, a ball winding up in bin 11 must have bounced to the left 1 time and to the right 11 times. Again, there are 12 different routes, depending on where the one bounce to the left occurred.

Figure 10.3 reports that there are 4,096 routes altogether. It also tells you what percent of these 4,096 routes leads to each of the 13 bins. The largest number of routes, 924, go to the middle bin. This is bin number 6, so you know that these balls must have bounced to the right exactly 6 times and to the left 6 times. A glance at the diagram will immediately convince you that there are many routes from the

FIGURE 10.3
Routes in the Pinball Probability Game

Bounces Right	Routes	Percent
0 (left bin)	1	0.02
1	12	0.29
2	66	1.61
3	220	5.37
4	495	12.08
5	792	19.34
6 (middle bin)	924	22.56
7	792	19.34
8	495	12.08
9	220	5.37
10	66	1.61
11	12	0.29
12 (right bin)	1	0.02
Total	4096	100.00

top into bin number 6, but you may be surprised to learn that there are fully 924 of them. This is 22.56 percent of the total of 4,096. The one route that goes all the way to the right is only about 0.02 percent of the total.

Another way to state this is to say that 1 out of every 4,096 balls will reach the far right. Of course, this is just a prediction about what will happen on average, and it does not mean that every 4,096th ball will hop over to bin number 12. If we run many thousands of balls, however, the average will be 1 out of 4,096. This is the same as saying that on average 0.02 percent of the balls will reach the far right, or 0.0002 if you express it as a simple proportion rather than a percent.

If you were to run tracer balls through the game for the whole afternoon, you would get a picture like the one at the bottom of Figure 10.2. Note, first of all, that a different trace is showing from the one in the top part of the illustration. The ball whose trace is shown at the top went into bin number 8, while the one at the bottom went into bin number 6. These are both rather common destinations. As we explained, on average 22.56 percent of the balls go to bin 6, while Figure 10.3 shows that 12.08 percent go to bin 8. In the bottom picture, bin number 6 is just about full, having received falling balls for some hours. Bin number 8 is closer to half full, having received just over half the number of balls as bin 6 over the same period of time.

The piles of balls in the bin reflect the probabilities of balls arriving in each, which are calculated as the proportion of routes going to each destination. Some of you who have taken a few social science courses will recognize something familiar about the distribution of probabilities. The distribution of balls is close to what statisticians call the normal distribution or **normal curve**. If you drew a curved line connecting the top balls in each bin, it would rise from the bottom at the left, getting steeper and steeper for a while. Then this curved line would begin to level off until it reached the middle bin. After that, it would fall off steeply to the right until the slope began to flatten out at the far right end, again back at the bottom of the bins. Thus, the piles in the bins give a rough picture of the famous normal curve.

To be precise, the distribution of routes is called the **binomial distribution** (Christensen and Stoup 1986:215). With 13 bins, the distribution of routes in Figure 10.2 roughly follows the normal curve. If I rewrote the program so that there were many, many bins and an appropriately greater number of arrowheads and routes, the distribution would come even closer to the perfect normal curve. And if we could somehow have an infinite number of bins, we would get the normal curve exactly.

Applying the Normal Curve: Statistical Significance in an Astronomy Test

One of the main uses of the normal curve, for social scientists, is helping us estimate the statistical significance of our results. We have already seen that chi-square is limited in its capacity to estimate the significance of correlations, and once we understand the normal curve we will be able to estimate statistical significance in an important new set of situations. We will consider this important application of the normal curve several times, from various perspectives, but we need at least a rough idea of the principles to start. Let me explain through an example.

Once upon a time, I invented a little astronomy quiz for one of my questionnaires. I wanted to see whether students who knew a lot about astronomy were scornful of astrology and other popular myths about the heavens, so I needed a simple test of astronomical knowledge. I wrote a set of eight true-false questions like these: "Pluto is the largest planet in the solar system." "Venus is the planet closest to the sun." "An eclipse of the sun is actually caused by the shadow of the moon." "The pull of gravity on the surface of Mars is less than the pull of gravity on the surface of the Earth." The first two of these statements are false, and the second two are true. Well, sad to say, my astronomy quiz bombed. The average score was about half right, and it appeared that

the overwhelming majority of the students responding hadn't the faintest idea what the correct answers were and just checked the true or false boxes at random.

At this point I gave up, but let's imagine that I persisted in this line of research and created a new and improved astronomy quiz, consisting of 12 true/false items. And now I give this test to you. You read each of the 12 items and check either the true or the false box after it. We add up your score and find that you got 9 right. Does this prove that you know something about astronomy?

We can use Figure 10.3 to get an insight into the depth of your astronomical knowledge, as revealed in this score of 9 right out of 12 true/false questions, because the table tells us how likely each possible score on the test is purely as a result of random guessing. If you decided which box to check by flipping a coin, you would have a 50-50 chance of checking the correct answer for each question. This is exactly the same thing the ball does in the pinball game when it bangs into an arrowhead. It has a 50-50 chance of going either way. Indeed, you could have let a ball answer my quiz. Run a tracer ball through and note whether it bounces left or right at each of the 12 arrowheads it hits. Let's say the boxes in my test were arranged like this: [ ] True [ ] False. True is on the left and false is on the right. So, whenever the ball bounces left, you check the True box, and whenever it bounces right, you check the False box.

To think most clearly about statistical significance, however, let's imagine that a bounce to the right means getting the question right. A bounce to the left means getting it wrong. Entirely at random, you have a 5.37 percent chance of getting 9 right, because 220 out of the 4,096 routes involve 9 bounces to the right. Another way of looking at this is to figure out what the chances are of getting a score this good or better. You do that by adding together the chances of getting 9, 10, 11, and 12 right. The total number of routes leading to these four bins is $220 + 66 + 12 + 1 = 299$. And 299 is 7.30 percent of 4,096. Thus, we would expect 7.30 percent of the students to do as well as you (or better) if they took this test simply on the basis of flipping coins.

Frankly, this is not very convincing evidence that you know any astronomy. You are part of a minority that did well on this test, but about 1 out of every 15 people would do as well as you, even if none of them knew anything about astronomy. Generally, no social scientist would be impressed by a finding that could come about purely by chance 1 out of every 15 times.

What we have just calculated is the *statistical significance* of your score. You have a 7.20 percent chance of having gotten a score this good (or better) by pure chance, without possessing a glimmer of astronomical knowledge. If we express this as a simple proportion rather than as a percent, we get 0.073. This could be stated as "statistical significance at the 0.073 level." If the figure were 5 percent, representing 1 chance in 20, social scientists might begin to take notice. As you know, we often speak of a research finding as "achieving the 0.05 level of statistical significance." This means we got 5 percent or less when we figured the probability that the results could have come about by pure accident.

More commonly, we like to see the 0.01 level of significance, representing only a 1 percent chance of dumb luck. If you examine Figure 10.3 carefully, you can see that a score of 11 right does better than the 0.01 level. There are 12 routes to a score of 11 right, and

1 route to 12 right, so the probability of getting a score as good as 11 by pure chance is 0.32 percent. I got that figure by adding the routes together $(12 + 1 = 13)$, dividing the result by the total number of routes $(13/4096 = 0.0032)$, and multiplying by 100 to get percent $(0.0032 \times 100 = 0.32)$. That is less than 1 percent, indicating a pretty good level of statistical significance and a low probability that a score of 11 was a pure accident.

A score of 12 certainly looks great, but there is always a small chance that any score was an accident. Only 1 time out of 4,096 (on average) can you expect pure accident to give you a perfect 12 score on a 12-item true/false test. That is a mere 0.02 percent, or about 2 chances in every 10,000 students (a 0.0002 chance). That surpasses the 0.001 level of statistical significance, a particularly impressive achievement among sociological researchers.

To do better than that, you would have to take a test with more than 12 items. As you have seen several times before, when we were drawing random samples, the larger your sample the more solid your results. The same thing is true for tests and surveys. It is a general rule in statistics that the greater the number of appropriate things you have measured (whether items on a test or respondents filling out a questionnaire), the more solid your results are.

I hope you can see a connection between statistical significance and sampling, because the two topics are closely related conceptually and we keep finding them together in this book. Whenever you run the game and let several balls run through, you get an approximate random sample of routes through the forest of arrows (though a route can be represented twice, and we seldom let people fill out our questionnaires twice!). Thus, the percentage distribution of the balls' destinations will be a reflection of the full percentage distribution of all 4,096 routes. The concept of "chance" or "probability" enters into both sampling and evaluations of statistical significance, and often you may gain insights by contemplating one of these issues in the light of the other.

Running Balls in the Pinball Probability Game

When you first run this program, I suggest you let a number of tracer balls (or slow balls) go through, watching them bounce and seeing them pile up in various bins. You can check how many you have run by looking for a message on the screen like "Balls: 20." The traces can be somewhat hypnotic—entrancing traces—but eventually you will have learned all you can by this, and it will be time to stop the computer. A message in the upper left corner of the screen tells you how: "Press a key to stop." Almost any ordinary key will do. You could hit (SPACE), the bar that makes spaces between letters in ordinary typing. I don't use this big key for anything special in my programs, but it is sitting right there at the bottom of the keyboard, where it is easy to reach.

When you leave the pinball game, the computer does a quick analysis and prints a table of data on the screen, like the one shown in Figure 10.4. (This table will be essentially identical, whether you used the plain or graphic versions of the game. The only difference is that the plain version will refer to "bounces upward," while the graphic version that I am discussing here will refer to "bounces to the right.") The top row of figures names the 13 bins in terms of the number of bounces to the right (or upward) it takes for a ball to get into each one. These numbers, 0 through 12, are the same as the numbers of the bins in the pinball picture. The next row of figures tells you how many balls did indeed get into each bin on the particular run.

Here we see the result of a particular run of 20 balls, 5 of which got into bin number 6. The bottom row of figures at the top of the screen turns these numbers into percentages of the total. For example, 5 balls is 25 percent of 20. Farther down on the screen are several summary statistics we shall consider later in this chapter, although you should already recognize the first one, the *mean*. This is simply the average number of rightward bounces across the 20 balls.

FIGURE 10.4
Results of Running 20 Balls through the Pinball Game

Bounces to the right:												
0	1	2	3	4	5	6	7	8	9	10	11	12

Number of balls:												
0	0	2	0	0	3	5	5	2	1	0	2	0

Percent:												
0.0	0.0	10.0	0.0	0.0	15.0	25.0	25.0	10.0	5.0	0.0	10.0	0.0

Mean $(\overline{X}) = 6.55$
Variance: $s^2 = 5.05$ $\sigma^2 = 5.31$
Standard deviation: $s = 2.25$ $\sigma = 2.31$
Variation ratio: $s/\overline{X} = 0.34$ $\sigma/\overline{X} = 0.35$

If you look at the distribution of balls that came from an actual run I did, you will see that it does not fit the ideal distribution given in Figure 10.3 particularly well. The middle bin, number 6, is pretty close. It is supposed to hold 22.56 percent of the balls, but, of course, you can't divide 20 balls up in such a way as to get this exact percentage, unless you take a saw or hatchet to the balls. To get 22.56 percent out of 20 balls, you would need 4 and 1/4 balls, plus some sawdust (assuming the balls are made of wood). This run put 25 percent into bin 6, or 5 whole balls.

But bin number 7 also holds 25 percent of the balls, when it is only supposed to get 19.34, 5 balls instead of slightly under 4. And bins 2 and 11, miraculously, got two balls each (10 percent), far more than either of them deserved. Naturally, we are looking at another demonstration of chance at work. Had we run a much larger number of balls, we should have gotten a distribution much closer to the ideal.

Options 2 through 8 on the pinball menu let us run balls fairly quickly, because they do not take the time to draw a trace of the ball's movements on the screen. The first of these choices, obtained by pressing the (2) key from the menu, runs only 10 balls, while pressing (8) gives you fully 4,000. The display will be identical to that for tracer balls, except, of course, that there will be no trace and no delay while you could examine it. Instead, on most computers you will see a light rain of flashing balls dropping through the game. They look like golden sand on my computer.

The bins fill up much more quickly than with the tracer balls, but if you get impatient running a large number of balls, you can press a key whenever you want to stop them and see the table giving the distribution of the balls you ran. If you let the machine go, it will run the number of balls you requested, then tell you it has reached the end, and you may press a key when you have examined the bins. If you plan to run more than 100 balls, prepare yourself for a wait. On most current computers, 4,000 balls takes a very long time.

If you want masses of balls, as quickly as the computer can provide them, select the final choice on the menu by pressing (9). This gives you 15,000 balls, but they run very quickly. To make room for all the balls, I have removed the pinball arrowheads from the graphics version and stretched the bins until they are as high as your screen. To make the balls go very fast, I have not attempted to draw them as they fall, but you can see them pile up in the bins. Again, to speed things up, I have not given you the opportunity to stop the game until a full 15,000 balls have dropped. You won't have to wait long, however, and it is fascinating to see the normal curve appear before your very eyes. (The plain version simply displays the numbers in the bins as they grow to a total of 15,000.)

Figure 10.5 shows the table I got once when I ran 15,000 balls. Although there is still some random fluctuation, the distribution is much closer to the ideal. We expect 22.56 percent of the balls to wind up in the middle bin, number 6. But the table in Figure 10.5 reports that 22.4 percent got there—pretty close but not exact. Actually, the computer has to round off the percentages to fit them all on the screen. For example, the 6 balls in bin number 0 represent 0.04 percent of the total 15,000; but this rounds off to 0.0, which gives the false impression that there were no balls at all in this bin. The next time, when I ran 15,000 balls, 22.8 percent wound up in bin number 6. Average these two times together, and you get 22.6, which is what you would expect on average. Combining the numbers from two runs gives you 30,000 balls, and a distribution that is apt to be slightly closer to the ideal than with 15,000 balls.

FIGURE 10.5
Results of Running 15,000 Balls through the Pinball Game

Bounces to the right:

0	1	2	3	4	5	6	7	8	9	10	11	12

Number of balls:

6	42	252	803	1788	2869	3361	2956	1821	839	215	46	2

Percent:

0.0	0.3	1.7	5.4	11.9	19.1	22.4	19.7	12.1	5.6	1.4	0.3	0.0

Mean $(\overline{X}) = 6.01$

Variance: $s^2 = 3.00$ $\sigma^2 = 3.00$

Standard deviation: $s = 1.73$ $\sigma = 1.73$

Variation ratio: $s/\overline{X} = 0.29$ $\sigma/\overline{X} = 0.29$

The more balls you run, the closer the result is to a perfect binomial distribution; and the more bins and bounces your pinball game has, the closer the result is to the famous normal curve. Figure 10.6 is a nice drawing of the ideal normal curve. It is often described as a bell-shaped curve, although as usually drawn it seems to me a little broad to be a bell. The very highest point on the normal curve is exactly at the mean, and the curve is perfectly symmetrical around this point.

The height of the curve represents how many cases there are with a particular value measured along the horizontal axis of the graph. The left and right extremes of the normal curve are called the *tails* of the distribution, and the farther you go either side of the mean, the closer the curve gets to the bottom of the graph. But the tails of a perfect normal distribution never quite get down to zero. Thus, a complete graph of the normal curve would have to use an infinitely wide piece of paper. In practical research, of course, there are real limits to how extreme the extreme cases are going to be, and we never have to worry about what happens a great distance out along the curve, very far above or below the mean.

A human characteristic that might be conceptualized in terms of the normal curve is weight. As you know, most people are close to the average in weight. A few people are very light, and a few people are very heavy. You could make a graph of how many are of each weight. Take 1,000 students, for example, and measure how much each one weighs. Then make a table that says how many people were of each weight, rounded off to the nearest pound. Graph this table, so that the horizontal axis of the graph is weight, with light people on the left and heavy people on the right. The vertical dimension would be how many people were in each weight bracket. The picture would probably look very much like the normal curve.

You should understand, however, that the normal curve is an abstract mathematical concept, and no set of real data will perfectly fit it. In addition to random fluctuations such as you get with our pinball game, there may be systematic departures from normality. For example, weight may not really fit the normal curve if your sample of people contains both men and women. Since women tend to be somewhat lighter than men, on average, you might want to separate people by sex before graphing their weights. There may be a normal curve for weight in men and another normal curve for weight in women. Put the two together, and you might get what we call a **bimodal distribution**.

Quick! Imagine a picture of a camel. How many humps does it have? One or two? In fact, there are two kinds of camels. The Arabic camel, also called a dromedary, has one hump. The Bactrian camel has two humps. Well, a bimodal distribution is like the Bactrian camel because it has two humps. The word *bimodal* implies that the distribution has two modes, two most-common values. Superimpose two normal distributions that have different means, and you get a bimodal distribution.

If you want to see quite a number of distributions that are variations on the normal curve, use the XTAB program to look at histograms for all the preference variables, such as number 26, sociology. Most of these histograms will look like roughly drawn normal curves, the highest bar in the graph being one of the middle values, while the extreme values are more rare. But many histograms are shifted a little to the left and right, and some are flatter and more spread out, while others peak more sharply near the center.

When the hump of a distribution is shifted to one side or the other, we call it **skewed**. The relative degree of peakedness or flatness of a distribution is called **kurtosis**. Elaborate computerized statistics packages include coefficients to measure the degree of skewness and kurtosis of a distribution, but we shall not worry about these details here. Other situations, far more difficult to describe, also make your distributions different from the normal curve. Later in this chapter, we will criticize inappropriate applications of the normal curve, which does not always approximate reality closely. For statistical analysis, however, it is a very useful abstract concept.

FIGURE 10.6
The Normal Curve

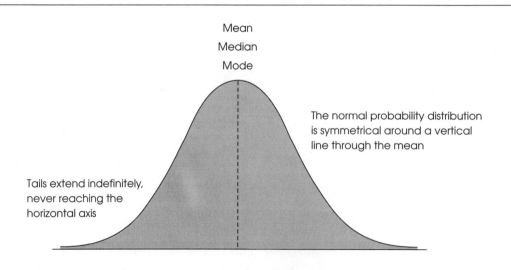

Mean
Median
Mode

The normal probability distribution is symmetrical around a vertical line through the mean

Tails extend indefinitely, never reaching the horizontal axis

Variance and Standard Deviation

The table that follows each run of the pinball game gives three sets of special statistics at the bottom: variance, standard deviation, and variation ratio. To make clear what these terms mean, I will show how to calculate and use them with a very simple example.

A Study of Sociology Departments

Consider for a moment how many full-time faculty there are in the sociology department of your college or university. Perhaps you don't know the exact number, but maybe you can guess. My current university, where I am writing this, has 20 full-time faculty in the sociology program, plus one affiliated professor who works mainly in the school of education. Some departments have just a few full-time faculty and many part-time faculty with joint, adjunct, or affiliated positions. Let's just worry about the full-time faculty, 20 in the case of my university.

Is that a lot, or is that an average number for a university sociology department that gives graduate degrees? To answer these questions, I need only reach for my copy of the 1988 *Guide to Graduate Departments of Sociology*, published by the American Sociological Association. This annual guide covers sociology programs in the United States, Canada, Australia, and England that have graduate students. It lists the names and specialties of their faculty members, as well as giving other useful information. Now, if I really wanted to know whether my department was of average size, I could count how many full-time faculty are in each of these 228 departments and calculate the average. But a smaller sample would be more manageable for our purposes here, so I'm going to focus on just the 17 sociology departments listed for California. My current department is not in California, and yours may not be either, but working with data on these 17 will be perfect for our present purposes.

These 17 California graduate sociology departments are listed in Figure 10.7. (Those of

you in the sociology department at Irvine should know that your university possessed a major program in social ecology and a social relations department, but not a sociology department as such at the time the 1988 guide to graduate departments was compiled.) The first eight are branches of the University of California. The next five have names beginning with *California State*. The first column of data is the number of full-time faculty in each of these 17 sociology departments, a total of 306. I am sure you know how to figure the mean (arithmetic average). Divide the total number of faculty (306) by the number of departments (17), and you get the mean. It happens to be exactly 18, very convenient for us because it will be much easier to calculate the variance without having to worry about fractions.

The second column of numbers in Figure 10.7 is this mean, listed 17 times, once for each department. Although this may seem a waste of time, it allows you to glance at each department and see if it is above average in size or below average. For example, the Berkeley department had 26 full-time faculty, which is 8 greater than the average of 18. The third column of numbers shows this comparison for all the departments. To calculate this column, I subtracted the mean from each of the department's faculty counts. For Berkeley, $26 - 18 = 8$. For Davis, $13 - 18 = -5$. Notice that the numbers in column three are often negative, showing that the particular department is smaller than the average.

Thus, calculating the mean allows us to see immediately whether a particular California department is bigger or smaller than average. And if anybody cared about how many faculty California graduate sociology departments had, on average, we could say 18. But it is often interesting to ask a slightly more subtle question: To what degree are departments spread out around the mean? If all we knew were the mean, it would be possible that every single

FIGURE 10.7
Full-time Faculty in California University Sociology Departments

University	Faculty	Mean	Difference	Difference Squared
U.C. Berkeley	26	18	8	64
U.C. Davis	13	18	−5	25
U.C. Los Angeles	35	18	17	289
U.C. Riverside	13	18	−5	25
U.C. San Diego	19	18	1	1
U.C. San Francisco	7	18	−11	121
U.C. Santa Barbara	25	18	7	49
U.C. Santa Cruz	17	18	−1	1
C.S. Dominguez Hills	15	18	−3	9
C.S. Fullerton	23	18	5	25
C.S. Hayward	14	18	−4	16
C.S. Los Angeles	16	18	−2	4
C.S. Northridge	20	18	2	4
San Diego State	24	18	6	36
San Jose State	8	18	−10	100
U. of Southern Cal.	20	18	2	4
Stanford	11	18	−7	49
Total	306	306	0	822

one of the 17 departments had exactly 18 members. In this case, there would be no distribution at all, and the departments would be all nailed right on the average. Or conceivably, the numbers of faculty could differ tremendously from the average. For example, 8 departments could have 5 faculty each, 8 departments could have 31 each, and 1 department could have 18, giving the exact same average of 18. Then, instead of the actual great variety in sizes of department, 16 of the 17 departments would be of very extreme sizes.

One way to measure the extent to which the 17 numbers are spread out (widely or narrowly) around the mean would be to take an average of their differences from the mean. One problem with this is that the total of the differences from the mean in the third column of Figure 10.7 is dead zero. Thus, the average of these 17 numbers is also zero. This is always true, not just an accident in this particular case.

We won't stop here to examine a mathematical proof, but you can try working with other sets of numbers, if you want. The sum of differences from the mean is always zero.

One solution would be to erase all the minus signs from the differences. This is called taking their **absolute value**. If you did this, the column of differences would add up to 96. Divide 96 by 17 and you get 5.65, the average absolute value of the difference from the mean. While some statistics textbooks talk about this approach, it is seldom used in social statistics.

Another way to get rid of the minus signs is not to erase them but to square the numbers. As you undoubtedly recall from high-school math, to square a number you multiply it by itself. A positive number (like Berkeley's 8) multiplied by itself gives a positive number: $8 \times 8 = 64$. And a negative number (like Davis's −5) multiplied by itself gives a positive number, too: $-5 \times -5 = 25$.

The fourth column in Figure 10.7 shows the squares of the differences. You should probably look down columns 3 and 4, checking that this is true and getting a clear picture of how we get from column 3 to column 4. Multiply each number in the "Difference" column by itself and you get the corresponding number in the "Difference Squared" column. The total of the 17 squares is 822. In a way, this 822 is the answer to our question. It does tell us how spread out around the mean the number of faculty are, in terms of the total squared difference. But it would be hard to compare this number with numbers derived from other data—for example, if we made a table of the departments in New York State—because the number of departments would be different.

So the final step in creating a really useful measure of how spread out the numbers are is to take an average of the squared differences from the mean. Take the sum of squared differences from the mean and divide it by the number of cases. Here, that means dividing 822 by 17, and the answer is 48.35. This is what we call the **variance**, which is defined as the average squared difference from the mean, for the particular variable.

You have undoubtedly heard the expression **standard deviation**. The standard deviation for a variable is simply the square root of the variance. Put the other way around, the variance is the square of the standard deviation: If you multiply the standard deviation by itself, you get the variance. Why would you bother? One way of thinking about it is that we squared the differences from the mean, partly to get rid of minus signs, and it would be nice to have a measure of deviation that got rid of that squaring. Standard deviation does that. This is a little like the situation when you buy a cat to get rid of mice that have infested your home. Then how do you get rid of the cat? Buy a dog? We squared partly to get rid of minus signs, and we take the square root to get rid of the squaring.

In our example of faculty in California sociology departments, the standard deviation is 6.95. If you have a calculator handy, you can verify that 6.95 times 6.95 is 48.35. The standard deviation is not an abstract measure but a very realistic one. In our example, the standard deviation is 6.95 *faculty members.* Standard deviation has the same units of measurement as do the raw numbers and the mean. This cannot be said for variance. Our variance of 48.35 refers to 48.35 *squared faculty members.* Now, I agree that some faculty members are pretty square, but the idea of squaring a faculty member (rather than squaring a number) sounds pretty painful, and maybe not very meaningful. Although both variance and standard deviation are very important in social statistics, standard deviation has a slightly more intuitive meaning. It is a direct measure of how widely spread out from the mean the cases are, and is therefore sometimes referred to as a *measure of dispersion.*

The mathematical formulas for variance and standard deviation are as follows:

$$s^2 = \frac{\Sigma(X_i - \overline{X})^2}{N} \quad \text{formula for variance}$$

$$s = \sqrt{s^2} \quad \text{formula for standard deviation}$$

We use the little letter s for standard deviation, and to remind us that the variance is the square of the standard deviation, we designate it s^2. The formula for variance has a Greek sigma (Σ), to indicate that we will be dealing with the sum of something. The X-bar (X with a line over it) stands for the mean across all the cases. The X_i stands for the value of a particular case, the number of faculty in a particular department in our example. It is the value of X for department i. To do the sum, you go through all the departments, from 1 to 17. For each of the 17 departments, you subtract the mean from the number of faculty in the department and square the result. The Σ indicates that you sum up all 17 of these squared differences. The N in the denominator refers to the number of cases, the 17 departments. Dividing by N gives you the averaged squared deviation from the mean, which is variance. From that, it is a short step to the standard deviation.

Variation Ratio and Coefficient of Variation

Occasionally, we go even a step further, calculating a pair of closely related numbers called the variation ratio and coefficient of variation. They make it easier to compare the standard deviations of two different variables with different means. To get some data to compare with the graduate sociology departments of California, I turn again to the 1988 directory. Massachusetts has only seven graduate departments of sociology (Boston College, Boston University, Brandeis, University of Massachusetts at Amherst, University of Massachusetts at Boston, and Northeastern). For these seven Massachusetts departments, the mean number of full-time faculty members is 25.39, and the standard deviation is 5.04. Recall that for the 17 California departments, the mean was 18 and the standard deviation was 6.95. The California standard deviation is larger, 1.38 times that for Massachusetts.

But that is probably not the right way to compare them. Because Massachusetts has a larger mean, we might expect it to have a larger standard deviation as well. One way of looking at this is to note that in Massachusetts there is more room between the mean and zero for small departments' faculty numbers. The **variation ratio** lets us take account of the differences in the means while we are comparing standard deviations.

To calculate the variation ratio, divide the standard deviation by the mean. For Massachusetts, the variation ratio is 0.20, because $5.04/25.39 = 0.20$. For California, it is 0.39. Thus, the variation ratio is almost twice as high for the California departments as for the ones in Massachusetts; a simple comparison of the standard deviations underestimates the difference between the two states. Relative to the means, the standard deviation is twice as big in California as in Massachusetts, and this is what the variation ratio tells us.

Some writers like to multiply the variation ratio by 100, by analogy with the way we calculate percentages, and they sometimes call the result the **coefficient of variation**. It would be 20 for Massachusetts and 39 for California. It represents the standard deviation expressed as a percentage of the mean.

You cannot validly calculate variation ratio and coefficient of variation for all variables for which standard deviation is appropriate. For the variation ratio to have clear meaning, the variable must be a ratio scale with a definite zero point. That is true for the number of faculty in a sociology department. Standard deviation and variance are meaningful even for interval-level variables that lack a good zero point, because both are figured in terms of distances from the mean rather than from zero. When you divide the standard deviation by the mean, however, you assume that the mean is counted upward from a zero point, which may not be the case. For example, the preference variables in our XTAB dataset do not have zero points, and it would be incorrect to calculate variation ratios for them, even though the program quite validly calculates their variances and standard deviations.

The Sociology of Baseball

Baseball affords an excellent illustration of the value of calculating variance and standard deviation. In the good old days, before I and most of your parents were born, the very best sluggers sometimes achieved batting averages of .400, but this has not happened since Ted Williams hit .406 in 1941. Were the baseball pioneers giants of such stature that modern players cannot hope to match their successes? Or have the rules of baseball changed enough over the years that a season record of .400 has become an absolute impossibility?

Stephen Jay Gould (1983, 1986, 1988) has argued that neither of these theories is correct, but that a third explanation based on analysis of variance really tells the story. Batting averages reflect not only how good a hitter is, but how good the opposing pitchers are. Thus, batting averages have social causes. If the quality of players varies greatly, then a given player will often be batting against weak opponents and find it easier to score hits. In the good old days, it may not simply have been that Ty Cobb and Babe Ruth were great, but also that many of the pitchers they faced were poor. To state these ideas as a theoretical proposition: The greater the variation in quality of baseball players, the higher the batting average of the very best players.

Another way of thinking about Gould's theory is to note that generations of players have been working to perfect baseball. He notes that shortstops and outfielders did not know exactly where to stand in the early days, but now they do. In 1897, Wee Willie Keeler achieved a batting average of .432 by "hitting 'em where they ain't." Apparently he had found gaps in the typical fielding defense that subsequent generations of outfielders have plugged. As baseball has become more of a science and (perhaps) less of an art, play has become largely systematized, and the difference between the worst players and the best players has narrowed.

Gould supported his thesis with statistics taken from the *Baseball Encyclopedia*. In the 1870s, the standard deviation of batting averages for regular players was 0.0496, while in the 1970s it was 0.0317. This is a substantial reduction in variation of batting averages, showing that, indeed, the worst and best players are closer together now than in the past. Can you think of any other statistic we might want to check?

Gould himself notes that these changes might simply result from changes in the mean batting average. Other things being equal, if the mean drops, the standard deviation and the variance will drop, too. Gould has looked at the ups and downs in mean batting average, which are often caused by changes in rules, such as alterations in the distance between home plate and the pitcher's mound, or the liveliness of the ball. Over the century under study, the mean has fluctuated around .260, and it does not seem to explain the general trend toward lower standard deviations.

One can look at this more closely, as Gould himself did, by calculating the coefficients of variation, thus correcting the standard deviations for changes in the means. Recall how to do this. The coefficient of variation is 100 times the standard deviation divided by the mean. Thus it tells us what percent the standard deviation is of the mean. In the 1870s, the coefficient of variation was 19.25. It dropped steadily through the 1930s until stabilizing around 12.2. For the 1970s it was 12.13. The total drop, from 19.25 to 12.13, is substantial. For the past 50 years, professional baseball has been a fully developed social system, but in its early days it was less standardized, a fact that was reflected both through greater variation in batting averages and by the number of .400 hitters.

Variance and Standard Deviation from Samples

The formulas we have been using for variance and standard deviation are perfectly correct when you want to know what these measures are for your particular data. However, we often want to infer the variance and standard deviation of a population when all we have are data about a simple random sample, and a slight modification of the variance formula will accomplish that. Below are the two versions of it:

$$s^2 = \frac{\Sigma(X_i - \overline{X})^2}{N} \quad \text{variance of data}$$

$$\sigma^2 = \frac{\Sigma(X_i - \overline{X})^2}{N - 1} \quad \begin{array}{l}\text{population variance,} \\ \text{estimated from sample}\end{array}$$

To symbolize this new version of the variance, I have used the Greek letter σ (small sigma) instead of the letter s. In various statistics books, you will see these letters used in various ways to distinguish the sample from the population, and other statistics texts use still other symbolism—for example, putting a little circumflex "hat" ("∧") over the s, something I cannot do on your nongraphics IBM-compatible computer screen.

Often, sociologists are able to do their research with data on an entire population, or we want to work with a certain dataset without worrying about exactly how it relates to the population from which it is drawn. For that, s^2 is perfectly appropriate. Having already used s^2 for the ordinary variance, I use σ^2 to signify a corrected version of it, mindful that textbooks differ in which symbol they use for which kind of variance. This corrected version of the variance formula produces a corrected standard deviation and variation ratio.

If the number of cases is very great, as when you run 15,000 balls through the pinball game, s^2 and σ^2 will be essentially identical. In Figure 10.5, you will see no apparent difference at all between the two, although one would appear if we ran the variances out to more decimal places. It is when you are dealing with very small samples that s^2 and σ^2 will be significantly different. Figure 10.4 shows the results of running just 20 balls through the game: the variances are 5.05 and 5.31, substantially different.

Sociologists like to use large numbers of cases, and when there is a wealth of data there may be little reason to worry about the difference between the two formulas, because results will come out the same either way. However, a small sample will tend to underestimate the variance of the population; putting $N - 1$ in the denominator, instead of just N, gives an appropriate correction. Note that this correction assumes you did a simple random sample. If your sample was drawn from the population following a more complex procedure, you will need to use more elaborate correction procedures.

Standard Scores (z-scores)

Often it is useful to standardize data in terms of the normal curve, using what are called z-scores. For example, suppose you wanted to compare the largest sociology departments of California and Massachusetts in terms of the other departments in their own states. The 1988 *Guide to Graduate Departments of Sociology* says that UCLA has 35 full-time faculty, while the biggest department in Massachusetts was

the University of Massachusetts at Amherst, with 28. That is, UCLA is 1.25 times as big as U. Mass., Amherst. Clearly, UCLA has the bigger sociology department in absolute terms, but considering each department relative to the others in its own state is something different from direct comparison of the numbers of faculty between the two schools.

We could compare the departments in terms of what percent each is of the mean for its state. The mean department size in California is 18, so UCLA, with 35, is 17 larger than the mean for its state. In percentage terms, UCLA has 194 percent of the mean in its state. The mean department size in Massachusetts is 20.43. With 28 full-time faculty, the sociology department at U. Mass., Amherst is 137 percent of the mean for its state, so UCLA is still relatively larger. By this measure it is 1.42 times as big. But the California scores are more spread out than the Massachusetts scores, in general, as reflected in their standard deviations of 6.95 and 5.04. An alternate way to compare the departments is in terms of the number of standard deviations each one is above its mean, thus comparing in terms of the relative position each has in its own state.

We just said that UCLA is 17 faculty members larger than the mean for California. That state's standard deviation is 6.95, and 17 is 2.45 times 6.95. That is, UCLA is 2.45 California standard deviations bigger than the mean size in its state. U. Mass., Amherst is 7.57 faculty larger than the Massachusetts mean. The standard deviation for Massachusetts is 5.04, and 7.57 is 1.50 times 5.04. Therefore, the U. Mass., Amherst department is 1.50 times as big as the standard deviation for its state. However you figure it, UCLA has not only a bigger sociology department in terms of the absolute number of faculty. It is also bigger in comparison to the other departments in California than is U. Mass., Amherst in comparison to other Massachusetts departments.

When we transform raw numbers into standard deviations above or below the mean, we are creating z-scores. The formula for z-scores is quite simple:

$$z_i = \frac{X_i - \overline{X}}{s}$$

X_i stands for the particular number we want to turn into a z-score, the number of faculty in sociology department "i." As usual, the X with a bar over it stands for the mean of the data that include X_i. The denominator of the formula, s, is the standard deviation. If X_i is greater than the mean, then z_i will be greater than zero. If X_i exactly equals the mean, then z_i will be zero. And if X_i is less than the mean, z_i will be negative. This equation expresses formally just what we did to figure standard scores for the UCLA and U. Mass., Amherst departments.

Standard scores have a number of uses. In Chapter 12, we will learn how z-scores can be used to calculate the statistical significance of Pearson's r and gamma correlation coefficients. And in Chapter 14, we will see how z-scores can be used to standardize a set of variables that have very different distributions, before combining them into a multivariable index. The following section describes another use of standardization. one that is somewhat more controversial.

_____ Limitations of the Normal Curve

Despite its great mathematical elegance and the multitude of uses to which it is put in statistical analysis, the normal curve is not always an appropriate standard of judgment. Your particular data may have a very different distribution, and if so you should be wary of relying upon standard deviations and other measures based on the normal curve. An excellent example of overuse of the normal curve is that highly controversial concept, IQ.

Fallacies in Research on Intelligence

Although many educational psychologists blithely employ IQ tests to measure "intelligence," many sociologists are convinced the tests are heavily biased, especially against people from social and cultural backgrounds different from those of the test writers, and that the tests may do more harm than good. Without completely rejecting the idea of aptitude testing, sociologist Jane Mercer (1973) has subjected IQ tests to severe criticism, and we shall follow her analysis here.

IQ stands for *Intelligence Quotient,* and the word *quotient* refers to the result of dividing one number by another. We can explain the meaning more fully by imagining that you have set out to measure the intelligence of schoolchildren with a pencil-and-paper test you have written. In practice, new IQ tests are usually based on existing tests, and a great lot of work goes into the items. To make things easy for you, however, let's say you just begin writing test questions out of the blue.

Each item is like a little puzzle. Here is a sequence of numbers: 1, 4, 9, 16, 25. . . . What is the next number in the sequence? If you said 36, you are right, because the numbers in my sequence are the squares of the ordinary sequence of integers—1, 2, 3, 4, 5, 6—and 36 is the square of 6. Here's another sequence: 3, 1, 4, 1, 5. . . . What is the right answer to this one? Did you guess 1? Wrong! The answer is 9. Hah, hah! You thought the sequence was an alternation of 3, 4, 5, 6, and the number 1. The answer is 9 because the sequence I was thinking of was the digits of π (pi), the ratio of a circle's circumference to its diameter. And π, to 14 decimal places, is 3.14159265353979. Every intelligent person should know that, right?

Well, maybe not. The answers to the questions in an IQ test may be very obvious to the people who write the test. The test writers define themselves as intelligent, so whatever questions they can answer, but many other people cannot, must measure intelligence—they think. People from a background similar to that of the test writers approach a test with about the same set of assumptions and information as the test writer, and thus they have a great advantage over people from different backgrounds who may have invested their intellectual energy in learning a very different set of facts and skills. For purposes of this discussion, however, we will let you put whatever items you want into your IQ test, although we suspect your tests will be biased to prove that you are intelligent and that people who think very differently from you are "dummies."

Now you inflict your test on a few hundred schoolchildren, and you count how many questions each person got right. Perhaps your test has 111 items, and the average kid got 73 right. So far, we do not have the information necessary to compute IQ. First, you have to separate the tests according to the ages of the children who took it. You make several big piles on your work table, one for all the tests of 10-year-olds, another for 11-year-olds, another for 12-year-olds, and so forth. Then you figure the average score in each pile. Let's say you got something like the results shown in Figure 10.8.

Now you can figure the IQ of any particular student. Let's start with young Roger Manning, who is just 10 years old. We call his age in years his *chronological age.* Suppose Roger got a score of 99 on the test. This is almost exactly the average for 12-year-old kids on this particular test, so we can say that Roger has the mind of a 12-year-old. We call this his *mental age.* So,

FIGURE 10.8
Hypothetical Average Intelligence-test Scores of Children

Average Age	Test Score
12	98.6
11	81.0
10	73.1
9	56.9
8	43.5

Roger has a mental age of 12 and a chronological age of 10. His IQ is his mental age divided by his chronological age, with the result multiplied by 100. This is exactly like figuring what percentage his mental age is of his chronological age. Roger's IQ is 120, because 12 divided by 10 is 1.2, and 1.2 times 100 is 120.

Suppose Roger had scored only 44 on the test. Because this is the average for 8-year-olds, Roger would have a mental age of 8. His chronological age would still be 10, and his IQ would be 80. Or, if Roger had scored right at the average for his own age group, 73 right answers, his IQ would be 100. This is how 100 is defined. An IQ of 100 means that a person scored right at the average of his or her age group for the test.

When this procedure is actually followed for children, with rather more attention paid to writing good questions but applying the same statistical methods to the test scores, it turns out that the IQ scores for kids of any given age tend to approximate the normal distribution. Note that the normal distribution was not in any way built into the statistical procedures, so many psychologists can be forgiven for feeling that the tendency of the data to fit the normal curve is a major empirical discovery about the human mind. However, the shape of the distribution says nothing about what is being measured, and sociologists might have much to criticize about the meaning and the content of the test.

Whatever the problems of the procedures we have described so far, things get immeasurably worse when intelligence testing is applied to older children and adults. The last time I took an IQ test was 20 years ago, when my chronological age was 28. Now, my chronological age is greater, but I doubt that I would do any better on the test than I did two decades ago. Have I gotten "dumber"? Maybe, but we cannot expect adults to gain in intellectual capacity from year to year the way children do. Therefore, we can't define IQ any more in terms of mental age and chronological age.

One way IQ is commonly computed for adults is to *assume* that the distribution of adult intelligence fits the normal curve exactly. This is a big leap from the empirical observation that the distribution of test scores for children fits the normal curve approximately, but many test makers leap to this assumption.

Here's how you would apply your test to adults. You give it to hundreds of them, perhaps (if you can afford it) to a random sample of the population. Let's say that the average score for adults is 81. This immediately becomes an IQ of 100. By definition, the average IQ is 100. Now the problem is to decide how to count IQ points up and down from 100. The solution test makers have used is to count each standard deviation equal to 15 points. An adult whose test score is one standard deviation above the mean will get an IQ of 115. An adult whose score is one standard deviation below the mean gets only 85.

Computationally, this is neat. You just figure the distribution of the test scores, consult a table of z-scores, and write out how many standard deviations and fractions of standard deviations each score is above or below the mean. Then, counting a standard deviation as equal to 15 IQ points, you quickly assign IQs to the people who took your test. One of the most brilliant aspects of this whole procedure is that few people, other than social scientists, are ever taught about the normal curve and standard deviations. So you can appear to be a very wise technical expert on human intelligence—thus a very intelligent person yourself—if you know how to figure people's IQs.

Figure 10.9 shows the rough distribution of percentages that this statistical definition of IQ produces. Notice that about 68 percent of the population falls within a standard deviation of the mean. Why? Because the normal curve defines it that way. Another 13.6 percent are between one and two standard deviations above the mean. What shall we call the people in this group? These aren't "geniuses," but that they are above the "normals" suggests we call them "high normals." Do you think it is artificial to distinguish these people from the 68 percent immediately below them? Sure, it is artificial. People may really differ in native intelligence,

FIGURE 10.9

Separating the Population into Groups by IQ Score

IQ	Percent	Description
131+	2.3	Abnormally high
116–130	13.6	High normals
85–115	68.2	Normals
70–84	13.6	Low normals
69–	2.3	Abnormally low

and conceivably your test measures those differences. But establishing categories into which to place human beings, purely on the basis of standard deviations, is completely artificial.

Above an IQ of 130, we have some very proud people who may be described as "abnormally high." Perhaps you have heard of a social club called Mensa, which accepts only people who have IQs two standard deviations or more above the mean. The Mensa meetings I attended revealed these people to be far more friendly and liberal-minded than you might expect for people who have such a rigid qualification for membership in their group. (Incidentally, the founder of the Process cult, discussed in Chapters 2 and 3, was a member of Mensa.) As a sociologist, however, I came to suspect that Mensa members tended to be underachievers who were not as well rewarded for their brains as they felt they deserved. Whether or not Mensa members tend to suffer from *status inconsistency*, as sociologists call an imbalance between different aspects of social status, remains to be determined by a future research project, but they certainly did not seem to be geniuses whose brains were enabling them to take the world by storm.

There is even a club called the Four Sigma Society, which is exclusively for people scoring four standard deviations above the mean. The president of the "ΣΣΣΣ" Society writes the test that is the entrance exam, and it looks to me like a silly set of trivial puzzles. Naturally, the president of ΣΣΣΣ passed his own test. I think it's dumb, and it certainly illustrates for us the potential absurdity of taking the normal curve too seriously.

When we start counting standard deviations below the mean, we leave the realm of silly pretensions and enter that of tragedy. By the statistical definition of intelligence, 13.6 percent of the population are "low normals," and 2.3 percent are "abnormally low." This 2.3 percent are also defined as adult mental retardates. Let the words *mental retardate* roll off your tongue, and think how shameful and damaging they are. To be considered mentally incompetent is about the worst shame that a member of our society can suffer (Edgerton 1967). When IQ is defined in terms of the mental age of children, then the metaphor expressed in these words is revealed: a kid is retarded if his or her mental age has lagged (been retarded or slowed down) far behind his or her chronological age. The 1860 United States census attempted to count all the mentally retarded in the country, officially calling them "idiots." Either term is cruel, and if based on an inflexible application of the normal curve to test scores, identification as mentally retarded can be a great injustice.

Mercer (1973:7) notes that the statistical definition of mental retardation makes it impossible to cure the problem. "With this model, there will always be abnormals in a population because there are always two extreme tails to any distribution. Abnormality is intrinsic to the model." Suppose you had invented "smart pills" that double the intellectual capability of anybody who takes them. Everybody does take

them. What, then, is the proportion retarded in the adult population? Again, it is 2.3 percent. Although the norms have moved up, the bottom 2.3 percent will be defined as retarded regardless of how smart they might be in terms of today's standards. Science-fiction author Cyril Kornbluth wrote a stunningly sarcastic story, "The Marching Morons," about a future century in which everybody is excruciatingly stupid. What, then, would be the average IQ and the proportion retarded? Again, 100 IQ points and 2.3 percent. Change reality, and the distribution merely shifts to produce exactly the same proportions in each standard-deviation category.

Ignorant of these problems, the American Association on Mental Deficiency used to apply standard deviations below the mean quite mechanically, to produce several subcategories of retardation: mildly retarded, moderately retarded, severely retarded, and profoundly retarded (Mercer 1973:5). Mental retardation is a very real problem, a terribly sad one for the families with members severely affected by it. But Mercer and other social scientists have shown that a substantial portion of those labeled mentally retarded are merely victims of unfair labeling and insensitive application of the normal curve to scores from tests of often dubious validity. The statistical tools introduced in this book are potentially very powerful. Power may be misused, however, and you should be careful to avoid imposing the normal curve on people and data for which it is not appropriate.

Analysis of Variance

Closely connected to the concept of variance is a very useful set of techniques for assessing the statistical significance of a set of means, known as **analysis of variance**, or **ANOVA** for short. There are many varieties of ANOVA, some of them very complex, and we will consider only some of the simplest aspects here. ANOVA is very commonly used to evaluate the statistical significance of differences among the various groups of subjects in an experiment, but it has other applications as well.

For our purposes, ANOVA is educationally useful because it bridges from the nonparametric measures used for crosstabs to the parametric measures we will begin discussing in the following chapter. The XTAB program has an option that does ANOVAs on any pair of variables you select from that dataset. It works pretty well, and I decided it was a more practical way of including analysis of variance in our software than creating an entirely new program with a dataset that would be absolutely perfect for ANOVA.

Standard Error and Confidence Interval

Back in Chapter 7, we considered the related concepts of sampling error and margin of error in surveys in which a simple random sample was drawn from a population. Recall that we imagined drawing a very large number of such samples, and then we were able to see that results from the samples varied in a predictable way that allowed us to estimate how different a single sample was likely to be from the population itself. Now that we have established the concept of normal curve, we can go through a similar line of thinking here. The mathematics of this business can be a bit complicated, however, so we will touch only on highlights that are especially useful for you to know.

Suppose we are drawing random samples from a population that has some characteristic, say the weights of the people in the population, and that the population has a normal distribution. Let's say the mean weight of people in the population is 130 pounds. Certainly, we would expect the mean in a random sample from this population to be about 130 as well, but few samples would have means of exactly 130. If we drew a very large number of random samples, what would the average mean weight across these samples tend to be? And how much would these mean weights be spread out around this average mean? Well, if you guessed that the average mean from a large number of random samples would be 130, the mean weight in the population itself, you were right. The variance of the mean weights in the samples depends on the variance of weights in

the population and the size of each sample. Put formally,

> If repeated random samples of size N are drawn from a normal population, with mean μ and variance σ^2, the sampling distribution of sample means will be normal, with mean μ and variance σ^2/N. (Blalock 1972: 177)

Size N refers to the number of cases (people) in each sample. If the number of people surveyed in each sample is 1000, then N = 1000. The symbol μ is simply the Greek letter for m, called "mu," and it stands for the mean, in particular the mean of the population. The little Greek sigma squared, σ^2, stands for the variance in the population. If you know the variance of the population and the number of cases in each sample, you can easily figure the variance of all the means of the samples by σ^2/N. One very important fact is that the variance of these sample means is very small if N is very large, because you divide by N to calculate it. Thus, a sample with a large N is likely to give a better estimate of the population that does a sample with a small N; in exercises using the SAMP program connected with Chapter 7, you can verify empirically that large samples tend to agree with each other better than do small samples.

It is also important to note that the sampling distribution (the distribution of the means in the samples) will fit the normal curve if the distribution in the population itself has a normal distribution. But what happens if the population does not have a normal distribution, or if you do not know what distribution it has? Here is where the **central-limit theorem**, a very important principle of statistics, comes in:

> If repeated random samples of size N are drawn from any population (of whatever form) having a mean μ and a variance σ^2, then as N becomes large, the sampling distribution of sample means approaches normality, with mean μ and variance σ^2/N. (Blalock 1972: 181)

Again we see an advantage to a large sample. If your many random samples all have large numbers of cases, then their distribution will very nearly fit the normal curve, and you can easily estimate the mean and variance of their distribution (if you know the mean and variance in the population). The central-limit theorem is thus a marvelous tool of analysis. Well, maybe. Do you see any problems with it? It seems to require you to take many very, very large samples, and it expects you to know the mean and variance in the population. But taking hoards of samples is extremely expensive to do, and you certainly do not already know the mean and variance in the population; if you did, there would be no point to your survey.

The whole value of this line of thought is that one can, in a sense, work backward along it. If you have surveyed one large random sample, then you can use these principles to estimate not only the mean and variance of the population, but also the probable sampling error in your estimate.

Earlier, we saw the formula for population variance (σ^2), estimated from a sample:

$$\sigma^2 = \frac{\Sigma(X_i - \overline{X})^2}{N - 1}$$

The standard deviation in the population (σ) is therefore estimated as

$$\sigma = \sqrt{\sigma^2}$$

Using a sample of size N, the **standard error** (S) of your estimate of the population's mean (or other number describing the population) is

$$S = \sigma/N$$

Standard error is a concept very much like standard deviation. If you draw many random samples of size N from the population, about 68 percent of them will be within one standard error of the true figure. In our weight example, for instance, about 68 percent of the samples would have a mean weight no farther from 130 than the standard error. The set of numbers within a particular distance of some particular number is called an **interval** around that number. Suppose we had calculated the standard error and found it was 5. Then about 68 percent of the samples would have been in the interval from 125 to 135 ($130 - 5 = 125$; $130 + 5 = 135$). Again, the fact that we calculate the standard error by dividing by N indicates that the larger the sample size, the smaller the error tends to be.

Another way of interpreting the standard error is to say that you are about 68 percent confident that the real mean for the population is within one standard error of the mean for your sample. But this is not a great deal of confidence. You might prefer to be about 95 percent sure. As it happens, about 95 percent of all cases in a normal distribution are within two standard deviations of the mean, and about 95 percent of your hypothetical samples will be within two standard errors of the mean (or other number) you are trying to estimate. Thus, if the mean weight of people in your random sample was 130 and the standard error was 5, you could be 95 percent sure the mean weight in the population from which you drew your sample was between 120 and 140. (Because the standard error is 5, twice the standard error is 10: $130 - 10 = 120$; $130 + 10 = 140$.) Naturally, in real studies you have to calculate the mean and standard error on the basis of the data your random sample provides, and you can't expect nice round numbers like 130 and 5.

An interval around a number, like this 120–140 interval around 130, is called a **confidence interval**. We have a certain confidence that the population mean lies within it. When the interval is two standard errors wide, we call it the *95-percent confidence interval.* Strictly, this means that about 95 percent of the random samples would fall within it, but more loosely we may say that we are 95 percent confident that the population mean falls within the interval. Because a confidence interval that is three standard errors wide contains more than 99 percent of the random samples, it is called the *99-percent confidence interval.*

Confidence intervals are just a short step away from the concept of statistical significance. Suppose we hypothesized that the average human being weighed more than 100 pounds. We drew a large sample and found that the mean was 130. Clearly, that is evidence in favor of our hypothesis, because the sample's mean weight is definitely more than 100. But there is always some chance that our particular sample just happened to be especially heavy, the result of pure chance in the sampling process. If the standard error is 5, however, then we should immediately feel very confident in our hypothesis, because 100 is more than two standard errors below 130. Indeed, it is six standard errors below. Therefore, our level of confidence is even greater than 99 percent. To put it another way, the difference between 130 and 100, in this hypothetical study of weight, is *statistically significant* at the 99-percent level.

Replicating the Bennington College Study

Let's begin our discussion with a famous example of classical social science research, the Bennington College study by Theodore M. Newcomb (1943). Five times, from the fall of 1935 through the spring of 1939, Newcomb surveyed the students at a small women's college in Vermont, examining the changes in their political views that occurred from the freshman to senior years. The heart of the questionnaire was a set of 26 agree-disagree items, 14 that political liberals might agree with and 12 that political conservatives might accept. The key finding, reported widely in textbooks ever since, was that the students tended to become

more liberal with the passage of time, presumably because the intellectual environment of the school encouraged development of liberal sentiments.

Written during the Great Depression, the items reflected the political and economic issues current at the time. They were also subtle, requiring some thought and education on the part of the respondents. For example, here are two of the liberal items: "The depression occurred chiefly because the working classes did not receive enough in wages to purchase goods and services produced at a profit." "Our government has always been run primarily in the interests of big business, and so it is those interests which were chiefly responsible for the depression." And two of the conservative items were: "You can't expect democracy to work very well as long as so many uneducated and unintelligent people have the vote." "The vast majority of those in the lower economic classes are there because they are stupid, shiftless, or both." In terms of today's political spectrum, the items present rather extreme political ideologies, and I can't imagine what results you would get if you were to replicate the study now.

We have data at hand, however, that can be used in a study rather similar to Newcomb's Bennington College research. One of the questions in the student dataset attached to the XTAB program determines what year in school each respondent is, and the preference questions certainly include many that relate to contemporary social and political issues. The obvious way to do this is simply to crosstab variable 69 (student category) by other variables, such as number 71 (conservatism). However, our task here is to learn about analysis of variance, so we will use that option of the XTAB program instead.

First, I should stress that our research design is considerably more modest than the one Newcomb employed. He surveyed the same students, year in and year out, doing what we call a **panel study**. This is by far the best way to learn if students change as they go through the four years of college. Our design will simply compare different groups who are freshmen, sophomores, juniors, or seniors at one particular point in time. Any difference we find among the years might merely represent political shifts in the larger society. Respondents might be more or less liberal depending on when they were born, and they might not change at all over the four years of college. For present purposes, however, the data give an excellent opportunity to practice statistical analysis of data comparable to those of the Bennington College study.

In what follows, I am not going to assume you are sitting at the computer, ready to work with the actual data. A project at the end of this chapter expects you to do that. Rather, I will report a small part of what I found when I ran XTAB on my machine; if you wish, you can try it yourself later.

First, I had to recode variable 69 slightly. As the dataset stands, 20 respondents are graduate students or fall into an "other" category, which is composed mainly of special students or those who have unusual numbers of credit hours behind them and thus are unsure what year they belong in. These 20 had to be removed, because I wanted to compare just the four regular categories of undergraduates. The way to get rid of them is to recode their values to zero, or simply to use the select-reject option to reject them. After doing so, I was left with 131 freshmen, 127 sophomores, 108 juniors, and 126 seniors.

Next, I selected option 5 on the XTAB menu, analysis of variance. As with crosstabs themselves, the computer then asked me to type in the numbers of two variables. Analysis of variance treats the independent and dependent variables quite differently, so you have to be careful to tell the computer which is which. The way you do this is simply to tell it the number of the independent variable first, thus making it variable X. So I first told the computer I wanted to work with variable 69 (student category) as variable X, and then gave it variable 71 (conservatism) for variable Y. Swiftly, the screen filled with a pair of tables. One of the tables, which appears in the top-left corner of the screen, is

FIGURE 10.10
College Year and Political Conservatism

Value	Y Cases	X Cases	Y Mean
7	6	0	—
6	40	0	—
5	89	0	—
4	50	126	3.56
3	104	108	3.20
2	157	127	3.16
1	46	131	3.08

rather simple, and I have included it here as Figure 10.10.

In part, this table is just a condensed version of the frequencies tables for the two variables. The left-hand column is simply the values the variables might take, from 1 through 7. The second column is the number of respondents who gave each possible answer to the political question, variable Y. The "6" at the top of the second column tells us that 6 students said they were "extremely conservative," the response that has the value 7. The "46" at the bottom of the column refers to the 46 extreme liberals.

The third column gives the frequencies for variable X, student category. Because of my recoding, no student has values of 5, 6, or 7. In the row for value 4, we see the number 126, telling us that there were 126 students in year 4 of their college work, the 126 seniors. Below them are the 108 juniors, the 127 sophomores, and finally the 131 lowly freshmen.

The last column of the table in Figure 10.10 gives means for variable Y in each category of variable X. Let me say that in ordinary English, so you will know what I mean. Do you see the number 3.56 on the row for value 4? That is the average political conservatism score for the 126 seniors. Because 3.56 is on row 4, to the right of value 4, we know it refers to the 126 students who have value 4 on the X variable, which is year in school. Again, these are the 126 seniors. The computer figured the average score these

126 had on the political conservatism scale and reported that it was 3.26.

Similarly, the average score on the political conservatism scale for the 108 juniors (value 3 on variable X) is 3.20. For sophomores, the mean conservatism score is 3.16, and for freshmen it is 3.08. Whatever two variables you choose, this is how the table works. For each value on variable X, the table shows the number of respondents having that value on X in the third column, and the average score for variable Y among that group of respondents in the fourth column.

Think for a moment about what these means suggest: seniors = 3.56, juniors = 3.20, sophomores = 3.16, freshmen = 3.08. The bigger the number, the more conservative the student is. The seniors thus appear more conservative than the freshmen. Indeed, each year is more conservative than the ones before it. Wait a minute! Isn't that the exact opposite of what Newcomb found at Bennington College? He found that students became more liberal over time, not more conservative.

I am not about to rush into print with these findings. They are based on just one political question, and I would want to check other political items in the survey to see if seniors give more conservative responses to them, too, than do freshmen. And again, a panel-study design would be better than our one-shot survey, for it would employ several surveys over time to chart changes in the same group of students. Well, I'm not about to do a panel study right now. It would delay this textbook by three years, and we have another question about the finding that we can answer right now. Are the political differences between classes of students statistically significant?

The version of analysis of variance we will present now is a technique for determining the statistical significance of differences in means. It looks at the dispersion in the data across the categories of respondents, and decides how likely it is that the differences in means would appear by pure chance.

The X variable is a set of two or more categories that need not be in any particular order.

Because analysis of variance is often used in experiments, the X variable frequently is simply the different experimental and control groups that were used. Here, the four student categories are in a definite order, freshman through senior, and they form an ordinal scale. They do not have to, however, for analysis of variance to work. The X variable could be nominal. For example, we could be comparing the political orientation of Protestants, Catholics, Jews and atheists, four categories of religious affiliation that we cannot simply arrange in an order from high to low. In analysis of variance, the Y variable must be an interval or ratio scale. That is, it must be mathematically proper to calculate a mean value for Y. Often, Y is a continuous variable that can take on any value, including fractions, over its entire range. For example, we might be comparing the economies of the United States and Canada by looking at the average incomes of samples of Americans and Canadians in dollars and cents. In much practical social research, however, the Y variable merely has a number of values over its range. For example, Newcomb combined the 26 items in his political survey to make a scale that ranged from 26 (extremely liberal) to 130 (extremely conservative), covering every possible whole number in-between these extremes. Our conservative scale is much rougher, having only 7 steps instead of 105.

Now you can see why I feel that analysis of variance is a good bridge from the discrete, discontinuous variables of crosstabs to the continuous interval or ratio scales of r correlations and regressions that we will introduce in the next chapter. In a sense, analysis of variance is a hybrid, because it requires very different kinds of variables for its X and Y.

The chief result of analysis of variance is a number called F. This is similar in function to the chi-square we have been using for several chapters. F is not a very interesting number in itself, but if you look up the F from a particular analysis in a table called the **F distribution**, the table will tell you how significant the results are. This is exactly how you use chi-square, of course.

As its name implies, analysis of variance works with the variance in the data. So let's remind ourselves how we would calculate the variance for the political question, for all four student categories combined. With the graduate students and others thrown out, we are working with 492 respondents. Let's call this "N," so N = 492. Now we would calculate the mean score on the political question for these 492. It is 3.37. Next, we would go through all 492 cases and subtract the respondent's value from the mean and square the result. Finally, we would divide this by the number of cases. If you wish, you can check the formula for variance above. Again, variance is defined as the average squared deviation from the mean. The variance in political conservatism for these 492 respondents happens to be 3.35.

To save a step in calculating, analysis of variance actually stops just before getting the final result in this series of calculations. It works with the sum of the squared deviations rather than with the variance itself. In our example, the sum of these squares is 1647.40. Again, you get this by subtracting the political score from the mean for all 492 respondents, squaring each of these differences, and summing them all up.

The sum of squares for variable Y, 1647.40, ignores that the students are divided up into four categories of variable X. Now we can introduce that slight complication. You can think of all the variation of the Y variable as having two parts. One part of the variation is the variation *within* each of the four groups on variable X. The other part is the variation *between* the four groups on variable X. We will consider the "within" part first.

Consider just the 126 seniors. Their average political conservatism score is 3.56. You could also calculate the variance of scores among the seniors. Or, short of that, you could figure the sum of squared deviations from the mean for seniors. You could do the same for the juniors, calculating their sum of squared deviations from the mean for juniors. And ditto for sophomores and freshmen. Then you could add these four numbers, getting the sum of squared

deviations *within* the four groups. The total happens to be 1022.62.

The sum of squares *between* groups can be figured in a similar way. Start with the seniors. The mean for their group is 3.56, and the mean for all 492 students is 3.37. The difference between these two means is 0.19. As usual, square this number: $0.19 \times 0.19 = 0.0361$. That gives you the squared deviation of the senior mean from the mean for all students. Because we are creating another sum of squares, we have to sum something up. This 0.0361 belongs to each of the 126 seniors, so we add up an 0.0361 for each of them. This is the same thing as multiplying 0.0361 by 126. The result is about 4.55. Do this for all four categories of students and you have the sum of squares *between* groups.

Actually, you don't have to go to all this labor. The total sum of squares, which we already figured, is exactly that, the *total*. If you add the sum of squares between groups and the sum of squares within groups, you get this total. So you really have to do only two of these three lengthy calculations, then add or subtract to get the third. And in truth, we make the computer do this work, not you. The results are given in a table that would appear at the bottom of your screen, as shown here in Figure 10.11. The first column of numbers gives the sums of squares we have just been discussing.

As with complex chi-square, figured on crosstabs with more than two rows or columns, analysis of variance requires us to deal with degrees of freedom. The total degrees of freedom is simply one fewer than the number of cases: $429 - 1 = 491$. The degrees of freedom between groups is one fewer than the number of groups: $4 - 1 = 3$. By analogy, this is like the way we figured degrees of freedom for a crosstab, where we subtracted 1 from the number of rows and 1 from the number of columns. As with the sums of squares, the total degrees of freedom is the sum of the degrees of freedom between groups and the degrees of freedom within groups.

The next step is to calculate what are called the *mean squares*. This is simply the sum of squares divided by the degrees of freedom. The

FIGURE 10.11
Analysis of Variance of Student Politics

Source of Variation	Sum of Squares	Degrees of Freedom	Mean Square	F	Significance
Between groups	17.65	3	5.88	2.49	n.s.
Within groups	1154.60	488	2.37		
Total	1172.25	491			

sum of squares between groups is 17.65, and there are 3 degrees of freedom between groups, so the mean square between groups is 5.88, because 17.65/3 = 5.88. And the mean square within groups is 2.37, because 1154.60/488 = 2.37. Finally, F equals the mean square between groups divided by the mean square within groups. In our example, F = 2.49, because 5.88/2.37 = F.

I have in front of me a set of statistical tables, and I turn to the pages for the F distribution. It is a complicated table, with rows and columns for the number of degrees of freedom, which in this case are 3 and 488. After making sure I have found the right section of the table, I see that an F of about 2.62 would achieve the .05 level of statistical significance, and an F of about 3.82 would achieve the .01 level. But because our F is only 2.49, it fails to achieve the .05 level of significance. So our findings are NOT solid support for the hypothesis that students tend to become more conservative as they progress through college. Certainly, however, our results run counter to Newcomb's finding that students become more liberal.

This is a good point for a reminder of how statistical significance is used to accept or reject hypotheses. Let's leave Newcomb out of this and just think about the idea that students become more conservative. We should compare two hypotheses. One hypothesis states that the mean conservatism of students increases with increasing school year. The other hypothesis, often called the **null hypothesis**, states that the years do not differ significantly in conserva-

tism. Our data do show apparently increasing conservatism from the freshman to senior years, but the analysis of variance indicates that the difference is not statistically significant. This means that we cannot reject the null hypothesis.

We must, however, make a further point about the null hypothesis. Strictly speaking, the null hypothesis that analysis of variance uses is the hypothesis that the means for the different groups are equal. Thus, analysis of variance will reject the null hypothesis if the means of the four groups are highly unequal in some complex pattern, not merely if the seniors have a much bigger mean than the freshmen. It is possible that the means for freshmen are equal to those of the seniors, yet F will come out significant, if the means for sophomores and juniors are very different from those for freshman and seniors. Any strong pattern of means may be significant, not just the ones that progress in a regular way from freshmen to seniors.

Indeed—and this bears stressing—analysis of variance does not "know" that the values for X are in any particular order. As I said earlier, analysis of variance can be done for nominal X variables (such as Protestants, Catholics, Jews, and atheists). Thus, if you are using ANOVA to test an hypothesis that does place the groups in a particular order (such as freshmen, sophomores, juniors, and seniors), you must examine the means carefully to see how they run. In the present example we had a nice, smooth rise in conservatism from freshmen to seniors. If the pattern of means is irregular, however, then ANOVA may not be the technique to use.

The computer software will do most of this work for you, except of course the thinking about hypotheses and theories. Because of the limitations in memory space that I worked within as I wrote the programs, however, the reports about statistical significance will be only approximate. For example, I did not include the full table of the F distribution on the computer disk, just a couple of rough guidelines for the computer to follow in making an approximate report to you. It will give you one of four messages about significance: ".01," ".05," "n.s.," or "???." The first two are levels of significance; "n.s." means not significant, and "???" means that the figures were outside the range for which the computer could decide, even approximately. If you want more precise estimates of statistical significance, use the information about degrees of freedom and F to find the answer in a printed table of the F distribution.

Analysis of variance is important enough that it deserves a second example. Not wanting to waste examples from the XTAB dataset that you might want to study yourself, I shall take one from a class I am currently teaching.

Grades and Class Attendance

Unexpectedly, I found myself teaching an extra course in the sociology of deviance this semester, because the scheduled instructor had died. This has been a bit of a challenge, because I did not see the assigned textbooks until five days before classes began. It has not been my habit to take attendance, but I have noticed that many students skip class pretty regularly. The course meets during the first period of the morning, and it is possible that I have been less entertaining than usual because I've had to struggle with somewhat unfamiliar material. In any case, however, the students don't come to lectures as often as I think they should. Has that hurt their performance?

On one Tuesday, I gave a 30-question multiple-choice exam based almost entirely on the

textbook. By the next class period, on Thursday, the exam was all graded and individual student score-sheets were ready to be picked up. Students rushed up and grabbed their score-sheets, but quite a pile of them remained on my desk. Later, I examined the remaining score sheets and found that only 21 of the 48 had been picked up, leaving me with 27 that belonged to students who had skipped class. Well, Thursday had brought the first snowfall of the year, and it was the class right after the exam, so it might not be too surprising that attendance was low.

On the second class meeting after the test, I had a little quantitative analysis ready for the students. I had calculated the mean scores of the students who had picked up their exams the time before, versus those who had not. I explained that having picked up the exam was my operational definition of attending class frequently, and that I was interested in whether coming to class was associated with better grades. Apparently so! The average grade for all 48 students who took the test was 20.1458. The average for those who had attended class was 20.9048, compared with only 19.5556 for those who had not. See! It pays to come to class, even for tests that are primarily based on the textbook.

There's an hypothesis for you. Attending class is associated with higher grades. The means seem to support it, but let's assess the statistical significance of the difference in means. Figure 10.12 shows the actual scores achieved by students in the two groups, along with some steps in calculating F.

The left-hand section of the table is for the 21 students who attended class on that snowy Thursday, while the right-hand section is for those who did not. In each section, the first column of figures is simply the scores the students got on the 30-item test. The second column is the difference between that score and the mean for the group. The mean was 20.9048 for the left-hand section and 19.5556 for the right-hand section. The third column is the square of each of these differences, and the totals at the bottoms of the third columns

FIGURE 10.12
Analysis of Variance of Class Test Scores

Students Who Attended Class			Students Who Did Not Attend Class		
Score	Score-Mean	Squared	Score	Score-Mean	Squared
21	0.0952	0.0091	19	− 0.5556	0.3087
25	4.0952	16.7710	20	0.4444	0.1975
21	0.0952	0.0091	18	− 1.5556	2.4199
20	− 0.9048	0.8186	18	− 1.5556	2.4199
14	− 6.9048	47.6763	17	− 2.5556	6.5311
24	3.0952	9.5803	18	− 1.5556	2.4199
17	− 3.9048	15.2475	19	− 0.5556	0.3087
24	3.0952	9.5803	10	− 9.5556	91.3095
28	7.0952	50.3419	22	2.4444	5.9751
24	3.0952	9.5803	23	3.4444	11.8639
24	3.0952	9.5803	19	− 0.5556	0.3087
19	− 1.9048	3.6283	12	− 7.5556	57.0871
24	3.0952	9.5803	16	− 3.5556	12.6423
25	4.0952	16.7710	17	− 2.5556	6.5311
21	0.0952	0.0091	20	0.4444	0.1975
19	− 1.9048	3.6283	24	4.4444	19.7527
25	4.0952	16.7710	23	3.4444	11.8639
16	− 4.9048	24.0571	14	− 5.5556	30.8647
25	4.0952	16.7710	19	− 0.5556	0.3087
10	− 10.9048	118.9147	24	4.4444	19.7527
13	− 7.9048	62.4859	25	5.4444	29.6415
			22	2.4444	5.9751
			20	0.4444	0.1975
			27	7.4444	55.4191
			19	− 0.5556	0.3087
			19	− 0.5556	0.3087
			24	4.4444	19.7527
	Total = 441.8114			Total = 394.6669	

	Attended Class	Missed Class
Mean	20.9048	19.5556
Difference from grand mean	0.7590	− 0.5902
Difference squared	0.5761	0.3483
Number of cases	21	27
No. cases times difference squared	12.0977	9.4051

Source of Variation	Sum of Squares	Degrees of Freedom	Mean Square	F	Significance
Between groups	21.5028	1	21.5028	1.1825	n.s.
Within groups	836.4783	46	18.1843		
Total	857.9811	47			

are the sums of squared differences from the group means. For the students who attended on Thursday, the sum of squares is 441.8114. For the stay-at-home students, the sum of squares is 394.6669. Add these two numbers together, and you get the sum of squares within groups.

To get the sum of squares between groups, you do the calculations in the middle of Figure 10.12. First, you figure the mean for each of the two groups, 20.9048 and 19.5556. Then you subtract from each of these numbers the mean for the whole class of 48 students, which is 20.1458. To help us keep straight which mean we are talking about, we often use the term *grand mean* for the mean across all of the cases, and I have labeled it as such in the table. Next, you square each of these differences. Then you multiply each of these squared differences by the number of cases in its group. Finally, you add the two results together to get the sum of squared differences between groups: $12.0977 + 9.4051 = 21.5028$.

At the bottom of Figure 10.12 you can see the final steps. Divide the sums of squares by the appropriate degrees of freedom, and you get the mean squares. Divide the mean square between groups by the mean square within groups, and you get F, which here equals 1.1825. I should mention that this is written out to too many decimal places. I should probably have put simply 1.18, to avoid implying more precision in my data than is warranted. But my computer programs carry out their calculations to many decimal places. Only when they get to the last step and are about to print a result do they round it off to a couple of decimal places. This avoids adding errors to the calculation that might arise if the computer rounded off all the intermediary numbers as they were being calculated. Accuracy aside, sad to say, an F of 1.18 for this pattern of degrees of freedom is just not significant. It would take an F of around 4.05 to achieve the 0.05 level of significance.

Well, I didn't tell my class that the difference in mean scores was not statistically significant. They should remember the moral lesson that coming to class is good for them. I'll bet that F

would be significant if I had used attendance figures for all the days of the semester and the final grade from all the tests. And I'll bet F would have been significant if my class had been larger. I'll bet!

Seriously, this analysis does not prove that attendance doesn't matter. It merely fails to provide a secure basis for rejecting this null hypothesis. Among the best ways to improve a test of an hypothesis is to collect data highly sensitive to the effect under study and consisting of a large number of cases. A single test with just a few questions does not measure learning very precisely. Attendance on a single, snowy day may not predict general attendance habits very accurately. But there is no getting around the results of this analysis of variance. Although the difference in means is in the direction my theory about class attendance and grade predicted, the difference is not large enough to be statistically significant.

t-test on the Difference Between Means

When you have only two groups to compare, as is often the case in experiments, and especially when the number of cases is small, you should consider a somewhat simpler method, the **t-test**. Analysis of variance is pretty complicated, as you saw from our calculations, and not easy to capture in a single, intelligible formula. But the formula for t is easy enough:

$$t = \frac{(\bar{X}_1 - \bar{X}_2)}{\dfrac{\Sigma x_1{}^2 + \Sigma x_2{}^2}{N_1 + N_2 - 2}\left(\dfrac{1}{N_1} + \dfrac{1}{N_2}\right)}$$

The numerator is just the difference between the means in the two groups. X_1 is the mean for one group, and X_2 is the mean for the other group. In the example of my deviance class, the means were 20.9048 and 19.5556, so the difference between them is 1.3492. N_1 and N_2 are the number of cases (students) in the two groups, which are 21 and 27.

The only hard part of the formula is $\Sigma x_1^2 + \Sigma x_2^2$. These are the sums of the squares of the scores in each group. The sums of the squares of the scores in the group of 21 students who attended the snowy Thursday class, Σx_1^2, is 9619. And the sum of squares of the group of 27 who failed to come to class, Σx_2^2, is 10720. Note that you get these numbers by squaring each *score* and adding the results. Unlike in analysis of variance, we do not worry about the differences between the scores and the group means.

When I put the class grading data through this formula, I got $t = 0.22$. As with F from analysis of variance and chi-square from cross-tabs, there is a statistical table for the t distribution. It is closely related to the normal curve but makes adjustments for small numbers of cases. Recall that we had two versions of the variance formula, one for the population and one for small samples. The t distribution is like a normal distribution figured for small samples.

As with F and chi-square, we have to figure out degrees of freedom. Part of the formula for t gives this: $N_1 + N_2 - 2$. This says to add together the number of cases in the two groups and subtract two from the result: $21 + 27 - 2 = 46$. Checking a table of the t distribution for 46 degrees of freedom, I find that t would have to be 1.68 to achieve the .05 level of statistical significance, so my 0.22 is not even close.

We have tried two different methods of assessing the statistical significance of the difference in these means, analysis of variance and the t-test. Both times we bombed out. Usually, a finding that falls short of statistical significance by one appropriate test will fail other tests, too. However, because the tests make at least somewhat different assumptions, and rounding errors in your calculations may go one way or the other, it can sometimes happen that a finding achieves significance by one test and falls slightly short by another. It is very bad practice to fish around, trying one test after another in a search for significance. If your results are right on the margin of statistical significance, however, you can report the exact level achieved (such as .06, for example), or even give both of the two slightly contradictory test coefficients you got. Always, the point should be to inform the reader of your scientific report, never to mislead the reader. It is a good practice to publish the value of t (or F or chi-square) you got, as well as the significance it achieves in the statistical table.

 ## t-test Option of the XTAB Program

When using the XTAB program, you do not have to do anything special to get a t-test. It will appear automatically, along with analysis of variance, if your X variable has just two values. So, select analysis of variance and give the computer the variables you want. We have been plagued by insignificant findings quite enough, so let me offer an example that achieves statistical significance: sex and soap operas.

Yes, I know, there is lots of sex in soap operas, or at least hints about sex. But I mean the question of whether the sexes differ in their appreciation of this kind of television drama. I hypothesize, purely on the basis of a comparison between my wife's tastes and my own, that women tend to like soap operas better than men do. Figure 10.13 shows the analysis of variance display for sex as variable X and soap operas as variable Y, along with the t-test information at the bottom. When the X variable has only two values and the t-test material appears, the table

FIGURE 10.13
Sex and Soap Operas

Value	Y Cases	X Cases	Y Mean	Sum of Squares
7	27	0	—	—
6	26	0	—	—
5	46	0	—	—
4	52	0	—	—
3	71	0	—	—
2	90	255	2.36	2065
1	199	256	3.02	3374

Source of Variation	Sum of Squares	Degrees of Freedom	Mean Square	F	Significance
Between groups	56.76	1	56.76	17.17	.01
Within groups	1682.38	509	3.31		
Total	1739.15	510			

Difference of means: 0.67
t: 2.30   df: 509
Significance: .05

at the top of the display will include the sum-of-squares information that goes into the formula for t.

Whether you look at the F-test from ANOVA or the t-test, the difference between the sexes in their appreciation of soap operas is statistically significant. The two tests do not agree exactly, giving .01 and .05, but both support the hypothesis that the means differ significantly. You have to look at the means themselves to confirm that their difference supports the hypothesis, because F and t do not come with plus and minus signs the way correlation coefficients do. And indeed, women give soap operas an average preference rating of 3.02, compared with 2.36 for men.

The t-test is mainly used with experimental data and whenever the number of cases is small. Because the t-distribution is based on modifications to the normal curve, it seemed appropriate to include it in this chapter. The full importance of the normal curve and of related concepts will become apparent only as we develop the material on correlations and regressions that will be the topics of the next three chapters.

P R O J E C T S   F O R   C H A P T E R   1 0

The projects for this chapter illustrate important features of the normal curve and of probability distributions in general. The pinball probability game in the GRAF program is the focus of the first two projects, which examine in a fresh way the question of the proper size of a random sample. They also provide practice working with means and standard deviations, as does project 3, which employs the XTAB program. The remaining three projects also use the XTAB program, affording practice with analysis of variance (ANOVA) and t-tests.

1. Varying Numbers of Cases and Variance. Using the GRAF program, run the pinball probability game seven times, once for each of the following numbers of balls: 20, 50, 100, 500, 1000, 4000, 15000. Each time, write down the mean and both versions of variance, standard deviation, and variation ratio. When done, arrange these numbers in a neat table that compares your results for the seven different numbers of balls.

You might consider each of these seven runs as a sample, drawn from a larger population—as if the numbers were based on responses to a survey question, for example. Now write a brief essay discussing how the number varied across the seven runs and suggesting what the differences imply for techniques of survey sampling.

2. Small Samples versus Large Ones. Run the probability pinball game 11 times. Do one run with 1000 balls and 10 runs with 100 balls each. Write down the statistics the computer gives at the end of each run, and construct a big table comparing the means, variances, standard deviations, and variation ratios for the 11 runs.

How do the percentage distributions in the 1000-ball run and each of the 10 100-ball runs compare with the ideal distribution given in Figure 10.3? How do the means compare? Remember, the ideal mean is exactly 6.00. Next, calculate the average of the 10 means from the 100-ball runs. Is it closer to 6.00 than are many of the 10 means themselves? Is this average mean (from 100-ball runs) closer to 6.00 than is the mean from the 1000-ball run? In principle, which should be closer to 6.00, the mean from a single 1000-ball run or the average mean from 10 100-ball runs?

3. Means and Standard Deviation. Using the XTAB program, examine the means and standard deviations for a number of the preference questions in the dataset. On the basis of what you find, select 10 of these items that have interesting standard deviations. For example, you would want to include the most extreme standard deviations—the largest and smallest ones. You might also want to include two variables with essentially the same means but somewhat different standard deviations.

Provide a table listing the items you have found interesting and giving the means and standard deviations. Then write a brief essay stating why you found this particular list interesting and explaining any differences or other interesting facts that you found.

4. The Bennington College Study. This chapter used the famous Bennington College study to illustrate analysis of variance. Read the appropriate section above and you will see how we used the XTAB program to analyze the changing political orientation of students as they progress from being freshmen to being seniors. Although we used just one political variable, a conservatism scale, the XTAB dataset has many other political questions. Identify all the questions you consider to be political—having liberal or conservative answers—and use the analysis of variance option in the XTAB program to test hypotheses about changing student politics.

If you study the example given in the chapter, you will see that your first step will be to recode variable 69 (student category) to get rid of 20 graduate students and others. Then you will do analysis of variance for each of the political questions you find in the survey. Each time, student category (freshman, sophomore, junior, and senior) will be the X variable, and the political item will be the Y variable. In addition to tables giving the statistical results, write a brief essay explaining your research methods and the findings they produced.

5. Randomness and ANOVA. Do 40 ANOVAs, using each of the first 40 XTAB preference variables as variable Y. The X variable should be either of the two random variables, number 80 or number 81. Each time, write down the F value and the message about statistical significance that goes along with it. How many of the 40, if any, achieve the .05 level of statistical significance? How many would you expect would achieve this level entirely by chance? If you were to do this 100 times, using the first 50 preference variables and both random variables, how many Fs would you expect to achieve the .05 level of statistical significance? The .01 level?

6. Sex Differences in Average Preferences. Employ the t-test part of the analysis of variance module in the XTAB program to evaluate the statistical significance of sex differences in 10 preference items. First, select 10 preference items from the XTAB survey on which you think men and women will differ. To get each t-test, select analysis of variance, with sex (variable 70) as X and the selected variable as Y.

Write a brief report, giving your predictions and evaluating each in the light of the t-test result. For each of the 10 items, explain why you expected the mean for one of the sexes to be higher than the other. Was it? If so, is the difference statistically significant, according to the t-test?

CHAPTER SUMMARY

Research studies often show weak effects—small differences between groups or correlation coefficients close to zero—and researchers need a tool to decide how much confidence to place in such findings. This chapter examines the concept of statistical significance in several ways, laying the foundation for discussions of parametric measures in later chapters.

The GRAF program includes a probability pinball game that illustrates the origins of the normal curve and helps explain variance and standard deviation. There are actually two versions of the game, one that will work on any IBM-compatible computer, while the other requires a graphics capability. It runs as many as 15,000 balls through a series of bumpers in the shape of arrowheads. When a ball hits an arrow, it has an exactly 50-50 chance of bouncing either way. After 12 such bounces, the ball comes to rest in one of 13 bins. There are 4,096 different routes a ball might take, with the largest number of routes, 924, going to the middle bin. From a consideration of probabilities, it is easy to estimate what fraction of the balls should wind up in each bin. The distribution of routes is the *binomial distribution,* and the result approximates the *normal curve.* The pinball game illustrates how the normal curve can be used to calculate statistical significance.

The normal curve is an abstract mathematical concept, which no set of real data will perfectly fit. In addition to random fluctuations, there may be systematic departures from normality. For example, a distribution may be *bimodal,* having two humps rather than one. When the hump of a distribution is shifted to one side or the other, the distribution is *skewed.* The relative degree of peakedness or flatness of a distribution is called *kurtosis.*

Variance and standard deviation are extremely important concepts related to the normal curve. The *variance* of a variable is the average squared difference from the mean. The *standard deviation* for a variable is the square root of the variance. Both are measures of dispersion around the mean, expressing the extent to which cases are spread far above and below the average. In comparing the dispersions of two or more variables, it is important to correct for the fact that they may have different means. The *variation ratio* is the standard deviation divided by the mean, and the *coefficient of variation* is the variation ratio multiplied by 100.

Research on baseball provides an illustration of the utility of these measures. Stephen Jay Gould observed that batters never achieve season batting averages of .400, as a few did in the old days, and he suggested this was because baseball had become more standardized than it originally was. The greater the variation in quality of baseball players, the higher the batting average of the very best players. He tested his theory by examining the standard deviations and coefficients of variation of batting averages over the decades.

Formulas for calculating variance and standard deviation for samples are slightly different from those used for populations. Often it is useful to standardize data in terms of the normal curve, using what are called z-scores. We illustrate this with a study of the sizes of sociology departments at universities and colleges.

Despite the multitude of uses to which it is put in statistical analysis, the normal curve is not always appropriate, in part because particular data may have a very different distribution. An excellent example of overuse of the normal curve is that highly controversial concept, IQ. This "Intelligence Quotient" is often calculated by applying the normal curve to results from mental tests, and categories of mental ability are artificially defined in terms of standard deviations above and below the mean.

Analysis of variance (ANOVA) is a very useful set of techniques for assessing the statistical significance of a set of means. Although ANOVA is very commonly used to evaluate the statistical significance of differences between the various groups of subjects in an experiment, it has other applications as well. We illustrate ANOVA by replicating the study that surveyed the students at Bennington College in Vermont. This study examined the changes in students' political views that occurred from the freshman to senior years. The key finding was that the students tended to become more liberal with the passage of time, presumably because the intellectual environment of the school encouraged development of liberal senti-ments. The original research was a *panel study*, while we use data from a question-naire administered at one point in time to students in different classes. The XTAB program includes an ANOVA procedure, employing the *F distribution* to evaluate statistical significance in much the way that we earlier used chi-square. Our results fail to replicate the Bennington College study.

The XTAB program also includes the t-test on the differences between means, which we illustrate by doing a little study on class attendance and grades in a so-ciology course.

KEY CONCEPTS FOR CHAPTER 10

normal curve   322
statistical significance   323
variance   329
standard deviation   329
variation ratio and coefficient of
    variation   332

standard scores (z-scores)   334
analysis of variance (ANOVA)   338
standard error   339
confidence interval   339
t-test   348

CHAPTER

Geographically Based Rates

CHAPTER OVERVIEW

Much of the information on which sociologists base their research was collected by government agencies and therefore can be called official data. Although these data have several drawbacks and limitations, they have the great advantage of being cheap (or even free), and they offer information on many phenomena about which it is very difficult for the sociologist to collect fresh data. Among the standard methods for analyzing such data are ecological (or geographic) correlations based on rates for cities, metropolitan areas, or states.

For a century and a half, one of the favorite techniques of social scientists has been statistical analysis of rates for various geographical areas. When you hear that the crime rate correlates with the unemployment rate, research of this kind is being reported. Among the terms used for this approach are **human ecology** and **social ecology**, and I will occasionally use the term *ecological* in this chapter. These words do not refer to research on air pollution or damage to wildlife, but simply to studies on how areas of the city or country differ. The ecology in question is not the biological environment but the social environment.

Between the two world wars, the center of human ecology was the sociology department at the University of Chicago. There and at other institutions Chicago influenced, literally dozens of sociologists used a wide variety of methods to study the nature of different social environments. Among them was analysis of statistical rates describing various features of communities, such as the crime rate or the percent of residents who lived in rented apartments. Today, we often ignore the other research methods used at Chicago and the theories about city life that justified them, and we describe any research employing geographically based rates as ecological.

This chapter begins by explaining how raw government data can be used to create rates; then it considers a number of examples, such as radio ownership in 1930, to show how we can interpret geographic variations. With our experience evaluating associations between variables by means of crosstabs, which I

explained in earlier chapters, we are ready to visualize relationships between variables that take any number of values. Examples that help us understand parametric correlations include the positive correlation between urbanism and income and the negative correlation between religion and suicide. Problems with this kind of research include biases in the collection of official data, the ecological fallacy, and Galton's problem. Some sociologists also feel that the use of rates can introduce autocorrelation.

The MAPS program creates maps and scattergrams (even on computers lacking graphics) of 255 variables across the 50 American states. The program also generates statistics on any variable, ranks the states, and calculates correlations and regressions in connection with the scattergram. The substantial dataset, and the ease of operation, make this program an excellent introduction to parametric correlations and regressions. This program also explains how we create variables based on official or geographic data.

_____ Ecological Rates

Which city is wilder, New York or Las Vegas? Both have somewhat unsavory reputations in the rest of the country, but both are exciting places to visit (Galliher and Cross 1983). Imagine you are a sociologist living in Normal, Illinois, and you want to decide which of these abnormal cities is safer to visit. One way to tell is to compare official statistics for suicides and homicides. In 1980, according to the annual federal summary *Vital Statistics of the United States,* 842 people killed themselves in the New York metropolitan area, compared with only 101 in metropolitan Las Vegas. And the *Uniform Crime Report* of the FBI says that 1,902 people died of murder and non-negligent manslaughter in New York, but just 108 in Las Vegas. So it appears that Las Vegas is a far safer place to visit than the Big Apple.

But this analysis neglects an important fact: New York is a far bigger city than Las Vegas. In 1980, the populations of the metropolitan areas were 9,120,346 and 463,087, a size difference of almost 20 to 1. We would expect to see more of almost everything in New York, because there are so many people. Before we can compare, we have to adjust for the population difference. The most familiar way to do this, of course, is to express each number as a percent. With rare events like suicide and murder, however, this can lead to awkward numbers. For example, in 1980 about 0.009 percent of New Yorkers killed themselves. Round off to the nearest tenth of a percent, and you get 0.0 percent, giving the false impression that there were no suicides at all.

Percent literally means "per hundred." Ten percent of Chicago's population was 65 years old or older in 1980. This means that 10 out of 100 Chicagoans were in this older age group. You can express the same fact in many different ways: 10 out of 100 is the same as 100 out of 1,000, as 1,000 out of 10,000, as 10,000 out of 100,000, and as 100,000 out of 1,000,000. When a phenomenon is as rare as suicide thankfully is, we generally express it in terms of cases per 100,000 or per 1,000,000. In 1980, New York had 92 suicides per million people, while Las Vegas had 218 per million. Thus, residents of Las Vegas had over twice the chance of killing themselves as did New Yorkers.

To get percent, you divide the cases by the population, then multiply the result by 100. We must remind ourselves of what the various parts of this simple calculation are called, something you probably learned in high-school math. When you divide one number by another, you are calculating a *ratio*. The number that does the dividing, in this case the city's population, is called the *divisor* or the *denominator*. The number it divides into, here the number of suicides, is called the *numerator*. And the number you multiply the ratio by to get your final result, in this case 100, is often called the *base*. Any statistic that expresses a ratio in terms of a base—such as percent or per million—is called a **rate**. Because we will occasionally use these familiar terms throughout this chapter, it is good to remember clearly what each of them means.

Let's compare the rates for our two cities. The first two columns of Figure 11.1 give the actual numbers of suicides and six crimes that local police departments reported to the FBI: murder and non-negligent manslaughter, forcible rape, robbery, aggravated assault, burglary, and larceny-theft. Clearly, New York had far more of each of these problems than did Las Vegas, in terms of numbers of cases.

The right-hand columns of the table express the data in terms of rates per million population. To get New York's murder rate, you divide the number of cases (1,902) by the city's population (9,120,346), and multiply the result by 1,000,000. This gives the rate per million (209). A slightly easier way, if you are calculating several rates for each city, is to express the population in millions to start with. The New York metropolitan area had about 9.12 million people. So the murder rate per million would simply be $1,902/9.12 = 209$ per million. Las Vegas had only about 0.463 million people. Its murder rate is $108/0.463 = 233$ per million. Look through Figure 11.1 carefully. Which of the rates are higher for New York? For Las Vegas? The comparison between cities is not so clear-cut now, but the rates give you a much better basis for judging their relative safety than the raw numbers did.

FIGURE 11.1

Crime and Suicide in New York City and Las Vegas, 1980

	Number of Cases		Rate per 1,000,000	
	New York	Las Vegas	New York	Las Vegas
Suicide	842	101	92	218
Murder	1,902	108	209	233
Rape	3,925	352	430	760
Robbery	103,457	2,915	11,344	6,295
Assault	45,955	1,932	5,039	4,172
Burglary	240,956	16,681	26,420	36,021
Larceny	304,777	21,781	33,417	47,034

With this brief introduction, we can turn to the computer program and dataset prepared for this chapter and begin doing our own ecological research using 255 rates for the 50 states of the United States.

The MAPS Program

When you select the MAPS program, the computer will prepare to show you dynamic maps, charting the geographic variations in 255 different characteristics of the American states. After all these data have been loaded into the computer, the main menu will appear:

```
[1]  Map of the 50 states
[2]  Map of the 9 divisions
[3]  Map of a variable
[4]  Statistics about a variable
[5]  Rank states on a variable
[6]  Scattergram of two variables
[7]  Partial correlations
[8]  Three variable regression
[9]  Switch map display (currently: monochrome)
[ESC]  Quit or switch programs
```

Options 7 and 8 will be explained in Chapter 13. Each allows you to examine the statistical association operating among three variables at once, and we will not really be able to understand them until after Chapter 12 explains correlation and regression more deeply.

Before you do anything else, you should check the final option by switching the map display. The program draws two different kinds of maps. If your computer has a color monitor, the states can appear as solid, colored shapes. But if you have a monochrome monitor—one that shows everything in one particular color (typically green, amber, black, or white)—the computer must draw the states using different shadings of a single color. The program always starts out assuming your monitor is monochrome, but if you press the (9) key once, the maps will appear in color on a color monitor. You can easily tell if your monitor is color, because the ordinary printing on the screen will appear in various colors if it is.

If you have selected color and want to switch back to monochrome, just get the main menu on your screen and press (9) again. Under some circumstances, you might want to select monochrome on a color monitor, or vice versa. A few monochrome monitors automatically represent the different colors as shadings, and you might prefer the result to the shadings built into the program. Set the program for color and see what the maps look like. Occasionally, if your computer has a printer attached, you might want to print out a map, using the PrintScreen command. If you have a color monitor, switch the menu option to monochrome, get the map you want, then give the command. (To print the contents of a text screen on the original models of IBM, hold down the shift key and press (PrtScr).) The printed map may not be pretty, and some printers won't do the job at all, but with luck you will have a readable copy of the map on the screen.

Although I am sure you know what a map of the United States looks like, it will be useful to have one at hand to consult while working with this program, so I built a couple in. To see a map of the 50 states, select the first choice on the main menu by pressing (1). The U.S. census bureau often groups states in nine "divisions," which the second menu option identifies for you. When you are through looking at a map or at other data produced by this program, press (ENTER).

Each map has a title in the upper-right corner, telling you what it shows. Between Michigan and Maine is the word *State* followed by a blinking cursor. If you type in the two-letter postal abbreviation for a state, that state will start flashing on the map. Don't press (ENTER) after the postal code, or the computer will think you are through with the map. Just type the two letters, such as CA for California or NY for New York.

Figure 11.2 is a map of the 50 states, showing the postal abbreviation for each one. It is drawn to duplicate the one on your computer screen. I suppose this is the place to apologize, on behalf of your computer, for the ugliness and imprecision of our maps. You see, many of the IBM-type college computers around today lack the capacity to display high-resolution graphics, so I had to write all the programs in this set to work without that luxury. The only way to draw a map of the country without high-resolution graphics is with little boxes. Although this distorts the shape of each state, I think you can recognize them all. Alaska and Hawaii are the two rectangles in the lower-left corner of the screen. This crude map has the advantage, however, that the computer can change it very rapidly, and even if your machine had super-high resolution graphics, this added speed would be of great benefit when you wanted to inspect several different maps.

Map of a Variable

The third choice on the menu gives you a map of any variable in the dataset. When you press (3) to select it, the computer needs to know what variable you want. The way you tell it is the same for several other options on the menu, so pay attention while I explain it now.

When the computer needs to know the variable you want, the following message will appear at the bottom of the screen: "Type the variable number and press ENTER." Do that, and you have selected the variable. The variables are numbered 1 through 255, and it is by this number that you will tell the computer which variable to work with. They are listed in Appendix C, along with detailed information that will help you understand clearly what they mean.

For your convenience, we also have a way of displaying the variable names on the screen. There are so many that I can't show all their names at once, so I have divided them into four groups. When it is asking you for a variable number, the computer will put this near the bottom of the screen: "Display: (A) Demographics (B) Problems (C) Miscellaneous (D) 1920–1930 variables." You can press one of these four letter keys—(A) or (B) or (C) or (D)—to see part of the list of variables.

FIGURE 11.2
The Fifty States

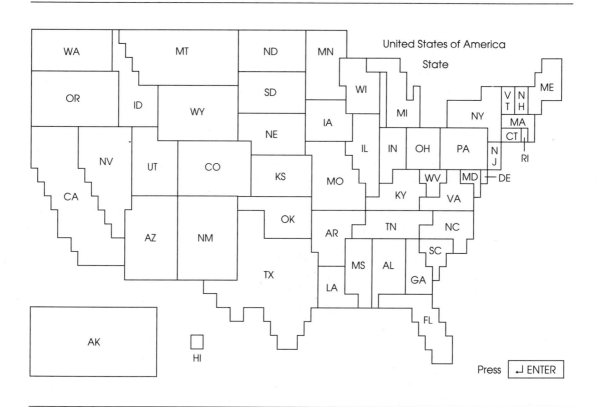

If it turns out you selected the wrong one, simply press a different letter to see another set.

The variables are divided into four groups of 64 or 63 each, the first three focusing on the 1980 census and the final one on the 1930 census. Group A is called "Demographics" and includes the most general census data, such as the populations of the states or the percent under age 18. Group B, "Problems," contains information on crime rates, poverty, suicide, divorce, and other topics often considered in sociology courses about social problems. Group C consists of miscellaneous variables. Group D, "1920–1930 variables," is comprised of 63 items mainly from the 1930 census, plus data on church membership in 1926.

You may find it more convenient to locate variables in Appendix C of this book, rather than on your computer screen. Indeed, you may plan a bit of research around a list of variables, and then it would make sense to write down all their names and numbers. In that case, you can ignore the four letter commands and just type the variable numbers from a written list you prepared.

The fact is, you can type in the number of any variable, even if it is not listed in the group you selected. The group listings are just for your convenience. Also, if you have been working with a variable and want to use the same variable for something different on the menu, simply press (ENTER) when the computer asks which one you want. To select a new variable, type a number from 1 through 255 and press (ENTER). If you are in the mapping option, the correct map will appear almost instantly.

The title of the map, printed in the upper-right corner of the screen, will be the name of the variable you selected. Near the lower-right corner is a key explaining the coloring or shading of the states. To make the map, the computer divides the states into four groups. The states high on the variable are depicted with the color or shading next to the word *High* in the key. For example, if you had selected the murder rate as your variable, the states with the highest rates of murder would have this color or shading.

Because there are 50 states, and 50 cannot be divided evenly into 4 parts, the computer will put the 12 states with the highest rates into the High group. The Medium High and Medium Low groups consist of 13 states each. The 12 states with the lowest rates will go into the Low group.

When you are working with data from 1920 to 1930, you will have information about only 48 states, because Alaska and Hawaii had not achieved statehood back then. This newest pair of states will not show up on the map, and the computer will divide the 48 states into four equal groups of 12.

Again, you can make a state flash on the map by typing in its two-letter postal abbreviation (but *don't* press (ENTER)). Once it has started blinking, look at the bottom of the screen. You will see the name of the state followed by its rate for the chosen variable. Pressing (ENTER) will take you back to the main menu.

For an interesting example, let's consider variable 239, "Radios (families)." Because this variable is taken from the 1930 census, we will have information about 48 states. The 1930 census counted 29,904,663 American families, and 12,048,762 possessed radio sets, about 40.3 percent. These were the very early days for radio, and television would not be perfected until the end of the 1930s. Families in some states were much more likely to have radio sets, partly because the first radio stations were concentrated in certain parts of the country. But variations across the states also reflected economic differences and perhaps the tendency of some states to be especially fast to adopt novelties.

To see a map of radio ownership, select the "Map of a variable" option from the menu, and tell the computer you want variable number 239. Just type 239 and press (ENTER) when the computer asks you which variable you want. Figure 11.3 shows what the map will look like. Notice that there are three separate bright areas, representing states with high levels of radio ownership. Can you explain these three areas? A hint is to think about what big cities are in the high-radio areas. In the 1940s, the early development of television centered on stations in New York, Philadelphia, Chicago, and Los Angeles.

Again, you can make a state flash by typing in its postal code. For example, if you type IL for Illinois while the radio map is on the screen, Illinois will begin to flash, and at the bottom center of the screen "Illinois: 55.6 percent" will appear. This means that 55.6 percent of the families in Illinois had radio sets in 1930.

FIGURE 11.3
Percent of Families with Radios in 1930

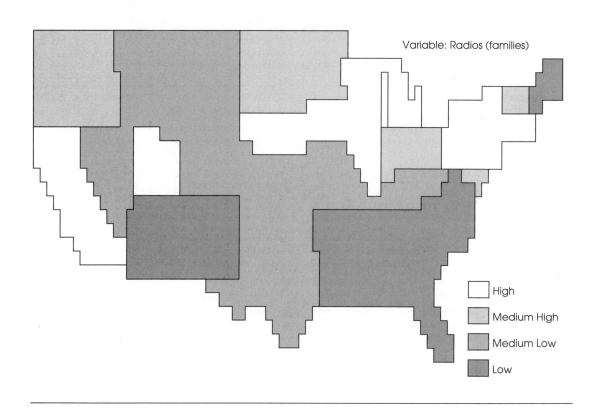

Variable: Radios (families)

☐ High

◻ Medium High

▨ Medium Low

▩ Low

 ## Statistics about a Variable

The fourth option on the main menu lets you see various information about a variable. After pressing (4), select a variable in the same way as when getting a map, described above. For example, Figure 11.4 shows what you get when you select variable 26, "Hispanic."

At the top of the screen is a heading that announces which variable you chose, and all the information is arranged below it. First, you see the name of the variable and the group it belongs to ((A) Demographics, (B) Problems, (C) Miscellaneous, or (D) 1920–1930 variables). The next line explains further what the variable measures. In the case of "Hispanic" it says, "Persons of Spanish heritage per 100,000."

For most variables, the number of valid cases is 50, but for those from 1920–1930 it is 48. The valid cases are simply the cases for which you have data, either 50 states or 48.

FIGURE 11.4
Statistics on Variable 26

Name of variable: Hispanic   Group: (A)Demographics
(Persons of Spanish cultural heritage per 100,000)
Valid cases: 50
Mean: 4.29 percent
Variance: 42.60
Standard deviation: 6.53
Range: from 0.4 percent (Maine)
           to 36.6 percent (New Mexico)

Mean, variance, and standard deviation are measures of central tendency and dispersion discussed in the previous chapter. The table of statistics ends with the range for the variable. The Hispanic variable ranges from a low of 0.4 percent in the state of Maine up to 36.6 percent for New Mexico.

For many variables, the computer will print a little message after the mean and range figures—for example, "percent," "per 100,000," "per million." This gives the base on which the rate was figured. If the computer does not print out such a message, it is a hint to read the variable's explanation on the screen or check this same information in Appendix C. Many of the variables have special bases, and some, like population size itself, are not rates.

Rank States on a Variable

Option 5 on the main menu will show you the rate each state has for a selected variable, ranking them from highest to lowest. Select the variable, as usual, and the screen will fill with the names of the states, their postal abbreviations, and the data for each state. Between the data and the name is a number in parentheses—(1) through (48) or (50)—giving the **rank** of the state. We will look at two examples, starting with variable 239, families with radio sets in 1930. You can check this on your computer, but Figure 11.5 shows what it would look like.

The state where the largest proportion of families owned radios was New Jersey, at 63.4 percent. New York comes second, with 57.9 percent. You cannot always find good explanations for the exact order the states are ranked in, but these two make sense to me. New York City was the largest metropolis in the country, with much research in electronics and early commercial radio broadcasting. All of New Jersey was within the range of stations in New York City, while some upstate parts of New York State may have been out of range.

The Boston stations served Rhode Island as well as Massachusetts. Chicago stations served Illinois, while Connecticut enjoyed stations from both New York City and Boston. Los Angeles and San Francisco stations served California. Radio was moving fast across the land, and the 24 states with higher than average rates

FIGURE 11.5
Ranking on Variable 239: Percent of Families with Radios, 1930

63.4	(1)	New Jersey NJ	39.2	(25)	Maine ME	*Ranking 48 states*
57.9	(2)	New York NY	38.9	(26)	Kansas KS	*on variable 239*
57.6	(3)	Massachusetts MA	37.8	(27)	Colorado CO	*Radios (families)*
57.1	(4)	Rhode Island RI	37.4	(28)	Missouri MO	
55.6	(5)	Illinois IL	34.1	(29)	Wyoming WY	
54.7	(6)	Connecticut CT	31.9	(30)	Montana MT	
52.0	(7)	California CA	30.6	(31)	Nevada NV	
51.0	(8)	Wisconsin WI	30.3	(32)	Idaho ID	
50.6	(9)	Michigan MI	23.3	(33)	West Virginia WV	
48.5	(10)	Iowa IA	21.6	(34)	Oklahoma OK	
48.1	(11)	Pennsylvania PA	18.6	(35)	Texas TX	
47.9	(12)	Nebraska NE	18.3	(36)	Kentucky KY	*Data are given as*
47.7	(13)	Ohio OH	18.2	(37)	Virginia VA	*percentages*
47.3	(14)	Minnesota MN	18.1	(38)	Arizona AZ	
45.9	(15)	Delaware DE	15.4	(39)	Florida FL	
44.6	(16)	Vermont VT	14.3	(40)	Tennessee TN	
44.4	(17)	New Hampshire NH	11.5	(41)	New Mexico NM	
44.2	(18)	South Dakota SD	11.2	(42)	North Carolina NC	
43.5	(19)	Oregon OR	11.2	(43)	Louisiana LA	
42.9	(20)	Maryland MD	9.9	(44)	Georgia GA	
42.3	(21)	Washington WA	9.5	(45)	Alabama AL	
41.6	(22)	Indiana IN	9.1	(46)	Arkansas AR	
41.1	(23)	Utah UT	7.6	(47)	South Carolina SC	
40.9	(24)	North Dakota ND	5.4	(48)	Mississippi MS	*Press (ENTER)*

were the Northeast, Middle West, and four in the Far West: California, Oregon, Washington, and Utah. The Deep South and the Southwest states of Arizona and New Mexico had the lowest rates.

The states are listed in two columns on the screen. The column on the left is the states with above-average rates. Those on the right have lower than average rates. You can compare this ranking with Figure 11.3, which shows a rough version of it in map form. The top 12 states in the ranking are the "High" states on the map, and the bottom 12 (numbers 37–48) are the "Low" states.

When two or more states have the same rates, as North Carolina and Louisiana do with their identical radio-ownership rates of 11.2 percent, their relative order in the ranking does not mean anything. When states are tied, the computer might draw them on a map in different shades, and it is worth glancing at the state ranking to interpret any map you find interesting.

One final use for the state ranking is to remind you of each state's two-letter postal code, so you can make the state flash on a map. Perhaps the easiest way is to ask the computer for a ranking in terms of variable 0—yes, just type the zero (not the "Oh") when the computer asks what variable you want for the ranking. The states will appear in alphabetical order, so you can quickly spot the name of the state you want. Its postal code follows the name.

For a second example of ranking the states, see Figure 11.6, which shows the per capita personal income in 1980. The numbers are in dollars, so 1980 incomes ranged from an average of $12,759 in Alaska down to $6,557 in Mississippi. Now we have data on 50 states rather than just 48, and it is interesting to see Alaska at the head of the list. Hawaii, in 13th position, just misses joining Alaska among the 12 high-income states when you map this variable. Compare Figure 11.5 with Figure 11.6, and you will find many states in roughly the same positions in the ranking. Apparently, states that were too poor to afford radios and radio stations in 1930 were still economically low a half-century later!

A casual impression received by glancing over a couple of sets of figures like these, however, is not strong scientific evidence. Clearly, we need a systematic procedure to help us judge how similar the patterns are for 1930 radios and 1980 incomes. Earlier chapters have given us a number of approaches useful when one or both variables are measured in terms of a small set of categories. But now, each state may have a unique value, and a crosstab would have to be huge to hold all the cells necessary. With 50 states, it would need 2,500 cells.

One approach would be to recode the data, collapsing the states into a small number of categories for each variable. For example, we can follow the

FIGURE 11.6
Ranking on Variable 82: Per Capita Income, 1980

12759	(1)	Alaska AK	9119	(26)	New Hampshire NH	*Ranking*
11692	(2)	Connecticut CT	9086	(27)	Nebraska NE	*50 states*
10935	(3)	New Jersey NJ	9066	(28)	Oklahoma OK	*on variable*
10929	(4)	California CA	8993	(29)	Florida FL	*82: per*
10875	(5)	Wyoming WY	8924	(30)	Indiana IN	*capita*
10723	(6)	Nevada NV	8865	(31)	Missouri MO	*income*
10479	(7)	Illinois IL	8814	(32)	Arizona AZ	
10477	(8)	Maryland MD	8652	(33)	Montana MT	
10355	(9)	Washington WA	8626	(34)	North Dakota ND	
10291	(10)	Delaware DE	8456	(35)	Louisiana LA	
10252	(11)	New York NY	8176	(36)	Idaho ID	
10118	(12)	Massachusetts MA	8041	(37)	Georgia GA	
10091	(13)	Hawaii HI	7878	(38)	New Mexico NM	
10033	(14)	Colorado CO	7868	(39)	Maine ME	
9967	(15)	Michigan MI	7832	(40)	North Carolina NC	
9864	(16)	Kansas KS	7818	(41)	South Dakota SD	
9765	(17)	Minnesota MN	7814	(42)	West Virginia WV	
9528	(18)	Texas TX	7810	(43)	Vermont VT	
9460	(19)	Ohio OH	7702	(44)	Tennessee TN	
9429	(20)	Rhode Island RI	7681	(45)	Utah UT	
9427	(21)	Pennsylvania PA	7662	(46)	Kentucky KY	
9413	(22)	Wisconsin WI	7434	(47)	Alabama AL	
9406	(23)	Virginia VA	7265	(48)	South Carolina SC	
9310	(24)	Iowa IA	7185	(49)	Arkansas AR	
9296	(25)	Oregon OR	6557	(50)	Mississippi MS	

procedure the computer used to produce maps, dividing the 48 states with radio data into four groups, each containing 12 states. Then we could look at how those groups of states were doing economically, 50 years later. For example, you could see how many states in each of the four groups were in the top half for per capita income in 1980. It turns out that 11 out the 12 states highest in 1930 radio ownership were in the top half for 1980 income. Only one of the states in the bottom quarter for radio ownership was in the top half for income 50 years later.

When you collapse categories, however, you lose information. Far better to use a method that gives a clear, easily understood result without collapsing. Back when we introduced crosstabs, in Chapter 8, we noted that the correlation coefficient known as r had many advantages. Among them is that it can readily be calculated without first putting the cases into a crosstab. A limitation of r is that, ideally at least, the data have to be at the interval or ratio levels of measurement. Ordinal data will give somewhat uncertain results with r, and nominal data (unless there are only two categories) cannot be used with r at all. But our state dataset fully meets this criterion for the use of r, and we will find that along with the obvious advantages of the r coefficient itself comes a whole crowd of related techniques that are of tremendous value for the social researcher.

Scattergram of Two Variables

A **scattergram** (sometimes called *scatter diagram* or **scatterplot**) is a graph that shows where all the cases stand in terms of two variables, X and Y. It is the equivalent of a crosstab but is designed for continuous variables, and it resembles many graphs you must have seen. Like a crosstab, it has various statistics attached to it, including a correlation coefficient.

When you select the scattergram option from the menu, the computer will ask you what variable you want. As soon as you tell it, it will ask again. This is because a scattergram needs two variables, X and Y. The first variable you pick will be variable X, the second Y.

Perhaps the best way to explain a scattergram is through an example. If you are at the computer, select the scattergram option. For your first variable, select number 27 (urban population), and for your second pick number 116 (per capita income). In a moment, the picture shown here in Figure 11.7 will appear on your screen.

Notice that most of the screen is covered with a scattering of small squares. This is the scattergram proper. To the right of it are the statistics. If you have the patience, you can count the squares, and you will discover that there are 50, one for each state. Each tiny square represents the position of a state.

Now look at the brief messages at the four corners of the scattergram. At the lower left you see, "Low Y, Low X." At upper left, "High Y, Low X." At upper right, "High Y, High X." And at the lower right is the message, "Low Y, High X." Can you guess what these mean? States near the top of the screen are high on variable Y, while those at the bottom are low on variable Y. States on the right are high on variable X, while those at the left are low on variable X.

Although you are probably familiar with graphs like this, it is worth going slowly and thinking through your first few scattergrams. This one has a lonely square at the

FIGURE 11.7
Scattergram of Urban and Income

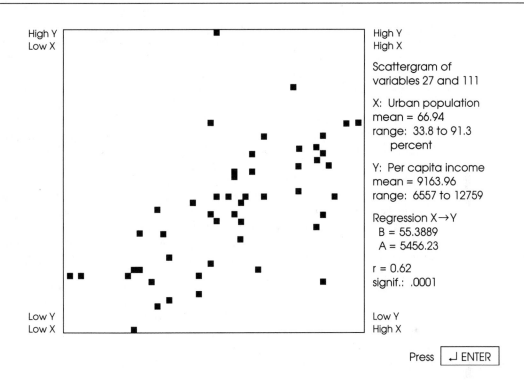

top center. Because it is at the very top, it must represent the state that is highest on variable Y. Recall that Y is per capita income. Therefore, this state is the one with highest per capita income, and a glance at the ranking of states for this variable (shown here in Figure 11.6) reveals that it is Alaska. But the tiny square representing Alaska is about in the middle from left to right in the scattergram. This means Alaska is about in the middle on variable X, which is percent urban.

Printed graphs, and some designed for computers with high-resolution graphics, will have numbers all around the edges and a grid of straight lines, so you can directly read the X and Y values for each case. We simply do not have room for such numbers and grid lines here. Of course, if you want to see where each state stands exactly, you can easily check the state rankings for each variable. Our scattergram is intended to convey only a general impression.

The extreme states, those high or low on variables X and Y, will always be at the extreme edges of the scattergram. That is, the diagram covers the full range for each variable and nothing beyond the range. You don't have to check the rankings or the statistics on each variable if you want to know the means and ranges. They are printed at the right-hand edge of the scattergram.

For variable X, percent urban, the range is 33.8 percent to 91.3 percent. Therefore, the tiny squares covering the scattergram go from 33.8 percent, at the left, to 91.3 percent at the right. There is no room on the scattergram for 20 percent urban or 95 percent urban, but since no states have these values, the graph is complete. And per capita income ranges from $6,557 to $12,759. Thus, the bottom edge of the graph represents an income of $6,557, and the top edge represents $12,759. There isn't room on the scattergram for $5,000 or $15,000, but no states had such extreme per capita incomes in 1980.

The means for the two variables are not necessarily in the exact middle of the scattergram. The exact middle is the midpoint of the ranges, 62.55 percent in the case of urban population, and $9,658.00 in the case of per capita income. The means are 66.94 percent and $9,163.96. For some variables, the mean and the midpoint of the range are quite different. You can usually spot them because most scattergram squares are bunched near an edge or corner.

When it is drawing the scattergram, the computer does its best to display all the states. If the computer wants to put a state at a particular point but one is already there, it puts the new state slightly above or below where it is supposed to be. When three or more states are supposed to go in the same place, however, the computer can't show all of them. On many scattergrams, such as the one shown in Figure 11.7, all the states are visible. You are more likely to lose a few states when their values are bunched together.

If you want to see real scattergram disasters, check out variables 189 through 192. These are the variables for geographic region, and there are only two values for each, 1 and 0. Obviously, scattergrams are not designed for such dichotomous variables. A two-by-two table would be better. But for most of our state dataset, the scattergram does an admirable job of showing graphically how two variables are associated.

Correlations and Regressions

Among the most important pieces of information, to the right of a scattergram, are a correlation coefficient and a regression. We have seen r correlations before, although we have not discussed them in detail, and regressions are closely related. Although the following chapter is devoted almost exclusively to these marvelous little numbers, a few words about each are in order now.

Ecological Correlations

Near the lower right in Figure 11.7, you see "r = 0.62, signif.: .0001." This is the same r

correlation coefficient we introduced in Chapter 8. You recall that a correlation of 0.62 indicates a pretty big positive association. Clearly, the per capita income tends to be higher in states with greater proportions of their populations living in urban areas. City incomes are high, compared to rural incomes. This 0.62 correlation is strong evidence that a major factor determining the per capita income of a state is how urban the population is.

When we first encountered correlations, in two-by-two tables and crosstabs, we noticed that a big correlation produced a clear pattern for our eyes to see. So, too, here. Most of the tiny squares in Figure 11.7 run in a fairly narrow band from the lower left-hand corner upward to the right. They don't point quite as high as the upper right-hand corner. If you had to draw a line through the squares (something we'll do a lot of in the next chapter), it would run from the lower-left corner to about where the words "X:Urban population" are to the right of the scattergram. Only one square is near the lower-right corner, and none is near the upper-left corner. Just as with our crosstabs, this is a picture of a positive correlation.

Although most of the squares cluster tightly in this band, a few are outside it, notably the one at the top center representing Alaska. We call cases like this **outliers**. In some cases, one or two outliers can seriously distort the r, and occasionally researchers feel it necessary to remove them and see what the correlation would be like without them in the dataset. The extreme cost of living in Alaska (high energy and shipping bills), and the money to be made in extractive industries like oil, give it a high per capita income despite only moderate urbanism, so Alaska may not contribute to a fair test of the theory that urbanism determines income. The formula for r gives a lot of weight to extreme values, and thus may give undue influence to outliers.

An example from real research concerns not Alaska but New Mexico. My colleague Rodney Stark and I did a number of ecological research studies to test our theory that deviant religious cults were a response to weakening of standard religious denominations. We thus predicted strong negative correlations between the rate of conventional church membership and various measures of cult activity. At one point, Stark looked at the home states of 501 cults listed in J. Gordon Melton's (1978) massive *Encyclopedia of American Religions*. For all 50 states, the correlation was -0.37 between the percent of the population who were church members and the number of cult headquarters per million. But nine of the states lacked cult headquarters, even though we knew there was considerable cultic activity in each, so Stark tried the correlation with the remaining 41 states and got a correlation of -0.49. Then he looked at the

scattergram and saw that New Mexico was an extreme outlier.

In terms of religious traditions, New Mexico is like two states. Many counties are very religious and have extraordinarily high rates of church membership. A few counties have low rates, but the overall rate for the state is high. In the 1971 data we were using, about 65 percent of New Mexico residents were members of churches, compared with 56 percent for the nation as a whole. And New Mexico's cult rate was 9.1 per million, compared with 2.3 per million for the nation as a whole. It turned out that New Mexico's cults were located in counties of low church membership. Thus, Stark felt justified in trying an analysis without New Mexico, based on just 40 states, and the correlation came out even more strongly on the negative side, -0.61 (Stark and Bainbridge 1985:441).

It is important to note that discarding outliers can be abused. It is against the rules of the scientific game to throw away data that contradict your theory and then announce that the data support your theory. Thus, when Stark and I reported the above analysis, we made sure to give the correlation for 50 states as well as for 40 and 41. It is essential to give the reader the information necessary to judge the correctness of the author's conclusions. If you want to see a scattergram in which New Mexico is the outlier, try one with variable 26 (Hispanic) or variable 32 (speaking a foreign language at home).

Another point about ecological correlations concerns how big they tend to be. In survey data, we really have to struggle to find an r as big as -0.61 or 0.62, but they are much more common with data like our state dataset. Ecological data are **aggregate data**. This means that information about many individuals was combined to make each rate. Aggregate data tend to have less noise in them than individual data.

Noise is a technical term in information theory. We need not concern ourselves with the details, but the concept is easy enough to grasp. When you are trying to tune in a distant radio station, the static that interferes with the program is the *noise,* and the program itself is called the *signal.* The best results come when there is a "high signal-to-noise ratio," that is, when the signal is strong and the noise is weak. Sociological correlations are a kind of signal, a message about society we are trying to tune in with our research methods, and noise is any factor that obscures the signal. In survey research, noise can enter the data in several ways. Many things, including pure chance and the emotional whim of the moment, can induce a respondent to check one box or another on the questionnaire. The effect of the noise is to reduce the correlations. In ecological research, however, the random or meaningless factors that affect individual responses are greatly canceled out when we combine information from many different people.

Before you quickly decide that aggregate data are superior to individual data, however, I must mention that the typically greater magnitude of ecological correlations can also herald problems in the analysis (Hannan 1971; Roberts and Burstein 1980). Methodologists have invested much time in trying to determine how individual-level correlations compare with aggregate-level correlations, and they have identified a number of distortions produced in aggregation that can inflate or deflate ecological correlations. Later in the chapter, we will consider a few limitations of this approach.

A First Glance at Regressions

Regressions, which are related to r-type correlations, are of very great use in the social sciences. The first difference worth noting between a regression and an r is that regressions clearly distinguish the independent variable from the dependent variable. Recall that one of the statistics attached to our crosstab analysis in Chapters 8 and 9 did this: Somers' D. At that time we called it an asymmetrical coefficient, and we used a little arrow to show which variable was which: X→Y. This arrow means that X is the independent variable that may influence variation in the dependent variable,

Y. The numbers a regression analysis produces let you predict what the value of the dependent variable will be if you know the independent variable.

Beneath "Regression X→Y" in Figure 11.7 is "B = 55.3889." This is the part of the regression analysis that is comparable to the correlation coefficient, r. It certainly doesn't look like r, because it is much larger than 1.00, and we have seen that correlations can't get this big. The simplest way to understand it now, before we undertake a full explanation in the next chapter, is in terms of the particular variables in Figure 11.7.

The 55.3889 refers to the number of dollars that each percentage point in urban population is worth. If one state has 50 percent of its residents in urban areas, and a second state has 51 percent, the per capita income should be $55.39 higher in the second state. In others words, two states that differ by 1 percent in urbanism are predicted to differ $55.39 in per capita income.

This can be extended to wider comparisons, for example between two states that differ 10 percent in urbanism. Simply multiply $55.3889 by 10, to get $553.889. We don't worry about fractions of a cent, of course, so we can say that two states differing by 10 percent in urbanism are predicted to differ $553.89 in per capita income. And states that differ 100 percent—one that was completely rural compared with one that was completely urban (0 percent versus 100 percent)—would differ by 55.3889 times 100, or $5,538.89.

Although B helps you predict differences in per capita income, it doesn't say how much people earn. That's where A comes in. It predicts what the per capita income might be in a state that was 0 percent urban, a completely rural state. Figure 11.7 reports that A = 5456.23. This means that the per capita income in a completely rural state should be $5,456.23. We just used B to estimate that a completely urban state should have a per capita income that was $5,538.89 higher than this. Add $5,456.23 and $5,538.89 together, and you get $10,995.12, the estimated per capita income for a completely urban state in 1980.

Of course, no state was completely rural or completely urban in 1980, but these extreme figures show how you can estimate the per capita income for any state on the basis of the percent of its population that is urban. To do so, take A from the scattergram and add the right number of Bs to reach the state you want. Consider Ohio, for example. If it were 0 percent urban, we would predict a per capita income of $5,456.23, but it was 73.3 percent urban. For each 1 percent, you should add $55.39. So, multiply 73.3 by $55.39, which gives you $4,060.08. Add that to $5,456.23, and your prediction for Ohio's per capita income is $9,516.31. In fact, Ohio's per capita income was $9,460, so our prediction is off by $56. But that's not bad at all, equivalent to being off only 1 percent in urban population.

The point of regressions is not merely to predict statistics for particular cases. That can be very useful if you don't have actual information for that particular case, which can be a common problem with some kinds of data. Rather, regressions are an especially powerful way to express the association between two variables.

Finding the Right Rate

Now that we know how to operate the program and have a little more insight into some statistical measures, we should consider the variables a little more closely. Note that our rates have a variety of denominators as well as numerators. Per capita income means the number of dollars per person. The data on radios in 1930 concerned the percent of families with radio sets, not individual persons having radios. Often we are concerned with certain age groups. Back in Chapter 4, for example, we had data on persons over age 20 who could not read and write, while the 1930 information on illiteracy concerned persons age 10 and over who could not read and write. When we work with data on the number of people in various occupations, we often divide by the number of employed persons rather than by the total population, to get a reasonable measure of how the occupations compare.

Consider fertility. One way to calculate the birth rate is simply to count how many children are born during a given year and divide by the total population at that time. We know, however, that men don't have babies, and the proportion of the population that is male varies from state to state. If we keep the men in the denominator, even though none of them is giving birth, our correlations will partly reflect the balance of the sexes, rather than births. We would get a better rate if we divided by the female population, but little girls don't have babies, and older women can't either. Social scientists who study population trends, **demographers**, often use the female population aged 15 through 44 as the denominator, because it better reflects the segment of the whole population that might have babies.

We call a denominator like this the **population at risk**. This is not to imply that babies are dangerous. The term is merely a way of pointing out that some people have a chance of contributing to the numerator in our rates and others do not. For the denominator, it is best to select only those who can contribute to the numerator, so the denominator should be as close to the population at risk as you can make it.

Suppose you wanted to compare states in terms of how dangerous they were for police. You could collect data on how many police suffered on-the-job injuries during the past year, and these numbers would be the numerators for your rates. What do you use for the denominators? The total population of the state would not be good, because states differ in what proportions of their residents are cops. Because the population at risk is the police, you should use the number of police as the denominator.

The Suicide Rate

The variety of ways we can calculate rates can be a bit bewildering. It takes serious thought and hard examination of available data to decide which rates are the best ones for a particular project, and often you have to accept some compromises along the way. An excellent example concerns the classic work on suicide by the French sociologist Emile Durkheim (1897).

Durkheim's study is a classic not only because it was done nearly a century ago, but also because it was a major step in the development of sociology as an autonomous discipline. Seeking to explain variations in suicide rates in terms of sociological variables, Durkheim rejected explanations based in other disciplines, such as psychology. To use a French expression, it was a tour de force. Suicide seemed the most lonely of acts, an individual taking the ultimate separation from society. If sociology could explain suicide, then the scope of our field must be vast and its significance great.

Perhaps the most famous of Durkheim's findings was that suicide rates were much higher in Protestant countries than in Catholic countries, and some of his data indicated that the same was true for the two religious traditions within certain nations. In Protestant areas of Europe, there were on average 190 suicides per million, compared with only 58 in Catholic areas (Durkheim 1897:152). The Protestant-Catholic difference in suicide rates has been taken as such a well-established fact that it has been called "sociology's one law" (Pope and Danigelis 1981). Some have criticized Durkheim's research methods, however, and today there is good reason to doubt that Protestantism and Catholicism really differ in their capacity to produce or prevent self-murder.

To start with, Durkheim was not really interested in comparing Protestants with Catholics. Instead, the part of his theory that drew in religion focused on the concept of **egoism**, which can be defined as weakness of social integration of the groups of which the individual forms a part (Durkheim 1897:209). Egoism is equivalent to excessive individualism and social disorganization; its opposite is social cohesion and stability. Cut off from the social support of the group, an individual is susceptible to many hazards, including suicide. A church can counteract egoism because it constitutes a more or less cohesive society, and Durkheim believed the Catholic church was a much more strongly integrated community than the Protestant church.

Thus, Durkheim might have preferred to work with data directly about the degree to which people were integrated into society through their churches, but no such data were available to him. Based on his assumption that Protestant and Catholic churches differed in social integration, he could use religious tradition as an indirect measure of integration. Today, somewhat more direct measures of religiously based social integration are available to us, notably the rate of membership in a church of any kind. Belonging to a church of either tradition certainly should provide more social integration than belonging to no church at all.

Actually, the alleged Protestant-Catholic difference in suicide rates was well known long before Durkheim wrote. Durkheim took much of his data directly from a book by Henry Morselli, who called "the influences of religion" among "the strongest motive powers which act on the will of man" (Morselli 1882:119). Writing about the same time as Morselli, Thomas Masaryk (1881) argued that suicide was stimulated by an historical process called **secularization**, the decline of religious faith and of the influence of the churches. (Incidentally, Masaryk received a rare honor for a sociologist when he was commemorated on United States postage stamps in 1960. However, this was for being the first president of the Czechoslovakian republic, rather than for his social research.)

For both Morselli and Masaryk, Protestantism was but one phase in secularization. These earlier authors believed that many aspects of religion, including the faith and hope it can give, prevented suicide. Thus, when Durkheim reduced religion to a mere indicator of social cohesion, he was making a sharp break with the research tradition in which he was working.

One problem with the quantitative research of a century ago was that the statistical techniques did not make it easy to handle several variables at once, something we will really begin doing in Chapter 13. If European countries differed in their suicide rates, which characteristics of those countries were responsible? Perhaps it was the level of economic and technical development, not the status of religion. In the 19th century, the nations most advanced in science and technology happened to be Protestant, while three centuries earlier the Catholic countries had been in the lead. Although Durkheim's work did not rest on ecological rates alone, all aspects of his work have been criticized for selective use of data to support his position (Pope 1976), and every aspect of the alleged Protestant-Catholic differences might be wrong.

American data on suicide and church membership have been available since the beginning of this century. In 1906, just nine years after Durkheim wrote, the Bureau of the Census did a special count of church members, and the government also published suicide statistics for 75 cities with populations over 50,000. Similar data were collected in 1916 and 1926, so we can test Durkheim's theory at three points in time (Bureau of the Census 1910, 1912, 1918, 1919, 1929, 1930; Bainbridge and Stark 1981).

The American religious data are incredibly rich. In 1926, information on a total of 232,154 churches representing 212 separate denominations with 54,576,346 members was tabulated. Published volumes contain numerous useful tables that are ready for secondary analysis, including sections giving membership for every single denomination in each city with 25,000 inhabitants, as determined by the previous decennial census. These volumes even provide membership figures for each county, and some of the state-level data are included in the dataset on your computer disk. How shall we turn all this information into rates?

The first step, always, is to think carefully about the theory being tested. Durkheim compared areas where Protestants predominated with areas where Catholics predominated, and

although he occasionally discussed other groups, the key comparison is Protestants versus Catholics. Most people in Europe or America identify themselves with one of these great traditions, but we can get much closer to Durkheim's theoretical analysis if we count only people actually participating in their religious denomination. The best way to do this is to focus just on the church members the census counted and to ask what proportion of them are Protestants or Catholics.

By far the easiest way to do the arithmetic is to calculate what proportion of the church members are Catholics. This is because there is only one Catholic church, so you can look just at two columns of figures, Catholics and the total of all denominations (which the census bureau was kind enough to add up for us). To get the number of Protestants, you would have to add up something like a hundred columns of figures, one for each separate denomination! So our first independent variable is the ratio of Catholics to all church members—that is, the proportion of church members who are Catholic.

I suggested, however, that one could get even closer to Durkheim's original theory, closer than he himself was able to get, by ignoring denomination and focusing instead on church membership. To do so, we calculate a church-member rate—that is, the proportion of all people who are members of a religious denomination. We can get the population figures from other publications of the census bureau and divide them into the total number of church members for all denominations listed in the religion censuses. Similarly, we can calculate a simple suicide rate from the number of suicides and the population figures.

The two religion rates are quite independent of each other. A high rate of church membership can be achieved with any mixture of Protestants and Catholics. One tradition or the other could predominate, regardless of how strong or weak religion was in the area. This would not be so if we had used total population as the denominator of the Catholic rate. Then the Catholicism variable would have been an integral part of the church-membership variable. It is essential to pick the right numerator and denominator for each of your rates, as we have done for our particular study.

Figure 11.8 shows the r correlations for 75 large American cities for the three years 1906, 1916, and 1926 (Bainbridge and Stark 1981). Note that both versions of Durkheim's theory predict negative correlations. Catholicism should be associated with low rates of suicide, and the social integration church membership affords should give it a negative association with suicide as well. The data support one of these two predictions but not the other. The church-member rate does have substantial negative correlations with the suicide rate, but the correlations for Catholicism are close to zero. What is worse, two of the correlations are positive and thus on the wrong side of zero. Taken together, the data from the three decades indicate that the proportion of church members who are Catholic has nothing to do with the suicide rate, thus disagreeing absolutely with Durkheim's empirical claim. However, his underlying theory that social integration prevents suicide is entirely supported by the powerful negative correlations between church membership and suicide.

It is often both possible and desirable to calculate rates that take into account more subtle qualities of the variables. The effort in creating the rates is greater, but the result is a closer measurement of real social factors. For example, the data for 1926 permit calculation of

adjusted rates, which are slightly better than the **raw rates** used for Figure 11.8 because they take into account two problems in the data on church membership.

First, in 1926 information on the number of Jews in each community was collected and tabulated by a trusted "special agent" hired by the Bureau of the Census, rather than by each separate congregation, as was the case for the Christian denominations. Because of this, and to satisfy Jewish concerns about privacy, data were not reported in as great detail as for other groups, and the published figures are estimates of the total number of persons with Jewish ethnic background, rather than actual counts of members of Jewish religious congregations. The role of Jews in Durkheim's theory is a bit complex anyway, and one doesn't know whether to include them in the analysis of Protestants and Catholics, leave them out, or do an entirely separate analysis of their connection, if any, to suicide rates.

In calculating an adjusted 1926 church-member rate, I chose to subtract the Jewish estimates from both the numerator and the denominator. Doing so is equivalent to assuming that the rates of active religious participation are about the same for Jews and Christians, an assumption that was probably not far wrong for the 1920s.

The second reason for creating adjusted rates is that denominations differed in whether they counted small children or only those who had experienced baptism or confirmation

FIGURE 11.8
Religion and Suicide in 75 Cities, 1906–1926

	Correlation (r) with the Rate of	
	Catholics/ church members	Church members/ population
1926 Suicides/population	− 0.18	− 0.56
1916 Suicides/population	0.07	− 0.32
1906 Suicides/population	0.03	− 0.40

in adulthood or the teenage years. The 1926 census tried to compensate for this problem by asking each church how many of its members were aged 12 or less, and how many aged 13 and above. For example, while only 4.3 percent of the 1,289,966 Northern Baptists and 6.1 percent of the 3,524,378 Southern Baptists were under 13, fully 28.2 percent of the 18,605,003 Roman Catholics were below this age.

Therefore, it seems best to concentrate on only the church members aged 13 and over. This means that the denominator of the church-member rate should be the number of people in the general population aged 13 and over in 1926, which one can estimate in a straightforward but tedious fashion from the censuses of 1920 and 1930. It makes sense to use the same denominator for the suicide rates, since few small children commit suicide.

Once we have calculated these adjusted rates, we can compare the results with those for raw rates. As it happens, data were available for 78 large cities in 1926. The average raw church-member rate is 56.1 percent, while the adjusted rate is 54.6 percent, almost the same. The correlation between these rates is 0.96, indicating that they are almost perfectly associated. Figure 11.8 reports results for 75 cities rather than 78, but even so the correlations are very similar. Using adjusted rates, the correlation between Catholicism and suicide is an insignificant − 0.11, while the correlation between the church-member rate and suicide is a substantial − 0.50.

Your dataset has both raw and adjusted church-member rates, variables 214 and 215, but the adjusted rate makes only the correction for Jewish population, not the one for age.

Sometimes a tiny adjustment is not worth the trouble, and you can check some scattergrams for these two variables to see whether it was in this instance.

When Stark, Doyle, and Rushing (1983) set out to do a parallel analysis with more recent data, they faced a similar challenge to calculate the best possible rates. Their data on church membership came from a private survey of denominations done in 1971, which was not nearly so complete as the ones the census bureau had done decades earlier. Not only did the survey miss Jews entirely; it left out large black denominations, too. However, estimates of the number of ethnic Jews in various cities are published every year in the *American Jewish Year Book,* and surveys provide a rough guide on how to estimate rates of active religious participation. After studying a number of surveys, Stark (1980) became convinced that black churchgoing patterns and white patterns were very similar, and thus that a procedure like the one we used for Jews in 1926 would work for blacks in 1971. And the results were about the same. Although there was a correlation of − 0.37 between church membership and suicide for 217 metropolitan areas, there was no correlation between the suicide rate and the proportion of church members who were Catholic.

As you can see, there are often many decisions to make in creating rates. Because the results were about the same using the raw and adjusted rates for 1926, we can be especially confident in them. But the aim is always to get the very best rates you can; then you can use them with confidence in testing social theories.

Opportunities for Secondary Analysis of Official Data

As we explained in Chapter 4 in our discussion of historical sociology, sources of data can be divided into primary and secondary sources. An example of a primary source was the manuscript census schedules on which the census takers wrote their information as they collected it. An example of a secondary source is the official published summary of a census, filled with tables calculated from the original data. A standard approach to official statistics is called secondary analysis. **Secondary analysis** is the use of published information for purposes beyond those of the original researchers (Hyman 1972). Much of this chapter is devoted to one of the most common ways of putting old data to new uses: correlational analysis of rates for different states or cities. But there are other approaches as well, all requiring a little imagination but few demanding much mathematical expertise.

Here's an example from my own research on religion (Bainbridge 1989c). The college library had decided to throw out its copies of the older Australian censuses; like many books produced at the turn of the century on paper with high acid content, they were crumbling into what looked like corn flakes. Nobody used them, and there seemed no point in saving them. But because I'm a glutton for old data, I carried home a crumbling pile of ancient Aussie censuses.

To get a census-based story into the newspaper, you probably have to use the most recent data. "If it ain't new, it ain't news," is the journalistic motto. Science is not journalism, however, and scientific laws can be tested as well with old data as with new. I was especially interested in the social factors that produce or prevent minority opinions about religion, and I have always regretted that the U.S. census does not ask citizens what their religious affiliations are. But other nations do ask this, notably Canada, Australia, and Germany.

The 1911 Australian census identified a bewildering array of minority religious affiliations (Knibbs 1914). There were Spiritualists and Theosophists, Sikhs and Shintos, in addition to the usual Presbyterians, Baptists, and Methodists. Of particular interest were seven minority categories: atheist, agnostic, freethinker, no religion, other (indefinite), objectors, and Adventists. Atheists are convinced God does not exist, while agnostics believe it is impossible to know. Freethinkers often believe in God, but they refuse to let organized churches speak for them, and they are often vocal in their condemnation of conventional religion. Those who answered "no religion" to the census-taker's

question included many who were indifferent to religion as well as some who were hotly opposed to it. The "other (indefinite)" category was mainly Spiritualists and members of other cults. Objectors were people who objected to the question about religion and refused to answer it. Seventh-Day Adventism was one of the most active radical religious sects in Australia at the time.

These groups can be described as categories of religious deviance, because only small numbers of Australians belonged to them, and the typical citizen may have been a bit suspicious of them. Sociologists of religion believe that geographic migration greatly stimulates religious deviance. That is, people who move from one place to another will be more likely to adopt a strange religion or to abandon religion altogether than will people who stay put. To move means to leave one's church congregation, and one may not join another congregation near the new home. Also, people who move are generally freer from social factors, such as the influence of close friends, that prevent them from trying novel alternatives of all kinds, including orientations to religion.

The 1911 census listed how many men and women of each deviant religious category there were in each Australian state. But it did more: it stated where all of them had been born. And this information allows us to look at the data in a very different way from that of the Australian census department—in terms of migration. Figure 11.9 shows just a small part of one of the tables about the state of New South Wales in the census report, and it can help us understand the different ways the data can be analyzed. The original table in the 1911 census volume reports numbers of males giving each of 30 different responses to the census-taker's question about religious affiliation, for each of 75 answers to the question about birthplace. Adding in totals and subtotals, the table had fully 2,573 cells, and this was but one of 27 similar tables in its section of the census volumes!

As you can see in Figure 11.9, 51 of the atheists were born in New South Wales. Eleven had been born in Victoria, 6 in Queensland, and so

FIGURE 11.9
Male Residents of New South Wales, Australia, in 1911

State of Birth	Atheists	Agnostics	No Religion	Total
New South Wales	51	265	683	608,517
Victoria	11	75	197	42,701
Queensland	6	18	35	11,018
South Australia	6	15	75	13,005
Western Australia	1	1	4	1,253
Tasmania	6	11	26	5,209
Northern Territory	0	0	0	12
Same state	51	265	683	608,517
Other states	30	120	337	73,198

on. One way to analyze these data would be to add the figures together: $51 + 11 + 6 + 6 + 1 + 6 + 0 = 81$. Apparently, 81 native-born Australian male atheists were living in New South Wales in 1911. The right-hand column in the table shows how many native-born men of all religious persuasions were living in New South Wales, a total of 681,715; and 608,517 of them had been born in the state. To figure the rate of atheistic men per hundred thousand, divide 81 by 681,715 and multiply the result by 100,000. The answer is about 12 atheists per hundred thousand men *living* in New South Wales.

That is a perfectly valid way to analyze the data. Another is to focus on where the men were born, rather than where they live. To do this, you would have to go through eight census-report tables about men's religion and birthplace, counting the atheists born in New South Wales and also the total number of men born in that state. For example, the table for the state of Victoria showed 13,273 of its male residents had been born in New South Wales, and 3 of them were atheists. Adding the numbers from all the tables reveals that 661,079 men were born in New South Wales, and 68 of them were atheists. That works out to a rate of just over 10 atheists per hundred thousand men *born* in New South Wales.

Far more interesting for my research purposes was a third way of analyzing the data. Rather than focus on men living or born in a particular state of Australia, I could compare the rate for men living in the state where they were born with the rate for men living in a different state from the one they were born in—looking at the whole nation rather than any one state. The figures at the bottom of Figure 11.9 do this for the New South Wales data. In that state, 51 atheistic men had been born in state, and 30 had moved in from other states. The data for the state of Victoria show 58 atheistic men who had been born in that state and 10 who had been born elsewhere in Australia before moving to Victoria.

One goes through the tables adding together all male atheists born in the same state they currently reside in, and the total is 141, including the 51 in New South Wales and the 58 in Victoria. One also counts up all the men of all religious categories born in their state of residence, 1,588,162, and divides this number into 58, then multiplies the result by 100,000 to get the rate. It is about 9. Then one does the same for atheistic men born in a different state from the one they currently reside in, and the total for them is 97. The total of all religious categories who have moved since birth to a different state is 226,735. So the rate of male atheists for these migrants is (97/226,735) × 100,000 = 43.

Now we can compare the atheism rate for men born in state with that for men who have moved since birth. The rate for those born in state is 9 per 100,000, compared with 43 for the migrants. The male atheism rate for migrants is 4.8 times as big as the rate for those born in state. This is a very substantial difference, and it supports the theory that migration encourages religious deviance. But the analysis does not stop with male atheists. I had to do similar calculations for women, and for the six other categories of religious deviance. The results, shown in Figure 11.10, could not be more consistent, giving very solid support to the theory. In every case the rate for migrants is higher than that for those still living in their state of birth.

This is a good point to reaffirm some of the logic of formal operational science, stated in Chapter 1. We *start with a theory*, that migration permits or stimulates religious deviance. From this we *derive an hypothesis*, that rates for the seven categories of religious deviance will be higher for native-born Australians who live in a different state from the one they were born in than rates for native-born Australians living in their state of birth. Then we *systematically examine data* that we took from the published volumes of the 1911 census. The data are completely in line with the hypothesis, and therefore they support the theory.

But note! If we merely look at the rates, they do not tell us that migration causes religious deviance. They show a strong association, but not which variable is the cause and which the effect. It might be that religious deviance causes migration—perhaps angry neighbors chase young atheists away from their birthplaces, or atheists feel sufficiently uncomfortable surrounded by believers they have known

FIGURE 11.10
Geographic Mobility and Religious Deviance in Australia, 1911

| Religion | Number | Rate per 100,000 population | | Ratio of other/same |
		Born in same state	Born in other state	
MALES:				
Atheist	238	9	43	4.8
Agnostic	1,294	53	203	3.8
Freethinker	1,451	59	226	3.8
No religion	4,049	183	507	2.8
Other (indefinite)	1,963	95	203	2.1
Objectors	39,119	2,009	3,179	1.6
Adventists	2,014	104	163	1.6
FEMALES:				
Atheist	47	2	6	3.0
Agnostic	394	18	53	2.9
Freethinker	330	16	39	2.4
No religion	1,289	68	103	1.5
Other (indefinite)	1,479	77	126	1.6
Objectors	22,816	1,252	1,394	1.1
Adventists	2,014	138	302	2.2

all their lives that they go voluntarily—or that both migration and religious deviance are caused by some third factor about which we have no data.

The point cannot be made too often. Correlation does not prove causation. If you have stated a causal theory, however, and the data are in line with hypotheses derived from it, then you are justified in saying that your correlations support your theory about causes. But sometimes everything goes very wrong, as the following story illustrates.

_____ A Story of Scientific Scandal

Soon after the 1840 census of the United States was published, numerous readers discovered that data on rates of insanity appeared to demonstrate slavery was good for blacks. _The Southern Literary Messenger_, a highly influential periodical published in Richmond, Virginia, made the case in its issue for June, 1843. A table extracted from the census showed the number of whites and blacks in each state, the number of insane and "idiots" (the seriously mentally retarded), and their proportions to the populations. A simple calculation showed that there was one insane or idiotic white for every 978 whites. In the slave states, there was one insane or idiotic black for every 1,605 blacks, but in the free states the proportion was 1 in 143.

It used to be common to present statistics in this way, as ratios in which the cases of interest are expressed as a numerator of 1, and the total population as whatever figure gives the right ratio. There are 100 U.S. senators, and one of them, Daniel Patrick Moynihan, happens to be a sociologist. So we could say there is 1 sociologist for every 100 senators. But the whole Congress, House and Senate combined, has 535 members, so that is 1 sociologist for every 535 members of Congress. And there is about 1 senator for every 5 members of Congress (100 out of 535). We got this last figure by dividing 535 by 100, getting 5.35, and throwing away the fraction. Today, of course, we use a different method: comparing rates that all have the same denominators and bases. For example, instead of dividing 535 by 100, we divide 100 by 535 and often express the result as a percent.

Figure 11.11 is based on the table published in _The Southern Literary Messenger_, and expresses the data as rates per 100,000 blacks. The top of the table lists 15 states in which less than 10 percent of blacks were enslaved. Indeed, these were "free states," and the tiny numbers of slaves in them may have been visiting in the company of their owners. Altogether, there were 171,523 blacks in these free states, and 1,189 of them were diagnosed insane or idiotic, producing a rate of 693 per 100,000. The bottom of the table lists 13 slave states in which more than half of all blacks were enslaved. Their combined black population was 2,755,988, with 1,702 insane or idiotic, for a rate of 62 per 100,000. Correlation coefficients had not yet been invented in 1840, but this simple analysis of rates shows a clear difference between the free and slave states.

The Southern Literary Messenger argued that this proved slavery was good for blacks. It is hard to think of a more shocking example of apparently scientific research than this, and I hope you can hang on until we tell the end of the story, paying serious attention to the research methods involved.

The magazine's analysis went so deeply as to argue that climate could not be the cause of the differences in rates of insanity, because states with similar climates still showed very different rates if one was slave and the other free. In terms of the social-scientific standards of the day, the article was well reasoned, and it drew upon several sources of empirical data to make its case. The anonymous author claimed to detest slavery, yet professed to be convinced by his data and by the testimony of history that "it is extremely difficult, if not impossible, for two races to prosper together of different

FIGURE 11.11
Slavery and Insanity among Blacks in the 1840 Census

State	Black Population	Percent Slaves	Black "Insane" and "Idiots"	
			Number	Rate per 100,000
Maine	1,355	0.0	94	6,937
Vermont	730	0.0	13	1,781
Massachusetts	8,669	0.0	200	2,307
New York	50,031	0.0	194	388
Ohio	17,345	0.0	165	951
Indiana	7,165	0.0	75	1,047
Illinois	3,598	0.0	79	2,196
Michigan	707	0.0	26	3,678
Pennsylvania	47,918	0.1	187	390
New Hampshire	538	0.2	19	3,532
Rhode Island	3,243	0.2	13	401
Connecticut	8,122	0.2	44	542
New Jersey	21,718	0.3	73	336
Wisconsin	196	5.6	3	1,531
Iowa	188	8.5	4	2,128
Delaware	19,524	13.3	28	143
Washington, D.C.	13,055	36.0	7	54
Maryland	151,815	59.1	141	93
Louisiana	193,954	86.9	45	23
Virginia	498,859	90.0	384	77
North Carolina	268,549	91.5	221	82
Kentucky	189,575	96.1	180	95
Tennessee	188,583	97.1	152	81
Florida	29,584	97.2	12	41
Missouri	59,814	97.4	68	114
South Carolina	335,314	97.5	137	41
Arkansas	20,400	97.7	21	103
Georgia	283,697	99.0	134	47
Mississippi	196,581	99.3	82	42
Alabama	339,263	99.4	125	37

civilization, and distinguished by ineffaceable marks, unless one is subordinate to the other" (anonymous 1843, p. 348).

These findings were powerful ammunition for slavery's greatest defender, John C. Calhoun, then secretary of state of the United States. In a letter concerning admission of Texas as a slave state, which he wrote to Lord Richard Pakenham, the British ambassador, on April 18, 1844, he claimed that the data proved the necessity of slavery for blacks, especially where their numbers are great and it would be impossible to deal with the vast increase of insanity and other social problems that he felt would inexorably follow their emancipation (Calhoun 1855, Vol. 5, p. 337). Calhoun claimed the combined rate for the deaf and dumb, blind, idiotic, and insane was seven times as high for blacks in the free states as in the slave states, and on another occasion he is said to have remarked, "Here is proof of the necessity of slavery. The African is incapable of self care, and sinks into lunacy under the burden of freedom. It is a mercy to him to give him this guardianship and protection from mental death" (quoted in Jarvis 1873: 135).

Quantitative social-scientific research appeared to support the institution of slavery, and high government officials were basing public statements upon this evidence (Litwack 1961:40–46). Thus it was important for the society, as well as for the development of sociology, when Edward Jarvis demolished the empirical basis upon which these claims rested. In a series of journal articles, he demonstrated that the tabulations of the 1840 census contained numerous errors that tended to inflate rates of insanity and idiocy for blacks.

Conducted years before mechanical data tabulation was available, the 1840 census depended upon the census takers themselves to do much of the adding. The data forms consisted of huge grids of rows and columns, into which the census taker wrote the numbers of persons in each category. Both in the data collection and in adding town totals, it was all too easy for him to place a number in the wrong column. Similar errors could occur at the state level and when the printed volumes were prepared. Errors that moved a few blacks into the white column in Northern states would not much distort the white totals, because they were large numbers, but moving a few whites into the black column could grossly distort its total, and thus substantially inflate a rate calculated upon it.

The first error that Jarvis noticed was for Worcester, Massachusetts. The 1840 census stated that 151 of the inhabitants of this town were black, and 36 of these were under age 10. Yet with equal confidence the census reported that 133 of these blacks were insane—88 percent of all the blacks and 116 percent of those aged 10 and over! Jarvis quickly found that the 133 white inmates of the Worcester State Asylum had been mistakenly moved into the column for black insane when the data were tabulated. Five Massachusetts towns were

counted as having no blacks at all, but 10 insane blacks! A dozen Michigan towns lacked blacks but were reported to have insane blacks. Dryden, New York, had no blacks, but 2 of them were insane and 2 were blind. The census was crazy, not the blacks.

One version of the story trivializes Jarvis's discovery and deserves to be refuted. According to Albert Deutsch, "as luck would have it, a broken leg and a curious mind resulted in a startling discovery regarding inaccuracies in the 1840 census. The broken leg and curious mind both belonged to Dr. Edward Jarvis, a versatile physician . . . with a growing passion for statistical research. . . . In 1842, Dr. Jarvis found himself confined to his bed with a broken leg. His active mind requiring exercise, he picked up the printed census of 1840 and started examining the figures and the methods used in compiling them" (Deutsch 1944:474, cf. Grob 1978:45). Based on and embellishing an earlier attribution of the discovery to a broken leg (Wood 1885:10), this story misses the crucial process by which Jarvis in fact made the discovery, one of great interest from the standpoint of the sociology of science.

Jarvis did indeed break his leg. The accident occurred when a boy's firecracker startled Jarvis's horse as he was returning home after delivering a manuscript to the editor of the *Christian Examiner* in Cambridge, Massachusetts (Jarvis 1873:133). But this occurred on June 13, 1843, after Jarvis had already published his first essays on the flaws in the 1840 census. His recuperation merely gave him extra time to continue work he had already begun. Jarvis turned to the 1840 census not out of boredom, but with a professional interest and hope that analysis of the great trove of data might illuminate sources of social problems like insanity. Indeed, Jarvis was one of the first to discover the apparently high rates of insanity among free blacks, saying they "had staggered him from the moment he saw the report" (Jarvis 1873:135). At first he not only took those data at face value but believed they strongly supported his theories about social causes of mental illness.

In July, 1842, while he was still a resident of Louisville, Kentucky, Jarvis submitted to the *Boston Medical and Surgical Journal* an article on the census, which the journal published in its September 21 issue (Jarvis 1842a). He began with three tables giving data on insanity of white and "coloreds" for both free and slave states, including proportions he had calculated that were similar but not identical to the ones given the following year by the *Southern Literary Messenger.* They indicated that 1 colored out of 162.4 was insane in Northern states, but only 1 in 1,558 in Southern states. Before attempting to explain the differences, Jarvis noted that the census reports had failed to identify a substantial portion of the cases of the insane, and he cited several higher estimates the states themselves had made. He expressed the hope that errors were evenly distributed, and thus that scientific use could be made of the statistics despite their incompleteness. He commented upon the slavery finding, not to support the institution of slavery but to find in its effect a general rule about social causes:

> Slavery has a wonderful influence upon the development of moral faculties and the intellectual powers; and refusing man many of the hopes and responsibilities which the free, self-thinking and self-acting enjoy and sustain, of course it saves him some of the liabilities and dangers of active self-direction. If the mental powers and the propensities are kept comparatively dormant, certainly they must suffer much less from misdirection or over-action. So far as this goes, it proves the common notion, that in the highest state of civilization and mental activity there is the greatest danger of mental derangement; for here, where there is the greatest mental torpor, we find the least insanity. . . . It is a common and a probable theory, that the development of insanity has kept pace with the progress of civilization; and that the great disproportion between the number of lunatics among the free whites and the slave blacks in the United States, surely

tends to corroborate this doctrine. (Jarvis 1842a:119, 121)

The proposition that civilization increased insanity was long one of Jarvis's favorite theories, and he published many articles arguing that people of any race would show high rates of insanity if their minds were unsettled by too much education and too many freedoms in life. Jarvis was in favor both of education and freedom, and he viewed insanity as an unfortunate but necessary price of progress. Although he detested slavery, Jarvis was thoroughly committed to theories about the human mind that seemed amply supported by the data from the 1840 census. Thus it was a remarkable turnabout, in the November 30 issue of the Boston journal, when Jarvis (1842b) retracted his analysis. Delving deeper into the data, he had discovered profound flaws.

Over the following months, Jarvis continued to document errors in the census volumes. In January 1844, he published in *The American Journal of the Medical Sciences* an expanded analysis that noted the continuing spread of the false news of slavery's mental benefits. This piece was published again and again in journals, magazines, and newspapers, in Europe as well as America. Then Jarvis called for a congressional investigation to determine the source of the errors and to explore the possibility of retabulation in case most mistakes turned out to have been made after the enumerators had finished their work.

Jarvis's discovery soon became known to the free black community, through the work of James McCune Smith, a black physician who had obtained his degrees in Glasgow, Scotland, because American universities were not yet open to people of his color. Writing to the *New York Tribune*, Smith remarked, "Freedom has not made us mad; it has strengthened our minds by throwing us upon our own resources, and has bound us to American institutions with a tenacity which nothing but death can overcome" (quoted in Litwack 1961:44). A mass-meeting of blacks in New York voted approval of his memorial to the Senate of the United

States, pointing out the errors and requesting that the census be officially reexamined (Morais 1976:32).

Jarvis himself wrote a memorial to the House of Representatives, documenting gross census errors in education and occupation statistics, as well as in those for insanity and idiocy, and formally requested an investigation (Jarvis, Thornton, and Brigham 1845). Directed by the House of Representatives to consider the challenge made by Jarvis and his associates, on February 8, 1845, Calhoun replied that an examination done at his direction confirmed the high rates of insanity among free blacks (Calhoun 1855, Vol. 5, p. 459). This cynical and scientifically unsupported defense of the pro-slavery thesis, however, apparently did not convince anyone.

It is noteworthy that the prime pro-slavery propaganda volume, *Cotton Is King* (Elliott 1860) contained an essay claiming high crime rates for free blacks, but said nothing about rates of insanity and idiocy. A Southern congressman told Jarvis, however, "that the census was in error in this respect, 'but,' he added, 'it is too good a thing for our politicians to give up, and many of them have prepared speeches based on this, which they cannot afford to lose' " (Jarvis 1873:136).

An article from a New York newspaper, reprinted a decade after the census in the *American Journal of Insanity* (anonymous 1851), prompted Jarvis to set the record straight once more, adding further evidence to his case and stating: "The refutation was complete and satisfactory. The errors of the census, and the thorough groundlessness of the theory of the preponderant liability of the free African, or colored race, to insanity or defect of vision, hearing or voice, over the slave African, was demonstrated beyond all question" (Jarvis 1852:270). Nonetheless, variants of the pro-slavery thesis continued to appear until the 20th century (Thomas and Sillen 1972; Warheit, Holzer, and Arey 1975; Williams 1986). Jarvis had refuted it, and he devoted much of his subsequent career to establishing official data collection on a sound basis that might prevent a recurrence of this scientific scandal.

The Necessity of Care in Using Official Data

If you collect your own data, through interviews or other means that you can monitor personally, you will be aware of the limitations of your information. Unfortunately, however, researchers sometimes place too much confidence in officially collected data. The story of Jarvis and the 1840 census illustrates that we cannot be too careful in checking out official data in every possible way, and that we should not place undue weight on findings based on them.

The story also illustrates that unless the researcher is very careful to subject his or her own conclusions to sharp criticism, personal biases can distort scientific research. The supporters of slavery who quickly accepted the connection between freedom and insanity were certainly guilty of political bias. And Jarvis himself almost fell prey to a scientific bias, because the data seemed to support his favorite theory. But his questioning mind forced him to delve deeper when he found an error, and he eventually uncovered the myriad errors that rendered the insanity data completely useless. When the issue is of great social significance, such as the effects of slavery, researchers have a special responsibility to be careful.

Jack D. Douglas (1967) asserted that official suicide rates were so severely flawed as to render them useless in sociological research. With Durkheim's famous study in mind, he argued that low rates in Catholic areas reflected a Catholic tendency to hide suicides. Assuming that Catholicism was more strongly against suicide than was Protestantism (something that Durkheim himself denied), it would be impossible to tell whether the negative correlation between Catholicism and suicide reflected a real difference in the rate of self-murder or merely a difference in the likelihood that a suicide would be counted as such. The irony, as noted earlier, is that there probably isn't a negative correlation in the first place.

That one can imagine a way in which official statistics could be flawed does not prove that the data are lousy. After all, it was statistical research using official data, not Douglas's unsupported charges, that cast the greatest doubt on the alleged difference between Catholics and Protestants on suicide. As a budding researcher, you should think about criticisms like Douglas's and use every scientific means at your disposal to ensure that both your data and your methods are as good as possible, but you should not become paralyzed by doubt.

The best course is to do what some sociologists call **triangulation**, a word we first encountered in Barbara Heyl's life-history research. This is a metaphor; we are not referring to real triangles. If you are lost and are trying to find out where you are using maps and other navigation aids, one of the best ways is to take sightings on various landmarks and "triangulate" your position, which basically means drawing triangles based on two or more landmarks. In sociology, triangulation means using two or more research methods to attack the same question. If, for example, surveys and ecological studies both support a given theory, then the theory is in pretty good shape.

Often, however, this is not practical. It is very difficult, for example, to find out the religious beliefs of people who have killed themselves. Even whether or not they were churchgoers is tough to determine, because their friends and relatives may exaggerate the suicides' closeness to God as part of their coping with grief, and thus may not give correct answers to your questions.

A few questionnaires, including the General Social Survey, have included questions about attitudes toward suicide, but the vast majority of people answering will never come close to taking their lives, and their answers are hypothetical in the extreme. A correlation—or the lack of one—may tell you nothing about which people might ever actually kill themselves. Just for fun, I did include such questions in a survey I administered to 1,465 college students. Catholics expressed slightly less acceptance of suicide than did Protestants, but the big difference was between the respondents who described themselves as religious and those who did not. Acceptance of the idea of suicide was greatest by far among respondents with no religion, but those findings are about attitudes so far removed from actual suicide that I don't take them seriously, and I have never published them.

One response to the question about official statistics is to accept it as a research challenge. Donald Black (1970) studied police encounters in the field, investigating the process by which a dispute produced an official record. He found that a crime was more likely to be registered officially if it was serious, and that the behavior of the person complaining about the incident was also a factor. Black found no evidence of racial discrimination, although one might guess that this could be a factor in some parts of the country. Indeed, whatever the factors that shape the collection of official statistics, they have to operate differently in different communities to have any effect on correlations based on their rates. If exactly half the burglaries that happened in each state were reported to the FBI, correlations based on the FBI's rates would be exactly the same as if they were based on all of the burglaries. And if reporting does vary from place to place, it ought to be possible to measure that variation and take it into account in quantitative analyses.

Sociological criticisms of official data have usually centered on disreputable phenomena like suicide and crime, which some people might want to hide. Also, city officials sometimes question whether the census has counted their populations correctly—an important issue for them because federal funding and legislative apportionment rest on census counts—usually arguing that the census has missed members of minority groups and highly mobile people. But many ordinary census variables seem as solid as any data a sociologist is ever likely to get.

Not all rates used in ecological analyses are based on government data. With a certain amount of effort, a sociologist can count listings of various kinds of businesses in the yellow pages of telephone directories, for example, something I have spent many hours doing. In one study (Bainbridge 1989a),

I tabulated addresses of Christian Science Healers, Transcendental Mediators, and Scientologists from lists the organizations themselves provided, and I counted "New-Age" spiritual centers and gay bars that advertised themselves in traveler's guidebooks. Once we have good numbers, however, our problems may not be over, as the following section illustrates.

Methodological Problems with Research Using _____ Ecological Rates

A century and a half of experience with statistical rates has made us aware of two difficulties that we must be alert for, the *ecological fallacy* and *Galton's problem*. We must also address the issue of *autocorrelation*. Often, we can prevent these problems or solve them if they arise, and the following is meant as advice on how to do good work of the kind described in this chapter, not as a warning to avoid using these often effective research techniques.

The Ecological Fallacy

The most infamous error in statistical comparison of rates between different geographical areas is called the **ecological fallacy**. This is the mistake of assuming that individuals have the typical characteristics for their areas. For example, household servants tend to live in rich towns. The ecological fallacy would be to conclude that household servants are rich. We know they aren't. Rather, they live in rich towns because their employers are rich.

The most famous example of the ecological fallacy concerns immigration and illiteracy in the 1930 census (Robinson 1950; cf. Hannan 1971). Early in this century, vast numbers of people came to the United States each year, and a relatively high proportion of them were unable to read and write. In 1930, only 1.5 percent of native-born whites aged 10 and older were illiterate. At the same time, however, 9.9

percent of foreign-born whites aged 10 and over were unable to read and write.

But if you check the correlation between the illiteracy rate (variable 244) and the immigration rate (variable 231), using our software, you will get a surprise. Instead of a positive correlation, you will find a big negative one!

A number of sociologists claim that the ecological fallacy is so serious a problem that it makes research using geographically based rates utterly meaningless. But most of these scholars, I think, are opposed to quantitative research of any kind and merely use the ecological fallacy as ammunition in their attack on numbers. As we saw in Chapter 7, survey research also has its problems, and the issue of response bias is probably as serious a problem for surveys as the ecological fallacy is for correlational analysis of rates. The problems are not insuperable, however, by any means.

In Chapter 13, we will suggest that the ecological fallacy is nothing but an example of **spuriousness**, the distorting effect of an unmeasured third variable on the correlation between two other variables. In any case, the ecological fallacy can apply only when the researcher attempts to test theories about individuals on the basis of rates for groups. Often this is the intent of research using geographically based rates, but often it is not. Instead, our theory may concern characteristics of the community, not characteristics of the individual. For example, some researchers employ variables that describe the degree of division of labor in different communities—such as how many different industries there are in town or how evenly distributed across various occupations the workers are—variables that have nothing to do with individuals (Frisbie 1984).

An example from my own research concerns the question of whether traditional religion prevented women from entering elite careers (Bainbridge and Hatch 1982). Some writers had suggested that religion prescribed very traditional roles for women and thus blocked their opportunities to enjoy highly rewarding careers in such fields as medicine and law. To test this theory, we assembled three datasets based on the U.S. and Canadian censuses. The independent variable was the rate of church membership. Dependent variables included the percent of doctors who were women and the percent of lawyers who were women.

The theory we were testing was not simply that religious women might be forced by their own personal beliefs to avoid seeking medical and legal careers. Rather, the religiousness of the entire community was the issue. A woman's career is affected not only—or even primarily—by her own feelings. Opposition to women entering elite careers on the parts of parents, friends, educators, potential employers, and other members of the community may be even more important. Thus, we felt the ecological fallacy was not an issue. The theory being tested concerned the characteristics of communities, not individuals.

But even if you are using rates to test theories about individual traits and behaviors, moderate care in selecting and analyzing variables is probably sufficient to defeat the problem of the ecological fallacy. Researchers have turned up few really striking examples of it in the nearly 40 years since sociologists were alerted to the example of immigration and illiteracy. The possibility of the fallacy should warn researchers using all methodologies, qualitative as well as quantitative, to avoid the sin of arrogance. Each study and each research method can contribute at most a few pieces to the puzzle, and we should recognize the modesty of our individual scientific accomplishments.

Galton's Problem

The error of wrongly assuming that each of your cases is completely independent of the others is often called **Galton's problem**, after the person who first identified it. It raises the general question of what is a proper case in ecological studies.

Here is a silly example, but one that gets the idea across. Suppose we did a study in northwestern Europe on the effect of alcoholic beverages on human speech. Wine drinkers, it turned out, spoke through their noses, sounding as if they suffered nasal congestion. And beer drinkers made a lot of wet sounds deep in their throats, like *ach* and *och*. Does this prove that wine produces nasal congestion, while beer erodes the throat? Not at all. It might merely reflect that the French drink wine, the Germans drink beer, and their languages differ in the funny sounds they make.

Part of the problem is that the scientists doing this research project might believe their results were highly statistically significant, when in a sense they were not. Even if we studied 1,000 little towns across the border between France and Germany, and interviewed 10,000 people, we are really only comparing two nations. Instead of an N of 1,000 or 10,000, in a sense we have only 2 cases.

Of course, one way to find out what's really happening in a study like this is to include a question about the language spoken or the nation the respondent resides in. That is, we can treat Galton's problem as one of spuriousness, and hunt for the hidden variables that will reveal the truth. But Galton's problem has caused concern for ecological researchers throughout this century.

Melvin Ember (1971) has studied the seriousness of the problem using anthropological data on hundreds of societies around the world. One of his examples concerns the connection between cattle herding and the custom of bride price. In traditional European societies, the family of a bride often was expected to provide her with a dowry, valuable things that would become her husband's property (or at least be shared with the husband) when they married. Other societies of the world required almost the reverse, the husband having to pay the bride's family for the privilege of marrying her. This payment, called bride price, appears more common among societies that make a substantial portion of their livelihood out of herding cattle.

It would be wrong to leap to the conclusion that these societies treat women like cattle, to be bought and sold, and anthropologists have identified a number of social functions that the custom may serve. One explanation, however, dismisses the connection between bride price and cattle herding as a mere historical accident. Some have suggested that bride price just happened to be the custom of cattle-herding societies of the Middle East, and that these two features of society spread from there to adjacent parts of Africa and other nearby areas. To investigate this, Ember compared the results from datasets in which each case was a very different culture, with results from datasets in which many cases represented very similar cultures, as indicated by their having historically related languages. In his particular study, Galton's problem proved unimportant, but we can never be sure the same is true of our own data.

A standard solution in ecological research is to select a unit of analysis that maximizes the distinctness of the cases. The unit of analysis in our present dataset is probably not the best. We have already noted that New Mexico might be better considered two states, and one can make a good case for breaking California, New York, Florida, and Texas into more logical pieces. At the other extreme, New England looks to me like two states rather than six. There's the coast from Portsmouth to Greenwich, and there's the back country north and west of that. Cities may be better units of analysis than states, but many urban areas are artificially divided into many crazily drawn political

entities. So that it could collect and analyze data for areas that most closely approximated natural economic and social units, the census bureau invented Standard Metropolitan Statistical Areas—SMSAs—each one carefully assembled out of cities and counties.

Autocorrelation from Rates

The final problem we shall discuss probably does not really exist, but the rumor that it does is so firmly established within quantitative sociology that we shall have to discuss it. According to this rumor, it is invalid to rely upon correlations between variables that are rates with the same denominator (Schuessler 1974; Bollen and Ward 1979). For example, there may be a modest positive correlation between the percent who are female and the percent who attend church, because many studies have found that women are slightly more likely to attend church than are men. In this example, the X variable is the number of women in the state divided by the total population. The Y variable is the number of churchgoers divided by the total population. So each variable has the population in it, and thus we might expect a correlation merely because X and Y partly measure the same thing.

To understand this better, we must discuss **autocorrelation**, the tendency of two variables to correlate with each other simply because they contain some of the same data. Suppose I said that Catholics are more religious than Protestants, and that you can tell this because there is a correlation between the percent Catholic and the percent who are members of churches. You can test this with our state data. Look at a scattergram of the following two variables from the year 1926: Catholics/population (variable 216) and Church members RAW (variable 214). You will find a very strong correlation between Catholicism and church membership. Are you convinced that Catholics are more religious?

Don't be. Instead, consider what the two variables mean. The number of Catholics and the number of church members are both taken from a survey of American churches the census bureau carried out back in 1926. The percent Catholic is based on the number of members Catholic churches reported. The percent church members is based on reports from more than 200 denominations, of which one is the Roman Catholics. That is, we have counted Catholics in both variables—percent Catholic and percent church members. And Catholics are a substantial part of American church membership. When you correlate Catholics with church members, you are partly correlating Catholics with Catholics. This is autocorrelation.

Now, that's a clear example, but the problem was that we had Catholics in the numerators of both rates. Is autocorrelation a problem whenever your two variables are rates with the same denominator? Careful empirical and mathematical studies have shown that this is not the case (MacMillan and Daft 1979; Long 1979). Here is a simple analysis showing that correlation of rates generally does not have this defect.

Consider cases when variable X has the population in it and variable Y does, too. Something always has a positive correlation with itself. Therefore, if it is true that having the same denominator makes two rates correlate, the correlation will be a positive one.

Take the specific example of the positive correlation between the percent female and the percent church members. Is it a mistake, merely the result of autocorrelation between the denominators of the two rates? The answer can be found by looking at the correlation between the percent male and the percent church members. If autocorrelation is a fault, this correlation should also be positive. Try this with our software package, and you will find that there is a *negative* correlation between percent male and percent church members. In fact, it is exactly the same size as the correlation for females, but negative instead of positive. Autocorrelation would produce a positive correlation for both, or at least shift both a little bit in the positive direction. We see no evidence of this.

P R O J E C T S   F O R   C H A P T E R   1 1

The following six projects with the MAPS program help you learn the key principles of research with geographically based rates. The first project asks you to describe one of the 50 American states, while the second contrasts two ways of ranking the states, and the third describes the nine regional divisions of the nation. Project 4 lets you test classical theories of the effects of social instability, while the fifth lets you rummage through the dataset in search of interesting variables, and the sixth explores religion in its dual roles as independent and dependent variable. The principles of analysis are not very different from those used for interpretation of survey data, but these projects give you experience working with official government data and increasing your facility with computer analysis.

1. Describing a State. Select 20 variables in the MAPS dataset that you feel give a good picture of the social characteristics of a state. Also select one of the 50 states, perhaps the one your class is being taught in. Using information on the 20 variables, write a brief essay describing the state.

If this is done as a class project, everybody could be assigned the same state, or the various states of a region, or states expected to contrast strongly with each other. Then, each person can report to the class on one or two variables, not only reporting the information about the state but also defending the choice of variables and explaining why they are socially important.

2. Contrasting Two Rankings. Select two MAPS variables that give very different rankings of the states. Make a list of the states, either alphabetically or by region, and write the rankings of each state for the two variables after its name. Then write a brief essay explaining why the states ranked approximately as they did, contrasting the explanations for your two variables. You may find that maps of the two variables will help suggest ideas to you, as will the rankings themselves.

3. Describing the Nine Divisions. Switching back and forth between the map of the nine divisions (or "regions"), the map showing individual states (or Figure 11.2), and maps for various variables, try to develop a set of contrasting descriptions for the nine divisions. Everybody has a sense, for example, that New England differs from the Pacific divisions, but what chief characteristics most clearly distinguish them?

If this is done as a project for reports in class, it might be good to divide the class into nine teams or committees, each given the mission to describe one of the regions. Naturally, it may be that some of the lines dividing divisions are purely artificial, and you might want to conclude that there is nothing at all special about certain parts of the country. But I think you can achieve a distinctive description of each division if you can find the right variables.

4. Effects of Social Instability. Mindful of the discussion of suicide earlier in this chapter, propose a theory explaining why certain social phenomena will be more common in states with high levels of social instability, and uncommon in areas of stability. Find variables in the MAPS dataset that measure instability (or stability) and others that measure the phenomena that result from instability. Run the appropriate scattergrams to test your theory.

Your report should consist of a statement of the theory, a table of data reporting the r correlations you found, and a brief discussion of your findings. Do the data support your theory?

5. Finding Large, Interesting Correlations. Using the scattergram, find 10 really large correlations, either positive or negative, that are interesting to you. Then briefly explain (a sentence or a paragraph for each) why they are interesting.

An interesting correlation is one that teaches us something. An uninteresting correlation results simply from the way the variables were created, or is otherwise so thoroughly expected that it is not worth thinking about. The correlation between a variable and itself is uninteresting. Which ones are interesting is partly a matter of taste. For example, I find the 0.81 correlation between percent of the population that is urban (variable 27) and percent of dwelling units with public sewers (variable 176) to be interesting, but you might feel it is pretty obvious. Make a case for the interest you find in each of 10 big correlations.

6. Religion as Independent and Dependent Variable. Working entirely with the variables in group D (1920–1930 variables), find six variables that correlate significantly with the RAW church member rate (variable 214). For three of them, church membership should function as the independent variable, explaining some of their variation. For the other three, church membership should function as the dependent variable, its variation being explained by these other variables.

Write a paragraph about each of the six correlations, giving a brief justification for calling church membership either the independent or the dependent variable.

Such justifications have to be based on a theoretical interpretation of how church membership relates to the other variable, but we do not expect you either to get deeply into a theory or to draw upon any sociological literature. Instead, use your own common sense to analyze how religion might influence other variables or be influenced by them.

CHAPTER SUMMARY

Social scientists analyze rates for geographical areas, an approach called *human ecology* and *social ecology* because it examines the social environment. *Percent* means "per hundred," and percentages are the most familiar rates used in social science. Dividing one number by another produces a *ratio*. The number that does the dividing is the *divisor* or the *denominator*. The number it divides into is the *numerator*. The *base* is the number multiplied by the ratio to get the final result—100 for percentages. Any statistic that expresses a ratio in terms of a base—such as percent or per million—is called a *rate*. Rates allow one to compare two groups that are of different sizes. For example, we can compare New York with Las Vegas to see which one really is wilder.

The MAPS program is an extensive statistical module, comparable to XTAB, which is designed for analyzing rates. It can project maps of the 50 American states on the screen, even if the computer lacks graphics capability, and it contains 255 variables describing the states. Maps of particular variables display the rates in four categories (high to low), either as different colors or shadings. Data on the percent of families that owned radios in 1930 illustrate how one can interpret such maps.

The program shows statistics for any variable, including further information about what the variable means. In the case of "Hispanic" it says, "Persons of Spanish heritage per 100,000." States can be ranked from high to low, and inspection of rankings for several variables can provide hints about how the variables are related. For example, states with few radios in 1930 were poor in 1980.

The MAPS program will generate scattergrams for pairs of variables. A *scattergram* is a graph that shows where all the cases stand in terms of two variables, X and Y. It is the equivalent of a crosstab but is designed for continuous variables. A scattergram of urban population and per capita income illustrates a positive correlation, and the scattergram program displays both *correlation* and *regression* coefficients. Cases that stand far from the others in a scattergram are *outliers*, as Alaska is for these two variables.

Ecological data are *aggregate data*, which combine information about many individuals to make each rate. Such data tend to produce larger correlations than variables based directly on individuals.

Regressions are related to r-type correlations, but they distinguish the independent variable from the dependent variable, allowing one to predict the value of the dependent variable for a particular case if one knows the value of the independent variable. A regression analysis in which X is the independent variable and Y the dependent variable produces two numbers, A and B. A represents the predicted value of the dependent variable if the value of the independent variable is zero. B represents the increase in the dependent variable for every unit increase in the independent variable. For example, if we know how much of the state of Ohio is urban, we can predict the average per capita income of the state from a regression analysis for these two variables.

Note that our rates have a variety of denominators as well as numerators, and it is important to pick the right ones for research studies having particular aims. For example, when we work with data on the number of people in various occupations, we often divide by the number of employed persons rather than by the total population. *Demographers* often use the female population aged 15 through 44 as the denominator in calculating birth rates, rather than the total population, because it better reflects the segment of the population that might have babies.

Durkheim's analysis of suicide rates was a classical study done following the ecological approach. Finding that rates were higher in Protestant areas than in Catholic areas, Durkheim developed theories of egoism and anomie to explain this difference. He worked with European data, but American data generally tend not to show Protestant-Catholic differences. One must be careful to calculate the most accurate rates, often adjusting for deficiencies in the original numbers. Secondary analysis of the 1911 Australian census provides another example of how to calculate and use rates in social research.

A story of scientific scandal concerns how the 1840 census was misused to support the institution of slavery in the South. When the 1840 census was published, several readers saw that rates of insanity among enslaved African-Americans were low compared to those for blacks in free states. Early American sociologist Edward Jarvis was able to show that the differences in rates were an illusion.

In social research, we must use triangulation before we can have great confidence in results. This means using two or more research methods to attack the same question, each compensating to some extent for the limitations of the other.

Several common methodological problems with ecological research have been the focus of concern for sociologists. The *ecological fallacy* is the mistake of assuming that individuals have the typical characteristics for their areas. *Galton's problem* is the error of wrongly assuming that each of one's cases is completely independent of the others. Some sociologists believe it is invalid to rely upon correlations between variables that are rates with the same denominator, because this introduces *autocorrelation*. This fear is unfounded.

KEY CONCEPTS FOR CHAPTER 11

Correlations and Regressions

CHAPTER OVERVIEW

This chapter provides further practice working with official data and geographically based rates, while teaching the elementary aspects of Pearsonian correlations and two-variable regressions. The chief novelty is the effective use of the computer to make the concepts come alive and to provide correct intuitive understandings. A new dataset consists of 48 variables on religion for the nine regions (or divisions) of the United States. The small number of cases makes it easy to calculate the

coefficients, especially with the help the computer provides, so students can gain comfortable experience arriving at interesting quantitative results.

The GRAF program includes two modules that work with the regional religion dataset. One shows how the coefficients are calculated, giving all the steps for associations between any pair of variables you select. The other, which requires a computer with simple graphics capability, shows a scattergram of nine data points graphing a pair of variables for the nine regions. A straight line appears, running through the points, which you can rotate around the intersection of the two means. Numbers on the side of the screen give you the changing equation of this line as you rotate it, along with the equation for the regression line that runs closest to the data points, and a resid- ual distance from the points to the line. You can rotate the line either by eye or by watching the residuals—both a calculated residual distance and actual pictures of the residual lines (if you wish them)—until it matches the regression line. This beautifully illustrates what linear regressions are.

The Regional Dataset

Thirty-three of the 48 variables in the regional dataset came from research Rodney Stark and I did for our book *The Future of Religion*. Because our conclusions were somewhat controversial, I feel it appropriate to report that the book won the 1986 Outstanding Book of the Year award of the Society for the Scientific Study of Religion. The controversy came from the fact that we had a mixture of good news and bad news for those interested in religion. First, our theoretical analysis and empirical findings convinced us that religion had a future and would continue to be influential in human affairs. This was good news for the majority of the population who consider themselves religious, although I doubt that these folk really needed us to bolster their faith. But it was bad news for, and hotly contested by, some of our colleagues in sociology. As it happens, sociology is about the most secularized intellectual field there is, and outside of the sociology-of-religion associations, most sociologists who publish extensively seem to be atheists or agnostics.

Second, our work also forced us to the conclusion that the religion of the future would be significantly different from the religion of today. Specifically, some of the groups that are commonly called "cults" would be far more important in the future, and the traditional churches of today would lose influence. In the long run, we expected wholly new religious traditions to rise to prominence, perhaps even replacing the great world religions of today. You can see that this was bad news for readers of the book who had strong commitments to the old religious traditions, balancing off the good news we had for them. For present purposes, of course, you don't need to agree with us on any of these points. The full exposition of our theory and research is found in a pair of books (Stark and Bainbridge 1985, 1987).

An important part of the empirical research used the statistical techniques of the previous chapter and this one to analyze various religion variables expressed as rates for states, cities, and metropolitan areas. Our key proposition was that cults tend to emerge and rise to prominence wherever the standard churches have lost their grip. Thus we collected all the data we could on the geographical distribution of cults, and we employed whatever data we could find on the relative strength of standard churches in different parts of the United States, Canada, and Western Europe.

An important issue in the sociology of religion is secularization. This term has many competing definitions, almost as many as there are scholars who have used it. Most, however, consider **secularization** to be the historical process in which people come to have less and less faith in religion, and the churches come to have ever weaker influence. Some believe this will lead, sooner or later, to the death of religion (Wallace 1966). Our research seemed to contradict this theory, suggesting instead a different conception of secularization. At any given time in history, the most prestigious religious organizations and traditions are losing their faith in the supernatural and are moving closer to the dominant secular institutions of the society. So far, this sounds like the standard secularization thesis.

But although some parts of religion are gradually losing their grip on the supernatural and starting to wither away, other parts are gaining faith and strength. Some of these are vigorous religious organizations that have broken away from the failing, liberal churches and are reestablishing faith on a conservative basis; sociologists often call these *sects.* Other sources of religious renewal are novel religious innovations, at the extreme even wholly new religious traditions with fresh beliefs and practices; these may be called *cults.*

I must stress that the news media frequently use the term *cult* for weird, usually dangerous groups that violate public morals, but some of the groups that the news media call cults are really sects. Others are not religious at all, and only a tiny proportion of real cults fit the terribly negative stereotype of cults that the news media have been spreading for some years. Some scholars use the term *cult* to refer to any systematized ritual practice, even for very standard practices such as reverence for the Virgin Mary in Catholicism, and these scholars imply no disrespect at all when they use the word *cult* this way. Other scholars use the word to refer to groups that have powerful, charismatic leaders. But many in the sociology of religion, myself included, use the term *religious cult* to mean formal religious groups with novel or exotic beliefs and practices. Most of the groups so designated are quite harmless.

This confusion over the word *cult* illustrates an important point about empirical sociological research, when one is testing a theory that another scholar has proposed. When operationalizing concepts, it is essential to follow the definitions of key words that the theorist has provided. If you redefine the words, then you are no longer testing the theory you set out to test. Of course, it may sometimes be hard to operationalize concepts exactly as the original theorist intended them, and some theorists are painfully vague about what they really mean. Therefore, the researcher often has to work a bit on the theory before testing it. Any extensions to a theory, however, including derivations of testable hypotheses, have to be made very explicit in your research report. And major redefinition of words is generally a very bad practice.

Our theory suggested that sects were the short-term religious response to secularization, reviving the standard religious traditions of the society. But cults are the long-term response to secularization, and even though the vast majority of cults die shortly after being conceived, a very few of them rise and develop into major new religious traditions. Perhaps you can see why *The Future of Religion* is controversial, but my point in introducing these ideas here is to prepare us to analyze some of the data.

First, we need some measures of the strength of traditional religion, especially measures that vary from one region of the country to another. Note that our theory does not assume that some parts of the society are significantly weak in religious faith or in individual religious practice. This may or may not be the case, but unlike proponents of the secularization thesis, we do not predict it. However, if we find that traditional religious organizations are stronger in some areas than in others, then we can perform an empirical test of part of our theory. We predict merely that cults will be strong where the conventional churches are weak. If the churches are weak in some places, then we can use geographical analysis to test this prediction.

One very good measure of the strength of traditional churches is the rate of church membership, the percent of the population who are formal members of religious organizations. A survey of most major denominations, done in 1971, provided much of the data needed to calculate such rates (Johnson et al. 1974). Because the survey missed some black and Jewish groups, it was necessary to perform some minor corrections (Stark 1980), as outlined in the previous chapter, but we wound up with what we felt were pretty good measures of the percent of church membership for each region, state, and metropolitan area. Nationally, 56 percent of Americans were members of churches in 1971, but the variation by region was marked. Seven of the nine regions were above the average, the highest being the West South Central division at 65 percent, with New England in second place at 63 percent. The Mountain region was slightly below average, having a church member rate of 53 percent, still a majority. The Pacific region was the really deviant case. There, only 36 percent of people are members of conventional religious organizations, according to our estimate.

The five states with the lowest rates are the five states of the Pacific region: Hawaii, Alaska, California, Oregon, and Washington. States with high rates are not especially concentrated in the Old South but are spread across the other regions. Thus, in terms of formal church membership at least, we found no evidence of a Bible Belt. Instead, we found an unchurched belt, or perhaps we should say a cliff, because rates dropped way down to the shores of the Pacific ocean. I like to call it the Pacific Abyss. Five metropolitan areas had rates below 30 percent: Eugene (Oregon), Santa Rosa (California), Tacoma (Washington), Salinas (California), and Seattle (Washington). Thus, the church-member rate shows substantial variation, and it is ready to work for us in analyzing the geography of American religion.

The full list of variables, starting with the church-member rate, is given in Figure 12.1. Several other measures of standard religion were drawn from national surveys (Glock and Stark 1966; Greeley 1975; McCready and Greeley 1976). For some of these, we might not expect to find substantial regional variation. For example, belief in the existence of God does not reveal a Pacific Abyss. On average, across the nation, 84 percent of people polled professed belief. The proportion is slightly lower in the Pacific region, 81 percent, but this is within the margin of error for the survey. And the East South Central region, proverbially part of the Bible Belt, has exactly the same level of belief as the Pacific region, 81 percent. New England and the Middle Atlantic region come in at 82 percent, essentially an identical figure.

The first 11 variables measure various aspects of conventional religion. Variables 12 and 13 measure opposition to atheism, and thus reflect antagonism to antireligious views. Variables 14 and 15 are measures of the number of sects and cults with their headquarters in each region, data taken from *The Encyclopedia of American Religions* (Melton 1978). This massive set of volumes describes something like 1,200 formally incorporated American religious denominations, 417 of which we were able to identify as sects, and 501 as cults. Incidentally, the Process (from Chapters 2 and 3) was among the cults listed in this very thorough encyclopedia. For all of these groups, except one sect, a supplementary volume of the encyclopedia listed the address of the official national headquarters, which for several cults was the only branch. We counted how many of the sect and cult headquarters were in each of the nine regions and divided by the populations of the regions to get the rates in your dataset. Variable 16 was the percent of the encyclopedia's 501 cults that were founded before 1930.

Variables 17 through 30 are other cult measures, derived from a great variety of address listings. Four came from editions of the *Spiritual Community Guide* (Singh 1974, 1978). This was a very well-produced directory of what can be called "New Age" groups, including many religious cults of Oriental derivation and a variety of businesses that serve people with a similar perspective. The 1974 edition contained a classified listing of 2,470 such establishments around the United States, and Variable 17 is based on them. Slightly more than half of these (51.5 percent) were centers "devoted to the spiritual path, raising one's consciousness, transmitting higher knowledge or promoting universal love and unity" (Singh 1974:110). A further 3.4 percent were communities, residential centers that welcome friendly guests. I combined these two categories, which are very similar to religious cults in most respects, to make Variable 18.

Three other classified categories provide services to the general public and superficially appear very different from religious cults: bookstores, food stores, and restaurants. Of the total 2,470, 10.2 percent are bookstores "specializing or providing metaphysical, spiritual,

FIGURE 12.1
The Regional Variables

1. Church members (percent)
2. Attend church more often than once a month (percent)
3. Never attend church (percent)
4. Believe in the existence of God "as I define Him" (percent)
5. Reject the existence of God (percent)
6. Say God's love is behind everything that happens (percent)
7. Feel very close to God most of the time (percent)
8. Sure there is life beyond death (percent)
9. Pray at least once a day (percent)
10. Say "my prayers are heard" (percent)
11. Felt as though they were very close to a powerful spiritual force that seemed to lift them out of themselves (percent)
12. Think an acknowledged atheist should not teach in a public high school (percent)
13. Think an acknowledged atheist's book ought to be removed from a public library (percent)
14. Sect headquarters (per 10,000,000)
15. Cult headquarters (per 10,000,000)
16. Cults founded before 1930 (as percent of all cults)
17. 1974 *Spiritual Community Guide* listings (per 1,000,000)
18. 1974 *Spiritual Community Guide* centers (per 1,000,000)
19. 1974 *Spiritual Community Guide* stores (per 1,000,000)
20. 1978 *Spiritual Community Guide* listings (per 1,000,000)
21. *Organic Traveller* listings (per 1,000,000)
22. *International Psychic Register* listings (per 1,000,000)
23. *Who's Who in the Psychic World* listings (per 1,000,000)
24. 1950s *Fate* stories (per 1,000,000)
25. 1960–1979 *Fate* stories (per 1,000,000)
26. November 1979 *Fate* subscribers (per 100,000)
27. 1970 Transcendental Meditation initiates (per 100,000 urban)
28. 1975 Transcendental Meditation initiates (per 10,000 urban)
29. Transcendental Meditation teachers (per 1,000,000)
30. Metropolitan astrologers (per 1,000,000 metropolitan population)
31. 1926 Christian Scientists (per 10,000)
32. 1926 Theosophists (per 100,000)
33. 1926 Spiritualists (per 100,000)
34. Born in state of current residence (percent of native-born)
35. Lived in same house in 1975 (percent of those age 5 or over)
36. Graduated from high school (percent of those age 25 or over)
37. Had four or more years of college (percent of those age 25 or over)
38. Families in poverty (percent of all families)
39. Live in urban area (percent)
40. Black African-American (percent)
41. Spanish origin (percent)
42. Ever divorced (percent of ever married)
43. Inmates of mental hospitals (per 10,000)
44. Inmates of home for the aged (per 1,000)
45. Inmates of college dormitories (per 1,000)
46. Foreign-born (percent)
47. Engineers (per 1,000 employed persons)
48. Farmers (per 1,000 employed persons)

esoteric, devotional, natural life style books." Food stores, specializing in "natural" foods, constituted 25.7 percent. The restaurants, 5.5 percent, offer vegetarian or macrobiotic meals. Variable 19 is based on these three classifications, and it is an open question whether they are part of the world of deviant cults.

Variable 20 is based on all 943 listings in the 1978 edition of the guide; the number is much smaller than for the previous edition in part because the guide had begun charging a fee for each listing. Variable 21 is based on listings in *The Organic Traveler* (Davis and Tetrault 1975), a guide to organic, vegetarian, and health-food restaurants. The next two variables were based on two other guides that list professional psychics and others providing similar cultic services: *The International Psychic Register* (McQuaid 1979) and *Who's Who in the Psychic World* (Finch and Finch 1971).

Since 1948, when it began publication, *Fate* magazine has been the central publication of the occult subculture in America. Among its features are two letter columns where readers write in to report their contacts with death and with supernatural forces: "My Proof of Survival" and "True Mystic Experiences." Conveniently enough for the geographic researcher, these stories always include the name and town of each contributor. I was able to obtain copies of 79 issues published in the 1950s containing 748 such stories. A total of 2,086 stories were published in all 237 issues from January 1960 through September 1979. In addition, I was able to obtain from the publisher the numbers of mail subscribers as of November 1979 living in each state; a total of 79,907. These data produced variables 23 through 25.

A student of mine, Daniel H. Jackson, requested the Transcendental Meditation organization to give us statistics on initiations to their group, and he successfully obtained a fabulous wealth of data. One computer printout lists the numbers of persons initiated from 1967 through 1977 whose homes were in each of 5,629 urban areas, a total of 735,280 meditators. Although it has fallen on hard times, "TM" was highly successful in the 1970s, presenting itself not as a weird Asian cult but as a practical way people might improve the level of their physical and mental functioning. TM was solidly based in the religions of India, however, and several courts judged it a religious organization, despite its own insistence that it was really a scientific discipline rather than a religion. The regional dataset includes rates for both 1970, when TM was still small, and 1975, when it was at its peak. Also, TM publications gave us the numbers of TM teachers, the people who instructed others in how to meditate, in each region.

Data on astrologers came from classified telephone directories. Except in Pennsylvania, where astrology was defined as illegal fortune-telling, the yellow pages list professional astrologers, and you can count how many there are in different places. I was able to find copies of phone books for every metropolitan area in the United States—except for a dozen small cities, and an assistant of mine simply called the phone companies in these cities and asked the person who answered to look in the yellow pages for us. I had to make sure that every astrology listing was placed in the correct area and that none was counted twice if listed in more than one directory, as often happens for large metropolitan areas. To get regional rates, I divided the number of astrologers in each region's metropolitan areas by the metropolitan population. Because Pennsylvania books did not list astrologers, the data for the Middle Atlantic region are based on just New York and New Jersey.

The 1926 survey of churches carried out by the United States Census covered three religious organizations with relatively novel beliefs: Christian Science, Theosophy, and Spiritualism (Bureau of the Census 1930). Keeping in mind that we define a "cult" as a religious organization with novel beliefs and practices, these three groups certainly qualify, although they are quite well established in American society. By including them in our dataset, we can see how stable the geography of American religious innovation has been over nearly half a century.

I included variables 34 through 48 simply to add variety. Taken from the 1980 United States Census, they offer a range of opportunities for statistical exploration quite outside the sociology of religion. All 48 variables are at your disposal in the GRAF program.

Correlation and Regression in the GRAF Program

In Chapter 10, we introduced the GRAF program, which has two modules demonstrating the meaning and calculation methods of correlations and regressions. One of these modules is a scattergram that requires your computer to have graphics capability, and as Chapter 10 explained, the software will not display it if your machine lacks graphics. Without graphics, the GRAF menu looks like this:

```
[1] Pinball probability game (Normal Curve) PLAIN version
[2] Regression analysis of two regional variables
[ESC] QUIT or change programs
```

The first option goes with Chapter 10, where we learned about the normal curve, so it should not concern you now. If your machine possesses a graphics capability, the menu will be longer:

```
[1] Pinball probability game (Normal Curve) PLAIN version
[2] Regression analysis of two regional variables
[3] Pinball probability game (Normal Curve) GRAPHIC version
[4] Scattergram of two regional variables
[ESC] QUIT or change programs
```

The first and third of these options go with Chapter 10, and the second and fourth go with this chapter. When you select either regression analysis or the scattergram, the computer will ask you to enter the numbers of two variables out of the 48 in the regional dataset.

The Equation of a Line

Before we can understand regression, we need to review some simple mathematics that you probably studied in high school, beginning with the concept of the slope of a line. Figure 12.2 consists of six little graphs, each showing a diagonal line drawn from the point labeled A to the point labeled A'. Near each line is a message saying what its slope is. For example, the slope of the first line, in the upper-left corner, is 1.0.

Put simply, slope is a measure of how steep a line is. Specifically, the **slope** of a line expresses how many units the line rises for each unit it runs forward. If you like mnemonics—acronyms or catch phrases that help you remember things—then you might memorize the phrase *slope is rise over run*. Personally, I find that pictures like those in Figure 12.2 stick in my memory better. Each of the six A-A' lines in Figure 12.2 is drawn inside a pair of axes, at right angles to each other, measuring the line in the left-right and down-up dimensions. The

FIGURE 12.2
Slopes of Lines

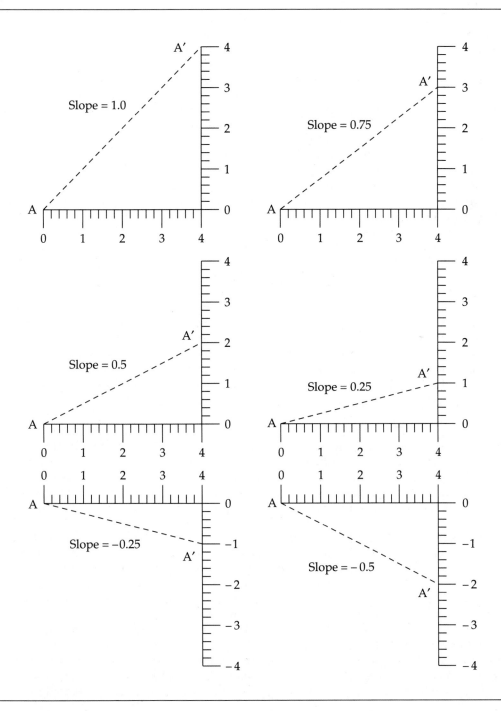

first line, for example, goes 4 units to the right and 4 units up. To calculate its slope, simply divide 4 (the rise) by 4 (the run), and you get 1.0, which is the slope. This means that the line rises 1 unit for every 1 unit it runs forward.

The A-A′ line at upper right in Figure 12.2 rises 3 units and runs 4 units to the right. Thus, its slope is ¾ or 0.75. The two lines in the middle of the figure have slopes of 0.5 and 0.25. Can you see how these slopes were calculated?

At the bottom of the figure are two examples of lines with negative slope. The A-A′ line at lower left drops 1 unit, which is the same as rising − 1 unit. It runs forward 4 units, just like the other lines in the figure. Therefore its slope is − ¼ or − 0.25. And the A-A′ line in the lower right drops two units (rises − 2 units) while running to the right 4 units, so its slope is − ²⁄₄ or − 0.5. Thus, slopes can be negative as well as positive. They also can be greater than 1.0. For example, a line could rise 2 units for every 1 unit it ran to the right. Its slope would be ²⁄₁ or 2.0. Similarly, a line that fell 2 units for every unit it ran forward would have a slope of − 2.0.

Figure 12.3 also shows a diagonal line, along with various points, and the slope of the line is 0.77. That is, it rises 0.77 units for every unit it runs to the right. Although the line is framed by two scales, just like the A-A′ lines in Figure 12.2, it does not go from one corner to another, or from one whole-number mark on an axis to another. The reason is that the line is based on actual data, and it passes neatly among the nine tiny diamond marks in the graph, each of which represents one of the nine regions of the United States.

To make sense of this, we need to review how to plot points on a graph. Our data happen to concern two variables from the regional dataset: variable 18 (1974 SCG centers per 1,000,000) and variable 19 (1974 SCG stores per 1,000,000). We described these data above. Both variables are counts of listings in the *Spiritual Community Guide* (Singh 1974). One is spiritual centers such as meditation groups; the other is stores such as occult bookstores. Although the two variables came from the same sources, they

are quite independent, in that no one business or organization is counted in both rates.

Let's plot a point. It will be an important one: the means for both variables. The mean SCG centers rate across the nine regions is 6.6 per million. The mean stores rate is 5.4. The scale for SCG centers runs from left to right, so we read across to 6.6 on that scale. The SCG stores scale rises from bottom to top, so we read up to 5.4. The plus sign ("+") on the graph marks the point that is 6.6 units to the right and 5.4 units up. *Plotting a point* means to find it on a graph and mark it. That's what I did with the "+."

I did the same for the nine separate regions, plotting the points that represented each one's value on the pair of variables. For example, the rates for the Pacific region are 19.1 and 14.1, and the tiny diamond near the A′ end of the diagonal line represents this point. In a conventional graph, the horizontal scale represents the X variable, which is variable 18 in this case. The vertical scale represents the Y variable, which is variable 19. So the rates for the Pacific region are X = 19.1, Y = 14.1. The point on the graph representing these rates can be described in the same way: X = 19.1, Y = 14.1.

The diagonal line in the graph is very interesting. It passes through the point marked with the plus sign, which is at the mean for both variables, and it passes very close to the nine diamond dots that mark the data for the nine regions. In a way, it summarizes the data. More importantly, it represents the association between the two variables in a way that would let you predict the value for Y if you already knew the value for X.

Imagine, for example, that we wanted to add Canada to this graph. No, Canadians, I am not suggesting merging the two countries. But suppose we knew how many spiritual centers there were per million in Canada, but we did not know how many "New Age" stores there were. We could read an estimate of the stores off of the graph. Say, just for the sake of example, that Canada's centers rate was 6.0 (I don't know the actual rate). We would look across the horizontal scale until we reached 6.0, then

FIGURE 12.3
Scattergram of Variables 18 and 19

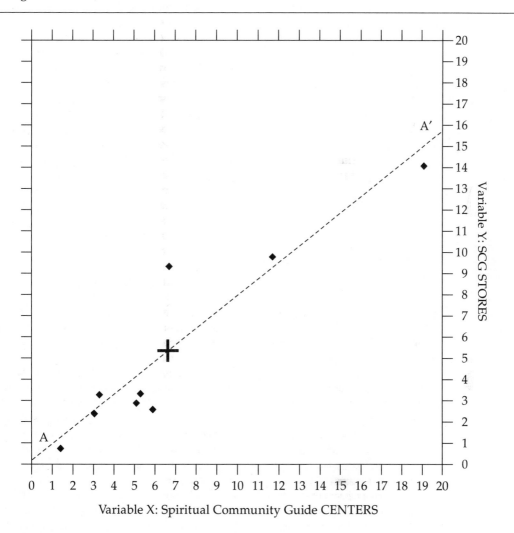

Variable X: Spiritual Community Guide CENTERS

look straight up until we bumped into the line. That would be at a point about 4.9 units up from the bottom. So, we would estimate that Canada, having 6.0 centers per million, would have 4.9 New Age stores per million. This assumes that the line A-A' properly expresses the association between the two variables, X and Y.

Another way to think about this line is in terms of its equation. Every straight line on a graph like this can be expressed as an equation of the following form:

$$Y' = A + BX$$

Y' is the line's estimate of variable Y for a given value of variable X. B is simply the slope of the line. A is the value of Y where the line crosses the X axis, where the line has a value for X of zero. Look at the left end of the line A-A', where it hits the left edge of the graph right above the 0 on the X scale. It happens that this point is 0.32 units up on the Y axis. We call this point the **Y-intercept**, because this is the point at which the line intercepts (or intersects) the Y axis. That is, the point is plotted at X = 0, Y = 0.32. The A in the equation above is the value of Y at this point, or 0.32. We said that the slope of the line is 0.77, so we now know the values of both A and B in the equation: A = 0.32, B = 0.77. Thus the equation for the particular line is

$$Y' = 0.32 + 0.77X$$

If you knew X and wanted to estimate Y using this equation, you would simply plug X into the formula and calculate the result. A moment ago I did this for a value of X = 6.0. Put this in the formula: Y' = 0.32 + (0.77)(6.0). My pocket calculator tells me that this is 4.94, or about 4.9. Shortly, we will learn how to calculate the equation of a line like this from the original data, the basis of regression analysis. But first, if your computer has graphics capability, we can use the scattergram option of the GRAF program to become familiar with lines and their equations.

A Dynamic Regression Line

If you are at your computer and it has graphics capability, select the GRAF program and follow the directions below to work with a graph like that shown in Figure 12.3. If your machine does not have graphics, or you are not working with your machine right now, look back at Figure 12.3 frequently and use a little imagination in reading what follows. In addition, Figures 12.4 and 12.5 will show parts of what the computer would display.

Start GRAF and select the scattergram option. When the computer asks you to choose a couple of variables, select variable 18 first, and then variable 19. This means that variable 18 will be X and variable 19 will be Y, just as in Figure 12.3. In a moment, the same picture will appear on your computer screen, except that the regression line will be horizontal. That is, everything looks the same—the tiny diamonds and the plus sign are in the same positions—except that the line itself is completely flat. It still goes through the plus sign, which represents the intersection of the means for X and Y, but it has no slope.

If you look in the upper-right corner of the screen, you will see this information: B = 0.00, A = 5.4. This is the equation for the horizontal line. Its slope is 0.00, represented by B. The Y-intercept is 5.4, which is the mean for Y. A horizontal line will always intersect the Y axis at the mean for Y. Indeed, the value of Y' is always the mean of Y for a horizontal line, regardless of what X is. This is a nice line, but it does not provide a good estimate of Y for different values of X, other than for the mean of X.

The problem is that the line has the wrong slope. The computer lets you rotate the line around the plus sign, which represents the intersection of the two means, until it fits best through the data points. To do this, press either the up-arrow key or the down-arrow key: (↑) or (↓). If you press (↑), the right-hand end of the line will go up. If you press (↓), it will go down. Try this a few times, rotating the line counterclockwise for a little while by pressing [↑] over and over, and rotating it clockwise by pressing [↓].

Note what happens to B and A, in the upper-right corner of the screen, as you do this. As the right-hand end of the line rises, the slope grows progressively larger, moving substantially above zero. As the right-hand end drops, the slope decreases, even going below zero. Once you have gotten practice rotating this line, move it until it seems to fit best among the nine data points, passing among them so that it is as close to them on average as you can get it. Don't worry about the mathematics of this right now; just rotate the line to get what your eye sees as the best fit.

With the line rotated into this position, glance at B in the upper-right corner of the screen. I'll bet it is close to 0.77. That is the slope of the line in Figure 12.3. Indeed, 0.77 is the slope of the best line, as indicated by the results of a regression analysis I will explain shortly. The mathematical approach saves us the trouble of rotating the line by eye, something very hard to do if you lack a computer with this particular software! It also gives a far more accurate result than trying to fit the line by eye.

Information about the ideal line is given at the right side of the screen, where it says, "Best line." There you see the information "Best line: $B = 0.77$, $A = 0.3$." The means for the two variables are given right below that, along with the variable numbers in case you have forgotten them.

In rotating the line A-A', you are trying to get it as close to the nine points as you can. This is the same as trying to get the distances between the line and the points as small as possible, but it is very important to understand how we should measure those distances. We are trying to find a line that will best help us predict the Y values of the points, assuming that we know the X values. Therefore, we are interested in the vertical (Y) distance between each point and the line, not the horizontal (X) distance. To make this as clear as possible, the computer will draw in the lines representing these distances, if you want.

Press (ENTER) to get away from the graph, back to the list of variables. Look at the bottom of the screen, and you will see a command, (E)rror:No. If you press (E) it will change to (E)rror:Yes. This means the graph will display the lines representing the errors in the line's predictions of the Y values of the data points. You do not have to type in the names of the variables in order to return to the graph; simply press (ENTER). (If, instead, you wanted to quit the program or change the part of the program you were working with, you would press (ESC).)

Now you will get a picture like that shown in Figure 12.4. The line A-A' is horizontal, and nine vertical lines connect it with the nine data points. This horizontal line represents the mean on the Y variable, which is 5.4. Therefore, the vertical lines represent how far each of the data points is from the mean of all nine. If you knew nothing except the mean value for the nine regions, 5.4 SCG stores per million, and somebody asked you how many such establishments there were per million in the Pacific region, your best guess would be the mean. In fact, the Pacific region is farthest from the mean of all the nine data points: the diamond at the far right of the picture, which represents the Pacific region, is well above the mean.

Because we really do know the SCG stores rate for the Pacific region, 14.1 per million, we can see how far off this guess would be. It is off by 8.7 per million because $14.1 - 5.4 = 8.7$. We could do worse. If we guessed the Pacific rate out of the blue, without any data to go on, we might say 100 per million, or 0.1 per million. But by rotating the regression line, we can do better still.

FIGURE 12.4
Residuals from the Scattergram Line

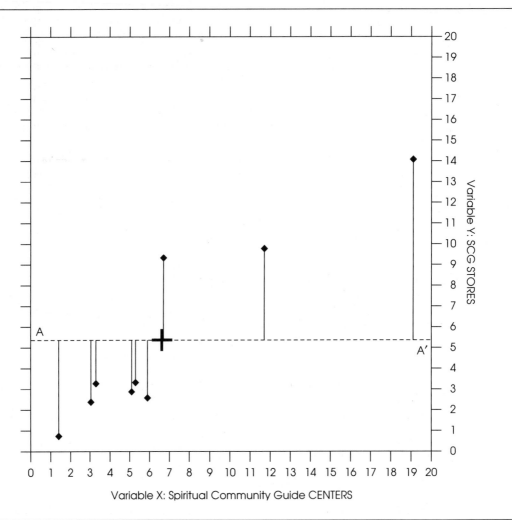

Figure 12.5 shows how the picture looks when you have rotated the line until it fits best the data points. Notice that the error lines are still vertical, but now they are shorter. The error line for the Pacific region is only 0.9 units long now, a great improvement over the 8.7 we started with.

Our estimate of one of the points has hardly improved at all. I mean the one right over the plus sign that represents the intersection of the two means. That data point represents New England. Its SCG centers rate, 6.7, is almost identical to the mean for the nine regions, which is 6.6; but its stores rate, 9.3, is considerably above the mean, which is 5.4.

FIGURE 12.5
Residuals and the Regression Line

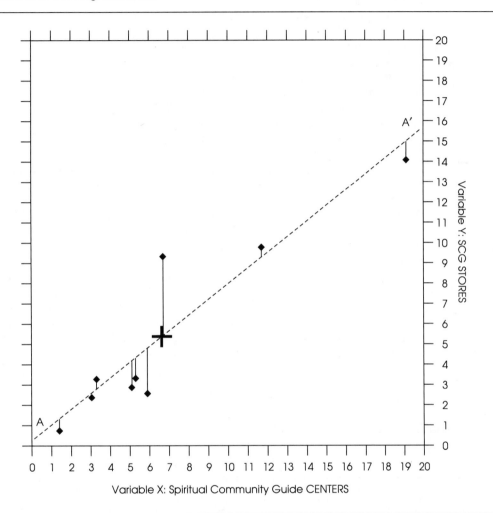

Variable X: Spiritual Community Guide CENTERS

Wayward data points like this, which wind up some distance from the line of best fit, are often sociologically quite interesting. Remember that in the previous chapter we discussed Alaska and New Mexico as outliers in some scattergrams. New England is not especially high in deviant religious groups, but it is high in milder forms of spiritual exploration. The SCG centers are in many respects similar to full-fledged religious cults, and many are actual branches of unusual religious groups. The "New Age" bookstores, food stores, and restaurants are less strange, counting among their customers many rather conventional people. Often, a wayward data point that is far from the line is a challenge to the sociologist, demanding both a theoretical explanation and further research to test that new hypothesis.

Calculating the Residuals

To understand exactly how the equation for the line of best fit is calculated, we need to examine the final option on the GRAF program. Note that this option does not require your computer to have a graphics capability. As usual, however, we will show you here what the results would be, in case you don't happen to be working at your computer right now.

If you are looking at a graph on your computer screen, press (ESC) to return to the menu of the program, and select "regression analysis of two regional variables." The computer will again ask you for the two variables you want to work with, but if you have already told it a pair of variables, pressing (ENTER) will get you directly to the regression analysis. A vast table, like that in Figure 12.6, will fill the screen.

Because we have only nine cases, the nine regions, it is possible to show you the entire calculation process, something I could not practically do with the 50 states or 512 respondents in other datasets. The first column gives the X values for the nine regions, the rates for variable 18, 1974 SCG centers per 1,000,000. The second column, labeled Y', is the predicted values of Y that result from plugging the X values into the regression equation: $Y' = 0.32 + 0.77X$. The third column of figures gives the actual Y values.

The fourth column gives the difference between the predicted and actual Y values, which is $Y' - Y$ and which I call δY, because δ is the Greek version of our letter d and stands for "difference" or "distance." So, the fourth column, δY, is the lengths of the nine vertical lines that represent the differences between the predicted Y value and the actual Y value for each of the nine regions. Another name for these numbers is residuals. The word *residual* comes from *residue*, meaning

FIGURE 12.6
Regression Analysis of Variables 18 and 19

Region	X	Y'	Y	δY	$(\delta Y)^2$	X^2	Y^2	XY
New England	6.7	5.5	9.3	−3.8	14.77	44.89	86.49	62.31
Middle Atlantic	5.3	4.4	3.3	1.1	1.18	28.09	10.89	17.49
East North Cent	3.0	2.6	2.4	0.2	0.05	9.00	5.76	7.20
West North Cent	3.3	2.9	3.3	−0.4	0.20	10.89	10.89	10.89
South Atlantic	5.1	4.2	2.9	1.3	1.77	26.01	8.41	14.79
East South Cent	1.4	1.4	0.8	0.6	0.35	1.96	0.64	1.12
West South Cent	3.9	3.3	2.6	0.7	0.51	15.21	6.76	10.14
Mountain	11.7	9.3	9.8	−0.5	0.26	136.89	96.04	114.66
Pacific	19.1	15.0	14.1	0.9	0.74	364.81	198.81	269.31
	59.5		48.5		19.83	637.75	424.69	507.91
	ΣX		ΣY		$\Sigma(\delta Y)^2$	ΣX^2	ΣY^2	ΣXY

X is variable 18 (1974 SCG centers per 1,000,000)
Y is variable 19 (1974 SCG stores per 1,000,000)

something left over, and a **residual** is the difference between the results of an empirical observation and the results of a computation from a formula. Residuals are an important concept in themselves, and we will encounter them again in the next chapter. In a sense, they are the part of the variation in the data that remains unexplained after the regression formula has done its work.

This is a good time to remember a few things about variance. Variance is a measure of how far the data points are from the mean, which is represented in our graph by a horizontal line. Now we need a measure of how far they are from a line that has a slope. Remember that in calculating variance we *squared* the difference between each value and the mean. We will do the same thing here, working not with the simple distances but with their squares. The fifth column of numbers in Figure 12.6 gives the squared Y differences from the line. The difference for New England is -3.8, because the predicted rate is 5.5, the actual rate is 9.3, and $5.5 - 9.3 = -3.8$ The square of -3.8 is 14.77. Oh well, if you try this on a hand calculator, you won't get exactly this answer, because of rounding error. My computer program works with very exact numbers, to many decimal places, and then rounds them off for display.

The fourth column is labeled $(\delta Y)^2$, meaning that the numbers in it are the squared distances from the regression line. Below the bottom of the column you will see 19.83, which is the total of these nine numbers and which we therefore call $\Sigma(\delta Y)^2$. When you rotate the A-A' line, in the scattergram part of the GRAF program, you will see a number near the upper-right corner of the screen, labeled "residuals." This name is just an abbreviation for "sum of the squares of residuals," or $\Sigma(\delta Y)^2$.

When you rotate the scattergram line, and its slope gets very close to the slope of the regression line itself, then "residuals" will get very close to the $\Sigma(\delta Y)^2$ given in the regression table for your particular pair of variables. Indeed, you can find the best position for the line A-A' by watching the residuals, rather than from eyeballing how close the line is to the nine points. As the slope of A-A' gets close to that of the regression line, the residuals will get smaller and smaller. Then as you rotate the line past the correct slope, the residuals will begin to get bigger again. This graphically demonstrates that the regression line itself fits most closely to the data points.

Figure 12.7 gives the residuals you will get as you rotate the line for variables 18 and 19 past the right slope. At the bottom of this table, you see that a line with slope 0.59 (B = 0.59), passing through the intersections of the means, will cross the Y axis at 1.5 (A = 1.5), and that the total of squared residuals is 27.1. As you rotate the line step by step, increasing the slope gradually, the residuals drop until they reach 19.9 at a slope of 0.75. Because the line rotates by jumps, you can't inspect the residuals at slopes of 0.76 or 0.77. At a slope of 0.78, however, the sum of squared residuals is again 19.9. With slopes greater than 0.78, the residuals number rises again beyond 19.9. This tells us that the slope of the line of best fit is about 0.75 or 0.78. A regression analysis, of course, has already told us the best slope is 0.77.

The particular numbers all depend upon the actual data you have, and different pairs of variables from the regional dataset will give different results. Also, you will get different numbers if you pick variable 19 to be X and 18 to be Y. Remember that the XTAB program included a measure of association called Somers' D. When we introduced Somers' D, we said that it was an asymmetrical measure, giving

FIGURE 12.7

Equations and Residuals of a Rotating Line

Slope (B)	Y-axis Intercept (A)	Sum of Squared Residuals
0.94	−0.8	27.0
0.91	−0.6	24.6
0.88	−0.4	22.7
0.84	−0.2	21.3
0.81	0.0	20.3
0.78	0.2	19.9
0.75	0.4	19.9
0.72	0.6	20.4
0.69	0.8	21.3
0.66	1.1	22.8
0.63	1.3	24.7
0.59	1.5	27.1

different results if you switched the independent and dependent variables. B, the slope of the line, is also an asymmetrical measure. When using regression analysis, you must always be clear about which are your independent and dependent variables. X is always the independent variable, and Y is the dependent variable. The regression equation allows you to estimate Y if you already know X.

Calculating the Slope of the Regression Line

The last three columns of Figure 12.6 show steps in calculating the slope of the line of best fit. They are the key computations in doing a regression analysis and in calculating the r correlation coefficient we encountered in earlier chapters. Here is the formula for figuring the slope, B:

$$B = \frac{N(\Sigma XY) - (\Sigma X)(\Sigma Y)}{N(\Sigma X^2) - (\Sigma X)^2}$$

If you think back to Chapter 9, you will remember that the formulas for Somers' D, gamma, and various taus all looked a little like this. There was a numerator in the formula that

subtracted one thing from the other, and this numerator was divided by a denominator that contained some of the same elements. Thus, a similar logic is at work here. Correlation coefficients should range from −1.00 through 0.00 to +1.00. Both the subtraction in the numerator, and the whole formula being a ratio, help achieve this.

The first column of numbers in Figure 12.6 gives the X values for the nine regions, and the total is shown at the bottom: 59.5, which we call ΣX. Notice that ΣX appears twice in the formula for B, once on the right-hand side of the numerator and once as the right-hand side of the denominator, where it is squared.

The third column of numbers in the table gives the Y values: their total, ΣY, is 48.5. The right-hand part of the numerator says to multiply this by the sum of the X values, $(\Sigma X)(\Sigma Y)$, and the result of doing this is 2885.75.

The final or eighth column of numbers is the product of the X and Y values—that is, $X \times Y$. These are called the *cross products*. To get them, you multiply values *across* the two variables. Their total, ΣXY, is 507.91. The left-hand part of the formula's numerator says to multiply this by N, the number of cases, which is 9: thus, $507.91 \times 9 = 4571.19$. Then $N(\Sigma XY) - (\Sigma X)(\Sigma Y)$ equals $4571.19 - 2885.75$, or 1685.44. So this is the numerator of the equation: 1685.44.

Now we must calculate the denominator. The sixth column of numbers in Figure 12.6 gives the squares of the X values, or X^2. The sum of these squares, ΣX^2, given at the bottom of that column, is 637.75. The formula says to multiply this by N, which is 9, and $N(\Sigma X^2) = 5739.75$. The rest of the denominator is $(\Sigma X)^2$, which means ΣX times ΣX itself, and $59.5 \times 59.5 = 3540.25$. Thus, the whole denominator, $N(\Sigma X^2) - (\Sigma X)^2$ is $5739.75 - 3540.25 = 2199.50$.

Finally, to get B, you divide the numerator by the denominator: $1685.44 / 2199.50 = 0.77$. A lot of work! Thank heaven the computer did it for us. This result is the slope of the regression line, which is the line of best fit among the nine data points.

The formula for B deserves some justification. Essentially, it is the covariance of X and Y divided by the variance of X. We know what variance is, but what is *covariance*? As the word implies, **covariance** is a measure of how X and Y vary together. Before we can go further, we must remind ourselves of the formula for variance:

$$s^2 = \frac{\Sigma(X - \overline{X})^2}{N} \quad \text{variance of X}$$

In this formula, s^2 is the name we give to variance, because variance is also the square of the standard deviation, which we notate by s. X is the value of variable X for any given case, going through the nine regions one at a time. Altogether, the formula gives us the average of the squared differences of the X values from their mean. Often, while writing

these programs, I used a version of this formula that is somewhat easier for the computer to calculate, thus speeding up the computations a bit. Although this formula is mathematically equivalent to the version just given (Christensen and Stoup 1986:90–91), it does not express the conceptual meaning of variance quite so clearly:

$$s_x{}^2 = \frac{\Sigma X^2 - (\Sigma X)^2/N}{N} \quad \text{variance of X}$$

Notice that the left-hand side of the equation has a little x in it, indicating that this is the variance for the X variable: $s_x{}^2$. The formula for the variance of Y has the same structure:

$$s_y{}^2 = \frac{\Sigma Y^2 - (\Sigma Y)^2/N}{N} \quad \text{variance of Y}$$

Finally, the formula for the covariance of X and Y is a hybrid of these two formulas:

$$s_{xy}{}^2 = \frac{N(\Sigma XY) - (\Sigma X)(\Sigma Y)/N}{N} \quad \begin{array}{l} \text{covariance} \\ \text{of X and Y} \end{array}$$

Notice that the numerator of this formula is almost identical to the one in the formula for B, which we gave above. If you divide the formula for the covariance of X and Y by the formula for the variance of X, and work through the algebra a bit to get rid of extra Ns, you get exactly the formula for B, the slope of the regression line.

If we had wanted a regression line in which Y was the independent variable and X the dependent variable, we would use the same approach, except that we would divide the covariance of X and Y by the variance of Y. Again, if you check back to our discussion of Somers' D in Chapter 9, you will find parallel logic.

Calculating the Y-intercept of the Regression Line

We now know how to figure the slope of a regression line, and perhaps we are content to let the computer do that work for us in the future, but we need one other piece of information before we can draw the line on the graph or complete the full regression equation. It is not enough to know the angle at which a line is tilted; we also have to know the exact location of at least one point it passes through.

If we know the means for the two variables, then we do know the location of one such point, because the regression line passes through the point that represents both means, the one indicated by the plus mark on our graphs. The regression equation is far easier to handle, however, if we nail down a different point, where the line crosses the Y axis of the graph, otherwise known as the Y-intercept or A. Look again at the formula for any straight line on a graph:

$$Y' = A + BX$$

This can be rewritten to give us A:

$$A = Y' - BX$$

To figure A, we simply put the value of the mean for X into X in this formula, and we put the mean for Y in the place of Y'. The mean for X happens to be 6.6, and the mean for Y is 5.4, as we noted earlier. And, of course, we have calculated that B = 0.77. The formula then becomes

$$A = 5.4 - (0.77)(6.6)$$

Or, A = 0.32. When you ask the computer to show you a regression analysis, the bottom-right corner of the screen will have this information ready for you to see. It will remind you of the general equation for a line: $Y' = A + BX$. And it will show you the specific formula for the two variables you chose, which in our example is $Y' = 0.32 + 0.77(X)$. Just to reinforce this, there will be a box near the center bottom of the screen containing, among other things, the values for B and A. The lower-left corner of the screen will give you a summary of the information from which all this was calculated, including the covariance of X and Y and the variance of X.

Calculating Pearson's r

I must remind you that the regression coefficient, B, is asymmetrical and is not limited to the range from -1.00 to $+1.00$. Closely related to it is a correlation coefficient that is symmetrical and that stays within this range, Pearson's r. We used this correlation coefficient, alongside the nonparametric coefficients, in the XTAB program and in our analysis of MAPS data, but we did not fully explain it. We can do that now.

We want a coefficient in which X and Y play completely equal roles. They do so in the numerator of the formula for B, but X dominates the denominator. Remember, the denominator of B's formula is essentially the variance of X. If we could just replace it by something that gave equal influence to Y, then we would have the coefficient we want.

Variance, as we have said so many times, is the square of the standard deviation. Therefore "(variance of X)" could be replaced by "(standard deviation of X) × (standard deviation of X)," and we can give Y an equal role by replacing one of these duplicate statements by "standard deviation of Y." Indeed, Pearson's r is the covariance of X and Y divided by the standard deviation of X times the standard deviation of Y. After doing a little algebra, its formula looks like this:

$$r = \frac{N\Sigma XY - (\Sigma X)(\Sigma Y)}{\sqrt{[N\Sigma X^2 - (\Sigma X)^2][N\Sigma Y^2 - (\Sigma Y)^2]}}$$

Although I have dropped a couple of unnecessary parentheses to make this complex formula look a little simpler, you should recognize that it has the same numerator as does the formula for B. The denominator clearly gives equal roles to X and Y, and r is completely symmetrical. It doesn't matter which of our two variables is dependent and which independent; r comes out the same either way. For the variables we are working with, SCG centers and SCG stores, here is how the final calculation goes, using some of the numbers from Figure 12.6 and plugging them into the formula for Pearson's r:

$$N = 9$$

$$\Sigma XY = 507.91$$

$$\Sigma X = 59.5$$

$$\Sigma Y = 48.5$$

$$\Sigma X^2 = 637.75$$

$$\Sigma Y^2 = 424.69$$

$$r = \frac{9(507.91) - (59.5)(48.5)}{\sqrt{[9(637.75) - (59.5)^2][9(424.69) - (48.5)^2]}} = 0.94$$

The computer also provides us with the variance of X, the variance of Y, and the covariance of X and Y, allowing us to calculate B and r using the following simple formulas, which I described above:

$$B = \frac{\text{covariance of X and Y}}{\text{variance of X}}$$

$$r = \frac{\text{covariance of X and Y}}{(\text{standard deviation of X})\,(\text{standard deviation of Y})}$$

The information required to calculate B and r, when X is variable 18 and Y is variable 19, is given in the lower-left corner of the regression-analysis display on your screen:

$$\text{variance of X} = 27.2$$

$$\text{variance of Y} = 18.1$$

$$\text{covariance of X and Y} = 20.8$$

$$B = \frac{20.8}{27.2} = 0.76$$

The standard deviation of X is the square root of the variance of X, or 5.22; and the standard deviation of Y is the square root of the variance of Y, or 4.25. Thus:

$$r = \frac{20.8}{(5.22) \times (4.25)} = 0.94$$

The value of B, 0.76, differs from the 0.77 we got earlier merely because of tiny errors introduced when the computer rounded numbers off for display on the screen. But this approach makes it easy for us to compare a regression in which the same two variables play different roles, X being the independent variable, as here, or the dependent variable. The value of r would not change at all, while the value of B would. The formula and calculations with Y as the independent variable and X as the dependent variable would be as follows:

$$B = \frac{\text{covariance of X and Y}}{\text{variance of Y}}$$

$$B = \frac{20.8}{18.1} = 1.15$$

This example proves that B can be greater than 1.00, depending on the data you are working with. Although regressions and r correlations should be far more clear to you now, another example may help you consolidate what you have learned.

 ## Negative Slopes and Correlations

We have been working with the example of a highly positive correlation and a regression line with a positive slope, but negative slopes are just as common. Our 48 regional variables provide many examples, but a particularly instructive one is an analysis in which X is variable 37, the percent of persons age 25+ who had four or more years of college, and Y is variable 38, the percent of families in poverty.

One might hope that education would reduce poverty. Thus, one would predict a negative association between college education and the poverty rate. The data and the steps in calculating B and r are given here in Figure 12.8, just what you would get if you asked the computer to show you the regression analysis of

FIGURE 12.8
Regression Analysis of Variables 37 and 38

Region	X	Y'	Y	δY	(δY)²	X²	Y²	XY

X is variable 37 (4+ years college % (age 25+))
Y is variable 38 (Families in poverty %)

Region	X	Y'	Y	δY	(δY)²	X²	Y²	XY
New England	19.2	7.8	7.4	0.4	0.16	368.64	54.76	142.08
Middle Atlantic	16.6	9.6	9.2	0.4	0.13	275.56	84.64	152.72
East North Cent	14.5	11.0	7.9	3.1	9.52	210.25	62.41	114.55
West North Cent	15.3	10.4	8.2	2.2	5.03	234.09	67.24	125.46
South Atlantic	15.7	10.2	10.7	− 0.5	0.28	246.49	114.49	167.99
East South Cent	12.1	12.6	14.8	− 2.2	4.77	146.41	219.04	179.08
West South Cent	15.5	10.3	12.1	− 1.8	3.22	240.25	146.41	187.55
Mountain	18.8	8.1	8.9	− 0.8	0.70	353.44	79.21	167.32
Pacific	19.4	7.7	8.4	− 0.7	0.55	376.36	70.56	162.96
	147.1		87.6		24.35	2451.49	898.76	1399.71
	ΣX		ΣY		$\Sigma(\delta y)^2$	ΣX^2	ΣY^2	ΣXY

these two variables. The r correlation between variables 37 and 38 is − 0.69, a substantial negative association. The slope, B, is − 0.68, and the Y intercept, A, is 20.83. Therefore the formula for the regression line is Y' = 20.83 + −0.68(X). Or, we could drop the plus sign and restate this Y' = 20.83 − 0.68(X).

Other information the computer gives, which you would find in the lower-left corner of the screen, allows us to do a quick calculation of B and r:

$$\text{variance of } X = 5.2$$

$$\text{variance of } Y = 5.1$$

$$\text{covariance of } X \text{ and } Y = -3.6$$

$$B = \frac{-3.6}{5.2} = -0.69$$

Notice that the covariance of X and Y is negative in this case, and this gives B its negativity. Again, rounding error produces a slightly different result than when we let the computer do all the calculating at high precision. To figure r, we need to take the square roots of the variances to get the standard deviation. For X, the standard deviation is about 2.28, and the standard deviation of Y is approximately 2.26. So r can be calculated like this:

$$r = \frac{-3.6}{(2.28) \times (2.26)} = -0.70$$

Again, because of rounding error we are slightly off the computer's result. The graph you would get if you looked at the scattergram in the GRAF program would be like Figure 12.9. Note that the line A-A' is lower on the right than on the

FIGURE 12.9
Regression Line with Negative Slope

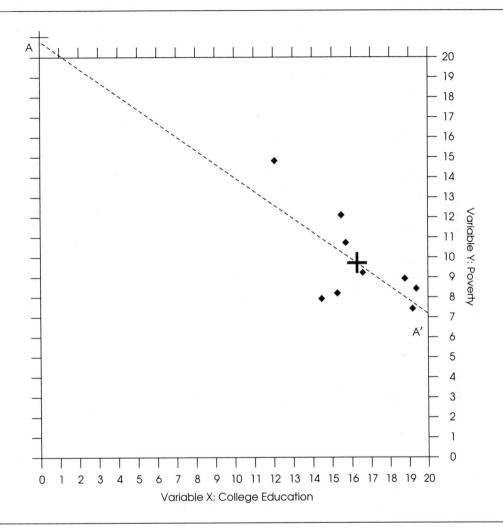

left, indicating a negative slope. I selected this pair of variables not only because it illustrates negative slope and negative correlation, but also because it allows me to discuss a few other features of the scattergram part of the GRAF program.

The regression line intercepts the Y axis up outside the square area of the graph that would appear on your computer screen. This often happens. You should rely upon the actual value of A, rather than an eyeball estimate of it from glancing at the graph on the computer screen, to determine the Y-intercept of the line.

Also, you will note that the data points are clustered rather closely together, compared to the nice scatter across the graph we had with variables 18 and 19. An option in the program allows you to adjust this, to some extent.

Adjusting the Scattergram Range

When the scattergram part of the GRAF program starts, it is set to display only a certain part of the picture. It goes from 0.0 for both X and Y, the intersection of the X and Y axes of the graph, up to the maximum value taken by a case on either value. For example, consider again variables 18 and 19. The highest value for either of the *Spiritual Community Guide* rates is 19.1, the centers rate for the Pacific region. Therefore the graph will cover the area from 0.0 on X to 19.1 on X, and from 0.0 on Y to 19.1 on Y.

The area display in the scattergram part of the GRAF program will always be square. This is not the case for the scattergram in the MAPS program, because that diagram covers the full range for each variable separately. This difference should cause you to think deeply about the shapes of graphs, and to pay attention to both the horizontal and vertical scales when you are trying to interpret such a picture.

The figures in this chapter showing what the graphs look like on the computer screen have been framed by rather complete ruler scales, giving all the whole numbers from 0 to 20. I did not have room to do this on the screen itself, where you will find only the extreme values, 0.0 and 19.1 in this case. The scattergram of variables 37 and 38 will cover the territory from 0.0 up to 19.4, because the highest value on either variable is 19.4.

To adjust this area, get to the point in the program where the computer is asking you what variables you want for the scattergram, and note the command in the bottom-left corner of the screen: (G)raph:0–top. This means that the computer is ready to show you the area on the graph from 0 to the top value for either variable. To change it, press (G).

When you do this, the command will change to two other options: (G)raph: 0–100% and (G)raph:Range. The latter option makes a nice picture with variables 37 and 38 and covers the ranges of both variables, which run from 7.4 to 19.4.

Variance, Regression, Correlation

It should be clear by now that the tremendously useful techniques of regression and r correlation are based on the concepts of variance and standard deviation, introduced in Chapter 10. Further connections deserve mention now.

It is extremely easy to turn the B from a regression calculation into the r from a correlation calculation. To explain how, I must first introduce a commonly used notation. Let B_{yx} stand for the result when X is the independent variable and Y is the dependent variable in a regression analysis. In Chapter 9, I used a notation for Somers' D that I found more intuitive: $D(X{\rightarrow}Y)$, with the arrow running from the independent variable to the dependent variable. Many statistics books express the same thing like this: D_{yx}. A regression in which Y was the independent variable and X was the dependent variable would produce a result called B_{xy}.

Now consider the following four formulas, keeping in mind that the subscript $_{yx}$ means $X{\rightarrow}Y$, and $_{xy}$ means $Y{\rightarrow}X$.

$$B_{yx} = r \times \frac{\text{Standard deviation of Y}}{\text{Standard deviation of X}}$$

$$B_{xy} = r \times \frac{\text{Standard deviation of X}}{\text{Standard deviation of Y}}$$

$$r = B_{yx} \times \frac{\text{Standard deviation of X}}{\text{Standard deviation of Y}}$$

$$r = B_{xy} \times \frac{\text{Standard deviation of Y}}{\text{Standard deviation of X}}$$

Let's work this through with a simple example, using the first two variables in the regional dataset, the percent of the population who are church members and the percent who attend church at least once a month. With variable 1 (church membership) for X and variable 2 (church attendance) for Y, you get the following results: B = 1.18, r = 0.76. The variances of X and Y are 67.7 and 162.9, so the standard deviations are 8.23 and 12.76. Divide the standard deviation of Y by the standard deviation of X, and you get 0.64. Multiply B, which is 1.18, by 0.64, and you get 0.76, which is r.

You can try the three other formulas yourself. Together, they show a very close connection between regressions and correlations. Indeed, in the context of a regression analysis, r is often called the **standardized regression coefficient**; another term you will encounter is **beta weights**. Remember that Chapter 10 mentioned the use of z-scores, based on standard deviations, to standardize the values of a variable, such as is done in transforming "intelligence" test scores into IQ scores. In the following chapters, we will again mention the standardization of individual variables. Here, we have shown that r is a version of B, standardized in terms of standard deviations.

Another way of getting a standardized regression coefficient is to standardize the variables before doing the regression calculation. In the following chapter I will explain how and why I standardized the FBI crime-rate variables in the MAPS dataset. Suffice it to say now that variables 79 (Z murder) and 80 (Z rape) are standardized versions of variables 65 (Murders)

and 66 (Rapes), transformed by means of z-scores. That is, the values for "Z murder" are the values for "Murders" expressed in terms of numbers of standard deviations above and below the mean.

For the 50 states, the correlations between the murder rate and the rape rate is 0.68, and the B with rape dependent is 2.0812. But a regression done with the standardized versions of these two variables produces a B of 0.68, which is identical to the r between the unstandardized versions of these two variables. Thus, the standardization can be done either before or after the regression calculations are made.

Yet another formula connecting B and r will take us back to our earlier work on nonparametric coefficients. Pearson's r, the standardized regression coefficient, can be expressed as the harmonic mean of the two unstandardized regression coefficients. To calculate the ordinary average of two numbers, the *arithmetic mean*, you add the numbers and divide by two. To get the *geometric mean*, you multiply the two numbers and take the square root of the result, as in the following formula:

$$r = \sqrt{(B_{yx}) \times (B_{xy})}$$

What links this discussion to nonparametric coefficients is the fact that exactly the same relationship exists between tau-b and Somers' D. Recall that there are two versions of D between any two variables, just as there are two versions of B, depending upon which of the two is independent and which is dependent: D_{yx} and D_{xy}. And the following is true:

$$\text{tau–b} = \sqrt{(D_{yx}) \times (D_{xy})}$$

Standardized regression coefficients (rs) are usually far more convenient than unstandardized coefficients (Bs) when you want to compare two or more of them. For example, you might wonder about the connection between divorce and participation in church. There is an r of − 0.62 between church membership (variable 1) and divorce (variable 42), and only − 0.39 between church attendance (variable 2) and divorce. This suggests that frequency of church attendance is not as important as sheer membership in a church in preventing divorce. It is quite appropriate to compare the -0.62 with the -0.39. In the following chapters, we will make great use of this comparability of standardized coefficients when we work with more than two variables at once.

Finally, there are versions of variance and standard deviation that are based on the scatter of data points around the regression line, rather than around the mean. Consider the following two formulas:

$$\frac{\Sigma(Y - \overline{Y})^2}{N} = \text{variance of } Y$$

$$\frac{\Sigma(Y - Y')^2}{N} = \text{variance of the estimate of } Y$$

The formulas are almost identical, except that the first one focuses on the difference between each Y score and the mean for Y, while the second focuses on the residual—the difference between the actual value (Y) and the value predicted by the regression line (Y'). When I was explaining how the dynamic line in the GRAF scattergram worked, I explained that you could rotate the line until the total residuals were at a minimum. Here, that total is divided by the number of cases to give the average squared difference between Y and the Y' predicted by the regression line.

The square root of this variance of the estimate of Y is analogous to the standard deviation, and it is called the **standard error**. This term is appropriate, because the difference between Y and Y' is the error the regression equation makes in predicting Y.

If you look back at Figure 12.6, regression analysis of variables 18 and 19, you will see that the sum of squared differences from the regression line, $\Sigma(\delta Y)^2$, is 19.83. Divide this by 9, the number of cases, and you get 2.20, which is the variance of the estimate of Y. The square root of that is 1.48, which is the standard error. Near the center bottom of your computer screen, when you have done a regression analysis, right under the values of B, A, and r, you will see a message about SE, or standard error. For the analysis we did with variables 18 and 19, the message reads, "SE = 1.48."

Statistical Significance of Regressions and Gamma

In Chapter 10, we explained in general terms how the normal curve can provide tests of statistical significance, and we also introduced the concept of z-scores. Now, we will build on the concepts developed there to show how the statistical significance of r can be evaluated.

Do you recall the probability pinball game we played back in Chapter 10? Both graphics and nongraphics versions of it are in the GRAF program we have just been working with, if you want to try it again and refresh your memory. Balls bounced off 12 arrowheads, with a 50-50 chance of going this way or that way at each bounce, and the result of running many balls was a rough picture of the normal curve.

To get to either extreme tail of the distribution, a ball had to bounce the same way many times in a row. This is rare. We used the pinball game to help us analyze results in a 12-item true-false test. By chance, on the basis of pure guesses, you might expect a person to get six right; but if you have many people answer the test at random, perhaps by flipping coins, you would not expect all of them to get six right. In fact, you would expect to get the distribution reflected in the pinball game. It would be a very rare person who got all 12 questions right. We used this fact to decide whether a person who got 11 or 12 right should be considered really to know the right answers to the test, rather than merely being the beneficiary of lucky guesses.

Now the problem is not to evaluate a single individual's score on a test, but to evaluate a correlation coefficient based on data from several cases. Because there are only nine cases in it, the regional dataset is really not good for that purpose, and as you have already learned, statistical significance is facilitated by a large number of cases. The XTAB dataset, with its 512 survey respondents, is far better.

Imagine that the 512 respondents were the entire student population of a college, and you were surveying them by means of a random sample. What you really want to learn are the correlations linking various variables in the entire population, but you are dealing with a mere subsample of this population. There is some chance that you would get a big correlation between two variables, simply because of bad luck in drawing your random sample, rather than because the two variables really correlated in the complete population of 512.

If you want, you can try an experiment. Pick two variables in the XTAB dataset that do not correlate at all, a pair with a Pearson's r of something very close to zero. One choice would be to use the two items based on completely random numbers, variable 80 (Random data 1) or variable 81 (Random data 2). In any case, you've selected two variables, X and Y, that just don't correlate in the population of 512.

For the experiment, do the following a number of times. Draw a random sample of 50 respondents out of the 512, using the part of the XTAB program that lets you do this. Look at the crosstab between X and Y. Write down the r. To get back to the full population of 512, cancel the random sample. Draw another random sample of 50. Again, write down the r between X and Y. Continue until exhausted.

Some of those random samples will indicate really big correlations between X and Y. In one sample, conceivably, luck might give you 25 people who rate both X and Y at the very top of the preference scale, and 25 who rate them both at the bottom. The r in that sample of 50 would be 1.00. But another sample could have an r of

−1.00. If you draw a very large number of samples, the average correlation in them should be the same as the actual correlation in all 512 respondents, but the correlations in these samples will have a distribution, as well. Indeed, it will be a normal distribution.

Here, we have gone from the population to the sample. Statistical significance, however, thinks the other way: from the sample to the population. If we get a correlation of 0.50 between variables A and B in a sample of 50 respondents, what is the chance that the correlation in the population from which the sample was drawn is really zero? Because the distribution of A-B correlations across a large number of samples has the normal distribution, we can use z-scores to assess the probability of getting this 0.50 correlation purely by chance. A simple formula will transform a correlation coefficient (r) into z-scores:

$$z = r \sqrt{N - 1}$$

In our example, $r = 0.50$ and $N = 50$, the number of cases in a sample. $N - 1$ then is 49; the square root of 49 is 7.00, and the correlation times that square root is 3.50. So, in this particular example, $z = 3.50$. At this point, you might have to pull out a book of statistical tables and look at the table for the normal curve (z-score distribution). It will tell you that a z of 3.50 achieves the .001 level of statistical significance. Thus, a correlation of 0.50 will show up in a sample of 50 cases less than once out of every 1,000 times, purely by chance. True, this will happen occasionally. If you look at only one correlation coefficient in only one sample, however, the z of 3.50 would be a sound basis for betting that variables A and B have a correlation greater than zero in the population from which you drew the sample, as well as in the sample.

Because the XTAB and MAPS programs calculate the statistical significance of r correlations automatically, you don't have to worry about it, and they do so in the way I just described. I should tell you that this method assumes the sample has at least about 30 cases in it; if you are working with smaller samples than that, you will have to consult a conventional statistics textbook for a method of evaluating statistical significance of a correlation using a t-test. A t-test employs distributions comparable to the normal curve, adjusted for small numbers of cases, so the concepts we have just discussed are sufficient background for you to understand the general principles.

We should consider one fine point of evaluating the statistical significance of correlations: one-tailed and two-tailed tests. The tails in question are the two tails of the normal distribution, the ends of the curve where it swoops down close to the X-axis of its graph. Again, suppose you get a correlation of 0.50 between A and B in your sample. We could express the question of significance, somewhat sloppily, as, What are the chances the coefficient in the population from which the sample was drawn is really 0.0?

But we might better state the question in one of the two following ways: If the correlation in the population is zero, what is the chance of getting a correlation this far from zero in the sample? If the correlation in the population is zero, what is the chance of getting a correlation this high above zero? Do you see any difference between those two questions? One talks about "far from zero," while the other talks about "high above zero."

If you start out with no particular theory about the relationship between variables A and B, you would be just as interested in a correlation of − 0.50 as in one of + 0.50. That is, you have to worry about both tails of the normal distribution. The correlation has two chances to surprise you, either by crawling to the right into the tail of the distribution where the strong positive correlation coefficients dwell, or by crawling in the opposite direction where the strong negative coefficients are. Thus, a two-tailed test of statistical significance would take account of both tails of the distribution. By a two-tailed test, a z-score of about 3.3 achieves the 0.001 level of significance.

In contrast, you might start out with a very definite hypothesis about the correlation

between A and B. For example, deductions from your favorite theory might tell you that A should correlate positively with B. If so, you don't have to worry about the negative tail of the normal distribution, and you would do a one-tailed test. By a one-tailed test, a z-score of about 3.1 achieves the 0.001 level of significance. If the correlation comes out the exact opposite of what you predicted, − 0.50 for example, you cannot stick with a one-tailed test, and your theory has clearly failed in any event.

The estimates of significance provided by the XTAB and MAPS programs are based on two-tailed tests. I don't know what theories you have, or even whether you have any theories at all, so I couldn't employ one-tailed tests.

If you are using the XTAB program, you will notice that I give you z-scores not only for Pearson's r but also for gamma. Even though gamma is not parametric itself, random samples from a population will give a normal distribution of gammas. The following formula is an approximate method for transforming gamma into z-scores:

$$z = G\sqrt{\frac{N_s + N_d}{N(1 - G^2)}}$$

In this formula, G stands for gamma. Both N_s and N_d have the same meaning as in the formula for gamma. If you tell the XTAB program to show you how it calculated gamma, it will give you the other information you need to figure z, but I suggest you not worry about this formula and trust the software to give you the right answer. The z-score from gamma is interpreted in the same way as the one from r.

The statistical significance of unstandardized regression coefficients can simply be taken from the significance of the standardized co-efficient. Some sociologists like to work with the standard error, however, and you will occasionally see journal articles reporting that the unstandardized regression coefficient is twice the standard error, instead of reporting statistical significance per se. This is done often for studies that used ecological analysis. Many authors are reluctant to use the words *statistical significance* when analyzing data that are not from random samples.

The logic of statistical significance is inextricably intertwined with the concept of random sampling. Recall our discussion of drawing samples of 50 from a population of 512 college students. What happens when your data are based on the entire population?

There are only 50 American states. Here, the word *population* would refer to the number of states that existed, not to the numbers of people in them. Our ecological state dataset is therefore not a sample drawn from a population. True, it does not include the Australian states, the Canadian provinces, the British counties, or the French departments, but it is not a random sample of political units from around the world. If you get a correlation of 0.50 between two state-rate variables, X and Y, that's it. You can't ask what the chances are that the correlation in the population is really zero. The correlation in the population is 0.50, because you are working with the population itself. The logic of random sampling and statistical significance breaks down.

Some sociologists stop at this point and say, "Okay. So, we won't talk about statistical significance when using datasets that are based on the entire population." Others simply ignore the problem and report whatever the computer tells them the statistical significance is. The computer doesn't know how many states exist—how big the population is—and the formulas for statistical significance need only the size of the sample, not the size of the population. If the computer says "0.001 level of significance," these sociologists dutifully copy the message into their journal articles.

A few sociologists have sought justifications for using statistical significance with populations as well as with samples. One line of thinking goes like this. There is a certain distribution of values for the variable X in the population. There is another distribution of values of Y. Imagine that each state was assigned an X value at random out of the X distribution. Then imagine that every state was independently assigned a Y value from the Y distribution, again

entirely at random. Now, how likely is our 0.50 correlation to arise from random assignment of values like this?

Sociologists simply don't agree about this issue, so expect to see different messages about significance attached to correlations and regressions based on data about entire populations. In my own publications, I like to offer standard errors or significance levels, and then let the reader decide whether to pay attention to them. It seems only polite to provide the information, which the reader can always ignore.

This is a good time to reemphasize that statistical significance is not the same as substantive importance. Look back at the formula for transforming a correlation into a z-score. It has two factors, r and N, the size of the correlation and the number of cases. A trivially small correlation can be statistically significant if the number of cases is high enough. And a huge correlation, one that may express a tremendously powerful social influence, may be statistically insignificant if your number of cases is very small.

One way to assess the importance of a correlation is to compare it with other correlations, as we shall do in the next chapter. Certainly, a correlation of 0.50 is bigger than a correlation of 0.25. We would like to say it is twice as big. Remember, however, that all our coefficients are abstract mathematical results. Some of them may not have simple interpretations in terms of the real world. Before comparing r correlations, and before evaluating the importance of a single coefficient, it is best to square. And r^2 has a simple meaning: it is the proportion of the variance explained by the association between the two variables.

So, to compare correlations of 0.50 and 0.25, we should square them. Do so, and you find that the bigger one explains not twice the variance of the smaller one, but four times. A correlation of 0.50 is not five times as important as a correlation of 0.10, but 25 times. With 512 respondents, as in the XTAB dataset, a correlation of 0.15 achieves the 0.001 level of statistical significance, but it explains only 0.02 of the variance!

_____ Caution in the Use of r Correlation and Regression

An inherent limitation of r correlation and regression techniques is that they assume the data are at the interval (or ratio) level. They are based on the concept of variance, which in turn is based on the concept of mean. Note that the formulas contain the numerical values (X and Y), which is not true for Somers' D, gamma, and the taus, which use instead the counts of cases in cells of a crosstab. The variables in the regional dataset indeed all achieve the interval level of measurement, and r correlation and regression techniques are therefore appropriate. The XTAB variables may or may not meet this criterion, although the program goes ahead and calculates Pearson's r for any crosstab you request. The manual for the popular statistics package SPSS contains the following instructive footnote:

> There has been much debate in recent years concerning whether measures such as mean and standard deviation can be used in practical research with variables of ordinal as well as interval levels of measurement. This manual is clearly not the place in which to enter into this complicated debate. Some researchers and methodologists regularly utilize statistics formally assuming interval level of measurement with ordinal variables. Others refuse to do so. SPSS provides no check for the level of measurement of a variable. Whether or not to utilize statistics assuming interval measurement with ordinal data is left totally to the judgment of each researcher. (Nie et al. 1975:185)

Furthermore, r and regressions assume that the values of the variables in the population have a normal distribution. This is not true for the nonparametric correlations, which are also called _distribution-free_. With sociological variables, it is often an unwarranted leap of faith to assume that population parameters are normally distributed. Many clearly are not. But usually, all we know is the distribution for some sample, which is hardly ever exactly normal.

One of the more interesting new techniques to appear in sociology is **bootstrapping**, a nonparametric technique for estimating standard errors (Dietz, Frey, and Kalof 1987). It is a little like the method the TABL program used to simulate the chi-square distribution through random data. Requiring a computer program employing random numbers, it does a tremendous number of calculations.

Suppose you have a sample of 50 cases. The computer takes a random sample of the same size from these 50, with replacement. This means that some cases may appear many times in the sample, while others will be missing. Think of it this way. You write the numbers 1 through 50 on ping-pong balls, representing the 50 questionnaires you collected, and place the balls in a hat. Then you take a ball out, write down the number on it, and replace it in the hat. Out comes another ball. You write down its number and replace it. And so on, until you have a list of 50 numbers. Your dataset will consist of 50 questionnaires, some of them being photocopies of other questionnaires in the set. You enter the data into the computer and calculate a regression coefficient.

Then you go through the whole process again, not once but 100,000 times. You wind up with 100,000 regression coefficients, and you figure their standard deviation, which is your estimate of the standard error for the regression coefficient. Of course, this technique sounds absurd if we imagine doing it by hand. But the computer can do the work in a matter of minutes, so the advent of cheap computers makes bootstrapping eminently practical. Similar techniques are beginning to be used in sociology to extend statistical techniques like correlation and regression to data that do not meet traditional criteria such as having normal distributions.

The aim of these new techniques is improved estimates, more accurate coefficients and statistical tests on which to base our evaluation of theories. In the past, sociologists were not very careful in selecting statistical methods that were mathematically correct for the particular kind of data. Methodologists have both warned us about inappropriate use of analytic techniques and developed new techniques appropriate for the kinds of data available. Consequently, our standards have been getting higher and higher.

I have heard it said that the students of some leading methodologists are unable to do any sociological research, because no conceivable data from the real world could perfectly meet all the restrictions their teachers have taught them concerning the statistical techniques. This rumor is unfair. The best methodologists understand that their techniques are tools for the accomplishment of practical tasks, designed to measure effects and help us evaluate theories. When doing research, we inevitably have to bend a few of the purists' rules, or sociology would be paralyzed. But as new methods and fresh perspectives on older methods have been developed over the years, a progressively higher standard in the application of statistical techniques has become feasible as well as ideally desirable.

Testing a Theory about Religion

At the beginning of this chapter, I explained that most of the data accompanying the GRAF program came from a study in the sociology of religion done by Rodney Stark and myself. An important part of our research concerned the geography of religious cults. Now, journalists often use the term *cult* simply to refer to groups they consider unendurably weird. As I have explained, however, sociologists of religion use the term more neutrally to refer to any novel or exotic religious group, and there is no implication that such groups are in any sense evil or crazy. Some novel religious groups may be very dangerous, but most certainly are not.

Our geographical analysis used many different units of analysis, including cities, metropolitan areas, American states, and Canadian provinces (Stark and Bainbridge 1985; Bainbridge 1989a). Here we will use the nine regions, so that you can see exactly how the calculations were made, by replicating the same analyses on your computer. We will seek to test an important hypothesis: "Cults are more common where the standard churches are weaker."

This hypothesis predicts a negative correlation between, for example, the rate of membership in standard churches (variable 1) and the rate of SCG centers (variable 18). If you check the regression analysis, you will find an r of -0.89 and a B of -0.56. Our hypothesis identifies church membership as the independent variable and cultism as the dependent variable.

The theoretical explanation behind this hypothesis has several elements. First, it argues that religion provides hope and thus serves universal human needs. Everybody faces death, and everybody must come to terms with more limited forms of loss and destruction. All people have unfulfilled desires and unresolved frustrations. True, some social forces work against religious faith. To cite a nearby example, sociology trains students to be skeptical of ideologies, and thus it works to erode belief. So, not everybody will possess religious faith, but there is a tendency for people to seek hope beyond the limits of earthly existence, and thus people will tend to be open to religion.

Where the rate of membership in conventional churches is low, apparently the standard denominations are failing to reach people. This may be because the particular community has a very high rate of geographic migration. When people move from one place to another, they lose social ties to whatever church they used to belong to, and ties to a new religious congregation may be slow in building. Unconventional religions may be very good at reaching out to such migrants. In any case, a weakness of standard churches leaves many people's religious need unmet, and novel religious groups therefore have a better chance of recruiting these people.

Also, the standard churches, almost by definition, set the norms of religious conventionality. If the standard churches are very strong and the majority of people belong to them, then novel religions will be seen as especially strange and deviant because they violate the prevailing religious norms. But if the standard churches are weak, then the norms themselves will be weak or vague. Under such circumstances, there will be less social penalty for experimenting with unconventional religions.

Thus, there are two mutually supportive explanations for why cults may flourish where the churches are weak. First, unmet religious needs create a substantial market for whatever form of religion can reach people. Second, the inhibitions against religious experimentation are reduced.

The nine regions of the United States do, in fact, differ substantially in rates of church membership and church attendance. In our regional dataset, 63.0 percent of New Englanders formally belong to one of the conventional denominations, compared with only 36.0 percent of residents of the Pacific region. And 54.0 percent of New Englanders attend church at least once a month, compared with 32.0 percent of those living near the Pacific Ocean.

Figure 12.10 shows the regression and correlation information from 14 statistical analyses done using the GRAF program. In each, the rate of church membership is X, and one of the cult rates is Y. You should probably look most closely at the r correlations, because they permit comparison across the dependent variables. Each one is substantial and negative. Together, they provide very powerful support for the hypothesis and the theory that lies behind it.

It might occur to you that there is a potential problem with this analysis. In Western societies, unlike many Eastern and Third-World societies, people belong to only one religious group at a time. You can't be a member of the Process cult, discussed in Chapters 2 and 3, and

FIGURE 12.10
Church Membership and Cults

| | Correlation and Regression Coefficients with the Church Membership Rate | | |
Cult Rate	B	A	r
15: Cult headquarters per 10,000,000	− 2.08	141.49	− 0.90
18: 1974 *SCG* centers per 1,000,000	− 0.56	38.55	− 0.89
19: 1974 *SCG* stores per 1,000,000	− 0.38	27.02	− 0.73
20: 1978 *SCG* listings per 1,000,000	− 0.38	26.48	− 0.85
21: *Organic Traveller* per 1,000,000	− 0.13	9.53	− 0.79
22: *Psychic Register* per 1,000,000	− 0.30	20.02	− 0.93
23: Psychic *Who's Who* per 1,000,000	− 0.18	12.51	− 0.88
24: 1950s *Fate* stories per 1,000,000	− 0.44	30.25	− 0.92
25: 1960–79 *Fate* stories per 1,000,000	− 0.67	48.71	− 0.83
26: *Fate* subscribers per 100,000	− 1.13	100.63	− 0.82
27: 1970 TM initiates per 100,000	− 0.48	38.84	− 0.48
28: 1975 TM initiates per 10,000	− 0.32	32.69	− 0.45
29: TM teachers per 1,000,000	− 1.13	77.49	− 0.80
30: Astrologers per 1,000,000	− 0.16	13.11	− 0.72

also consider yourself a Baptist in good standing. Thus, you might think a negative correlation is built into these analyses, almost by definition. However, this is not true.

First of all, several of the measures are not logically incompatible with membership in conventional churches. For example, anybody can subscribe to *Fate* magazine, both Baptists and Processeans. Anybody can visit organic restaurants and occult bookstores. For a long time, Transcendental Meditation claimed not to be religious in nature, and it was very popular among the liberal Protestant denominations. Many Episcopal clergy, for example, tried TM. Thus, it was not a foregone conclusion that the correlations between church membership and the cult rates would be strongly negative.

In a study of data from 1926, I found powerful negative correlations between the rate of church membership and the rates of various cults (Stark and Bainbridge 1985:449), despite the fact that members of the cults were actually included among the church members, and thus one might have expected positive correlations.

This discussion illustrates a fine point of correlational analysis. The two variables must be conceptually distinct, or the correlation will be uninformative no matter how big the coefficient is. If I had included the rate of people who are not members of churches in the dataset, it would have produced the following regression and correlation information with the rate of those who are church members: $B = -1.00$, $A = 0.00$, $r = -1.00$. But no competent social scientist would have said that these numbers told us anything we did not already know.

In the case of the negative correlations between the church-member rate and the cult rates, we do learn something new. For one thing, an alternative hypothesis predicts that the correlations should be positive, not negative. It springs from the theory that some parts of contemporary society are more secular than others. The secular communities don't much want religion of either kind, and in the most religious areas the cults might flourish as deviant reflections of the standard churches. If you cannot frame two competing hypotheses, each one with at least some claim to plausibility, then quantitative analysis may not be very informative.

Let there be no mistake. I do not consider these correlations to be conclusive proof of our theory. There are no conclusive proofs in sociology or in any other science, but other data often are in line with the theory as well. We get similar ecological correlations in Canada and Western Europe. Several survey datasets show lower levels of openness to occult ideas among people who strongly identify with the standard religious tradition than among those who profess no religion. However, there is ample room for argument. You are certainly invited to suggest alternative theories to explain the correlations you will find in the regional dataset. It is only fair to ask you, however, to suggest ways of empirically testing your theories in competition with ours. If you get that far in your sociological analysis of secularization, then maybe you should do the imagined research, publish it in the scientific journals, and take your place among professional sociologists!

PROJECTS FOR CHAPTER 12

The seven projects that follow use the GRAF program and its data on nine regional divisions to perform pilot studies that could later be done more thoroughly with data for all 50 states or with smaller units of analysis, such as metropolitan areas, cities, or counties. Here, we restrict ourselves to just nine cases so that you can see exactly how the calculations are done. The first two projects ask you to hunt for the

Bible Belt and the Pacific Abyss, by inspecting data on religion for the nine geographical divisions. The next three relate religion to migration, social class, and social change. The final pair of projects focuses on the calculation of regressions, visually by rotating the regression line (if you have a computer with graphics capability) and mathematically by calculating coefficients yourself from information provided by the computer.

1. Hunting for the Bible Belt. For this project you will use the following option on the GRAF program's menu: "regression analysis of two regional variables." However, you will ignore the complex parts of the analysis and focus instead just on the rates for the nine regions. Select a number of religion variables, and determine whether the rates for the three southern regions are much different from those for the other six regions. Write a brief report summarizing your findings. If you find some variables for which the southern rates are very different, say so and attempt to explain why. And if you find a number of variables for which you would expect different rates in the South, but the rates you found were about the same as in the North, see if you can explain these findings as well. To the extent that you find a Bible Belt, how can you describe the aspects of religion in which it seems to exist?

2. The Pacific Abyss. Perhaps the most striking feature of American religious geography is what I call the Pacific Abyss, a sharp drop in church membership in the Pacific region and parts of the western Mountain region of the United States. The same feature is found in Canada, because British Columbia (and to a lesser extent Alberta) has much lower rates of church involvement than does the rest of the nation.

Follow the same instructions as for project 1, above, but focus your attention instead on the features of the Pacific Abyss. You may want to emphasize the first 15 variables in the regional dataset, which concern some general features of religions. Do they all show a marked drop for the Pacific region, compared with the rest of the country? Write an essay, supported by statistics from the regional dataset, reporting what you found.

3. Migration and Religion. Two variables in the regional dataset concern geographic migration. One is variable 34, "Born in state % (native)," which is the percent of native-born Americans who were born in the same state where the 1980 census found them. The other is variable 35, "Same house five years % (age 5+)," the percent of people over age five who were living in the same house five years before. Clearly, these are both measures of low migration or of residential stability. I suggested that geographic migration might reduce the rate of conventional church membership and increase the rate of involvement in cults.

Using the GRAF program, test these hypotheses. You must select appropriate measures of church membership and cultism, perform a correct statistical analysis, and discuss your findings in a brief report.

4. Social Class and Religion. Consider the theory that low social class encourages church membership and conventional religious faith. In our regional dataset, variables 36 through 41 might be considered measures of social class, whether direct or indirect. Variables 1 through 10 might be considered measures of conventional religious involvement, although they cover a wide range of phenomena and might not show exactly the same correlations with social class.

First, construct a plausible theory explaining why social class might correlate negatively with conventional religion, and identify which of the variables I mentioned are appropriate measures to test it. Then conduct a statistical test, reporting your results both in the form of a table and a written discussion of whether hypotheses derived from the theory were supported.

5. Persistence of Unusual Religion. Three variables in the regional dataset, numbers 31 through 33, were taken from a survey of church members done in 1926 (Bureau of the Census 1930), and reflect regional acceptance of novel religious expressions. Christian Science has become a familiar if small and rather unusual Christian denomination, while Spiritualism and Theosophy are greatly outside the Christian tradition. All have unusual beliefs and practices, and all were quite novel when they appeared at various points in the 19th century. Thus it might be appropriate to call them *established cults,* so long as we understood that the term *cult* was not meant as criticism but merely to express the unusual character of these groups.

Use these three variables, in conjunction with more recent cult variables in the regional dataset, to explore the geographic stability of unusual religions over the space of half a century. After doing appropriate statistical analysis using the GRAF program, write a brief essay stating whether the distribution of cults in 1926 was about the same as it was around 1980. NOTE: You may find that some of the rates have very different geographic distributions. If so, say so, and document the differences statistically.

6. Rotating Regression Lines (for classes with access to computers with graphics capability). Explore the regional dataset, using the scattergram option in the GRAF program, looking for pairs of variables that give a variety of scatters of data points across the graph and a variety of regression-line slopes. Select eight pairs of variables that this exploration shows give eight very different pictures. Draw rough sketches of each of the eight graphs, with the regression line rotated to the right position, and write a one-paragraph description explaining why each picture looks the way it does.

7. Calculation Practice. Select any pair of variables you wish from the regional dataset, copy down all the information provided by the computer, and show exactly how to calculate B, A, r, and standard error.

CHAPTER SUMMARY

This chapter explains how to calculate correlations and regressions, working with a simple dataset that has only nine cases—the nine official "divisions" of the United States. The GRAF program includes two modules for explaining these statistical tools, one requiring a computer with graphics capability, the other not.

Thirty-three of the 48 variables in this regional dataset came from research Stark and Bainbridge did for their award-winning book *The Future of Religion*. Their theory argued that the decline of traditional churches stimulates first revival (in the form of religious sects), then innovation (in the form of religious cults). The GRAF program lets students replicate the findings while learning the logic of the analytical tools.

We review some simple high-school mathematics. The *slope* of a line expresses how many units the line rises for each unit it runs forward. Every straight line on a graph like this can be expressed as an equation of the following form: $Y' = A + BX$. Y' is the line's estimate of variable Y for a given value of variable X. B is the slope of the line. A is the value of Y where the line crosses the X-axis, where the line has a value for X of zero.

The GRAF program has a demonstration of a dynamic regression line, which may be seen on computers possessing graphic capability. First one selects two variables from the 48-variable regional dataset. Then a graph of the nine data points appears on the screen, with a horizontal line running through the point where the means intersect. By pressing the [↑] or [↓] keys, the student can rotate this line until it seems to pass closest to the nine data points. The equation for the line appears on the right side of the screen, changing as the line rotates. Also shown are the residuals, the little lines that go vertically from the data points to the moving line. When the residuals are minimized, the moving line matches the calculated regression line, the A and B of which are shown in a box on the screen. This program demonstrates vividly the meaning of the equation of a line, the concept of residuals, and the value of finding the line that fits best through the data points, allowing one to predict Y if X is known.

A formula calculates the regression line from the data. The formula for B is the covariance of X and Y divided by the variance of X. To calculate A, we put the value of the mean for X into X in this formula, and we put the mean for Y in the place of Y'. Negative slopes are illustrated with two regional variables, the percent of persons aged 25+ who had four or more years of college, and the percent of families in poverty.

B is asymmetrical and is not limited to the range from −1.00 to +1.00. Closely related to it is a correlation coefficient that is symmetrical and that stays within this range, Pearson's r. The concept of standard deviation is used to show further connections between regressions and r correlations. The standard error of an estimate is analogous to standard deviation. Statistical significance of r and gamma can be estimated using z-scores. Among the newest techniques to appear in sociology is *bootstrapping*, a nonparametric technique for estimating standard errors.

The regional dataset can be used to test the Stark-Bainbridge theory, which predicts that cults are more common where the standard churches are weaker. The nine regions of the United States differ substantially in rates of church membership and church attendance. They also differ in a number of measures of cult activity. If the theory is correct, there should be strong negative correlations between church membership and these cultic variables. There are.

KEY CONCEPTS FOR CHAPTER 12

slope of a line   398
regression line   402
residuals   407
Y-intercept   409

covariance   409
Pearson's r   410
standard error   416
bootstrapping   420

CHAPTER

13 Multiple Variable Analysis

CHAPTER OUTLINE

CHAPTER OVERVIEW

The key to modern quantitative research methods is the simultaneous analysis of three or more variables. There are many ways of combining variables in a statistical analysis, but one distinction is between approaches in which the variables compete with each other and approaches in which they cooperate. This is the chapter for competition between variables; cooperation comes in the next and final chapter.

Here, we will be concerned with situations in which two or more independent variables are seeking to explain variation in one dependent variable. Often, we want to compare

independent variables, to see which has more explanatory power. At other times, we investigate the possibility that a particular independent variable does not really explain anything about the dependent variable, even though it may initially appear to. Instead, a third **extraneous variable** is really responsible, a situation called spuriousness.

The classic hypothetical example concerns fires and firefighters. Presumably, if you study accidental fires at homes and businesses, you will discover that there is a positive correlation between how many firefighters go to the blaze and the dollar amount of damage done. This can lead to the conclusion that the firefighters cause the damage, chopping madly with their axes and squirting floods of water from their hoses, and that we should stop paying their salaries. But a more reasonable analysis says that the real cause of damage is the fire itself. The bigger the fire, the more damage. The bigger the fire, the more firefighters are sent to battle it. So it is wrong to blame the firefighters for the damage. The correlation between the number of firefighters and the amount of damage is the spurious result of the varying magnitude of the fires.

One approach to this problem is to construct three-variable tables that examine the associa-tion between two variables, X and Y, for each value of variable Z. Just as we can calculate gamma for a single crosstab, we can calculate partial gamma for the set of crosstabs that makes up a three-variable table. Partial r and multiple regression are the equivalent methods for parametric (continuous) variables. These methods are not without problems, however, which include collinearity and heteroscedastic-ity, not to mention response bias and the eco-logical fallacy.

The XTAB program, using the select/reject option, can provide the raw material for three-variable tables and partial gamma. The MAPS program has modules for partial r and for three-variable regression.

_____ Three-Variable Tables

One of the classic methods for controlling for one variable while looking at the association between two others is the three-variable table. An example I have always found fascinating is an analysis of cigarette smoking and juvenile delinquency by Travis Hirschi (1969:167), from the questionnaire study that inspired our SAMP program described in Chapter 7. Hirschi argues that youth who reject the status of child and behave more like adults are especially apt to commit acts of delinquency, such as theft, vandalism, and assault. It is not that adults nec-essarily steal, but that youth who reject the sta-tus of child are less likely to be under effective social control. Hirschi's favored theory of devi-ance is called **control theory**, the view that de-viant behavior will readily occur unless suppressed through strong bonds to the legiti-mate social order.

In recent years, cigarette smoking has come under increasing attack, and many communi-ties have enacted laws to restrict it. In a sense, then, cigarette smoking is today treated as slightly deviant, although a substantial portion of the population engages in it. In the 1960s, however, when Hirschi did his survey, there was nothing deviant about adults smoking cig-arettes. There were no health warnings on ciga-rette packs. There were cigarette advertisements on television. Few restaurants had no-smoking sections, and smoking was permitted in essen-tially all public buildings. However, there were laws prohibiting sale of tobacco to minors, and considerable efforts were made to keep kids from smoking.

Hirschi had included two smoking items in the survey he administered to high-school boys. One simply asked if the high-schooler smoked, and 24 percent of 1,250 respondents said they did. Another question was an agree-disagree item using the statement, "It is none of the school's business if a student wants to smoke outside the classroom." Among the smokers, 72 percent agreed with this pro-smoking state-ment. Among the nonsmokers, only 29 percent agreed. Clearly, these two smoking items are correlated. On theoretical grounds, how-ever, Hirschi felt these two items should be considered separately. One is about behavior— actual smoking—while the other expresses an attitude. We have seen much evidence that behavior and attitudes are very different phe-nomena, and they may often diverge in wholly unexpected ways.

Among the 1,250 high-school boys, 1,076 gave a definite agree or disagree answer to the attitudinal question about the school's right to restrict smoking outside of class. Of these, 216 both smoked and felt that it was none of the school's business. And in this group of 216, 73 percent had committed one or more delinquent acts such as theft or vandalism. At the opposite extreme were 534 boys who did not smoke and who rejected the statement limiting the school's right to prohibit smoking. Among them, only 32 percent admitted ever committing a delinquent act. We can analyze these figures more flexibly with a simple table, Figure 13.1.

In a way, this table is a compressed form of four tiny tables. The 73-percent figure in the upper-left cell of the table refers to 157 delinquent boys among the 216 boys who both smoke and agree with the pro-smoking statement. You can imagine a little table that is just for these 216, reporting that 157 of them (73 percent) had committed one or more delinquent acts, while 59 of them (27 percent) had not. There would be three similar tiny tables for the other percentages in Figure 13.1.

A three-variable table, such as Figure 13.1, allows us to see the effect of two independent variables, separately and in combination. To see the effect of smoking, while holding constant the effect of attitudes toward school control of smoking, compare across the two columns. You will note that 73 percent is much bigger than 44 percent—29 percentage points bigger, in fact.

FIGURE 13.1
Smoking Behaviors and Attitudes Predicting Delinquency

Pro-smoking Statement	Smokes	Does Not Smoke
Agree	73%	44%
Disagree	59%	32%

The numbers are percent in the specified group who committed one or more delinquent acts.

And 59 percent is 27 percentage points bigger than 32 percent.

To see the effect of ideological differences, while controlling for the actual behavior of smoking, compare the numbers across the two rows. Note that 73 percent is 14 percentage points bigger than 59 percent, and 44 percent is 12 percentage points bigger than 32 percent.

Finally, to see the effect of the two independent variables in combination, compare the upper-left number with the one in the lower-right corner. And 73 percent is fully 41 percentage points greater than 32 percent. Thus smoking—both the behavior and the attitude—is strongly associated with delinquency among Hirschi's high-school boys. And together, the behavior and the attitude contribute greatly to an explanation of delinquency.

Hirschi concluded, however, that the behavior was more important than the attitude. The previous paragraphs show that the percentage differences across the columns are better than twice as big as the percentage differences across the rows. To Hirschi, this fact indicates that premature adulthood encourages delinquency, even without the support of beliefs about the right to smoke. Indeed, to me the percentage differences suggest the ever-present sociological question of which comes first, attitudes or behavior.

Traditional sociology talks of norms and values as determinants of behavior, implying that these are relatively abstract verbal statements that shaped the person's thinking about potential lines of behavior. The alternative, that norms and values are minor constituents of human action that frequently provide a mere ideological gloss on already existing behavior patterns, is a view that has often challenged my own research. But one should not let one's imagination go theoretically too far afield in discussing the implications of a single research finding. The point here is to understand that a modest three-variable table can tell us a lot, not that it can tell us everything.

Among the many other classic examples of the three-variable table approach are studies of the factors leading to anti-Semitism (Glock and

Stark 1966; Lipset and Raab 1970). Glock and Stark examined the extent to which hostility toward Jews reflected certain kinds of religious commitment within the Christian tradition. Using data from their huge, well-designed survey they created an index of religious bigotry and discovered that persons expressing this unfortunate attitude were also very likely to be anti-Semitic. However, low levels of education also predicted anti-Semitism, and low education was associated with religious bigotry. Thus, lack of education might have been to blame, rather than religious bigotry as such.

To examine this possibility, Glock and Stark (1966:204) constructed a table in which the cells were various combinations of education level and religious bigotry, and the numbers in the cells were the percent of each group high on the anti-Semitism variable. Within each level of education, religious bigotry was associated with anti-Semitism; and within each level of religious bigotry, low education was associated with anti-Semitism. Later, Lipset and Raab (1970:441) tried something similar with their own data. They looked, for example, at Christians with college educations who were low in religious commitment and found that only 3 percent of them scored high on an index of anti-Semitism. Among college-educated persons who were high in religious commitment, however, 29 percent were high in anti-Semitism. For each level of education, religious commitment was associated with anti-Semitism, and for each level of religious commitment, low education was associated with anti-Semitism. Thus, these studies show that each of the independent variables (religion and education) predicts variation in the dependent variable, controlling for the other independent variable.

Sex, Race, and Delinquency

Hirschi's delinquency research, as you know, inspired the simulated survey in Chapter 7. To a limited extent, the associated SAMP program allows you to analyze three variables at once, to check for spuriousness. For example, suppose we found that hating school was associated with performing delinquent acts. In fact, Hirschi and his colleagues made much of this finding. But let's consider the possibility that Hirschi was wrong and that the correlation between hating school and delinquency was spurious.

Boys hate school, I know from personal experience. Girls, perhaps, hate school less. Boys are more apt to perform delinquent acts. Therefore, the variable of sex may be responsible for a spurious correlation between hating school and delinquency.

This is easy to check. First, look at the association between liking school and some of the delinquency variables in the survey, using a sample of 500 teenagers. Then do the same thing for a sample of 500 boys, and repeat the analysis for a sample of 500 girls. By looking at the sexes separately, you have controlled for sex. If attitudes toward school and delinquency are associated in a similar way for each sex separately, then the association cannot be the spurious result of gender.

The same thing can be done with race as your control variable, because it is possible to do samples of 500 white boys, 500 white girls, 500 black boys, and 500 black girls. I do not promise you that you will make any very exciting discoveries if you do this, because I did not build any complex interactions among these variables into the simulated dataset. The procedure I suggested, however, is a very valid way of approaching such problems, and you can try it with the SAMP program if you wish.

A Woman President?

Respondents to the XTAB survey were asked their views about whether a woman should become president of the United States, through variable 57, a preference question that asked how much they liked this idea. To be sure, many respondents might have wanted to tell me, "It all depends on who she is, what her political positions are, and who her opponent is!" So, you might wonder whether a simple question like this is too crude to capture people's opinions validly. But as we shall see, responses to this item correlate in interesting ways with other variables, and one of my graduate students pointed out to me that this item provides perfect material for an examination of three-variable analysis.

Women like the idea of a woman president more than men do. In the XTAB dataset, women gave a woman president an average preference score of 5.69, while men gave an average of 4.46. Expressed as gamma, the correlation between being male and liking the idea of a woman president is -0.51. You might note that men, on average, liked the idea, rating it slightly above the middle of the preference scale (4.46 compared with 4.00), so you should not say that men are against a woman president. Women, however, are much more strongly for it. In part, it is a women's issue.

But the gender of the respondent may not be the only factor influencing attitudes toward having a woman president. Although some women have achieved high positions in the Reagan and Bush administrations, and even back in the Eisenhower administration, there is a general feeling that conservatives are unenthusiastic about having a woman president, and the Democratic Party was the first of the two major parties to nominate a woman for vice-president. So we should examine political orientation as well as gender, and the gamma between being conservative (variable 71) and liking the idea of a woman president is -0.36.

As my student pointed out, however, men tend to score more conservatively on this item than women do, and the gamma with being

male is 0.33. Thus, it is possible that the key variable is gender. Being female makes one like the idea of a woman president, and being female makes one more liberal in general. This would be an example of spuriousness. The negative correlation between conservatism and liking a woman president might merely result from the fact that being female is strongly correlated with both of these variables. And, my student noted further, the select/reject option in the XTAB program makes it easy to test this hypothesis.

One way to check this possibility is to divide the sample of respondents into two groups, the men and the women. Then one can see if there is a negative correlation between being conservative and liking the idea of a woman president in each of these two groups. That is, by separating the respondents by sex, we control for the variable of gender. Figure 13.2 does this.

This table shows how the gammas were calculated, giving the numerator ($N_s - N_d$) and the denominator ($N_s + N_d$) for the final division that produces the gamma. For all 502 respondents who expressed a preference concerning having a woman president, gamma is -0.3584 between this preference and being politically conservative. I figured gamma to four decimal places, so you could see some of the details in what is to follow. Among the men, gamma is -0.3067, just 0.0517 smaller. And among the women, it is -0.3408, only 0.0176 smaller. Apparently, attitudes toward a woman president are not just a reflection of the respondent's gender, but also reflect political orientations within each gender. Thus, the negative

FIGURE 13.2

Conservatism and a Woman President, Controlling for Sex

Respondents	$N_s - N_d$	$N_s + N_d$	Gamma
502 Men & Women	-29295	81737	-0.3584
248 Men	-6416	20920	-0.3067
254 Women	-6100	17898	-0.3408
Contingent total	-12516	38818	-0.3224

correlation between being conservative and liking the idea of a woman president is not merely the spurious result of gender differences.

It might be nice to summarize this finding in a single number, rather than in separate gammas for the two sexes, and one could take the average of the two gammas for men and women: $(-0.3067 + -0.3408)/2 = -0.3238$. But an average like this ignores that there are not exactly the same numbers of both sexes, and in cases where the numbers in different groups were very different, this average would seriously distort the result. An alternative way of combining gammas from different subgroups among respondents is called **partial gamma**. Although not very widely used in sociology journals, it has a clear meaning, is easy to understand, and will prepare us to deal with slightly more complicated partial correlations later in this chapter.

Notice that Figure 13.2 gives us $N_s - N_d$ and $N_s + N_d$ for both groups. The final line of the table, labeled "contingent total," adds these parts of gamma together. For example, $N_s - N_d$ for the men is -6416, and for the women $N_s - N_d$ is -6100. Add these together and you get -125126. Similarly, the total of $N_s + N_d$ for both men and women is 388118. These contingent totals are the $N_s - N_d$ and $N_s + N_d$ for the crosstab of conservative and women president, with the influence of sex removed. Divide this $N_s - N_d$ by this $N_s + N_d$, and you get a new gamma, -0.3224. It is quite substantial in size, indicating in one coefficient that political orientation is strongly correlated with attitude toward a woman president, while controlling for sex of respondent. This *partial gamma* is only slightly different from the average of the gammas for the two sexes, but for some analyses partial gamma might wind up very different, and thus is to be preferred over the average.

At this point we might wonder whether we have our hypothesis about spuriousness backward. Perhaps political orientation is what matters, not sex. A moment's reflection, however, suggests something amiss with this notion. When we thought that sex might be the key

variable, it was quite reasonable to hypothesize that being female tended to make one become liberal. But the reverse of that is hard to believe. How could being politically liberal make one become female? Sex really cannot become a dependent variable, certainly not in ordinary analyses of survey data.

There are very good reasons, however, for trying an analysis in which we look at the correlation between sex and the attitude toward a woman president, controlling for political orientation. Most important, we will gain insight into how the three variables fit together. Here is one possibility: Perhaps sex influences political orientation, and political orientation shapes the attitude. If so, sex has its influence on the attitude only indirectly, through political orientation. This is what is called a *causal chain,* a set of three or more variables connected through a simple series of correlations that are assumed to reflect cause-and-effect relationships. We could express it this way: sex $\rightarrow$ politics $\rightarrow$ attitude. If this is how the variables fit together, then controlling for politics will erase the correlation between sex and the attitude.

An alternate possibility is that sex has two ways of influencing the attitude toward a woman president, both direct (sex $\rightarrow$ attitude) and indirect (sex $\rightarrow$ politics $\rightarrow$ attitude). If this is true, controlling for politics will leave a significant correlation between sex and the attitude. Thus, it would be interesting to try an analysis in which political orientation was the control variable, and we separately examined the crosstab between sex and preferences for a woman president for each value of the conservatism variable. This is done in Figure 13.3.

The gammas in Figure 13.3 are all for the crosstab of sex by preference for a woman president. The sex variable is coded so that males get a value of 2, while females get a value of 1. So the negative gammas show that men are less apt to like the idea of a woman president. Again, we have given $N_s - N_d$ and $N_s + N_d$ for each of the seven categories in the conservatism scale. In each case, except the seven extreme conservatives, the gamma between sex and

FIGURE 13.3

Sex and a Woman President, Controlling for Conservatism

Respondents	$N_s - N_d$	$N_s + N_d$	Gamma
502 Men & Women	− 26701	52835	− 0.51
7 Extremely conservative	5	5	1.00
39 Conservative	− 150	250	− 0.60
89 Slightly conservative	− 523	1573	− 0.33
51 Moderate	− 240	508	− 0.47
108 Slightly liberal	− 1314	2438	− 0.54
161 Liberal	− 2239	4755	− 0.47
47 Extremely liberal	− 251	387	− 0.65
Contingent total	− 4712	9916	− 0.48

preference for a woman president is negative, indicating that men like the idea less well. And the partial gamma is − 0.48, showing a substantial negative correlation even when controlling for political conservatism. This suggests that gender has a strong influence on attitudes toward a woman president, aside from the political differences measured by the conservatism scale.

You might wonder what was happening in the extremely conservative group to give so different a gamma, 1.00, which seems to indicate that extremely conservative men like a woman president better than extremely conservative women do. Well, there were only seven extreme conservatives, and just one of them was a woman. She gave a woman president a rock-bottom rating of 1 on the preference scale, as did one of the extremely conservative men. The five other extremely conservative men gave a woman president preference ratings greater

than 1. For this little crosstab, gamma looks at just five comparison pairs, pairing the one woman off with each of the five men who were not tied with her in rating a woman president at 1. In a sense, then, the gamma is really based on just the one extremely conservative woman respondent, and thus is not a good indication of how women feel in general.

We can summarize the two tables examining the interrelationships of the three variables. Within each sex, political orientation predicts attitudes toward having a woman president. And within each political category, except the tiny group of extreme conservatives, being female predisposes one toward wanting a woman president. Neither independent variable can simply be explained in terms of the other. Both gender and political orientation matter in determining respondents' attitudes toward having a woman president of the United States.

Partial r Correlations

Statistical techniques have been developed comparable to partial gamma for the other coefficients that are called correlations. Most important among them is the method of **partial correlations** using r, appropriate for

interval-level data. The seventh option in the menu of the MAPS program allows you to calculate the partial correlation between two variables while controlling for a third variable.

I'll start with a vivid example. Early in this century, social scientists and government officials alike were convinced that one of the chief causes of crime was immigration. Although this theory has largely been abandoned, one can make a strong prima facie case for it on the basis of official census and crime data. For the 50 American states, in 1980, there was a correlation of 0.50 between the percent of population who were foreign-born and the larceny rate, and the correlation between percent foreign-born and the assault rate was 0.28. Thus, both property crimes and violent crimes correlated with percent foreign-born, which is a pretty direct measure of immigration.

So watch out! Foreigners are dangerous! My wife happens to be foreign-born, so I should be especially careful she doesn't sneak up behind me as I am processing these words, bash me on the head, and steal my pocket change. Wherever the rate of foreign-born is high, expect high crime rates. It is a short step from this empirical observation to the conclusion that it is the foreigners, themselves, who are committing the crimes.

But let's think sociologically. Recall Robinson's (1950) warnings about the ecological fallacy. His chief example concerned the fact that areas with high rates of immigration tended to have above-average rates of literacy, thus producing a positive ecological correlation between immigration and literacy. But data based on individuals rather than areas showed that immigrants were more likely than native-born to be illiterate, rather than literate. Thus, if we interpret the correlations in terms of individuals, statistical analysis at the ecological level can lead us astray. And, as we shall consider again later in this chapter, the ecological fallacy can usually be understood simply as an instance of spuriousness, in which some unmeasured third variable has distorted the association between the two variables under consideration.

What third variable could be doing that here? Well, what about urbanism? Other things being equal, we may expect higher crime rates in urban areas, thus higher rates in states that are highly urbanized. Many immigrants head for big cities when they come to the United States, believing they can achieve better lives in urban centers and often drawn by substantial numbers of compatriots already living in the cities. Thus, we should analyze the associations linking three variables, not two: crime, immigration, urbanism.

The Partial-Correlations Option of the MAPS Program

From the menu of the MAPS program, press (7) to get partial correlations. The computer will then expect you to enter the numbers of three variables. We will call them X_1, X_2, and Y. X_1 and X_2 are two independent variables, like immigration and urbanism. Y is the dependent variable, such as crime. This is the order you should enter these variables: X_1, X_2, Y.

In our example, X_1 should be variable 29, the percent of the population that is foreign-born. X_2 should be variable 27, the percent of the population living in urban areas. And Y should be variable 70, the FBI report of larcenies per 100,000 people. So you would type (2)(9)(ENTER), (2)(7)(ENTER), and (7)(0)(ENTER). After you have done so, your computer screen will fill with quite a lot of information, actually two tables and two long calculations. To make things maximally clear, I have divided the screen up with lines, and we will look at each part of the analysis separately here.

FIGURE 13.4

Correlation Matrix, Basis of Partial-correlation Analysis

	Var 29	Var 27	Var 70
Var 29	1.00	0.72	0.50
Var 27	0.72	1.00	0.63
Var 70	0.50	0.63	1.00

The first thing to note, and the basis of all later calculations, is the correlation matrix of the three variables. For the variables in our example, it looks like Figure 13.4. I said that the correlation between variable 29 (foreign-born) and variable 70 (larcenies) is 0.50, and you see that fact in the correlation matrix. You also see that percent urban has even higher correlations with these two variables, 0.72 and 0.63. Generally, that is a big clue that this third variable may be responsible for a spurious correlation between the first two variables.

For urbanism to distort the association between immigration and larceny, it has to have a powerful connection to each of these other variables. If you wish, you can conceptualize this in physical terms. For urbanism to push immigration and larceny together, unnaturally, it has to have a firm grip on each and exert considerable force on it. This requires close connections between urbanism and immigration and between urbanism and larceny. The correlation matrix suggests it has such close connections, but only a statistical analysis can tell us if its grip is firm enough.

Calculating a Partial Correlation

The formula for calculating a partial correlation is based on the original correlation coefficients connecting the three variables. The correlation between X_1 and Y will be called $r[X_1,Y]$. The correlation between X_2 and Y will be called $r[X_2,Y]$. And the correlation between X_1 and X_2 will be called $r[X_1,X_2]$. Finally, we need a name for the partial correlation between X_1 and Y, controlling for the effect of X_2. We shall call it partial $r[X_1,Y].X_2$. Notice the little dot (".") between the $r[X_1,Y]$ and the X_2. Using that notation, the formula for partial r is

$$\text{partial } r[X_1,Y].X_2 =$$

$$\frac{r[X_1,Y] - (r[X_2,Y]) \times (r[X_1,X_2])}{\sqrt{(1 - (r[X_2,Y])^2)} \times \sqrt{(1 - (r[X_1,X_2])^2)}}$$

The numerator is simply the original correlation minus the product of the two other correlations. The original correlation between X_1 and Y is 0.50, and the two other correlations are 0.63 and 0.72. Multiply 0.63 by 0.72 and you get about 0.45. Subtract that from 0.50 and you get 0.05. Actually, when the computer does this, using very precise numbers before they were rounded off to two decimal places, it gets about 0.04 for the numerator of the formula.

The denominator requires more steps in calculation. When you call for this analysis in the MAPS program, you will get the information given here in Figure 13.5. The denominator works from the two correlation coefficients other than the one between X_1 and Y, so you can momentarily ignore the first row of the table and focus on the rows for $r[X_2,Y]$ and $r[X_1,X_2]$.

FIGURE 13.5
Steps in Calculating Partial Correlations

Items	r	r^2	$1 - r^2$	$\sqrt{(1 - r^2)}$
$r[X_1,Y]$	0.50	0.25	0.75	0.87
$r[X_2,Y]$	0.63	0.40	0.60	0.77
$r[X_1,X_2]$	0.72	0.52	0.48	0.69

Consider $r[X_2,Y]$, the correlation between X_2 and Y. It is 0.63. The square of 0.63—that is, $r[X_2,Y]^2$—is 0.40. The next step is to subtract that from 1, giving a result of 0.60. Then we take the square root of that, getting 0.77. To get the other part of the denominator, follow the same steps for $r[X_1,X_2]$, which gives you 0.69. Then, the denominator in the formula for partial correlation is the product of these two numbers, 0.77×0.69, or about 0.53.

Finally, you divide the denominator into the numerator, 0.04/0.53, and get a result of about 0.08. Again, the computer works with more precise numbers, and 0.08 is the answer it gets when it goes through all these calculations. So the partial correlation between foreign-born and larceny, controlling for urbanism, is 0.08. This is close to zero and is vastly lower than the 0.50 we started with. What does this mean?

Strictly speaking, it means that the apparent correlation between percent foreign-born and the larceny rate could very well be the spurious result of urbanism. A rough theoretical analysis would go as follows. Larceny is more common in the cities, and immigrants move to the cities. Through no fault of their own, immigrants wind up living in high-crime places. Immigrants have no more tendency to commit larceny than do native-born Americans. The impression that immigrants are criminals is an entirely false impression, the result of a spurious correlation.

But I must stress two things. First, the correlation itself is not spurious, only our original interpretation of it. Second, the analysis does not really *prove* that immigrants are innocent. Rather, it pretty well demolishes the original

case against them and leaves us with no sociological justification for claiming that they are guilty. Science is never conclusive, however, and some fourth variable might conceivably be introduced into the analysis that would restore some semblance of the original correlation.

Herbert A. Simon (1954) long ago argued that statistical analysis of spuriousness was shaped by the theories we bring to it. It is very plausible to argue that the correlation between urbanism and immigration results from the fact that immigrants move to the cities. In fact, I cannot think of another interpretation at the moment.

It is also plausible to argue that something about cities stimulates larceny. Cities have a lot of stores where there are nice things to steal. The problems of the cities may inspire more people to want to steal. The anonymity of the cities may give people greater freedom to violate the norms. We might need a whole chapter to discuss seriously the various ways that urbanism might stimulate larceny, but we could frame pretty good explanations without ever blaming immigrants.

One could argue, however, if one were in a particularly quarrelsome mood, that the reason cities have high crime rates is precisely that so many foreigners are there. Thus, an advocate for the original theory that many foreigners are thieves would not be entirely defeated by our partial-correlations analysis. True, we have seriously weakened the evidence for this theory, and in defense its advocate may have to claim that the correlation between urbanism and larceny is simply the spurious result of immigration.

This is easy to test, and the computer display gives you all the information necessary to do so. We can do another partial-correlation analysis, looking at the correlation between urbanism and larceny, seeing what happens when we control for percent foreign-born. This means to calculate the partial $r[X_2,Y].X_1$. The original correlation between urbanism and larceny is 0.63. When we use partial correlations to control for immigration, it drops a bit to 0.45, but this is still a substantial correlation. Thus, the correlation between urbanism and larceny is probably not the spurious result of immigration.

Now, the theory that the foreign-born tend to be thieves is on very shaky ground. Unless its advocates find a very different way of analyzing the data, perhaps introducing several other variables and a whole lot of good theoretical argument, we have to conclude that there is no evidence in favor of this theory.

We can try the same analysis for the violent crime I mentioned, assault. The original correlation between foreign-born and assault is 0.28, suggesting some tendency for immigrants to be assaultive. But controlling for urbanism with the partial-correlations method actually drives this correlation negative, to -0.09. Further analysis provides no support to the idea that the correlation between urbanism and assault is the spurious result of immigration. That correlation drops only slightly, from 0.46 to 0.40.

Now, I am very happy to see the theory accusing immigrants of criminality demolished, and I shall go back to trusting my immigrant wife. But I really need to stress that any empirical analysis, especially using statistical analysis of the interrelationships of several different variables, is somewhat tentative. We can think of this in terms of the warrant for claims.

In the absence of any evidence, the claim that immigrants tend to be criminal is entirely unwarranted. The original correlations provided some justification for asserting this theory. When we demolished that justification, using partial correlations, we rendered the claim that immigrants are criminal unwarranted again, but we did not achieve absolute certainty.

Science never does. We did arrive at a very plausible interpretation, entirely in line with the evidence. Most of us will consider that sufficient. If you want to believe from now on that immigrants are no more criminal than the rest of us, be my guest. That's what I believe myself. It is a very respectable belief scientifically, entirely in line with the evidence as we have analyzed it here. But there is always the possibility, remote as we may feel it is, that we would get a very different result if we added certain other control variables.

This raises two difficult, related questions: How do you know which variables to employ as controls? When do you stop controlling for other variables? Rosenberg (1968:37–40) lists three wrong answers to these questions:

1. Decide there is no point introducing controls at all, because one can never have complete confidence the relationship is real no matter how many controls one introduces.
2. Decide it is best not to interpret the relationship at all, because one can never be sure that an interpretation is not faulty and really the result of an extraneous variable you failed to consider.
3. Automatically control for just a limited number of very familiar variables, such as social class, age, and sex.

Instead, Rosenberg advises that we try control variables when (and only when) there is a theoretical or empirically based reason for believing that they account for the observed relationship. I believe we did that in this case, but an advocate of the original theory has the right to propose a new theoretical argument, introducing other controls the theory logically demands. However, the issue is not just one of theory and argument. Ultimately, the data rule, and we seldom encounter situations in which different statistical controls support competing theories equally.

_____ Multiple Regression

Partial correlations is but one of a collection of techniques for working with three or more variables at once. A closely related approach is **multiple regression analysis**, an expanded version of the regression analysis we have already considered, which employs two or more independent variables simultaneously. Our MAPS program allows you to do an analysis of this kind with two independent variables, but full-featured statistical analysis packages allow as many as seven or even more independent variables. Two independent variables and one dependent variable are quite sufficient to illustrate the general principle.

The Three-Variable Regression Option of the MAPS Program

When you select the three-variable regression option of the MAPS program, you will select three variables, just as you do for partial correlations: X_1, X_2, and Y. Computationally, there are many ways to approach multiple regression, but for ease of explanation I have chosen to use the one closest to the partial correlations module we just examined. As before, the computer first calculates a correlation matrix showing the Pearson's r associations among the three variables.

A good example that builds on our earlier work seeks to explain variations in the larceny rate across the 50 states. Recall that we found the percent urban to be a good predictor of the larceny rate. What other variable might add to our understanding? As it happens, the church-member rate explains part of the variation in larceny, but we don't have 1980 statistics on church membership in the state dataset, so we have to consider other options.

Recall Travis Hirschi's (1969) control theory, as briefly described in Chapter 7. It states that persons whose bond to society is weak or broken are especially likely to commit larceny. One way in which people's bond to the social order can be weakened is through geographic migration. When an individual moves from one place to another, his or her attachments to other people are often cut, and a recent migrant generally experiences weaker social influences from friends and neighbors that might prevent deviant behavior. A survey, such as the one simulated in the SAMP program connected to Chapter 7, may look at this issue at the individual level, for example comparing people who have moved recently with those who have not, to see if they are more likely to commit larceny. The MAPS program can look at the ecological level, to see if the larceny rate is higher in states with high rates of migration.

A good measure of migration is variable 31, "different house." It reports the percent of persons over age 5 who were living in a different house in 1980 from the one they lived in back in 1975. Our measure of larceny will again be variable 70, FBI-reported larcenies per 100,000 people. It turns out that the correlation between these two variables is 0.60, quite substantial, but the correlation between variable 27 (percent urban) and variable 70 was also substantial, 0.63. When you select a three-variable regression analysis in which X_1, X_2, and Y are variables 27, 31, and 70,

FIGURE 13.6

Correlation Matrix, Basis of Multiple-regression Analysis

	Var 27	Var 31	Var 70	r^2	Mean	Standard Deviation
Var 27	1.00	0.17	0.63	0.40	66.94	14.26
Var 31	0.17	1.00	0.60	0.36	47.89	7.14
Var 70	0.63	0.60	1.00	1.00	3133.64	765.74

you will first see these coefficients displayed in a small correlation matrix in the upper-left corner of the screen, similar to the one here in Figure 13.6.

In addition to the correlation matrix, your computer screen and Figure 13.6 will show the mean and standard deviation for each of the three variables, on the appropriate row of information, plus the square of the correlation with the dependent variable Y. Called r^2, the square of the correlation is the proportion of the variance in the dependent variable explained by the particular independent variable.

The correlation between X_1 (urbanism, variable 27) and Y (larceny, variable 70) is 0.63. The square of this is 0.40. So 0.40—or 40 percent—of the variance in larceny rates can be accounted for by variations in the percent urban. This is substantial, strongly supporting the theory that cities stimulate stealing. The correlation of 0.60 between X_2 (different house, variable 31) produces an r^2 of 0.36, only slightly smaller. Thus, urbanism explains 40 percent of the variance, and migration explains 36 percent. Does this mean that we have explained 40 + 36 percent of the variance, or 76 percent? Not necessarily.

It could be that the two independent variables overlap considerably. That is, urbanism and migration may be connected, for example if urban people tend to move around more than do other folks. If so, the two independent variables may be explaining substantially the same variance in the dependent variable, and it may be quite fallacious to add the r^2s as we just did. A glance at the correlation matrix in Figure 13.6 reveals that X_1 and X_2 (variables 27 and 31) have only a modest correlation between them, 0.17; so the overlap in explained variation is apparently not great. However, we should try a regression analysis employing both independent variables, to see precisely how great it is and to get a clearer picture of how urbanism and migration combine in explaining larceny rates.

One approach is to transform the correlations into standardized regression coefficients. When we were dealing with just a single independent variable, the Pearson's r was the standardized regression coefficient. But now we want a slightly different kind of standardized regression coefficient, comparable to r in every way but taking account of two independent variables simultaneously. For that, we need a new formula, very similar to the one that transformed ordinary correlations into partial correlations:

$$\text{Beta}(X_1, Y) = \frac{r(X_1, Y) - (r(X_2, Y)) \times (r(X_1, X_2))}{1 - (r(X_1, X_2))^2}$$

FIGURE 13.7
Variable 70 Explained by Variable 27 and Variable 31

	r	Beta	B
Var 27 Urban population	0.63	0.54	29.2241
Var 31 Different house	0.60	0.51	54.5158

Here, Beta(X_1,Y) means the standardized regression coefficient with X_1 as the independent variable and Y as the dependent variable, taking account of the other variable in the analysis, X_2. Beta is the Greek letter for B, and I might have put "β" instead of *Beta,* using the lowercase (little) Greek letter. Appropriately enough, this Beta is often called the standardized partial regression coefficient.

Figure 13.7 shows the summary of this analysis given by the MAPS program. Note that the urbanism-larceny r of 0.63 becomes a Beta of 0.54, a bit lower, and the migration-larceny r of 0.60 becomes 0.51. These are estimates of how the two independent variables correlate with the dependent variable, without any overlap between them. The overlap, the shared variance, is not thrown away but is apportioned between the two independent variables.

Apparently both urbanism and migration matter in shaping the larceny rate, and while they overlap slightly, their joint contribution is larger than the contribution of either independent variable alone. But how much larger? In the lower-left corner of the screen, the computer will provide several pieces of further information, including multiple R and R^2. The *multiple* R is, if you will, the combination of the two correlations between the independent variables and the dependent variable. The letter R is capitalized to show that it is not just a correlation between two variables but a kind of combination of correlations.

The original correlations are 0.63 and 0.60, and if you added them, you would get 1.23. The Betas are 0.54 and 0.51, which add together to make 1.05. No correlation (multiple or otherwise) should get over 1.00. Clearly, simply adding correlations or Betas is not the right way to get multiple R. I will explain one way to do it later on. For now, suffice it to say, the computer calculates that the multiple R for these variables is 0.81.

R^2 is the square of multiple R. It expresses the total amount of variance in the dependent variable explained by the combination of both independent variables. In this analysis, R^2 is 0.65. (If you square 0.81 you will get 0.6561, but the multiple R is actually slightly less than 0.81, which the computer rounded up to 0.81.). This 0.65 is the proportion of variance in larceny explained by urbanism and migration working together. It is much greater than the 0.40 r^2 of urbanism alone and the 0.36 of migration alone.

This analysis demonstrates one of the basic truths of modern sociology. Typically, we can best explain something through a combination of variables. Properly chosen, a set of independent variables will explain more than any single independent variable. The price we pay for this advance is that our theoretical explanations and our statistical analyses must be much more complex than formerly was the case in sociology. In paying this price, however, we gain immensely in our understanding of the social world.

Figure 13.7 includes not only r and Beta but also a "B" unstandardized regression coefficient for each of the independent variables. If you recall Chapter 12, you will remember that there was a simple way to transform standardized coefficients into unstandardized coefficients. Multiply the standardized coefficient by the ratio of the standard deviation of the dependent variable divided by the standard deviation of the independent variable. This can be applied to Betas as well as to rs. Here is the formula:

$$B = Beta \times \frac{\text{Standard deviation of } Y}{\text{Standard deviation of } X}$$

Let's try this for urbanism. Figure 13.7 tells us the Beta is 0.54. Figure 13.6 tells us the standard deviation for Y is 765.74, and the standard deviation for X is 14.26. All this information would be on your computer screen. Divide 765.74 by 14.26, and you get 53.70. Multiply this by 0.54 and you get about 29, or 29.2241 as the computer calculates all the steps precisely. So, unstandardized B for variable 27 (urbanism) is 29.2241. The corresponding unstandardized B for variable 31 (migration) is 54.5158.

Unstandardized B takes on its full meaning only in the context of a regression equation, a formula that allows one to predict the value of the dependent variable if one knows the values of the independent variables. As you recall, such a formula for one independent variable looks like this:

$$Y' = A + BX$$

With two independent variables, X_1 and X_2, we have to find room for two X variables, and each one needs its own B. So the formula becomes

$$Y' = A + B_1X_1 + B_2X_2$$

This is not, I submit, a very great complication over the equation with just one independent variable. The method of calculating A is the same as for the simpler formula, and in the case of the variables we are considering, A = -1433.17. Therefore, if we plug A, B_1, and B_2 into the general formula, we get a regression equation for predicting the larceny rate, on the basis of urbanism and migration:

$$Y' = -1433.17 + 29.2241(X_1) + 54.5158(X_2)$$

I really should not give A, B_1, and B_2 to so many decimal places, because to do so implies unreasonable precision in our estimates. But different variables will produce numbers that range widely, so I needed to provide room for significant figures in the estimates, wherever they came in relation to the decimal point. A more modest version of the same equation would be

$$Y' = -1433 + 29(X_1) + 55(X_2)$$

Take the percent urban (X_1) and multiply it by 29. Take the percent living in a different house (X_2), and multiply by 55. Add these numbers together and subtract 1433, and you have a fair estimate of the larceny rate for the particular state.

One way to check the results is to calculate this formula for the mean values. The scattergram part of the GRAF program showed you that the regression line passes through the point that represents the conjunction of the means of the two variables. Essentially the same is true with three variables. Try it yourself. Plug the values for the means of the two independent variables into this equation, solve it, and you will get a Y' that is equal to the actual mean for Y in the data. When I programmed the computer to calculate A, I simply worked backward from this fact.

Another comment about A is in order. Note what A means. It is the estimate for the Y variable when the values of both independent variables are zero. Our regression equation tells us that A = − 1433, approximately. This means that the regression equation predicts *minus* 1,433 larcenies per 100,000 in a state that had no cities and no migrants. Wait a minute! That's crazy! You can't have fewer than zero crimes.

True, and this is one of the quirks of regression analysis. It can predict less than zero of something, even when that is not meaningful. Conversely, it could predict a crime rate even for a state with zero population, if population were one of the independent variables. This is unreasonable.

Simply put, we are dealing here with inaccuracies in the estimate given by the regression equation. One source of inaccuracy is simply the data themselves, because there are always random fluctuations that might add up to a modest error in one direction or another. For one thing, there could be a couple of outlier cases that rotated the regression line. Or, tiny errors might be spread throughout the data, unnoticeable but distorting.

Another possible source of trouble is that the relationship between the variables might not be what we call linear. A **linear** relationship is one that can be represented well as a straight line; *linear* is simply the adjective form of *line*. Although the regression analyses discussed in this book are all linear, it is possible to do other kinds as well. That is a proper discussion for more advanced texts on regression. Wandering As are not the only way nonlinearity can manifest itself. Techniques exist for doing regressions with curved lines, and the alternative approaches are almost endless. Most publications using regression analysis in sociology, however, look for linear relationships by means of straight regression lines.

The particular A we have here, −1433, is a good illustration of a general principle with estimates: *Do not estimate too far beyond your data.* No state in fact has zero urban population or zero migrants. Indeed, in both cases 0.0 is very far away from the mean. Consider urbanism. On average, 66.94 percent of the state populations live in urban areas, and the standard deviation is only 14.26. This means that 0.0 is 4.7 standard deviations below the mean. That is far! And for migration, 0.0 is 6.7 standard deviations down. Clearly, A is so far away from the spread of data points that it does not make sense even to ask what the larceny rate would be. Apparently, −1433 is not a bad number to have as A in the equation when estimating values much closer to the means on the two independent variables.

Standard Error, Multiple R, and R²

When discussing regression with one independent variable, we introduced the concept of standard error, which is comparable to standard deviation, being measured from the regression line rather than from the mean. If you get further into regression analysis, you will encounter standard error frequently. The computer calculates it for the three-variable regression, too. One of its many uses is evaluating how good a job the regression equation does in helping us understand the social phenomenon under study.

Recall our examination of how urbanism and migration combined to explain much of the variation in the larceny rate. The standard deviation of the larceny rate is 765.74. The standard error from the regression equation is rather smaller, 591.32. This is one way of expressing the success of the regression analysis in improving our capacity to predict the value of the dependent variable, given the values of the two independent variables.

Another way of gauging the success of the theory expressed in the regression equation is to consider the correlation between the actual values of the dependent variable and the predicted values. That is, we could examine the correlation between Y and Y'. This is the multiple R, which we mentioned above. In our example, multiple R equals 0.81. And R^2 is the square of that, or 0.65. Thus, the combination of urbanism and migration explains 65 percent of the variance in the larceny rate, a very substantial proportion.

Another example will illustrate complete failure of a regression equation to improve our capacity to predict the dependent variable. The MAPS dataset has two random variables, variable 187 and variable 188. For each, the computer assigned states numbers at random in the range 0–999. I saved these meaningless variables on your disk, rather than having the computer calculate them afresh each time, and you thus will get the same results each time you use them. A third sociologically meaningless variable is variable 0—yes, zero—which simply ranks the states in alphabetical order. Let's see what happens when we select the two random variables to be X_1 and X_2, and have alphabetical ranking be Y.

The correlation between the two independent variables is only 0.08, essentially zero, so they are not going to influence each other's capacity to explain Y. Variable 187 has a corre-

lation of -0.04 with variable 0, while variable 188's correlation is 0.03. I said we were going to explore the depths of predictive failure!

Regression analysis gives betas of -0.04 and $+0.04$, essentially the same as the rs. The regression equation is

$$Y' = 25.62 - 0.0020(X_1) + 0.0017(X_2)$$

Simple inspection of the values for B usually does not tell you much, unless you already have a sense of the distributions of the variables and can intuitively weigh the influence suggested by particular values of B. One quick hint of the lack of success of the analysis can be gained by comparing A with the mean for the dependent variable. While A here is 25.62, the mean for Y is 25.50, almost the same. Of course, if Y has a very narrow distribution around this mean, then the regression equation could still be explaining a substantial portion of the variation. If the mean were very close to zero, we would not expect A to differ from it much, but, of course, the mean is not relatively close to zero for these variables. And the standard deviation for the dependent variable is 14.43. The difference between A and the mean, 0.12, is only a tiny fraction of this standard deviation, about 1 percent. This casts deep gloom over the regression.

Another way to get a rough picture of the explanatory success of the regression is to compare the standard deviation with the standard error. If the regression line is closer to the data points than is the horizontal line representing the mean, then the standard error should be much smaller than the standard deviation. We have just seen that the standard deviation is 14.43. The standard error from this regression analysis is 14.41, fully 99.9 percent as big. This is another sign of failure.

Finally, one can examine the multiple R and R^2, which are 0.05 and 0.00, respectively. Here we see final, conclusive proof that the two random variables do not help us predict the ranking of a state in terms of alphabetical order. I certainly hope your theories do not result in such total empirical failure, but when you do get results as dismal as this, please remember that science progresses as much by falsifying theories as by finding data in support of them.

Regression with Many Independent Variables

Our three-variable regression analysis is the simplest version of multiple regression. In principle, there is hardly any limit to how many independent variables may be used. The sociological literature is filled with examples. So that the material will be familiar, however, I will stick to the two multiple-regression studies on religion I did while working on this textbook, both mentioned earlier (Bainbridge 1989a, 1990a).

We have discussed Emile Durkheim's analysis of suicide, and you may recall my statement that the rate of church membership was a powerful predictor of the suicide rate. Several studies have found that suicide rates are low where the church-member rate is high. Imagine my surprise, therefore, when I tried the usual sort of analysis with data from 1980 and found something quite different.

I was working with the 75 largest American metropolitan areas outside New England, ignoring the four largest cities in that region simply because the data on church members were all at the county level and could not generate good rates in the one part of the nation where Standard Metropolitan Statistical Areas (SMSAs) are not simply combinations of counties. In 1980, there had been 14,153 suicides in those 75 SMSAs, for an average rate of 12.3 per 100,000. The top section of Figure 13.8 reveals that there was a correlation of -0.37 between the church-member rate and this suicide rate, supporting the traditional theory that religion deters suicide.

But other variables also had considerable power to explain variations in the suicide rate. As control theory predicts, and we have stated several times, geographic migration should stimulate deviant behavior like suicide, by reducing the restraining influence of social bonds.

FIGURE 13.8
Explaining the 1980 Suicide Rate

	1980
Correlations:	
Church members	-0.37
Different house	0.53
Divorced	0.64
Age 65+	0.17
Betas:	
Church members	0.11
Different house	0.20
Divorced	0.58
Age 65+	0.26
$R^2 = 0.48$	
Betas:	
Church members	-0.01
Different house	0.53
$R^2 = 0.28$	

The proportion who had moved to a different house in the past five years correlated 0.53 with the suicide rate. One might expect suicide to result from family dislocation, such as divorce, and indeed the correlation between the divorce rate and the suicide rate was quite substantial, 0.64. There was also a small correlation, 0.17, between the suicide rate and the proportion aged 65 and over, hinting at a connection between despair of aging and suicide.

With its -0.37 correlation, the church-member rate explains only 14 percent of the variance in suicide rates. The middle of Figure 13.8 shows a far more successful analysis, its R^2 of 0.48 explaining fully 48 percent of the variance. The coefficients reported are betas—standardized regression coefficients from an analysis that used all four independent variables simultaneously. The particularly surprising fact is that the coefficient for religion has hopped across zero, from -0.37 to $+0.11$.

On the face of it, my study fails to replicate studies done with earlier data that had shown church membership to have a negative coefficient with suicide even after controlling for other variables. When a coefficient resists such controlling, we call it *robust.* In the 1980 data, the effect of religion on suicide did not appear robust at all.

But I cannot stress too often that blind manipulation of statistics is not a sure way of doing social science. We also have to think, and we have to have well-developed theories to think with. Although the three other independent variables in Figure 13.8 are all reasonable choices, their relationships with religion may not be simple.

Consider divorce. Traditional religion may still have the power to deter divorce. Divorce encourages suicide. Therefore, religion may still inhibit suicide indirectly, through its effect on divorce. If the only way religion reduced suicide was through divorce, then statistical control for divorce would make the religion-suicide association vanish. Rather than refuting the power of religion, such an analysis would have specified that religion had its effect entirely through divorce.

But the bottom section of Figure 13.8 shows that even just one of the other independent variables, our "different house" measure of migration, is sufficient to drive the religion-suicide association from -0.37 to -0.01, effectively to zero. The R^2 is not so impressive, only 0.28; but all of that 0.28 can be attributed to migration, and thus to social instability, and none to church membership. The best understanding of suicide rates I achieved has three independent variables (migration, divorce, age). Religion plays no role.

I must emphasize that no one sociological study proves anything. We need a series of studies done by different people with different methods on different data, before we can be really sure we understand a phenomenon. In the case of church membership and suicide rates, we are in the uncomfortable but stimulating situation of having a few studies that do not agree. Under such circumstances, it would be useful if someone would replicate all the studies with a consistent set of methods to make sure whether the disagreement between published studies was real or merely the result of

different techniques of analysis. This could be exciting, because if all the studies are trustworthy (not a foregone conclusion!), then church membership has lost a power it once had, and something very important has changed about the role of religion in American life.

If the negative correlation between church membership and suicide is the spurious result of social instability, then social instability must have a strong association with church membership. If so, it may help explain church membership itself. In studies of religion and suicide, suicide is the dependent variable and religion is an independent variable; however, we can place religion in the role of dependent variable and seek to explain it. Look at the following equation:

$$Y' = 46.9 + 0.36(X_1) - 0.19(X_2) + 0.00(X_3) - 0.33(X_4) - 0.19(X_5) + 0.59(X_6)$$

This is a regression equation with fully six independent variables. It came from an analysis of data on 288 metropolitan areas. Y is the rate of church membership. The independent variables are

X_1: the percent of native-born who were born in the same state

X_2: the percent who lived in a different house five years before

X_3: the population of the metropolitan area

X_4: the percent of adults who graduated from high school

X_5: the per capita income

X_6: the percent under age 18

This is far from my favorite regression equation explaining church membership. I chose it merely because it illustrates the possibility of having many independent variables in one equation. We still have just one A, the Y-intercept, which is 46.9 in this case. For each independent variable (X_n), there is an unstandardized regression coefficient (B_n). In principle, one could go on endlessly, adding more and more independent variables. Actually, you have to stop before the number of independent variables equals the number of cases, which is 50 for this dataset, or the mathematics go crazy. But usually, even six independent variables is too many, because some of them contribute almost nothing to your ability to estimate the dependent variable.

With all six independent variables, the R^2 is 0.45. The equation makes it clear that variable X_3 (population) does not matter, because B_3 is 0.00. One can explain church membership almost as well dropping per capita income out of the analysis, because its beta is only 0.01. The measure of migration has the greatest single power to predict the church-member rate (beta = 0.42), and three or four variables do a very good job.

Technical Difficulties

I think you get a sense that multiple regression is a terribly useful technique, but there are several things to be careful about. As a general rule, the more complex your analytical techniques become, the more careful you have to be in using them. Complexity gives error many routes to enter. The following sections introduce two of them, collinearity and heteroscedasticity. This is also an appropriate time to think more deeply about spuriousness.

Collinearity

The word **collinearity** is obviously based on the word *linear,* referring to regression lines. Collinearity is a problem that can affect the independent variables, and it can distort partial-correlations analysis as well as multiple-regression analysis. **Collinearity** is the situation when two or more independent variables are highly correlated with each other. I suppose an easy interpretation of the word is to say it refers to situations when independent variables are lined up with each other. It is a very common problem in multiple-regression analysis (Johnston 1972; Chatterjee and Hadi 1988).

At the extreme, collinearity could cause the computer program to crash. Here is that extreme. Suppose that X_1 and X_2 had a correlation of 1.00 and you tried to use both of them to explain Y. Look back at the formula for Beta we gave earlier. The denominator of this formula is $1 - (r[X_1,X_2])^2$. Here, $r[X_1,X_2]$ stands for the correlation between X_1 and X_2, which is 1.00. The square of 1.00 is still 1.00. Subtract 1.00 from 1 and you get zero. What happens when you divide a number by zero? Remember we were just figuring the denominator of the Beta formula, which means we divide it into whatever the numerator would be. Well, your computer can't divide by zero. If I make it try, the program will crash, so I wrote all the divisions in this software package so that the computer would skip them if their denominators were zero.

This proves that a correlation of 1.00 between two independent variables would be a disaster, but correlations close to 1.00 can be pretty bad, too. At worst, the computer's result may say nothing at all about the data, and merely be a magnification of the unavoidable small errors in the way the computer does its calculations. Short of that, tiny noise in the data may be amplified until it completely dominates the results.

Here is an example from the 1920–1930 data in the MAPS program. Variables 214 and 215 are slightly different—*very* slightly different—estimates of the church-member rate for 1926. Variable 216 is an estimate of the percent of the population who are members of the Roman Catholic Church. To be sure, the Catholics were counted among the other church members, so these three variables are all autocorrelated. The raw (unadjusted) rate of church membership, taken directly from publications of the Census Bureau, correlates 0.51 with the proportion Catholic. An adjusted rate, a slightly altered version of the raw statistics, correlates 0.49. The correlation between the two church-member rates is a huge 0.99.

A partial-correlation analysis would reveal the following. Controlling for the adjusted rate, the correlation between the raw church-member rate and the Catholic rate would drop from 0.51 to 0.33. Controlling for the raw rate, however, the correlation between the adjusted church-member rate and the Catholic rate would drop from 0.49 to −0.27. Yes, it would swing far over to the minus side of zero. This happens because the two church-member rates are highly collinear.

When introduction of a control variable causes such a huge whiplash effect as this, sociologists are cautioned to suspect collinearity, and they can have little confidence in the results. Our field has not agreed upon any fixed set of criteria to decide when excessive collinearity vitiates our findings (Finke and Stark 1989), and all I can do is urge caution. When there are several independent variables, and several of them correlate highly with each other, we speak of multicollinearity; in such situations it can be even harder to decide how much confidence to have in the results. Some statistics textbooks say that multiple-regression analysis ideally assumes no correlations at all among the independent variables, but in the social sciences this is almost never the case, and we must take care at least that the correlations are only modest.

Another example, using 1970–1980 data, involves variables 1, 2 and 3 of the MAPS dataset. Variable 1 is the 1970 population of the state; variable 2 is the 1980 population; and variable 3 expresses population growth through the 1980 population as a percent of the 1970 population. There is a correlation of 0.99 between the 1970 population and the 1980 population, and these variables have correlations of −0.31 and −0.23 with the rate of population growth. That is, big cities grew less than did small cities.

In a partial-correlation analysis controlling for 1980 population, the correlation between the 1970 population and growth over the decade changes from −0.31 to −0.61. A partial-correlation analysis controlling for 1970 population swings the correlation between 1980 population and growth from −0.23 around to 0.58. That is about as extreme an example of the wild effect of collinearity as we will ever see, short of crashing a program with a correlation of 1.00.

NOTE: The MAPS program will refuse to do these calculations for you. Sorry, but I felt a warning about collinearity was more important than a glimpse of meaningless numbers. There is a block in the program that prevents further analysis if the correlation between independent variables is greater than 0.90. If you select independent variables with such a high collinearity, the program will print the correlation matrix, give you a warning, and refuse to go further in either a partial-correlation or three-variable regression analysis.

Other than avoiding analyzing data altogether, when independent variables are highly correlated, there are a couple of approaches you can take. One is simply to be quite candid with the reader of your report, and let him or her judge if the correlations are too high. Another is to try your analysis several ways, with various independent variables in or out of the equation, carefully checking to see if results are relatively stable and interpretable.

Another approach is to think carefully about the meaning of the independent variables that are highly correlated, and consider combining them into an index. The following chapter discusses multiple-variable indexes at length, so a brief example will serve here.

An article I published in *Social Forces* (Bainbridge 1990a) sought to explain the 1980 church-member rate in 288 American metropolitan areas. Among the independent variables were 12 items that were indicators of three concepts: social stability, urbanism, and social class. Variables that measured the degree of social stability were our "different house" measure, the percent population growth, the percent of native-born Americans born in the same state where the 1980 census found them, and the so-called "sex-ratio" (number of males per 100 females). The urbanism measures included the percent of the population who lived in urban areas, the percent living in the central city of the metropolitan area, the population of the city, and the population density per square mile. Social-class indicators were the percent high-school graduates, the percent college graduates, the per capita income, and the percent of families below the official poverty line.

Clearly, within each group of four, independent variables could be highly correlated. The percent of natives born in the state correlated −0.68 with the percent who moved in the past five years, and the two education variables correlated 0.61. These were the highest correlations among my independent variables, not very big by the standards for collinearity many sociologists use, and all the other correlations were far lower. Still, I was concerned about the issue, so I tried an analysis combining the items into three indexes.

As was the case for its component variables taken separately, the social stability index predicted church-membership rates quite well. The more stable the social life of the community, the higher the rate of church membership. Urbanism seems irrelevant, but class may have a role to play—especially the education variables that correlated negatively with church membership. Although the stability and urbanism indexes were not correlated with each other, the class index achieved a modest correlation with each of the other two. These inter-index correlations were low enough to avoid any new problems of collinearity.

Heteroscedasticity

Even though collinearity can vastly distort betas, A, and unstandardized B, heteroscedasticity generally does not (Bohrnstedt and Carter 1971:124), but it may affect standard errors or other measures of statistical significance. The problem identified with the jaw-breaker word *heteroscedasticity* concerns the possibility that the errors in our data are not random but correlate with one or more variables, some of which might be in our dataset or be associated in some way with variables that are. The opposite is *homoscedasticity*, the situation when the

distribution of Y scores has the same variability for each X score. But if the actual values of Y are bunched close to the regression line for some values of X, and spread far from it for other values of X, we have heteroscedasticity. As with extraneous variables that are implicated in spuriousness, variables implicated in heteroscedasticity may be hard to find and may not even be measured in the dataset you are working with. They become a practical problem, however, only when they are in some way connected to the X variables you are working with in a particular analysis. I think the example of my article on church membership will again help communicate the concept.

Data on the church-member rate came from a survey of denominational headquarters done by the Glenmary Research Center in 1980 (Quinn et al. 1982). For each county, it provided rough estimates of the numbers of members in churches of several Christian and Jewish denominations, but by no means all. Data for the counties could be combined into metropolitan areas. There were many sources of error, however, and probably the errors were relatively larger for the metropolitan areas with small populations. The range of populations was huge, from 62,820 to 9,120,346, a factor of 146.

In some small cities, one of the denominations that the survey did not cover might have held a substantial fraction of the church members in town. Furthermore, the membership statistics for any single church or denomination were probably somewhat rough. In large cities, the random errors in the individual church membership may have balanced off, while in small cities with fewer churches, this would not be the case. This is simply another application of the law of large numbers in sampling. A big city is like a big sample; a small city is like a small sample.

Let me rephrase what I have just said, in terms of an hypothesis about correlation: *There is a negative correlation between population size and the errors in the church-member rates.* A correlation between one variable and the errors in another variable is **heteroscedasticity**. A lack of such correlations in the data is called *homoscedasticity*. In regression analysis, error is the scatter of data points around the regression line, and social scientists often assume that the size of these residuals tends to be the same regardless of the values of the independent variables—that the scattering is homogeneous, hence the term *homoscedasticity*. Heteroscedasticity is uneven scattering that correlates with one or more independent variables, thus violating this common assumption (Younger 1979).

A number of methods have been proposed for determining if heteroscedasticity is a problem in a given set of data (Goldfeld and Quant 1965). For our present purposes, I like Glejser's (1969) technique. We have just predicted a negative correlation between city size and the residual errors, the differences between the actual Y values and the Y' predictions from the regression equation. Glejser suggested correlating the independent variable that was under suspicion with the absolute values of the residuals from the regression analysis.

The best regression equation in my study to explain the church-member rate had seven independent variables. The variable I have implicated in heteroscedasticity, population size, was actually not one of them, because population of the 288 metropolitan areas did not correlate with the rate of church membership. However, it was still worth checking. The correlation between the population and the absolute value of residuals from my regression analysis was − 0.13. This is negative, just as predicted, indicating that the errors were smaller for large cities. But it is not a big correlation, and thus it tells us that heteroscedasticity was relatively small. I decided, however, that it was still worth doing something about.

One tactic is to use more advanced regression techniques. The approach I have incorporated in our software is sometimes called "ordinary least-squares regression." A more complex alternative, "weighted least-squares regression," allows the researcher to weight data points in terms of the variable implicated in heteroscedasticity. Obviously, this is not the right place to go deeply into advanced techniques like that, but there is a simpler solution.

You can separate your analysis into two or more parts, in terms of the variable implicated in heteroscedasticity. In the case of church membership, we have already seen that the culprit is population size. So I separated the 288 metropolitan areas into three groups: the 96 with the largest populations, the 96 with medium populations, and the 96 with the smallest populations. Then I did my final analysis separately within each of these subgroups of cities. Glejser's test revealed essentially no heteroscedasticity within each of these three groups.

Although heteroscedasticity can be a problem, worrying excessively about possible flaws hidden in your analysis can be disastrous, too. For example, you might contemplate applying Glejser's test to all the variables in your dataset, a big job in itself. And as is the case with ordinary correlations, check enough times and pure chance will give you an association big enough to worry about. Wesolowsky (1976:136) warns against this, saying, "Deduction of a link by study of the pattern of residuals can be dangerous, especially if the regression sample is small. Spurious patterns are notoriously easy to discern if one is looking for patterns."

In order to impress upon you the importance of issues such as this, I have added Glejser's test to the three-variable analysis of variance in the MAPS program. You will find the word *heteroscedasticity* in the lower-left corner of the screen, followed by the correlation between population and the absolute value of residuals from the regression equation. Earlier in this chapter we did a partial-correlation analysis, explaining the larceny rate (variable 70) by the percent foreign-born (variable 29) and the percent urban (variable 27). Glejser's measure of heteroscedasticity for that analysis comes out dead zero: 0.00. When you explain larcenies by percent urban and by the "different-house" variable (variable 31), you get a heteroscedasticity of − 0.08, very small but suggesting a slight tendency for errors to be less for states with greater populations.

When you are working with variables from the 1970–1980 period, the computer evaluates heteroscedasticity in terms of 1980 population. But when any of your variables date from the 1920–1930 period, it will use 1930 population. It is easy to tell which it has done. In the very lower-left corner of the screen, the computer will tell you how many states are reflected in the analysis, 48 or 50. If the number of states is 48, at least one of the three variables was from the 1920–1930 period, when there were only 48 states, and heteroscedasticity is figured in terms of 1930 population. The 1980 population is used when all 50 states participate in the analysis.

Spuriousness and Suppression

We generally use the term **spuriousness** for situations in which a hidden variable creates the false impression that there is a causal relationship between two other variables. Extraneous variables can affect coefficients in ways other than merely inflating them. Most interesting, but rather rare in actual research, is the possibility that a hidden third variable can artificially reduce the apparent correlation between two variables that really are related causally.

As Morris Rosenberg (1968:85) defines it, a **suppressor variable** "is one which weakens a relationship, which conceals its true strength." In other words, suppressor variables "intercede to cancel out, reduce, or conceal a true relationship between two variables." Here's an example from my experience as director of the undergraduate sociology program at the University of Washington. I don't know about your college, but at many schools sociology is considered a "gut major." We got some very fine, hardworking undergraduates in sociology at UW, but we also got some who wanted to graduate as painlessly as possible and didn't want the abysmal stigma of a degree in General Studies.

So it wasn't a great surprise when I found that the grade-point average (GPA) of sociology majors was lower than that for the university as a whole. I also discovered that about two-thirds of our majors were women. Before you leap to a spurious interpretation, let me report that the average GPA of women at the university was actually higher than the GPA of men.

Thus a positive correlation existed between being female and majoring in sociology, and between being female and having a high grade-point average. Just on the basis of these two facts, you might expect a spurious positive correlation between majoring in sociology and having a high grade-point average, but I had discovered that sociology majors tended to have low GPAs. That is, a negative correlation existed between sociology and GPA, rather than the positive one that spuriousness would have produced.

When I re-examined the association between sociology and GPA while controlling for sex, the negative correlation became even more negative. The truth was that sociology had a substantial negative correlation with GPA. That being female correlated positively with both variables pulled the apparent sociology-GPA correlation in the positive direction, making the situation seem better than it actually was.

This is an example of suppression, with sex acting as a suppressor variable. Note that suppression is not defined as pushing a correlation in the negative direction but as artificially pushing it closer to zero than by rights it ought to be. Other examples can be found in your MAPS dataset.

We have discussed several variables that shape the larceny rate. One variable, which on the surface has nothing to do with larceny, is population density. Variable 28 is the population per 10 square miles, and its correlation with variable 70 (larcenies) is an insignificant − 0.03. We have already found that it is sometimes wise to control for the percent of the state's population that is urban (variable 27). If we use the partial-correlations method to do this, the insignificant correlation of − 0.03 becomes − 0.49.

One way to interpret this is to say that urbanism had suppressed a strong negative correlation between population density and larceny. Control for urbanism, and a substantial association appears where previously there was none. It is risky, however, to leap to such a conclusion without a compelling theoretical argument to explain why the variables are related in the way they are. I leave it to you to suggest one.

Response Bias

In Chapter 7 we discussed **response bias**, the tendency of a respondent to answer questions in a particular way, regardless of what the question specifically is about. Among the varieties of response bias is **acquiescence,** the tendency of a respondent to agree or disagree with whatever a survey item says, regardless of its content. A tendency to agree is called **yea-saying,** and a tendency to disagree is called **nay-saying** (Couch and Keniston 1960, Block 1965, Berg 1967). The tendency of a respondent to give socially acceptable answers to questions, putting himself or herself in a good light, is called **social desirability bias** (Crowne and Marlow 1960, Edwards 1967, Phillips and Clancy 1972).

Response biases can produce spurious correlations between other variables in a questionnaire. People vary in their tendency to admit deviant behavior, for example. Suppose you are interested in the connection between use of mild illegal drugs, such as marijuana, and stealing. You have noted that hard-drug addicts often steal to support their habits, and you theorize that the drug subculture has made stealing one of its norms. From this you hypothesize that even users of inexpensive, mild drugs will steal, in accordance with the norms of the drug subculture. So you administer a questionnaire, asking respondents whether they use marijuana and whether they steal, and you find a significant positive correlation.

But it could be spurious. It may be that no causal relationship exists. People vary consistently in their willingness to admit deviance, and the correlation really represents nothing but their variation in response bias. Problems such as this, which are very real in questionnaire research, have stimulated survey methodologists to develop various ways of measuring the biases so that their effects on

other variables can be determined. But for some of the most interesting examples—notably the entire field of social problems and social stigma—conclusive solutions remain to be found.

Ecological Fallacy

Like response bias, the ecological fallacy, introduced in Chapter 11 and discussed already here, is largely a problem of spuriousness. If two rates have a statistically significant correlation, then they must be associated in some meaningful way. Something is going on; the only question is what. As we have seen, spuriousness is not really a problem of the statistics themselves but of our interpretation of them. Often, two variables may correlate simply because a third, unmeasured variable is connected to each of them. The task, then, is to search for other variables that might play this deceptive role, and include them in the analysis. This chapter and the next show us how to work effectively with many variables at once in statistical analysis. Project 6 at the end of this chapter asks you to examine the example of illiteracy and immigration yourself, through a small piece of research you can do with our dataset.

When you are analyzing the correlations between rates, it is good to imagine what possible problems of spuriousness might exist, and to include any variables you think might be confusing the picture. If you are concerned that variable Z might be the cause of the correlation between X and Y, check to see if Z correlates with X and with Y. If it doesn't, then it can't be the link between X and Y.

No one researcher has the obligation to be infinitely resourceful in finding all the possible variables that might be distorting the results. Science is a social process. One sociologist publishes a journal article reporting that X and Y are correlated and basing a theoretical analysis on the fact. Then other sociologists are free to publish their own articles, bringing in other variables. The hope of the scientific method is that the truth will sooner or later be clear. The original but necessarily incomplete journal article can be an important contribution even though it did not conclusively prove its theoretical interpretations.

Furthermore, as we explained in Chapter 1, empirical research is often designed to evaluate theoretical statements, following a systematic and logical approach. A theory has been proposed. We derive hypotheses that predict how certain data should behave. We examine the data. If they are in line with the theory-based hypotheses, then our confidence in the theory is strengthened. If they contradict them, then we lose confidence in the theory. But no one set of data, however carefully collected and analyzed, can prove a theory conclusively. The flip side of this principle is that a study deserves respect if it was conducted carefully and honestly, even though we might be able to imagine flaws such as extraneous variables that might have produced false interpretations of the statistical findings.

A Troubling Research Example

I am going to direct your attention to a very troublesome and disturbing topic, reflected in three variables of the MAPS dataset: rape. I chose this example both because some very interesting things are going on among the relevant variables, but also because the topic reminds us of what Edward Jarvis learned long ago: there can be serious ethical issues even when the data you are analyzing were collected not by you but by official agencies of the government.

Variable 66 is the number of rapes per million population, as reported to the FBI by local police departments. There are very good reasons to suspect the validity of this variable. Even today, with our more enlightened understanding of the plight of the victim, many rapes go unreported. This means that variations in the rate from one state to another are strongly affected by factors that influence reporting, as well as by variations in the actual commission of this terrible crime. Having made those observations, let's proceed (for educational purposes)

as if the rape rate really were a good measure of the crime itself.

Who commits rape? Well, men do. A very few women may be guilty of violent sex crimes, but they are not counted as rapists, and it is clear that the overwhelming majority of sex criminals are men. An awareness poster was recently put up on bulletin boards around my university. In large white letters on a black background were printed the words "MEN RAPE." Then, in scrawled white letters meant to look like an editing change, the words "can stop" were inserted between the two printed words: "MEN can stop RAPE." I suppose the message here was not merely that those few males personally guilty of rape could end the crime by stopping doing it, but also that something about American masculine culture encourages mistreatment of women, including rape. Clearly, we can raise many sociological questions about this sad topic, and despite the strong negative emotions that such ideas may cause, it is the duty of sociologists to study social problems scientifically, to understand them, and to contribute to their solution, if possible.

Okay, men rape. This suggests that the rape rate should be higher wherever the proportion of males in the population is high. On average, across the 50 states, 48.9 percent of the population is male, and the variation is not great, as indicated by a standard deviation of only 1.0 percent. But the correlation between the percent male (variable 15) and the rape rate (variable 66) is 0.31, not huge by ecological standards but definitely a positive association.

There are other ways of interpreting this positive correlation. For example, here's a crude but logical explanation. Where there are many women, the men have no trouble finding sexual partners legitimately. Therefore, the rape rate will be low. Where men are in excess, however, many of them will be unable to find willing partners, and they will resort to rape. Not a pleasant line of thought, but it fits the data, as we have analyzed them so far.

What about other variables? Let me suggest divorce. I will propose two theories. Divorce Theory 1: Divorced men have a grudge against women, because of the bad experience they had in marriage, and some of them will express this through rape. Divorce Theory 2: A high rate of divorce indicates that something is wrong in the social life of the community, particularly in relations between the sexes, and this strain between the sexes will manifest itself in many ways, including rape. The correlation between the divorce rate (variable 93) and the rape rate (variable 66) is 0.46.

If you analyze the two independent variables (percent male and divorce rate) by either partial correlations or three-variable regression, the correlation between percent male and rape drops from 0.31 to 0.04, essentially zero. Thus, controlling for divorce demolishes the correlation. One might then conclude that the correlation between percent male and rape was spurious.

However, this interpretation might be too hasty. There can be no doubt that rapists are men, because we have lots of other evidence of the fact, and the idea of the ecological fallacy warns us to be cautious about making individual-level conclusions on the basis of ecological findings. Thus, no reasonable sociologist is going to reject that rapists are men, merely because controlling for divorce wiped out the correlation.

But sociologists might feel that the collapse of the correlation when controlling for divorce renders less convincing the theory that rape results from the inability of men to find female partners legitimately in areas where men are numerous. This second theory is stated at the ecological level of analysis. That is, this theory directly concerns the proportion of the population that is male; it is about characteristics of the community rather than of the individual.

Both theories that predict a positive correlation between the percent male and the rape rate survive this collision with the data. This is because we did not state a logical justification for controlling for divorce. Controlling for extraneous variables is not just a matter of throwing other plausibly independent variables into the equation. One also has to explain why they should be related to the other independent

variable in such a way as to be responsible for spuriousness. I have not done this.

The theories about percent male are weakened in their power to convince, but in the absence of a compelling argument about how the spuriousness works, we cannot confidently reject them. And the undeniable fact that rapists are men, despite the collapse of the relevant correlation, should be a warning that a statistical control for divorce might not be appropriate.

We stated two theories about how divorce might produce rape. One of them implied that divorced men should be especially likely to be rapists, but we do not have data about that. It would be an ecological fallacy to conclude confidently that divorced men are rapists, on the basis of a robust correlation between divorce and rape.

The other theory about divorce considers it to be a reflection of wider problems in the society, from which elevated rates of rape might also come. Stated at the community level, this is a particularly appropriate theory for testing with ecological data.

To some degree, the data support both of the theories about divorce. Both theories predicted a positive correlation, and we found one. Controlling for percent male does not reduce it significantly, so we can call it a robust correlation. But the second divorce theory is stated at the ecological level, while the first is not, so the data provide more support for the second than for the first.

Thus, statistical controlling is not a simple, mechanical process. It takes judgment to interpret the results. The standing of a theory rises or falls, not merely as a result of the coefficients we get, but also depending upon our judgment of how good a test of the theory the particular empirical analysis was.

Finally, I should note the powerful ethical dimension in research on such topics. Sociologists, I said, have an obligation to investigate unpleasant topics such as rape, and to do so in as intelligent, skeptical, and careful a manner as possible. The correlation between divorce and rape does not immediately send me to the newspapers, announcing in a press conference that divorced men are rapists. That is simply too strong a conclusion for the data to bear. Sociologists should be judicious in reporting their findings, because incorrect findings based on bad research can only increase the harm of a social problem that is already quite terrible.

Dummy Variables

Although regression analysis is designed for variables that achieve the interval level of analysis, it is possible to incorporate nominal variables into regression equations. In earlier chapters, we saw that Pearson's r could be calculated for variables that were dichotomies. Take sex, for example. In survey data, we could assign the value 1 to members of one sex and 0 to members of the other, and proceed to use this gender variable in regression equations whose other variables were at the interval level. For example, we might want to examine the effect of sex and years of education on income of men and women, thus doing a three-variable regression analysis.

A variable limited to values of 0 and 1 raises no questions about equal intervals—there is only one interval, and it is bound to be equal to itself—so it is definitely at the interval level. We might worry about the fact that regression analysis assumes the values are normally distributed in the population, but sociologists generally go ahead anyway and employ dichotomous variables in regressions. Of course, it is essential to explain to the reader of the research report exactly what was done, so that he or she can evaluate the research methods and results in terms of his or her own standards.

The way to employ nominal (or ordinal) variables that have more than two categories is to collapse the categories into two. A dichotomous variable that was created by collapsing categories in the raw data is called a **dummy variable**.

Suppose you had a religious-affiliation variable with four categories: Protestant, Catholic, Jewish, and None. There are many ways you could collapse these four categories into two, and each way might produce a different dummy variable. For example, you could assign the value 1 to Protestants, and give 0 to members of the other three groups. This gives you a variable that should be called "Protestant," because it measures whether the respondent is Protestant or not. Similarly, one could create a "Catholic" variable by giving Catholics a 1 and everybody else a 0; and you could combine the Protestants and Catholics, giving respondents in both of the categories the value 1 and assigning the value 0 to members of the two other groups. This dummy variable could properly be named "Christian."

The MAPS dataset includes four dummy regional variables. Recall that the United States is divided into 9 "divisions," but the Census Bureau also likes to work with 4 "regions" that are created by combining divisions. For example, the West region combines the Pacific division with the Mountain division. Variable 192 (West region) gives a value of 1 to each state in that region and a 0 to all other states. The other regions are South (combining West South Central, East South Central, and South Atlantic divisions), North Central (combining West North Central and East North Central), and Northeast (combining Middle Atlantic and New England).

The four region variables are mutually exclusive. That is, a state that has a value of 1 for one of these variables will have values of 0 for the other three variables. This is essential if regional variables are to be used together in the same regression analysis.

For example, one could try to explain larceny purely in terms of regional variables. Let's work with variable 192 (West region), variable 191 (South region) and variable 70, the larceny rate. States in the West have a higher larceny rate than do states in other parts of the country, as evidenced by a correlation of 0.64 between variables 192 and 70. The South seems to have a low rate of larceny, because variables 191 and 70 have a correlation of − 0.34. By definition, however, Southern states cannot also be Western. No, I am not denying that Arizona is south and west of Maine, but we defined the South region so that it would not overlap the West region. There is a correlation of − 0.41 between the two region variables.

This means that it is worth doing a partial-correlations analysis, looking at whether the negative correlation between South and larcenies is greatly due to the association each of these variables has with West. And, indeed, if you use partials to control for the effect of West on the − 0.34 correlation between South and larcenies, the coefficient weakens considerably to − 0.11. Thus, the South is really not very low in its larceny rate. Rather, the West is spectacularly high in larcenies, and other regions will have negative correlations with the larceny rate merely by contrast with the West. You can check the other two regions for yourself.

Another analysis using the West and South regions as independent variables can be done to explain variations in variable 18, the percent of the population that is African-American (black). Although there are many citizens of African descent in various parts of the West—for example, in Los Angeles—they are rare in other sections of the region. The correlation between West and percent black is − 0.43. In contrast, the correlation between South and percent black is 0.73. And, as in the previous analysis, the correlation between the two regional variables is − 0.43.

This time, we can try a three-variable regression analysis. With West for X_1, South for X_2, and percent black for Y, the regression equation looks like this:

$$Y' = 5.78 − 3.2194(X_1) + 13.1378(X_2)$$

The Betas for West and South are − 0.15 and 0.67, respectively, and R^2 is 0.56. Thus, the regression equation does a pretty good job of predicting the percent of the population of African descent, but the South variable does most of the work, and West adds only slightly to our capacity to predict. If you want to work through another example, try using variable 151 (percent of employed persons over age 16 in manufacturing industries) as the dependent variable, with regions as the independent variables.

PROJECTS FOR CHAPTER 13

The six projects below employ the XTAB and MAPS programs to show how researchers can profitably work with three or more variables at once. The first project asks for a three-variable crosstabulation, while the second is limited to two-variable regression, and the rest encourage you to handle three variables and more. Several projects test interesting theories in areas such as education, ethnic geographical distribution, and social problems. In so doing, they show how important it can be to look beyond a single independent variable as the complete explanation for a dependent variable. The final project, on the ecological fallacy, lets you attack a classic problem that has been influential in sociology for decades. Again, you gain familiarity with methods of sociological analysis while working on real questions.

1. Three-Variable Tables. This chapter showed how one might use three-variable tables to explore the possibility of spuriousness between two variables in the

XTAB dataset. Avoiding the particular example given in this chapter, find two other sets of variables in the XTAB dataset that might benefit from analysis with three-variable tables. Do the analyses, and write a report both justifying your choice of variables and interpreting the results you got.

2. Explaining Education. Variables 140 through 150 in the MAPS dataset concern secondary and post-secondary education. Particularly interesting are variable 147 (High-school dropout), variable 149 (High-school grads), and variable 150 (4 or more years of college). If you examine the state rankings, you will see that states vary in these important measures of the level of education. Develop a theory, using other variables in the dataset, to explain variations in education, and test it with two-variable regression.

Your report should not only present your findings, including tables of the statistical results. It should also state the theory, explaining why the selected independent variables should predict differences on the education variables, and discussing any surprises that appeared during your analysis.

3. Explaining the Geographic Distribution of Three Ethnic Groups. Use three-variable regression to explain the 1980 distribution of Hispanics, Chinese Americans, and Japanese Americans. Thus, you must arrive at three good regression equations to explain variation in the following three dependent variables: variable 26 (Hispanic = persons of Spanish cultural heritage per 100,000), variable 20 (Chinese Americans = Chinese Americans and Chinese per 100,000), and variable 22 (Japanese Americans = Japanese and Japanese Americans per 100,000).

You should think clearly about possible social factors that might draw members of these groups to particular parts of the country, but you should also not overlook the obvious. For each of these three variables there is an extremely powerful independent variable that might seem sociologically uninteresting but still must be included in your analysis.

4. Explaining a Social Problem. Select one of the following social problems measured by a variable in the MAPS dataset: murders, families in poverty, divorces, abortion, or the unemployed. Develop a theory to explain variations in the particular social problem, a theory whose key concepts can be operationalized in terms of independent variables in the dataset. Test the theory using partial correlation and three-variable regression. Your report should state both the theoretical argument and the empirical results.

5. Residential Characteristics. Consider variables 173 through 178 from the MAPS dataset: air conditioning, old houses, apartments, public sewer, and home owners. First examine information about these five variables to understand what they mean. Then develop a theory or theories to explain why these five dependent variables vary across the 50 states. Identify the appropriate independent variables and do the statistical analysis to test your hypotheses. Are these five dependent variables just five separate phenomena, or can some of the same independent variables and theories explain two or more of them? That is, do the physical conditions we live under have one simple explanation, or must they be understood in terms of a variety of factors?

6. The Ecological Fallacy. Recall that a classical example of the ecological fallacy concerns immigration and illiteracy. As the 1930 census showed, immigrants were more likely to be illiterate than were native-born citizens. But the ecological correlation between immigration and illiteracy is negative, not positive. Perhaps we can explain this with a simple theory: Immigrants are attracted to cosmopolitan areas and to economic opportunity. Therefore, they tend to live in areas where the rest of the population is highly educated. They are not attracted to the parts of the country where there are high rates of illiteracy. Thus, it is not surprising that immigration correlates negatively with illiteracy, even though immigrants are more likely than natives to be illiterate.

The 1930 variables in our state dataset contain all the information necessary to evaluate this theory, and there are several ways to approach the issue. I suggest you identify which variables in group D (variables 193–255) are relevant to it, and look at maps of them, which will help you think through their relationships. Then check out several scattergrams of pairs of variables, noting the correlations. Next, you may want to try partial correlations or three-variable regressions. Finally, write an essay of about five pages attacking the issue. You will want to state your research problem, briefly say how you went about studying it, report the correlations you found, and evaluate the theory in light of your findings.

CHAPTER SUMMARY

This chapter concerns situations in which two or more independent variables are seeking to explain variation in one dependent variable. Social scientists are often concerned that a research finding may be *spurious*, the situation when an apparent association between variables X and Y is really caused by an extraneous variable Z. One of the classic methods for controlling for one variable while looking at the association between two others is the three-variable table, illustrated by data from Travis Hirschi's famous study of juvenile delinquency.

To a limited extent, the SAMP program allows one to analyze three variables at once, to check for spuriousness. Hating school is associated with performing delinquent acts, but conceivably this is the spurious result of sex, because boys may hate school more than girls, and boys are more often charged with delinquency. One can control for sex by looking at the sexes separately. If attitudes toward school and delinquency are associated in a similar way for each sex separately, then the association cannot be the spurious result of gender.

Respondents to the XTAB survey were asked whether a woman should become president of the United States, and political conservatives were less enthusiastic than were political liberals. But women are more likely to be liberals, and women tend to support the idea of a woman president. The select/reject option in the XTAB program makes it easy to test this hypothesis. Each sex, separately, shows a strong negative correlation between being conservative and wanting a woman president, so attitudes toward a woman president are not just a reflection of the respondent's gender, but also reflect political orientations within each gender.

A more advanced tool for investigating spuriousness is partial r correlations, which the MAPS program can calculate. We consider the strong correlation between percent foreign-born and the larceny rate, which (if we ignore the possibility of the ecological fallacy) appears to indicate that foreigners steal. But the partial correlation between foreign-born and larceny, controlling for urbanism, is close to zero. This means that the apparent correlation between percent foreign-born and the larceny rate could very well be the spurious result of urbanism.

Closely related to partial correlations is *multiple-regression analysis,* an expanded version of the regression analysis we have already considered, which employs two or more independent variables simultaneously. Using the three-variable regression option of the MAPS program, we learn that both migration and urbanism combine to explain variations in the larceny rate. We are cautioned to avoid extrapolating very far beyond our data with multiple regression, and we see that it is possible to calculate standard errors even for complex regression equations.

Regression analysis may employ many independent variables at once. For instance, a recent study of the church-member rate used six: the percent of native-born who were born in the same state, the percent who lived in a different house five years before, the population of the metropolitan area, the percent of adults who graduated from high school, the per capita income, and the percent under age 18.

Despite its great utility, regression analysis has problems and limitations. *Collinearity* arises when two or more independent variables are highly correlated with each other, and it can render results highly unstable. *Heteroscedasticity* comes about when errors in our data are not random but correlate with one or more variables that are either in the dataset or are unmeasured. *Spuriousness* appears when a hidden variable creates the false impression that there is a causal relationship between two other variables; *suppression* is the opposite situation, when an extraneous variable gives the illusion that a relationship is weaker than it actually is. *Response biases* in surveys and the *ecological fallacy* in analysis of geographically based rates are both examples of spuriousness. They can often be handled effectively by locating appropriate measures of the extraneous variable and controlling for this variable. Examination of explanation for the rape rate illustrates methodological problems and reminds us there can be serious ethical issues even when the data being analyzed were collected by official agencies of the government.

K E Y   C O N C E P T S   F O R   C H A P T E R   1 3

CHAPTER

14

Advanced Methods of Measurement

CHAPTER OUTLINE

CHAPTER OVERVIEW

This chapter covers a variety of advanced methods of measurement, beginning with an examination of the issues of validity and reliability, which lead to the split-halves method and Cronbach's alpha. The construction of indexes from nonparametric data is followed by indexes with standardized variables. Methods for finding clusters of items in a set of many variables include factor analysis (illustrated with data on fantasy movies).

A new dataset is introduced, based on a survey in which 512 college students expressed

their opinions of 90 possible goals that the space program might serve. The challenge is to find clusters of these narrow goals that express more general values that people may find in spaceflight. This illustrates the general problem of identifying meaningful general dimensions of variation in a dataset.

The XTAB program illustrates index construction with nonparametric variables. The NASA program employs the space-goals survey to illustrate both theory-based index construction and empirical exploration of item clusters in a dataset. Its options include statistics on an item, correlates of an item, creation of an index, statistics on an index, histogram of an index, correlation matrix, correlating an index with items, and two-dimensional scaling.

_____ **Validity of Measures**

Among the most important issues in scientific measurement are the reliability and validity of the measures themselves. Reliability and validity, though related, are not the same thing. For example, it is quite possible for a measure to be reliable but not valid. **Reliability** is the quality of a measure that gives consistent results. A reliable questionnaire item tends to get the same response if administered twice, so long as the relevant circumstances have not changed. **Validity** is the quality of a measure that measures the phenomenon it purports to measure. A valid questionnaire item accurately reflects the desired aspect of the respondent's thoughts, behavior, or characteristics. If we return to the logic of the first chapter, the validity of a measure has to do with how well it operationalizes an abstract concept.

Many studies have investigated the validity of people's reports about their physical health. Are such self-reports valid measures of people's actual health? In the 1950s, Edward Suchman, Bernard Phillips, and Gordon Streib (1958) surveyed more than 1,000 retired men, asking them several questions about their general health and specific health problems. When they compared the men's responses with doctors' reports about them, they found striking disparities. For example, of the 635 men who the doctors said were in good health, 23 percent described themselves as in bad health. Of the 361 who the doctors said were in bad health, fully 61 percent described themselves as in good health.

You might think the solution to the problem is to ask better-focused questions that zero in on specific health problems. Consider these two apparently clear yes/no questions: "Do you have any trouble with your hearing?" "Did a doctor ever say you had varicose (swollen) veins?" A fifth of the men with normal hearing said they had trouble hearing. Three-quarters of the men with varicose veins denied having them. The researchers dryly observed that "the self-rating of health by a respondent . . . is subject to a great deal of error."

The health self-ratings were not useless, however. They did tend to correlate strongly with doctors' ratings, and thus they could be used in statistical studies if care were taken in interpreting the results. These self-ratings were also better predictors of the person's attitudes about health than were doctors' diagnoses. For example, self-ratings predicted very well which men would constantly "worry about health." Thus validity really refers to our interpretation of an item: does it measure what we think it does?

If validity is a problem with questions about physical health, the difficulties are much worse with questions about mental health and emotional conditions. A number of psychological survey **instruments** have been created, sets of items that together are believed to measure particular pathological psychological states and psychiatric syndromes. A common way to validate such a questionnaire is to administer it to a group of normal people and to a group of disturbed people, then see whether the scores from the instrument discriminate the two groups. If the survey describes healthy people as ill and gives mentally ill people a clean bill of health, the items clearly are not valid.

Mental health questionnaires have been evaluated in this way many times. For instance, this validity test has been applied to the Leighton instrument, a questionnaire given through interviews (Moses et al. 1971). One hundred outpatients at a psychiatric clinic were compared with a random sample of 100 members of the general public. The average scores were very different, and only a small minority of the general public scored as badly as the typical patient. Of course, some members of the general public undoubtedly are in bad shape and have merely missed getting into treatment for some reason or another. But, though we want our research tools to be as good as possible, no survey item or index is perfectly reliable or valid.

We use the term **criterion group** for a group of people known (on the basis of conclusive, independent evidence) to have the characteristic an item or index is supposed to measure. An item that correctly distinguishes the criterion group from other people is said to have **criterion validity**.

We seldom have a perfect standard with which to compare our questionnaire items, however. Usually, we compare our surveys with judgments other people have made, or we compare results from two or more different questionnaire items. In contrasting mental patients with the general public, we are relying upon the judgments of doctors that the patients were in need of help, and perhaps upon the judgments of the patients themselves that they wanted help. This evidence of emotional problems may be very convincing, but it is not perfect.

When Travis Hirschi (1969) administered his huge questionnaire to high-school students, he asked whether they had performed various delinquent acts. His correlations showed that boys who said they were very close to their parents were far less likely to report performing delinquent acts than boys who were not close to Mom and Dad. However, it could be that boys close to their parents had simply learned to lie about the bad things they had done, and thus Hirschi's major research conclusions could have been false.

This is a question about the validity of Hirschi's items on delinquent behavior. Do they validly reflect behavior, or are many of the boys lying? Anticipating this problem, Hirschi had also gone to the police to get information about which boys had been picked up by the authorities, a very different indicator of

delinquency. To be sure, trouble with the police is far from a perfect measure of delinquency. Fully 66 percent of the boys admitting theft on the survey had escaped the notice of the police. Some of these may have done their delinquent deeds in a different town and gotten into the files of a different police department, and some may have been picked up by the police prior to the two-year period of the records Hirschi examined. So, validating questionnaire responses by comparing them with official records is not an ideal method, but often it is the best we have.

Hirschi was able to take another step: to make sure that his main research conclusions were especially well-grounded. When he did his analysis, he did not rely on the questionnaire items alone. Instead, he did a parallel analysis using the police records as his indicator of delinquency. For example, he shows that boys who are close to their parents are much less likely to answer "yes" to the theft item than are boys who are estranged from their parents. Then he also shows, in a separate analysis, that boys who are close to their parents are less likely to have had trouble with the police.

Thus, one general solution to the problem of validity in sociological measurement is to develop separate indicators that have their own different strengths and weaknesses. You can inspect correlations between them to see if they support each other, and you can run parallel analyses of the relationships between your indicators and the other variables of interest. In fact, Hirschi and his associates have worked constantly on these problems, and they have concluded that different measures of crime and delinquency give very much the same results in research, thus supporting each other's validity (Hindelang, Hirschi, and Weis 1979).

A good example of how to assess the validity of an index is provided by research on self-esteem conducted by Morris Rosenberg (1965). Ten items, in a four-response agree-disagree format, comprised the index of self-esteem:

1. On the whole, I am satisfied with myself.
2. At times I think I am no good at all.
3. I feel that I have a number of good qualities
4. I am able to do things as well as most other people.
5. I feel I do not have much to be proud of.
6. I certainly feel useless at times.
7. I feel that I am a person of worth, at least on an equal plane with others.
8. I wish I could have more respect for myself.
9. All in all, I am inclined to feel that I am a failure.
10. I take a positive attitude toward myself.

If you look through this list, I think you will agree that half of these statements express a positive feeling about oneself and half express a negative feeling. Combined in the right way, they make a scale of self-esteem that has considerable **face validity**. This means that each item looks like a reasonable indicator of the concept Rosenberg wanted the scale to measure. Upon reflection, most of us would say that each item primarily expresses high or low self-esteem.

But Rosenberg wanted more than just a strong personal conviction that his scale measured what he wanted it to. He sought independent evidence. If the index were an obesity index, he could easily see if objectively fat people got high scores on it while skinny ones did not. The physical weight of the respondents would be the criterion against which we could evaluate the validity of questionnaire items about obesity. But it is not so easy to identify people having high or low self-esteem. If there were a definite group of people objectively known to have high self-esteem and another group known beyond the shadow of a doubt to have low self-esteem, then Rosenberg could give his questionnaire to both groups and see if the scale was successful in identifying which group each respondent belonged to. This would establish the scale's criterion validity.

With psychological conditions that do not drive a person into psychiatric treatment, it is hard to say what objective evidence we could get to prove that a person was in a particular category. You can weigh people to see if they are heavy and check their bank accounts to see if they are rich. You can't look inside their heads to see if they have self-esteem. But it certainly is possible to get independent evidence to compare with a self-esteem scale and improve one's basis for evaluating it.

Fifty average citizens who answered the ten questions were observed by hospital nurses, who then rated each person's apparent mood. None of those scoring high on the self-esteem scale were said by the nurses to be "often gloomy," while a third of those scoring low on self-esteem were described in this way. The nurses judged that only 4 percent of those scoring high had been "frequently disappointed," compared with exactly half of those scoring low.

Often we compare the results of one scale with the results of another scale we think should be related to it. Quite logically, Rosenberg argued that people low in self-esteem should be depressed as well, and many clinical observers report that depression and low self-esteem go hand-in-hand. When self-esteem and depression scales were given to 2,695 respondents, a powerful connection was found. Only 4 percent of those high in self-esteem scored as "highly depressed," compared with fully 80 percent of those scoring low in self-esteem (Rosenberg 1965:21).

If you think deeply for a moment about this, you might come up with a couple of serious questions. First of all, if low self-esteem is strongly connected to depression, who is to say they are not really the same thing? The capacity of an item or index to measure something different from what other scales measure is called **discriminant validity**. That is, if an index can be clearly discriminated statistically from other indexes that already exist, then it must be measuring something of its own and thus deserve a special name.

On the other hand, if we are assessing the validity of a questionnaire item by examining its correlations with another item in the same survey, aren't we really just measuring the *reliability* of both items, the consistency with which they give a particular result? At the beginning of this chapter, it was said that validity and reliability were two different qualities we seek in a measure. These questions suggest that we cannot complete our understanding of validity until we have also considered reliability.

Reliability and Construct Validity

A reliable item or index gives consistent results. Most simply put, the result we get one time will be the same as the result we get another time. On occasion, we actually put a given item in a questionnaire twice, separated by many other items so the respondent doesn't notice the duplication, and check to see if we get the same answer both times. However, reliability can become a rather complex topic if we push the concept to its extremes.

Psychologists often speak of **test-retest reliability**. This refers to consistent results when we give the same set of items to a person twice, with some gap of time between the two administrations. Indeed, psychological experiments sometimes begin by giving a questionnaire to the research subjects. Then subjects get whatever experiences the experimenter wants to inflict upon them, followed by the questionnaire again. Of course, the second administration of the survey is designed to see if anything has changed as a result of the experiment.

If the survey is not reliable, then it will give different results a second time even if the experiment has no real effect on the research subjects. A standard experimental approach, of course, is to divide subjects at random into two or more groups that undergo different experiences. There might be a control group to whom nothing happens except that the same number of hours go by between first and second administrations of the questionnaire as for the groups to whom something is done. Then changes in the experimental group can be compared with changes in the control group, compensating for any instability in the measuring indexes.

Often the mere fact that a person has seen the survey before can produce different responses the second time. With tests of skill or knowledge, this is often called the **practice effect**. Having taken the test once makes it possible for you to do better the second time, whether because you have actually learned how to handle the problems or simply because you are less anxious the second time.

Thus, test-retest reliability is more than just a quality of the items; it also reflects changes in the respondents. Therefore, it may be better to speak of test-retest *stability* than of reliability. And if you want to assess the pure reliability of your items, giving the test twice may not be the best way.

Another approach assesses **parallel-forms reliability**. The survey researcher creates two equivalent forms of an index. For example, you could make one index of 10 items that reflect the extent to which the respondent is generally suspicious of other people, then create another index of 10 different items that also measure suspiciousness. Both indexes can be placed in the same survey, even right next to each other. Because each is supposed to measure the same thing, there should be a strong correlation between scores on them. If not, one or both of the indexes is unreliable.

Essentially the same thing is achieved with the **split-halves reliability** approach. You create a 20-item index of suspiciousness. When you have data from a number of respondents, purely to test reliability you create two 10-item indexes out of the 20—two subindexes of suspiciousness. A common method is to create one subindex out of all the odd-numbered items and make the other subindex out of all the even-numbered items. Because each half of the index is supposed to measure the same thing as the whole index, they should correlate highly with each other.

If all the items of an index reliably measure the same thing, they will stick pretty well together. But if they easily divide into blocks of correlations, and if a few stray items fail to correlate at all with the others, then the index is not a reliable unit. Perhaps it contains what we call **subscales**, sets of items that measure somewhat different things. Each subscale might be reliable, but if they measure very different phenomena, the combination of subscales might not be a reliable measure of anything.

There is room here for differences of opinion. Should an index always measure just one narrow phenomenon, or is it appropriate to combine somewhat distinct subscales to measure a wider tendency? For example, there might be several kinds of political conservatism. Religious conservatism is different from economic conservatism; conservatives who believe in free enterprise are different from conservatives who believe in strong military preparedness. It is possible to create an index to measure each one of these, then to combine them into an overall conservatism index. If the index gives reasonable results when used in research, then it must have some validity. But the attitudes we label "conservatism" may differ so much that it only causes confusion to combine them, and the best course may be to study each separately (Hicks and Wright 1970).

One standard finding in the sociology of religion is that there are several different dimensions of religiousness. Glock and Stark (1965) suggested five ways of being religious: believing, observing religious practices, having religious experiences, knowing the facts about one's religious tradition, and behaving as a religious person in one's daily life. Although these correlate with one another and it is quite possible to combine them in an index of overall religiousness, groups of people differ greatly in which of these five are important to them. Studies have shown that the aspects of religion can be measured through reliable, valid indexes (Hilty and Morgan 1985), and the decision to study religion as one or many dimensions is best made in terms of the particular scientific goal a researcher wishes to achieve.

One concept, very popular a few years ago with social scientists but deeply suspected of unreliability and invalidity today, is *modernity*. The assumption behind this concept is that people differ in how modern they are. People in preindustrial and developing societies were believed to have different values and personalities from the educated folk who inhabit industrial societies. One interview survey of 1,060 people in Guatemala found adequate reliability in a modernity index, but the researcher remained unconvinced that what the index was measuring had much to do with achieving economic development in the country (Portes 1973). Another study found that a set of modernity indexes achieved statistical reliability but could not easily be distinguished from indexes of other concepts such as "alienation" and "anomie" (Armer and Schnaiberg 1972).

This brings up the possibility that some indexes may be perfectly reliable without being completely valid. An index that does not allow you to predict anything about the respondents lacks criterion validity, and an index that correlates too well with other indexes adds nothing to what you can learn without it.

The ideal is an index that is both coherent and distinct. It should be coherent in the sense that its items cohere—stick together—as revealed by consistent correlations connecting them. It should be distinct in the sense that its items correlate much more with one another than with items from a different index with a different name. An index with both of these good qualities is sometimes said to have **construct validity**.

A **construct** is a concept we use to understand a phenomenon that cannot be observed directly. For example, to speak of some people as having an "authoritarian personality" is to suggest that there is a characteristic or dimension of authoritarianism that can help us understand human behavior. Some people have authoritarianism, and others do not. Or, more subtly, perhaps, people vary in how authoritarian they are. But you cannot just look at a person and see authoritarianism; its existence has to be inferred on the basis of survey results. Authoritarianism is a construct.

If possible, you would like to validate a concept like authoritarianism with respect to some readily observed criterion. But for many concepts in the social sciences, this cannot be done. If research finds a group of variables that cohere as a reliable index, however, and this index is distinct from other indexes, then *it must be measuring something.*

Commonsense interpretation of the variables can suggest what we should call the index. And if the variables do seem to share meaning, then the index has face validity. If an index is reliable and distinct statistically and expresses a meaningful concept, then it has construct validity (Cronbach and Meehl 1955). Although we might like to find appropriate, readily observable data to assess its criterion validity, we may have to be satisfied with construct validity. And, since the early 1950s, psychologists have been convinced that construct validity is a very strong indication of the value of a survey index.

Construct validity sounds very much like simple reliability, and it was said at the very beginning of this chapter that reliability was not the same thing as validity. So I must emphasize that distinctness from other indexes is an essential attribute of an index that has construct validity. And I would add the requirement that the index reflect some clear theoretical concept before I would be convinced it had construct validity. Therefore, it is vitally important to work out your theoretical assumptions and make explicit the precise concepts you are using if you want to claim construct validity for an index you have created. If you do all this, you will find other social scientists very sympathetic toward your index, even if you cannot conclusively establish criterion validity.

Before you make your own index, you should gain a little familiarity with the basic methods for combining several variables into one. An *index* is a created variable assembled from several other variables. If sociologists do their work properly, each index will have a single root concept. Each of the variables comprising the index will tap one or another aspect of that concept and thus will be a valid and reliable **indicator** of it. The variables can be of any kind, including those of the nominal or interval levels of measurement, and the methods of combining them into an index range from simply adding together their scores to performing more complex manipulations of the data.

Indexes from Nonparametric Data

The procedures in the NASA program are designed for interval-level data, but researchers often need to combine ordinal-level data into indexes, so I have provided you with several examples.

In the SAMP program, we simulate writing and administering a questionnaire based on Hirschi's research on delinquency. Among the items are five (variables 34 through 38) that ask the respondent whether he or she has committed various specific delinquent acts: stolen inexpensive items, stolen valuable items, driven a car without permission, vandalized property, and beaten someone up. The last two items in the dataset (variables 39 and 40) were created by counting how many of the five offenses the respondent admitted to. If the respondent claims to be innocent of any wrongdoing, he or she will have a value of 0 on both these items. If one or more of these five delinquent acts is admitted to, the person gets a 1 for item 39, "committed one or more such acts." And if the person has done two or more, he or she gets a 1 for variable 40, "committed two or more such acts."

This is approximately the way Hirschi created a delinquency index in the original study. Variable 39, "committed one or more such acts," distinguishes respondents who have been involved in any kind of delinquency from those who have not. Variable 40, "committed two or more such act," counts the variety of delinquency. An individual might have beaten up dozens of people, but if he or she has never done any of the other things, he or she will still get a 0 for this variable. But someone who once beat someone up and once drove a car without permission will get a 1, having performed two of the five delinquent acts, thus appearing more delinquent.

The last five variables in the XTAB dataset, variables 83 through 87, were created by combining other variables in the set in such a way that the new variables could be used in crosstabs. The methods of building these variables avoid the assumption that the component variables are of interval level.

For example, variable 83 is called "Apple fan." It is constructed from responses to preference questions 63 ("IBM PCs") and 64 ("Apple PCs"). By this point, you should have developed a feeling about personal computers in general, but you may not have had enough experience to allow you to compare Apple brand computers with IBM personal computers and the various brands called "IBM-compatible" or "IBM clones." Among some microcomputer users, IBM has a reputation as a powerful near-monopoly corporation that imposes its unimaginative decisions on much

of the industry, while Apple claims to be "the computer for the rest of us," more friendly, more humanistic, and more creative. These images may be false, but they are sufficiently widespread that respondents to our questionnaire might be influenced by them, and "Apple fan" may measure a preference for democracy in computer technology, as opposed to dictatorship. It might interest you to know that the software for this textbook and software package was written on an IBM-compatible made by the Zenith company, while the text was written on an Apple.

Figure 14.1 shows how the Apple fan variable was created. A value of 3 means the person rated Apple more highly than IBM. A value of 2 means the ratings were identical. A value of 1 means the person rated IBM higher than Apple. The respondent has a value of 0 if he or she has missing data on item 63 and/or item 64, and, of course, the XTAB program treats a value of 0 as missing data.

Another index is variable 84, "spaceflight support." This is a scale in which each respondent starts out with one point. A point is added each time the person gives a highly pro-space response in items 72 through 77, which concern the space program. That is, the person gets one point for checking the "increased" box when asked, "Should the amount of money being spent on the U.S. space program be increased, kept at current levels, decreased, or ended altogether?" Another point is earned for saying "important" in response to the question "Do you think that putting civilians into space is

FIGURE 14.1
Apple Fan—Variable Measuring Preferences for Apple over IBM

Responses to Preference Items about IBM PC and Apple PCs	Coded	Cases	Percent
Like Apples better than IBMs	3	157	31.1
Like the two brands equally	2	235	46.5
Like IBMs better than Apples	1	113	22.4
Failed to respond to an item	0	7	Missing

important—or is it too dangerous?" Another point is earned by saying that it is important to maintain a manned space program rather than concentrating on unmanned missions like the Voyager probe. Another is earned by saying that the United States should build a permanently manned space station in orbit around the earth over the next few years. Another point comes from saying that research should continue on a system of space satellites to defend against nuclear attack. Finally, a point is earned by favoring an attempt to land people on Mars.

Figure 14.2 shows the value frequencies for spaceflight support, along with three other indexes to be described shortly. The range of the spaceflight support index is 1 through 7. A value of 1 means that the person did not answer any of these 6 questions in a way supportive of the space program. A value of 7 means that he or she gave a pro-space response to each one. Note that the six spaceflight items are ordinal at best, but the index based on them is an interval scale. Each step in the index means that the respondent gave one more response in favor of the space program, and counting things one at a time produces an interval scale.

Variable 85, the next index, measures love for the physical sciences. Again, each respondent starts out with one point. One point is added each time a person gives a 7 rating, the highest possible, to one of the following five items: 2, Astronomy; 9, Physics; 10, Geology; 15, Mathematics; and 25, Engineering. Variable

86, life sciences, is constructed in a similar manner from the following five items: 1, Botany; 12, Biology; 19, Nursing; 28, Medicine; and 29, Zoology. Finally, variable 87, social sciences, is assembled from responses to items 5, Political science; 16, Economics; 18, Anthropology; 23, Psychology; and 26, Sociology. These three indexes have ranges from 1 through 6, although because a value of 6 requires the respondent to show extreme enthusiasm for all five items in the index, such a score is rare.

No respondents have missing values for the index of spaceflight support. If they failed to answer a space question or failed to give a pro-spaceflight response, then they did not get a point for it; if they gave a pro-space response, they got a point.

The three indexes for types of science do have missing values, however. Each science index was calculated so that a person who failed to rate any one of the five items that comprise it was given a 0 for the index as a whole, thus having a missing value because the XTAB program treats 0 as missing. When constructing your own indexes with elaborate statistical software packages, you will have to decide how to handle missing values. The decisions I made are quite reasonable, and you may want to guess what my justifications were. But when you make your own indexes with your own data, you will have to consider carefully how to proceed.

Figure 14.2 shows that these indexes can be treated like any other variable and are of the

FIGURE 14.2
Four Indexes Based on Crosstab Variables

Index	Range	Mean	Mean for: Men	Mean for: Women	Gamma with Being Male
Spaceflight support	1–7	4.31	4.84	3.79	0.42
Physical sciences	1–6	1.93	2.12	1.75	0.21
Life sciences	1–6	1.82	1.73	1.91	− 0.13
Social sciences	1–6	2.46	2.30	2.62	− 0.19

interval type. The figure gives the range, mean, mean for each sex, and gamma with being male for each of the four. Note that men have a tendency to support spaceflight more than do women, something found in practically every poll taken on the subject. Men also tend to prefer the physical sciences, while women on average give higher ratings than men do to the life and social sciences. You may want to use the XTAB program to check the individual variables that make up one of these indexes, because we would expect to find the same sex differences on most of the component variables.

Indexes with Standardized Variables

Every year, the Federal Bureau of Investigation publishes a book reporting a tremendous amount of information about crime, including "crimes known to police" in a number of categories. Our MAPS dataset gives rates for the fifty states of seven crimes for the census year of 1980: murders, rapes, robberies, assaults, burglaries, larcenies, and car thefts.

Recent reports also list cases of arson, but the arson statistics are probably even less accurate than the often-criticized data on the other seven offenses. Many cases of arson are "white-collar" crimes in which, for example, the owner of a clothing store seeks to escape mounting debts by burning up some overinsured merchandise. White-collar crimes often are not reported by their victims, and in the case of arson the insurance company may not even be sure it has been victimized if all the evidence is destroyed in the conflagration.

In addition to reporting how many crimes of each type were known to police forces in each state, the FBI gives overall numbers for three categories: violent crime, property crime, and all crimes. Indeed, the seven crimes in our dataset are often called "index crimes" because they are used to make up these indexes of crime. Every year, the news media trumpet the results: the crime rate is going up, or the crime rate is going down. Sometimes the violent crime rate is doing something different from what the property crime rate is doing. The violent crimes are murder, rape, robbery, and assault. The property crimes are burglary, larceny, and auto theft.

There are serious methodological problems with these three crime indexes, however. They are created by simply adding together the number of crimes in the appropriate categories, then dividing to get rates per 100,000. But some crimes are far more common than others and thus dominate the final rates. Larcenies are extremely common, and when you talk about "the crime rate," you really mean "larceny with a few other things thrown in." Murders are far less common than assaults, so they contribute far less to the rate of violent crime, even though murder is more serious than assault.

One solution, of course, is to keep separate statistics on the seven crimes and not combine them into an index at all. Certainly, many kinds of crime are not covered by the FBI reports, including common fraud and drug offenses, so it is deceptive to refer to an index made by adding the seven crimes together as "the crime rate." Still, it may be useful to combine different offenses for various purposes, and exploring a different way of doing so can serve our present educational purposes.

Our problem is the difficulty of combining variables that have very different means and standard deviations. A very common way of dealing with this is to standardize the variables before combining them so that their means and standard deviations will be the same. Thus, when combined into an index, the individual variables will each be given the same weight. A frequently used method of standardization was introduced in Chapter 10 and mentioned again in Chapter 12—transforming the values on the variable into z-scores.

With the help of a computer, this is easy to do. First, you calculate the mean and standard deviation for the variable, then you go through the cases one by one, transforming each value. If a value is X, you subtract the mean from it and divide the result by the standard deviation. This gives you a new variable, which always has a mean of 0.0 and a standard deviation of 1.00. There are generally about as many scores less than 0 as there are scores above 0 in this standardized variable, even if all the scores were positive before standardization.

The MAPS dataset has two versions of the seven crime rates. Variables 65 through 71 are the rates as reported by the FBI. Variables 79 through 85 are the same variables in standardized form. Because the MAPS program is not comfortable with negative numbers, I added one little twist: 10. That is, after standardizing each variable into z-scores, I added a constant 10 to each value. This will not affect correlations you do with these variables; the mean for each of the seven standardized crime rates is 10.0, and the standard deviation is 1.0.

The dataset also contains two versions of each of the three crime indexes. Variable 76 through 78 are indexes made by adding the rates for the component variables. Variables 86 through 88 were made by first standardizing each crime rate, then taking an average of the rates that make up each index. The reason for averaging rather than simply adding was to get three indexes with the same means, although this does not ensure that the indexes will have the same standard deviations.

One way to compare these two methods of creating indexes is to look at the correlation between the larceny rate and the overall crime rate. We should expect a very strong correlation with either index. Larcenies will be reflected in both crime rates; furthermore, larceny rates correlate significantly with several other crime rates, perhaps because similar social factors influence both larceny and other crimes. In our dataset, the correlation between the larceny rate and the unstandardized crime rate is 0.89, substantially higher than the correlation of 0.64 between larceny and the standardized rate. In terms of explained variance, calculated by squaring these numbers, the first correlation is about 1.93 times as big as the second.

Whenever you combine variables to create an index, you should contemplate whether standardization or some other preparation is required. For example, your questionnaire might have 10 items about political conservatism, 5 items about religious conservatism, and 5 items about economic conservatism. If you simply combined these 20 into a "conservatism index," it would be unbalanced because there are more political items than either religious or economic ones. You might consider counting each religious or economic item twice or deflating the political items in some way—for example, by multiplying their scores by 0.5. The technique you adopt should be suited to the data and to your theoretical purposes.

A different way of conceptualizing the issue is in terms of "truth in advertising." An index should measure what you say it does. So long as we understand that the FBI's crime index was created simply by adding together the numbers for the seven index crimes and we are aware that larceny dominates the total, there is nothing wrong. It is when we give an index an inappropriate name or ignore the precise way it was created that we lead our readers astray.

Finding Structure in Data

To explain a few principles for finding structures of meaning in existing data, I will use the example of classic horror, fantasy, and science fiction movies. You may have seen some of the 36 films in question, and I am sure you have seen many of their type. The data come from a questionnaire administered to 379 participants in a major convention of science fiction editors, authors, artists, and dedicated fans. This extravaganza was held in 1978 in a futuristic hotel in Phoenix, Arizona, that boasted a rotating restaurant on its top (a TV movie broadcast a few weeks later depicted a comet smashing into that very building). The weirdly costumed participants staged ray-gun fights in the plaza, and a noted author was displayed in a plastic bubble in the lobby, where he wrote a story right before the participants' eyes. Another questionnaire I administered at this convention led to my book on the ideological structure of science fiction literature (Bainbridge 1986), but the data on movies have never been published.

The questionnaire included a section of preference items asking respondents to rate how much they liked each of 67 movies on a scale from 0 (do not like) to 6 (like very much). Some of the movies had been seen by only a few respondents, and some respondents had seen few movies. To get a solid core of data based on knowledgeable respondents and familiar films, I will focus here on the 200 respondents who rated at least 45 of the 67 films and on the 36 best-known movies. Figure 14.3 lists the movies along with the dates they were made, the average score each got on the 0-to-6 preference scale, and the percent of the 200 knowledgeable respondents who had seen each one. They are arranged in descending order of average preference.

There are many ways of searching for structure in data such as these, but we can first distinguish approaches that start with theory from approaches that start with data. Ultimately, both approaches employ both theoretical and empirical analyses, but we can distinguish them in terms of where each starts.

A *theoretical* approach starts by considering the meaning of the items and hypothesizes **a priori** about the ways they may be connected. Here, the term *a priori* means that we would work deductively from a set of theoretical principles. For example, you might start with the theory that fear is one of the primary human emotions. You can then define a horror movie as one that generates fear in its audience. If you

happen to have seen a number of the movies in our list of 36, you can use your own judgment to decide which ones are in the horror category, perhaps on the basis of which ones struck fear into your own heart. I've seen all of them, and I think they can be divided into several groups, including a large number of horror films. However, I also see other dimensions of meaning in the films, and several films combine horror with other qualities. It may be those other qualities that impress many viewers, so we cannot be sure that all of the films that look like horror to you or me really belong in that genre.

Once you have stated a theory about the structure of meanings represented by these films and have framed hypotheses about the individual movies, then you can turn to the data to test your theoretical analysis. A statistical analysis intended to test a theory about the structure of the data is often called a **confirmatory analysis**, even if in fact it disconfirms the original theory. The key principle is that movies you place in the same category should correlate with one another. If they do, then you know that your theory of the meaning structure does capture well the way members of our culture react to the movies. If some of the movies you place in a given group do not correlate highly, however, you have probably made a mistake in your theoretical analysis.

The second way of uncovering structure, the *empirical* approach, is to start with the data. Employing one or another statistical technique, you examine the correlation matrix (or some other matrix showing empirical relationships linking all the items) and try to find dimensions, variation, or clusters of items in it. An analysis of the structure of the data that does not start with any theoretical assumption is called an **exploratory analysis**. The statistical procedures are usually pretty mechanical, requiring no human judgment. However, once they have given you dimensions or clusters, you have to decide what each one means, and here both human judgment and abstract theory play important roles. We shall try both the theoretical and the empirical approach with the movie data.

FIGURE 14.3
Thirty-six Horror, Fantasy, and Science Fiction Movies

Movie	Date	Average on 0-to-6 Scale	Percent Rating It
1. *Star Wars*	1977	5.45	100.0
2. *The Day the Earth Stood Still*	1951	5.25	97.5
3. *2001—A Space Odyssey*	1968	5.17	99.0
4. *Forbidden Planet*	1956	5.09	99.0
5. *Dr. Strangelove*	1964	4.78	95.5
6. *Close Encounters of the Third Kind*	1977	4.70	96.5
7. *Young Frankenstein*	1974	4.64	95.5
8. *War of the Worlds**	1953	4.63	97.5
9. *The Andromeda Strain*	1971	4.59	98.0
10. *King Kong**	1933	4.56	98.0
11. *The Wizard of Oz**	1939	4.47	99.0
12. *Sleeper*	1973	4.46	88.0
13. *Silent Running*	1972	4.23	96.5
14. *Psycho*	1960	4.18	88.0
15. *Invasion of the Body Snatchers**	1956	4.19	88.0
16. *20,000 Leagues Under the Sea*	1954	4.16	97.0
17. *Fahrenheit 451*	1966	4.04	97.0
18. *Fantastic Voyage*	1966	4.00	98.0
19. *Westworld*	1973	3.89	95.5
20. *Yellow Submarine*	1968	3.85	89.5
21. *When Worlds Collide*	1951	3.86	94.5
22. *The Seventh Voyage of Sinbad*	1958	3.84	89.5
23. *Planet of the Apes**	1968	3.76	98.5
24. *Jason and the Argonauts*	1963	3.73	88.0
25. *The Thing**	1951	3.64	88.0
26. *Soylent Green*	1973	3.50	93.0
27. *The Bride of Frankenstein*	1935	3.42	87.5
28. *Flash Gordon**	1936	3.36	91.0
29. *Logan's Run**	1976	3.31	96.5
30. *Omega Man*	1971	3.31	91.5
31. *Rollerball*	1975	3.09	92.0
32. *The Creature from the Black Lagoon*	1954	2.95	97.0
33. *The Fly**	1958	2.76	90.5
34. *Godzilla**	1955	2.73	95.0
35. *Rosemary's Baby*	1968	2.62	88.0
36. *The Land That Time Forgot*	1974	2.49	88.5

*There was either a subsequent remake of the movie or a television program.

The Theoretical Approach to Structure

What in a horror movie can cause fear? It cannot be simply a sense of danger, because all good adventure films produce that feeling. Instead, there must be a sense that an unknown, unexpected, inexplicable, inescapable doom is stalking us. This doom may be supernatural in origin, as in *Rosemary's Baby*, it can come from another planet, as in *Invasion of the Body Snatchers*, or its origin may be the dark recesses of the human soul, brought forth by madness, as in *Psycho*. Other films on the list scared me as well. *Forbidden Planet* is the home of monsters from the "id," the portion of the human mind that knows only lust, neither reason nor mercy. *The Bride of Frankenstein, King Kong*, and *The Creature from the Black Lagoon* involve monsters, one created by science and the other two discovered by it, that are plausibly frightening and certainly bizarre, all three encompassing psychological horrors of distorted sexuality.

I have hypothesized that these seven movies have much in common, together expressing various qualities of the horror film. If so, they should correlate with one another; that is, people should respond somewhat similarly to these seven. A person who likes scary films should rate each of the seven more highly on the preference scale than would somebody who does not enjoy horror. Figure 14.4 gives the actual correlations for the seven movies, along with the average correlation linking each of the seven with the other six and associations to two other films we shall consider below.

Focus first on the top part of the table, which shows the correlations linking the seven movies. Do all seven items hold together? One way to answer this question is to take an average of all the correlations, excluding the seven 1.00 correlations between each item and itself. This average is 0.31, which looks like a solid enough correlation. But looks can deceive, and we need a strict criterion for deciding.

One of the most widely used measures of the reliability of an index composed of several items is **Cronbach's alpha** (Cronbach 1951; Carmines and Zeller 1979). Later, I will explain how you can conceptualize alpha, but first let's learn how to calculate it—which is very easy—and how to use it. One formula for calculating Cronbach's alpha asks you first to calculate the average correlation between items in your list,

FIGURE 14.4
Correlations Linking Selected Horror Films

Movie	Rosemary	Invasion	Psycho	Forbidden	Bride	King
Rosemary	1.00	0.31	0.54	0.07	0.42	0.34
Invasion	0.31	1.00	0.48	0.12	0.43	0.33
Psycho	0.54	0.48	1.00	0.06	0.43	0.34
Forbidden	0.07	0.12	0.06	1.00	0.26	0.17
Bride	0.42	0.43	0.43	0.26	1.00	0.52
King	0.34	0.33	0.34	0.17	0.52	1.00
Creature	0.31	0.32	0.33	0.16	0.41	0.36
Average	0.33	0.32	0.33	0.16	0.41	0.36
Fly	0.35	0.36	0.36	0.17	0.42	0.29
Thing	0.21	0.20	0.15	0.35	0.50	0.46

as we have just done, getting 0.31. It also asks you to count the number of items, which is 7. Then you figure alpha (α) like this:

$$\alpha = \frac{NR}{1 + R(N-1)}$$

In this formula, N is the number of items and R is the average correlation between them. The numerator, NR, is $7 \times 0.31 = 2.17$. The denominator, $1 + R(N-1)$ is $1 + 0.31(6) = 2.86$. And alpha (α) is $2.17/2.86 = 0.76$. Generally speaking, an alpha of 0.70 or greater is considered quite good, so this scale of seven items is satisfactorily reliable as measured by Cronbach's alpha.

You might wonder what alpha's range is; that is, how low and how high can alphas get? If the average correlation is zero, alpha will be zero, too, and if the average correlation is 1.00, alpha will be 1.00 as well. You can verify these facts by checking what the formula will give you for average correlations of 0.00 or 1.00. However, as our example showed, alpha will not be the same as the average correlation and in fact tends to be bigger.

One of the best ways to understand alpha is to think of the problems behavioral scientists (especially psychologists) had in assessing reliability before alpha was devised. Suppose you have an index composed of 10 items and want to check its reliability. As mentioned earlier, one standard technique used to be the *split-halves* approach. You would split the index into two halves, each consisting of 5 items. Each of these 5-item indexes would be a miniature version of the original 10-item index. If the original was reliable, then these two miniature indexes should be measuring the same thing, and there should be a high correlation between them.

Researchers actually used to go through these steps. They would split their index into equal halves, perhaps taking the odd-numbered items to make one 5-item index and the even-numbered items to make the other 5-item index. The researchers would actually compute the two miniature indexes and calculate the correlation between them. Then they would have to do something called "correcting for attenuation." **Attenuation** is a decline in a coefficient because of a reduction of the number of items in an index, reflecting the fact that an index with many items tends to be more reliable than one with few items (Bainbridge 1989b:223). The result of all this work—tremendous labor in the old days before computers—was something called the *split-halves reliability coefficient*.

The chief flaw in this procedure is that you get somewhat different results if you split the original index in different ways. For example, instead of putting all the odd-numbered items of your original index in one miniature index and all the even-numbered items in the other, you could put the first five items in one and the last five in the other. The reliability coefficients would come out differently depending on which you chose to do. This is quite unsatisfactory because you want an objective measure of reliability that cannot be pushed up and down by tinkering with the precise way you calculate it. *Cronbach's alpha* offers this objectivity because it is the average of all the possible split-halves reliability coefficients.

At this point, you might be satisfied with our horror movie index. Alpha came out 0.76, which is higher than the 0.70 that marks a really reliable index, and we now understand that alpha is a quite appropriate tool for evaluating reliability. Aside from laziness, one good reason for stopping the analysis now is that we have done what we set out to. On a priori grounds, we selected movies to be in the index, and we evaluated its reliability, which proved satisfactory.

But we may not have the best possible index; it may include one or more films that do not really belong, and it may exclude some that do. Look back at Figure 14.4; scan across the row of average correlations and see if one of the items has a much lower average correlation with the other six. Indeed, the coefficient for *Forbidden Planet* is only 0.16, while the other average correlations are all greater than 0.30. It is easy enough to figure out what the alpha would be for a horror index based on six of these films, dropping out *Forbidden Planet*.

The average correlation among items in this six-item index turns out to be 0.37, and alpha is 0.78.

Thus, the six-item index is better than the seven-item index. Its alpha is slightly higher, and it has the advantage of requiring fewer calculations to create because it includes fewer items. Of course, the fewer items an index contains, the less reliable it will tend to be. But in this case, throwing out an item that did not correlate highly with the others actually boosted the alpha. Apparently, I was wrong to believe that the chief quality of *Forbidden Planet* is horror, and I will have to see that film again to contemplate what its dominant characteristic really is.

Our work is still not over because we have not considered what other films might be added to the index. Looking through the list of films again, I found that I had been a bit sloppy in making up the original list of horror flicks, leaving out *The Fly,* in which a scientific experiment accidentally combines magnified parts of a fly with parts of a man, and *The Thing,* in which a sinister being crashes in a flying saucer near an arctic base and begins drinking human blood.

(Both of these films were remade in recent years; I am referring to the originals.) These two have a correlation of 0.35 between them, and the bottom part of Figure 14.4 gives their correlations with the other items in question.

The items in this eight-item horror index have an average correlation of 0.36, and the index's alpha is 0.82. Note that the average correlation is actually slightly lower than in the six-item index—0.36 compared with 0.37—but alpha is a bit higher. The size of alpha is affected both by the average correlation and by the number of items, as the formula for alpha makes clear. I think we can be satisfied with this horror movie index, and we can use this set of eight items again in other studies to measure people's appreciation of horror movies. We started on the conceptual level, thinking about what *horror* meant, and selected movies for the initial seven-item index on the basis of whether I felt they had it. Then empirical analysis caused us to drop one of these movies, and reconsideration of the full list made us add two, arriving at an eight-item index with a very good reliability, as measured by Cronbach's alpha, of 0.82.

_____ The Empirical Approach to Structure

An alternative way of uncovering the structure of meanings in our movie dataset is to start with the data. I have in front of me the full correlation matrix for the 36 films, a huge table consisting of 1,296 coefficients covering several pages of big-paper computer printout. A few minutes of scanning through this table and I discover that the largest correlation is 0.77—about as big a correlation as you will ever find in preference survey data—between *The Seventh Voyage of Sinbad* and *Jason and the Argonauts.* These two movies are so similar in style that the second is practically the sequel of the first, even though the legends on which they are based come from different cultures. Although the story of Sinbad comes to us through Islamic society, it probably originated in Ancient Egypt

as much as two thousand years before the birth of Islam. Jason and the good ship *Argo* derive from Ancient Greece. Both movies feature extremely realistic stop-motion animated mythological monsters, and they were created by the same crew under the close direction of Ray Harryhausen.

The second-highest correlation is 0.54, between *Rosemary's Baby* and *Psycho. Omega Man* and *Soylent Green* come next at 0.53, followed by *The Bride of Frankenstein* and *King Kong* at 0.51 and *The Bride of Frankenstein* and *The Thing* at 0.50. *Omega Man* and *Soylent Green* both star Charlton Heston, focusing very closely on the vantage point of his character, and both are set in decayed future societies devoid of hope. (For you real horror fans,

Omega Man is a remake of the rather fine *Last Man on Earth,* starring Vincent Price.) The others in this group look like the tip of the horror iceberg. Thirteen other correlations range between 0.42 and 0.48. Figure 14.5 shows one way of graphing them.

Figure 14.5 looks like a conventional bar graph, but it isn't, and you should avoid thinking of it as one. Note the list of 19 movies along the left-hand edge, all those that participate in correlations above 0.42. Across the top is a scale of correlations increasing to the right, covering the range of correlations from 0.40 to 0.77. The horizontal lines, most of them dashed for much of their length, represent the movies. A short,

dark vertical line connecting two of the movies is a correlation between them. Look first at the lines for *Sinbad* and *Jason.* Way at the right edge of the picture, they are connected by a vertical line representing the 0.77 correlation between them. If you look at the scale along the top of the diagram, you will see that this line is right below the 0.77 point. Thus, the further to the right two of the movies' lines are connected, the higher is the correlation between them. To make the connections between movies stand out, I have shaded the space between them, to the left of the correlation line.

Consider first the four pairs of movies connected in this way and the triplet. I have

FIGURE 14.5
Correlations among Movies

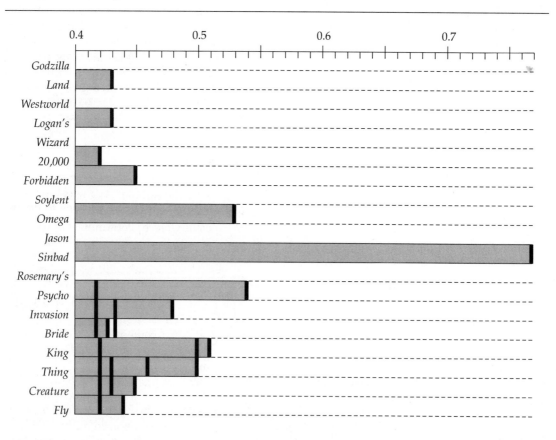

already explained why *Sinbad* and *Jason*, and *Omega* and *Soylent*, were correlated. *The Land That Time Forgot*, based on a novel by Edgar Rice Burroughs, and *Godzilla* both feature dinosaurs. *Logan's Run* and *Westworld* both focus on sinister, contained societies in which "the system" has gained control over the lives of human beings. Exactly why *Forbidden Planet*, *20,000 Leagues Under the Sea*, and *The Wizard of Oz* go together I cannot say.

The bottom of the chart is filled with eight movies that are connected closely together, each correlating above 0.42 with at least two of the others: *Rosemary's Baby, Psycho, Invasion of the Body Snatchers, King Kong, The Bride of Frankenstein, The Thing, The Creature from the Black Lagoon,* and *The Fly*. These are the same eight films that wound up in our horror movie index when we began with theoretical principles and revised our list only slightly on the basis of the correlations. Apparently, horror movies constitute a major genre within the films included in our questionnaire.

The process we just followed, building up a picture of the structure in the data by charting the correlations in descending order from the highest, is sometimes called **cluster analysis**. This term is also used more widely to cover a range of techniques that accomplish similar results. Unfortunately, many datasets do not have a very clean structure of correlations. There may be a very definite structure, but simple inspection of the biggest correlations will not reveal it. Perhaps the alternative statistical approach most popular with social scientists is called **factor analysis**.

This is not the place to explain factor analysis fully. It is very complicated, and the researcher has many different choices concerning exactly how the analysis will be done. It has some affinities with multiple regression, covered in the previous chapter. We can, however, savor a taste of factor analysis, and you can learn the details later on, either in a more advanced course or when you consider using this collection of techniques in your own research and consult some texts in the library specifically about factor analysis. The brand of cluster

analysis we have just considered considers only a few of the coefficients in the factor analysis, while factor analysis is based on all of them. It produces a set of *factors*, which I like to explain as *phantom variables*.

We are working with 36 movies, but these movies may reflect a small number of clusters, one of which, we suspect, is horror. Imagine that there were a perfectly typical horror movies—let's call it *Horror Movie*—and all of the other horror movies would correlate with it to a greater or lesser extent. Indeed, because *Horror Movie* would be perfectly typical of the genre, we could use correlations with it to measure the extent to which each of the 36 movies in our list is of the horror type. This would be great; the correlation between, say, *The Fly* and *Horror Movie* would reflect how heavily loaded with horror *The Fly* is. Unfortunately, *Horror Movie* is a phantom; it does not exist, and we have no data about it.

Factor analysis of the type I shall use below produces a table of *factor loadings,* coefficients that in essence tell us how closely each of the real movies correlates with each of the phantoms. The loading *The Fly* gets on the horror factor (if there is one) tells us how heavily loaded with horror *The Fly* is, even though we do not have *Horror Movie* in our list. Perhaps we can explain best by actually looking at a table of loadings. Figure 14.6 shows some of the loadings I got when I told a factor analysis program in a statistical software package to do an analysis looking for six phantom variables. To simplify things, I have left off the last three factors, and I have limited the table to the films that achieved loadings of 0.40 or greater with one of the factors. The original table on the printout in front of me has loadings for all 36 movies and all 6 factors, a total of 216 loadings. Figure 14.6 is thus only an excerpt of the full analysis, having 26 movies and 3 factors, a total of 78 loadings.

I have arranged the movies in a way that highlights their division into factors. The first 10 load highly on factor 1. The next 9 load on factor 2, and the final 7 load on factor 3. Factor 2 is clearly the phantom variable we

FIGURE 14.6
Factor Analysis of Movies

	Movie's Loading on:		
Movie	Factor 1	Factor 2	Factor 3
Logan's Run	0.67	− 0.04	− 0.05
Soylent Green	0.61	0.12	0.04
The Andromeda Strain	0.59	− 0.02	0.07
Omega Man	0.58	− 0.10	− 0.05
Westworld	0.57	0.11	0.03
Fantastic Voyage	0.52	− 0.14	0.12
The Land That Time Forgot	0.50	0.16	0.05
Silent Running	0.48	0.06	0.05
Fahrenheit 451	0.44	0.22	0.16
Rollerball	0.43	0.05	− 0.07
Psycho	− 0.11	0.68	− 0.02
The Bride of Frankenstein	− 0.06	0.65	0.29
Rosemary's Baby	0.02	0.59	0.12
The Fly	0.15	0.59	0.16
King Kong	0.01	0.54	0.33
Invasion of the Body Snatchers	0.12	0.51	0.16
The Creature from the Black Lagoon	0.20	0.47	0.39
Young Frankenstein	0.09	0.44	− 0.02
Godzilla	0.16	0.41	0.12
20,000 Leagues Under the Sea	0.10	0.14	0.68
Forbidden Planet	0.00	0.08	0.60
The Wizard of Oz	− 0.18	0.30	0.54
The Day the Earth Stood Still	0.11	0.07	0.52
The Thing	− 0.08	0.35	0.48
When Worlds Collide	0.36	0.25	0.47
War of the Worlds	0.35	0.12	0.40

have been discussing, *Horror Movie.* The 9 films in the middle of the table consist of 7 of the 8 in our horror index, with two others added. Their loadings on factor 2 range from 0.41 to 0.68. Again, to simplify, we can imagine that these loadings are correlations with the phantom variable, *Horror Movie*—the perfect but nonexistent representative of the horror genre.

So far, factor analysis has given us essentially the same result we got before. But what

about factor 1 and factor 3? How can we interpret these factors?

Most movies in the first group depict depressing future versions of our own world in which misuse of technology and tyrannical regimentation have created what social philosophers call a *dystopia*—the opposite of a utopia. Thus, we can imagine a phantom variable, a movie called *Dystopian Movie,* that perfectly embodies these qualities. The loadings on factor 1 could then be interpreted approximately as correlations with this phantom.

My interpretation is not completely certain, however. Indeed, interpreting factors is a pretty uncertain process, requiring some intuition as well as thorough familiarity with the meaning of the items in the dataset. Different social scientists will come to somewhat different conclusions when making such interpretations.

A couple of the movies in the first 10 do not seem to fit the dystopian description perfectly. *The Land That Time Forgot* is set at the time of the First World War rather than in our future. A submarine brings warring Germans and Americans to a lost land inhabited by dinosaurs, and eventually all are killed except the hero and heroine. It does depict 20th-century technology at war with nature, and it ends with near total disaster, so it might fit the description but not comfortably.

Fantastic Voyage concerns a trip through the bloodstream of a scientist taken by a miniaturized submarine with miniaturized people aboard. It has a sinister mood, and technology seems threatening, in a struggle with the nature of the human body. Depressing distortions of biology are also themes in *Soylent Green* (in which humans are chemically processed into food biscuits), *The Andromeda Strain* (in which a mutated microorganism threatens all human life), *Omega Man* (in which a plague transforms into vampires those few it doesn't kill), and *Silent Running* (in which the last forests of the world are scheduled for destruction).

So, do we rename this factor *Biohazard Movie*, to express the interest in biological hazards shared by a number of the films highly loaded on it? There is no clear answer to this question, and it points to some of the problems of interpreting factors that were created purely empirically, without an initial theoretical basis. Sometimes it is hard to see a common quality shared by all the items loaded highly on a factor. As in this case, we may see two qualities (*Dystopian* and *Biohazard*), each of which seems to fit approximately but that do not express exactly the same concept. One slightly awkward solution is to call this phantom variable the *Dystopian-Biohazard Movie*. I will mention other solutions after we consider factor 3.

Frankly, I cannot see what emotional or intellectual quality runs through all or most of the films in factor 3. If you happen to have seen some of these nine films, then you can try to find your own interpretation. Having seen all of them, however, I cannot find the shared characteristic. *When Worlds Collide* and *War of the Worlds* were both produced by George Pal and involve extraterrestrial threats to human existence; in the first, our world is accidentally smashed by another planet, and in the second, the Martians attack us. *The Day the Earth Stood Still* and *The Thing* both concern tragic difficulties of dealing with alien visitors. But the three most heavily loaded on the factor seem to share nothing with the others. In general, when interpreting factors, you should give the greatest weight to the most heavily loaded items. But with factor 3, that does not clarify its meaning.

A different possibility emerges if you look at the dates when the movies were made. Three of the movies in factor 3 were made in 1951, and the average date for all seven is also 1951. Except for *The Wizard of Oz*, made in 1939 and re-released in the 1950s, the films were made between 1951 and 1956. Perhaps this factor is simply movies from the early fifties!

Immediately, this makes us worry about our interpretations of the first two factors. The average date of the 10 movies in factor 1 is 1972, while the average for factor 2 is 1955. Is it possible that all three factors are nothing but different periods in which movies were made? A clue can come from the standard deviations of the dates, because they will tell us how narrowly bunched in time the films in each group are.

The standard deviations for the three factors, in order, are 3.4, 13.5, and 5.5. Thus, the middle factor, the one we called *Horror Movie*, is not narrowly situated in time, and therefore it probably does not represent merely films made in a particular band of years. We can continue to consider it to have very clear meaning, expressing horror. But the other two factors are narrowly spaced in time and thus may merely express particular time periods, the early 1970s and the early 1950s.

A glance at the full list of 36 films reveals that some movies made in the early 1970s or early 1950s did not wind up in factors 1 and 3, however. Also, I examined correlations between respondents' ages and their preference for particular films, finding nothing of interest. Thus, it is not simply the year of production that places a film in factor 1 or 3. Instead, I suggest, it is something about the content or style of the film, reflecting the orientations of filmmakers in the two periods. I believe that the early 1970s were indeed a time of great concern about societal regimentation, uncontrolled technology, and environmental degradation. These concerns were reflected in the fantasy and science fiction of films of that period. This conjunction of topics and the tenor of the times give us factor 1.

I am less confident, still, about factor 3, but perhaps there were conventions of filmmaking centered in the early 1950s that tie these movies together. You decide.

The fact that we were able to learn something by looking at the dates of the films implies that we might learn more by bringing in other variables; that is one of the chief ways of overcoming the judgmental difficulties of interpreting factors. I have been describing factors as phantom variables. Indeed, it is possible to create new variables in your dataset, indexes based on the items that load heavily on each factor. The simplest approach would be simply to add together each respondent's scores for the films in factor 1 and give this new variable a name, such as *Dystopian*. Then you would add together each respondent's scores for the films in factor 2 and call the resultant new variable *Horror*. You would do the same for the other factors as well.

I mentioned earlier that one should give greater emphasis to the items more highly loaded on each factor, and there may not be a good justification for ignoring completely the lowest-loaded items. Thus, you might want to create a variable based on weighting the loadings of all the items in the set. This is usually done through **factor scores**, numbers that are by-products of a factor analysis created by the computer especially to make it possible to create new variables, one for each factor. If you do this, the phantom variables will come to life and can be treated the same as any real variable. For example, you can correlate them with other variables in your dataset that might help interpret the factor.

Factor scores confirm our interpretation of factor 2. People who like the films in this factor have highly significant tendencies also to like "horror and weird" fiction, ghost stories, and the literature of H.P. Lovecraft and Edgar Allan Poe, preeminent writers of horror stories. Unfortunately, the variables I happened to include in the questionnaire did not offer much help in interpreting factors 1 and 3.

This brings us to a pair of warnings about factor analysis, especially when it is applied to data that were not collected to test particular theories. First, it can be very risky to accept interpretations of factors unless they are undeniably clear or backed up with other information, such as correlations linking factor scores with other variables. Second, you cannot expect all real-world data to possess clear structure.

The world is messy. Some aspects of human culture but not others may be neatly divided up into categories, and you have to be prepared for the possibility that the particular cultural phenomena of interest to you lack simple structure. Movies may be a good example. To be sure, filmmakers work in somewhat separate genres. The structure is probably even more clear for television programs. Situation comedies and soap operas may share some common elements—for example, a concern for problems in family relations—but they are produced by different people following a clear distinction between the genres. J.R. Ewing does not often stick his tongue out on *Dallas,* and there is no laugh track (simulated audience laughter) on that program. It is a soap opera, not a situation comedy.

Whether cultural phenomena of interest to you divide naturally into neat categories is an empirical question. Used carefully, such techniques as cluster analysis and factor analysis can be used to evaluate the clarity of the structure of this culture, and if it is clear, they will help identify its parts. But you cannot apply these statistical techniques blindly, assuming without good reason that whatever results you get reflect a definite structure.

The Space-Goals Study

As I explained in Chapter 8, the XTAB dataset used for Chapters 8 and 9 came from a study of the ideology of the American space program (Bainbridge 1990b). In the spring of 1986, two months after the explosion of the space shuttle Challenger, 1,007 students at Harvard University completed a survey that included preference and opinion items and gave us the XTAB data. However, the heart of that survey was actually some pages of open-ended items that sought respondents' views on the possible goals of the space program.

Over the summer of 1986, I analyzed the tremendous amount of material respondents wrote in and developed a new questionnaire consisting primarily of 125 statements suggesting goals for the space program. Each goal was based on ideas contributed by at least two—and often dozens—of the respondents to the spring survey. Administered to about a thousand other students in the fall of 1986, the questionnaire collected data for an analysis that would show how the many specific goals fitted together into a few general goals.

These general goals would be comparable to the concept of societal values. When many sociologists speak of "American values," they mean a coherent set of very general beliefs that certain things are good. This system of values is widely held in American society, perhaps by about everybody, and is different from, say, the values held by Russians. Undoubtedly, you have heard many lectures in sociology classes on values, and the concept arises frequently in publications, especially those published a few years ago.

Today, many sociologists doubt the validity of the notion of societal values. Some argue that the various subgroups in society are in conflict with one another, and although each group might have a set of values, the entire society does not. Other sociologists, and I must count myself among them, doubt that the behavior of individuals is organized by a few overarching abstract principles, instead suspecting that most people are incoherent bundles of attitudes, beliefs, and feelings.

But social movements often adhere to strict ideologies, and spaceflight was promoted over the years by a radical group of engineers and dreamers such as the rocket pioneer Wernher von Braun and the science fiction author Arthur C. Clarke (Bainbridge 1976). There exists no manifesto of the spaceflight movement, no sacred book that exactly states its beliefs and values, but years of sociological research on the topic convinced me that a spaceflight ideology did exist and that it had achieved some influence outside the confines of aerospace organizations. A chief aim of my survey research was to determine the intellectual structure and content of this spaceflight ideology as expressed through educated young people outside the social movement itself.

I am not the first person to do survey research on spaceflight attitudes, although my study was by far the most complex one. Back in 1960, Raymond A. Bauer polled 1,717 readers of the *Harvard Business Review*, asking them a number of questions about the value of spaceflight, including one that required them to rank five possible space goals. They are listed in Figure 14.7, along with the percentages rating each one highest among Bauer's 1,717 respondents, among 3,300 respondents to a subsequent poll of the same population (Furash 1963), and among the Harvard student respondents who provided the data for our NASA dataset.

You can contemplate these five justifications for the space program and decide which ones carry the most weight with you, too. But perhaps you can think of other justifications as well. I do not assume that you are a fan of the space program. Sociologists often study ideologies and other aspects of culture that they do not personally like. Whatever your own private feelings, you should be able to think of a range of purposes, both broad and narrow, that some people might wish the space program to serve. Perhaps you can list many kinds of potential "tangible economic payoffs and research results for everyday life on Earth" that might best be considered separately rather than covered by this rather general statement in Bauer's very short list of goals.

Think for a moment about the second and fifth justifications given in Figure 14.7: "control of outer space for military and political reasons" and "winning the prestige race with the Soviet Union." Are these two really separate? The reason for massive American investment in the space program back in the 1960s was to compete with the Soviet Union, which had

taken an early lead in space (Van Dyke 1964; Logsdon 1970). But that competition combined propaganda battles for the admiration of the world with technical developments that might have direct military application. Thus, Bauer's list of objectives may not offer an ideal analysis of the ultimate values of the space program; perhaps it separates things that ought to be combined and combines things that ought to be separated.

Our NASA program and dataset will allow you to do your own study of the ideology of the space program. It consists of responses to 90 different specific goals of the space program, each one judged by 512 college students. My book reports analyses of a slightly larger dataset, 125 questions and 894 respondents, along with much other information, both quantitative and qualitative. So that it would fit on your disk and in your computer, I had to trim the dataset down somewhat: items that did not play important roles in my analysis were dropped, and I took an essentially random

FIGURE 14.7
Ranking of Five Possible Objectives for the Space Program

	Percent Rating the Objective Highest		
	Harvard Business Review		Harvard Students 1986
	1960	1963	
Pure science research and gaining of knowledge	47%	43%	55.4%
Control of outer space for military and political reasons	31	31	4.1
Tangible economic payoffs and research results for everyday life on Earth	14	18	30.5
Meeting the challenge and adventure of new horizons	8	8	9.2
Winning the prestige race with the Soviet Union	3	5	0.8

sample of respondents. Within these limits, no data are missing, and every one of the 512 respondents answered every one of the 90 questions.

The item format was very simple. Each specific space goal was followed by a scale of seven numbers, 0 through 6. The instructions called them "justifications for the space program" and said: "On the following pages we have listed 125 reasons for continuing the space program that 1,007 Harvard students mentioned in response to the survey that we administered last spring. You will probably feel that some reasons are much better than others. Don't worry about all the aspects of each one, but make an overall judgment of it. After each statement is a scale from 0 (not a good reason) to 6 (an extremely good reason). For each justification, please circle the ONE number that expresses how good a reason you feel it is for supporting the space program."

The 90 justifications from this list of 125 that we will be using are listed in Appendix D at the back of this book. The questionnaires presented these space goals in random order. Indeed, there were five different random orders in five different editions of this questionnaire, a precaution to avoid statistically significant but meaningless correlations arising merely from the placement of items.

The NASA program will allow you to examine how the 90 goals fit together into clusters on the basis of their intercorrelations, and each cluster will represent a very general value that might be served by a vigorous space program. We need not assume that these ultimate values of spaceflight are universally accepted by any one group of people. Indeed, the fact that relatively weak correlations across groups of items separate them into clusters suggests that different people endorse different values. Although you are cordially invited to read the book I wrote detailing my own analysis, I hope you will enjoy using the NASA program to explore spaceflight ideology yourself, learning some of the ways we can use statistical techniques to measure the contours of an ideology or a subculture.

 ## Running the NASA Program

When it starts, the NASA program will load the responses of 512 college student respondents to the 90 spaceflight ideology items and offer you the following menu of choices:

```
[1] Statistics on an item
[2] Correlates of an item
[3] Create an index
[4] Statistics on an index
[5] Histogram of an index
[6] Correlation matrix
[7] Correlate an index with items
[8] Two-dimensional scaling
[ESC] QUIT or change programs
```

Choices 4 through 8 cannot be selected until you have created an index from several individual items, something done with option 3. If you try one of these later options without first creating an index, the computer will beep at you and exclaim, "You must create an index before selecting this option." The first two options help you prepare to create an index.

Statistics on an Item

When you decide to look at statistics on one of the 90 items, the computer will give you a list of them, shown here in Figure 14.8. As in other programs, you simply type the item's number and press (ENTER). The names of the items are abbreviated versions of them; you should check Appendix D for the exact wording of any items you are seriously interested in.

For my example, I will pick a justification for the space program that is both very familiar and very controversial, item 24 ("Military"). Its full wording is "There are great military applications of space." Many citizens, including probably a majority of sociologists, have been very suspicious of the militarization of space, seeing it as dangerously destabilizing and contributing little to the general welfare. However, military justifications for the space program are popular in some quarters, and I think the topic will be of interest to you, whatever your personal feelings about it. The summary statistics for this item are shown in Figure 14.9.

The display of statistics on an item is very similar to that in the XTAB program. One difference is that here the item's extreme values are labeled "bad reason" and "good reason," to express the meaning of the scales in this particular dataset. Another difference is the range itself, which goes from 0 to 6 rather than from 1 to 7, as in the XTAB dataset. Because all the space ideology items meet the criteria of

FIGURE 14.8
The Variable Names in the INDEX Dataset

1	Imagination	24	Military	47	New energy	70	Know universe
2	Adventure	25	Tests theories	48	Waste disposal	71	Broaden horizons
3	Travel to stars	26	Space resources	49	Expand species	72	World peace
4	Food supply	27	Morale and hope	50	Navigation	73	Triumph pride
5	Longterm benefit	28	Learn origins	51	Origin of life	74	Encourage people
6	Rivalry outlet	29	Predict weather	52	Should explore	75	Business
7	New medicines	30	We must expand	53	Physics	76	Noble endeavor
8	Curiosity	31	Spread life	54	Medical research	77	It's there
9	Technology	32	Unite world	55	Inspire faith	78	Defense
10	Respect Earth	33	Need to discover	56	Faith in man	79	New worlds
11	Comsats	34	Fun	57	Future in space	80	Alternate home
12	New frontier	35	Dreams	58	National unity	81	Unexpected
13	Education tool	36	Space probes	59	Employ talents	82	New societies
14	Earth resources	37	Move pollution	60	Earth photos	83	Beyond trivia
15	Space cities	38	Electronics	61	Practical info	84	Improve TV
16	Exciting mission	39	Beauty of space	62	Jobs for people	85	Boldly go
17	New perspectives	40	Control pollute	63	Overpopulation	86	Raw materials
18	Recon satellites	41	Solar power	64	Know ourselves	87	Space telescope
19	Advance science	42	Colonize moons	65	Inspire youth	88	Learn humility
20	Tech spin-offs	43	Understand world	66	Missile defense	89	Goal for humans
21	Int. coop.	44	National pride	67	Industry	91	Human spirit
22	Economy	45	Map Earth	68	Manufacture		
23	Unselfish quest	46	New challenges	69	Medical care		

FIGURE 14.9
Statistics for Variable 24: Military

	Value	Cases	Percent	Mode?
Good reason	6	24	4.7%	
	5	20	3.9	
	4	39	7.6	
Range: 0–6	3	73	14.3	
	2	65	12.7	
	1	61	11.9	
Bad reason	0	230	44.9	Yes

Mean: 1.58
Variance: 3.29
Standard deviation: 1.81
Variation ratio: 1.15

both an interval scale and a ratio scale, I have dropped median and dispersion, adding variation ratio in their place.

A glance at the distribution reveals that respondents are not very enthusiastic about the military justification for the space program. The modal response, including nearly half the respondents, is a zero—"not a good reason." Substantial numbers of respondents do favor military justifications, however, and we have enough variation of the item to explore its correlations with others in the set.

Correlates of an Item

When you select this option, the computer will again present you with the list of 90 items and ask you to pick one. We will stick with number 24 (Military). As usual, just type in this number and press (ENTER). In a moment, the computer is working away, figuring all 89 of the coefficients correlating this item with each of the others. As it does so, it begins displaying intermediary results along the left side of the screen. Its goal is to find the 20 items having the highest correlations with the selected item, arranged in descending order of coefficients. As it works, it will keep inserting items according to their correlations. Figure 14.10 shows the final result for item 24 (Military).

The top two items have astronomically high correlations, as survey data go, with the Military item: 0.72 and 0.71. This suggests they are almost synonymous with it. Indeed, they are: "78. The space program contributes to our defense." "66. A space-based anti-missile system, part of the Strategic Defense Initiative, could reduce the danger of war and nuclear annihilation." Certainly, it made sense to include the item about SDI. Many of the respondents to the earlier survey, which collected the open-ended responses that generated the items in the NASA survey, had mentioned the idea, some in approving tones. Many respondents to the earlier open-ended survey had mentioned "military" justification, and others had spoken

FIGURE 14.10
Correlates of Item 24 (Military)

Rank	r		Item
1	0.72	78	Defense
2	0.71	66	Missile defense
3	0.39	44	National pride
4	0.36	18	Recon satellites
5	0.34	75	Business
6	0.32	67	Industry
7	0.27	15	Space cities
8	0.25	80	Alternate home
9	0.24	22	Economy
10	0.23	26	Space technologies
11	0.23	9	Technology
12	0.22	86	Raw materials
13	0.22	38	Electronics
14	0.22	20	Tech spin-offs
15	0.21	73	Triumph pride
16	0.20	58	National unity
17	0.20	31	Spread life
18	0.19	79	New worlds
19	0.19	84	Improve TV
20	0.19	37	Move pollution

of "defense." I had seriously considered combining these into one item, but I thought it would be worth keeping them separate in case the different connotations of the words might elicit different reactions.

The very high correlations linking item 78 (Defense) and item 66 (Missile defense) with item 24 (Military) are certainly no surprise, but they confirm that our research method is working. Items that are based on the same or similar concepts are rated similarly. Respondents who like one will tend to like the others, and those who hate one will tend to hate the others. The three items reflect the same set of beliefs and values, the assumption that military strength is essential in the troubled modern world and that the space program can contribute to it.

It is a big jump down to item 44 (National pride), which correlates only 0.39 with Military, and item 18 (Recon satellites), which achieves 0.36. Their full wording is "The space program builds national pride" and "Reconnaissance satellites help prevent war and nuclear attack." Clearly, national pride is not the same thing as militarism, although some brands of nationalism combine the two. Also, strictly speaking, reconnaissance satellites are not military because they are a major part of the "national technical means of verification" that are at the base of recent treaties to limit armaments. Thus, it is quite reasonable to find these two variables correlating strongly with Military but lower on the list than Defense and Missile defense.

The next two items, item 75 (Business) and item 67 (Industry), are intriguing. In full, they are "Space has great commercial applications and many opportunities for business" and "The space program has great benefits for industry." Neither of these items says anything about militarism explicitly, yet both correlate above 0.35 with Military. To many sociologists, these two items appear to measure allegiance to capitalism, and thus their correlations demonstrate a connection between capitalism and militarism. It is harder to explain the inclusion of other items lower on the list of 20 correlates.

You will notice that the NASA program does not include any measures of statistical significance. For many applications, a test of statistical significance can be used to define a cut-off point, below which we would ignore correlation coefficients. For example, if correlations had to be 0.20 or greater before they were statistically significant, we could limit our attention to only the top 17 items in the list of 20, all achieving this 0.20 threshold. Partly because of the large number of respondents, this approach won't work very well for the present dataset. In fact, a correlation of 0.19, at the bottom of the list, achieves the 0.001 level of statistical significance with a two-tailed test.

When the computer lists the top 20 correlates of an item, it gives you the mean correlation for the 20 plus the mean of all 89 coefficients linking the target items with each of the others. For Military, the means are 0.29 (mean r of 20) and 0.14 (mean r of 89), and even 0.14 achieves the 0.01 level of statistical significance with a two-tailed test or 0.001 with a one-tailed test.

The reason for this is very simple. All 90 items are to some extent measures of general support for the space program. On top of this component shared by all the items in respondents' ratings of them is a unique component based on each item's individual meaning. And many subgroups of items may also measure concepts that express particular values that the space program might serve, more general than those captured in any one item but less general than simple support for the space program, concepts that can be measured through indexes composed of several items.

Create an Index

You can create an index containing as few as 2 items and as many as 12. When you select the menu choice to do this, the computer will present the standard list of items, asking you to type the number of the first item and press (ENTER). For example, you might want to create a Military index starting with item 24, so you would type (2)(4)(ENTER).

The list of items will remain on the screen but with the "24" of item 24 highlighted, and the computer will direct you to enter the next item. For my example, I will create a Military index based on our analysis of correlations between item 24 and the others. I next enter the item 78 (Defense). (As you work, entering items, you can glance at the screen to see which have already been entered because their numbers will all be highlighted.) Then I enter items 66 (Missile defense), 44 (National pride), and 18 (Recon satellites).

You might want to add items 75 (Business) and 67 (Industry), which have correlations above 0.30 with Military. If so, your resulting index might measure attitudes toward the "Military-Industrial complex," the allied forces of the military and industrial sectors of society, which President Eisenhower warned might have gained too much influence. However, I decided to leave these two items out of the index. This leaves me free, if I wish, to create a separate Capitalism index, using other items as well as these two, and see how it correlates with the Military index.

When you have selected all the items you want, press (ENTER) again. If you select 12 items, the computer will automatically quit without the necessity of your pressing (ENTER) once more. At this point, the computer asks you to wait while it creates the index. Even on relatively slow computers, this wait seldom lasts longer than fifteen seconds.

The computer is doing a tremendous amount of work while you are waiting, so please do not resent the slight delay. For one thing, it creates a new variable, which is the index itself. To do this, it goes through the whole set of 512 respondents one at a time. For each respondent, it adds together the ratings that person gave to each item in the index. That total becomes the respondent's score on the index. For a 12-item index, the computer has to add 12 numbers together 512 times. Truth to tell, those 6,144 additions don't take it long, but it has other work to do as well.

The computer's main job is to create a correlation matrix showing all the correlations linking the index items. For the maximum 12 items, that means a matrix of 144 correlations. Twelve of these are just each item's correlation with itself, and I programmed the computer simply to stick a "1.00" in the table at that point rather than to bother actually computing it. Half of the remaining 132 correlations are identical to the other half (the correlation between X and Y is identical to the correlation between Y and X), so it really has to figure only 66 correlation coefficients. But each one is based on 512 respondents, and that means a lot of calculating.

It might be instructive to tell you how I programmed the computer to calculate so many correlations so quickly. The secret hinges on the fact that there are no missing data in this dataset. If you look back at the formula for Pearson's r in Chapter 12, you will see that it includes the sums for both variables and the sums of the squares for both variables. In creating a correlation matrix, the computer will use these same numbers over and over again. So, rather than have the computer calculate these same numbers repeatedly, I figured the sum and sum of squares for each of the 90 variables ahead of time and saved them on your disk. In creating a correlation matrix the computer only has to calculate the cross product (ΣXY) for each correlation, then combine it with numbers it already has, to get the coefficient very quickly.

On top of that work, if the index is not the first one you created during the run, the computer has to figure the correlation between the new index and the old one, which it does an instant before it replaces the old index with the new one. (The computer recalls only one index at a time.) And there are a few minor housekeeping tasks to do. Fifteen seconds does not seem a long time to do all that, despite some programming tricks, and shorter indexes compute even faster. When it's finished, the computer returns you to the menu.

Statistics on an Index

Once you have created an index, you will want to check its summary statistics. When you do so, the computer will remind you of the items that comprise the index—in our example, 24 (Military), 78 (Defense), 66 (Missile defense), 44 (National

FIGURE 14.11
Statistics on Index Number 1

Items:: 5
Possible range: 0 to 30
Actual range: 0 to 29
Mean: 10.48
Variance: 5.79
Standard deviation: 2.41
Max. r: 0.72
Min. r: 0.33
Cronbach's alpha: 0.83

pride), and 18 (Recon satellites). The right side of the screen contains the quantitative information shown in Figure 14.11.

The heading of the table tells you how many indexes you have created during the run and allows you to identify the index by its number. Of course, it is best defined by the set of items included in it, but if you are writing down data by hand, it may be useful to identify indexes by number as well.

An index created by adding scores for two or more individual items will have a greater possible range than any one item, and the actual range of values will tend to be greater as well. Our items range from 0 through 6, so a five-item index will range from 0 through 30. It can reach the minimum only if at least one respondent rates all the component items at 0. It can reach the maximum only if at least one respondent gives all five items the maximum score of 6. Note that $5 \times 0 = 0$ and $5 \times 6 = 30$. In the case of our Military index, at least one person did rate all five items at 0, but nobody rated all five at 6 because the actual top of the range is 29, not 30.

The mean, variance, and standard deviation were all calculated in the same way as for individual items. The maximum correlation is the highest positive correlation in the correlation matrix, other than the 1.00 correlations between each item and itself. The minimum correlation is the lowest one in the matrix, which on rare occasions can be less than 0 for this dataset.

Unless the index is the first one you have created in the computer run, you will also see the correlation between it and the previous index you created. This is the chief tool for examining how indexes relate to one another. The speed at which the computer works allows you to invent a whole set of indexes—not sharing any items between them, it is hoped—and check their correlations to see how distinct they are from one another and to learn which indexes group together into more general concepts.

Cronbach's alpha, described earlier in this chapter, was calculated from the correlation matrix. You should expect to see some very high alphas in this dataset, and it may not be appropriate to use the conventional criterion of 0.70 to decide if an index is a good one. Yes, indexes with high alphas are reliable, but they are not necessarily valid. Remember that all our items measure general support for the space program to some extent. Thus, the alpha of 0.83 for the Military index partly reflects the fact that all five items measure support for the space program and partly expresses their military aspect. Thus, the 0.83 cannot be taken as conclusive proof that the index validly measures militarism rather than general support for the space program.

Perhaps this observation is just a quibble, because there can hardly be any doubt that this index does a good job of measuring military justifications for the space program. The component items certainly have face validity in that they obviously measure attitudes about military applications of space, and the program has other means of evaluating this index, which we shall discuss shortly.

The general approach we should use in determining the groupings of items from our 90 into specific indexes is comparative. Cronbach's alpha can be used to compare two indexes based on different items but each containing the same number of items. Or it can help us decide whether to add one more item to a particular index by noting how much alpha improves (if it does) when we add the item. Especially with datasets containing such high correlations as ours, it is possible to get a high alpha from a group of items that would really be best split into two indexes. Suppose we have put together 12 items, but they really represent two concepts, each with 6 items. Within each group of 6, the correlations may be so high that the average correlation is enough to give a big alpha despite low correlations across the two groups of 6. But it is easy to check for such a possibility, either by eyeballing the correlation matrix itself or by letting the computer do so with its two-dimensional scaling option.

This is a good time to remind you that there are two general approaches to creating an index: empirical and theoretical. In our military example, we followed the empirical approach, letting the computer find the items that correlated most highly with the Military item. But some theoretical judgment entered when we decided how far down the list to go in including items. The theoretical approach would be to select a list of items entirely on the basis of the meaning of the survey items, by reading the items' wordings given in Appendix D and thinking about the concepts they had in common. Contemplation of current issues in aerospace policy would certainly suggest that one factor would be military applications, and the debate continues—both inside and outside government—on how much to emphasize military applications of space compared with the wide range of nonmilitary space goals.

Histogram of an Index

A graphic picture of the distribution of scores in an index can be had by inspecting the histogram. Figure 14.12 shows two graphs, one for the Military index (Index 1) and one for an expanded version of it that we will consider later (Index 2). The graph itself is a forest of thin bars reaching various distances up the screen. There can be as many as 73 bars, representing the full range of 0 through 72 that a 12-item index can achieve. When a bar is missing, reflecting the fact that no cases have that particular value, it will be replaced by a tiny dot, so you will be able to count across to determine the value represented by each bar.

At the right of the computer screen will be a little key telling you how tall is the tallest bar in the histogram. For the Military index (Index 1), the tallest bar is

FIGURE 14.12
Histograms of Two Military Indexes

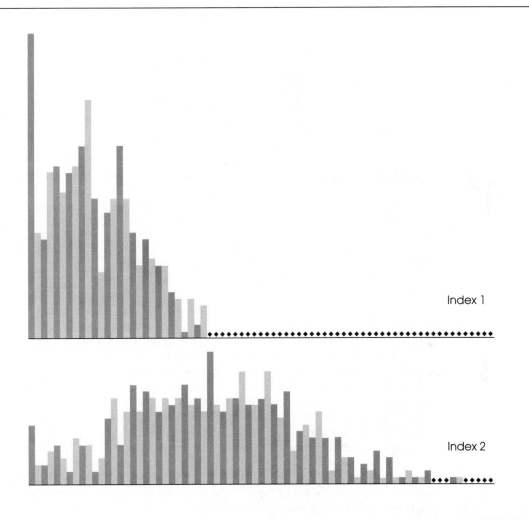

Index 1

Index 2

46 cases high. The highest possible score shown on the histogram is 72, but the Military index cannot reach it because its maximum is only 30.

For some indexes, especially those composed of just two items, it may not be possible to display the histogram at the same scale as for the others. A tiny message at the right edge of the computer screen will tell you whether this is so. For the two indexes in Figure 14.12, the message reads "☐ = 1 case." This means that each tiny square that the bars are made out of represents one case. But, if necessary, each square might represent two cases (☐ = 2 cases) or even three (☐ = 3 cases).

FIGURE 14.13

Correlation Matrix for the Military Index Items

	Var. 24	Var. 78	Var. 66	Var. 44	Var. 18	
Var. 24	1.00	0.72	0.71	0.39	0.36	Military
Var. 78	0.72	1.00	0.69	0.40	0.48	Defense
Var. 66	0.71	0.69	1.00	0.36	0.47	Missile defense
Var. 44	0.39	0.40	0.36	1.00	0.33	National pride
Var. 18	0.36	0.48	0.47	0.33	1.00	Recon satellites

Correlation Matrix

After an index's statistics and histogram, the next thing to check is the correlation matrix. For indexes with many items, there is not room on the screen to list their names, so the correlation matrix table gives just their numbers. The correlation matrix for a 12-item index completely fills the screen. Figure 14.13 gives the one for our five-item military index, with the names of the items added.

The first thing you will note about the matrix is that the two defense items (Defense and Missile defense) correlate highly, their 0.69 being almost identical with the 0.72 and 0.71 they each achieve with the Military item. However, I see something even more interesting in the matrix. The Recon satellites item correlates more highly with the two defense items (0.48 and 0.47) than with the Military item (0.36). Although reconnaissance satellites have played roles in warfare, and reports suggest that both the United States and the Soviet Union shared spy satellite pictures of troop movements with the sides they were supporting in the 1973 Mideast war, their chief purpose is to warn of preparations for attack, thus improving their nation's capacity to defend itself. At some time in the future, an international system of reconnaissance satellites may provide such information to all nations, thus contributing to world peace in a manner that few could deny.

You may often want to inspect correlation matrixes for items whose meanings have little to do with one another and thus cannot validly combine in an index. Well, create an index out of them anyway, remembering that you do so only to get them into the same correlation matrix.

Correlate an Index with Items

Once you have an index you like, you can check its correlations with as many as 20 individual items, selected in the usual manner from a list the computer displays. This has several uses, including the important one of helping you decide whether you have exactly the right set of items in the index. Indeed, an important way of checking an index is to look at the correlations between each item included in it and the index itself. Figure 14.14 gives these correlations for the five military items.

The first three index items achieve very high correlations with it (0.82, 0.85, and 0.84), while the other two have somewhat lower but still high coefficients (0.64 and 0.69). Keep in mind that the correlation between an index and one of the

FIGURE 14.14
Military Index Correlated with 12 Items

Item	r	Mean	Variance	Std. Dev.
24 Military	0.82	1.58	3.29	1.81
78 Defense	0.85	2.14	3.50	1.87
66 Missile defense	0.84	1.79	4.24	2.06
44 National pride	0.64	2.27	3.49	1.87
18 Recon satellites	0.69	2.69	3.77	1.94
6 Rivalry outlet	0.33	1.73	2.86	1.69
21 Int. coop.	0.20	3.46	3.14	1.77
32 Unite world	0.13	2.75	‚3.67	1.92
58 National unity	0.36	2.59	3.14	1.77
7 World peace	0.21	2.38	3.71	1.93
73 Triumph pride	0.36	2.10	3.03	1.74
76 Noble endeavor	0.22	2.43	3.55	1.88

items that comprise it is partly an **autocorrelation**; that is, the item is partly being correlated with itself, because it constitutes one fifth of the index. Thus, we expect high correlations, but they will differ because the items have various associations with one another.

If one item in an index has a distinctly lower association with the index than the others, you should consider dropping it. Naturally, the meaning of the item, and the meaning you want the index to have, should be important considerations as well.

Figure 14.14 includes seven other items that I selected entirely on the basis of their meanings. I felt they related in some way to the issues raised by the military items, and their wording will suggest these possible connections to you: "6. Competition in space is a constructive outlet for nationalistic rivalries that otherwise would take the form of aggression and conflict," "21. Joint space projects between nations improve international cooperation," "32. The common cause of space exploration unites the peoples of the world and could eventually create a world community," "58. The space program generates national unity, encouraging cooperation between numerous sectors of society," "72. The space program contributes to world peace," "73. Space triumphs give us justified pride in our achievements," and "76. Spaceflight is a noble endeavor, expressing the hopes and aspirations of humankind."

Some of these items seem almost the opposite of the military items, speaking of international cooperation rather than international conflict. I wondered whether national unity was more strongly connected with international conflict or international unity. The item on pride from triumph reminds me that the word "triumph" originally referred to the ceremonial procession of a victorious Roman general who had vanquished a foreign enemy. Perhaps today many people give the word a less military meaning, and thus the item might fit poorly with our first index. However, concepts of triumph and nobility have been linked with militarism in the past, and it will be interesting to see if our contemporary respondents do so.

By their correlations, item 58 (National pride) and item 73 (Triumph pride) are more closely connected to the military index than are the others. Of course, the fact that all the items partly reflect enthusiasm for the space program causes some positive correlation with military applications of space for the whole list, even for item 72 (World peace), item 21 (International cooperation), and item 32 (Unite world).

We might guess that several of the items with the lowest associations with Military would have negative coefficients with it if they did not share this general pro-spaceflight aspect. One way to handle this situation would be to create an index of general spaceflight support and use partial correlations or some similar method to control for general spaceflight enthusiasm in looking at correlations linking our 90 specific justifications. Such a spaceflight index should ideally be based on items outside our list of 90, measuring such things as the respondent's willingness to increase funding for the space program, and we cannot use this approach here. Instead, we can compare the magnitudes of the positive correlations we've got, collecting the items into a number of indexes that are internally highly correlated but relatively separate from one another.

The table of correlations between the index and individual items includes each item's mean, variance, and standard deviation, along with the mean of these means (2.33 for the items in Figure 14.14) and the mean correlation with the index (0.47 for this dozen items). Note that the most popular justification in this set is item 21, "Joint space projects between nations improve international cooperation." Its mean of 3.46 on the 0-to-6 scale is much higher than the 1.58 mean for item 24 (Military). Thus, our particular group of college student respondents is far more enthusiastic about peaceful goals of the space program than about military ones. As you work with the dataset, you will find many highly popular space goals, and you will quickly see the vast range of ideas about the space program that garner much stronger support than do the ones in the military index.

Item 66 (Missile defense) has the highest variance (4.24) and thus the highest standard deviation (2.06) among the dozen. At the time of the survey, the Reagan administration's plan to develop a partially space-based defense against nuclear missiles was one of the most hotly debated political issues, and sometimes even good friends would come to blows over it. It was discussed earlier in this book, and a related item is in the dataset for the XTAB program. The high variance reflects the extreme division over this question.

As you work with the space-goals dataset, you will find many clusters of items glued together by strong correlations, and you will note that many of these clusters do not correlate strongly with each other at all. However, I can't give you a strict rule on how to decide when to separate items into different clusters and when to combine them into a single index. The statistics will help you to make such decisions, but you will also have to rely upon your own judgment, relevant sociological theories, and the implications of the particular ideas you want to explore. A couple of metaphors will help communicate some general principles.

Imagine you are making a geological map of the Hawaiian islands, not one designed to guide tourists but one that will help us understand the geophysical processes that created the islands. Sitting at a drafting table, you start to draw the outlines of the islands. But wait, these outlines are based on something that may not have much to do with geology: the particular amount of water in the Pacific

Ocean. If the water happens to rise, as it may if recent warnings about global warming are correct and the polar ice sheets begin to melt, the shorelines of the islands will climb up the hills, and the islands will get smaller. And if the ocean dries up, the shorelines will grow until some of the islands begin to merge, all the water between them having evaporated away.

Even though the Pacific ocean may remain right at the level it is presently, this line of thought suggests that the current coastlines might not be very important for your geological maps. You might want to include information about what is under the water right now, part of the island chain, as well as information about geological features that are currently on dry land. So you might draw a set of contour maps showing the outlines of the islands at several levels, including sea level. Some of these contour maps will merge two or more islands into one, while others, drawing altitude lines high up the hills, will split each island into several, each being a hilltop.

You can think about space goals in the same way. At one level, they form a complete unity, all 90 being measures of support for the space program. At another level, they are 90 distinct concepts. And at various levels in between, they clump into more or fewer clusters that can be studied using the NASA program.

Another way to think about this is in terms of the scale of a map. A globe of the world depicts only the largest features, while a detailed street map of your town may have room even to show the building you live in. The social maps we considered in Chapter 2 come in even closer and can show such details as the furniture in a single room. Between the globe-level and city-map-level of cartography are several other potential levels. A map of the United States and Canada shows the borders of the states and provinces; a map of a single state or province may show the county boundaries; and a map of a county may depict the townships or other subdivisions.

Thus, there is no one "right" level or scale at which to draw your map. Each may be valid depending upon your interest. You can lump space goals together or you can split them apart—not arbitrarily but in accordance with the statistical analysis—arriving at an understanding of the conceptual structure of spaceflight ideology that examines a few major groupings of many ideas or many small clusters of items.

It is said that all people can be split into two groups, lumpers and splitters. Lumpers like to understand things in terms of a few conceptually large categories, while splitters like to make many fine distinctions. (But then, lumpers tend to say that people cannot be split into lumpers and splitters, while splitters say that two groups is hardly enough.) If your research interest defines a level at which to do the analysis, then follow its guidelines. In my book (Bainbridge 1990b) based on an analysis of all 125 space goals, I found it convenient to work at several different levels. Most of the space goals could be considered in terms of four large groups, of which the smallest was the Military cluster, and these four groups conveniently produced four book chapters, one about each. But then, within each chapter I looked at subgroups and subsubgroups.

The fact that there is no one statistical standard to decide when to lump and when to split emphasizes the fact that quantitative sociological research must always draw upon theory and qualitative analysis as well as simply working with the numbers. In the end, sociological research relies upon human judgment as well as computers.

Two-dimensional Scaling

The final option on the menu of the NASA program offers you a picture of the correlations linking the items in an index you have created. It is a graphic way of looking at the correlation matrix, and it may suggest ways you might want to split the index apart. I call it "two-dimensional scaling," in tribute to a general set of methods called "multidimensional scaling," but it is really not a perfect example of any standard method, merely a rough technique I developed to produce a reasonable map from the space data without requiring your computer to have high-resolution graphics capability.

Many statistical techniques are capable of producing two-dimensional maps. For example, many factor analysis programs will crank out maps if you ask them, each based on the item's loadings on a pair of factors. Or you could draw a map of 88 of the 90 space items in which one axis of the graph was each item's correlation with item 24 (Military) and the other axis was each item's correlation with item 72 (World peace). If the distinction between war and peace was a major dimension of spaceflight ideology, then most of the 88 items would be spread in a rough line from one corner (pro-Military, anti-Peace) to the opposite (anti-Military, pro-Peace).

To illustrate the rather crude (but effective) approach used by the final option of the NASA program, I will create a new index (Index 2) composed of all 12 items listed in Figure 14.14, the 5 items of the Military index plus the other 7. Index 2 correlates 0.78 with Index 1, and they do have 5 items in common. Its possible range is 0 through 72, but the actual range is 0 to 67. If you create the index yourself and check the statistics on it, you will find its mean (27.91), variance (5.79), and standard deviation (2.41). The bottom part of Figure 14.12 shows what its histogram looks like.

Now, I do not suggest that these 12 items ought to fit together. Quite the contrary; I think that they reflect two or more groups of items that ought to be split into separate indexes. The computer-generated map will help us decide. When I asked the computer to do two-dimensional scaling, it gave me a map like that shown at the top of Figure 14.15.

Do not try to make sense of this map. When the two-dimensional scaling module of the program begins, it places the index items at random on the screen. Although you cannot see it, there is a checkerboard pattern of 625 tiny squares, 25 squares by 25 squares, on the computer screen. Each item is placed at random into one of these squares, and you can see its number there. *Note:* If you work with the same index, you will get a very different starting arrangement because yours will be a different random placement of items.

Two-dimensional scaling works as follows. The computer starts with the items in a random arrangement, then fiddles with their positions until they are arranged in the way that best expresses the correlations between them in a simple two-dimensional map.

The computer gives you two commands: (R)un 25 times, (S)earch. There are two versions of the Search command: (S)earch:Global and (S)earch:Local. The command starts out at (S)earch:Global, and we will examine it with that version in effect. If you press (R), the computer will run for 25 turns.

This is like a game played by the 12 items: each one gets 25 turns, in order. On a turn, the computer calculates how well the item fits with the others—is it close

FIGURE 14.15
Scaling Diagram

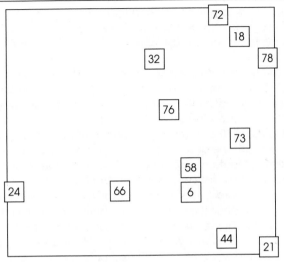

Beginning: Stress = 10,519

End: Stress = 507

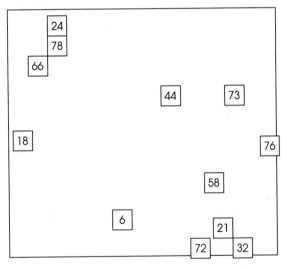

to items it correlates strongly with and far away from items it has only a weak correlation with? The computer picks another spot on the screen and does the same calculations for that spot. Then the computer compares the two spots, the one where the item actually is and the other spot taken entirely at random, and it decides where the item fits best. If the fit is better where it is, then it stays put. If it would fit better at the other spot on the map, then the computer moves it.

How does the computer calculate how well the item fits at a particular spot? A valid question, but not so easy to answer. To make the process work within the limitations of a 25 × 25 array of squares, I had to make some arbitrary decisions. Put simply, the two items that have the highest correlation in the correlation matrix "want" to be right next to each other, on adjacent squares. The two items that have the lowest correlation in the correlation matrix "want" to be 25 squares apart.

Thus, each item "wants" to be at certain distances from the other eleven items. On each turn, the computer calculates how "dissatisfied" the item is with its position vis-à-vis each of the others and adds these numbers together. The total dissatisfaction is called the *strain*. The total strain for all 12 items as arranged at the top of Figure 14.15 is 10519. This number is roughly analogous to the total residuals from the straight line described by a regression equation. Because the practicalities of working without graphics on the IBM forced me to use a technique that is not standard, we shall not worry about exactly how this measure of strain is calculated.

As the program runs, the total strain will decrease. Every time you press (R), it will run 25 turns ahead and tell you the new total strain at the end of those 25. The bottom part of Figure 14.15 shows the arrangement I got after running 150 turns. The strain had dropped from 10519 to 507, and running on to 200 turns did not change things any, so this was the best arrangement I could get.

Note: The final arrangement you get when you try this with the exact same items will be somewhat different, perhaps mainly rotated one way or another and flipped over backward but with minor variations as well. Recall that the initial arrangement is random, and there is no perfect final outcome for most indexes.

Now I should explain the difference between (S)earch:Global and (S)earch:Local. These two variants describe how the computer searches for a spot for an item to move to. When set on Global, the program picks one spot entirely at random in the full field of 625 boxes. When set on Local, it picks one of the spots immediately next to the spot the item is currently on, whether it is a spot to the side, directly above or below, or diagonally adjacent to the spot occupied by the item. Thus, Global makes the items take big jumps, while Local makes them creep around the screen in tiny steps.

I find the best approach is to start with Global, run for 100 turns or so, then switch to Local for the finish. This way, Global lets the items quickly rearrange themselves into roughly the right arrangement, while Local provides the final adjustments to get them in the best possible positions. It can be fun to use Local from the very beginning, because you can watch the items crawling around each other like a scrambling herd of beetles. Usually, however, this takes more turns than if you start with Global and switch to Local at the end.

One problem with using only a Local search is that items can get stuck. Suppose item 72 (World peace) starts out in one of the corners and 24 (Military) and 78 (Defense) are right near that corner. Item 72 might desperately want to get away from the two military items, and the only way it can do this under Local search is to press hard into the corner. Global search would let it hop out of the corner, to the opposite end of the screen, thus escaping militarism.

Even though you eventually reach a point beyond which no further movement happens and the strain does not drop any further, the map is not necessarily the best that could be drawn. A second try, starting with a different random arrangement, might work slightly better. And, of course, we could reduce the strain still further if we drew the map in three dimensions rather than just two.

Suppose you had three items in your scale that all wanted to be exactly 10 squares apart from one another. Ignoring the effect of other items, the three could form a perfect equilateral triangle on the screen and be quite happy with their positions vis-à-vis one another. But if there were four such items, they could not do this. A square would hold pairs of items at opposite corners too far apart. They would be happy if arranged like the corners of a tetrahedron (a pyramid composed of four equilateral triangles), but that would require three dimensions, not two.

Serious statistical approaches, like factor analysis and multidimensional scaling, can work with three or more dimensions, and they give you the option to decide how many you want. But here I think you will find that our rough-and-ready maps do a pretty good job of depicting associations among a dozen items in just two dimensions. Look at the bottom of Figure 14.15, for instance.

Crammed close together, cheek by jowl, are items 24, 78, and 66, the three items most closely associated in the Military index we first created. Keeping some distance from these three, but still closer to them than any of the other items, are items 18 (Recon satellites) and 44 (National pride). Closest to item 44 (National pride) is item 73 (Triumph and pride). (The name for a group of lions is a "pride," and I am resisting calling these two pride items a pride of items.) Item 58 (National unity) is also close to 44 (National pride), two nationalist items.

Very close together, at the opposite end of the map from the military trio, are item 21 (International cooperation) and item 32 (Unite world), and not far away is item 72 (World peace). I think we have found the seed of another index. One of the projects at the end of this chapter will ask you to explore the indexes that might be made by combining this "international peace and cooperation" trio of items with others from the list that share common meaning.

Now, I don't know if this map excites you at all, but it does me. We didn't ask the 512 respondents to draw maps. We didn't even ask them to judge how the 90 different space goals fitted together. We merely asked them to say how good a reason each one was for supporting the space program. Different people have different values and beliefs. They respond to different subsets of items in terms of meanings common to those items that are relevant for disagreements among different groups of respondents. And after some statistical manipulations, we get a map that makes absolutely perfect sense. Magic? No, sociology!

PROJECTS FOR CHAPTER 14

The first six projects below use the NASA program, while the seventh uses XTAB, and all of them teach you to use multiple variables to measure an abstract or underlying concept. The first project merely familiarizes you with the dataset, while projects 2 through 5 have you construct and evaluate different indexes that may reflect very different values people may hold relevant to the space program. Project 6, which uses NASA, and project 7, which uses XTAB, ask you to look for dimensions of complexity that may exist in sets of variables. These final quantitative projects of the book may seem very remote from the simple, qualitative projects we did at the beginning. But really, they focus on the same issue: how can we extract clear truths from the complex social world? Thus, in addition to giving practical experience with multi-item indexes, these projects encourage conceptualization and observation.

1. Popularity of the 90 Items. What are the most popular reasons for supporting the space program? Examine the information about each item provided by the NASA program, writing down the mean score of each of the 90.

Write a brief report, including a table of the 90 popularity scores, stating which justifications for the space program are most successful in garnering support and which are least successful. To do this, you will have to identify the most popular items and contemplate what many of them may have in common. Do the same for the least popular items as well. Your findings might be valuable for the National Aeronautics and Space Administration, but they will also suggest what ideas to stress in a propaganda campaign designed to boost space support.

2. A World Peace Index. Use the empirical approach to create an index starting from variable 72 (World peace). Thinking about the meaning of each item and examining the quantitative measures, arrive at the best index for measuring respondents' acceptance of the value of the space program in promoting world peace.

Your report should list the steps you went through to create the index, including descriptions of earlier versions of it and your attempts at adding and subtracting items, and should explain how you might use this index in future research.

3. An Interstellar Flight Index. Item 3 in the space-goals dataset concerns the possibility of travel out of the solar system and into the galaxy: "Eventually, interstellar travel could be possible, taking people to distant stars." Presumably, this item measures one aspect of far-out, unlimited hopes for the space program. However, a serious scientific periodical, *The Journal of the British Interplanetary Society*, has outlined the technology required to build a primitive starship, so such a voyage may in fact be possible during your lifetime.

Starting with the item about interstellar travel, construct an index measuring respondents' acceptance of such long-range plans for the space program. When you have completed the index, write a brief report explaining the steps you went through and giving your analysis of what the index means. Which other items correlate most highly with the one about interstellar travel? What common values do these items share?

4. A Spin-offs Index. One standard justification for the space program is expressed in item 20 of the space-goals dataset: "Technological spin-offs (advancements developed for the space program, then applied to other fields) improve everyday life." Following directions given for the two previous projects, create a spin-offs index and explain what general value of the space program it seems to express.

5. A Health and Ecology Index. Several items suggest the space program has a positive role to play in improving people's health and the world's ecology. Three items are clearly medical: 7 (New medicines), 54 (Medical research), and 69 (Medical care). Others have clear implications for ecology: 37 (Move pollution),

40 (Control pollute), 41 (Solar power), and 48 (Waste disposal). You might want to add item 10 (Respect Earth) to this group as well. Two others concern problems of world demography: 4 (Food supply) and 63 (Overpopulation).

Consider whether these items belong together in a Health-Ecology index. If not, can they be the basis of two or three indexes, perhaps combined with other items I have not mentioned? Use the full power of the NASA program, plus the power of your mind analyzing the meaning of the items, to explore these issues. Your report should communicate both your thinking and the methodological steps you took.

6. Dimension of Space Ideology. There may be several different ideological dimensions among the 90 in the NASA dataset, but exploration of the relations among the following dozen will allow you to find at least three dimensions:

15 Space cities
22 Economy
42 Colonize moons
49 Expand species
56 Faith in man
62 Jobs for people
67 Industry
75 Business
76 Noble endeavor
79 New worlds
89 Goal for humans
90 Human spirit

Use the tools of the NASA program to discover subgroups of items from this list that express particular values of the space program. Write a brief report giving the research steps you took and explaining the different aspects of space ideology that you found.

7. The Three Ideologies of Science Fiction. When I introduced the XTAB questionnaire items at the beginning of Chapter 8, I explained that 12 of them were taken from a study of science fiction literature that found that authors and readers were somewhat separated into three ideological factions with different perspectives on science, technology, and society. Hard-science science fiction is optimistic about the future and oriented toward technology and the physical sciences. New Wave is more interested in the social sciences, literary experimentation, personality development, and possible dooms for the human species. Fantasy relies on magic rather than science and postulates supernatural beings that dwell in a realm of myth and legend. Science fiction fans tend to be drawn to one or another of these styles; however, research on the special subculture of science fiction fans and authors does not tell us how people in general might feel.

Pick two of these three science fiction ideologies and concentrate on the eight items that express them (four for each of the two you choose), analyzing them with the crosstab option in the XTAB program. Using r as your measure of association, see whether the four items for each science fiction ideology correlate with one another, as they ought to do if each is a coherent unit. Then check whether some of the items in one set of four correlate with items in the other set. If our student respondents are like science fiction fans, the four items in one set will correlate together and the four items in the other set will correlate together, but there will not be high correlations across the two sets. If you have access to a hand calculator, you can easily calculate Cronbach's alpha for both correlation matrixes.

CHAPTER SUMMARY

This chapter examines ways we can combine individual variables to create indexes with wider meanings and often with greater precision of measurement. It begins by noting the importance of ensuring that our measures are both valid and reliable. *Reliability* is the quality of a measure that gives consistent results. *Validity* is the quality of a measure that measures the phenomenon it purports to measure. Examples show that validity is a problem with surveys of physical and mental health.

A number of ways of assessing and improving validity and reliability have been developed. A *criterion group* is a group of people known to have the characteristic an item or index is supposed to measure, and an item that correctly distinguishes the criterion group from other people has *criterion validity*. If each item in a scale looks like a reasonable indicator of the concept we want to measure, the scale has *face validity*. The capacity of an item or index to measure something different from what other scales measure is called *discriminant validity*. *Test-retest reliability* refers to consistent results when we give the same set of items to a person twice, with some gap of time between the two administrations. *Parallel-forms reliability* is achieved when two equivalent forms of an index, created from different items, give substantially the same results. The *split-halves reliability* of an index is evaluated by dividing the items into two subsets; because each half of the index is supposed to measure the same thing as the whole index, they should correlate highly with each other. An index that is both coherent and distinct in terms of its items' correlations has *construct validity*.

Some variables in the SAMP dataset are indexes created from nonparametric variables. Among the items are five that ask the respondent whether he or she has committed various specific delinquent acts, and two other items in the dataset were created by counting how many of the five offenses the respondent admitted to. Five variables in the XTAB dataset were created by combining other variables in the set in such a way that the new variables could be used in crosstabs. The methods of building these variables avoid the assumption that the component variables are of interval level.

It may be necessary to standardize items before combining them into an index. This may be true when one wants to create an index of crime from the annual data published by the FBI, because the published overall crime rate adds together trivial common crimes (like theft) with rare serious crimes (like homicide), counting each crime equally.

Methods for finding structure in data are illustrated with a study of science fiction and horror movies, from a survey administered at a science fiction convention. The *theoretical* approach starts by considering the meaning of the items and hypothesizes *a priori* about the ways they may be connected, working deductively from a set of theoretical principles. The *empirical* approach starts with the data and employs statistical techniques to find dimensions, variation, or clusters of items in them. A statistical analysis intended to test a theory about the structure of the data is a *confirmatory* analysis, while an analysis of the structure of the data that does not start with any theoretical assumptions is called an *exploratory* analysis.

The NASA program affords experience in creating and evaluating indexes. It incorporates data from a fresh survey of 512 college students who were asked to judge a variety of justifications for the space program, goals that spaceflight might conceivably serve. A set of items can be correlated with one another, and a two-dimensional scaling procedure automatically seeks structure in the correlation matrix. This research offers insight into the technological values of American culture.

KEY CONCEPTS FOR CHAPTER 14

Epilogue:
The Future of Sociology
and Computer Methods

This textbook and software package has introduced you to many of the chief methods of sociological research practiced by professionals. Now you are ready for advanced courses on one particular method or another and further courses in social statistics, if you wish to take them. You are even ready to undertake a variety of actual research projects. Your future in sociology is greatly up to you, and you have made a good beginning in the vast, exciting field of sociological research.

If you continue your sociological studies, you should soon become familiar with a standard statistical analysis package. Do not become alarmed when you first glance at the instruction manual for such a package. Each of the major ones includes many different statistical procedures, only a few of which are used by any particular researcher. Thus, the instruction manuals are not designed to be studied from start to finish; rather, you read the introduction and then hop to the chapters on the particular research methods you want to use. Several good statistical packages are available for microcomputers, and versions designed recently for minicomputers or mainframes are not much more difficult to use.

You should also consider other kinds of computer software that may help you in sociological research. There are data management programs, spreadsheets, graphics programs, and many other types. I drew the illustrations for this book using MacPaint on the Macintosh,

and many other programs exist to help you turn data into pictures. With a little imagination, even a word processing program can be used to manage data and do a variety of kinds of analysis. Microsoft Word, the one I used to write this book, will sort paragraphs, and you can use this feature to analyze qualitative data by typing in each separate piece of information as a single paragraph and simply putting a key word or number at the beginning of it for the computer to use in sorting.

At present, some colleges and universities have extensive microcomputer laboratories or other facilities that make computers widely available to students. A few even require students to have their own machines. But many others lack adequate microcomputer equipment, some still having hardly any. Furthermore, schools vary greatly in the machines they have. This presented a great challenge for me when I set out to write the 10 programs in this package. After examining the machines available on a number of campuses, I decided to write the programs in Turbo Pascal 5.5, the most recent version of a highly developed language popular with programmers, that would run on almost any IBM-compatible microcomputer. Then I was forced to limit the use of graphics because so many of the IBMs currently available on campuses lack graphics capabilities altogether. But, as you have seen when you ran the programs, there are ways of "faking" graphics and getting quite a lot of visual performance without demanding that machines have true graphics capabilities.

The development of academic microcomputing is at an awkward point. The IBM computer standard for which I wrote these programs has come to dominate the market, but it is highly limited. Far better would have been the Macintosh II, which would have permitted splendid visual effects, but hardly any schools have this machine. In a few years, the standard IBM-type computer will have very high resolution color graphics, huge internal memory, the capacity to draw on vast databases, pictures, and even music from laser discs, and a standardized user interface that will simplify students' work. At that time, a true revolution in academic computing will occur.

Few colleges and universities have caught up to today's technology, however, and many are falling far behind the leaders. The cost of outfitting all schools with the machine this software is written for is huge, and schools are still caught in the dilemma of whether to buy cheap, basic machines today or wait for the next generation, which will inevitably be expensive when they first come out. I do believe, however, that the current, ordinary generation of microcomputer can make an educational revolution, however nice it would be to have the power of the most expensive machines of today or their successors tomorrow. The software in this teaching system does introduce you to social research methods and statistics with a clarity and richness never possible before. The datasets are certainly big enough, and the calculations go quickly enough, for any introductory educational purpose, and we have found many ways of turning the microcomputer into an effective learning tool.

Sociology teaching at almost all institutions has not even caught up with the hardware that is common today. Compare sociology with chemistry; at my university, introductory sociology is three credit hours, and introductory chemistry is four. The difference is that chemistry requires a three-hour laboratory meeting every week. That, dear friends, makes chemistry a science. Science without laboratories is mere scholasticism, the mere memorization of ancient lore. Introductory sociology should have its lab period each week too, done with microcomputers. Anything less makes ours a highly inferior discipline. Here I speak of introductory courses; advanced courses will vary, of course, some naturally requiring no empirical work. But perhaps half of all sociology courses logically demand laboratory or field work.

What does a decent computer cost today? Well, they vary, but $2,000 will provide one that is more than adequate for the 10 programs in our set. It is an open question whether each individual student needs one, but if computer work is being done in laboratories, then two to five students can put in their lab time each day on one computer, and if each student has on average only about one lab course in a given semester, then more than a dozen can be comfortably accommodated on a single machine. And the machines last several years. True, one needs a room, with appropriate furniture, security, and lab personnel, but if the laboratory gives students regular course credit, the school has to provide some facilities anyway. Furthermore, appropriately designed software does not require lab personnel to do any significant troubleshooting, and one faculty member or teaching assistant can handle 20 or more students. When I assigned the present software in my courses, I often sat in the lab for a few hours, and my help was definitely not needed. Occasionally a student wanted a tiny boost to get started, but after that my only role was to rejoice with students as they discovered fascinating things in their work.

This brings up a very tricky point about the future of education. Perhaps I shouldn't even mention it, but I think it is an issue that will become important in the future, and you might want to think about it now. Do all courses need teachers? Other than to keep professors off the unemployment lines, do we really need class meetings and instructors for all subjects? Frankly, I think we could dispense with conventional teaching altogether for some subjects, reserving faculty for advising and leading early orientation meetings.

Why should you sit and listen to lectures when the material is all in your book, anyway? Well, some of my colleagues believe students need the discipline that an instructor can impose. At the crudest level, this implies that students can't read, so the instructors have to digest the readings for them and crack the whip.

A series of research projects using well-designed software can provide the needed "discipline" and pacing for a course. A single weekly class meeting or individual advising can provide the warm human contact, a double-check that the work is being done correctly, and the chance to share new ideas not encompassed by the assignments. This would not work for many kinds of subject matter, and we will have to develop the techniques and learning materials for the appropriate classes over a series of years.

If I may get personal for a moment, let me admit to you that I have never taken a course in computer programming. Many of the best programmers and most innovative leaders of the computer industry have not, either. I simply bought a microcomputer in 1983, an Apple II it was, and read the simple instructions on how to prepare the computer to program in the BASIC language. A set of manuals from Apple told me what the commands were in BASIC, and the computer would beep at me if I did something very wrong. Reading and trying, trial and error. When I got an IBM personal computer two years later, I soon paid a whole $100 for a version of the Pascal language, and Pascal programs were running successfully within a few hours. To learn to program well in Pascal took months, but they were private months shared by me and my computer, and no teacher was involved at any point in the process.

We are used to only two models of formal education. One is the ancient "Socratic," tutorial, or apprenticeship method. An individual student works directly with a teacher to learn a particular subject. The arts and some of the humanities are probably best learned in this way, although it is awfully expensive to hire one teacher for every student. The other traditional model is the large lecture, in which the teacher recites a mostly prepared speech before frequently bored and slumbering students. Seminars are mixtures of these two traditional approaches.

Not all learning is social. For example, much about research methods can be learned through computerized tutorials. I cannot now guess how many standard sociology topics can be learned effectively by an individual outside the traditional teacher-led model, and I certainly agree that several cannot. Also, it is very useful to have other people check over one's individually done learning from time to time to make sure one is not going off on a tangent. The real barrier to individual learning in college is not technical, educational, or motivational; it is political.

Anything that upsets the status quo threatens professors—and I mean that it really threatens them, not merely that they feel threatened. Especially in difficult economic times, college administrations are always looking for ways to increase class size or teaching load. A department that finds a way to teach more efficiently will lose faculty, because the administration will use the innovations and the retirement of a senior professor to reduce the number of faculty slots allocated to the department. State legislatures talk a lot about the need to support education, but when a crunch comes, the state colleges are cut first and most.

But forget that sad reality for a moment. Imagine this: we create a really good software package for individual learning of a particular subject within sociology. Professor X adopts the package, and with permission of the departmental curriculum committee, he or she redesigns the course. The thirty students never meet as a class; instead, they are given access to computers, and the professor adds the ordinary class time to his or her office hours, allocated specifically for members of the class. Each week an assignment is due, and the professor can call in any individuals who need help but are not coming for it. When the material is mastered, the course is over. If the software is designed correctly, the students will have little need for the professor's office hours, and the professor can concentrate on a different course, perhaps a seminar in social theory that demands much personal contact.

Perhaps I am all wrong about this, but an underlying point is clearly valid: if computers become an effective new means of education, they may demand a new structure through which education is done. In particular, I would like us to get away from old models of *teaching*, in which the authoritative teacher tells the students what's what, and move toward *facilitated learning*, in which college faculty members become assistants in the students' own self-directed learning. From its ancient Latin roots, the word *education* implies that the teacher *leads* the student. I hope for a time when new tools, such as computers and advanced software, make it possible for us to become helpers rather than teachers, assisting you in your own individually charted course of learning.

And new tools are coming. Statistical analysis packages have been available for a generation, but completely new approaches are continually being invented. Previously, much of the software focused on crosstabs, correlations, and the like, but I foresee many completely different areas in which new computer methods can make great contributions. For example, several sociologists have recently offered microcomputer software for doing sociometry, and the field of social network analysis is expanding rapidly.

The two-dimensional scaling option of the NASA program achieves very efficient and visually clear analysis of data, and it illustrates a very basic analytical procedure that was not possible before computers. Technically, it has the funny name *greedy algorithm*. The computer program starts with some messy data and goes through a series of steps to get the data into more meaningful shape. At each step, the computer has the data in a particular form. At random, it rearranges something in the data, generating a second form; then it compares the two forms to see which is closer to the goal. It throws away the form farther from the goal

and keeps the one closer to the goal, then prepares to go through the same step again. Many variants of the greedy algorithm exist, but these are the essential ideas.

I think the greedy algorithm is an incredibly basic and useful tool, almost as basic as addition and subtraction and even more basic than long division and square roots. Correlations may play a role in such an analysis, as they do in the NASA program, but they need not, and many methods are suitable. The possible future applications in sociology are vast, and even our theories may evolve as we take ever greater advantage of analytic possibilities like this.

A current buzzword in computer science is *artificial intelligence*, often called AI. This is an obnoxious term because it implies that computers are taking over the mental functions previously performed only by human beings. Indeed, even though many software companies advertise excitedly that their products use "artificial intelligence," it is not at all clear what the term means. One proverb among software programmers is "Once we understand it, it isn't artificial intelligence anymore." But among the techniques recently developed under the banner of AI are some that may make tremendous contributions to sociological research methods, including expert systems and neural nets.

In general, *expert systems* are combinations of programs and datasets that put in highly accessible form the knowledge developed by human experts. Usually, the program works primarily with linkages between separate facts, often creating complex networks of ideas and information. The chief use of expert systems has been in providing knowledge bases for professionals in such fields as medicine, but they have just begun to be applied to analysis of sociological data—for example, as a radically new approach to survey data (Carley 1985).

Neural nets are computer programs, often written for specially designed computers, that emulate the elements of a biological nervous system. One reason why traditional computers have a great deal of difficulty duplicating the power of the human brain is that they are built on entirely different principles. The computers for which the present software was written have central processing units (CPUs), one per computer. Not so the brain. New computers, just now being built, employ *parallel distributed processing* (PDP), in which data are processed simultaneously and independently by many processing units, even thousands of them (Rumplehart and McClelland 1987). This not only allows the computer to do certain calculations much faster—such as ordinary correlations—but it also facilitates very different approaches.

The classic area in which neural networks were programmed is perception. For two decades, programmers and engineers have been working with neural nets to get machines to see, and considerable success has been achieved. One feature of neural nets is that the programs start out incredibly stupid, incapable of accomplishing anything; then, through trial and error, they learn to perform better and better. I can imagine a project to train a neural net to interpret scattergrams, for example. We program another computer to flash all the possible scattergrams from the MAPS dataset at a neural net PDP computer. After it has seen all of them, it will understand their patterns better than we do, and it will have knowledge about the data that could never be gained simply from inspecting all the correlation coefficients.

Wadsworth Publishing Company and I have already published software incorporating neural nets that run successfully on ordinary computers in *Sociology Laboratory* (Bainbridge 1987c). Designed to aid teaching of social theory, the programs also permit computer-assisted explorations that take social theory in somewhat new directions. The use of AI techniques in sociology has only just begun, and it is impossible to predict with confidence how they will be used a decade or so from now. There have been many exaggerated claims and dashed hopes in the brief history of artificial intelligence, but AI—expert systems, neural nets, and other approaches—promises much for sociology.

For one thing, our statistical analysis packages can be programmed to advise the user as well as simply crank out coefficients. It is trivially easy to tell the computer at what level of measurement each variable is and make the computer suggest which statistics would be most appropriate for the given variable or even for sets of variables of different types. Software is just coming on the market that does this.

Computer programmers and scientists in several fields have struggled for decades to create computers that understand human speech, and they have not yet fully succeeded. When adequate computer methods have been developed to do this, automatic analysis of interviews and other verbal data will be possible. At present, computers can help with this work, but the crucial judgments of meaning and connections among ideas in the material under analysis are made by human beings.

Computers also have a role to play in theory construction and in the logical analysis of theories. Chatting about *Sociology Laboratory* over lunch with me one day, George Homans said that he had once hoped to write a third book in the spirit of *The Human Group* and *Social Behavior*. To be called *A Toy Society*, it would start from his set of simple axioms and build a miniature society operating according to principles logically derived from the axioms and through its realism, demonstrating that Homans's approach could indeed explain the chief features of human society. Unfortunately, Homans said, he could not find the means to produce a functioning toy society. Computer simulation, he agreed, could be that means. Unavailable to Homans, modern computer simulation techniques make possible a variety of experiments with toy societies, leading ultimately to a grand test of the logical coherence and sufficiency of any theory of human behavior constructed along the lines proposed by Homans.

Before a theory can be used as the basis of a computer program, it must be stated rigorously. Too often, sociological theories are metaphors that lack logical structure and clarity. But if even a few fragments of standard theory can be explicitly formalized, they can form the basis of exploratory simulations, which in turn may contribute to further formalization of the theories. A formal scientific theory is a set of abstract rules describing how a system of real phenomena operates. Ideally, formal theory is capable of mathematical proof: given a certain set of axiomatic assumptions, particular consequences follow. Of course, a given theory might be logically consistent and still fail to describe the world we humans inhabit; empirical research will always have a key role to play. But, as Homans observed, sociologists have done too little to formalize their theories and to build deductive logical structures.

A computer program, like a mathematical proof, is an algorithm: a set of rules for solving a problem in a finite number of steps. If we write a computer program to simulate a particular aspect of social reality, the results may increase our comprehension of the theoretical issues associated with that fragment of reality and offer hints on how to build more complete theoretical explanations. A computer simulation can be based on a particular, limited set of propositions from sociological theory. When the program runs, fresh propositions, other than those programmed in, will emerge in the results. These derived propositions were generated through a process analogous to mathematical deduction. Many social scientists have already investigated the value of computer simulations as tools for advancing theory, and *Sociology Laboratory* (Bainbridge 1987c) offers you a set of programs to explore this for yourself.

Ultimately, when all the computing is done and the machines are switched off, the sociologist makes the final conclusions in his or her own mind. I hope the projects you have done with this textbook and software package have taught you much about sociological research and statistics. Designed to give you realistic experience in research and quantitative analysis, the programs have introduced you to the very human activity of doing sociology. You are cordially invited to become a professional sociologist, adding your sociological imagination and human wisdom to the facts and findings provided by raw data and sophisticated computing machines.

Introduction to a Complete Learning System

This textbook and the computer software that accompanies it put you in command of a complete system for learning social research methods and statistics. The software consists of 10 computer programs and several datasets. Some of these programs are simulations that create imaginary data to illustrate certain principles of research methods, but the disks contain much real data from surveys, interviews, observations, and official government studies such as the United States Census. Several chapters of the textbook are supported by their own programs, while others share programs that contain especially rich choices for research projects.

The first two programs, CULT and TALK, illustrate methods of qualitative field research based on a study I did of the Process Church of the Final Judgement (Bainbridge 1978). This more-or-less Satanic cult offered me a tremendously exciting adventure when I performed ethnographic field research on it, and I believe it offers you a pretty interesting experience too, as you encounter it through these programs. Because the group was extremely exotic, you start out in the CULT program knowing and understanding nothing about it. Your familiarity with other religious groups will not help you; therefore, you have to learn everything about it through research, simulated through the software. The first program is a set of dynamic social maps that allow you to enter the cult's headquarters and gain information about rituals, social status, and the secrets locked away in several rooms of the Process chapter house. The second program allows you to interview members of the group and learn their beliefs, histories, and cult activities.

The third program, named HIST for HISTory, puts the 1860 census of Baton Rouge, Louisiana, at your disposal. By modern standards, Baton Rouge in 1860 was every bit as sinister and exotic as the cult. You can look at the actual census records, which give everybody's name, and learn which families owned slaves. There are actually three datasets for this program: 340 inmates of the Louisiana penitentiary (complete with information on their crimes), 1,024 white citizens of the city, and 328 free nonwhite residents. The program allows you to find out the numbers and percents in each category—such as what percent of rich kids versus poor kids went to school—thus introducing the first step in quantitative analysis.

The fourth program, named XPER for eXPERiments, shows you the logical structure of several kinds of social experiment and simulates the actual running of both the original experiments and replications you can do yourself. The experiments range from a modest one done with schoolchildren by Pitirim A. Sorokin many years ago to the massive, million-dollar TARP experiment done more recently with hundreds of released convicts.

Program 5, TABL, uses real data, some of it coordinated with the two previous programs, to show how social scientists use two-by-two tables in quantitative analysis. You will learn about simple chi-square, phi, and Yule's Q. The program shows you exactly how to calculate these statistics; once you understand them, the statistics introduced in later chapters will be relatively easy to comprehend. To demonstrate the concept of statistical significance, the program can quickly generate 100 or 1,000 random tables similar to any particular table you are examining and let you see how your table's chi-square compares with those produced from random data.

The sixth program is named SAMP for SAMPle. Inspired by Travis Hirschi's classic work on juvenile delinquency, it simulates the entire process of creating, administering, and analyzing a survey questionnaire. Your survey can include as many as 20 items taken from a list of 40; you decide which city to do the survey in, how big the random sample should be, and whether to sample all youth or only those of one sex or race. The computer allows you to administer the same survey to several different populations and samples, keeping two of them fresh in its memory so you can compare them for any of the items. Among other things, this vividly illustrates sampling variations and helps you see why large samples are generally preferred over small ones.

Program 7, named XTAB for crosstabs, is one of two major programs with many options and a substantial dataset. Working with an 87-item survey responded to by 512 college students, this program teaches you the main principles of cross-tabulation. Included are the following statistical procedures: Pearson's r, Kendall's tau, gamma, Somers' D, complex chi-square, variance, standard deviation, analysis of variance, and t-tests. The capacities to recode any of the variables, to select or reject subsets of respondents on any variables, and to draw a random sample from the full set of respondents add immeasurable flexibility and educational benefit to this program.

The eighth program, GRAF (graph), is designed to illustrate two areas of social statistics that are made most clear with detailed graphic displays, the normal curve and regression lines. It includes two versions of a "probability pinball game" that illustrates the concept behind the normal distribution and prepares you to understand how statistical significance is often calculated for parametric statistics. One version of the pinball game requires your computer to have a graphics display capacity, and the other does not. Two other parts of the program employ a dataset of 48 rate variables for the nine geographic divisions (regions) of the United States, illustrating the concept of regression. Again, one of these modules requires your computer to have graphics, and the other does not. This is the only program in the set of 10 that even partially requires graphics, and you can get most of its educational benefit even without a computer that can display high-resolution graphics.

Program 9, MAPS, is the second major program in the set, using a massive dataset of 255 rate variables for the 50 American states. It illustrates correlations, scattergrams, linear regression, partial correlations, and multiple regression. Capable of doing many kinds of real research, it provides excellent material for two of the textbook's chapters. Its simplest displays consist of vivid dynamic maps of the states, shaded or colored (depending on whether your computer has a color monitor) to show variation on any of the variables. These maps do not require your computer to have graphics capability.

The tenth and final program, NASA, possesses its own survey dataset based on responses by 512 college students to 90 questions about the value of the space program. It is designed to give you experience in creating multi-item indexes, evaluating their reliability, and analyzing the structure of correlation between items using cluster analysis techniques. The most advanced of the programs, this one completes our survey of research methodologies. After working with each of the 10 programs, you will be ready to undertake real data collection projects and move up to serious statistical analysis packages.

That is our goal: to prepare you for real research, for serious statistical analysis, and for advanced courses in these subjects. I have often taught courses using instructional software programs I wrote, and thus I am well aware that students come to a course like yours with a wide range of backgrounds. Rest assured that I assume no special familiarity with computers. Those of you who have used computers extensively should pay attention while reading even the most elementary instructions in this book; you might learn something.

Headings for some sections of this textbook begin with a little symbol that looks like a floppy disk. This means that the section concerns the computer. However, I have tried to write all parts of this book so that they will make sense even if you are far away from the computer and cannot try the instructions out immediately. For example, I have included quite a number of illustrations of how the computer screen might look if you were working at it. The sections that most directly discuss working at the computer will have this little computer-screen symbol in their headings.

We will begin at the beginning. No, not how to plug the computer in—how to communicate with it by pressing its keys.

The Computer Keyboard

Many of you are unfamiliar with personal computers, and some of the rest of you will be unfamiliar with the particular type of computer you will be working with, so a few words about the computer's keys are in order. I wrote this book on an Apple Macintosh computer, which is different in several respects from the IBM-type with which I wrote the programs, and I still get a little confused when I switch from one to the other. Also, as if to add to our troubles, different models of IBM-type microcomputer have somewhat different keyboard arrangements.

To minimize confusion and make it possible for you to start running my programs right away without spending any time learning to use the IBM, I have avoided many of the strange keys. For example, most IBM-type machines have a number of "function" keys with messages like "F1," "F2," "F3 . . . " on them. Forget them. We don't use them. Almost all the keys we shall use are the friendly old letter and number keys of a typewriter.

Most of the time, you will control my programs very simply by pressing a single key. For example, the screen will often display a list of choices, what we call a computer *menu* because it resembles a restaurant's menu of choices, like this:

[A] Abuse your professor
[B] Beep the beeper
[C] Count the crocodiles
[D] Demolish the computer lab

This menu is fictional, and you won't ever get this set of choices, but they will help me explain how to control the computer. If you wanted the computer to abuse your professor (perhaps electrocuting him or her or merely printing an insulting comment about professors on the computer screen), you would press the [A] key. Whenever I show a letter like this inside brackets—[A]—it is meant to be a picture of one of the computer's keys, so when you see such a picture on the computer screen, you will know you can press the appropriate key to make something happen. Pressing [B], the B key, would cause the computer to beep. If we had any crocodiles and you pressed [C], the computer would count them. Similarly, pressing [D] would demolish your college's computer laboratory.

Let me hasten to add that my software does not, in fact, have the power to demolish the computer lab; in fact, it can't do anything dangerous at all. So don't worry about pressing the wrong key. It will happen sometimes, but the result won't be laboratory demolition. Indeed, with this particular software, mistakes are quite harmless. The worst that will happen is that you might lose five minutes' worth of your own work. Most of the time, however, the computer will ignore wrong keys as if they had never been pressed. Just to complain to you, the computer might beep when you press a wrong key. If this happens, thank the computer for telling you that you have pressed the wrong key, and look for the right one.

Sometimes there will not be a complete menu of choices on the screen but just one or two little messages stuck down at the bottom or over in a corner, like this: [B]eep. This message combines the word "beep" with a picture of the B key: [B]eep. Guess what happens if you press the B key while this message is on the screen? That's right, the computer will beep. Well, you won't ever see this beep message, but other, similar ones appear in several programs. Whether they are part of a formal menu or are merely stuck in various corners of a picture on the computer's screen, pictures of keys like [B] tell you how to make something happen.

When you are considering pressing a letter key to give one of these simple commands, don't worry about whether you should type a capital letter or a little letter. My programs don't care—just press the key.

Many of my menus use numbers rather than letters to tell you which number keys to press to get a particular result, like this:

[1] Abuse your professor
[2] Beep the beeper
[3] Count the crocodiles
[4] Demolish the computer lab

Here, you would press [1], the 1 key, to abuse the professor and [2] to make the computer beep. Don't use the L key for "1," as you might on a typewriter; it won't work. And don't press the key for the letter O (Oh!) when the instructions tell you to press the zero key. Most of the computers you will be using have two sets of number keys, and it is important which set you use. I strongly advise you to use the number keys up above the letters, right where the number keys on a typewriter are found. Do not use the extra set of number keys over at the right of most keyboards.

The square-shaped block of number keys on the right side of most computer keyboards is the *numerical keypad.* This set of keys is designed for very rapid entry of quantitative data, and the numbers are arranged like those on a pocket calculator. You won't be entering very big sets of numbers into this software because I have already done this job for you, and the number keys above the letter keys are very convenient for selecting menu choices because they are arranged in a straight line, just as are the choices on the screen.

The problem with the numerical keypad on many IBM-type computers is a design flaw in the original IBM-PC personal computer. Wanting to conserve space on the keyboard, IBM decided to make these keys do double duty. In particular, the designers needed to fit in some keys that would move you around on the computer screen, so they combined them with the keys on the numerical keypad. When you want to use these keys for numbers, you press a special key called the [NumLock] ("Number Lock") key before doing so. And to use these keys to move around on the screen, you press [NumLock] again. This is especially confusing for people who are not used to computers with this clumsy feature. My Macintosh does not have this flaw, and of course pocket calculators do not, either. So I urge you to avoid the numerical keypad when you want to press a number key. The number keys up above the letters work just fine.

In some of my programs, however, you need the keys of the numerical keypad in order to move around the screen. For example, four of the keys at the right of many IBM-type keyboards have these symbols on them: [→], [↓], [↑], [←]. These are called *cursor control keys.* If you press one of these keys, the *cursor,* a flashing rectangle that sometimes appears on the screen, will move in the indicated direction. For example, pressing [↓] moves the cursor (flashing rectangle) downward. Some IBM-type machines have separate arrow keys that are not part of the numerical keypad. Look for the arrow keys on your particular computer.

Other useful keys often found in the keypad have other messages on them: [PgUp], [PgDn], [End], [Home]. In one of my programs, you get to see actual pages from the 1860 census of Baton Rouge, Louisiana, on the computer screen. [PgUp] and [PgDn] let you move up a page ("PageUp") or down a page ("PageDown") in these census records. The [End] key would take you to the end of the records, the very last page. The [Home] key might better be called the "beginning" key, because it takes you to the very beginning of the census records. I don't use these special keys very much, however, and the appropriate chapter in this book will alert you when they are needed.

In addition to the letter and number keys as on a typewriter, and in addition to the cursor control keys, computers have other useful keys. One found on most typewriters is the backspace key. Again, when I refer to specific keys in this book, I put their names or symbols in brackets to make a crude picture of the key itself, so [BACKSPACE] refers to the backspace key. Sometimes you have to type a two-digit or three-digit number into the computer, and if you hit the wrong number key while doing this, you can use [BACKSPACE] to correct the error. Many IBM-type computers have an arrow pointing left on the backspace key rather than the word "backspace."

Another key on many computers has a similar left-pointing arrow but with a hook on the right-hand end. This key is right below the backspace key, and, unfortunately, it is easy to confuse them. There are several awkward problems with the original IBM keyboard; some computer manufacturers have attempted to correct them, so not all keyboards are alike. The key that can be confused with backspace is the "enter" or "return" key. Instead of an arrow, it may have "ENTER," "RETURN," or even "RETRN" on it. This is a very important key. Some typewriters have an analogous key that makes the carriage return and moves the paper up so you can type on the next line.

[ENTER], as I designate this important key in this text, basically tells the computer to go ahead and do something. What it does depends on the particular software program you are running. Usually, the computer will start its next task, whatever that may be.

Finally, a very powerful key is the escape key. It usually sits near the upper left corner of the keyboard, and it may have "ESC" written on it. Often you will see this key depicted as the last choice on a menu: [ESC]. Usually, it is followed by some message like "QUIT or change programs." If so, of course you should pay attention to that message. But the chief purpose of [ESC], as its name implies, is to let you escape a given situation, such as escaping from one program so you can enter another. My programs do not contain many traps, so you won't have much need for escape hatches. Mostly you just need to pay attention to the simple instructions in this book and on the computer screen. If all else fails, you can try pressing [ESC] and see what happens.

Preparing to Run the Social Research Programs

It is very easy to run the 10 computer programs on the two disks enclosed with this textbook, but you need to do a couple of things to get ready, and you might like some basic information about the software. If you have no experience whatsoever working with a microcomputer, you might need some help at the beginning. To start with, you will want to make extra copies of the two program disks, and disk copying can be hazardous if you are not familiar with it.

The programs were written to run on any standard IBM-type microcomputer, and we have tested them on many. Your computer does not need special graphics capability for 9 of the programs, and the two parts of the GRAF program that use graphics are not essential. If your machine has a color display, the programs will be slightly more attractive, but color is not needed for any of the work you will be doing. Nor do you need a lot of computer memory; 256K should be enough.

Your two program disks are not copy-protected. That means you can transfer the programs and data to a hard disk (or "fixed disk," as IBM likes to call it) or to one of the new 3.5-inch microdisks. Most important, it means you can make personal backup copies in case an accident ruins the original disks. You should not fail to do this. If in doubt about how to make backup copies, read the instructions for your computer's operating system or ask somebody knowledgeable.

If you copy these programs onto a hard disk, you should probably put them in their own directory. There is always the possibility that some other file of your own has the same name as one of ours, and you don't want to erase it accidentally, or confuse the computer about which one it should work with. Each of the 10 programs is separate from all the others, so you could copy 1 program, or 2, or any number up to 10, onto the same disk (so long as there is room). However, there are innumerable datasets that belong to various programs, plus two helper programs called XXX.TPU and YYY.TPU that are needed by each of the 10. Therefore, you are best advised to copy all of either or both disks rather than just parts.

Although the programs in the set allow you to explore many kinds of sociological research and are often quite sophisticated in their use of data, they will not save any new files on your disks. Therefore, you need not worry if the disks provided with this textbook appear full. Indeed, they *are* full, crammed with some exciting adventures in social research!

To use one of the disks or an identical copy of it, start up the computer with its disk operating system (DOS). DOS is a kind of program that allows the computer to run other programs, such as the ones in this set of software. If you are not familiar with the machine, consult briefly with someone who is. If the computer has a hard disk, DOS may already have been loaded onto it. If so, you need only switch it on.

If the computer does not already have DOS on a hard disk, you will need to place a disk containing DOS in the disk drive called drive A, which is almost invariably the left-hand disk drive (if there are two drives side by side) or the top drive (if there are two, one above the other). Only then can you turn the machine on.

When the machine starts, it will load DOS into its memory, quickly check itself over, and ask you for the date and time. My programs do not need that information, so if you do not plan to switch to other software later, simply press [ENTER] in response to these questions.

Shortly, the screen of the computer will show one of the following brief messages: A>_ or C>_. If it shows C>_, you should type A: and then press [ENTER]. (That is the letter A followed by a colon (":"), followed by [ENTER].) Then the screen should say A>_. At this point, put the program disk you want to work with in the main disk drive (drive A).

Naturally, if you have transferred the programs to a disk that is not going to be in disk drive A—for example, to a hard disk, which is probably called drive C—you will have to decide exactly which commands are appropriate to get the software going.

To start any of the 10 programs, make sure you have the right disk in the machine and type the four-letter name of the program, followed immediately by [ENTER]. For example, the first program is called CULT, so you would type CULT[ENTER]. The contents of the two disks are as follows:

DISK 1:
CULT: Observational field research on a deviant cult

TALK: Interviews of individual cult members
HIST: The 1860 census of Baton Rouge, Louisiana
XPER: Research designs for social experiments
TABL: Two-by-two statistical tables analyzing data
SAMP: A delinquency survey and random sample

DISK 2:
XTAB: Analysis of a survey on college preferences
GRAF: The normal curve and regression analysis
MAPS: Map and data on the 50 American states
NASA: A survey on the values of the space program

After you have finished working with a program, it will take you back to DOS. After that, you could start a different one of the 10 programs, begin work with entirely different software, or stop working with the computer altogether. Incidentally, my software does not care if you simply switch the computer off without quitting to DOS. If your computer is part of a larger system, however, there is the possibility that simply switching off could cause trouble for somebody else, so check before doing this.

Copyright Notice

Guidelines for the Use of Software[*]

Software enables us to accomplish many different tasks with computers. Unfortunately, in order to get their work done quickly and conveniently, some people justify making and using unauthorized copies of software. They may not understand the implications of their actions or the restrictions of the U.S. copyright law. Here are some relevant facts:

1. Unauthorized copying of software is illegal. Copyright law protects software authors and publishers, just as patent law protects inventors.
2. Unauthorized copying of software by individuals can harm the entire academic community. If unauthorized copying proliferates on a campus, the institution may incur a legal liability. Also, the institution may find it more difficult to negotiate agreements that would make software more widely and less expensively available to members of the academic community.
3. Unauthorized copying of software can deprive developers of a fair return for their work, increase prices, reduce the level of future support and enhancement, and inhibit the development of new software products.

Respect for the intellectual work and property of others has traditionally been essential to the mission of colleges and universities. As members of the academic community, we value the free exchange of ideas. Just as we do not tolerate plagiarism, we do not condone the unauthorized copying of software, including programs, applications, data bases, and code.

Questions You May Have About Using Software

a. *What do I need to know about software and the U.S. Copyright Act?* Unless it has been placed in the public domain, software is protected by copyright law. The owner of a copyright holds exclusive right to the reproduction and distribution of his or her work. Therefore, it is illegal to duplicate or distribute software or its documentation without the permission of the copyright owner. If you have purchased your copy, however, you may make a backup for your own use in case the original is destroyed or fails to work.
b. *Can I loan software I have purchased myself?* If your software came with a clearly visible license agreement, or if you signed a registration card, *read the license carefully* before you use the software. Some licenses may restrict use to a specific computer. Copyright law does not permit you to run your software on two or more computers simultaneously unless the license agreement specifically allows it. It may, however, be legal to lend your software to a friend temporarily as long as you do not keep a copy.
c. *If software is not copy-protected, do I have the right to copy it?* Lack of copy-protection does *not* constitute permission to copy software in order to share or sell it. "Non-copy-protected" software enables you to protect your investment by making a backup copy. In offering non-copy-protected software to you, the developer or publisher has demonstrated significant trust in your integrity.
d. *May I copy software that is available through facilities on my campus, so that I can use it more conveniently in my own room?* Software acquired by colleges or universities is usually licensed. The licenses restrict how and where the

*This section was originally published by EDUCOM, a nonprofit consortium of colleges and universities committed to the use and management of information technology in higher education, and ADAPSO, the computer software and services industry association. For additional copies of the original brochure, contact EDUCOM, Software Initiative, P.O. Box 364, Princeton, NJ 08540 or ADAPSO, 1300 North 17th Street, Suite 300, Arlington, VA 22209.

software may be legally used by members of the community. This applies to software installed on hard disks in microcomputer clusters, software distributed on disks by a campus lending library, and software available on a campus mainframe or network. Some institutional licenses permit copying for certain purposes. Consult your campus authorities if you are unsure about the use of a particular software project.

e. *Isn't it legally "fair use" to copy software if the purpose in sharing it is purely educational?* No. It is illegal for a faculty member or student to copy software for distribution among the members of a class without permission of the author or publisher.

The Survey of College Student Preferences

Preferences for College Subjects

Following is a list of various subjects that are taught at universities. Please tell us how much you like each one of them, whether you actually have taken a course in it or not.

Please circle the number 1 if you do not like the subject at all. Please circle the number 7 if you like it very much—if it is one of your very favorite subjects. Otherwise, please circle the *one* number in between that best indicates how much you like it.

		Do Not Like					Like Very Much	
1.	Botany	1	2	3	4	5	6	7
2.	Astronomy	1	2	3	4	5	6	7
3.	A foreign language	1	2	3	4	5	6	7
4.	Law	1	2	3	4	5	6	7
5.	Political science	1	2	3	4	5	6	7
6.	Music	1	2	3	4	5	6	7
7.	History	1	2	3	4	5	6	7
8.	Classics (ancient civilization)	1	2	3	4	5	6	7
9.	Physics	1	2	3	4	5	6	7
10.	Geology	1	2	3	4	5	6	7
11.	Business	1	2	3	4	5	6	7
12.	Biology	1	2	3	4	5	6	7
13.	Chemistry	1	2	3	4	5	6	7
14.	Art	1	2	3	4	5	6	7

		Do Not Like					Like Very Much
15.	Mathematics	1	2	3	4	5	6	7
16.	Economics	1	2	3	4	5	6	7
17.	Education	1	2	3	4	5	6	7
18.	Anthropology	1	2	3	4	5	6	7
19.	Nursing	1	2	3	4	5	6	7
20.	Oceanography	1	2	3	4	5	6	7
21.	Social work	1	2	3	4	5	6	7
22.	Drama	1	2	3	4	5	6	7
23.	Psychology	1	2	3	4	5	6	7
24.	Communications	1	2	3	4	5	6	7
25.	Engineering	1	2	3	4	5	6	7
26.	Sociology	1	2	3	4	5	6	7
27.	Literature	1	2	3	4	5	6	7
28.	Medicine	1	2	3	4	5	6	7
29.	Zoology	1	2	3	4	5	6	7
30.	Architecture	1	2	3	4	5	6	7
31.	The sciences, in general	1	2	3	4	5	6	7
32.	The humanities, in general	1	2	3	4	5	6	7

General Preferences

Following is a list of several very different things. They are highly varied, but most are kinds of art or fiction you might like. Please tell us how much you like each one of them, just as you did for college subjects above.

Please circle the number 1 if you do not like the thing at all. Please circle the number 7 if you like it very much—if it is one of your very favorite subjects. Otherwise, please circle the *one* number in between that best indicates how much you like it.

		Do Not Like					Like Very Much
33.	Spy and detective stories	1	2	3	4	5	6	7
34.	Stories of love and romance	1	2	3	4	5	6	7
35.	Science fiction stories	1	2	3	4	5	6	7

		Do Not Like					Like Very Much	
36.	Television soap operas like "Dallas" and "Dynasty"	1	2	3	4	5	6	7
37.	War stories	1	2	3	4	5	6	7
38.	Fiction based on the physical sciences	1	2	3	4	5	6	7
39.	Fiction based on the social sciences	1	2	3	4	5	6	7
40.	Stories about magic	1	2	3	4	5	6	7
41.	Stories in which there is a rational explanation for everything	1	2	3	4	5	6	7
42.	Avant-garde fiction that experiments with new styles	1	2	3	4	5	6	7
43.	Tales of the supernatural	1	2	3	4	5	6	7
44.	Stories about new technology	1	2	3	4	5	6	7
45.	Fiction that is critical of our society	1	2	3	4	5	6	7
46.	Myths and legends	1	2	3	4	5	6	7
47.	Stories about scientific progress	1	2	3	4	5	6	7
48.	Fiction that deeply probes personal relationships and feelings	1	2	3	4	5	6	7
49.	Fantasy stories involving swords and sorcery	1	2	3	4	5	6	7
50.	Factual science articles	1	2	3	4	5	6	7
51.	Poetry	1	2	3	4	5	6	7
52.	Utopian political novels and essays	1	2	3	4	5	6	7
53.	Feminist literature	1	2	3	4	5	6	7
54.	The holy Bible	1	2	3	4	5	6	7
55.	Essays critical of American society	1	2	3	4	5	6	7
56.	President Ronald Reagan	1	2	3	4	5	6	7

	Do Not Like					Like Very Much
57. Electing a woman as president of the United States	1	2	3	4	5	6	7
58. The Republican party	1	2	3	4	5	6	7
59. The Democratic party	1	2	3	4	5	6	7
60. Investment in South Africa	1	2	3	4	5	6	7
61. The Equal Rights Amendment	1	2	3	4	5	6	7
62. Advanced technology	1	2	3	4	5	6	7
63. IBM personal computers	1	2	3	4	5	6	7
64. Apple personal computers	1	2	3	4	5	6	7
65. Driving very fast in a car	1	2	3	4	5	6	7
66. Complete personal security	1	2	3	4	5	6	7
67. Taking physical risks	1	2	3	4	5	6	7
68. Taking risks in your relationships with people	1	2	3	4	5	6	7

Miscellaneous Questions

For the first two, please check the *one* appropriate box.

69. Which category of student do you belong to?

[1] Freshman   [3] Junior   [5] Graduate

[2] Sophomore   [4] Senior   [6] Other

70. Your sex is:

[1] Female   [2] Male

71. We hear a lot of talk these days about liberals and conservatives. Below is a seven-point scale on which the political views that people might hold are arranged from extremely liberal (point 1) to extremely conservative (point 7). Where would you place yourself on this scale? Please circle the *one* number that best indicates your general political views.

1 Extremely liberal

2 Liberal

3 Slightly liberal

4 Moderate, middle of the road

5 Slightly conservative

6 Conservative

7 Extremely conservative

Space Opinion Questions

Following is a set of eight questions, some taken from national polls. First, check the *one* box that comes closest to your own personal opinion. Then write a brief comment explaining your answer in the space below the question, giving us a bit of your thinking on the particular issue.

72. Should the amount of money being spent on the U.S. space program be increased, kept at current levels, decreased, or ended altogether?

[1] Increased   [2] Kept at current levels   [3] Decreased   [4] Ended

_____

_____

_____

_____

73. Do you think that putting civilians into space is important—or is it too dangerous?

[1] Important   [2] Too dangerous   [3] Don't know

_____

_____

_____

_____

74. Some people say the United States should concentrate on unmanned missions like the Voyager probe. Others say it is important to maintain a manned space program as well. Which comes closer to your view?

[1] Unmanned program only
[2] Manned as well as unmanned program
[3] No opinion

_____

_____

_____

_____

75. Do you think the United States should build a permanently manned space station in orbit around the earth over the next few years or not?

[1] Yes   [2] No   [3] No opinion

_____

_____

_____

_____

76. Recently, there has been much talk about building a system of space satellites to defend us against nuclear attack. Do you think research on this idea should continue, or should research stop?

[1] Research should continue
[2] Research should stop
[3] No opinion

_____

_____

_____

_____

77. There has been much discussion about attempting to land people on the planet Mars. How would you feel about such an attempt—would you favor or oppose the United States' setting aside money for such a project?

[1] Favor   [2] Oppose   [3] No opinion

_____

_____

_____

_____

78. If you were asked to go along on the first rocket trip to the planet Mars, would you want to go or not?

[1] Yes   [2] No   [3] No opinion

_____

_____

_____

_____

79. Do you think we should attempt to communicate with intelligent beings on other planets, perhaps using radio?

[1] Yes, definitely   [2] Yes, perhaps   [3] No   [4] No opinion

_____

_____

_____

_____

NOTE: VARIABLES 82 THROUGH 87 WERE CREATED IN THE COMPUTER AND ARE NOT SIMPLY ITEMS IN THE SURVEY.

Totally Random Data

Variables 80 and 81 are not items from the actual questionnaire but are two variables with completely meaningless data produced by a random-number generator in the computer.

82. Liberalism. This item is identical to item 71 (Conservatism) and is based on exactly the same data, except that the responses are coded in the reverse way, as follows:

    7 Extremely liberal
    6 Liberal
    5 Slightly liberal
    4 Moderate, middle of the road
    3 Slightly conservative
    2 Conservative
    1 Extremely conservative

83. Apple fan. This variable is a combination of variables 63 and 64, preference for IBM personal computers and preference for Apple personal computers. The respondent has a value of 0 if he or she has missing data on item 63 and/or item 64. A value of 1 means the person rated IBM higher than Apple. A value of 2 means the ratings were identical. A value of 3 means the person rated Apple more highly than IBM.

84. Spaceflight support. This is scale in which each respondent starts out with 1 point. A point is added each time the person gives a highly pro-space response in items 72 through 77.

85. Physical sciences. In this scale, each respondent starts out with 1 point. One point is added each time the person gives a 7 rating to one of the following items: 2, Astronomy; 9, Physics; 10, Geology; 15, Mathematics; and 25, Engineering.

86. Life sciences. This is a scale in which each respondent starts out with 1 point. One point is added each time the person gives a 7 rating to one of the following items: 1, Botany; 12, Biology; 19, Nursing; 28, Medicine; 29, Zoology.

87. Social sciences. In this scale, each respondent starts out with 1 point. One point is added each time the person gives a 7 rating to one of the following items: 5, Political science; 16, Economics; 18, Anthropology; 23, Psychology; 26, Sociology.

NOTE: THE FOLLOWING ITEMS ARE NOT IN YOUR XTAB DATASET BE-
CAUSE THEY ARE OF THE OPEN-ENDED VARIETY. HOWEVER, THEY CON-
TRIBUTED THOUSANDS OF VERBAL RESPONSES THAT FORMED THE BASIS
FOR THE ITEMS IN THE LATER "NASA" SURVEY.

Ideas about the Space Program

The following questions ask you to write brief statements expressing your
thoughts. Unlike the questions above, these seem to assume you have a favorable
attitude toward the space program—but please do not be put off by this. The purpose of this section is to collect many ideas about why people might support the
space program or various space projects. All these ideas will be sifted carefully,
compared with one another, and incorporated in a future questionnaire that will
assess the enthusiasm (or lack of enthusiasm) that students have toward each of
them. Thus, we would greatly appreciate your responding to these questions
whether or not you personally support the space program.

88. Please briefly describe a future space project that you would like to see
    carried out.

    _____
    _____
    _____
    _____

89. In your opinion, what is the most important reason why we should continue
    the space program?

    _____
    _____
    _____
    _____

90. Can you mention a very different benefit of the space program?

    _____
    _____
    _____
    _____

91. Some perfectly valid and important justifications for the space program are often ignored and deserve greater mention than they commonly receive. Can you give us such a justification?

    _____

    _____

    _____

    _____

92. Can you mention a possible long-range result of a vigorous space program that would eventually be significant for humanity?

    _____

    _____

    _____

    _____

93. What is the most important reason for exploring and settling the planet Mars?

    _____

    _____

    _____

    _____

94. Can you mention another reason for exploring and settling the planet Mars?

    _____

    _____

    _____

    _____

95. What do you think the main consequence would be for people on our planet if a research project did in fact succeed in picking up and understanding radio signals from other planets?

    _____

    _____

    _____

    _____

Variables in the State Dataset

The following pages list the names of the 256 variables in the MAPS dataset, numbered 0 through 255, with descriptions of those variables. Most were taken from federal publications, notably the censuses of 1930 and 1980.

0   Alphabetical order
     The numbers 50-1 assigned in alphabetical order

1   1970 population
     1970 population in thousands of persons

2   1980 population
     1980 population in thousands of persons

3   Population 1980/1970
     1980 population as percent of 1970 population

4   Under age 5
     Percent of population under 5 years old

5   Age 5-13
     Percent of population age 5-13 years

6   Age 14-17
     Percent of population age 14-17 years

7   Age 18-24
     Percent of population age 18-24 years

8   Age 25-44
     Percent of population age 25-44 years

9   Age 45-64
     Percent of population age 45-64 years

10   Age 65-74
     Percent of population age 65-74 years

11   Over age 74
     Percent of population over age 74

12   Under age 18
     Percent of population under 18 years old

13   Age 18-64
     Percent of population age 18-64 years

14 Over age 64
Percent of population over age 64

15 Males
Percent of the population that is male

16 Females
Percent of the population that is female

17 Whites
Percent of population that is white

18 Blacks
Percent of population that is African-American

19 American Indians
American Indians per 100,000 persons

20 Chinese Americans
Chinese and Chinese Americans per 100,000

21 Filipino Americans
Filipino and Filipino Americans per 100,000

22 Japanese Americans
Japanese and Japanese Americans per 100,000

23 Asian Indian Amers.
(Asian) Indians and Indian Americans per 100,000

24 Korean Americans
Koreans and Korean Americans per 100,000

25 Vietnamese Americans
Vietnamese and Vietnamese Americans per 100,000

26 Hispanic
Percent of population of Spanish cultural heritage

27 Urban population
Percent of population living in urban areas

28 Population density
Population per 10 square miles

29 Foreign born
Percent of population that is foreign born

30 Born in state (nat.)
Native persons: percent born in state of residence

31 Different house
Age 5+: percent living in different house in 1975

32 Foreign language
Age 5+: % speak lang. other than English at home

33 In-county movers
Moved 1975-80 within same county, percent

34 In-state ct movers
Moved 1975-80 in-state, different county, percent

35 Moved into state
Moved 1975-80 from outside the state, percent

36 Income < $10,000
% households with income less than $10,000

37   Income $10000-$19999
     % households with income $10,000-$19,999

38   Income $20000-$29999
     % households with income $20,000-$29,999

39   Income $30000-$39999
     % households with income $30,000-$39,999

40   Income $40000-$49999
     % households with income $40,000-$49,999

41   Income $50,000+
     Percent of households with income $50,000+

42   Small farms
     Percent of farms with less than 50 acres

43   Big farms
     Percent of farms with 500 or more acres

44   Resident farmers
     Percent of farm operators residing on farm

45   Work off farm
     % farm operators who work off farm 100+ days

46   Farms as % of land
     Percent of all land that is in farming

47   Farms $/acre
     Average value of farms per acre

48   Farm sales $40,000+
     % farms ($2500+ sales) with $40,000+ sales

49   Crops %farm sales
     Percent of farm sales that are from crops

50   Stock %farm sales
     Percent of farm sales that are from livestock

51   Birth rate 1960
     1960 birth rate per 100,000 population

52   Birth rate 1970
     1970 birth rate per 100,000 population

53   Birth rate 1980
     1980 birth rate per 100,000 population

54   Heart disease
     Heart disease deaths per million

55   Malig. neoplasms
     Malignant neoplasm deaths per million

56   Cerebrovascular
     Cerebrovascular deaths per million

57   Accidental deaths
     Accidental deaths per million

58   Pulmonary deaths
     Chronic pulmonary deaths per million

59   Pneumonia + flu
     Pneumonia + flu deaths per million

60 Diabetes deaths
Diabetes deaths per million

61 Liver deaths
Chronic liver + cirrhosis deaths per million

62 Artherosclerosis
Artherosclerosis deaths per million

63 Suicides
Suicides per million

64 Perinatal deaths
Perinatal deaths per million

65 Murders
FBI report: murders per million people

66 Rapes
FBI report: rapes per million people

67 Robberies
FBI report: robberies per million people

68 Assaults
FBI report: aggravated assaults per 100,000 people

69 Burglaries
FBI report: burglaries per 100,000 people

70 Larcenies
FBI report: larcenies per 100,000 people

71 Car thefts
FBI report: car thefts per 100,000 people

72 Male prisoners
Male federal-state prisoners per 100,000 males

73 Female prisoners
Female federal-state prisoners per 100,000 females

74 Prisoners
Federal and state prisoners per 100,000 persons

75 F/M (prisoners)
Female prisoners as a % of male prisoners

76 Violent crimes
FBI report: violent crimes per 100,000 people

77 Property crimes
FBI report: property crimes per 100,000 people

78 Crimes
FBI report: crimes per 100,000 people

79 Z murder
Murder rates standardized by z scores on 10

80 Z rape
Rape rates standardized by z scores on 10

81 Z robbery
Robbery rates standardized by z scores on 10

82 Z assault
Assault rates standardized by z scores on 10

83 Z burglary
Burglary rates standardized by z scores on 10

84 Z larceny
Larceny rates standardized by z scores on 10

85 Z care theft
Car theft rates standardized by z scores on 10

86 Z violent crime
Violent crime rates standardized by z scores on 10

87 Z property crime
Property crime rates standardized by z scores on 10

88 Z crime
Crime rates standardized by z scores on 10

89 In old age homes
Inmates of home for the aged per 100,000

90 Living alone (60+)
Percent living alone among persons age 60+

91 Two parents (0-17)
Age 0-17: percent living with two parents

92 Marriages
Marriages per 100,000 persons

93 Divorces
Divorces per 100,000 persons

94 Hotel % of service $
Hotel etc. $ as percent of service $

95 Amusement $ services
Amusement + recreation $ as percent of services $

96 Jail + prison
Adults in jail or prison per 100,000 adults

97 Parole
Adults on parole (1+ year, not county) per 100,000

98 Probation
Adults on probation per 100,000 adults

99 % births mom <20
Percent of births to mothers under age 20

100 Abortions (women)
Abortions per 100,000 women age 15-44

101 Abortions (births)
Abortions as a percent of live births

102 Ever married (w.24-)
% of women age 15-24 who have ever been married

103 Mother unmarried
% of kids (moms 15-24) whose mom never married

104 Matrifocal families
% of families, female-headed, kids 17-, no husband

105 Police & fire
Police & firefighters per 1000 employed

106   Property taxes $
      Average property taxes in dollars

107   SSI monthly $
      Average monthly supplemental security income $

108   Social security
      Average monthly social security payment $

109   M labor force (16+)
      Percent of males age 16+ who are in labor force

110   F labor force (16+)
      Percent of females age 16+ who are in labor force

111   F labor force (kids)
      % of females (age 16+ with kids) in labor force

112   Unemployed
      Percent unemployed among civilian labor force

113   Workerless families
      Percent of families with no workers

114   Food stamps
      Percent of population receiving food stamps

115   Incomplete plumbing
      Percent of housing units with incomplete plumbing

116   Per capita income
      Per capita annual income in dollars

117   Household income
      Median household income in dollars

118   Family income
      Median family income in dollars

119   Families in poverty
      % of families with income below poverty level

120   Physicians
      Physicians per 100,000 civilian population

121   Dentists
      Dentists per million civilian population

122   Hospital beds
      Hospital beds per million population

123   Schools local $
      Percent of local government $ spent on education

124   Highways local $
      Percent of local government $ spent on highways

125   Welfare local $
      % of local government $ spent on public welfare

126   Health local $
      % of local govt $ spent on health & hospitals

127   Police local $
      Percent of local government $ spent on police

128   Mental inmate
      Inmates of mental hospitals per 100,000

129 Year of statehood
Year in which the state achieve statehood

130 Employed, % female
Percent of employed who are women

131 Work force, % female
Percent of civilian labor force who are women

132 Work out-county
% workers who work outside home county

133 Drive alone to work
Percent of workers who drive alone to work

134 Car-pool to work
Percent of workers who car-pool to work

135 Use public transit
% of workers age 16+ who use public transportation

136 Church members
Percent of population who are church members, 1971

137 Sect HQs
Sect headquarters per million, 1978

138 Cult HQs
Cult headquarters per million, 1978

139 Sect + cult HQs
Sect + cult headquarters per million

140 M. college students
Percent of males enrolled in college

141 F. college students
Percent of females enrolled in college

142 College students
Percent of population enrolled in college

143 Males (col.stu.)
Percent of college students who are male

144 M/F college rates
College enrollment: $100 \times$ male-rate/female-rate

145 Private (col.stu.)
Percent of college students in private colleges

146 Part-time (col.stu.)
Percent of college students who are part-time

147 High school dropout
Civilians 16-19 not high school grad or student

148 Students (age 18-24)
Percent of persons age 18-24 enrolled in school

149 High school grads
Persons age 25+: percent high school graduates

150 4+ years of college
Age 25+: % completed 4+ years of college

151 Manufacturing worker
Employed age 16+: % in manufacturing industries

152   Managers
        Executive and managerial per 1000 employed

153   Engineers
        Engineers per 1000 employed

154   Natural scientists
        Natural scientists per 1000 employed

155   School teachers
        School teachers per 1000 employed

156   Sales occupations
        Sales occupations per 1000 employed

157   Computer operators
        Computer operators per 1000 employed

158   Secretaries
        Secretaries, typists per 1000 employed

159   Financial processors
        Financial records processors per 1000 employed

160   Food service
        Food service occupations per 1000 employed

161   Farm operators
        Farm operators & managers per 1000 employed

162   Farm workers
        Farm workers per 1000 employed

163   Construction trades
        Construction trades per 1000 employed

164   Precision production
        Precision production occupations per 1000 employed

165   Vehicle operators
        Motor vehicle operators per 1000 employed

166   Mining employees
        Mining employees per 1000 employed

167   Publishing
        Printing, publishing etc. per 1000 employed

168   Electrical machinery
        Electrical machinery workers per 1000 employed

169   Transport equip.
        Transportation equipment workers per 1000 employed

170   Railroad workers
        Railroad workers per 1000 employed

171   Banking + credit
        Banking + credit workers per 1000 employed

172   Entertainers
        Entertainers + recreation per 1000 employed

173   Air conditioning
        Percent of housing units with air conditioning

174   Old houses
        Percent of housing units built before 1940

175   Apartments
      % of housing units with structures with 5+ units

176   Public sewer
      Percent of housing units with public sewer

177   Home owners
      % of occupied housing units owner lives in

178   Housing growth
      Percent growth in housing units 1970-80

179   >1 person per room
      % housing units with more than 1 person per room

180   Gas heat
      Percent of housing units with gas heat

181   Electric heat
      Percent of housing units with electric heat

182   Oil heat
      % housing units with fuel oil or kerosene heat

183   Private school
      % of K-12 school children in private schools

184   Government employees
      Government employees as % of civilian labor force

185   Self-employed
      Self-employed as % of civilian labor force

186   Factories are big
      Percent of factories with 20+ employees

187   Random number 1
      Random numbers in the range 0-999

188   Random number 2
      Random numbers in the range 0-999

189   Northeast region
      "1" means the state is in the Northeast region

190   North Central region
      "1" means the state is in the North Central region

191   South region
      "1" means the state is in the South region

192   West region
      "1" means the state is in the West region

193   1920 population
      Residents of the state in thousands, 1920

194   1930 population
      Residents of the state in thousands, 1930

195   Population 1930/1920
      1930 population as a percent of 1920 population

196   Males
      Percent of population who are males

197   Age under 5
      Percent of the population under 5 years of age

198   Farm population
      Farm population as a percent of total population
199   Urban
      Percent of population living in urban areas
200   Single (men)
      Percent single among males age 15 or over
201   Married (men)
      Percent married among males age 15 or over
202   Widowed (men)
      Percent widowed among males age 15 or over
203   Divorced (men)
      Percent divorced among males age 15 or over
204   Ever-married (men)
      Percent ever-married among males age 15 or over
205   Single (women)
      Percent single among females age 15 or over
206   Married (women)
      Percent married among females age 15 or over
207   Widowed (women)
      Percent widowed among females age 15 or over
208   Divorced (women)
      Percent divorced among females age 15 or over
209   Ever-married (women)
      Percent ever-married among females age 15 or over
210   Men (single)
      Percent of single persons who are male
211   Men (married)
      Percent of married persons who are male
212   Men (widowed)
      Percent of widowed persons who are male
213   Men (divorced)
      Percent of divorced persons who are male
214   Church members RAW
      Church members as % of population, 1926
215   Church members ADJ
      Church members as % of population, 1926 adjusted
216   Catholics/population
      Catholic church members as % of population, 1926
217   Catholics/Christians
      Catholic church members as % of Christians, 1926
218   Jews/population
      Ethnic Jews as % of population, 1926
219   Christian Scientists
      Christian Scientists per million persons
220   Theosophists
      Theosophists per million persons

221   Chiropractors
       Chiropractors per 100,000 employed persons

222   Healers
       Non-medical healers per 100,000 employed persons

223   Inventors
       Independent inventors per 100,000 employed persons

224   Illiterate (pop)
       % illiterate among population age 10+

225   Illiterate (nat.wh.)
       % illiterate among native whites age 10+

226   Illiterate (for.wh.)
       % illiterate among foreign-born whites age 10+

227   Illiterates (black)
       % illiterate among blacks age 10+

228   Black/white illit.
       Ratio of black to native white illiteracy as %

229   Native-born whites
       Percent of population who are native-born whites

230   Blacks
       Percent of population who are African-Americans

231   Foreign-born whites
       Percent of population who are foreign-born whites

232   School attendance
       Percent of children aged 7-13 who attend school

233   Left state
       % born in state & living in different state

234   Entered state
       % of natives born in other states

235   Left state (wh.)
       % whites born in state & living in different state

236   Entered state (wh.)
       % of native whites born in other states

237   Left state (bl.)
       % blacks born in state & living in different state

238   Entered state (bl.)
       % of native blacks born in other states

239   Radios (families)
       Percent of families having radio set

240   Radios (urb.fam.)
       Percent of urban families having radio set

241   Citizens (for.bor.)
       % of foreign born who are naturalized citizens

242   New (immigrant)
       Percent of foreign born who arrived 1925-1930

243   Employed (boys)
       Percent gainfully occupied among boys age 10-15

244   Employed (girls)
      Percent gainfully occupied among girls age 10-15

245   Employed (sing.wo.)
      % gainfully occupied among single women age 15+

246   Employed (mar.wo.)
      % gainfully occupied among married women age 15+

247   German
      German-language foreign born per 100,000

248   Scandinavians
      Scandinavian-speaking foreign born per 100,000

249   Italians
      Italian-speaking foreign born per 100,000

250   Yiddish speakers
      Yiddish-speaking foreign born per 100,000

251   Irish
      Irish-born per 100,000 residents

252   Chinese
      China-born per 100,000 residents

253   Japanese
      Japan-born per 100,000 residents

254   Canadians
      Canada-born per 100,000 residents

255   Mexican
      Mexico-born per 100,000 residents

APPENDIX

Space-Goals Survey

These 90 space goals were rated by 512 Harvard students as explained in Chapter 14. For each, they circled a number (0–6) to indicate how good a reason they thought it was for supporting the space program: from "0" (not a good reason) to "6" (an extremely good reason). The numbering of items is arbitrary, and the space goals were presented in five different random orders in five editions of the actual questionnaire.

1. Space stimulates the creative human imagination.
2. Space exploration fulfills the human need for adventure.
3. Eventually, interstellar travel could be possible, taking people to distant stars.
4. Farms in space and advances in terrestrial agriculture aided by the space program could increase our food supply.
5. The long-term, ultimate benefits of the space program could eventually be important.
6. Competition in space is a constructive outlet for nationalistic rivalries that otherwise would take the form of aggression and conflict.
7. New medicines could be manufactured in the zero gravity and vacuum of space.
8. Investigation of outer space satisfies human curiosity.
9. The space program contributes much to our technology.
10. Space travel makes us realize that Earth is a fragile, unique, unified world that deserves more respect and better care.
11. Satellites link all corners of the globe in a complete information and communication network.
12. Space is the new frontier.
13. The space program is an educational tool, helping us to learn from each other.
14. Observations from orbit help us find new sources of energy and minerals on Earth.
15. We could establish manned space stations, communities in space, and space cities.
16. Space missions are exciting.
17. The space program gives us new perspectives on ourselves and our world.

18. Reconnaissance satellites help prevent war and nuclear attack.
19. The space program contributes to the advancement of science.
20. Technological spin-offs (advancements developed for the space program, then applied to other fields) improve everyday life.
21. Joint space projects between nations improve international cooperation.
22. The space program stimulates the economy and has direct economic benefits.
23. The exploration of space is an unselfish quest that could benefit all mankind.
24. There are great military applications of space.
25. Space research tests our scientific theories and promises conceptual breakthroughs.
26. We could find new mineral resources on the moon, Mars, or the asteroids.
27. The exploration of space lifts morale and instills a sense of hope and optimism.
28. We could discover our own origins, learning about the history of the universe and Earth.
29. Meteorology satellites are great aids for predicting the weather and understanding atmospheric patterns.
30. Earth is too small for us, so we must expand off this planet.
31. Humans should spread life to other planets.
32. The common cause of space exploration unites the peoples of the world and could eventually create a world community.
33. Humans have an innate need to search and discover.
34. Space travel is fun.
35. Space gives people something to dream about.
36. Space probes increase our knowledge of space, planets, comets, and the entire solar system.
37. We could preserve Earth's environment by moving the most polluting industries into space.
38. The space program produces better computers, calculators, and electronics.
39. The beauty of space creates a sense of wonder.
40. From space, we could find new ways to control pollution and clean up our environment.
41. Solar power stations in orbit could provide clean, limitless energy to Earth.
42. We could colonize the moon, Mars, and other satellites or planets of our solar system.
43. We could gain greater understanding of the world we live in.
44. The space program builds national pride.
45. Satellites are useful in surveying and mapping Earth.
46. Space offers new challenges, and civilization would stagnate without challenges.
47. New fuels found in space or the development of fusion power in space could help solve Earth's energy problem.
48. The moon or the sun could be used for safe disposal of toxic materials and nuclear wastes.
49. Space offers room for the expansion of the human species.
50. Satellites are an important component in navigation systems.
51. Through the space program, we could learn the origin of life.
52. We should explore the unknown.

53. Space research benefits physics—in studies of the nature of matter, for example.
54. Medical research performed in space could benefit human health.
55. New experiences and perspectives gained in space inspire art, music, and literature.
56. Spaceflight reaffirms faith in man's abilities.
57. Our future ultimately lies in space.
58. The space program generates national unity, encouraging cooperation between numerous sectors of society.
59. The space program employs many engineers and scientists who otherwise would not be able to utilize their talents.
60. Satellite photography of Earth contributes to geology, oceanography, and archaeology.
61. Space research provides valuable, practical information.
62. The space program provides jobs for thousands of people.
63. Space settlements could ease the growing problem of overpopulation.
64. We could gain knowledge about ourselves.
65. The space program inspires young people to study the sciences.
66. A space-based antimissile system, part of the Strategic Defense Initiative, could reduce the danger of war and nuclear annihilation.
67. The space program has great benefits for industry.
68. In the weightlessness and vacuum of space, we could manufacture new and better alloys, crystals, chemicals, and machine parts.
69. Some medical problems could be treated more effectively in the weightlessness of space.
70. We could gain a better understanding of the universe as a whole and how it functions.
71. We must broaden our horizons.
72. The space program contributes to world peace.
73. Space triumphs give us justified pride in our achievements.
74. The space program encourages people to make achievements and solve problems.
75. Space has great commercial applications and many opportunities for business.
76. Spaceflight is a noble endeavor, expressing the hopes and aspirations of humankind.
77. We should go into space for the same reason people climb Mt. Everest—because it's there.
78. The space program contributes to our defense.
79. We could find new worlds we can live on or transform a planet to make it habitable.
80. We need an alternate home planet in case Earth is destroyed by a natural catastrophe or nuclear war.
81. Space could offer many unexpected benefits we cannot now foresee.
82. In space, we could create new cultures, lifestyles, and forms of society.
83. The space program allows people to think beyond the triviality of earthbound conflicts and concerns.
84. Communication satellites improve television transmissions.

85. We should boldly go where no man or woman has gone before.
86. We could use raw materials from the moon and planets when natural resources are depleted on Earth.
87. An orbiting space telescope could give astronomers a much better view of the stars.
88. In space, we see how small our world is and thus learn humility.
89. The space program provides a goal and a feeling of long-term purpose for humanity.
90. Space exploration is a human struggle, expressing the unconquerable human spirit.

Bibliography

Abrahamson, Bengt
   1970 "Homans on exchange: Hedonism revived." American Journal of Sociology 76:273–285.

Adler, Alfred
   [1927] Understanding Human Nature. Greenwich, Conn.: Fawcett. 1954
   [1929] Individual Psychology. Totowa, N.J.: Littlefield, Adams. 1968

Akers, Ronald L.
   1985 Deviant Behavior: A Social Learning Approach. Belmont, Calif.: Wadsworth.

American Sociological Association
   1989 "Code of ethics." Washington, D.C.: American Sociological Association.

Anderson, Barbara A., Brian D. Silver, and Paul R. Abramson
   1988a: "The effects of race of the interviewer on measures of electoral participation by blacks in SRC national election studies." Public Opinion Quarterly 52:53–83.
   1988b "The effects of the race of the interviewer on race-related attitudes of black respondents in SRC/CPS national election studies." Public Opinion Quarterly 52:289–324.

Anderson, Nels
   1923 The Hobo. Chicago: University of Chicago Press.

Andrews, Edward Deming
   1953 The People Called Shakers. New York: Oxford University Press.

Anonymous
   [1828] A Defense of the Order, Government and Economy of the United Society Called Shakers against Sundry Charges and Legislative Proceedings. New York: Egbert, Hovey and King, 1846.

Anonymous
   1843 "Reflections on the census of 1840." Southern Literary Messenger 9:340–352.

Anonymous
   1849 Report of the Examination of the Shakers of Canterbury and Enfield before the New-Hampshire Legislature at the November Session, 1848. Concord, N.H.: Tripp.

Anonymous
   1851 "Startling facts from the census." American Journal of Insanity 8:153–155.

Armer, Michael and Allan Schnaiberg
   1972 "Measuring individual modernity." American Sociological Review 37:301–316.

Ayllon, T. and N.H. Azrin
   1964 "Reinforcement and instructions with mental patients." Journal of the Experimental Analysis of Behavior 7:327–331.

Babbie, Earl R.
   1973 Survey Research Methods. Belmont, Calif.: Wadsworth.
   1986 The Practice of Social Research. Belmont, Calif.: Wadsworth.

Bainbridge, William Sims
   1976 The Spaceflight Revolution. New York: Wiley.
   1978 Satan's Power: Ethnography of a Deviant Psychotherapy Cult. Berkeley: University of California Press.
   1982 "Shaker demographics 1840–1900: An example of the use of U.S. census enumeration schedules." Journal for the Scientific Study of Religion 21:352–365.
   1984a "The decline of the Shakers: Evidence from the United States Census." Communal Societies 4:19–34.
   1984b "Religious insanity in America: The official nineteenth-century theory." Sociological Analysis 45:223–240.
   1985a "Cultural genetics." Pp. 157–198 in R. Stark (ed.) Religious Movements. New York: Paragon House.

1985b "Utopian communities: Theoretical issues." Pp. 21–35 in P.E. Hammond (ed.), The Sacred in a Secular Age. Berkeley: University of California Press.

1986 Dimensions of Science Fiction. Cambridge: Harvard University Press.

1987a Interview with George C. Homans. Sociology Lives 3(3):5–11.

1987b Interview with David Riesman. Sociology Lives 3(4):5–14.

1987c Sociology Laboratory. Belmont, Calif.: Wadsworth.

1989a "The religious ecology of deviance." American Sociological Review 54:288–295.

1989b Survey Research: A Computer-Assisted Introduction. Belmont, Calif.: Wadsworth.

1989c "Wandering souls: Mobility and unorthodoxy." Pp. 237–249 in G.K. Zollschan et al. (eds.)., Exploring the Paranormal. Bridport, Dorset, England: Prism.

1990a "Explaining the church member rate." Social Forces, in press.

1990b Goals in Space. Albany, N.Y.: SUNY Press.

Bainbridge, William Sims, and Laurie Russell Hatch
1982 "Women's access to elite careers." Journal for the Scientific Study of Religion 21:242–254.

Bainbridge, William Sims and Rodney Stark
1980 "Sectarian tension." Review of Religious Research 22:105–124.
1981 "Suicide, homicide, and religion: Durkheim reassessed." Annual Review of the Social Sciences of Religion 5:33–56.

Bales, Robert F.
1950 Interaction Process Analysis: A Method for the Study of Small Groups. Cambridge, Mass.: Addison-Wesley.
1953 "The equilibrium problem in small groups." Pp. 111–161 in T. Parsons et al. (eds.), Working Papers in the Theory of Action. New York: Free Press.
1962 "Attitudes toward drinking in the Irish culture." Pp. 157–187 in D.J. Puttman and C.R. Snyder (eds.), Society, Culture, and Drinking Patterns. New York: Wiley.
1970 Personality and Interpersonal Behavior. New York: Holt, Rinehart and Winston.

Bales, Robert F. and F.L. Strodbeck
1951 "Phases in group problem solving." Journal of Abnormal and Social Psychology 46:485–495.

Bales, Robert F., F.L. Strodbeck and T.M. Mills
1951 "Channels of communication in small groups." American Sociological Review 16:461–468.

Bart, Pauline and Linda Frankel
1986 The Student Sociologist's Handbook. New York: Random House.

Batson, C. Daniel
1977 "Experimentation in psychology of religion: An impossible dream." Journal for the Scientific Study of Religion 16:413–418.

Becker, Howard S.
1963 Outsiders. New York: Free Press.
1970 Sociological Work. Chicago: Aldine.

Benedict, Ruth
1934 Patterns of Culture. Boston: Houghton Mifflin.

Benson, J. Kenneth and James Otis Smith
1967 "The Harvard drug controversy." Pp. 115–140 in G. Sjoberg (ed.), Ethics, Politics, and Social Research. Cambridge: Schenkman.

Berg, Irwin A. (ed.)
1967 Response Set in Personality Assessment. Chicago: Aldine.

Berk, Richard A. and Joseph M. Adams
1970 "Establishing rapport with deviant groups." Social Problems 18:102–117.

Bertaux, Daniel and Martin Kohli
1984 "The life story approach." Pp. 215–237 in R.H. Turner (ed.), Annual Review of Sociology, vol. 10. Palo Alto: Annual Reviews.

Beveridge, William Ian Beardmore
1950 The Art of Scientific Investigation. New York: Vintage.

Bezilla, Robert (ed.)
1988 America's Youth, 1977–1988. Princeton, N.J.: Gallup.

Black, Donald J.
1970 "Production of crime rates." American Sociological Review 35:733–748.

Blalock, Hubert M.
1970 Social Statistics. New York: McGraw-Hill.
1989 "The real and unrealized contributions of quantitative sociology." American Sociological Review 54:447–460.

Blinn, Henry C.
1901 The Life and Gospel Experience of Mother Ann Lee. East Canterbury, N.H.: Shakers.

Block, Jack
1965 The Challenge of Response Sets. New York: Appleton-Century-Crofts.

Blumer, Herbert
1969 Symbolic Interaction: Perspective and Method. Englewood Cliffs, N.J.: Prentice-Hall.

Bohrnstedt, George W. and T. Michael Carter
1971 "Robustness in regression analysis." Pp. 118–146 in H.L. Costner (ed.), Sociological Methodology 1971. San Francisco: Jossey-Bass.

Bollen, Kenneth A. and Sally Ward
1979 "Ratio variables in aggregate data analysis: Their uses, problems, and alternatives." Sociological Methods and Research 7:431–450.

Bond, Kathleen
1978 "Confidentiality and the protection of human subjects in social science research." The American Sociologist 13:144–152.

Booth, Andrew B.
1920 Records of Louisiana Confederate Soldiers and Louisiana Confederate Commands. Spartanburg, S.C.: Reprint (1984).

Boyle, Richard P.
1970 "Path analysis and ordinal data." American Journal of Sociology 75:461–480.

Bragg, Jefferson Davis
1941 Louisiana in the Confederacy. Baton Rouge: Louisiana State University Press.

Braithwaite, Richard Bevan
1953 Scientific Explanation. London: Cambridge University Press.

Buley, R. Carlyle
1967 The Equitable Life Assurance Society of the United States 1859–1964. New York: Appleton-Century-Crofts.

Bureau of the Census
1910 Religious Bodies: 1906. Washington: U.S. Government Printing Office.
1912 Mortality Statistics: 1909. Washington: U.S. Government Printing Office.
1918 Mortality Statistics: 1916. Washington: U.S. Government Printing Office.
1919 Religious Bodies: 1916. Washington: U.S. Government Printing Office.
1929 Mortality Statistics: 1926. Washington: U.S. Government Printing Office.
1930 Religious Bodies: 1926. Washington: U.S. Government Printing Office.

Burgess, Ernest W.
1930 "Discussion." Pp. 184–197 in C.R. Shaw (ed.), The Jack Roller. Philadelphia: Albert Saifer.

Burnham, J.C.
1968 "New perspectives on the prohibition 'experiment' of the 1920s." Journal of Social History 2:51–68.

Burt, Ronald S.
1982 Toward a Structural Theory of Action. New York: Academic Press.

Bushell, Don and Robert L. Burgess
1969 "Characteristics of the experimental analysis." Pp. 145–174 in R.L. Burgess and D. Bushell (eds.), Behavioral Sociology. New York: Columbia University Press.

Calhoun, John C.
1855 Reports and Public Letters of John C. Calhoun. New York: Appleton.

Cannell, Charles F., Peter V. Miller and Lois Oksenberg
1981 "Research on interviewing techniques." Pp. 389–437 in S. Leinhardt (ed.), Sociological Methodology 1981. San Francisco: Jossey-Bass.

Carden, Maren Lockwood
1969 Oneida: Utopian Community to Modern Corporation. Baltimore: Johns Hopkins University Press.

Carley, Kathleen
1985 "An approach for relating social structure to cognitive structure." Journal of Mathematical Sociology 12:137–189.

Carmines, Edward and Richard Zeller
1979 Reliability Assessment. Beverly Hills, California: Sage.

Catton, Bruce
1961 The Coming Fury. New York: Washington Square.
1963 Terrible Swift Sword. New York: Washington Square.
1965 Never Call Retreat. New York: Washington Square.

Chatterjee, Samprit and Ali S. Hadi
1988 Sensitivity Analysis in Linear Regression. New York: Wiley.

Chirot, Daniel
1976 Social Change in a Peripheral Society. New York: Academic Press.

Chirot, Daniel and Charles Ragin
1975 "The market, tradition and peasant rebellion: The case of Romania in 1907." American Sociological Review 40:428–444.

Christensen, Larry B. and Charles M. Stoup
1986 Introduction to Statistics for the Social and Behavioral Sciences. Pacific Grove, Calif.: Brooks/Cole.

Clark, Terry Nichols
1973 Prophets and Patrons: The French University and the Emergence of the Social Sciences. Cambridge: Harvard University Press.

Clarridge, Brian R., Linda L. Sheehy and Taissa S. Hauser
1977 "Tracing members of a panel: A seventeen-year follow-up." Pp. 185–203 in K.F. Schuessler (ed.), Sociological Methodology 1978. San Francisco: Jossey-Bass.

Cloward, Richard A. and Lloyd E. Ohlin
1960 Delinquency and Opportunity. New York: Free Press.

Cohen, Albert K.
1955 Delinquent Boys. New York: Free Press.

Coleman, James S., Elihu Katz and Herbert Menzel
1966 Medical Innovation: A Diffusion Study. Indianapolis: Bobbs-Merrill.

Cook, Thomas D., James R. Bean, Bobby J. Calder, Robert Frey, Martin L. Krovetz and Stephen R. Risman
1970 "Demand characteristics and three conceptions of the frequently deceived subject." Journal of Personality and Social Psychology 14:185–194.

Couch, Arthur and Kenneth Keniston
1960 "Yeasayers and naysayers: Agreeing response set as a personality variable." Journal of Abnormal and Social Psychology 60:151–174.

Crane, Diana
1972 Invisible Colleges. Chicago: University of Chicago Press.

Crockett, Harry J. and Lewis Levine
1967 "Friends' influences on speech." Sociological Inquiry 37:109–128.

Cronbach, Lee J. and Paul E. Meehl
1955 "Construct validity in psychological tests." Psychological Bulletin 52:281–302.

Crowne, Douglas P. and David Marlow
1960 "A new scale of social desirability independent of psychopathology." Journal of Consulting Psychology 24:349–354.

Davis, James A.
1961 Great Books and Small Groups. New York: Free Press.

Davis, James A. and Tom W. Smith
1986 General Social Surveys, 1972–1986: Cumulative Codebook. Chicago: National Opinion Research Center.

Davis, Maxine W. and Gregory J. Tetrault
1975 The Organic Traveler. Syracuse, N.Y.: Grasshopper Press.

Davis, Phillip W.
1984 "The social organization of lie-detector tests." Urban Life 13:177–205.

Dawson, Sarah Morgan
1913 A Confederate Girl's Diary. Boston: Houghton Mifflin.

Demerath, N.J. and Richard M. Levinson
1971 "Baiting the dissident hook: Some effects of bias on measuring religious belief." Sociometry 34:346–359.

Desroche, Henri
1971 The American Shakers. Amherst: University of Massachusetts Press.

Deutsch, Albert
1944. "The first U.S. census of the insane (1840) and its use as pro slavery propaganda." Bulletin of the History of Medicine 15:469–482.

Deutsch, Morton and Robert M. Krauss
1960 "The effect of threat upon interpersonal bargaining." Journal of Abnormal and Social Psychology 61:181–189.

Dietz, Thomas, R. Scott Frey and Linda Kalof
1987 "Estimation with cross-national data: Robust and nonparametric methods." American Sociological Review 52:380–390.

Dillman, Don A.
1978 Mail and Telephone Surveys. New York: Wiley.

Dollard, John
1935 Criteria for the Life History. New Haven: Yale University Press.

Dornberger, Walter
  1952 V2—Der Schuss ins Weltall. Esslingen am Neckar, W. Germany: Bechtle.

Douglas, Jack D.
  1967 The Social Meanings of Suicide. Princeton: Princeton University Press.

Downie, N.M. and R.W. Heath
  1970 Basic Statistical Methods. New York: Harper and Row.

Durkheim, Emile
  Suicide. New York: Free Press. [1897]
  The Elementary Forms of the Religious Life. New York: Free 1965 Press. [1915]

Edgerton, Robert B.
  1967 The Cloak of Competence. Berkeley: University of California Press.

Edwards, Allen L.
  1967 "The social desirability variable: A review of the evidence." Pp. 48–70 in I.A. Berg (ed.), Response Set in Personality Assessment. Chicago: Aldine.

Eister, Allan W.
  1972 "A theory of cults." Journal for the Scientific Study of Religion 11:319–333.

Elliott, E.N. (ed.)
  1860 Cotton Is King. Augusta, Ga.: Pritchard, Abbott, and Loomis.

Ember, Melvin
  1971 "An empirical test of Galton's problem." Ethnology 10:98–106.

Emerson, Robert M.
  1987 "Four ways to improve the craft of fieldwork." Journal of Contemporary Ethnography 16:69–89.

Evans-Pritchard, E.E.
  1937 Witchcraft, Oracles and Magic among the Azande. London: Oxford University Press.

Everitt, Brian
  1974 Cluster Analysis. London: Heinemann.

Eysenck, Hans J.
  1965 "The effects of psychotherapy." International Journal of Psychiatry 1:99–144.

Faris, Robert E.L. and H. Warren Dunham
  1939 Mental Disorders in Urban Areas. Chicago: University of Chicago Press.

Festinger, Leon and J. Merrill Carlsmith
  1959 "Cognitive consequences of forced compliance." Journal of Abnormal and Social Psychology 58:203–210.

Festinger, Leon, Stanley Schachter and Kurt Back
  1950 Social Pressures in Informal Groups. New York: Harper.

Finch, William J. and Elizabeth Finch
  1971 Who's Who in the Psychic World. Phoenix, Ariz.: Psychic Register.

Finke, Roger and Rodney Stark
  1989 "Evaluating the evidence." American Sociological Review 54:1054–1056.

Finkel, Norman J.
  1976 Mental Illness and Health. New York: Macmillan.

Flexner, Stuart Berg
  1960 "Introduction to the appendix." Pp. 596–608 in H. Wentworth and S.B. Flexner (eds.), Dictionary of American Slang. New York: Crowell.

Fogel, Robert William and Stanley L. Engerman
  1974a Time on the Cross: The Economics of American Negro Slavery. Boston: Little Brown.
  1974b Time on the Cross: Evidence and Methods. Boston: Little Brown.

Foster, Lawrence
  1981 Religion and Sexuality. New York: Oxford University Press.

Fox, William F.
  1898 Regimental Losses in the American Civil War. Albany: Brandow.

Frank, Jerome D.
  1961 Persuasion and Healing. New York: Schocken.

Frank, Ove
  1981 "A survey of statistical methods for graph analysis." Pp. 110–155 in S. Leinhardt (ed.), Sociological Methodology 1981. San Francisco: Jossey-Bass.

Freedman, Jonathan L.
  1969 "Role playing: Psychology by consensus." Journal of Personality and Social Psychology 13:107–114.

Friendly, Michael L. and Sam Glucksberg
  1970 "On the description of subcultural lexicons." Journal of Personality and Social Psychology 14:55–65.

Frisbie, W. Parker
  1984 "Data and methods in human ecology." Pp. 125–178 in M. Micklin and H.M. Choldin (eds.), Sociological Human Ecology. Boulder, Colo.: Westview.

Furash, Edward E.
1963 "Businessmen Review the Space Effort," Harvard Business Review (September-October): 14–32, 173–190.

Gaede, Stan
1976 "A causal model of belief-orthodoxy." Sociological Analysis 37:205–217.

Galliher, John F. and John R. Cross
1983 Morals Legislation without Morals. New Brunswick, N.J.: Rutgers University Press.

Gallup, George
1976 The Sophisticated Poll Watcher's Guide. Ephrata, Pa.: Science Press.

Garfinkel, Harold
1967 Studies in Ethnomethodology. Englewood Cliffs, N.J.: Prentice-Hall.

Geer, Blanche
1964 "First days in the field." Pp. 322–344 in P.E. Hammond (ed.), Sociologists at Work. New York: Basic Books.

Giallombardo, Rose
1966 Society of Women. New York: Wiley.

Glejser, H.
1969 "A new test for heteroskedasticity (sic)." American Statistical Association Journal 64:316–323.

Glock, Charles Y. and Rodney Stark
1965 Religion and Society in Tension. Chicago: Rand McNally.
1966 Christian Beliefs and Anti-Semitism. New York: Harper and Row.

Goffman, Erving
1959 The Presentation of Self in Public Places. Garden City, N.Y.: Doubleday.
1961 Encounters. Indianapolis: Bobbs-Merrill.
1963 Behavior in Public Places. New York: Free Press.

Goldfeld, Stephen M. and Richard E. Quandt
1965 "Some tests of homoscedasticity." American Statistical Association Journal 60:539–547.

Golding, Stephen L. and Edward Lichtenstein
1970 "Confession of awareness and prior knowledge of deception as a function of interview set and approval motivation." Journal of Personality and Social Psychology 14:213–223.

Goode, Erich
1972 Drugs in American Society. New York: Knopf.

Gorden, Raymond L.
1969 Interviewing: Strategy, Techniques, and Tactics. Homewood, Ill.: Dorsey.

Gould, Peter and Rodney White
1974 Mental Maps. New York: Penguin.

Gould, Stephen Jay
1983 "Losing the edge." Vanity Fair (March): 120, 264–278.
1986 "Entropic homogeneity isn't why no one hits .400 any more." Discover (August): 60–66.
1988 "Trends as changes in variance: A new slant on progress and directionality in evolution." Journal of Paleontology 62:319–329.

Gouldner, Alvin W. and Richard A. Peterson
1962 Notes on Technology and the Moral Order. Indianapolis: Bobbs-Merrill.

Granovetter, Mark
1976 "Network sampling." American Journal of Sociology 81:1287–1303.

Greeley, Andrew
1972 That Most Distressful Nation: The Taming of the American Irish. Chicago: Quadrangle.
1975 The Sociology of the Paranormal: A Reconnaissance. Beverly Hills, Calif.: Sage.

Green, Calvin and Seth Y. Wells
1823 A Summary View of the Millennial Church, or United Society of Believers. Albany, N.Y.: Packard and Van Benthuysen.

Grob, Gerald N.
1978 Edward Jarvis and the Medical World of Nineteenth-Century America. Knoxville: University of Tennessee Press.

Gusfield, Joseph R.
1963 Symbolic Crusade. Urbana: University of Illinois Press.

Gutman, Herbert H.
1975 Slavery and the Numbers Game. Urbana: University of Illinois Press.

Gutman, Jonathan and Robert F. Priest
1969 "When is aggression funny?" Journal of Personality and Social Psychology 12:60–65.

Haas, Mary R.
1964 "Men's and women's speech in Koasati." Pp. 228–233 in D. Hymes (ed.), Language in Culture and Society. New York: Harper and Row.

Hammond, Kenneth R. and James E. Householder
1962 Introduction to the Statistical Method. New York: Knopf.

Hannan, Michael T.
1971 Aggregation and Disaggregation in Sociology. Lexington, Mass.: Lexington.

Hardy, Melissa A.
1989 "Estimating selection effects in occupational mobility in a nineteenth-century city." American Sociological Review 54:834–843.

Harvey, O.J.
1953 "An experimental approach to the study of status relations in informal groups." American Sociological Review 18:357–367.

Heider, Fritz
1958 The Psychology of Interpersonal Relations. New York: Wiley.

Heinkel, Ernst
1953 Stürmisches Leben. Stuttgart, W. Germany: Mundus.

Heyl, Barbara
1979 The Madam as Entrepreneur. New Brunswick, N.J.: Transaction.

Hickey, Joseph, William E. Thompson and Donald L. Foster
1988 "Becoming the Easter bunny." Journal of Contemporary Ethnography 17:67–95.

Hicks, Jack M. and John H. Wright
1970 "Convergent-discriminant validation and factor analysis of five scales of liberalism-conservatism." Journal of Personality and Social Psychology 14:114–120.

Hilty, Dale M. and Rich Morgan
1985 "Construct validation for the Religious Involvement Inventory." Journal for the Scientific Study of Religion 24:75–86.

Hindelang, Michael, Travis Hirschi and Joseph G. Weis
1979 "Correlates of delinquency: The illusion of discrepancy between self-report and official measures." American Sociological Review 44:995–1014.

Hirata, Lucie Cheng
1979 "Free, indentured, enslaved: Chinese prostitutes in nineteenth-century America." Signs 5:3–29.

Hirschi, Travis
1969 Causes of Delinquency. Berkeley: University of California Press.

Hirschi, Travis and Rodney Stark
1969 "Hellfire and delinquency." Social Problems 17:202–213.

Holland, Paul W. and Samuel Leinhardt
1983 "An omnibus test for social structure using triads." Pp. 302–325 in R.S. Burt and M.J. Minor (eds.), Applied Network Analysis. Beverly Hills, Calif.: Sage.

Hollingshead, August B. and Frederick C. Redlich
1958 Social Class and Mental Illness. New York: Wiley.

Homans, George C.
1941 English Villagers of the Thirteenth Century. Cambridge: Harvard.
1950 The Human Group. New York: Harcourt, Brace and World.
1967 The Nature of Social Science. New York: Harcourt, Brace and World.
1974 Social Behavior. New York: Harcourt Brace Jovanovich.

Hostetler, John A.
1974 Hutterite Society. Baltimore: Johns Hopkins.
1980 Amish Society. Baltimore: Johns Hopkins.

Hovland, Carl I. (ed.)
1957 The Order of Presentation in Persuasion. New Haven, Conn.: Yale University Press.

Hovland, Carl I., Irving L. Janis and Harold H. Kelley
1953 Communication and Persuasion. New Haven, Conn.: Yale University Press.

Howard, George Elliott
1918 "Alcohol and crime: A study in social causation." American Journal of Sociology 24:61–80.

Howard, William F.
1987 "Lee's lost orders: Special Orders No. 191 and the Maryland Campaign of 1862." Civil War Quarterly 9 (June): 27–33.

Hyman, Herbert H.
1972 Secondary Analysis of Sample Surveys. New York: Wiley.

Inhelder, Bärbel and Jean Piaget
1958 The Growth of Logical Thinking from Childhood to Adolescence. New York: Basic Books.

James, William
1911 "The moral equivalent of war." Pp. 267–296 in Memories and Studies. New York: McKay.
1963 Pragmatism and Other Essays. New York: Washington Square Press.

Jarvis, Edward
 1842a "Statistics of insanity in the United States." Boston Medical and Surgical Journal 27:116–121.
 1842b "Statistics of insanity in the United States—II." Boston Medical and Surgical Journal 27:281–282.
 1852 "Insanity among the colored population of the free states." American Journal of Insanity 8:268–282.
 1873 Autobiography of Edward Jarvis. Unpublished manuscript in the Harvard College Library.

Jarvis, Edward, J. Wingate Thornton and William Brigham
 1845 "The sixth census of the United States." The Merchants' Magazine and Commercial Review 12:125–139.

Johnson, Douglas W., Paul R. Picard and Bernard Quinn
 1974 Churches and Church Membership in the United States. Washington, D.C.: Glenmary.

Johnson, Eugene C. and H. Gilman McCann
 1982 "Acyclic triplets and social structure in complete signed digraphs." Social Networks 3:251–272.

Johnson, Paul
 1980 Ireland: Land of Troubles. London: Eyre Methuen.

Johnson, R. Christian
 1978 "A procedure for sampling the manuscript census schedules." Journal of Interdisciplinary History 8:515–530.

Johnston, J.
 1972 Econometric Methods. New York: McGraw-Hill.

Jones, Maldwin Allen
 1960 American Immigration. Chicago: University of Chicago Press.

Kandel, Denise B.
 1974 "Inter- and intragenerational influences on adolescent marijuana use." Journal of Social Issues 30:107–135.

Kandle, Denise B., Donald Treibman, Richard Faust and Eric Single
 1976 "Adolescent involvement in legal and illegal drug use." Social Forces 55:438–458.

Kanter, Rosabeth Moss
 1972 Commitment and Community. Cambridge: Harvard University Press.

Karmel, Madeline
 1969 "Total institution and self-mortification." Journal of Health and Social Behavior 10:134–140.

Katz, Daniel
 1942 "Do interviewers bias poll results?" Public Opinion Quarterly 6:248–268.

Kennedy, Joseph C.G.
 1860 Instructions to U.S. Marshals. Washington: Bowman.
 1864 (ed.) Population of the United States in 1860. Washington: Government Printing Office.

Kern, Louis
 1981 An Ordered Love. Chapel Hill: University of North Carolina Press.

Keyser, Daniel J. and Richard C. Sweetland (eds.)
 1984 Test Critiques. Three volumes. Kansas City, Mo.: Test Corporation of America.

Kish, Leslie
 1965 Survey Sampling. New York: Wiley.

Knibbs, G.H. (ed.)
 1914 Census of the Commonwealth of Australia. Melbourne: McCarron, Bird, and Co.

Langley, Pat, Herbert A. Simon, Gary L. Bradshaw and Jan M. Zytkow
 1987 Scientific Discovery: Computational Explorations of the Creative Process. Cambridge: M.I.T. Press.

Larson, Albert J. and A.P. Garbin
 1967 "Hamlets: A typological consideration." Sociological Quarterly 8:531–537.

Larson, Richard F.
 1968 "The clergymen's role in the therapeutic process." Psychiatry 31:250–263.

Leary, Timothy
 1983 Flashbacks. Los Angeles: Tarcher.

Leavitt, Harold J.
 1951 "Some effects of certain communication patterns on group performance." Reprinted as pp. 279–300 in P.V. Crosbie (ed.), Interaction in Small Groups. New York: Macmillan, 1975.

Lee, Brother Basil Leo
  1943 Discontent in New York City 1861–1865. Washington: Catholic University of America Press.

Leinhardt, Samuel
  1983 "Prologue." Pp. xi–xviii in Sociological Methodology 1983–1984. San Francisco: Jossey-Bass.

Lévi-Strauss, Claude
  1970 The Raw and the Cooked. New York: Harper.

Linn, Lawrence S.
  1968 "Social identification and the seeking of psychiatric care." American Journal of Orthopsychiatry 38:83–88.

Lipset, Seymour Martin and Earl Raab
  1970 The Politics of Unreason. New York: Harper and Row.

Litwack, Leon F.
  1961 North of Slavery. Chicago: University of Chicago Press.

Livermore, Thomas L.
  1957 Numbers and Losses in the Civil War in America. Bloomington: Indiana University Press.

Loether, Herman J. and Donald G. McTavish
  1976 Descriptive and Inferential Statistics. Boston: Allyn and Bacon.

Lofland, John
  1966 Doomsday Cult. Englewood Cliffs, N.J.: Prentice-Hall.

Lofland, John and Rodney Stark
  1965 "Becoming a world-saver: A theory of conversion to a deviant perspective." American Sociological Review 30:862–875.

Logsdon, John M.
  1970 The Decision to Go to the Moon. Cambridge: MIT Press.

Long, Susan B.
  1979 "The continuing debate over the use of ratio variables: Fact and fiction." Pp. 37–67 in K.F. Schuessler (ed.), Sociological Methodology—1980. San Francisco: Jossey-Bass.

Luft, Joseph
  1970 Group Processes. Palo Alto, Calif.: Mayfield.

MacMillan, Alexander and Richard L. Daft
  1979 "Administrative intensity and ratio variables: The case against definitional dependency." Social Forces 58:228–248.

Magdol, Edward
  1986 The Antislavery Rank and File. New York: Greenwood.

Malinowski, Bronislaw
  1927 Sex and Repression in Savage Society. New York: Meridian.
  1929 The Sexual Life of Savages. New York: Harcourt, Brace and World.
  1961 Argonauts of the Western Pacific. New York: Dutton.

Malone, Dumas (ed.)
  1943 Dictionary of American Biography. New York: Scribner's.

Marshall, Mary (Mary Dyer)
  1847 The Rise and Progress of the Serpent from the Garden of Eden to the Present Day. Concord, N.H.: Marshall.

Masaryk, Thomas
  [1881] Suicide and the Meaning of Civilization. Chicago: University of Chicago Press, 1970.

Maslow, Abraham
  1969 The Psychology of Science. Chicago: Henry Regnery.

Matthews, Glenna
  1976 "The community study: Ethnicity and success in San Jose." Journal of Interdisciplinary History 7:305–318.

McCall, George J. and J.L. Simmons
  1969 Issues in Participant Observation. Reading, Mass.: Addison-Wesley.

McCready, William C. and Andrew Greeley
  1976 The Ultimate Values of the American Population. Beverly Hills, Calif.: Sage.

McDougall, Walter A.
  1985 . . . the Heavens and the Earth: A Political History of the Space Age. New York: Basic Books.

McGregor, Douglas
  1960 The Human Side of Enterprise. New York: McGraw-Hill.
  1966 Leadership and Motivation. Cambridge, Mass.: MIT Press.

McQuaid, Donald A.
  1979 The International Psychic Register. Erie, Pa.: Ornion Press.

Melko, Matthew
  1989 review of The Dynamics of Deterrence, by Frank C. Zagare. Contemporary Sociology 18:566–568.

Melton, J. Gordon
  1978 Encyclopedia of American Religions. Wilmington, N.C.: McGrath (A Consortium Book).

Mercer, Jane R.
  1973 Labeling the Mentally Retarded. Berkeley: University of California Press.

Merton, Robert K.
  1968 "Social structure and anomie." Pp. 131–160 in Social Theory and Social Structure. New York: Free Press.
  1970 Science, Technology and Society in Seventeenth-Century England. New York: Harper.

Mommsen, Hans
  1972 "The political effects of the Reichstag fire." Pp. 109–149 in H.A. Turner (ed.), Nazism and the Third Reich. New York: Quadrangle.

Moore, Ward
  1972 Bring the Jubilee. New York: Avon.

Morais, Herbert M.
  1976 The History of the Afro-American in Medicine. Cornwall Heights, Pa.: Publishers Agency.

Morselli, Henry
  1882 Suicide: An Essay on Comparative Moral Statistics. New York: Appleton.

Moses, Lincoln E., Alan Goldfarb, Charles Y. Glock, Rodney W. Stark and Morris L. Eaton
  1971 "A validity study using the Leighton instrument." American Journal of Public Health 61:1785–1793.

Mueller, Hohn H., Karl F. Schuessler and Herbert L. Costner
  1977 Statistical Reasoning in Sociology. Boston: Houghton Mifflin.

Murray, Henry A.
  1938 Explorations in Personality. New York: Oxford University Press.
  1981 Endeavors in Psychology. New York: Harper and Row.

Nagel, Ernest
  1961 The Structure of Science, New York: Harcourt, Brace and World.

National Science Foundation
  1990 "Instrumentation and laboratory improvement—Program announcement and guidelines." Washington, D.C.: National Science Foundation.

Newcomb, Theodore M.
  1943 Personality and Social Change. New York: Dryden.

Nie, Norman H., C. Hadlai Hull, Jean G. Jenkins, Karin Steinbrenner and Dale H. Bent
  1975 SPSS: Statistical Package for the Social Sciences. New York: McGraw-Hill.

Nietzsche, Friedrich
  1872 Die Geburt der Tragödie (The Birth of Tragedy). Munich: Goldmann.
  1885 Also Sprach Zarathustra (Thus Spoke Zarathustra). Stuttgart: Kröner.

Nordhoff, Charles
  1875 The Communistic Societies of the United States. London: John Murray.

Noyes, John Humphrey
  1870 History of American Socialisms. Philadelphia: Lippincott.

Noyes, Pierrepont
  1937 My Father's House: An Oneida Boyhood. New York: Farrar and Rinehart.

Ogburn, William F.
  1922 Social Change. New York: Huebsch.

Onions, C.T.
  1966 The Oxford Dictionary of English Etymology. London: Oxford University Press.

Opler, Marvin K. and Jerome L. Singer
  1956 "Ethnic differences in behavior and psychopathology: Italian and Irish." International Journal of Social Psychiatry 2:11–22.

Ornstein, Barbara (ed.)
  1981 Tod's Point: An Oral History. Greenwich, Conn.: Greenwich Library.

Osgood, Charles E.
  1976 Explorations in Semantic Space. The Hague, Netherlands: Mouton.

Osgood, Charles E., George J. Suci and Percy H. Tannenbaum
  1957 The Measurement of Meaning. Urbana: University of Illinois Press.

Osgood, Charles E., William H. May and Murray S. Miron
  1975 Cross-Cultural Universals of Affective Meaning. Urbana: University of Illinois Press.

Ouchi, William G.
1979 "A conceptual framework for the design of organizational control mechanisms." Management Science 9:833–848.
1980 "Markets, bureaucracies, and clans." Administrative Science Quarterly 25:129–141.
1981 Theory Z: How American Business Can Meet the Japanese Challenge. New York: Avon.

Ouchi, William G. and Alfred M. Jaeger
1978 "Type Z organization: Stability in the midst of mobility." Academy of Management Review 3:305–314.

Ouchi, William G. and Jerry B. Johnson
1978 "Types of organizational control and their relationship to emotional well-being." Administrative Science Quarterly 23:293–317.

Peabody, Andrew P.
1885. "Memoir of Edward Jarvis." Boston: Clapp.

Perlmann, Joel
1979 "Using census districts in analysis, record linkage, and sampling." Journal of Interdisciplinary History 10:279–289.

Phillips, Derek L. and Kevin J. Clancy
1972 "Some effects of 'social desirability' in survey studies." American Journal of Sociology 77:921–940.

Piliavin, Irving M., Judith Rodin and Jane Allyn Piliavin
1969 "Good Samaritanism: An underground phenomenon." Journal of Personality and Social Psychology 13:289–299.

Platt, A.M.
1969 The Child Savers: The Invention of Delinquency. Chicago: University of Chicago Press.

Pope, Whitney
1976 Durkheim's "Suicide." Chicago: University of Chicago Press.

Pope, Whitney and Nick Danigelis
1981 "Sociology's 'one law.'" Social Forces 60:495–516.

Popper, Karl R.
1959 The Logic of Scientific Discovery. New York: Harper and Row.
1962 Conjectures and Refutations. New York: Basic Books.

Portes, Alejandro
1973 "The factoral structure of modernity." American Journal of Sociology 79:15–44.

Psathas, George
1968 "Ethnomethods and phenomenology." Social Research 35:500–520.

Quine, Willard Van Orman
1982 Methods of Logic. Cambridge: Harvard University Press.

Quinn, Bernard, Herman Anderson, Martin Bradley, Paul Goetting and Peggy Schriver
1982 Churches and Church Membership in the United States, 1980. Atlanta, Ga.: Glenmary Research Center.

Rachman, S.J. and G.T. Wilson
1980 The Effects of Psychological Therapy. Oxford, England: Pergamon.

Rand Corporation
1955 A Million Random Digits with 100,000 Normal Deviates. Glencoe, Ill.: Free Press.

Regan, Opal G.
1973 "Statistical reforms accelerated by sixth census errors." Journal of the American Statistical Association 68:540–546.

Reid-Green, Keith S.
1989 "The history of census tabulation." Scientific American 260 (February): 98–103.

Reynolds, Paul Davidson
1979 Ethical Dilemmas and Social Science Research. San Francisco: Jossey-Bass.
1982 Ethics and Social Science Research. Englewood Cliffs, N.J.: Prentice-Hall.

Riabchikov, Evgeny
1971 Russians in Space. Garden City, N.Y.: Doubleday.

Rice, Stuart A.
1929 "Contagious bias in the interview." American Journal of Sociology 35:420–423.

Richardson, James T. and Mary Stewart
1977 "Conversion process models and the Jesus movement." American Behavioral Scientist 20:819–838.

Richter, Maurice N.
1972 Science as a Cultural Process. Cambridge: Schenkman.

Roberts, Karlene H. and Leigh Burstein (eds.)
1980 Issues in Aggregation. San Francisco: Jossey-Bass.

Robinson, Charles Edson
1893 A Concise History of the United Society of Believers. East Canterbury, N.H.: United Society of Believers.

Robinson, John P., Robert Athansiou and Kendra B. Head
1969 Measures of Occupational Attitudes and Occupational Characteristics. Ann Arbor, Mich.: Institute for Social Research.

Robinson, John P., Jerrold G. Rusk and Kendra B. Head
1968 Measures of Political Attitudes. Ann Arbor, Mich.: Institute for Social Research.

Robinson, John P. and Phillip R. Shaver
1969 Measures of Social Psychological Attitudes. Ann Arbor, Mich.: Institute for Social Research.

Robinson, Louis Newton
1911 History and Organization of Criminal Statistics in the United States. Boston: Houghton Mifflin.

Robinson, W.S.
1950 "Ecological correlation and the behavior of individuals." American Sociological Review 15:351–357.

Rogers, Carl and R. Dymond
1954 Psychotherapy and Personality Change. Chicago: University of Chicago Press.

Rosenberg, Morris
1965 Society and the Adolescent Self-Image. Princeton, N.J.: Princeton University Press.
1968 The Logic of Survey Analysis. New York: Basic Books.

Rossi, Peter H., Richard A. Berk and Kenneth J. Lenihan
1980 Money, Work, and Crime. New York: Academic Press.
1985 "Saying it wrong with figures," American Journal of Sociology 88:390–393.

Rossi, Peter H. and James D. Wright
1984 "Evaluation research: An assessment." Pp. 331–352 in R.H. Turner (ed.), Annual Review of Sociology, vol. 10. Palo Alto: Annual Reviews.

Rothman, David J.
1971 The Discovery of the Asylum. Boston: Little, Brown.

Rumplehart, David E. and James L. McClelland
1987 Parallel Distributed Processing. Two Volumes. Cambridge: MIT Press.

Schofield, William
1964 Psychotherapy: The Purchase of Friendship. Englewood Cliffs, N.J.: Prentice-Hall.

Schuessler, Karl
1974 "Analysis of ratio variables: Opportunities and pitfalls." American Journal of Sociology 80:379–396.

Schuman, Howard and Lawrence Bobo
1988 "Survey-based experiments on white racial attitudes toward residential integration." American Journal of Sociology 94:273–299.

Schuman, Howard and Stanley Presser
1978 "The assessment of 'no opinion' in attitude surveys." Pp. 241–275 in K.F. Schuessler (ed.), Sociological Methodology 1979. San Francisco: Jossey-Bass.

Schutz, Alfred
1967 The Phenomenology of the Social World. Evanston, Ill.: Northwestern University Press.

Schwartz, Richard D. and Jerome H. Skolnick
1964 "Two studies of legal stigma." Pp. 103–117 in H.S. Becker (ed.), The Other Side. New York: Free Press.

Sedlack, R. Guy and Jay Stanley
1991 Social Research: Theory and Methods. Boston: Allyn and Bacon.

Shannon, William V.
1963 The American Irish. New York: Macmillan.

Shaw, Clifford H.
1930 The Jack-Roller. Philadelphia: Albert Saifer.

Sharpless, John B. and Ray M. Shortridge
1975 "Biased underenumeration in census manuscripts." Journal of Urban History 1:409–439.

Sherif, Muzafer and Carolyn W. Sherif
1969 Social Psychology. New York: Harper and Row.

Sherif, Muzafer, B. Jack White and O.J. Harvey
1955 "Status in experimentally produced groups." American Journal of Sociology 60:370–379.

Silverman, Irwin, Arthur D. Shulman and David L. Wiesenthal
1970 "Effect of deceiving and debriefing psychological subjects on performance in later experiments." Journal of Personality and Social Psychology 14:203–212.

Simmel, Georg
1950 The Sociology of Georg Simmel. New York: Free Press.

Simon, Herbert A.
1954 "Spurious correlation: A causal interpretation." Journal of the American Statistical Association 49:467–79.

Singh, Parmatma (Howard Weiss)
1974 Spiritual Community Guide 1975–76. San Rafael, Calif.: Spiritual Community Publications.
1978 Spiritual Community Guide 1979. San Rafael, Calif.: Spiritual Community Publications.

Smith, M. Brewster, Jerome S. Bruner and Robert W. White
1956 Opinions and Personality. New York: Wiley.

Sociology Writing Group
1991 A Guide to Writing Sociology Papers. New York: St. Martin's.

Somers, Robert H.
1962 "A new asymmetric measure of association for ordinal variables." American Sociological Review 27:799–811.

Sommer, Robert
1969 Personal Space. Englewood Cliffs, N.J.: Prentice-Hall.

Sorenson, E. Richard
1974 "Anthropological film: A scientific and humanistic resource." Science 186:1079–1085.

Sorokin, Pitirim A.
1930 "An experimental study of efficiency of work under various specified conditions." American Journal of Sociology 765–782.

Stark, Rodney
1980 "Estimating church-membership rates for ecological areas." National Institute of Juvenile Justice and Delinquency Prevention, LEAA, U.S. Department of Justice. Washington: U.S. Government Printing Office.
1989 Sociology. Belmont, Calif.: Wadsworth.

Stark, Rodney and William Sims Bainbridge
1985 The Future of Religion. Berkeley: University of California Press.
1987 A Theory of Religion. New York: Peter Lang.

Stark, Rodney, Daniel P. Doyle and Jesse Lynn Rushing
1983 "Beyond Durkheim: Religion and suicide." Journal for the Scientific Study of Religion 22:120–133.

Stephan, Karen H. and G. Edward Stephan
1973 "Religion and the survival of utopian communities." Journal for the Scientific Study of Religion 12:89–100.

Strauss, Alselm, Leonard Schatzman, Rue Bucher, Danuta Ehrlich and Melvin Sabshin
1964 Psychiatric Ideologies and Institutions. New York: Free Press.

Suchman, Edward A., Bernard S. Phillips and Gordon F. Streib
1958 "An analysis of the validity of health questionnaires." Social Forces 36:223–232.

Sutch, Richard
1975 "The treatment received by American slaves." Explorations in Economic History 12:335–438.

Sutherland, Edwin H.
1937 The Professional Thief. Chicago: University of Chicago Press.

Sutherland, Edwin H. and Donald Cressey
1974 Principles of Criminology. Philadelphia: Lippincott.

Sweetland, Richard C. and William O'Connor (eds.)
1983 Tests. Kansas City, Mo.: Test Corporation of America.

Tatum, Georgia Lee
1934 Disloyalty in the Confederacy. Chapel Hill: University of North Carolina Press.

Taviss, Irene
1972 "A survey of popular attitudes toward technology." Technology and Culture 13:616–621.

Taylor, A.M.
1967 Imagination and the Growth of Science. New York: Schocken.

Temple, William F.
1949 Four-Sided Triangle. London: J. Long.

Thomas, Alexander and Samuel Sillen
1972. Racism and Psychiatry. New York: Brunner/Mazel.

Thomas, Emory M.
1979 The Confederate Nation. New York: Harper.

Thrasher, Frederic M.
1927 The Gang. Chicago: University of Chicago Press.

Truzzi, Marcello (ed.)
1974 Verstehen: Subjective Understanding in the Social Sciences. Reading, Mass.: Addison-Wesley.

Tsuya, Noriko O.
1986 "Retention of ethnic cultural values and assimilation: Japanese Americans in Chicago." Nanzan Review of American Studies 8:23–59.

Tubbs, Stewart L.
1988 A Systems Approach to Small Group Interaction. New York: Random House.

Tuma, Nancy Brandon
1985 "Prologue." Pp. xi–xx in Sociological Methodology 1985. San Francisco: Jossey-Bass.

U.S. Army
1945 The Story of Peenemünde. Mimeographed documents carrying catalogue number KG6114 in the Harvard University library system.

Van Dyke, Vernon
1964 Pride and Power: The Rationale of the Space Program. Urbana: University of Illinois Press.

Vigderhous, Gideon
1977 "The level of measurement and 'permissible' statistical analysis in social research." Pacific Sociological Review 20:61–72.

Wallace, Anthony F.C.
1966 Religion: An Anthropological View. New York: Random House.

Warheit, George J., Charles E. Holzer and Sandra A. Arey
1975 "Race and mental illness: An epidemiologic update." Journal of Health and Social Behavior 16:243–256.

Warner, W. Lloyd
1941 The Social Life of a Modern Community. New Haven: Yale University Press.

Wax, Murray L.
1972 "Tenting with Malinowski." American Sociological Review 37:1–13.

Webb, Eugene J., Donald T. Campbell, Richard D. Schwartz and Lee Sechrest
1966 Unobtrusive Measures. Chicago: Rand McNally.

Weil, Andrew
1972 The Natural Mind. Boston: Houghton Mifflin.

Welch, Kevin W.
1981 "An interpersonal influence model of traditional religious commitment." Sociological Quarterly 22:81–92.

Wesolowsky, George O.
1976 Multiple Regression and Analysis of Variance. New York: Wiley.

White, Harrison and Cynthia A. White
1965 Canvases and Careers. New York: Wiley.

White, Harrison C., Scott A. Boorman and Ronald L. Breiger
1976 "Social structure from multiple networks." American Journal of Sociology 81:730–780.

White, Leslie
1959 The Evolution of Culture. New York: McGraw-Hill.

White, Lynn
1962 Medieval Technology and Social Change. London: Oxford.

Whitworth, John McKelvie
1975 God's Blueprints. London: Routledge and Kegan Paul.

Whyte, William Foote
1943 Street Corner Society. Chicago: University of Chicago Press.
1984 Learning from the Field. Beverly Hills, Calif.: Sage.

Williams, Donald H.
1986 "The epidemiology of mental illness in Afro-Americans." Hospital and Community Psychiatry 37:42–49.

Wines, Enoch C. and Theodore W. Dwight
1867 Report on the Prisons and Reformatories of the United States and Canada. Albany: Van Benthuysen.

Wines, Frederick Howard
1888 Report on the Defective, Dependent, and Delinquent Classes of the Population of the United States. Washington: Government Printing Office.

Winter, Frank H.
1983 Prelude to the Space Age—The Rocket Societies: 1924–1940. Washington: National Air and Space Museum.

Winters, John D.
1963 The Civil War in Louisiana. Baton Rouge: Louisiana State University Press.

Wittke, Carl
1956 The Irish in America. Baton Rouge: Louisiana State University Press.

Wolf, Eric
   1969 Peasant Wars of the Twentieth Century. New York: Harper and Row.
Wolfe, Tom
   1969 The Electric Kool-Aid Acid Test. New York: Bantam.
Wood, Robert W.
   1885 "Memorial of Edward Jarvis, M.D." Boston: T.R. Martin.
Wrightsman, Lawrence S.
   1969 "Wallace supporters and adherence to 'law and order.'" Journal of Personality and Social Psychology 13:17–22.
Wuthnow, Robert
   1981 "Two traditions in the study of religion." Journal for the Scientific Study of Religion 20:16–32.

Yeager, Chuck and Leo Janos
   1985 Yeager: An Autobiography. Toronto: Bantam.
Yeatts, John R. and William Asher
   1979 "Can we afford *not* to do true experiments in psychology of religion?" Journal for the Scientific Study of Religion 18:86–89.

Young, Michael W.
   1979 "Introduction" to The Ethnography of Malinowski. London: Routledge and Kegan Paul.
Younger, Mary Sue
   1979 Handbook for Linear Regression. North Scituate, Mass.: Duxbury.

Zablocki, Benjamin
   1971 The Joyful Community. Baltimore: Penguin.
Zeisel, Hans
   1982a "Disagreement over the evaluation of a controlled experiment." American Journal of Sociology 88:378–389.
   1982b "Hans Zeisel concludes the debate." American Journal of Sociology 88:394–396.
Zelditch, Morris
   1980 "Can you really study an army in the laboratory?" Pp. 531–539 in A. Etzioni and E.W. Lehman (eds.), A Sociological Reader on Complex Organizations. New York: Holt, Rinehart and Winston.

Tables

Normal Curve Areas

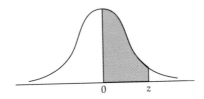

z	.00	.01	.02	.03	.04	.05	.06	.07	.08	.09
0.0	.0000	.0040	.0080	.0120	.0160	.0199	.0239	.0279	.0319	.0359
0.1	.0398	.0438	.0478	.0517	.0557	.0596	.0636	.0675	.0714	.0753
0.2	.0793	.0832	.0871	.0910	.0948	.0987	.1026	.1064	.1103	.1141
0.3	.1179	.1217	.1255	.1293	.1331	.1368	.1406	.1443	.1480	.1517
0.4	.1554	.1591	.1628	.1664	.1700	.1736	.1772	.1808	.1844	.1879
0.5	.1915	.1950	.1985	.2019	.2054	.2088	.2123	.2157	.2190	.2224
0.6	.2257	.2291	.2324	.2357	.2389	.2422	.2454	.2486	.2517	.2549
0.7	.2580	.2611	.2642	.2673	.2704	.2734	.2764	.2794	.2823	.2852
0.8	.2881	.2910	.2939	.2967	.2995	.3023	.3051	.3078	.3106	.3133
0.9	.3159	.3186	.3212	.3238	.3264	.3289	.3315	.3340	.3365	.3389
1.0	.3413	.3438	.3461	.3485	.3508	.3531	.3554	.3577	.3599	.3621
1.1	.3643	.3665	.3686	.3708	.3729	.3749	.3770	.3790	.3810	.3830
1.2	.3849	.3869	.3888	.3907	.3925	.3944	.3962	.3980	.3997	.4015
1.3	.4032	.4049	.4066	.4082	.4099	.4115	.4131	.4147	.4162	.4177
1.4	.4192	.4207	.4222	.4236	.4251	.4265	.4279	.4292	.4306	.4319
1.5	.4332	.4345	.4357	.4370	.4382	.4394	.4406	.4418	.4429	.4441
1.6	.4452	.4463	.4474	.4484	.4495	.4505	.4515	.4525	.4535	.4545
1.7	.4554	.4564	.4573	.4582	.4591	.4599	.4608	.4616	.4625	.4633
1.8	.4641	.4649	.4656	.4664	.4671	.4678	.4686	.4693	.4699	.4706
1.9	.4713	.4719	.4726	.4732	.4738	.4744	.4750	.4756	.4761	.4767
2.0	.4772	.4778	.4783	.4788	.4793	.4798	.4803	.4808	.4812	.4817
2.1	.4821	.4826	.4830	.4834	.4838	.4842	.4846	.4850	.4854	.4857
2.2	.4861	.4864	.4868	.4871	.4875	.4878	.4881	.4884	.4887	.4890
2.3	.4893	.4896	.4898	.4901	.4904	.4906	.4909	.4911	.4913	.4916
2.4	.4918	.4920	.4922	.4925	.4927	.4929	.4931	.4932	.4934	.4936
2.5	.4938	.4940	.4941	.4943	.4945	.4946	.4948	.4949	.4951	.4952
2.6	.4953	.4955	.4956	.4957	.4959	.4960	.4961	.4962	.4963	.4964
2.7	.4965	.4966	.4967	.4968	.4969	.4970	.4971	.4972	.4973	.4974
2.8	.4974	.4975	.4976	.4977	.4977	.4978	.4979	.4979	.4980	.4981
2.9	.4981	.4982	.4982	.4983	.4984	.4984	.4985	.4985	.4986	.4986
3.0	.4987	.4987	.4987	.4988	.4988	.4989	.4989	.4989	.4990	.4990

Source: Abridged from Table I of A. Hald, *Statistical Tables and Formulas* (New York: John Wiley & Sons, Inc.), 1952. Reproduced by permission of A. Hald and the publisher, John Wiley & Sons, Inc.

Percentage Points of the Chi-square
Distribution

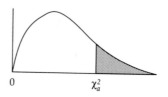

d.f.	$a = .995$	$a = .990$	$a = .975$	$a = .950$	$a = .900$
1	0.0000393	0.0001571	0.0009821	0.0039321	0.0157908
2	0.0100251	0.0201007	0.0506356	0.102587	0.210720
3	0.0717212	0.114832	0.215795	0.351846	0.584375
4	0.206990	0.297110	0.484419	0.710721	1.063623
5	0.411740	0.554300	0.831211	1.145476	1.61031
6	0.675727	0.872085	1.237347	1.63539	2.20413
7	0.989265	1.239043	1.68987	2.16735	2.83311
8	1.344419	1.646482	2.17973	2.73264	3.48954
9	1.734926	2.087912	2.70039	3.32511	4.16816
10	2.15585	2.55821	3.24697	3.94030	4.86518
11	2.60321	3.05347	3.81575	4.57481	5.57779
12	3.07382	3.57056	4.40379	5.22603	6.30380
13	3.56503	4.10691	5.00874	5.89186	7.04150
14	4.07468	4.66043	5.62872	6.57063	7.78953
15	4.60094	5.22935	6.26214	7.26094	8.54675
16	5.14224	5.81221	6.90766	7.96164	9.31223
17	5.69724	6.40776	7.56418	8.67176	10.0852
18	6.26481	7.01491	8.23075	9.39046	10.8649
19	6.84398	7.63273	8.90655	10.1170	11.6509
20	7.43386	8.26040	9.59083	10.8508	12.4426
21	8.03366	8.89720	10.28293	11.5913	13.2396
22	8.64272	9.54249	10.9823	12.3380	14.0415
23	9.26042	10.19567	11.6885	13.0905	14.8479
24	9.88623	10.8564	12.4011	13.8484	15.6587
25	10.5197	11.5240	13.1197	14.6114	16.4734
26	11.1603	12.1981	13.8439	15.3791	17.2919
27	11.8076	12.8786	14.5733	16.1513	18.1138
28	12.4613	13.5648	15.3079	16.9279	18.9392
29	13.1211	14.2565	16.0471	17.7083	19.7677
30	13.7867	14.9535	16.7908	18.4926	20.5992
40	20.7065	22.1643	24.4331	26.5093	29.0505
50	27.9907	29.7067	32.3574	34.7642	37.6886
60	35.5346	37.4848	40.4817	43.1879	46.4589
70	43.2752	45.4418	48.7576	51.7393	55.3290
80	51.1720	53.5400	57.1532	60.3915	64.2778
90	59.1963	61.7541	65.6466	69.1260	73.2912
100	67.3276	70.0648	74.2219	77.9295	82.3581

$a = .10$	$a = .05$	$a = .025$	$a = .010$	$a = .005$	d.f.
2.70554	3.84146	5.02389	6.63490	7.87944	1
4.60517	5.99147	7.37776	9.21034	10.5966	2
6.25139	7.81473	9.34840	11.3449	12.8381	3
7.77944	9.48773	11.1433	13.2767	14.8602	4
9.23635	11.0705	12.8325	15.0863	16.7496	5
10.6446	12.5916	14.4494	16.8119	18.5476	6
12.0170	14.0671	16.0128	18.4753	20.2777	7
13.3616	15.5073	17.5346	20.0902	21.9550	8
14.6837	16.9190	19.0228	21.6660	23.5893	9
15.9871	18.3070	20.4831	23.2093	25.1882	10
17.2750	19.6751	21.9200	24.7250	26.7569	11
18.5494	21.0261	23.3367	26.2170	28.2995	12
19.8119	22.3621	24.7356	27.6883	29.8194	13
21.0642	23.6848	26.1190	29.1413	31.3193	14
22.3072	24.9958	27.4884	30.5779	32.8013	15
23.5418	26.2962	28.8454	31.9999	34.2672	16
24.7690	27.5871	30.1910	33.4087	35.7185	17
25.9894	28.8693	31.5264	34.8053	37.1564	18
27.2036	30.1435	32.8523	36.1908	38.5822	19
28.4120	31.4104	34.1696	37.5662	39.9968	20
29.6151	32.6705	35.4789	38.9321	41.4010	21
30.8133	33.9244	36.7807	40.2894	42.7956	22
32.0069	35.1725	38.0757	41.6384	44.1813	23
33.1963	36.4151	39.3641	42.9798	45.5585	24
34.3816	37.6525	40.6465	44.3141	46.9278	25
35.5631	38.8852	41.9232	45.6417	48.2899	26
36.7412	40.1133	43.1944	46.9630	49.6449	27
37.9159	41.3372	44.4607	48.2782	50.9933	28
39.0875	42.5569	45.7222	49.5879	52.3356	29
40.2560	43.7729	46.9792	50.8922	53.6720	30
51.8050	55.7585	59.3417	63.6907	66.7659	40
63.1671	67.5048	71.4202	76.1539	79.4900	50
74.3970	79.0819	83.2976	88.3794	91.9517	60
85.5271	90.5312	95.0231	100.425	104.215	70
96.5782	101.879	106.629	112.329	116.321	80
107.565	113.145	118.136	124.116	128.299	90
118.498	124.342	129.561	135.807	140.169	100

From "Tables of the Percentage Points of the χ^2-Distribution," *Biometrika*, Vol. 32(1941), pp. 188–189, by Catherine M. Thompson. Reproduced by permission of the *Biometrika* Trustees.

Glossary/Index

a priori the quality of a line of analysis that works deductively from a set of theoretical principles. 471

absolute value the difference between a given number and zero, figured simply by ignoring any minus sign in front of the number. 330

abstract a short summary of an essay, stating its aims and findings; often a single paragraph in size and seldom longer than 300 words. 13

acquiescence the tendency of a respondent to agree with whatever a survey item says, regardless of its content. 213

adjusted rate a rate calculated in some complex but defensible way that is believed to measure a phenomenon better than would a raw rate. 374

administration the doing or running of an experiment, or the giving of a survey or interview. 137

aggregate data numbers describing groups that have been created by combining (aggregating) data about individuals. 369

analysis of variance a set of techniques for assessing the statistical significance of differences in a set of means. 338

anonymity keeping secret the identity of particular persons, while making public some information gained through research on them. 18

ANOVA see *analysis of variance.*

area sample a sample that selects locations and then accepts people found at those locations to be respondents. 225

artifacts material objects created by or used by the people under study and that may reveal much about them. 34

attenuation a decline in a coefficient because of a reduction of the number of items in an index, reflecting that an index with many items tends to be more reliable than one with few items. 474

attrition the loss of subjects from an experiment or other study over the course of the research. 147

autocorrelation artifactual correlation between two variables caused by their in some way containing or being contaminated by the same quantities. 387, 493

beta weight see *standardized regression coefficient.*

bimodal distribution a distribution that has two modes, two distinct "humps." 328

binomial distribution a distribution of cases across categories that approaches the normal curve if there are many categories. 323

bootstrapping a computerized, nonparametric technique for estimating standard errors; by extension, any of a variety of estimation techniques using computer-generated random samples from a dataset. 420

case a unit of the thing under study; often an individual person. 103

categorical sample a sample in which the researcher first identifies categories of people in the population, just as in quota sampling, and decides how many of each are needed; then, a random sample is drawn for each of these categories separately. 223

CATI Computer-Assisted Telephone Interviewing. 219

cell the smallest part of a crosstabulation table; the intersection of two or more variables defining a single value on each. 176

census a survey of the entire population rather than of a sample. 226

census manuscript schedules the forms on which the census-takers used to write as they went door-to-door. 99

central-limit theorem a principle of statistics stating the characteristics of the sampling distribution for large samples from a population. 340

chi-square a coefficient calculated from a table and expressing the degree to which the cell frequencies diverge from the distribution expected by chance; thus a step toward estimating the statistical significance of the departure from chance. See *complex chi-square.* 185

chronological confusion a lapse of memory, by an informant or interviewee, that confuses the time order of events. 67

closed-ended item a fixed-choice item. 75

cluster analysis a variety of techniques that seek clusters of items in a dataset, for example by grouping items in terms of their highest correlations. 477

cluster sample a sample in which individual respondents are geographically clustered together into groups. 224

coding assigning pieces of information to analytic categories that are often identified by distinct numbers. 78

coefficient of variation the variation ratio multiplied by 100. 332

collinearity the situation when two or more independent variables are highly correlated with each other. 447

collapse categories to recode a variable in such a way as to combine cases with two or more values and assign the same new value to them. 274

column percent percentages calculated within each column of figures in a table. 183

complex chi-square chi-square calculated for tables with more than two values for one or both variables. 299

confidence interval the interval within which a specified fraction of estimates from a series of random samples would fall. 340

confidentiality keeping secret some information concerning people who were studied by the researcher. 19

confirmatory analysis a statistical analysis intended to test a theory about the structure of the data. 471

construct a concept used to understand a phenomenon that cannot be observed directly. 465

construct validity the quality of an index that is both coherent and distinct. 465

contagion bias the tendency of data from an interview to be infected by the views of the interviewer. 73

contingent questions items that only a subgroup of respondents are supposed to answer. 220

continuous variable a variable that can take on a near-infinite number of different values within its range. 266

control group a group of subjects in an experiment to whom nothing special is done, used for comparison with one or more experimental groups. 136

control theory the view that deviant behavior will readily occur unless suppressed through strong bonds to the legitimate social order. 429

convenience sample is a subset of the population polled simply because they were easy to contact. 221

correlation see *negative correlation, positive correlation, measure of association.*

counterexample a case that contradicts a given theory. 48

counterfactual argument an assertation of what might have happened if certain factual events had not occurred. 124

covariance the variance shared by two variables; a measure of how X and Y vary together. 409

covert observation research done when the people under observation are unaware they are being studied, perhaps even actively deceived about the researcher's identity and purposes. 31

criterion group a group of people, known (on the basis of conclusive, independent evidence) to have the characteristic an item or index is supposed to measure. 462

criterion validity the quality of a measure that correctly distinguishes a criterion group from other people. 462

Cronbach's alpha a measure of reliability of items in an index equivalent to the average of all the possible split-halves reliability coefficients. 473

crosstab see *crosstabulation.*

crosstabulation a table that runs two variables across each other. 261

cursor the flashing rectangle on the computer screen that indicates where the computer is prepared to print a letter or do other work. 55

cursor control keys four computer keys printed with arrows, generally used to move the cursor on the screen. 55

cutting point a value on a variable that is used as the dividing line between categories of values. 201

D see *Somers' D.*

dataset a collection of information all of one type or from one source. 101

data subset a portion of a dataset consisting of cases that were selected from it. 110

debriefing discussing a research study with a subject, after the subject has participated, to leave this person with a proper understanding of its meaning and to minimize bad effects of the research on the subject. 164

deception the technique of giving research subjects false impressions of the nature of a research project to facilitate performing it. 163

deflation the mathematical process of compensating for oversampling to arrive at a good estimate of responses from the population. 223

degree of association the absolute value of a correlation coefficient (its size, ignoring the plus or minus sign), how far from zero it is. 285

degrees of freedom the number of cases, scores, or categories that are free to vary in calculating a measure such as chi-square from the cells of a table. 300

demand characteristics all the things brought by the researcher into a situation that might demand a particular set of responses from the research subject. 74

demography the social-scientific study of trends in the number of persons in the population, shaped by birth, death, and migration. 371

dependent variable roughly the effect in a cause-effect relationship, or a variable that is temporarily treated like the effect of a particular independent variable; variations in the dependent variable are said to be explained by variations in the independent variable. 135

diary of field notes a classic, anthropological research tool; a thorough chronicle of observations. 32

dichotomy divisions of things into a pair of categories. 173

direction of an association the sign on the correlation coefficient, whether positive or negative. 194, 285

discontinuous variable a variable whose values consist of a relatively small number of distinct categories. 266

discrete variable see *discontinuous variable.*

discriminant validity the capacity of an item or index to measure something different from what other scales measure. 463

dispersion of a variable the extent to which the cases are spread out across a variable's values. 303

domain a statement of the set of phenomena to which a proposition applies. 8

dummy variable a dichotomous variable that was created by collapsing categories in the raw data. 455

ecological correlation a correlation between two geographically based rates. 368

ecological fallacy the mistake of assuming that individuals have the typical characteristics for their areas. 385, 452

ecology study of the environment; social or human ecology is the study of the social environment. 355

egoism weakness of social integration of the groups of which the individual forms a part. 372

ego threat a phenomenon, such as an aspect of an interview, that threatens the self-esteem of a person. 66

ethics a set of formal standards of professional behavior, such as the Code of Ethics enacted by the American Sociological Association, which sets forth rules concerning authorship and plagiarism of publications, conflicts between teachers and students, ethical obligations of employers and employees, as well as matters relating to research. The Code also sets up procedures for dealing with ethical disputes. 17

ethnographer a trained, professional documenter of the culture of a group. 29

etymology the study of the origins of words and phrases. 82

evaluation research the assessment of the net effects of a social program. 144, 153

experiment a research study in which the researcher systematically takes some action and compares its result with the result of taking some other action. 136

experimental conditions the different circumstances experienced by different groups in an experiment. 136

experimental group a group of subjects in an experiment who receive a manipulation, compared with the control group, which does not. 136

explanation the process of showing that a research finding follows as a logical conclusion, as a deduction, from one or more general propositions under specified given conditions; *formal explanation* of a specific proposition consists of showing that it follows logically from one or more general propositions. 9

exploratory analysis an analysis of the structure of the data that does not start with any theoretical assumptions. 471

external corroboration information supportive of claims made by information, obtained other than from the informant. 84

extraneous variable a third variable, Z, that distorts the relationship between two other variables, X and Y, for example by creating the spurious semblance of a correlation between them. 428

F distribution a set of numbers used for evaluating the statistical significance of results from analysis of variance; comparable to chi-square in its use. 343

face validity the judgment that a measure is valid based on common-sense interpretation of it or its components. 463

factor analysis a set of statistical techniques for reducing a correlation matrix, extracting a set of dimensions that parsimoniously reflect the structure of the data. 477

factor score a created variable generated from a factor analysis reflecting each case's values for a particular factor. 480

falsifiability the quality of a theory or hypothesis that is logically capable of being disproven; when suitable data fail to falsify a theory or hypothesis, then we gain confidence in it. 7

field experiment experimental research done in natural settings. 152

field research research done in real-world settings, often but not always qualitative and observational. 25

field theorist a researcher who is primarily a theorist and uses real-world experiences to inspire his or her theories. 31

fixed-choice item a questionnaire item that presents people with a fixed set of choices to select from. 75

folk theories theories of events created by nonscientists, particularly by the people under study themselves. 93

forced-choice item a fixed-choice item. 75

formal-operational approach an approach to social research that states a theory, logically derives hypotheses from it, operationalizes these hypotheses, and then subjects them to empirical testing upon suitable data. 2

frequency the number of cases in a given category, value of a variable, or cell of a table. 182

Galton's problem the error of wrongly assuming that each of the cases in a dataset is completely independent of the others. 386

gamma a nonparametric measure of association, a correlation coefficient. See also *Yule's Q*. 289

gatekeeper a member of a group or organization with some special authority over access to the group or to information about it. 31

heteroscedasticity the situation when the residuals from a regression equation are not randomly distributed; it becomes a problem when they correlate with some variable implicated in the relationships under examination. 449

histogram a bar graph in which the height of each bar represents the number of cases of a given value. 256

hypothesis a somewhat specific statement, less general than a theory, that the researcher hopes to test empirically. 4

hypothetico-deductive research the stating and testing of an hypothesis about reality and the logical reasoning that deduces the empirical consequences of an hypothesis. Equivalent to the formal-operational approach. 2

impression management conscious projecting of a certain image to achieve a desired reaction from other people. 63

independent variable roughly the cause in a cause-effect relationship, or a variable treated temporarily like a cause with respect to a particular dependent variable; variations in the independent variable are said to explain some of the variations in the dependent variable. 135

indicator a variable or piece of specific information that reflects a more general, underlying reality. 201, 466

inductive research a form of research in which hypotheses are not stated at the outset but gradually developed from the data as they are collected. 11

inferential confusion coming to a false conclusion about the meaning of past events. 67

informant participant in an interview or survey who provides objective information. 72

information overload receiving more data than one can comfortably handle. 78

instrument a set of items in a survey that together are believed to measure a particular psychological or other phenomenon. 461

intake interview in medical settings, an interview prior to treatment to determine what the problem is and decide upon the proper course of treatment. 146

interaction process analysis   a system developed by Robert F. Bales for categorizing the communications in discussion groups. 44

internal consistency   a test of the reliability of information provided by an informant, focusing on whether data obtained at different times agree with each other. 84

interpretive-advocacy approach   a kind of sociology that seeks the human meaning of a social phenomenon while advocating the sociologist's values, politico-economic policies, or other personal commitments. 4

interval   the set of numbers within a particular distance of some particular number. 340

interval variable   a variable that measures a quantity along a scale consisting of equal steps or intervals. 265

interview schedule   a questionnaire written to guide interviews. 63

journal format   an outline for empirical research essays, favored by leading scientific journals, consisting of five parts: abstract, introduction, methods, results, discussion. 13

Kendall's tau   a nonparametric measure of association, a correlation coefficient; in fact, there are three tau coefficients: a, b, and c. 287

knee-jerk item   a questionnaire or interview item that elicits an almost automatic, conventional response from most respondents. 217

kurtosis   the relative degree of peakedness or flatness of a distribution. 328

level of measurement   the characteristic of a variable that determines which mathematical functions can legitimately be performed on it; four are generally distinguished: nominal, ordinal, interval, and ratio. 263

life history   an essay, typically based on interviews often supplemented with data from other sources, that describes and analyzes the development, conditions, and behavior of an individual over time. 83

linear relationship   an association between two variables that can be represented well as a straight line on a graph. 443

listwise deletion   dropping all the cases with missing values on any variable in a list. 275

manipulation   the different actions the researcher takes to different groups of people in an experiment. 136

marginals   numbers along the margins of a table expressing the total number of cases for each value of the variables. 182

margin of error   the range around a sample-based estimate in which 95 percent of samples would fall, if one drew a very large number of samples from the population. 242

mean   a measure of central tendency calculated by adding the values and dividing by the number of cases; commonly called *average*. 255

measurement   a step in the research process where concepts are operationalized, valid indicators are selected, phenomena are observed, and instances of the phenomenon the concept names are identified, counted, or quantified. 10

measure of association   a coefficient that expresses the strength and direction of an association between two variables. 194, 287

median   a measure of central tendency—the value for the middle case, if the cases are ranked in terms of their values. 255

mental set   the expectations a person brings to a situation that shape how he or she will interpret it. 16

menu item   a questionnaire item that asks the respondent to select from a list of various distinct alternatives. 211

misprision   a crime defined as concealment of treason or a felony by someone not guilty. 52

missing values   data that were not obtained but are expected by the analytical procedure, such as gaps caused by the failure of a respondent to answer a question. 274

mode   a measure of central tendency—the most common value. 256

multiple regression   techniques involving regression equations with two or more independent variables. 439

multistage sample   a sample produced by nesting samples at various aggregation levels, for example first drawing a sample of counties and then drawing samples of individuals from the selected counties. 225

native informant   a member of a group under study who is willing and able to provide the researcher with reliable information. 32

nay-saying   a form of response bias in which the respondent tends to disagree with agree-disagree items, regardless of their content. 213

necessary condition   a condition that must be met before some phenomenon can occur. 195

purposive sample a set of cases that the researcher has carefully considered and that in his or her judgment will serve the needs of the research. 221

Q see *Yule's Q*.

quota sample a sample that sets targets for how many people are to be included from each of several categories. 222

r see *Pearson's r*.

random sample see *simple random sample*.

rank to arrange a set of numbers in terms of their increasing or decreasing size; the position of a given number in a set after it has been ranked. 363

rapport a relationship marked by harmony, conformity, accord, or affinity. 63

rates proportions expressed in terms of the same denominator or base. 357

ratio variable a variable that measures a quantity along a scale consisting of equal steps or intervals, starting from a zero point. 266

raw rate a rate that has been calculated simply by dividing numbers from a dataset by a given base; contrasted with adjusted rate. 374

real number a continuous variable that can be expected to include fractions. 267

recidivism commission of new crimes after having been convicted. 153

recoding to change some of the values of a variable, following a systematic plan. 269

record linkage finding information about a case in two different places and bringing these two pieces of information together. 116

reflexivity the principle that results of sociological research are always shaped by the researcher's viewpoint; it states that the researcher is always part of the phenomenon under study, and it suggests that the researcher's own identity should be expressed in the results. 5

regression a statistical technique, analogous to correlation, that allows one to predict the value of one variable, Y, if the value of another variable, X, is known. 370

reliability the quality of a measure that gives consistent results; a reliable questionnaire item tends to get the same response from a respondent if administered twice, so long as the relevant circumstances have not changed. 461

replication repeating a previously completed scientific study, sometimes varying the method slightly, to see if the same results are obtained. 137

representative sample a sample that does a good job of capturing the pattern of responses one would get from the entire population. 221

research contract an agreement between an agency and an investigator by which the agency pays the investigator to perform research the agency designed. 15

research grant a payment of money by an agency to an investigator to perform research the investigator designed and proposed to the agency. 14

residual on the graph of a regression line, the distances between the actual Y values and the Y values predicted by a regression equation; the difference between the results of an empirical observation and the results of a computation from a formula. 407

respondent participant in an interview or survey who provides personal opinions, feelings, and attitudes. 72

response bias the tendency of a respondent to answer questions in a particular way, regardless of what the question specifically is about. 213, 452

response rate the fraction of people given a survey who actually complete it. 219

retention rate the proportion of cases that remain in a given status over a specified period of time. 120

row percent percentages calculated within each row of figures in a table. 183

sample a subset of people in the population under study, often selected by random numbers, whose responses to a survey are used to estimate how the entire population would have responded if it had all been surveyed. 221

scale an item or combination of items that measures a respondent characteristic along a graduated series of points, usually assumed to be equal distances apart. 214

scattergram a graph that shows where all the cases stand in terms of two variables, X and Y. 366

scatterplot see *scattergram*.

scientific theory a general statement that can generate two or more potentially testable hypotheses. See also *theory*. 4

screening questions items that separate people into subgroups that receive different contingent questions. 220

secondary analysis research based on data that were originally collected for another purpose. 210, 376

secondary source a source of historical information that was written by a later compiler, historian, or analyst. 127

secularization the decline of religious faith and of the influence of the churches. 372, 393

semantic differential a question format asking the respondent to pick a number indicating a judgment between a pair of opposites, such as good-bad. 216

setting the social cues that tell a person how to interpret a situation. 16

simple random sample a sample created using random numbers or other chance-based procedures, selecting individuals from the population at random; each member of the population has an equal chance of appearing in the sample, and every combination of a given number of individuals also has an equal chance. 222

skewness the quality of a distribution of cases in which the mean and the median are substantially different. 257, 328

slope how many units a line on a graph rises for each unit it runs forward. 398

snowball sample a subset of the population the researcher obtains by beginning with some individuals who are appropriate informants and then asking them for referrals to other appropriate informants. 221

social desirability bias the tendency of a respondent to give socially acceptable answers to questions, putting himself or herself in a good light. 213

social evaporation the process in which members of a group whose fortunes decline defect from it, leaving behind those members whose fortunes rise or remain constant. 148

social map a map of an area people use, showing who goes where and what they do there. 38

Somers' D an asymmetrical, nonparametric measure of association. 287

speech accommodation the tendency of a person to adjust his or her speech to conform to the style used by the people he or she is talking with. 74

split-halves reliability reliability of an index assessed by dividing the items into two groups and determining whether there is a high correlation between them. 464

spontaneous remission the lifting of a disease or other problem when no treatment was responsible for the cure. 145

spuriousness the distorting effect of an unmeasured third variable on the correlation between two other variables. 385, 451

standard deviation the square root of the variance. 331

standard error a measure of the dispersion of a sampling distribution, comparable to standard deviation. 340, 416

standardized regression coefficient a regression coefficient based on standardized scores, equivalent to Pearson's r. 415

standard score one of a set of quantities that has been expressed in terms of the number of standard deviations above or below the mean for the set. 335

statistical significance the evaluation of the probability that a certain pattern in the data occurred by pure chance. 184

stratified random sample a categorical sample. 224

subculture dictionary a document systematically presenting the special words used by a subculture, often with pronunciations and word origins included. 81

subject a person who is the object of study in scientific research. 136

subscale a subset of items from a measurement index that measures something identifiably different from the other items in the index. 465

sufficient condition a condition that, if met, will ensure that some phenomenon occurs. 196

suppressor variable an extraneous variable that weakens the apparent relationship between two other variables, thus concealing the true strength of the relationship. 451

syllogism a three-step argument; the first two statements are the *major premise* and the *minor premise,* while the third proposition in the syllogism, the *conclusion,* is deduced logically from the two premises. 9

systematic sample a cheap imitation of a random sample that follows a repetitive system to select names from a list. 222

tau see *Kendall's tau.*

tautology a statement that is true because of its logical form alone; thus it may seem trivial, containing no useful information. 298

technological determinism a perspective holding that technology is the source of all significant social change and that technology is self-generating and is not significantly shaped by nontechnological factors. 125

test-retest reliability   the quality of a measure that gives consistent results when performed twice, with some gap of time between the two administrations. 464

theory   in the interpretive-advocacy mode, a set of metaphors and analogies that place social phenomena in a humanly meaningful context; in the formal-operational mode, a set of formal propositions linked by a system of deductions showing how some propositions follow logically from others. See also *scientific theory*. 4

theory construction   the process of inventing and framing formal theories. 10

theory testing   the process of operationalizing concepts in an hypothesis derived from a theory and conducting empirical research to evaluate them. 10

tracking   record linkage across time; for example, looking a person up in two or more successive censuses. 117

triangulation   getting the best fix on an event by employing different perspectives concerning it. 84

T-test   a technique for evaluating the statistical significance of a difference between means, especially useful when there are relatively few cases. 347

unit act   the smallest piece of communication that can be unambiguously perceived. 44

unobtrusive research   gathering information without disturbing or influencing the people being observed. 26

valence   one of the categories of a dichotomy. 175

validity   the quality of an instrument that measures the phenomenon it purports to measure; a valid questionnaire item accurately reflects the desired aspect of the respondent's thoughts, behavior, or characteristics. 461

value   a distinct number or category, associated with a particular variable, that unambiguously describes cases. 105

variable   a quantity that may assume any one of a set of values. 105

variable name   brief description of a variable, often a single word, used to keep track of its meaning during computer analysis. 251

variance   the average squared difference from the mean of cases for a particular variable. 331

variation ratio   the standard deviation divided by the mean. 332

working paper   an essay that is constantly being modified, updated, and subjected to sharp criticism by the field researcher and the field researcher's colleagues; very useful in developing a theoretical analysis or complex empirical description. 34

yea-saying   a form of response bias in which the respondent tends to agree with agree-disagree items, regardless of their content. 213

Y-intercept   in a graph of a regression line, the point where the line crosses the Y-axis, equivalent to the point on the line with an X value of zero. 402

Yule's Q   a measure of association for two-by-two tables; equivalent to gamma. 194

Z-score   see *standard score*.

Software License Statement